TREASURY MANAGEMENT:
INTERNATIONAL BANKING OPERATIONS

Also by Alasdair Watson, FCIB
Finance of International Trade (3rd Edition 1985)
The Chartered Institute of Bankers

TREASURY MANAGEMENT: INTERNATIONAL BANKING OPERATIONS

by
Alasdair Watson
and
Ron Altringham

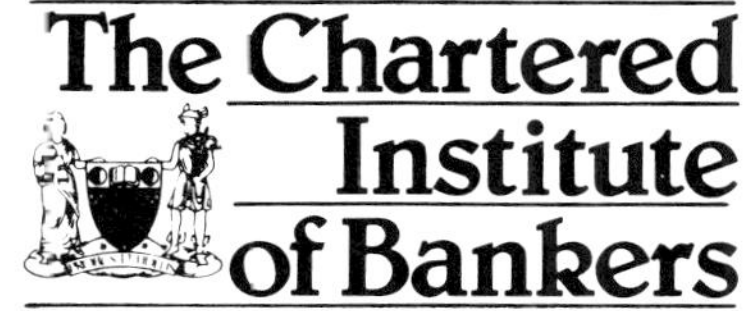

The Chartered Institute of Bankers

10 Lombard Street, London EC3V 9AS

First published January 1986
Reprinted November 1986 (with minor amendments)
Reprinted March 1988

Chartered Institute of Bankers (CIB) Publications are published by Bankers Books Limited under an exclusive license and royalty agreement. Bankers Books Limited is a company owned by The Chartered Institute of Bankers.

Enquiries should be sent to the publishers at the undermentioned address:

BANKERS BOOKS LIMITED
c/o The Chartered Institute of Bankers
10 Lombard Street
London
EC3V 9AS

 British Library Cataloguing in Publication Data

Watson, A.J.W.
   TREASURY MANAGEMENT: INTERNATIONAL BANKING OPERATIONS.
   1. Banks and banking, International
   I. Title   II. Altringham, R.   III. Institute of Bankers
   332.1.5   HG3881

   ISBN 0-85297-142-7

Typeset in 10 on 12pt Times
Cover: 118gsm Fleet Chromo, Text paper: 90gsm Fineblade
Printed and Bound: Grosvenor Press (Portsmouth) Ltd, England

Preface

This textbook was commissioned by The Institute of Bankers following the decision of the Council in 1984 to introduce the International Banking Diploma. It is designed expressly to meet the needs of students studying the *International Banking Operations* syllabus. The words "Treasury Management" in the title are designed to emphasise the Treasury and Treasury related functions described in the book. Both authors have many years practical management experience in the Treasury of major international banking groups, and it is their opinion that the book, whilst being written primarily for the international banker, will also be of considerable value to those engaged in the Treasury function of any multi-national enterprise.

For bankers and treasurers alike there is a clearly identified need to be able to understand the various financial instruments and markets, to know how they are handled and how they operate, to recognise and assess exposures and risk, and to control the related dealing and operating procedures concerned. This is of particular importance today with the many developments that are taking place bringing new instruments and techniques into play in the world's international and national markets. The book sets out to meet the needs of students and Treasury staff in this context from a practical rather than a theoretical standpoint.

Acknowledgements

The authors would like to express their gratitude to the following:

The Association of International Bond Dealers for their permission to reproduce the text of their Rules and Recommendations for dealing practice in Eurobonds.

The British Bankers' Association for their permission to reproduce relevant extracts from their booklets on 'Recommended Terms and Conditions for the London Interbank Market in Foreign Currency Options; Interest Rate and Currency Liability Swaps and Forward Rate Agreements'. (The BBA took the initiative in establishing standardised terms and conditions which have been readily accepted by the Market and are now in wide use.)

Mr. W. F. Batt for having kindly read and commented on the manuscript.

The Bank of England and in particular Mr. J. C. W. Osborn for the guidance provided.

Alan Orsich and Roy Haines for their support and encouragement.

Janet Power and Julia Stow for their patience, perseverance and perfection in superlative secretarial assistance.

The authors would also wish to express extreme gratitude to both Mireille and Celia for having done without their husbands for so long during the production period of this publication.

And finally, to National Westminster Bank PLC, Standard Chartered Bank PLC and The Institute of Bankers, without whose assistance this publication would not have been possible.

Contents

SECTION 1 – TREASURY OPERATIONS

CHAPTER ONE

An Introduction to the Treasury Functions in International Banking

Part I

The Changing Environment

Whilst it might be something of a generalisation, it is probably true to say that, until the mid 'sixties, international and multi-national banking was, at least by today's standards, a comparatively simple subject.

Prior to the Second World War international banking was in the main related to the finance of foreign trade. This activity was conducted by domestic banks in one country using the correspondent banking facilities of other domestic banks in various countries around the world, or the branches of international banks which had developed their activities in selected geographical regions of the world to service these requirements. In many instances these branches and offices of international banks extended their activities through internal branch netwcrks to provide retail banking operations within their country of domicile and still remain today as a major domestic banking force within many of those economies.

However, during the post war period of the 1940s and 1950s the internationalisation, or more properly the multi-national character, of banks did gather increased momentum consequent upon the substantial volumes of international trade taking place, post-war aid and reconstruction programmes, together with the provision of capital for the development of third world countries. Much of this expansion was in response to corporate demand with many banks joining the ranks as "international banks" through the development of overseas branches and operations to service the expanding international business requirements of their clients.

Up until the mid 'sixties these developments took place against a back-cloth of relative stability in both interest and exchange rate structures. An environment which encouraged bankers to accept both types of risk as inherent factors within the business of banking and each bank's head office structure tended to reflect this with its main components comprising functional and administrative responsibilities normally carried out by Chief Accountants, Advances, Inspection, Secretariat and Personnel Departments with often specialised branches caring for client's international trade requirements.

Prior to 1931 gold was the common denominator against which trading nations measured the value of their currencies. In 1931 the United Kingdom left the "gold standard", albeit that London was up to that time a major international centre within the "gold standard" system. Consequent upon this decision two major monetary areas emerged. First, the "Sterling Area" which then comprised those countries which geared the value of their currencies to sterling and, with one or two exceptions, maintained all their reserves in terms of sterling. Secondly, there was the so-called "Hard Currency" bloc, representing those countries which continued to denominate the value of their currencies in terms of the "gold standard".

During 1944 the international financial system was reviewed and, within the terms of the Bretton Woods Agreement, the rates of exchange for the major currencies, inclusive of sterling, were fixed against the US dollar with official intervention points established at three quarter percent either side of a published fixed dollar rate. The inclusion of sterling within this agreement effectively encompassed the "Sterling Area" and two major reserve currencies emerged: within the context of the "Sterling Area" or the "Scheduled Territories" as it was later defined by the 1947 Exchange Control Act,
– Sterling, but more importantly in the international context
– the United States dollar.
Although continuing as a reserve currency the role of sterling as a major medium of exchange in international trade diminished further during 1967 with the abolition of its use in third country trade which

2

left the US dollar as the dominant currency for financing international trade. Within the terms of the Bretton Woods Agreement the price of gold was pegged at United States dollars 35 a troy ounce with "official" holders of dollars being able to convert freely their holdings into gold.

The interbank foreign exchange market did not re-open in London after the Second World War until 1952 and its scope, at least until 1958, was strictly limited. The only major concern of companies, corporations and individuals with foreign exchange exposure was in regard to a significant devaluation or revaluation through a re-alignment of the relevant parity rates against the US dollar. A bank's primary activity in regard to foreign exchange at that time was to cover underlying commercial requirements.

During the late 'fifties and early 'sixties substantial international payment imbalances developed with both the United Kingdom and the United States running large deficits and it became increasingly apparent that first sterling and later the US dollar, the two major reserve currencies, were substantially over-valued in terms of the basic strength of the respective economies. At the same time, large external holdings of US dollars had developed as a result of the combined effects of the US payments deficits, the post-war outflow of aid from the US to Europe and the interest rate restrictions which existed within the US itself at a time when there was freedom to "export" the currency. A direct consequence of these factors together with political tensions and other considerations was the emergence of the phenomenon now known as the Eurodollar and of the market devoted to trading in this particular 'currency' – the "eurodollar market". The euro-market is essentially a market within which currencies – the dollar having subsequently been joined by several others – can be borrowed and lent and through the foreign exchange market converted into other currencies free of the restrictions and constraints which might otherwise operate within the respective national boundaries of those currencies. The very existence of these markets increasingly affected the stability of interest and exchange rates, both as a result of their direct impact upon individual nations' interest rate structures and via the substantial exchange of these funds between currencies for investment purposes, interest arbitrage and speculation against a possible re-alignment of a major currency's fixed parity rates.

The system of fixed parities, as established under the auspices of the International Monetary Fund by the Bretton Woods Agreement duly came under increasing pressure and the world moved from one currency crisis to another. On the 18th November 1967 sterling devalued against the US dollar by 14.3% and the French Franc devalued by 12.5% on the 8th August 1969. The Deutschemark was allowed to float upwards during September 1969 and was fixed again in late October 1969 at an effective revaluation of approximately 8.5%. The Canadian dollar which had previously floated between 1950 and 1962 floated again from May 1970. The Deutschemark floated for a second time, joined by the Dutch Guilder, in May 1971. During the same month the Swiss Franc floated briefly and revalued by 7.1% on the 9th May and on the same date Austria revalued by 5.1%.

Eventually, on the 15th August 1971, the United States dollar's convertibility into gold at US$35 per troy ounce was suspended and thereafter the major currencies were – subject to a greater or lesser degree of official intervention – floating against each other. This situation remained until December 1971 when the International Monetary Fund through the Smithsonian Agreement attempted to re-establish central rates against the US dollar with a wider fluctuation margin of 2.25% either side of parity. The United States re-established the official gold price at US$38 per troy ounce – an effective devaluation of 7.9% – but did not re-introduce the dollar's convertibility for official holders. Japan together with the major West European countries revalued their currencies. The Canadian dollar, however, continued to float.

Within the terms of the Smithsonian Agreement the member countries of the European Community agreed that, whilst collectively they would work within the new 4.5% band, each would maintain fluctuation margins of only 1.25% either side of their central rates with each other. This inner agreement, the European "snake" was the forerunner of the present European Monetary System.

4

The Smithsonian Agreement quickly collapsed. Sterling was unable to sustain its new central rate of US$2.61. On the 23rd June 1972 the British Government floated the pound and by the Exchange Control Amendment Act re-defined the Scheduled Territories which effectively disbanded the sterling area in its broader context. Many other countries were forced to introduce measures to stem the substantial movement of capital funds which was taking place. Finally, on the 13th February 1973 the United States announced a second devaluation, this time by 10% and raised the official gold price from US$38 to US$42.22. The foreign exchange markets closed briefly and when they re-opened all major currencies were floating against each other – the situation which has continued to date.

Within a floating rate structure the rate of exchange of one currency in terms of another should be determined entirely by market forces with official monetary policy or smoothing operations being implemented as necessary through open market intervention mechanisms. Whilst it is often implied in the broadest context that foreign exchange rates are floating this is often far from accurate. Exchange control regulations and other monetary directives, two-tier financial systems, constraints on capital flows, negative interest rates, reserve requirements, withholding tax, official exchange rate policy, alignment with another currency or basket of currencies and similar constraints or intervention, all limit to a greater or lesser extent not only the impact of market forces upon individual nation's foreign exchange rates but also individual's freedom of access to various international currencies on a competitive basis.

The 'seventies also witnessed the consequences of the two oil price shocks and the resultant disequilibrium they created within international balance of payment surpluses and deficits. This impacted substantially on the expansion of the eurocurrency markets and the involvement of individual banks as the intermediary in capital flows of funds to sovereign borrowers, an area which had in the main previously been the preserve of private investors, central banks, governments and their agencies.

It was during the late 'sixties and early 'seventies that the European foreign exchange markets and, in particular that of London, the centre of the eurodollar market, became increasingly competitive as banks in ever increasing numbers entered these markets. In terms of time zones the European financial centres are ideally situated being able to meet the requirements of the Far East during the mornings and the Americas during the afternoon. However, with increasing levels of volatility in both exchange and interest rates through the number of currencies moving from official parity rates or aligning themselves with a "free floating" base, the lifting of most interest rate restrictions in the United States and communication systems which facilitated the instant response to world events, commercial requirements and rumour, the European centres alone were insufficient to provide for global requirements and other major foreign exchange and eurocurrency markets developed around the world.

Not only were the international banks quickly able to respond to these developments but many traditionally domestic and regional banks also took this opportunity to internationalize themselves to keep apace with, and take part in, these new markets. Although the majority of the larger banks have established by choice a presence in most, if not all, of the major dealing centres, the necessity for many banks to develop "offshore" branches and operations outside of their own national boundaries was often prompted by the presence of domestic regulations which either prohibited and restricted access to these markets on a competitive basis or confined the extent to which domestic currencies could be utilised to finance international corporate requirements. The specific reasons that each bank required or desired access to these markets were varied; protecting existing business, funding domestic or international requirements, deploying surplus currency deposits, establishing a presence in the growing syndication market or in many cases simply trading for their own account in the substantial interbank deposit and foreign exchange markets which evolved.

Alongside these developments and having entered the international arena, strategic objectives were heightened and many banks developed international operations not only through branch expansion but also by mergers and acquisitions, thus establishing themselves as major multi-national corporations.

These developments were not without associated problems and casualties, for example :

- the secondary banking crisis of the early 'seventies in the UK

- substantial foreign exchange and funding losses incurred by several banks due to interest rate and exchange rate exposure in volatile or unregulated markets

- spectacular bank collapses

- the sovereign debt crisis which began to develop in 1982 and the ensuing banking crisis of 1984.

It was within this environment from the mid sixties that banks evolved specialised head office functions to care for their development and activities within these markets. International Banking Divisions, Treasury Divisions, Eurocurrency Lending and Syndication Departments, Financial Control Divisions, Business Development Departments, Strategic Research and Development Departments to name a few. The responsibilities of each type of department will vary from bank to bank and may not be recognisable within any particular heading already mentioned; therefore within the context of this publication, treasury management is better defined as a functional operation rather than a specific division or department of any particular bank.

Part II
The Treasury Function
In the larger bank it is probable that the Treasury function and the Financial Control function is segregated whereas in the smaller banking operation a single unit is more common.

The centralised Treasury operation of a bank is concerned with the following functions:

- Risk exposure management which embraces credit, country, liquidity and interest rate risk considerations together with those risks associated with trading and dealing in Foreign Exchange, Deposits, Securities, Gold, Commodities and various Financial instruments including futures and options.

- Asset and Liability management which incorporates both domestic and foreign currency wholesale and retail funds in various financial centres throughout the world, the funding of assets on the best possible terms, mobilisation of deposits and the utilisation of surplus resources. Within this process liquidity, interest rate structures and sensitivity together with future maturity profiles are major considerations in addition to the management of day to day funding requirements.

- The co-ordination of local money book management in various centres throughout the world.

- Control and development of dealing operations incorporating cash, forward, futures, options, interest rate and currency liability swaps and forward rate agreements in some or all of the following: foreign exchange, deposits, negotiable instruments, securities, gold and commodities.

- Responsibility for the judicious use of the bank's name.

- The funding of investments in subsidiaries and affiliates.

- Capital debt raising and loan stock administration.

- Control of investment portfolios and the utilisation of a bank's own liquid resources.

- Fraud protection.

Financial Control operations normally embrace the following functions:-

- Financial accounts

- Matters relating to international taxation

- Management information

- Budgeting and forecasting

- Capital appraisal

The principal functional responsibility of the international treasury of a bank is the funding of the bank's foreign currency business and investments. This embraces not only short- term liabilities and working capital raised by way of money market deposits and instruments on the widest possible range of money markets, but also the acquisition of long-term debt for balance sheet structural purposes. Resorting to any market in a haphazard fashion may reflect adversely on the borrower's name if it is perceived by others in the market that there exists a lack of planning and/or control in the way in which the borrower operates. To ensure that the bank obtains ready access to all available money markets, in order to continue to service its business, it is essential that the good quality of the bank's name is constantly protected by effective planning and control.

The 1984 banking crisis demonstrated just how fragile are the good names of highly respected financial institutions. Banks are vulnerable to sudden withdrawal of deposits, frequently prompted by self-prophetic rumours and, unless the liability structure of the bank is sufficiently diversified to withstand a run as confidence evaporates, the public assurance of a central bank and, perhaps, even a public insurance corporation such as the Federal Deposit Insurance Corporation (FDIC), still will not necessarily be able to save the bank from liquidation.

Good press coverage and continued payment of healthy dividends, can help to conceal fundamental management and structural defects in any organisation for a while. The size of a company is not a guarantee to its stability – its structure is all important. The quality of the debt acquired and the margin over funding costs are, and always have been, key factors in the continued success of a banking business. Growth of loans and investments must also be supported by growth in profits and capital adequacy.

It is well known that a bank's success depends, to a large extent, upon judicious approach to its lending and, more recently, in international terms, to the exposure in terms of country and sovereign risks. It is an equally important ingredient in the success formula of a banking business to have a fully co-ordinated treasury function and funding policy, and a management team which is aware of the need to remain flexible in the light of changing economic and business conditions.

With diminished margins and increased competition for high quality business there has been a drive for ways in which to increase profitability. This applies not only to banks but to most other commercial enterprises and the drive has been directed towards the buyers in industry to improve their sourcing. Likewise, in many banks an objective of the treasury function has been to achieve lower cost of funding, and various techniques such as interest rate swaps and currency swaps have been introduced which, at the same time as raising capital debt to improve gearing ratios, have enabled banks to reduce funding costs.

Large banks which have been created as the result of a number of mergers and acquisitions often have one or more major subsidiary banking and/or finance companies and, therefore, tend to have quite different structures. It is not unusual to find autonomous units each maintaining separate treasury and financial control functions and indeed there generally exists good legal and tax reasons for maintaining a completely arms length operation in certain centres abroad. There is also a recognised need for operational units of a large international bank to remain flexible in order to meet local regulations, get the best from local markets and provide a required level of service for customers in a very competitive international banking environment. Opportunities to streamline and centralise the group treasury function are often missed because it would require fundamental changes to systems, structures and personnel as well as additional investment for which no immediate return can necessarily be guaranteed and these changes are generally resisted. Extra branches and subsidiaries are tacked-on to an existing framework, new business schemes are promoted, and new markets developed where a policy of expansion and diversification is apparent. Structural changes may also be necessary to ensure that the group's international banking operations are properly co-ordinated and effectively controlled.

The centralised treasury function of an international bank is essentially one of policy formulation, group control, co-ordination of liabilities and dealing operations. Local treasury functions in branches of certain subsidiary banking companies and finance houses are usually responsible for foreign exchange operations, indigenous money market operations in the local market, eurocurrency market operations (where applicable) and funding of the branches or subsidiaries' associated business as written. The local treasury function would maintain a close liaison with the central or group treasury function in respect of group philosophy with regard to the following exposures: country/sovereign – individual names – foreign exchange – maturity – remittance/retention of profits. Local regulations may well be the determining factor regarding the retention of profits and fiscal regulations often have a bearing on the method of distribution. The amount of capital, or in the case of a branch quasi-capital, which is injected from head office, will be governed by the criteria laid down by the host country's regulations of the branch or subsidiary and the anticipated nature and level of the branch or subsidiary business. In the UK, for example, branches of foreign banks which receive loans from their parent do not enjoy tax deductability on interest payments made thereon since the Inland Revenue consider them to be of a "capital" nature rather than ordinary course interbank indebtedness on which interest paid is tax deductible.

The treasury function in local branches and subsidiaries will also maintain close liaison with the internal auditor on the subject of controls and with their local management with regard to both mandatory and prudential control requirements.

Control of dealing is an essential treasury feature and technical experience by those responsible for this function is imperative. In establishing guidelines, whether by way of a written manual or some less formal arrangement, it is necessary to know where to draw the line between sensible and effective controls and those which are merely oppressive and deny dealers the opportunity to function effectively in their market. It is common practice for the central treasury or group treasury function to make surprise visits to various dealing operations throughout the group, in addition to spot checks by the bank's internal audit or inspection team. It is essential for controllers to be aware of dealers' needs and to be familiar with market conditions. Good dealers are a valuable commodity and they know it! Uncontrolled markets are more open to abuse than those which are well regulated – dealers know this too and are sometimes tempted to exploit situations which go apparently unpoliced. The treasurer, or whoever is responsible in a branch or subsidiary for one or more dealing functions, is often an experienced ex-dealer who understands the markets and dealers, and it is normal practice for large international banks to have arrangements for the local man to have regular and ready access to the central treasury with whom a regular dialogue is maintained.

Risk exposure management inclusive of asset exposure in the areas of sovereign and country debt risk and industrial specialisation may also constitute part of the responsibilities of a central treasury function.

Banks have tended to focus their thinking on several key areas to achieve greater profitability, these include:

- Improving sourcing or funding techniques by accessing a more diverse range of markets and entities with liquidity and thereby being able to attract funds as cheaply as possible. The treasury function would certainly be directly involved.

- Tightening advances/investment control policies and spreading the asset portfolio more widely in both geographical and client terms. Only an indirect involvement by the bank's treasury function would be normal.

- Developing a greater proportion of fee income to interest income – a noticeable interest by banks has been seen in the 1980s in trade related activities, securities business, financial instruments and innovative credit lines all of which tend to generate "off balance sheet" income and perhaps improve the return on total assets. Developments in which a treasury function will often take the lead.

The next two chapters of this section describe the nature of the risks inherent in treasury activities and how asset and liability management can provide objective data on which appropriate policy decisions may be based.

Banks involved in international business are often more reliant on money market funds and instruments than on customer deposits to service their loan and investment portfolios – nowhere is this more apparent than in their eurocurrency business. Sections 3 and 4 describe some specific funding instruments and discuss the various financial markets within which banks may operate.

Market conditions, particularly in those capital markets in which the bank may wish to make an issue of long-term debt securities, are monitored by the treasury or similar function on a continual basis. A centralised treasury may also be responsible for the overall co-ordination of new capital debt issues, the negotiation of detailed terms and conditions and be responsible for the movement and employment of funds eventually raised. The range and depth of the markets and nature of market instruments are discussed in Section 5 and long-term debt raising matters by a bank in Section 6. The continuing administration of loan stocks until their redemption including the optional redemption, sinking fund or note purchase strategies and compliance by the bank with all covenants and warranties, are part of the capital raising responsibilities often centralised in a bank's group treasury function. The loan stock administration will also be responsible to ensure that all payments of interest and repayments of principal are made to the relevant principal paying agent when due, and that all information of importance/relevance to stock holders is properly published. These include, for example, notices of drawn bonds, and coupon amount payable, and interest rate applicable to forthcoming interest periods on floating rate securities.

Strategic and trading portfolios in government and other securities may be held by the bank and/or various subsidiaries worldwide. From a liability and asset management involvement as well as a dealing control overview it is a logical treasury function to monitor such group activities.

Evidence of fraud may well have a damaging effect on a bank's name and reputation, not necessarily because of any direct involvement by its own staff but because it may appear that its systems and security are inadequate. Frauds are less likely to occur if there exists within the control framework of the bank a high level of technical competence in market practices, procedures and developments, backed by proven systems and alert management. Section 2, in particular Chapter 8, focuses on this subject with specific reference to dealing operations where very substantial figures are involved and the daily turnover by major banks will run into astronomic sums.

CHAPTER TWO

Exposure Management

Sections 3, 4 and 5 of this publication explain many of the activities a bank might undertake within a wide range of foreign exchange, money and capital debt markets. Whether the purpose of these operations is related to a bank's own capital or investment requirements, trading for its own account, hedging structural positions, funding purposes or covering underlying commercial business, many elements of risk are involved. Some of these risks are unique to these particular markets, others are not and have in the past been accepted as traditional and inherent risks within the nature of banking. However, they now require increased attention and consideration due to the very volatile nature of interest and exchange rate movements. Other risk considerations evolve upon the expansion of international banking itself, particularly its role in the distribution and re-cycling of the substantial disequilibrium in international balance of payments surpluses and deficits. In many instances risk is not only confined to a bank's activities within the international and wholesale domestic markets but also impacts upon the totality of a banking institution's operation.

Chapter 5 considers the supervisory authorities' approach to the prudential supervision of individual banks together with certain guidelines related to risk exposure which may be applied and within which each bank falling under those authorities' control will be expected to operate. That chapter also identifies various weaknesses and inconsistencies in current supervisory arrangements. However, these considerations aside, ultimate responsibility for the management and control of risks and exposure, as with all the other activities a bank may undertake, rests with the board and management of each individual banking institution. It is their responsibility to consider and review the totality of that institution's exposure to each risk. In discharging this responsibility it is necessary to identify all the various areas of risk to which the particular institution is exposed, assess and evaluate the possible impact each type of risk could have upon its capital structure and the continued success of its operations. Thereafter it should quantify through approved limits and policy documents, taking cognizance of any official guidelines or statutory restrictions, the types and levels of exposure that that institution is prepared to accept relative to each type of activity and with each individual counterparty. It is also necessary for management to establish a suitable system of internal control and reporting requirements to ensure compliance with these objectives and facilitate frequent reviews and monitor actual exposure on a regular basis. The whole of this process comprises Exposure Management. These responsibilities extend not only to the activities of the parent but also to those of its overseas branches, subsidiaries and associate companies.

It is the authors' opinion that in undertaking these responsibilities in relation to its activities within the international financial markets each individual bank's management should not only be concerned with its own internal risk and exposure considerations but also ensure that their decisions are consistent with, and contribute to, the continued development of orderly and sound markets. In addition, management must be conscious of the impact of market forces upon their decisions. For example in reviewing credit risk exposures the effect of exchange rate movements must be considered. For a UK bank to give a credit line to a borrower in US dollars when the £$ rate is 2.40 implies an entirely different credit risk than if the £$ rate falls to 1.20 for if the customer was unable to repay then the cost to the bank in its own reported currency would be twice as much. Within this chapter the authors develop and consider the implications of some of the various types of special risk associated with a bank's dealing and treasury operations together with exposure management issues, elements of control, and internal reporting requirements related thereto.

Credit risk relates to the risk that individual counterparties or other creditors will be unable to meet their obligations. This risk continues to be as equally important a consideration in the context of a bank's operations within the international financial markets as it is within its traditional retail operations and no business should be allowed to be undertaken with any counterparty bank or other debtor which involves credit risk unless it is within an approved limit for that type of

16

business. The subject of basic credit analysis, which is already well documented, falls outside the reference terms of this publication and therefore comment is confined to credit risk issues related to counterparty limits within the interbank markets; criteria for assessing acceptable exposure levels on individual banks together with the format of counterparty limits which may be applicable to market related activities.

The largest volume of counterparty limits within the context of the interbank markets is established on an unadvised basis, in other words there is no underlying commitment to undertake business. As developed under reference to the Measurement of Capital Adequacy in Chapter 5, without additional information which is probably only known to each individual bank's management, it is difficult to undertake a meaningful appraisal of a bank's true financial strength merely based upon the information available in published accounts. However, such assessments are undertaken and unadvised limits established often without any direct discussion or contact with a counterparty but merely on the knowledge that the name in question is active in the markets. Consequently, within each bank it is important that management approve the parameters of approach and criteria upon which interbank credit assessment is to be based within its own institution. Whatever additional factors are taken into consideration the prime issue will be those related to published accounts, i.e. capital resources and capital/asset (gearing) ratios, albeit this latter measure has a further constraint insofar as acceptable ratios differ substantially from country to country and organisation to organisation. Other factors considered may incorporate overall size and world ranking, the standing of a bank in its own country, official supervision therein and its central bank's possible attitude to support and/or lender of last resort issues. Its reputation within the international financial markets is important. Caution will be exercised where a bank is considered to be over-trading or expanding the size of its operations without prudential consideration of its capital base. The most recently published financial results are reviewed in detail. Substantial losses or other adverse figures will impact upon the size of limit one bank is prepared to approve in favour of another. Known strengths and reputations of management are a further factor together with a bank's spread of activities. The overriding measurement as to the maximum level of exposure provided to any one name will be a function of the approving institution's own capital risk ratios.

Within the context of unadvised facilities it is important to emphasise that lines can be instantly withdrawn, subject to the proviso that current exposure will only be expected to be eliminated within the terms of each specific contract. Whilst this procedure may provide some internal comfort particularly in considering liquidity and country risk exposure issues, the opinion is expressed that the control of this facility places on each bank's management an added responsibility towards facilitating the continuance of orderly markets. Whilst prime considerations must be a bank's own interests, and prudency must prevail, many instances have been seen where unsubstantiated rumour relating to a particular bank has resulted in the indiscriminate withdrawal of unadvised facilities to that bank without due recognition or consideration being given as to the foundation of the rumour or the level and extent of official support that would be available if there was in fact a real problem. In many of these situations the action of cancelling lines has in itself precipitated a major liquidity crisis for the bank concerned.

For credit control purposes, limits in favour of another bank's subsidiaries or associate companies should normally be considered in isolation of the parent, based on the strength of the subsidiary or associate as a separate entity. A basic assumption of ultimate parental responsibility will not normally be given undue weighting within the assessment unless guarantees or other formal support are established. Subject to the considerations of local regulations or restrictions, overseas branch operations are normally considered on the basis of the parent institution. However, this is not always the case and for judicious reasons individual banks may not be prepared to extend facilities to specific branches of an international bank's operations so freely, particularly where claused confirmations, restricting repayment terms are in evidence or where there is particular concern in relation to primary country risk.

Each bank will have established policy for the level of internal authority required for the approval of limits, frequency of review, report and ratification by a bank's management or, as appropriate,

18

board. A bank may vary these policies for facilities which fall within its own established credit assessment criteria for banks and those that do not comply with such criteria. Differentials have in the past been drawn by some banks between requirements for banks in a selected top strata of world rankings and other institutions. However experience now proves that even some of the largest of banks can run into serious financial difficulties. This, together with the fact that accepted ratios for banks (together with the level of regulatory supervision to which they are subject) differ so considerably from area to area, makes it questionable as to whether this procedure has merit.

The type of credit limit which management have to consider applying to any particular counterparty, be it bank, corporate or other market participant with whom the bank deals within the international financial markets, will be dependent upon the nature of the underlying business it envisages undertaking; the manner in which it will be transacted together with market practice and settlement procedures related thereto.

Within both the interbank deposit and foreign exchange markets it is customary for each contract to be settled in full at maturity or value dates. However, in the commodity and precious metals markets, counterparties normally only settle the net difference of all contracts maturing with each other on any particular value or settlement date. Within futures markets, it is usual for a clearing house to stand at the centre of all trades thus relieving counterparties of credit risk issues on each other but replacing it with exposure to the clearing house. Upon granting an option the premium may be the only credit issue which a grantor has to consider. Conversely, the purchaser of an option will be concerned with credit exposure issues on the grantor during the life of the contract. If an option is exercised, both the grantor and purchaser may require to deliver. Within the secondary markets a bank will not only be concerned with credit risk considerations relating to the issuer of the underlying security but will also have to consider risks associated with the counterparty with whom the trade is transacted.

Within the deposit markets, both international and domestic, the major credit risk consideration is the ability of the counterparty to repay at maturity. Approved lending limits will clearly define loans which may be made available to a particular name and will usually incorporate time constraints. Larger limits will be given for shorter dated facilities and banks will differentiate between various periods when approving limits, e.g. overnight, call up to one month, up to three months, up to six months, and will, as appropriate, specify longer dated facilities which may be provided. Unadvised facilities which allow for loans beyond a six month period tend to be the exception rather than the rule. Loan approvals will also normally identify the types of business which may be written in a particular name, e.g. money facilities, CDs, acceptances, etc., and, in the absence of any inner constraint, limits will relate to total exposure whether transacted through the primary or secondary markets.

Credit risk considerations for foreign exchange limits differ from those for lending where a bank is concerned with the creditworthiness of a counterparty during the total period of a loan. A foreign exchange contract involves the receipt of one currency against the payment of another on the agreed value date, at which point each counterparty has a "delivery risk" which is the risk that it may pay away good value funds subsequently to find that it has not received the corresponding settlement. A "delivery" or "spot" limit is usually established to cover this exposure. Secondly, a counterparty "position risk" is to be considered in that prior to value date a counterparty's inability to meet future obligations is apparent. In this event actual exposure would be restricted to the possible cost related to closing out the counterparty's contracts at current exchange rate levels. Therefore in addition to a delivery risk limit, a limit will be placed on the total aggregate of outstanding purchases and sales with total exposure monitored thereto. However, in recognition that the real value of this latter risk is far less than the face value of the contracts, it is customary in most banks to apply only a percentage of this total limit and utilisation when considering and reviewing the actual credit exposure to a particular name. The applied percentage will be varied by management from time to time dependent upon the current volatility of exchange rates, and in normal circumstances will be between 10 and 25 per cent.

Where market practice calls for full settlement of each contract a corollary to the concept of delivery and total forward exposure is that consideration must also be given to the aggregate of purchase and sales that mature on any one value date in the future, to ensure that delivery limits are not exceeded by maturing forward contracts. These limits are frequently referred to as "valeur compensée" (V.C.) limits or future delivery risk limits and will not be greater than the delivery limit imposed for any one value date. In summary, the three types of limit which will normally be approved for foreign exchange activity together with figures by way of illustration are:

- "Delivery" or "spot" limit   US$10 million
- "V.C." or future value date limit   US$10 million
- Total aggregate forward
  outstandings, purchases and sales   US$100 million

To calculate credit exposure:
    Delivery limit   US$10 million
    Plus say 20% of the forward limit   US$20 million
             Total   US$30 million

Within several primary, secondary and security markets arrangements frequently exist to exchange simultaneously, either through a wire (electronic) or physical clearing facility or over the counter, the relative underlying security for good value payment. In these circumstances delivery limits are not normally established for counterparties. However, in other securities markets over the counter delivery may be made against anticipated receipt of good value funds or against an uncleared payment instruction. In these circumstances appropriate delivery limits will have to be established.

Within the gold and other commodity markets it is customary to net purchases and sales due between counterparties on any particular value date. In these circumstances ultimate delivery exposure continues to be an important consideration and suitable limits are established to cover this risk. However, valeur compensée limits are not applied as subsequent trades will affect the potential delivery risk for each future value date. It is also common practice in these markets

21

for a principal to establish the right to net a counterparty's long and short positions irrespective of value dates. Position limits are established within which the net open positions both physical and forward are monitored. If extant open positions exist in two or more commodities against the same counterparty limit these will, in the absence of any formal arrangements, normally not be netted but aggregated for monitoring purposes. Initial and/or variation margins are frequently called for, the latter being based on a daily 'mark to market' of open outstanding positions to establish profit or loss exposure due to or from each counterparty. As explained elsewhere within this publication, the basis of these calls when off exchange are subject to negotiation and agreement between individual counterparties. Margin calls may be made in full or be subject to profit and loss limits which when exceeded will trigger a margin call which, if not complied with, will provide the principal with the right to close out all outstanding positions and obtain legal redress for any shortfalls incurred.

In option trading, delivery limits will only be a consideration if ultimate delivery is requested or anticipated. Normally this type of transaction will be closed out with any resultant profit being paid by the grantor to the buyer of the option. Grantors of options may be the subject of margin requirements and in such instances appropriate profit and loss limits will be established. Where margin is not applicable, a buyer of an option will establish a credit limit to the extent to which he will accept the name of a grantor. Exposure under these limits will be by reference to the "in the money" value of any contract. A grantor will normally establish limits in respect of premiums due to him.

Country risk refers to the possibility that sovereign borrowers of a particular country may be unable or unwilling, and other borrowers unable, to fulfil their foreign currency obligations for reasons beyond the usual risks which arise in relation to all lending. Sovereign risk arises from the special risk associated with a sovereign loan which is a loan to, or one guaranteed by, a government. The special significance of sovereign risk lies in the risk that it might prove impossible to secure redress through legal action, i.e. the borrower might claim immunity from process or might not abide by a judgment. For country risk purposes, sovereign lending is treated as constituting part of a bank's total exposure and, although the subjects of sovereign and country risk are closely related, sovereign risk is ultimately a credit risk.

Resultant from the third world debt crisis, the subject of the management of country risk and exposure has assumed increased importance and attracted greater attention. An individual bank or banking group's country exposure is its total external claims on borrowers in individual foreign countries and it is incumbent upon a bank's management to ensure that it does not become disproportionately at risk if a particular country with whom it has exposure runs into economic difficulties. Each bank normally has a process of country risk assessment which, as with bank risk assessment, will require management to define the parameters of approach to this task. First considerations will evolve upon whatever statistical information is available. A country's current external debt, official reserves, balance of payments, exchange, interest and inflation rate trends together with its ability to, and record of, servicing and repaying its debt will be considered. Economic developments and potential social and political stability, the possible impact of external factors such as world recessions, conflict or natural disasters together with the impact of movement in basic commodity prices, particularly oil, will all play a role. These assessments and frequent reviews thereof will be considered in conjunction with the individual bank's own prudential considerations relating to capital etc., and thereafter a bank's management will establish maximum levels of exposure it is prepared to accept for each country, normally differentiating between short- and medium-term risk and perhaps incorporating various sub-divisions relating to its mix of business. Whilst country limits themselves will constitute part of the normal credit approval process, consolidated reports reflecting country limits, total commitments and utilisation will be frequently prepared and reviewed by management.

Country risk exposure is a complex subject which requires an examination of the totality of a bank's assets which cross national boundaries. Each parent bank will require to consider its treatment of the activities of, and its activities with, its overseas branches, subsidiaries and affiliates. Additionally, it will require to consider its own criteria in reviewing its exposure on the overseas branches, subsidiaries and affiliates of other institutions. Within the context of country risk it is necessary to consider both primary and transfer (or secondary) risk. The primary risk allocation is determined by the location of a borrowing entity. However, where the borrowing entity is itself an overseas branch, subsidiary or affiliate of a parent to whom the creditor bank could reasonably, in case of need, assume parental responsibility for a debt, there is also a transfer risk to be considered on the country of domicile of the parent. Conversely, where a parent bank accepts parental responsibility for the obligations of its branches, subsidiaries or associates, it will require to consider a primary risk against the country of domicile of that branch, subsidiary or affiliate. For example, if the Panama-based subsidiary of a London bank borrowed US Dollars from a Japanese bank in Tokyo against the London parent's guarantee, the Japanese bank would have a primary risk on Panama and a transfer risk on the United Kingdom. The London-based bank would have created a primary risk on Panama. A bank's management will, when reviewing country exposure, consider figures in relation to both primary and transfer risk.

There are extensive legal, economic and prudential implications concerning transfer risk and therefore considerations relating thereto are dependent upon the subjective views of the management of each bank and differences of opinion will occur. It has in the past been common practice to assume a parental transfer risk in relation to country risk issues associated with lending to overseas branches of a bank. However, the recent refusal of a major US bank with a branch in the Philippines to meet this assumed obligation has resulted in individual banks reviewing their stance and, whilst continuing to assume a transfer risk, it is quite common for banks to differentiate between other banks' overseas branches on primary country risk considerations.

The position of subsidiaries and associate companies is more definitive. In law a shareholder is only primarily liable to the extent of his capital commitment to a company, be it subsidiary or affiliate, except where any legally binding additional facilities have been extended or agreed to. Therefore when considering country risk as with credit risk a creditor of another bank's overseas subsidiary or associate should not assume a transfer risk and, similarly, the parent may not consider itself to have any legal obligations.

24

Whilst for prudential reasons banks are frequently required to consider the cross border liabilities of subsidiary and associate companies on a consolidated basis, this should not be taken to imply parental responsibility. Many subsidiaries of a large international bank may in their own right be substantial banks within the country of their operations. Negotiating advised facilities with another bank's subsidiary without any reference or advice to the parent institution of such discussions or arrangements, or alternatively, undertaking transactions within unadvised lines should be taken to imply that parental responsibility was not sought or expected.

It is usual, when considering both commitments and exposure in relation to country risk, to consider all balance sheet and off-balance sheet items, e.g. acceptances, commitments under a bank's own letters of credit, confirmations of other banks' credits, liabilities under guarantees and letters of comfort. Transfer risk can arise where no primary risk exists, e.g. lending to a branch of an overseas parent in domestic money markets.

Whilst the treatment of many items is readily apparent special attention requires to be given to unadvised lending limits, overdraft facilities and foreign exchange and other trading limits. It is reasonable to assume that for unadvised facilities commitment and current utilisation are the same. Inclusion of a commitment figure for overdraft facilities may range from current utilisation up to a total of all limits plus any excesses dependent upon internal policy and, where appropriate, agreement with supervisory authorities. Whilst it is recognised that an element of foreign exchange and other counterparty trading limits are related to country risk, it is a matter of subjective view as to whether it is necessary to incorporate them within the country risk analysis exercise as the main risk is a one day delivery situation whereas country exposure analysis is primarily related to short- and medium-term issues.

In June 1982 the Basle Committee issued a paper entitled "Management of banks' international lending: country risk analysis and country exposure measurement and control" which sets out for banks a number of considerations, recommendations and guidelines which the Committee consider banks should bear in mind when establishing or reviewing country risk assessment and control systems. The purpose of the report is also to encourage the development of a standardisation of approach by banks when considering these subjects, the advantages of which would be:

- to give banks some assurance that their system of measurement conforms at least to some minimum standards

- to allow aggregation in summary form for banking groups nationally and globally for the statistical reference of all participants in the market

- to enable individual banks to assess their own exposure in comparison with others – information which will be of value to both senior management and supervisors

Part I of the paper deals with banks' assessment of country risk, suggesting factors which require consideration. It recognises that country risk assessment cannot be an exact science, but an art in which a significant degree of unpredictability must be acknowledged. Part II covers subjects relating to a bank's measurement of country exposure, including primary and transfer risk considerations, consolidation of country exposure figures for each bank and includes suggestions for the break-down of certain balance sheet and off balance sheet items. Part III considers the establishment of limits and control systems. It emphasises that this process should take account of the size and nature of the bank itself, the perceived economic strength and stability of the borrowing country and the bank's spread of risk or existing portfolio diversification. Limits should be set on prudential grounds and not on marketing grounds. Finally this section touches upon the subject of rescheduling and additional considerations that may apply in this event. Section IV of the report covers the subject of the role of the banking supervisor in regard to country risk considerations.

Credit, country and sovereign risk considerations are all specifically related to exposure with individual counterparties. Other areas of risk which require to be considered within a bank's exposure management, concern those internal elements of risk created by, or inherent within a bank's asset/liability portfolio, inclusive of commitments and its dealing and trading activities. These subjects are associated with the impact of interest rate risk, maturity mis-match risk, liquidity risk, open position risk and currency risk, to which a bank is exposed in its day to day activities.

Whilst a bank is unable independently to control or influence the extent of price movements which give rise to some of these risks, it is able to quantify in absolute terms the total amount of assets/liabilities upon which it is prepared to accept this type of exposure. The main considerations in establishing such parameters are the relationship and possible adverse impact of each type of risk upon the bank's free capital base.

Increased volatility in both exchange rate movements, and more recently, interest rate levels have, on several occasions, precipitated substantial losses, and at times irretrievable situations for several banks. These movements have also resulted in increased attention being placed both upon asset/liability management and group strategy to contain these exposures. It is now quite common for banks with an extensive branch network to centralise (as far as possible) the management and control of asset/liability exposures at strategically placed treasury divisions and dealing centres, thereby following a policy within which all but very short-dated interest rate risks and mis-matched positions, together with a small element of foreign exchange business to cover customer requirements, are the responsibility of a specialist market-orientated unit.

Interest rate risk is the risk associated with applying different bases of interest rates to assets and corresponding liabilities – for example, lending or borrowing medium- or long-term funds at fixed rates of interest and funding such assets or utilising such liabilities against short-dated interest rate structures which will fluctuate throughout the period of the loan. Despite the maxim of banks not lending long and borrowing short, in an environment of controlled interest rate structures many banks in the past were able to develop substantial interest rate exposures within their advances/deposit portfolios without incurring losses: appreciation of this risk was only recognised when some of these markets moved to floating rate structures. The demise of many Savings and Loans Associations in the United States was as a result of mis-managed exposure to interest rate risks and more recently, some West German banks found themselves encountering a problem related to the same exposure with fixed rate medium- and long-term investment portfolios being funded with short-term and even overnight monies in an environment of rising interest rates.

In the context of its activities within the international financial markets, a bank as a matter of course would not accept this type of interest rate exposure as a part of its day to day activities and any risk of this nature would normally require the specific authority of senior management. Although an element of longer dated fixed rate lending is evident within the markets, this is normally funded by similar period, fixed rate liabilities or hedged with other financial instruments, e.g. futures. However, this does not mean that banks do not raise capital, invest and trade in, medium- and long-term fixed rate instruments as part of their investment, trading or business strategies.

Substantial fixed rate capital issues are frequently made by banks and substantial portfolios of fixed rate bonds and other securities are held. Whilst some banks will accept the interest rate risk on capital issues, particularly where there is a capital expenditure project directly related thereto, there is an increasing tendency to exchange such funds (if merely raised for capital gearing) for floating rate liabilities through the swap markets so that they should relate more closely to the yield of the underlying assets being funded. Portfolios may be developed through the management and investment of a bank's free capital and reserves where management criteria is to maximise rates of return thereon, the success of which is measured against opportunity cost criteria. In this context the subject of interest rate risk is not necessarily a prime consideration. Many banks operate fund management schemes at arms length in subsidiary companies and some relate to fixed rate instruments. However, the return to the investor is represented by the rate of return achieved by the fund managers and therefore the bank itself is not directly exposed to an interest rate risk. Another area of operation in fixed rate assets is within trading and underwriting portfolios. Those assets will for the purposes of exposure management be treated as an outright position in bonds, securities or other instruments in the same manner as foreign exchange or any other open position exposure.

There are also many areas of the world in which international banks operate where statutory requirements are such that banks require to have minimum holdings of specified investments, some of which are fixed rate medium- or long-dated stock in a quantity related to either their overall asset or liability position or their total statutory assets. As with other exposures of this nature, senior management within banks will require to be advised of these situations, and, as appropriate, they will authorise appropriate risk limits thus controlling in absolute terms the totality of that bank's exposure.

Maturity mis-match or 'gapping' risk is the risk associated with the movement in interest rates and interest rate differentials between assets and liabilities which are priced on the same basis, e.g. interbank or prime, but are mis-matched in time. As part of a dealing operation, it is normally accepted policy to provide treasury areas with authority to establish mis-matched positions to enable them to structure their various currency portfolios in anticipation of interest rate movements, allow an element of flexibility in managing short-dated liquidity positions and avoid pressure on balance sheet footings being created through excessive entry into the interbank markets for the purpose of maturity matching. Management will normally establish limits by currency within which these mis-matches are to be contained. Each limit will incorporate constraints as to the periods for which such mis-matches can be established and will normally include a net, by currency or aggregate, progressive figure which must not be exceeded.

As discussed in detail in Chapter 16, it is also common practice to run managed maturity mis-matches within a bank's spot and forward exchange portfolio. Whilst taking nostro, one day value, spot and forward positions together, a bank may have a square overall position, mis-matches in the value dates of individual contracts making up the forward portfolio will within established limits be permitted. This will enable positions to be structured to take advantage of interest rate movements as reflected by the differentials in the swap prices and facilitate the management of short-dated liquidity positions. The format of these limits will be similar to those for placings and deposits.

Open position dealing or trading risk is the risk associated with a bank being long or short for its own account, on an outright basis, of a foreign currency, bullion, commodity, stock, bond or other security in the physical or futures markets at any point in time in the course of its day to day operations. This exposure remains open until an opposite deal is undertaken to square or hedge the position. Within the international financial markets, even the briefest period can be sufficient time to transform a potentially profitable outright position into a substantial loss. An open or outright position is the resultant net difference of an actual asset or liability position in a particular instrument adjusted by the total extant commitment to buy and sell that currency, security or commodity in the future.

Within its consideration of open position risk, a bank is not concerned with the time mis-match between purchases and sales or the implied cost of carry as reflected by forward premiums and discounts, but with the absolute gross impact of subsequent price movements on a net long (overbought), or net short (oversold) outright position.

To control dealing risk exposure the management of each bank will establish appropriate limits within which outright open positions are to be contained in each type of instrument or currency traded. Separate limits will normally be approved for end of day positions and intra-day or daylight positions. The size of limits will differ considerably between banks dependent upon their size, the levels of risk they are prepared to accept together with their overall strategy towards trading activities. Many banks adopt a prudent and conservative stance towards these risks, preferring to rely on profitability from intra-day jobbing or spread trading expertise. Whilst accepting a reasonable level of outright exposure during the day, these banks will expect dealers to revert to end of day limits at levels which are square to near square.

Other banks take a more aggressive stance and will allow open positions to reflect short-dated views on exchange rate and other price movements, frequently in very sizeable amounts. This will be reflected within the end of day limits established but will also normally specify a senior officer or officers who approve each position taken.

Limits established for intra-day trading are generally much larger than those allowed for overnight positions and will frequently distinguish between the size of dealing positions that may be created in the normal course of a bank's own account trading and larger temporary positions which may be required to accommodate underlying customer interests. Some banks prefer not to establish intra-day dealing limits but to control outright exposure by placing limits on the maximum size of transactions permitted which must then be closed down within a specific time constraint. It is also increasingly common for management to place individual stop-loss limits on positions to ensure dealers close out a loss-making position rather than incur the risk that a position will further deteriorate.

Within the context of foreign currency exposure risk, a bank will also require to consider the impact of future exchange rate movements on both its foreign currency income flow and any corporate structural positions maintained. Until such time as foreign currency income, whether resultant from direct business activities, profit or dividend remittances, is sold or hedged, any exchange rate movement against the reported currency will impact upon profit and loss figures. Management will therefore formulate policy and strategy in relation to covering or hedging this risk with the objective of maximising its reported profits. This may be achieved within either one or a mix of the following: cash, futures, forward, currency swaps or option transactions. These considerations will include any current year's earnings even though some may ultimately be held as retained profits within operating subsidiaries.

Corporate structural positions are normally of a longer- term nature than dealing or income flow positions and usually relate to a bank's fixed and long-term currency asset and liability positions. A bank will not normally during the course of its daily activities borrow in one currency and lend in another without covering the exchange risk. However, outright structural positions may of necessity have to be established or created for a variety of reasons, for example:

- net capital investments in branch, subsidiary and affiliate companies.

- the utilisation of excess liquidity in another currency where a bank is unable satisfactorily to deploy resources within the appropriate domestic currency due to local laws or market conditions, and a forward swap market of sufficient depth is not available to cover the exchange risk related thereto.

- reserves or provisions maintained in currencies appropriate to the risk against which they are held.

As each bank's structural foreign exchange position will relate to these and other special situations, some of which in the case of banks falling within the supervisory authority of the Bank of England, would require the Bank's prior agreement to be treated as such, they will normally be considered and approved by senior management on a case by case basis and be outside the day-to-day control of the dealing room. Subsequent reviews and adjustments thereto will also be similarly subject to management's specific consideration. Within this process, management will consider the underlying reasons for the positions being created, evaluate as far as it can be determined the extent of the impact of exchange rate risk upon its reserves and consider whether or if, this could be minimised through a hedging strategy which may involve cash, future, forward or option positions, or by holding one particular currency with a close correlation to the base currency or through the deployment of a basket of currencies.

The revaluation and accounting principles for dealing, investment and structural positions are developed in Chapter 32. However, at this juncture it is pertinent to reflect briefly upon the impact of translation exposure. Translation exposure arises from the influence of exchange rate fluctuation on the consolidated balance sheet when incorporating the figures of foreign branches and subsidiary companies which maintain their assets and liabilities in foreign currencies. Although this exposure is a consequence of an accounting function, it can impact considerably upon the free capital base, ultimate balance sheet size and consequently the gearing ratios of a bank, particularly where a high percentage of a bank's free capital resources are main-

tained in the reported currency albeit the main asset/liability consti-
tuents of the balance sheet are in various currencies. The possibility
of such distortions make it necessary for management to consider the
viability of the establishment of structural positions by raising or
transferring capital resources between currencies to equate approximately with the currency mix of the underlying asset base or otherwise hedge against these movements.

There are also other special exposure risks to be considered in
relation to futures and option activities. In futures trading whether
for hedging or trading purposes the adverse impact on cash flow
projections through variation margin calls must not be overlooked.
During periods of high volatility in price movements these can be
substantial, and limits in absolute terms should be formulated within
which variation margin requirements are to be contained. The granting of call options on an uncovered basis exposes a bank to unlimited
risk on a rising market while the granting of put options gives rise to a
quantifiable but nevertheless substantial risk on a falling market.
Unless a bank is operating within the parameters of a proven pricing
and hedging module – a subject which is discussed in further detail in
Chapter 18 – all options granted should be considered in terms of
potential outright exposures. Additionally, as with futures, the impact of any negative margin requirements must also be quantified.

Liquidity risk is the risk related to a bank being unable to continue
to obtain funds to meet its commitments, or having to pay a substantial premium to do so, and is considered in conjunction with Asset
and Liability Management in Chapter 3. This risk is usually associated with the problems that a bank, through its activities, has incurred and which have detracted from its ability to continue to obtain
deposits. However, in terms of the international markets, liquidity
risk also has other implications not always relevant to the standing of
a particular bank. These are more particularly concerned with the
ability of the market to be able or willing to continue to meet the
increasing demands being placed upon it for funding purposes especially by banks lacking a substantial base in a particular currency. The
extent of maturity transformation which takes place within the euro
and other offshore markets continues to escalate. This results from
banks extending medium- and long-term facilities to customers upon

the basis of floating interest rate structures related to, and often dependent upon their continuing ability to obtain relatively short-dated market funds to cover these commitments. The euro markets do not have any formal lender of last resort facilities available to them and are interest rate-sensitive markets in which the level of liquidity may be erratic.

A bank's ability to obtain funds at the finest rates and indeed to retain the confidence of its depositors will depend to a large extent on management ensuring that its capital adequacy, balance sheet ratios and exposure to loss are maintained at acceptable levels. Cognizance must also be given to external forces. In particular the perception of investors and market participants to its country of domicile and major activities together with the implications of its reliance upon the continuing liquidity of specific markets. These objectives all constitute part of the exposure management process. In addition, a bank recognises the need to retain or improve the market's perception of the quality of its name since this is essential to ensure a healthy and continued access to its sources of funds.

Adverse credit exposure decisions will be reflected in increased debt provisions. Adverse dealing, maturity mis-matches, interest rate, currency and other exposure will lead to losses which will adversely impact upon either current profit and loss or reserves and can be very serious if they are allowed to occur. All of these factors will affect free capital ratios, diminish the return available on shareholders funds and restrict the expansion of a bank's business. These events will also influence other banks' perception of appropriate credit risk limits and this could precipitate liquidity problems. Although in the short-term a bank may be able to sustain the impact of running losses its inability to repay deposits immediately puts it out of business. Management will continually review consolidated figures to ensure that acceptable ratios are maintained and, if appropriate, strategies will be formulated to direct activities to achieve this objective by ensuring the retention of sufficient profits or raising additional debt or equity capital.

CHAPTER THREE

Asset and Liability Management

Current asset and liability management is one of the prime responsibilities of the treasury operations of a bank. The importance of this function has escalated over recent years for various reasons inclusive of:

- An increased reliance by banks on market-related sources for funding purposes.

- A greater awareness of the importance of adequacy of balance sheet ratios and gearing.

- The failure of several banks over the past decade to meet their obligations – often resulting from a lack of attention to asset and liability and other exposure management matters.

- Increased volatility in exchange and interest rate movements.

- Diminishing levels of margin and return on earning assets.

Within the internal process of asset and liability management, a bank is primarily concerned with three inter-related issues:

- Cash Management

- Interest Rate Sensitivity

- Liquidity

Considerations in relation to these separate issues may evolve upon both extant and projected positions and will incorporate the control of day to day cash positions in each currency, individual currency portfolios in both domestic and foreign currency, together with the totality of a bank's current asset and liability portfolio irrespective of currency. Where regulations allow, assets in one currency may be funded by obligations in another currency through simultaneous spot and forward transactions in the foreign exchange markets. However, most banks exercise strict controls and conservative judgment on the extent to which assets in one currency may be funded through liabilities in another even though there may be an offsetting forward transaction.

Within a large banking organisation responsibility for the generation and line management of many individual functions will probably be vested in various operational areas outside of the treasury, and therefore a continuous and instant flow of information is necessary for treasury purposes. The major issues in this context upon which the treasury will focus are:

- The mix of assets and liabilities

- The source of liabilities

- External cash balances

- The pricing structures of both assets and liabilities

- Maturity and cash flow profiles

- Liquifiable assets

- Mobilisation of deposits and the utilisation of internal liquid resources

- The funding of assets on the best possible terms

- Balance sheet considerations

- Judicious use of the bank's name

Where a bank has several treasury operations strategically placed around the world there are some elements of the asset and liability management processes, particularly those relating to the day to day control of cash positions where separate nostro accounts are maintained, that may be undertaken locally and sometimes with a degree of autonomy. However, interest rate sensitivity and liquidity have major strategic implications and will constitute both local and centralised issues.

A bank's liability and asset mix can be defined in various broad categories by type, period and pricing. Liabilities may include a mix of current account credit balances, savings account balances, wholesale and retail deposits, the proceeds of certificates of deposit and commercial paper issues, re-purchase agreements, capital debt instruments and shareholders equity. Assets will in the main comprise private, corporate and inter-bank lending together with sizeable holdings of marketable securities such as treasury bills, treasury bonds, local authority or municipal bills and bonds, bankers acceptances, government securities, certificates of deposit, capital debt instruments, investment in and the provision of working capital to other group areas.

The life or period of individual assets and liabilities may be measured in both terms of days to final maturity, repayment or redemption, or days to the next interest rate period on floating rate transactions. Deposits are taken for repayment on demand or at sight, at short notice or on a fixed-term basis for various periods. Capital debt instruments are frequently issued by banks for various periods and may or may not provide for early redemption. Similarly, assets will be a mix of those repayable on demand through to those repayable at various fixed or scheduled repayment dates in the future.

From the point of view of pricing, liabilities will comprise both non-interest bearing and interest bearing funds. Although the majority of assets will be interest bearing, an element of non-earning compensating balances may require to be held for working or statutory purposes. Additionally, some advances will constitute past due, doubtful or non-performing loans.

The pricing structure, i.e. the levels of interest rates applicable to both assets and liabilities will vary by account and transaction type.

Interest rates may be priced on fixed or floating rate structures related to or associated with advertised, base, prime or other similar retail banking or trade related rates. Alternatively, pricing may be at fixed or floating rates associated with various domestic or offshore market-related rates – for example interbank offered or bid, certificate of deposit, commercial paper, eligible, ineligible, trade and treasury bill rates. Other fixed rate pricing will be based upon perceived rates for longer dated monies as reflected in the medium- or long-term capital markets.

Within the context of asset and liability management the individual identity of the many items which make up these broad groups of assets and liabilities are of little significance to the treasurer, provided he is able to identify those main elements already mentioned, define them into maturity bands, quantify their impact upon day to day cash movements, consider the quality of marketable securities, the extent of future commitments to lend and differentiate between the source of funds.

Within liability management, the relative stability of a bank's deposit base is of prime importance and will, in addition to overall economic, financial, country, and market liquidity conditions, be influenced by both the depositors and the markets perception of that bank's creditworthiness. The likely volatility of deposits, particularly those of a short-term (retail) nature repayable at call or demand, may be different from those which are market related. The latter are likely to be more volatile and responsive to adverse factors or rumours related to a particular bank's standing. Consequently a major objective within liability management will be to attain a diversified deposit portfolio by source and maturity as both a prudent and protective measure.

Cash Management
During each day a bank's treasury operation will analyse the bank's daily actual and projected cash position in each of the currencies in which it operates. A bank's payments in various currencies on any one day may well comprise, among other things, drawdowns on overdrafts and loans, drawings on current accounts, repayment of de-

posits, the purchase value of any assets bought, interest payments, fees and commissions, operating expenses, taxation and dividends. Receipts may be represented by new deposits, repayment of loans or reductions in overdrafts, cleared credits to current accounts, the gross proceeds of any marketable assets sold together with any fee, commission interest or dividend income. Additionally, both assets and liabilities in each currency will be impacted upon by the net amount of any foreign currency exchange deals which are for settlement that day.

A bank's real end of day cash position is represented by cleared funds on its nostro accounts. For clearers in the United Kingdom, major money centre banks in the United States and banks with large domestic operations in other countries, nostro balances in domestic currencies will normally constitute their accounts held with, respectively, the Bank of England, the Federal Reserve or other central monetary authority. Other banks' domestic and each bank's foreign currency nostro balance will usually comprise the net cleared balance on their clearing or overseas correspondent bank account in each currency. Where more than one nostro account is held in a currency, the bank's true net cash position in that currency will be represented by the net of the balances on each account.

Within the cash management exercise a treasury is primarily concerned with the movement of funds in each currency outside of its own operations, i.e. funds being received by, or paid away from, its nostro accounts. The internal movement of funds within a currency between the bank and its clients, from client to client or between a client's different types of account do not constitute external cash movements. However, where more than one nostro account is maintained in a currency it is necessary within the cash management exercise to record separately the movements on each of these accounts in order that the balance of each is maintained within agreed guidelines at the end of each day. Where necessary, transfers between these accounts are arranged.

Each day the treasury will record and revise the assessed balances and for the major currencies of operation agreed cleared balances on each of its nostro accounts. These balances will be adjusted by any uncleared items anticipated to come into value that day: then, within the confines of agreed reporting lines and other internal procedures for trading, the treasury will monitor and control the deployment and funding of these accounts in each currency.

The objective of this exercise is to ensure that the bank's day to day cash positions are employed to the maximum advantage of the bank and that any shortfall positions are covered. At the end of each day the balance of each account will be expected to be maintained at the lowest possible levels within the agreed criteria for the establishment of the account. Such criteria will normally be clearly defined.

Nostro accounts maintained with correspondent banks or a bank's own overseas operations may be charged solely on a fee basis related to transactions processed or may require a specific level of compensating or other form of credit balance to be maintained. Some accounts will encourage credit balances as interest is payable thereon. The majority however require interest to be paid on debit balances, often at penal rates of interest. Where regulations or agreements permit overdrafts on nostro accounts, any utilisation will normally be related to the highest or closing overnight money market rates for a particular day. This procedure is to discourage banks from using such facilities as a convenience in periods of day to day liquidity shortages in the money markets.

Within a climate of relatively high and volatile interest rates the internal day to day management of a bank's cash position has become a specialised subject with major banks developing systems of instant internal communication to monitor movements. Also many banks have developed sophisticated computer and communication systems related to money transfer and balance reporting systems for the use of both their bank and commercial clients.

Throughout any particular day a bank can only estimate its anticipated cash position as at the end of that day on the basis of anticipated cash movements. During the day the actual accounts will reflect substantial swings from debit to credit as various payments and receipts are recorded. It is not until the end of a business day at the place where the account is maintained that the actual balance is apparent. The non-receipt of anticipated funds or receipt of funds which were not expected will result in lower or higher day-end balances on the accounts than forecast. Within the international and domestic financial markets it is normal practice to incorporate a value date on each payment order which instructs the correspondent of the exact date upon which a payment is to be made in cleared funds. Additionally many correspondent banks will accept value dated "receive instructions" and are prepared to monitor receipt of funds on behalf of the beneficiary bank and, as appropriate, investigate non-receipt. However, irrespective of these procedures funds frequently are not received or paid on the appropriate value date, and in these circumstances it is normally accepted practice to request or make payment with good value, or to claim for compensating interest directly from the bank's counterparty or client.

Where funds are being paid or received by mail or other form of paper transfer as compared to electronic transfers, i.e. cheques, travellers cheques, mail transfers, bills for collection, negotiations etc., it is not always possible to determine accurately when good value funds will be received or paid away from a nostro account. This is a particular feature where large retail foreign trade related operations are concerned. Usually in these circumstances the day to day cash management exercise will estimate an ultimate cash position based upon assessed mail and clearing collection periods, but this may still result in large surpluses or shortfalls over anticipated positions. Wherever possible arrangements will be made to compensate for these discrepancies. Many correspondent banks will now provide facilities whereby surplus resources at the end of each day will be employed within the local money markets and appropriate interest rates applied to these balances. In the United States of America the payment of credit interest on current account balances is prohibited. However, cash management facilities are available whereby such balances may be transferred to interest-bearing accounts.

From the above it is evident that the day to day cash movements of one bank can impact upon the daily cash flow of another and a similar situation exists with regard to large corporate clients. Therefore in practice, so long as no specific advice to the contrary is received, note will be taken of anticipated receipts and payments to cover individual client bank's positions and, whilst closely monitoring such movements, no action will be taken until an actual end of day net position becomes apparent. Additionally a regular dialogue is frequently maintained between bank officers responsible for these controls and their respective clients to determine ultimate end of day positions as accurately as possible.

It is appropriate at this point briefly to mention the role of a correspondent bank. The relationship between an account-holding and correspondent bank is no different from a normal creditor/debtor or bank/client relationship. Without any formal arrangements being made to the contrary there is no obligation whatsoever on the part of the correspondent bank to honour the drawings of its account-holding banks and there is no formal obligation upon a correspondent bank to pay funds which are uncleared. This point may be well illustrated in the Clearing House Interbank Payment System (CHIPS) which operates in New York. Under CHIPS rules no payments can be withdrawn from the system once they have been entered, and upon receipt are assumed by the recipient bank to be cleared. In view of this situation a system has been introduced by member banks of CHIPS whereby intra-day bilateral limits are imposed by each member upon other members, and similarly each member monitors the position of its client banks. Within these arrangements payments will only be effected up to an internally approved limit and thereafter receipts will be required prior to further payment instructions being effected through the CHIPS system. In this context it is pertinent to mention the right of the Clearing House to implement CHIPS Rule 13. This requires that the totality of transactions undertaken during any particular day would be unwound and each bank would be placed in the same position as it was at the commencement of that business day, irrespective of whether it had subsequently paid the funds away. Normally this rule would be applied only as a result of the collapse or default of a major bank where immediate support was not available. It is intended to expand the control of individual banks intra-day positions within both the CHIPS and Federal Wire payment systems with the introduction of "CAP" limits during 1986.

Interest Rate Sensitivity
The management of day to day cash positions and the consequential funding/utilisation of short/surplus resources is in itself simply

involved with the physical movement of monies in and out of an individual bank's system. Within this exercise the treasury is not concerned per se with the underlying period or pricing of these funds, but merely the funding or utilisation of any resultant day to day shortfall/surplus on the most beneficial terms to the bank.

However, as a separate exercise, the treasury function will also monitor, control and manage within pre-defined guidelines the elements of interest rate risk and sensitivity which exists within each separate currency portfolio in which it operates together with its aggregate overall exposure to this risk.

In considering interest rate sensitivity, the treasurer is primarily concerned with current interest rate periods. Within this process the treasurer will consider either directly or indirectly all current assets and liabilities inclusive of those "not in value", forward transactions and any applicable hedges upon which the level of interest rate and interest rate period has been established; but exclusive of any items which may comprise the base of separate specific trading or investment portfolios. The movements of assets and liabilities between interest rate periods is equally important, irrespective of whether or not the result is an external cash movement to that bank. For example a transfer of funds from a two day call account or a current account to a three month fixture, is equally as important as a new three month fixed deposit from external sources. Within this process of management the treasurer is not interested in either the original or ultimate life period of assets and liabilities, but merely the remaining period of the current interest rate commitments.

Areas of interest rate sensitivity are measured as time gaps between the effective date of interest rate changes on an equal and opposite amount of assets and liabilities. The extent of this sensitivity represents an interest rate exposure which can be impacted upon by any subsequent movements in interest rate levels and the higher the volatility of interest rates the greater the risk.

The internal approach which individual banks use to manage interest rate sensitivity will be dependent upon the size and spread of its operations, together with the sophistication of its internal procedures and systems. This approach may comprise or evolve upon either the internal transfer and centralisation of all individual assets and liabilities, or a money transfer pricing system. The latter procedure implies that the interest values of assets and liabilities are accounted to or from the central treasury at internally agreed interest rate levels and thereafter the treasury is responsible for interest exposure management.

Alternatively, a treasury may only concern itself with the net impact of assets and liabilities which are both equal in time and priced upon the same interest rate structure. For example, within retail banking operations most interest rates for both assets and liabilities are amended immediately a change takes place in base, prime or other form of advertised rate. The net impact on interest margins is compensated to the extent that such assets are equal and opposite to liabilities, provided the interest rate differential between the two remains the same. Therefore a central treasury function may only involve itself with the amount by which assets or liabilities exceed each other for various given interest rate maturity periods. Similarly if a bank is able to borrow and lend at the same fixed interest rate plus a margin, for exactly the same period inclusive of the same start and end dates, a net margin is secured and provided both transactions run to maturity, an interest rate or time mis-match does not exist.

In practice a common procedure is to net floating base related assets against an element of short-dated liabilities – usually up to seven days – inclusive of short call and current account balances. All other fixed rate period assets and liabilities, together with the surplus or shortfall funding requirement resultant from the procedure outlined, are centrally administered within the treasury operation either by a transfer pricing system, or the physical covering of transactions either individually or gross and categorised by interest period. However, in applying this strategy it must be recognised that any increase or decrease in interest rates will impact totally on returns from those interest-free funds included in the netting process. The subject of funding related to various types of assets is further developed in Chapter 4.

Whilst internal procedures may differ from bank to bank, the ultimate objective of this exercise is to manage and control the risk created by time mis-matches or gapping periods between the different interest rate maturity dates of assets and liabilities. To achieve this objective it is necessary to identify such time gaps. The most common procedure is to construct an interest rate maturity schedule or maturity ladder of assets and liabilities by interest rate maturity period. Within this matrix, current assets and liabilities are listed **in interest maturity date order**, with the net position for each day being identified and the net position from each day thereafter accumulated to provide the required net positions for various selected periods by week, month, quarters, etc., together with an aggregated overall position:

Interest Maturity Date	Demand Call	daily/weekly/monthly or other selected time bands
Assets		
Less Liabilities		
= Net mis-match		
+/− carried forward		
Aggregated or progressive position		

This maturity ladder usually starts with those net or gross assets and liabilities which may be liable to immediate change in interest rate or maturity, for example non-interest bearing accounts, overdrafts, savings account balances, and other demand items, followed by all other items in order of their respective interest rate maturity dates. From this process, periods of long and short exposure can be identified and assessments made within a bank's dealing strategy as to subsequent action to be taken.

Theoretically, should a bank wish to negate all of this risk, each individual deposit and loan would be matched exactly with interest rate periods by amount and time. In reality, this is rarely possible or desirable as it could require excessive market entry as a lender and borrower of funds for the purpose of eliminating interest or natural time gaps. This could place unacceptable pressure on balance sheet ratios, possibly adversely impact upon the market's perception of that bank's name and, more importantly, make it necessary to enter the market for deposit periods for which liquidity was not readily available. Furthermore the bank's lines with other banks on the interbank market would be filled up, and, very importantly, profitability of the deposit dealing operation would be drastically reduced or even eliminated.

An alternative to the procedure described above, is to compile reverse cumulative mis-match ladders. Within this process the matrix commences with total extant Assets and Liabilities and thereafter reduces as they fall away at maturity. This procedure allows a bank to measure the calculated rates they require to earn/pay in order to achieve desired returns.

Liquidity
Both cash management and interest rate sensitivity issues as described above devolve in the main upon considerations related to extant positions on a day to day basis incorporating the mobilisation of current resources and the funding of assets on the best possible terms within a managed and controlled environment.

It is not only essential that a bank meets its current obligations but equally important that it gives consideration to future liquidity profiles to ensure its continued ability to meet both its current and potential obligations as they fall due, and achieve similar or improved levels of profit margins. Maintenance of adequate liquidity can affect profitability particularly during normal periods of positive interest rate yield curves. However, the well known risk which has caused several bank failures, of borrowing short and lending long (the opposite of liquidity), must never be overlooked in this context. Greed should never obscure prudential common sense.

Historically a bank's liquidity was measured on the basis of a minimum percentage amount of defined elements of its total deposit base which by statute, convention or precedent it was expected or required to maintain in specified classes of assets which were defined as "liquid assets". This form of liquidity measure does not recognise the totality of a bank's overall obligations which not only relate to its capacity to repay deposits as they fall due but also its capacity to fund its commitments to lend. It is the authors' opinion that "true" liquidity should be perceived to comprise those elements which are held in excess of minimum statutory levels.

The best strategy for liquidity management is to ensure that a bank develops a prudent mix of assets and liabilities, in terms of quality, return and an acceptable maturity profile. This ensures a continuing certainty of access to its source of funds, at the finest rates, and without excessive exposure to sudden shortages of liquidity either by the market's perception of the borrowing bank's name or its country of origin or the result of a general shortage of liquidy within the market.

A bank's future obligations both to repay deposits and to meet commitments to lend will be provided from a mix of sources. These include:

- Funds received in repayment of maturing loans

- A bank's ability to continue to retain maturing deposits and attract new interbank and customer deposits more cheaply or without any additional margin cost

- Increased internal resources

- The realisation of liquifiable assets

The most usual technique used to measure, quantify, manage and control liquidity matters within a bank is by means of projected cash flows on a maturity ladder matrix.

A liquidity maturity ladder is similar in principle to that already described in regard to the management of interest rate sensitivity in that it provides both gross and net positions, by period, together with a progressive position throughout the portfolio. However, the data base is very different, as within various broad definitions assets are incorporated by reference to their ultimate or final maturity date, or in the case of liquefiable assets, by reference to their marketability. In this context the distinction between marketable and unmarketable assets relates to the existence of a secondary market of sufficient depth being available to realise immediately such assets, and would therefore include those and similar instruments as already described earlier in this Chapter under "Cash Management". Conversely, liabilities are incorporated by reference to their earliest possible repayment date. The schedule on the following page illustrates a typical matrix which may be used.

In addition to extant transactions, agreed but undrawn commitments and, where appropriate, contingencies, must also be incorporated. Theoretically liabilities will comprise the sum total of deposits, commitments to provide facilities, and contingent liabilities; the assets will comprise the sum total of current assets and any formal standby facilities available to that bank. Although it is usual to include formal standby facilities available in this measurement it must be recognised that, although such arrangements may constitute legal obligations, substantial resistance may be experienced at drawdown when there is a creditworthiness crisis, country risk issue or lack of overall liquidity within the markets.

All sight or demand deposits together with unutilised overdrafts and other commitments to lend if subject to immediate drawdown, followed by drawn overdrafts, cash and other liquefiable assets are normally incorporated within the maturity ladder as sight items. All other assets and liabilities would be included under the relative period by reference to their remaining life from the effective date of the matrix to ultimate maturity date or earliest possible realisation date if marketable. The original underlying period of such deposits and advances is of no significance within these considerations.

However, in practice there are various other important issues which must be considered within the compilation of a liquidity profile. Many of these matters will be decided upon by the subjective views of each bank in relation to its underlying activities. By way of illustration, the following typify subjects which will require specific consideration. Although in theory doubtful, non-performing and rescheduling loans may be recorded as repayable on demand, in practice it is known that repayment would not be forthcoming. It would therefore be appropriate to include such items towards the longer end

	Demand	2–8 days (by day)	8 days to 1 month	two months	three months	3–6 months	7–9 months	10–12 months	13–18 months	19–24 months	over 2 years
Liabilities											
Deposits											
Commitments											
Contingencies											
Less Assets											
Marketable											
Non-marketable											
Standby facilities available											
= Net position											
+/– Carried forward											
= Net progressive											

of the maturity ladder rather than at the beginning. Similarly, whilst performing overdrafts and other facilities may be repayable on demand, in practice this will not always be practicable and it would therefore be prudent to anticipate the reality of the situation by only incorporating a percentage as immediately recoverable and the remainder on an assessed scheduled repayment basis over selected periods of the maturity ladder.

Liquefiable assets will constitute both those held for trading and for investment purposes. However, as many of these instruments are normally arranged on a discounted price basis, their current value may well differ from that reflected as a book value and suitable adjustment will be required to indicate this fact. It is also unusual for a bank's total commitment to lend to be ever fully drawn and the realistic extent of such drawdowns would be assessed and again only a percentage of the total incorporated within the appropriate period of the liquidity profile. Contingent liabilities will also require examination and any of those upon which it is anticipated the bank's undertaking will have to be fulfilled, including note issuance facilities and revolving underwriting facilities, will be incorporated. Other issues which a bank will focus upon relate to its right of set off on various accounts, items in the course of collection and impersonal accounts which would impact upon the earlier dates of the maturity ladder.

Asset and liability maturity profiles will be continually reviewed, not only to determine and monitor interest rate mis-match or sensitivity by current maturities but also to monitor and anticipate cash flows as liabilities run off and assets, together with other commitments, continue to require funding. In the medium term alternative funding strategies may be developed in relation to a bank's asset structure such as capital issues, floating rate paper, diversification of its mix of liabilities with a bias towards those which are less interest rate or market sensitive, the development of a natural deposit base in various currencies, the introduction of commercial paper or certificate of deposit programmes, interest rate swaps and currency swaps, etc. These are all subjects which will be considered when reviewing liquidity exposure. Policy decisions related thereto will comprise strategy rather than specific limits upon particular types or areas of business.

CHAPTER FOUR

Funding Operations in a Multi-Currency Book

Introduction

A bank's mix of current liabilities for funding its ordinary banking business will depend on the scale of its operations in each currency and each country. The degree to which it can attract retail deposits or indeed wishes to attract retail deposits has traditionally been dependent upon the scale and geographical spread of its branch banking operations. Such deposits are an important source of domestic currency funding for both the major indigenous banks and those international banks with a wide spread of retail branch banking operations in various countries. Additionally, in those countries which are free from exchange control this type of operation usually attracts substantial deposits of a retail nature in a variety of foreign currencies. However, as private and corporate investors have become more sophisticated or aware of alternative homes for their money, and the tendency of many banks to concentrate on wholesale as opposed to retail business to avoid becoming over labour-intensive, there is now a greater reliance on market-related funds than on customer deposits in the form of current, savings and fixed deposit accounts received at advertised interest rates through retail operations. The overseas branch operations of many large international banks are often dependent upon interbank money sources, particularly in centres outside New York and London, and many branches of foreign banks in those centres also are largely reliant upon similar markets as their principal funding source. To supplement this, issues of Certificates of Deposit, commercial paper programmes and other similar funding instruments (which are discussed in Section 3) are commonplace.

It is a bank treasury function to mobilize all current liabilities and ensure that they are effectively employed. Typically, the assets into which such funds may be channelled include:

- Nostro Account balances
- Overdrafts
- Loans
- Negotiations of outward collections
- Commercial & Public Sector bill discounts
- Securities trading and investment portfolios
- Forfaiting

Within its multi-currency deposit activities a bank will wish to avoid any unnecessary exchange risk exposure on both its assets and liabilities and it is usual therefore for the funding of all assets to be matched by currency. Although in many instances lending in one currency may be funded by borrowings in another, the forward exchange rate risk will normally be covered through the foreign exchange markets. Thereafter funding strategy relative to various assets will be determined by subjective judgments related to many of the issues already discussed in Chapters 2 and 3 and in this context the above-mentioned assets are discussed below.

Nostro Account Balances
As explained under cash management in Chapter 3, nostro accounts occasionally are interest-bearing although by and large they are non-interest earning currency accounts and may in many cases require compensating balances to be maintained. A large or excessive balance, above that required, left on a nostro account is generally a sign of bad husbandry rather than a planned treasury operation. However, conversely it is equally as important that there is a sufficient balance maintained on the account to service the business transacted across the account. Nostro account management is an important aspect of treasury operations and it is therefore appropriate to elaborate further on some key features of the subject as follows.

It is imperative that the exchange control or other mandatory requirements of the host country or the account-holding correspondent are adhered to so far as the operation of the account is concerned, the most common requirement being to ensure that the account is kept in credit. It is normal for the authorities abroad to permit "temporary resultant overdrafts" where the bank with which the account is held is aware that funds are on the way but have not yet been received to cover a payment order which would otherwise overdraw the account. Apart from contravening the requirements of the authorities in some countries by overdrawing a nostro account, the bank would be charged overdraft interest by the bank with whom the account is held. As previously mentioned such a charge may very well be at penal rates and as a source of funds it is not a desirable nor necessarily an economic practice to adopt. Indeed, the only time it may seem profitable to resort to such a measure is when there is considerable pressure on the currency of the nostro account and the dealers have shortened their exposure to the currency by selling it in the foreign exchange market. In due course, after the currency has devalued, positions can be reversed. Major bear market operations against a weakening currency are not, however, favoured by central banks and most banks do not practice this type of operation in deference to central bank opinion.

An essential function of an international bank is the reconciliation of its nostro accounts and the daily identification of balances held thereon. Time differences in various centres around the world, coupled with the different practices of banks and dissimilar computer systems employed by them, give rise to the management of nostro accounts being less than a perfect science. Payments received as a result of, say, UK exporters' open account business may not be advised to the account holding bank before one or more days have elapsed. Many payments issued or authorised by a bank may not be debited to its nostro account for a while and the debit date cannot be determined at the time the transaction is originated.

As there is always a danger, if funds are not available in a nostro account, that payment instructions given to the account-holding bank might not be carried out, arrangements are frequently made for covering funds other than those related to value dated transactions to be transferred to the appropriate nostro account as soon as the underlying transaction is initiated. Telegraphic or electronic instructions can normally be funded on the nostro account with the value date of the covering funds matching the value date of payment.

Credits paid into nostro accounts with value before the credit advices are received on collections is a regular occurrence which can give rise to excessive balances on a bank's various nostro accounts around the world. Delays in receipt of information vary, sometimes only during the course of a day, or for one day, but sometimes for a longer period depending on the communications established between the two banks and, of course, their own internal systems. As previously mentioned, various cash management schemes have been established by correspondent banks for the benefit of their clients and instant communication systems developed for both internal and external cash management purposes. A proliferation of nostro accounts is usually considered uneconomic. Whilst correspondent banks are keen to obtain more correspondent accounts, the maintenance and control of several accounts in any one currency is not only uneconomical but can lead to funding problems, misunderstanding and reconciliation difficulties. Indeed the question whether more than one nostro account per currency is really necessary needs to be examined objectively.

Overdrafts

All overdraft facilities can be drawn down at the customer's option up to the agreed overdraft limit. Overdraft facilities are sometimes used by corporate clients as standbys and are most likely to be drawn at the least convenient time when there is a shortage of liquidity in a particular currency or interest rate period. The cumulative size of outstanding overdraft facilities should be closely monitored, particularly if the money base in the currency of the facility is thin, and funding sources are limited.

There are various interest rate formulae that may be applied to overdraft facilities and some offer alternative formulae for charging overdraft interest in certain currencies. The formulae bases include overnight euro-rates, base rate, prime rate and a variety of composite or other short-term money rates. The ability of customers to repay an overdraft at their own option as well as drawing funds when they want makes this type of facility a particularly flexible method of borrowing. However, without a similarly priced liability base being available or achievable within the drawn currencies, it is not always possible for a bank to realise its full profit potential and this factor is taken into account when pricing overdraft facilities. In other words the flexibility of an overdraft is usually reflected by the relatively high margin over the base, prime or other formula cost.

Where insufficient retail funds are available in the liability base by way of current, demand or short call liabilities it will be necessary for the treasury to obtain market-related funds at current rates to meet both present and anticipated obligations. In practice a mixture of both of these strategies may be adopted to fund these assets. However, for the purposes of interest rate risk and liquidity issues, such liabilities will normally be relatively short-dated obligations and will incorporate a spread of maturities for both bank's own day to day liquidity purposes. This also avoids excessive exposure to the vagaries of the substantial interest rate movements which may take place within the markets for funds in the very short-dated periods, due to liquidity shortages.

Within the above strategy any subsequent increase in overdraft rates would improve margins whereas, conversely, decreases would diminish margins. The results of 'round tripping', i.e. arbitrage activity by customers, is also a risk of funding overdraft facilities from market and fixed rate funds, as opportunities will be taken when money market rates are in excess of the effective base-related or composite lending rate for customers. They can then draw down on agreed overdraft facilities for the purpose of short-term investment at market-related rates, often with other banks. This practice increases a bank's funding requirements at a time of liquidity shortages and, immediately market rates return to below effective lending levels, overdrafts will be repaid and the bank whipsawed by its funding strategy unless express action has been taken within facility letters to exclude such practices.

Loans
Loans are provided as part of both the retail and wholesale operations of a bank and may be priced at a fixed rate of interest for the duration of the loan or on a floating rate basis at a margin over a predetermined formula based upon domestic or eurocurrency interest rates. Floating rate loans will comprise both those upon which the interest rates can be amended immediately or upon the expiration

of an agreed period of notice, e.g. 7 day call, and those which are primarily at a fixed rate of interest within pre-determined parameters for selected interest rate periods. Such interest periods may facilitate drawdown for one, three, six or even 12 month periods at the borrower's option.

As with overdrafts a bank will endeavour to fund its loan portfolio with liabilities of a similar period and interest rate structure, and where deemed appropriate, a bank will access the wholesale money markets to facilitate matched funding of part of these portfolios. The extent to which matched funding is desired will be dependent upon the depth and spread of its liability base, liquidity issues related to the funding of other assets and the bank's current dealing strategy. The level to which matched funding can be achieved is dependent on the extent to which market-related funds or suitable hedging instruments are obtainable for the period concerned.

Where fixed rate term-lending is undertaken for periods in excess of those for which liabilities are either available or obtainable from retail or market sources, for example in consumer credit or hire purchase activities, a bank will endeavour to achieve a spread of liabilities taking into consideration anticipated cash flows created by repayments and anticipated increased activity at the lowest attainable cost. Both the interest rate risk associated with funding this type of activity together with the high credit risk exposure should be recognised by the margins levied.

Negotiations of outward collections
Negotiation facilities involve a payment with recourse usually to the drawer of a trade bill drawn on an overseas importer. The exact period of finance is indeterminable at the time of negotiation due to the vagaries of collection periods. Proceeds of a three month negotiated term bill would not be received in three months' time but three months plus the collection period. On the assumption that the drawee pays promptly and that the collecting bank abroad can and does remit the funds without delay, it will still be a matter of several days before the negotiating bank can expect to receive notice that the funds have been credited to a nostro account either in the collecting bank's

country or elsewhere, or authority is given to debit the collecting bank's account, in reimbursement. When considering the funding of such items the negotiating bank can only rely upon its experience to estimate the likely collection period and arrange funding accordingly.

Bills presented for negotiation may be drawn in either domestic or foreign currency. Domestic bills negotiated are usually priced on the basis of domestic fixed rates whereas foreign currency bill rates generally are determined by the respective eurocurrency rates for the underlying period for which it is anticipated that the bank will be short of these funds. The beneficiary of a foreign currency bill, usually an exporter of goods or services, may receive the negotiated proceeds in foreign currency credited to a foreign currency account, but more likely will require the foreign currency to be exchanged immediately for domestic currency.

In the first instance, the modus operandi is similar to that applied for domestic negotiations to the extent that there is no exchange involvement. Within the negotiation the cost of the perceived funding requirements plus a margin will be deducted from the gross proceeds. However, should the negotiated bill be subsequently unpaid, a bank will expect to receive from its client the face value of the underlying instrument in the currency of the negotiation. If an exporter has subsequently sold the underlying currency for his base currency, any resultant exchange loss would be for his account as the currency would have to be purchased at the then spot rate to reimburse the bank.

Where a negotiation is converted into the home currency, it is normally the practice to undertake the exchange transaction with the customer at the current spot exchange rate and separately to deduct interest and commission charges to compensate with a margin for funding the underlying currency for the appropriate period. Should a negotiation be subsequently unpaid, then under the recourse arrangement the beneficiary will be expected to repay the full amount of foreign currency originally negotiated at the then current rate of exchange with any resultant shortfall again being for the client's account. Unpaid currency items must be taken into account if they are allowed to remain outstanding pending delayed but anticipated receipt of proceeds, and it will be necessary to make an adjustment for the cost of funding for any additional period in excess of what was originally anticipated at the outset of the negotiation.

Bankers Acceptances

Bankers acceptances together with the discount and rediscount of bills of exchange, is covered in detail in Chapter 11. Bankers acceptances in themselves are fee-generating contingent liabilities as far as the accepting bank is concerned and unless they are discounted by a bank they do not form part of a bank's asset portfolio or require funding.

When a bank discounts a bill it has the facility to either rediscount or hold it within its own portfolio, and funding issues will depend upon this decision. Where a discounted bill is immediately rediscounted there are no funding requirements as cash will be received. However, in practice there is a requirement to retire bills if they contravene market rules or their continuing validity is questionable.

The funding approaches adopted by banks for discounts and other similar short-term assets will probably depend on their policy on investment or trading in such assets. In the authors' opinion all properly **managed** portfolios should include an element of trading and therefore the portfolio manager should also be responsible for the under-pinning funding in the context of overall profitability of the portfolio.

Trading Portfolios

Funding decisions related to a security trading portfolio are different from those applied to fixed-rate loan and investment portfolios.

Within a trading portfolio it is essential that flexibility exists to trade in the underlying instruments and therefore funding applied for this purpose will normally be of a much shorter dated duration than that of the underlying assets comprising the portfolio. Such funds ideally will comprise a mix of liabilities from both retail and wholesale sources with the period of such funding being dictated in the main by considerations related to the time for which it is anticipated the various elements of the trading portfolio will be held prior to their sale. Many banks fund such trading positions on a mix of short period liabilities with maturities often peaking at three months. The assets (in theory) are marketable securities although a hardcore of "positions" held can be identified and funded for longer periods if interest rates are expected to rise.

Investment Portfolios

It is inevitable within a bank's investment portfolio, funded from retail or wholesale sources, that the average life of the assets will normally be substantially in excess of the funding cover. Within this type of operation funding issues are an integral part of the portfolio management and therefore requirements will be dictated by the fund manager with the treasury operation per se responding to his requirements.

Forfaiting

Forfaiting is the non-recourse discount of a series of bills of exchange or promissory notes and sometimes book debts. The forfaiting institution relies for its reimbursement on a separate guarantee or an aval on the bill of exchange or promissory note normally given by a bank of satisfactory standing to the forfaiter. The importer in the underlying contract will expect to issue/accept at given intervals a bill of exchange or a promissory note for payment. Such bills normally contain the agreed fixed financing cost that the importer is prepared to pay for the deferred terms of credit he is getting. Sometimes a separate series of bills covering the interest element is drawn although this is relatively uncommon in forfaiting propositions. The financing bank will make an outright purchase of the entire series of bills at a single rate for the package and the discounted proceeds will be paid straight away to the manufacturer without recourse.

Before this takes place, institutions in the forfaiting business will be asked to quote for the business in order that the manufacturer can complete the commercial contract with the buyer on the basis of a firm and fixed cost of finance. Whilst indication rates may be quoted and are, in practice, often required particularly where contracts involving a reasonably long manufacturing period are concerned, firm quotations are also sought and obtained from forfaiters for delivery of the obligations for periods up to six months or more ahead. It is customary within this market for the quotation to be firm on the forfaiter's side but not necessarily so on the manufacturer's as the latter may not get the contract. It is normal for firm quotes for future deliveries to be held for up to 48 hours on such an open-ended basis and then if the manufacturer wishes to use the facility the commitment to deliver the paper is a condition of the quotation.

In these circumstances if a manufacturer is awarded the contract he may find that interest rates within the 48 hour period have moved down in the meantime and the forfaiter will be asked to quote again. If interest rates move up the manufacturer will hold the forfaiter to an original firm quote and the transaction will probably go ahead with delivery of the obligations taking place as originally envisaged. From the forfaiter's point of view the obvious problem is funding costs. If he takes a market deposit to cover a firm quotation made and interest rates move downwards, he will be left with the deposit to re-employ in the market at a lower rate than he originally acquired it. On the other hand if he does not take a deposit and rates move upwards and funds are obtained in the market to cover the transaction as and when drawdown is made, the cost of such funding may well exceed the agreed return on the forfaited obligations. For protection the forfaiter can firm up the rates (which are usually based on the cost of funds in the respective money market for the currency concerned), when interest rates are thought to be relatively low and likely to rise between the date of the firm quotation and the anticipated date of drawdown. This protection for the "forward quote" for a firm discount rate may be built into the rate itself or taken as a separate commitment fee. When interest rates on the other hand are likely to fall for the currency concerned between the date of quotation and the drawdown date, protection may be considered unnecessary as it is unlikely that the original quotation will be taken – a matter of funding judgment.

Effective funding is of primary importance to a profitably run forfaiting investment portfolio. Some forfait institutions will not hold inventory at all. In other words they will endeavour to rediscount the paper to others in the market as soon as they have bought it. Therefore anticipated funding will merely be treated as a hedge and closed out when rediscount takes place. Other forfait institutions will maintain a portfolio of paper which, from time to time, they will endeavour to sell on the secondary market to other forfait institutions. The secondary market consists of some 35 banks, discount houses and licensed deposit takers in London as well as a number of financial institutions in Zurich, Vienna and Frankfurt. The secondary market, however, has little depth. Some forfaiters who run asset portfolios will wish, from time to time, to sell series of forfait paper to enable them, for example, to make head-room in their global limits for a particular country. Consequently, as with other trading portfolios, funding decisions will not only be related to the maturity bands but rather views on interest rate movements and anticipated sales. Therefore, when drawdown takes place on a firm forfait quotation, the bank may fund the paper on the basis of short-term money and even if rates have moved upwards since the firm quotation was given it is probable that the bank would still be able to fund the asset profitably if there exists a positive yield curve in that currency.

Looking at the total maturity structure of a forfait investment portfolio over a period of time, repayments of the portfolio will occur on a regular basis monthly or even daily depending on the size of the portfolio. Funding of a forfait investment portfolio should, therefore, be considered on the basis of the portfolio in total rather than each individual new asset as it is purchased. The dollar portfolio can, of course, be hedged against rising interest rates for given periods by taking out an interest rate futures contract. Funds can also be borrowed for fixed periods to be hedged against rising interest rates which would otherwise render the portfolio temporary unprofitable or the size of the portfolio reduced by the sale of the fixed interest earning assets before net income margins are eroded.

The following forfait proposition is provided by way of illustration:

Assume a manufacturer of agricultural machinery is in the process of negotiating a major contract and that the date is June 1985. Shipment is anticipated in December 1985 and 10% of the contract is payable on shipment. 90% of the contract amount will be payable over a six year period from the date of shipment in 10 equal instalments of principal which commence 18 months from the date of shipment. The buyer has indicated a willingness to pay $6\frac{1}{4}\%$ interest on the outstanding balances. The forfaiter makes a firm quotation for the entire parcel at a straight discount rate of 7% per annum, the total cost of goods delivered duty paid (DDP Zurich) SwFcs.32,344,800. The manufacturer intends to achieve a profit margin of 10% over this cost figure (SwFcs.3,234,480). The invoice price as calculated below shows a goods value of SwFcs.38 million DDP Zurich. The mechanics of the transaction are illustrated in the chart below:

Payment on shipment in December 1985	SwFcs. 3,800,000
Gross amount of bills to be discounted	SwFcs.42,215,625
Less discount charges	SwFcs.10,436,345
Net discount proceeds in December 1985	SwFcs.31,779,280

Total receipts for the package	SwFcs.35,579,280
of which costs amount to	SwFcs.32,344,800
and profits	SwFcs. 3,234,480

Date	Position	Principal amount	Balance Outstanding	Interest at $6\frac{1}{4}\%$ pa on balances outstanding	Straight Discount at 7% pa on note value	Net Values Principal plus Interest payable by buyer
June 85	Firm funding quote					
Dec 85	Shipment and 10% paid	3,800,000				
June 86			34,200,000	1,068,750		
Dec 86			34,200,000	1,068,750		
June 87	1st Note Due	3,420,000	34,200,000	1,068,750	695,756	6,626,250
Dec 87	2nd Note Due	3,420,000	30,780,000	961,875	613,463	4,381,875
June 88	3rd Note Due	3,420,000	27,360,000	855,000	748,125	4,275,000
Dec 88	4th Note Due	3,420,000	23,940,000	748,125	875,306	4,168,125
June 89	5th Note Due	3,420,000	20,520,000	641,250	995,006	4,061,250
Dec 89	6th Note Due	3,420,000	17,100,000	534,375	1,107,225	3,954,375
June 90	7th Note Due	3,420,000	13,680,000	427,500	1,211,963	3,847,500
Dec 90	8th Note Due	3,420,000	10,260,000	320,625	1,309,219	3,740,625
June 91	9th Note Due	3,420,000	6,840,000	213,750	1,398,994	3,633,750
Dec 91	10th Note Due	3,420,000	3,420,000	106,875	1,481,288	3,526,875
	Totals	38,000,000		8,015,625	10,436,345	42,215,625

Calculation of average life of the series:

Years		Note Amounts		Products of Series
1.5	×	6,626,250	=	9,939,375
2	×	4,381,875	=	8,763,750
2.5	×	4,275,000	=	10,687,500
3	×	4,168,125	=	12,504,375
3.5	×	4,061,250	=	14,214,375
4	×	3,954,375	=	15,817,500
4.5	×	3,847,500	=	17,313,750
5	×	3,740,625	=	18,703,125
5.5	×	3,633,750	=	19,985,625
6	×	3,526,875	=	21,161,250
37.5		42,215,625		149,090,625

$$149,090,625 \div 42,215,625 = \underset{\text{avg. life}}{3.531646} \text{ yrs}$$

In this illustration it is assumed that the manufacturer had as his starting point estimated the cost of his goods and perceived a profit margin of 10% thereon. No commitment, option or other fees have been included, although commitment fees may well have been charged to cover the forfaiter's risk of possible rising interest rates prior to drawdown. The formula given below can be used to enable the manufacturer to calculate his invoice amount taking into the figures the interest element to be paid by the borrower on a reducing balance basis. The formula gives rise to a factor which, when multiplied by the price required by the exporter (SwFcs.35,579,280), gives the final invoice value payable by the borrower.

$$\frac{1}{(1 - \frac{a}{100}) \times (1 + \frac{ir \times cp}{100}) \times (1 - \frac{dr \times al}{100}) + (\frac{a}{100})} = \text{Factor}$$

Where a = the amount payable on shipment (in % terms) = 10

ir = interest rate payable by the buyer (in % terms) = 6.25

cp = credit period (averaged in years) = 3.75

dr = discount rate charged by the bank (in % terms) = 7

and al = average life of the bills (see calculation) = 3.531646

The Factor =

$$\frac{1}{(1 - \frac{10}{100}) \times (1 + \frac{6.25 \times 3.75}{100}) \times (1 - \frac{7 \times 3.531646}{100}) + (\frac{10}{100})}$$

$$= \frac{1}{0.9 \times 1.234375 \times 0.75278478 + 0.1}$$

= 1.068037353 × SwFcs.35,579,280 (price required) = SwFcs.38 million

SwFcs.38 million is therefore the invoice value on which to base the calculations.

Some banks have established their forfaiting operation in a separate subsidiary company. Others have incorporated a forfait service within the main operating bank vehicle. From a funding view-point, the main operating bank vehicle would probably provide the better platform with a blend of retail deposits in various foreign currencies which can be employed behind forfaiting operations. In order to provide an effective and competitive forfait operation, the forfaiter must have a high degree of co-ordination between funding, credit control and the negotiators. Some banks have established their forfaiting units in branches or smaller subsidiary companies which can provide the essential flexibility and internal co-ordination for this merchant banking type of business. It is generally felt to be prudent, however, for a banking group to consider their credit and operational exposures on a group aggregated basis. This will naturally include any forfaiting subsidiary. From a control point of view, it is not advisable to increase the size of the cake just to undertake additional business via a subsidiary company, which might nevertheless expose the group to an increased level of risk where it may not be considered prudent to do so.

The Regulation and Supervision of Banks

Part 1

Regulation and Supervision

Each country normally has, either within its legislative framework or through the evolution of more informal developments, specific regulations and procedures relating to the application, licensing and establishment of banks and other forms of deposit-taking institutions. Additionally, authority will usually be vested in a designated body or bodies to undertake the roles of central banker, regulator and supervisor in regard to this industry.

There are two reasons for this heightened regulatory and supervisory process for banks. Firstly and primarily, the regulators are concerned with the protection of depositors and therefore with a bank's role, as custodian of other people's money. Secondly, as the controllers and managers of national and/or international monetary resources, it is important that governments establish a permanent framework within which they are able, as appropriate, to influence and direct the utilisation of those resources at the disposal of banks in the interests of official monetary and economic policy.

Although regulation and supervision are primarily involved with depositor protection, by implication the authorities responsible for their implementation must also be involved with the interests of banks and consider the totality of their operations and activities on a prudential basis to ensure that the security of adequate capital resources provides support for the risks related thereto. It is only through this process that a regulator or supervisor can be properly satisfied that depositor's funds are secure. In several countries these supervisory and regulatory responsibilities may extend to ensuring the development of orderly financial markets whilst in others this function is undertaken by separately appointed bodies. With regard to depositor protection in various countries, several authorities have mandatory requirements in respect of deposit insurance; others leave it to the discretion of the individual banks to subscribe to such schemes, whilst in many countries no such arrangements exist. Cover provided under these schemes is often confined to domestic deposits maintained with banks, and incorporates relatively low maximum liability limits. For example, in the US the Federal Deposit Insurance Corporation (FDIC) formally only provides cover for individual's deposits of up to US$100,000 placed with member banks, and only those banks are permitted to accept such deposits. However, it is worth mentioning that during the Continental Illinois crisis of 1984 the FDIC did issue unlimited support for all depositors including other banks. In the UK a Deposit Protection Fund which is administered by the Deposit Protection Board provides cover for 75% of sterling deposits up to a maximum of £10,000 per depositor with member banks. All recognised banks and deposit-taking institutions, other than some branches of foreign banks which obtain exemption, must subscribe to this scheme.

In the United Kingdom the Bank of England has developed responsibility as central banker, regulator and supervisor. However, this is not always the pattern of regulation adopted by other countries. For example, in the US the regulatory system is much more complex involving both federal and state legislature and authority. United States banks may apply for charter under either state or federal law. The state banking authority is the primary regulatory and supervisory body for state chartered banks and The Office of the Comptroller of Currency for federally chartered banks. The Federal Reserve have primary responsibilities for US bank holding companies, 'Edge Act' and 'agreement corporations' and specific responsibilities for its member banks which include both federal and state chartered banks. Essentially Edge Act banks are restricted from undertaking domestic banking operations but nevertheless are subject to all other appropriate regulatory and supervisory requirements of the Federal Reserve. Additionally, the Federal Deposit Insurance Corporation also supervises the activities of its member banks. In West Germany the regulatory and supervisory function is vested in the Federal Banking Supervisory Office in Berlin with the Bundesbank undertaking the role of central banker. In Switzerland these responsibilities are undertaken by the Federal Banking Commission and the National Bank respectively whilst in Japan there is a division of responsibility between the main supervisory bureaux of the Ministry of Finance and the central bank – Bank of Japan. In Hong Kong, the Commissioner for Banking is charged with responsibility for supervision but Hong Kong does not have an official central bank. The Hongkong and Shanghai Banking Corporation acts as the banker to other banks with matters relating to the Hong Kong Banking Ordinance, and banking in general, being considered by a Banking Advisory Committee which reports to the Governor.

The primary responsibilities of a central banking function are the custody and management of a country's official foreign exchange and other monetary reserves, the management and control of the domestic monetary economy inclusive of the development of orderly domestic money markets, and to act as bank of issue (for domestic currency notes and coin) and lender of last resort to the banking sector. Lender of last resort operations will normally be confined to routine day to day official funding operations for liquidity or monetary policy reasons. On occasions, however, the provision or arrangement of longer-term discretionary support may prove necessary for individual banks to prevent a default or liquidity crisis arising. This may be by way of direct involvement, the arrangement of support facilities from various other commercial banks, mergers or the appointment of caretaker managers.

In different countries the mechanism varies through which day to day funding operations are implemented. Some countries provide this facility through a selected market segment of specialised bankers who act as intermediaries between the central bank and the rest of the banking system, as has been the case with the Bank of England and the Discount Houses. Other central banks provide discount facilities directly to a broader segment of the banking industry. For example, within the United States the regional Federal Reserve Bank discount windows are open to their respective member banks. Facilities provided through these processes are usually on a fully secured, discounted, or sale and repurchase basis.

Within the regulatory and supervisory process each national authority has developed its own characteristics. Some countries like the

UK have favoured an informal approach to supervision which requires contact with individual bank's management and encourages the development of self-regulated markets. Other countries like the US have shown a preference for a more formal approach with many regulators and supervisors whose authority and responsibilities are defined and codified in law. Such legislation may also define the permissible business activities of the various segments of the financial sector. The extent and quality of the supervisory process in each country also varies. Most countries like the US and UK, historically have maintained a high level of control and supervision over their banking industry, the markets in which they operate, and range of services and activities they undertake; others like some of the so-called "Offshore Banking Centres" have developed with little, if any, formal regulatory or supervisory arrangements.

Within the regulatory and supervisory process the authorities will amongst other things consider:

- licensing and authorising procedures

- capital requirements

- statutory reserve and liquidity requirements

- business activities

- monitoring and inspection

Licensing and authorising procedures are usually additional rather than an alternative to a country's formal requirements for company formation or business establishment. They normally encompass all deposit-taking institutions inclusive of any foreign-owned subsidiaries, associates, branches or offices which are permitted to operate within that country but may provide for some specific exemptions. Through the licensing process many countries differentiate between specific segments of the financial sector. For example, the 1979 Banking Act in the UK distinguishes between Recognised Banks and Licensed Deposit-Taking Institutions but does exempt some Deposit-Taking Institutions, such as building societies, from the requirements of this Act. However, it is pertinent to mention that the abolition of this two tiered system is being considered. As already mentioned, in the United States banks must be licensed either as a national, state or Edge Act bank and may make separate application for membership of the Federal Reserve system and for insured status with the Federal Deposit Insurance Corporation. In Singapore merchant banks do not require to be licensed but do need to be approved by the Monetary Authority of Singapore.

Although some countries continue to prohibit the establishment or participation of foreign banks within their banking sector, many countries do facilitate their access in one form or another. This may be permitted through the establishment of a branch, subsidiary or affiliate or a combination of any of these entities.

Also, controls are exercised frequently over the branching activities of banks and this is particularly relevant to the development and structure of the banking industry in the United States. Both the McFadden Act of 1934 and the Bank Holding Company Act of 1956 have, among other things, confined the activities of US banks to one state. Also some individual states restrict the number of branches or geographical area of operations of banks therein. However, through the Edge Act of 1919 and subsequent amendments to the Federal Reserve regulation K under which Edge Act corporations are regulated, US banks, where state legislation permits, are able to provide multi-state international banking services.

Until 1978 branch activities of foreign banks were not subject to the restrictions of the McFadden or Banking Holding Company Act and were able to develop branches in several states. This competititve advantage was abolished by the International Banking Act of 1978 which required foreign banks' branches to require a federal or state charter and thereafter to be subject to the requirements of the McFadden Act, but branches already established could be retained.

Within their regulatory and supervisory system several countries have special criteria for the establishment of "offshore" banking operations. However, as these criteria and supervisory activities related thereto may differ considerably from those which are normally applied to other banking operations, they are considered separately in Chapter 6.

In considering applications, licensing authorities will usually satisfy themselves that the proposed company is both adequately capitalised and has reputable and capable management available to it. In most countries the establishment of banks is not just a formality provided corporate requirements are complied with, as the authorities will also consider economic need criteria. However, in any country once a bank receives a licence to commence business irrespective of its standing as a corporate entity, it assumes responsibility for its activities to that country's regulators and supervisors, and it must comply with their regulations and directives.

Universally there are no accepted standards of measurement for either initial capital requirements or continuing capital adequacy for banks, and each country applies its own criteria. Although some regulatory authorities do specify minimum capital requirements which must be complied with upon incorporation and maintained thereafter, most satisfy themselves on a case by case basis having regard to the size of each bank's proposed operations. Foreign banks' subsidiaries and affiliates will normally be expected to comply in full with the host country's capital adequacy requirements, and in addition some regulatory authorities may require letters of comfort, a guarantee or other support document to be provided by the parent bank or banks for part or all of the subsidiary or affiliate's obligations. Branches of foreign banks may require to be fully or partially capitalised to the extent of the host country's capital requirements through the provision of specified investments, deposits, fixed or working capital by the parent. Fixed or working capital funds may either have to be provided in total by the head office of the parent, or be allowed to comprise the net inter-group funds made available from external sources. However, other authorities are prepared to accept foreign bank branch operations entirely on the standing of the parent and do not expect a branch to be separately capitalised.

Most authorities also consider, within their regulatory and supervisory role, a bank's continuing capital adequacy. There are two distinct types of measurement which are used in this process and parent authorities may apply either or both of these in relation to a bank's consolidated or non-consolidated position. The first type of measurement, the Capital/Asset ratio, is based upon gearing ratios related to the level of capital required to support a bank's total liability or asset base. The second, the Capital/Risk ratio, is based upon the relationship between capital and risk assets. Some authorities will formally publish their minimum criteria, others will merely issue guidelines and consider their application on a prudential basis having regard to the nature of each individual bank's business. The procedures adopted within the second method of measurement involve applying different weightings to specified categories of assets and are illustrated by reference to the Bank of England's criteria for this measurement in Part 3 of this chapter. Within these considerations it is usual to review foreign banks subsidiary and associated companies established within the host country but it is not common practice to extend the risk asset measurement to foreign banks' branch operations in isolation of the parent.

Although the principle of these types of measurement will be similar from country to country, perceived ratios, the composition of risk assets, basis of weightings and even the definition of a bank's capital base are not. For capital purposes authorities will, as a general rule, include shareholders equity and reserves (including general provisions) but some will exclude all, an element, or a percentage, of any subordinated debt and redeemable preference shares. Consequently there are significant differences in application and banks in one country may be able to hold several times more total assets, current liabilities, or higher levels of risk assets, on the same capital base as their competitors or indeed their own group operations in another country. Furthermore, as some parent authorities only apply these measurements to a bank's operations within its home country, consolidated ratios of banks so assessed may be substantially out of line with its parent authority's criteria.

In the context of a bank's maintenance of its capital adequacy, several countries also impose constraints and restrictions in regard to both credit and country risk exposure by relating maximum exposure to any individual counterparty or country to an element of such bank's capital base, but again such regulations are not always applied on a consolidated basis.

Historically a bank's liquidity has been assessed upon the relationship between defined elements of its deposit make-up related to statutory, conventional or perceived levels of defined reserves which banks are required or expected to maintain within each country. The definition of reserves is not uniform and may include requirements for non-interest bearing deposits being maintained with central banks, low yielding investments, market related instruments or an element of long-dated government or quasi government securities. Typically they may include cash, deposits and balances held with the central bank, treasury bills, money with discount houses or money brokers, eligible bank bills, government stocks or bonds maturing within a specified time period or a percentage of such instruments with longer life periods, and authorities may further differentiate between those which comprise primary and secondary reserves. Similarly the measure upon which these requirements are applied differs between countries. Some require reserves to be provided on all defined deposits irrespective of currency whilst others only require reserves to be provided on defined deposits in its domestic currency. For example in the United Kingdom eligible banks are required to maintain liquidity related to eligible liabilities (ELs) to a minimum level as agreed between the Bank and individual institutions. These are:

- Eligible liabilities comprise the total of the following sterling liabilities as defined within the Bank of England Form B.S. returns:

- Sight deposits (except those of the reporting institution's own overseas offices)

- Time deposits of the UK monetary sector

- Time deposits, other than those of the UK monetary sector and overseas offices, with an original maturity of two years or less

- Certificates of deposit issued

- Promissory notes, bills and other short-term paper issued

- Items in suspense

- 60% of credit items in course of transmission to UK offices of the reporting institution and other monetary sector institutions in the UK

- Net sterling liabilities, if any, to overseas offices comprising -
  Sight and time deposits from overseas offices including
  working capital provided by them in the form of deposits
  Less balance with them, i.e.
  loans and advances to them,
  and investment in them in the form of deposits.
  (An overall net claim on overseas offices should be disregarded.)

Less :
the total of sterling of the following:

- Balances with Bank of England (excluding special deposits and cash ratio deposits)

- Secured money with the London Discount Market Association

- Unsecured money with the London Discount Market Association

- Secured money at call with money brokers and gilt edged jobbers

- Balances with, loans and advances to, other monetary sector institutions

- Certificates of deposit issued by other monetary sector institutions

- Promissory notes, bills and other short-term paper issued by other monetary sector institutions

- 60% of debit items in course of collection on UK offices of the reporting institution and other monetary sector institutions in the UK

and plus the total in other currencies of the following:

- Net liabilities, if any, in currencies other than sterling (Note: a net asset position is not included)

Monetary liquid assets (MLAs) which are described below must be retained for liquidity purposes.

- A non-interest bearing balance with the Bank of England calculated as a percentage of the average eligible liabilities over a 6 month period (the "cash ratio"). Normally this is $\frac{1}{2}$%.

- Special deposits with the Bank of England at either no interest or at a non-commercial rate. At present, no special deposits are required by the Bank of England.

- Secured money with members of the LDMA and/or secured call money with brokers and gilt-edged jobbers – all at market rates appropriate to the nature of the lending – such that:
  (i)   the total funds so held average a specified percentage of the bank's ELs (currently 5% over a particular period)
  (ii) the amount held in the form of secured money with members of the LDMA does not normally fall below a specified percentage of ELs on any one day (currently $2\frac{1}{2}$%).

In the United States banks are required under Regulation D of the Federal Reserve System to maintain with it non-interest bearing deposits comprising a percentage of reservable assets. They are currently applied at the rate of 12% on current (checking) account balances and 3% on time and savings deposits exclusive of the accounts of private individuals.

West Germany has similar regulations which call for non-interest bearing deposits of 10.15% on sight deposits, 7.15% term deposits and 4.5% savings account balances being placed with the Bundesbank.

In Hong Kong banks are required to hold minimum holdings of specified liquid assets primarily related to 100% of liabilities due to banks and deposit-taking companies (DTCs) in Hong Kong and 25% of other deposit liabilities. Of these requirements at least 15% must be held in highly liquid assets defined as

- Hong Kong dollar notes and coin or currency immediately re-mittable to Hong Kong

- Refined gold

- Money on demand or call with DTCs or banks in Hong Kong

- Marketable CDs issued by a bank outside of Hong Kong

- Treasury bills maturing within 93 days

The remaining 10% or less may include:

- Money at short notice with a DTC or bank in Hong Kong

- Certificates of Deposit with a maturity of less than three years issued by a bank in Hong Kong, but holdings are limited to 2% of deposit liabilities

- Bills payable outside of Hong Kong

- UK Government securities with less than five years to maturity

Although this type of reserve continues to be required in most countries it is normally applied only to domestic banking operations including branches of overseas banks, many authorities have also developed or are in the course of developing, additional liquidity measures related to broader criteria which involve an examination of the make up of all assets and liabilities on a consolidated basis, with particular reference to marketable assets, a bank's commitments to lend, and contingent liabilities. This subject is discussed earlier under Asset and Liability Management in Chapter 3 and is further developed as a supervisory issue in the context of Bank of England requirements in Part 3 of this chapter.

In some countries there are few constraints on the types of business which individual banks may undertake, but others impose rigid delineations between commercial and investment banking and also businesses which are perceived to relate to banking activities. For example, in the United States the Glass-Steagall Act differentiates between commercial and investment banking. Commercial banks are generally excluded from participating in securities-related activities other than government bonds and money market instruments. Consequently it is frequently found that a bank may undertake activities in one country which it is not permitted or able to conduct in another. Considerations relating to non-banking businesses are more complex. Various authorities impose total, partial or no constraints upon a bank's ability to invest or partake directly in non-banking businesses whilst others, relate to specific types of business which may not be undertaken, for example, insurance, property investment, commodity investment and trading, or any wholesale or retail trade other than banking. Additionally, although banks may not be constrained from undertaking certain financial sector functions, their entry into those markets is often limited by separate regulations or requirements for entry. For example, within the UK primary trading in gilt-edged stocks has previously been limited to a small number of specialised jobbers and also Stock Exchange rules have prohibited the entry of banks and other financial institutions into that market.

Business constraints may not necessarily be caused by permitted or restricted business activities, but can be created by other monetary directives. For example, specific foreign or domestic lending and investment constraints may be imposed from time to time on a bank's ability to lend to specific sectors of an economy or to non-residents. The imposition of artifical interest rate levels will restrict a bank's ability to be competitive and frequently results in a loss of deposits as such ceilings are reached and higher rates of return sought by depositors. Exchange control regulations may affect a bank's ability to hold foreign currency balances either in other domestic currencies or through the eurodollar markets.

Regulatory and Supervisory authorities will also monitor the activities of banks through various other processes. These include the submission of selected returns, review meetings with individual bank management and reaction to any adverse rumour or events which may impact upon a particular bank's name. Within this monitoring process the authorities will consider matters related to the quality of individual bank management, internal controls, procedures, review activities and performance. Supervisory authorities may also have authority to undertake inspections and examination of a bank's operations, and in some countries, require external auditors to provide independent reports on the status of a bank to them on an annual basis. The establishment of a formal relationship and reporting system between the Bank of England and individual reporting banks' external auditors is a major consideration following the Johnson Matthey Bankers collapse.

Reports and returns required by the authorities comprise a mix of those which are required for both supervisory and statistical purposes. Taking the principal reports of the Bank of England as an example they may typically include:

Form B.S. – a detailed balance sheet expressed in sterling but covering all currencies converted at current exchange rates which is submitted monthly and at end calendar quarters.

Form C.1 – country exposure report completed by UK registered banks on a consolidated basis submitted six monthly for monitoring country concentration risk.

Form Q.1 and Q.3 – Sector and industry analysis of defined items on the B.S. return submitted for both statistical purposes and for monitoring loan concentration risk by industry type. Required quarterly.

Form Q.7 – Analysis of Shareholders' Funds and certain other miscellaneous information. Submitted quarterly. Used in conjunction with Form B.S. the return provides the necessary information to establish the current capital base of a bank in regard to the measurement of capital adequacy and capital risk ratios.

Form S.1 – Relates to external claims and liabilities in sterling by country and is required to be submitted eight times per annum.

Form S.2 – Relates to external claims and liabilities in foreign currency by country and is required on a quarterly basis.

Form S.2 (Section 2) – Analysis of total foreign currency claims and liabilities and forward sales and purchases by currency, submitted quarterly.

Form S.3 – Analysis by currency on a consolidated basis of total assets and liabilities including forward purchases and sales, gold, financial futures and if appropriate, options, converted into sterling at current spot rates. The completed return provides the Bank of England with the open positions in each currency and the overall open position of a bank. Submitted monthly and used to monitor a bank's compliance with agreed foreign exchange exposure guidelines.

Form S.5 – An analysis by maturity on a consolidated basis of foreign currency assets and liabilities reported on the B.S. and in the same format as for Q.6 for sterling submitted quarterly.

Form W.1 – Weekly summary of B.S. figures (not submitted in the same week as B.S.). Used to help forecast money supply statistics.

Form H.1 – Overseas direct investment return.

Form EB – Eligible Banks: secured deposits.

In summary it is evident that on a global basis substantial disparities do exist between mandatory or prudential levels and assessment of capital and liquidity, the scope of business activities in which banks may be involved together with the extent, depth and quality of reporting and supervisory arrangements which are imposed by individual countries. Attention as a general rule is focused upon national rather than global considerations with many supervisory and regulatory bodies only concerning themselves with issues related to their own domestic currency and the activities undertaken by banks within their national boundaries or other defined areas of jurisdiction. Although these regulatory and supervisory arrangements have merit insofar as they leave independent integrity as a matter for each country, they tend to give rise to the following:

- Different standards of regulatory and supervisory control being applied to various areas of an international bank's operations.

- No single authority being responsible for the totality of a bank's international business.

These disparities and weaknesses have not escaped the authorities' attention. Following the secondary banking crisis, oil price shocks and their consequences, together with some spectacular foreign exchange losses suffered by several banks in the early 1970s, the supervisors' attention focused more upon the multi-national nature of banks and their activities within the international markets. A standing committee of bank supervisors, "The Bank Supervisors Committee", comprising the Group of Ten (France, West Germany, United Kingdom, Canada, Japan, USA, Sweden, Netherlands, Italy and Belgium) plus Switzerland, was formed under the auspices of the Bank for International Settlements to co-ordinate surveillance over the international banking system – developments which are discussed in detail in Part 2 of this chapter.

In considering the Regulation and Supervision of Banks it is pertinent to mention that at the time of this publication many of the barriers mentioned are being removed in regard to restricted business activities. De-regulation is taking place in the US. In the UK arrangements are already under way for the Bank of England to provide discount facilities on a direct basis with a broader range of banks and other financial institutions, the previous preserve of members of the London Discount Market Association being extended to a broader market segment of institutions who are prepared to be market makers at all times in money market instruments. The Stock Exchange has pre-empted official action and permitted market entry to other financial institutions by way of investment up to a maximum of 29.9% in Stock Exchange companies and the Stock Exchange Council have amended their rules to allow such investments to be increased to 100%. An extension to the number of market makers in government securities is being encouraged and an initial list of 29 applicants has been approved. Concurrent with these changes in the UK, the Bank of England is considering the future regulatory framework for the financial markets and again, following the Johnson Matthey Bankers collapse, the Government is giving consideration to formally extending the authority of the Bank. As part of these developments a Securities and Investments Board has been established as the regulatory body for security firms and investment companies and the Department of Trade and Industry is preparing instructions for a new bill on investor protection.

However, it is not only the regulators who must concern themselves with these new developments. As new markets and opportunities present themselves each bank's management must consider its potential involvement therein, the special risks associated with each and, as appropriate, formulate policy guidelines and limits to control and monitor these activities and measure their possible impact and contribution to overall results and balance sheet risks.

The EEC have also issued directives on various issues related to banking. Those which have particular relevance to this chapter are the "Directive on freedom of establishment and to provide services" which is intended to ensure that there are no restrictions on banks and financial institutions within the community establishing themselves in other member states; the "First banking co-ordination directive" which required each member state to have a system of authorisation of banks – this directive resulted in the formulation of the UK Banking Act of 1979 and also provides for the calculation of solvency and liquidity ratios for observation purposes.

Part 2
The Basle Concordat
During 1975 the Bank Supervisors Committee or the "Cooke Committee" as it is now often referred to, issued guidelines for the division of responsibilities between national supervisory authorities.

Subsequently in 1983 this document which became known as the "Concordat" was revised by a further paper entitled "Principles for the Supervision of Banks' Foreign Establishments" which was issued and distributed to supervisory authorities worldwide. The 1983 paper takes cognizance of understandings, agreed by the participants since 1975.

The 1983 paper was agreed by the Group of Ten plus Switzerland and Luxembourg with the principle that supervision of international banks' capital adequacy and risk exposure should be monitored on a consolidated basis; a principle which had been endorsed by their central bank governors in 1978. Prior to its issue members of the Offshore Supervisors Group representing all the major offshore countries had also been involved in the discussions leading up to the document and that group also endorsed its content. Subsequently most other supervisory authorities throughout the world to whom the document was circulated have endorsed the revised document, as they did the original Concordat.

The report sets out various principles which the Committee believes should govern the supervision of banks' foreign establishments by parent and host authorities. Whilst accepting the principle of consolidated supervision this does not imply any lessening of host authorities' responsibilities for supervising foreign bank establishments that operate in their territories, although it is recognised that the full implementation of the consolidation principle may well lead to some extension of parental responsibility. Consolidation is only one of a range of techniques, albeit an important one, at the disposal of the Supervisory Authorities and it is not applied to the exclusion of supervision of individual banking establishments on an unconsolidated basis by parent and host authorities. Moreover, the implementation of the principle of consolidated supervision presupposes that parent banks and parent authorities have access to all the relevant information about the operations of their banks' foreign establishments, although existing banking secrecy provisions in some countries may present a constraint on comprehensive consolidated parental supervision.

The report identifies two basic general principles. First, that no foreign banking establishment should escape supervision and secondly, that the supervision should be adequate. Whilst specific responsibilities of parent and host authorities are identified, the necessity for effective co-operation between host and parent authorities as a central prerequisite for the supervision of banks' foreign establishments is stressed.

The types of banks' foreign establishments are considered, e.g. branches, subsidiaries, joint ventures or consortium, and reference is made to other minority participations which may be held to be part of a bank's overall foreign banking operation, together with those situations where international banking groups may derive from an ultimate holding company which is not itself a bank. Thereafter the report emphasises that whatever the banking structure the general principles of supervision and the foreign establishments' treatment therein are the same when examining the three major aspects of solvency, liquidity, and foreign exchange operations and positions.

The report suggests that, while there should be a presumption by supervisory authorities that host authorities are in a position to fulfil their supervisory obligations adequately with respect to all foreign bank establishments operating in their territories, this may not always by the case. Therefore in order to ensure that no foreign banking establishment should escape supervision it is the responsibility of the parent authority to ascertain whether the host authority is able to undertake adequate supervision and the host authority should inform the parent authority if it is not in a position to do so. In cases where host authority supervision is inadequate the parent authority should either extend its supervision, to the degree that it is practicable, or it should be prepared to discourage the parent bank from continuing to operate the establishment in question. Problems may arise where the host authority considers that supervision of the parent institution of foreign bank establishments operating in its territory is inadequate or non-existent. In such cases the host authority should discourage or, if it is in a position to do so, forbid the operation in its territory of such foreign establishments. Alternatively, the host authority could impose specific conditions governing the conduct of the business of such establishments.

Gaps in supervision can arise out of structural features inherent in some international banking groups. Supervisory problems may arise where holding companies, while themselves not being banks, have substantial liabilities to the international banking system. Where holding companies are at the head of groups that include separately incorporated banks operating in different countries, the authorities responsible for supervising those banks should endeavour to co-ordinate their supervision of those banks, taking account of the overall structure of the group in question. Where a bank is the parent company of a group that contains intermediate holding companies, the parent authority should make sure that such holding companies and their subsidiaries are covered by adequate supervision. Alternatively, the parent authority should not allow the parent bank to operate such intermediate holding companies.

Where groups contain both banks and non-bank organisations, there should be where possible, liaison between the banking supervisory authorities and any authorities which have responsibilities for supervising these non-banking organisations, particularly where the non-banking activities are of a financial character. Banking supervisors, in their overall supervision of banking groups, should take account of these groups' non-banking activities; and if these activities cannot be adequately supervised, banking supervisors should aim at minimising the risks to the banking business from the non-banking activities of such groups.

The implementation of the second basic principle, namely that the supervision of all foreign banking establishments should be adequate, requires the positive participation of both host and parent authorities. Host authorities are responsible for the foreign bank establishments operating in their territories as individual institutions, while parent authorities are responsible for them as parts of larger banking groups where a general supervisory responsibility exists in respect of their worldwide consolidated activities. These responsibilities of host and parent authorities are both complementary and overlapping. Host authorities should ensure that parent authorities are informed immediately of any serious problems which arise in a parent bank's foreign establishment. Similarly, parent authorities should inform host authorities when problems arise in a parent bank which are likely to affect the parent bank's foreign establishment.

The allocation of responsibilities for the supervision of the solvency and liquidity of banks' foreign establishments between parent and host authorities will depend upon the type of foreign establishment.

For branches, the report recognises that their solvency is indistinguishable from that of the parent bank as a whole. So, while there is a general responsibility on the host authority to monitor the financial soundness of foreign branches, supervision of solvency is primarily a matter for the parent authority. The initial presumption is that primary responsibility for supervising liquidity rests with the host authority. Host authorities will often be best equipped to supervise liquidity as it relates to local practices and regulations and the functioning of their domestic money markets. At the same time, the liquidity of all foreign branches will always be a matter of concern to the parent authorities, since a branch's liquidity is frequently controlled directly by the parent bank and cannot be viewed in isolation from that of the whole bank of which it is a part. Parent authorities need to be aware of parent banks' control systems and need to take account of calls that may be made on the resources of parent banks by their foreign branches. Host and parent authorities should always consult each other if there are any doubts in particular cases about where responsibilities for supervising the liquidity of foreign branches should lie.

For subsidiaries, the supervision of solvency is a joint responsibility of both host and parent authorities. Host authorities have responsibility for supervising the solvency of all foreign subsidiaries operating in their territories. Their approach to the task of supervising subsidiaries is from the standpoint that these establishments are separate entities, legally incorporated in the country of the host authority. At the same time parent authorities, in the context of consolidated supervision of the parent banks, need to assess whether the parent institutions' solvency is being affected by the operations of their foreign subsidiaries. Parental supervision on a consolidated basis is needed for two reasons: because the solvency of parent banks cannot be adequately judged without taking account of all their foreign establishments, and because parent banks cannot be indifferent to the situation of their foreign subsidiaries. Primary responsibility for supervising liquidity rests with the host authority. Parent authorities should take account of any standby or other facilities granted as well as any other commitments, for example through comfort letters, by parent banks to subsidiaries. Host authorities should inform the parent authorities of the importance they attach to such facilities and commitments, so as to ensure that full account is taken of them in the supervision of the parent bank. Where the host authority has difficulties in supervising the liquidity of foreign banks' subsidiaries, especially in foreign currency, it should inform the parent authorities and appropriate arrangements will have to be agreed so as to ensure adequate supervision.

For practical reasons the supervision of joint ventures' solvency is normally the responsibility of the authorities in the country of incorporation. Banks which are shareholders in consortium banks cannot, however, be indifferent to the situation of their joint ventures and may have commitments to these establishments beyond the legal commitments which arise from their shareholdings, for example through comfort letters. All these commitments will be taken into account by the parent authorities of the shareholder banks when supervising their solvency. Depending on the pattern of shareholdings in joint ventures, and particularly when one bank is a dominant shareholder, there can also be joint responsibility of the authorities in the country of incorporation and the parent authorities of the shareholder banks. Primary responsibility for supervising liquidity should also rest with the authorities in the country of incorporation with the parent authorities of shareholders in joint ventures taking account of any standby facilities or commitments by shareholder banks to those establishments. The authorities in the country of incorporation of joint ventures should inform the parent authorities of shareholder banks of the importance they attach to such facilities and commitments so as to ensure that full account is taken of them in the supervision of the shareholder bank.

Within the framework of consolidated supervision, parent authorities will have a general responsibility for overseeing the liquidity control systems employed by the banking groups they supervise and for ensuring that these systems and the overall liquidity position of such groups are adequate. It is recognised, however, that full consolidation may not always be practicable as a technique for supervising liquidity because of differences of local regulations and market situations and the complications of banks operating in different time zones and different currencies. Parent authorities should consult with host authorities to ensure that the latter are aware of the overall systems within which the foreign establishments are operating. Host authorities have a duty to ensure that a parent authority is immediately informed of any serious liquidity inadequacy in a parent bank's foreign establishment.

The report concludes that the supervision of banks' foreign exchange operations and positions is a joint responsibility of parent and host authorities. It is particularly important for parent banks to have in place systems for monitoring their group's overall foreign exchange exposure and for parent authorities to monitor those systems. Host authorities should be in a position to monitor the foreign exchange exposure of foreign establishments in their territories and should inform themselves of the nature and extent of the supervision of these establishments being undertaken by the parent authorities.

"Concordat" deals exclusively with the responsibilities of banking Supervisory Authorities for monitoring the prudential conduct and soundness of the business of banks' foreign establishments. It recognises that in many countries the supervisory function is undertaken by authorities which are not central banks and therefore stresses that the paper does not address itself to the lender-of-last resort aspects of a central bank. Similarly, it is accepted that the principles set out therein are not necessarily embodied in the laws of the countries represented on the Committee, rather they are recommended guidelines of best practices in the area of supervision which all members have undertaken to work towards implementing, according to the means available to them.

To illustrate some of the implications of "Concordat", Part 3 of this chapter outlines the content of three papers issued by the Bank of England under the headings:

- Measurement of Capital

- Foreign Currency Exposure

- Measurement of Liquidity

Part 3
The Bank of England – Capital Adequacy

In the United Kingdom the 1979 Banking Act formally gave the Bank of England (the Bank) the statutory right to grant, or revoke, banking licences in Britain and to exercise prudential supervision over all banks operating from and within the United Kingdom. On the 5th September 1980 the Bank of England issued a paper on the subject of "The Measurement of Capital" which was the first in a series of three documents explaining the Bank's approach to prudential supervision. A second paper styled "Foreign Currency Exposure" was issued on the 24th April 1981 and the final paper "Measurement of Liquidity" was issued on the 20th July 1982. Each paper was published following extensive consultations with the banking community dating back to 1975. These papers respectively establish, for the purpose of the Bank's continuing supervision of banks, and as appropriate, deposit-taking institutions for which the Bank of England has supervisory responsibility under the 1979 Banking Act, a basis for:

- assessing the adequacy of capital to sustain a bank's business and as protection against the risk of loss

- measuring, monitoring and discussing exposure to movements in exchange rates

- the measurement of liquidity

These papers follow the three major aspects of the supervision of banks' foreign establishments as identified in the Basle Committee's 1983 paper:

- Solvency
- Foreign exchange operations and positions
- Liquidity

In general, the Bank of England's approach to the assessment of capital adequacy is flexible. It takes account of the particular character of each institution, and has regard not only to the interests of depositors with individual institutions but also to the maintenance of confidence in the system as a whole. It is concerned essentially with the capital needs of a continuing business. It also takes account of the acknowledged division of responsibilities among supervisory authorities internationally. Although the Bank prescribes capital adequacy targets it does not (at least publicly) issue minimum ratio requirements for the capital needs of all institutions or for groups of institutions as it considers this would be inappropriately inflexible. Such an approach would endorse overtrading by some companies and be harmfully restrictive to others. Furthermore, it is recognised that a sufficient flow of earnings is essential as a first defence against losses and as a source of fresh capital to allow a business to grow or even to maintain the scope of its operations during a period of inflation. The Bank consider profitability and other prudential considerations have their place within the assessment of capital adequacy so that, within a common framework for the measurement of capital applying to all institutions, the Bank's final assessment of the capital adequacy of a particular institution will involve qualitative judgments depending on the nature of its business. Within the field of supervised institutions there is therefore a range of capital ratios regarded as adequate.

In assessing the capital adequacy and risk exposure of banking groups the Bank of England recognises the principle of consolidated supervision which takes account of the business of all the branches at home and abroad and all the wholly-owned and majority-owned subsidiaries engaging in financial business. In the case of UK-incorporated deposit-taking businesses, it is thus the Bank's approach in assessing capital adequacy to take account of their worldwide operations on a consolidated basis. The Bank also considers that deposit-taking subsidiary companies in the United Kingdom should be adequately capitalised in their own right. In addition to a consolidated measure the Bank will thus also have regard for the capital adequacy of individual deposit-taking companies within a group.

The Bank identifies the following as the two most important objectives of capital ratios:

- to ensure that the capital position of an institution is regarded as acceptable by its depositors and other creditors, and

- to test the adequacy of capital in relation to the risk of losses which may be sustained.

As depositors and other creditors have to form judgments about the capital adequacy of an institution using published information and because their reaction to these judgments will have an important bearing on the stability of each institution, it is desirable that the first measure of capital to be employed by a bank should be constructed of elements, as far as possible, available to the public. The Bank concludes that this requirement is broadly met by relating current liabilities to capital resources – the free resources or gearing ratio. However, within its definition of the capital base for supervisory purposes it includes inner reserves and general debt provisions the existence of which may not be apparent to the public.

The Bank concludes that the second objective for supervisory purposes is the more important so that the risk measurement of capital adequacy should take precedence. However, the gearing measurement will also be considered by the Bank in ensuring that an institution is not running ahead of its probable capacity to sustain its business in normal circumstances. The risk measurement of capital adequacy has assumed increased importance as a result of the recent international debt crisis and its possible impact upon the international banking community.

Within the Measurement of Capital paper the Bank provides a basic definition of capital; a definition of capital and liabilities for the gearing ratio, and a definition of capital and risk assets for the risk asset ratio. For neither ratio is any specific numerical guideline established. The Bank takes the view that to publish such numbers would allow insufficient flexibility to take account of the different circumstances of particular institutions. Publication could also impair the ability of an institution to raise fresh capital when most in need. The Bank will discuss capital adequacy with individual banks in confidence and the guidelines that evolve are not intended to be inflexible. However, the Bank indicates that it is firmly of the view that over the longer term certain standards must pertain and it will therefore wish to be assured that in planning for expansion all deposit-taking institutions give due weight to maintaining an acceptable level of capital.

The capital for both gearing and risk asset ratios will comprise the equity capital base, viz:

- Paid up share capital -
  issued ordinary and non-redeemable preference shares.
  Share premium.

- Minority interests -
  When included in accounts as a result of the consolidation of subsidiary companies not wholly owned. However, where these interests contribute significantly to the consolidated capital base the Bank will examine them closely to consider whether some part of them should be excluded.

- Reserves -
  Balance on profit and loss account. General reserves, including "inner" reserves.

- Provisions -
  General bad debt provisions, less any associated deferred tax asset. (Provisions for specific bad debts and interest in suspence, and provisions for deferred and current taxation are not included.)

- *less* Goodwill

90

Surbordinated loan stocks comprise:
a) primary capital loan stocks.

Perpetual debt which is fully subordinated to the rights (in liquidation) of other creditors, and on condition that the loan agreement does not include any clauses which might trigger repayment of the debt and that there are no cross-default clauses and negative pledge. It must also have loss absorption capacity in the event of the issuer's liquidation.

b) non-primary loan stocks.

Loan stock which is fully subordinated to other creditors (including depositors) and does not have any restrictive covenants. Subject to straignt line "amortisation" in the last five years of life. Redeemable preference shares are treated as subordinated loan capital.

The total of (a) and (b) which may qualify for inclusion within the Bank's measurement of capital adequacy is subject to the following limits.

1. $\dfrac{\text{PRIMARY CAPITAL LOAN STOCKS}}{\text{EQUITY CAPITAL BASE}}$ = MAXIMUM 50%

2. $\dfrac{\text{NON-PRIMARY LOAN STOCKS}}{\text{PRIMARY CAPITAL BASE (Equity capital base plus primary capital loan stocks)}}$ = MAXIMUM 50%

3. $\dfrac{\text{TOTAL LOAN STOCKS (PRIMARY \& NON-PRIMARY)}}{\text{EQUITY CAPITAL BASE}}$ = MAXIMUM 100%

The following points should also be noted:

a) Any primary capital loan stocks which are surplus to the maximum permitted ratio in 1 above may be treated as non-primary loan stocks for the purposes of ratios 2 and 3.

b) The maximum ratios permitted in 1 and 2 above are overridden by that in 3.

For the purpose of the gearing measurement the following deductions will be made from the capital base to arrive at the adjusted

91

capital base. This will be measured against all other non-capital liabilities incorporated in the balance sheet apart from contingent liabilities and subordinated loan stocks, disallowed by the qualifying criteria for the capital base. The deductions are:

- Investments in subsidiaries and associated companies – when not consolidated within the parent's accounts and inclusive of subordinated debt issued by other banks. (Exceptions in respect of other banks subordinated debt will be made for selected banks which are market-makers in these instruments and to facilitate specialist institutions to hold issues of other banks' capital for up to three months from the date of issue.)

- Goodwill

- Equipment

- Premises

- Other fixed assets

The adjusted capital base for the risk measurement will be arrived at through making the same deductions as with the gearing measurement except that premises will not be deducted from the capital base but will be treated like other balance sheet assets. The increased emphasis the Bank devotes to this measure requires a detailed differential between the degrees of risk attaching to various categories of asset. Therefore the standard risk asset calculation utilised by the Bank takes into account three types of risk inherent in the assets themselves applying weightings to the different assets reflecting the extent to which they are susceptible to these risks. The three types of risk are:

- credit risk – the risk that claims on others may not be paid on the due date at their full book value.

- investment risk – the risk that marketable claims on others, or directly held assets, may depreciate below their book value.

● and as a further element within investment risk, the
forced sale risk – the risk that actual and additional losses may be
sustained because of the need to make untimely sales of assets
which, depending on the narrowness of the market, may yield
less than their quoted value.

The following schedule provides a classification of assets and risk
weightings held by UK offices of reporting banks as issued by the
Bank of England. Commercial advances are taken as a benchmark to
which a weight of unity is therefore ascribed. The risk asset ratio is
calculated by multiplying each balance sheet asset by its weight to
produce an adjusted total of risk assets and then establishing the
proportion of this total represented by the capital base as modified by
the items requiring a deduction.

Nil weight	Bank of England notes and UK coin
	Other sterling notes
	Balances with Bank of England
	Special deposits with Bank of England
	Debits in course of collection on banks in the United Kingdom
	Balances with overseas offices of the reporting bank
	Lending under special schemes for exports and ship- building
	Certificates of tax deposit
	Items in suspense
	Refinanced lending at fixed rates
	Gold physically held in own vaults
	Gold held elsewhere on an allocated basis
0.1 weight	Foreign currency notes and coin
	UK and Northern Ireland Treasury bills
0.2 weight	Debit items in course of collection on overseas banks
	Market loans with listed banks, discount market, etc.
	Market loans to UK local authorities and public cor- porations
	Balances with banks overseas with a maximum term of up to one year (including claims in gold)

Bills other than UK and Northern Ireland
Treasury bills

Other loans and advances to Northern Ireland Government, UK local authorities, public corporations and other public sector

British government stocks with up to 18 months to final maturity

Acceptances drawn on UK and overseas banks and UK public sector

Claims in gold on UK banks and members of the London Gold Market

0.5 weight British Government stocks with over 18 months to final maturity

Northern Ireland government stocks

UK local authority and other public sector stocks and bonds

Guarantees and other contingent liabilities

Note issuance facilities

Revolving underwriting facilities

1.0 weight Market loans placed with other UK residents

Other loans and advances, net of specific provisions for bad debts, but excluding connected lending

Assets leased to customers

Working capital provided for overseas offices of the reporting bank, both in the form of deposits and in other forms

Balances with banks overseas with a term of one year or over (including claims in gold)

Claims in gold on non-banks

Aggregate foreign currency position (to be defined in the Bank's paper on Foreign Currency Exposure)

Other assets, e.g. silver, commodities and other goods beneficially owned by the reporting bank

Other quoted investments, not connected

Acceptances drawn on other UK and overseas residents

1.5 weight   Connected lending (to be looked at case-by-case and to exclude market-type lending where this can be separately identified)

Unquoted investments (subject to case-by-case treatment)

2.0 weight   Property (includes all land and premises beneficially owned by the reporting bank)

It will be noted that this schedule covers only assets held by the UK offices of reporting companies. The Bank now attaches importance to assessing the adequacy of capital against the consolidated total of risk assets, on the basis of local equivalents provided there is no cross border element in the source basis and individual discussions take place with those banks affected in order to agree an appropriate statistical framework for the classification of assets held abroad.

In looking at the capital position of a particular institution the Bank will include in its assessment of the risk asset ratio, the perceived exposure to further risks such as fraud and other operational risk or concentrations of exposures on special sectoral and geographic exposures. This will involve a series of qualitative judgments and as a result there will be a range of ratios regarded as adequate according to the character of each institution's business. The assessment will also have regard for any marked divergence from the ratios which may obtain among similar institutions, and for changes over time in the ratios of particular institution. Final assessment of capital adequacy for each institution will also take into account the particular circumstances of each institution. For example, the large institution with a well diversified spread of high quality lending will inherently be less exposed to risk, and therefore requires relatively less capital cover against its assets, than the small specialist institution with a narrower customer base.

During April 1985 in Notice BSD/1985/2 the Bank announced its intention, and is in the process of considering the treatment of various off-balance sheet risks for purposes of assessing capital adequacy and liquidity management control. In particular this notice expressed concern regarding the obligations assumed by institutions which act as underwriters of note issuance facilities or revolving underwriting facilities and as reflected in the risk weighting schedule immediately included such obligations at a weight of 0.5 in the calculations of the risk asset ratio. Additionally, on the 22nd May 1985 the Bank of England issued a paper under the title "Consolidated Supervision: A Discussion Paper" on the subject of its approach to the supervision on a consolidated basis of banks which are part of a group of companies. The paper sets out the criteria for determining which companies should be included in consolidated returns for reporting purposes. These include the type of activities undertaken by the company, the company's size in relation to the bank, and the group management structure, the extent of funding provided by the bank and potential calls on, or other adverse circumstances for, the bank arising from the activities of the company. As a general rule it is proposed that all financial companies which are majority owned by a bank, either directly or through intermediate holding companies, should be consolidated.

Within Bank of England guidelines, banks in the UK are only normally expected to lend up to 10% of their capital base to any individual counterparty risk although in exceptional circumstances this may be increased to 25%.

As identified in Chapter 2 exposure to movements in exchange rates is only one of the many categories of risk to which banks are subject in the conduct of their foreign currency operations. However, the nature of foreign exchange risk is so significant in terms of potential loss that the Bank consider it justifies special consideration within the supervisory process.

The Bank of England's Foreign Currency Exposure paper sets out the basis on which the Bank will measure, monitor and discuss with banks and licensed deposit-taking institutions their exposure to movements in exchange rates. The Bank accepts that the primary responsibility for the control of exposures arising from foreign currency operations, as for any other aspect of a bank's business, must rest with a bank's own management. However, in the discharge of its supervisory responsibilities, the Bank needs to know the methods by which banks' management control such exposures, the extent of each bank's exposure, and its relation to other risks and to its capital. Satisfactory internal control procedures are considered essential and the Bank requires to be informed about the general arrangements within each institution for controlling its foreign currency trading.

The Bank of England is concerned with exposures arising out of any uncovered foreign currency position in any currency and considers each bank's exposure both in terms of its net position in any one currency and its overall position, i.e. the aggregate net position in all currencies. Net currency positions include the position held against sterling because the risk of loss arising from a net open position in sterling is no different from that arising from a position in any other currency. The net position in sterling is monitored separately and included in the assessment of each bank's overall exposure. Currency positions include gold and may also take positions in silver and foreign currency options into account. Foreign currency income and expense items which have accrued will be included but those which have not been accrued (including known future cash flows) need not be included, unless a bank wishes to do so because it has already covered them. For example future payments and receipts of interest on deposit swap transactions which are discussed in Chapters 15 and 16.

Within the context of supervision of Foreign Currency Exposure the Bank of England applies different arrangements for UK- incorporated banks and for branches of foreign banks, although both participate in the same reporting system. For UK-incorporated banks the Bank will not set any formal limits on the size of a bank's foreign currency positions, but will agree dealing position guidelines with each institution individually. These will take account of the institution's particular circumstances and expertise. The guidelines will be determined in terms of a relationship between the dealing position and the bank's capital, because it is ultimately from this source that any loss arising from the position has to be made good. However, for administrative convenience guidelines are normally set by the Bank as a specific amount in pounds sterling. As a general rule, for banks which are experienced in foreign exchange the Bank will expect to agree a figure within the following guidelines:

- Net open dealing position in any one currency: not more than 10% of the adjusted capital base, as defined in The Measurement of Capital for the risk assets measure.

- Net short open dealing position of all currencies taken together: not more than 15% of the adjusted capital base.

The Bank would expect banks less experienced in foreign exchange to operate within more conservative guidelines.

These arrangements and guidelines will apply to the operations of all the branches both in the United Kingdom and overseas of UK-incorporated banks. They do not, as at the date of this publication, extend to UK banks' subsidiaries either domestic or overseas. However, the Bank indicates that it will wish eventually to include in its consolidated assessment of capital adequacy foreign currency exposures of UK banks' subsidiaries and this will be the subject of further consultations with the banking community in due course.

The Bank accepts that there is a valid distinction between "dealing" positions which arise from a bank's daily or 'normal' banking operations and "structural" positions which are intended to be of a longer term nature and may conveniently be considered separately from dealing positions. The Bank will be prepared to exclude structural positions from the dealing guidelines agreed with each bank. However, this distinction does not mean that the Bank considers structural exposures are without risk, and the aggregate foreign currency position included in the risk assets ratio encompasses both dealing and structural positions.

Each bank has its own views on the categorisation of exposures as dealing or structural. The dividing line is not always clear and will depend on the particular circumstances of that bank. The Bank of England will wish to ensure, however, that the make-up of a structural position does not undermine the application of the guidelines for the dealing position. Therefore the Bank will wish to be consulted on whether any part of a position in any currency should be treated as structural. The Bank would normally accept, as structural, exposures arising from banks' fixed and long-term assets and liabilities, includ-

98

ing such items as loan capital, premises and investments in subsidiaries and associates. It might also be appropriate to treat, as structural, positions which banks are obliged to maintain as a result of laws or market conditions to which their overseas affiliates are subject, and positions which arise as a result of reserves or provisions being maintained in currencies appropriate to the banking risks against which they are being held.

Whilst the Bank of England has supervisory responsibility under the Banking Act for UK branches of foreign banks, it is enabled, under the Act, to place substantial reliance on the supervisory authorities in the country of origin to monitor foreign exchange exposure risk. However in order to carry out its responsibility under the Act and to see that foreign exchange markets in the United Kingdom are conducted in an orderly manner, the Bank does require returns to be made by UK branches of foreign banks.

In monitoring the foreign currency operations of foreign branches, the Bank will take account of a branch's own internal controls, those exercised by its head office, and the monitoring arrangements of its own supervisory authority in determining appropriate guidelines.

The Measurement of Liquidity paper issued by the Bank of England is less specific than those on Capital and Foreign Currency and primarily provides a framework for discussions with individual banks and licensed deposit-taking companies, and does not extend to the overseas branches or subsidiaries of UK parent institutions for which host authorities have primary responsibility. The Bank recognises that whilst the provision of MLAs, Reserve Assets or other mandatory liquidity requirements has the virtue of simplicity it does not take account of the development of liability or asset management techniques for controlling liquidity through cash flows. It also involves an over-sharp distinction between "liquid" assets and other assets, many of which will be capable of generating cash in particular circumstances.

The Bank of England's supervisory objective is to ensure that banks' management policies apply a prudent mix of different forms of liquidity appropriate to the circumstances of the bank and that these policies are sustained at all times. The Bank regards a prudent mix as one which offers security of access to liquidity without undue exposure to suddenly rising costs from liquefying assets or bidding for deposits.

The responsibility for ensuring the liquidity of a bank rests with its own management. The Bank does not seek to impose across-the-board liquidity ratio norms, just as it does not seek across-the-board capital adequacy ratio norms, and thereby to supplant the exercise of judgment by bank managements. Instead, in determining what is a prudent policy for a bank, the Bank will take full account of its particular characteristics and situation within the banking system. As part of its regular discussions with senior management, the Bank will require to be fully satisfied that banks have both prudent policies and adequate management systems to ensure that the policies are followed; and it will continue to monitor banks' liquidity management during the normal course of its supervision. The Bank will wish to examine the extent to which potentially immediate obligations (deposits at sight and short notice and commitments to lend) should be supported by cash and immediately maturing or liquefiable assets and their appropriate quality; and the extent to which banks have planned ahead to meet the maturing of deposits with fixed maturity dates.

With these principles in mind, the Measurement of Liquidity paper establishes a framework for measuring liquidity applicable to banks generally, that will serve as a first step towards a qualitative assessment of the adequacy of the liquidity of individual banks taking account of their particular circumstances.

In measuring liquidity in the United Kingdom a distinction has often been made between the position in sterling-denominated business and that in other currencies, although the positions in different foreign currencies normally have not been separately identified. Such distinctions may be appropriate because of the particular circumstances of a bank or its internal management policies. When this is the case, the Bank would expect to take account of these same divisions as a basis for its own monitoring. The Bank, however, also wishes to assess the liquidity of a bank's total business, undifferentiated as to currency denomination, since in principle, through the foreign exchange markets, obligations in one currency may be met by the availability of liquid funds in another.

The basis of measurement applied by the Bank is based on a cash flow approach, similar to that already discussed in Chapter 3, and normally taking liabilities and assets in all currencies together. The Bank provides the following format:

	Sight–8 days	8 days–1 month	1–3 months	3–6 months	6–12 months
Liabilities					
Deposits					
Commitments					
Less Assets					
Marketable					
Non-marketable					
Standby facilities available					
= Net position					
+/− Carried forward					
= Net cumulative position					

Liabilities and assets are inserted in a "maturity ladder", with the net positions in each time period being accumulated. In the first maturity bands on the ladder this measure, by comparing sight and near sight liabilities with cash and assets capable of generating cash immediately, is similar to a customary liquid assets ratio. Marketable assets are placed at the start of the maturity ladder, rather than according to their maturity date, but account is taken of limitations, if any, on their marketability and their susceptibility to price fluctuations. Commitments are recognised by being included as liabilities or as agreed in specific cases. The Bank also provides the undermentioned guidelines for preparation and presentation of the liquidity profile.

Deposits of all types are included according to earliest maturity. However, the Bank recognises that it may be appropriate for certain special categories of deposit, e.g. those where it is agreed that set-off should apply, to be netted off against specific assets and excluded from the calculation. The volatility of deposits, particularly call or notice deposits taken in aggregate, may be in practice tend to be more closely related to a bank's creditworthiness as perceived by depositors and to its position in the system or to current economic or financial conditions rather than to the precise terms of the deposits. It is recognised that for some banks, distinctions can be drawn between different types of deposit, for example, between retail and wholesale deposits. This stability and diversification of the deposit base will be taken into account in discussion of appropriate guidelines. Known firm commitments to make funds available on a particular date are included in the appropriate time band at their full value. Commitments which are not due to be met on a particular day, for example, undrawn overdraft and other facilities, are unlikely to have to be met in full and cannot be treated precisely. The extent to which undrawn facilities should be included as a liability will vary with their nature. This imprecision will be reflected by the inclusion of only a proportion of outstanding commitments in the first maturity band, the remainder being excluded. The appropriate proportion for each bank will be determined having regard to its past and prospective drawndown experience. Contingent liabilities are not included in the measurement, unless there is a reasonable likelihood that the conditions necessary to trigger them might be fulfilled.

Assets are measured by reference to their final maturity, unless, as in the case of overdrafts, they are repayable on demand, in practice only nominally, or unless they are marketable, or are known to be of doubtful value. Lending repayable on demand only nominally may yield some regular cash flow but this cannot be measured at all precisely. The Bank will wish to agree appropriate treatment with each bank. Possibilities which might be appropriate to normal circumstances would be for banks to treat some proportion of the total as generating an immediate cash flow or to treat it as repayable in instalments over a period. The treatment of marketable assets takes account of the extent to which they can be sold for cash quickly (or used as security for borrowing), incurring little or no cost penalty;

and of any credit or investment risks which may make their potential value less predictable. It is important that the market for the asset should be sufficiently deep to ensure a stable demand for it. An important factor in this is the willingness of the central bank to use the asset in its normal market operations. These considerations are recognised in the measurement by applying varying discounts normally against the market value of marketable assets, all of which are included at the start of the maturity ladder. Discounts for the majority of sterling assets are provided below.

Nil Discount: Treasury, eligible local authority and eligible bank bills.
Government and Government guaranteed marketable securities with less than 12 months remaining term to maturity.

5% Discount: Other bills and certificates of deposit with less than six months remaining term to maturity.
Other Government, Government guaranteed and local authority marketable securities with less than five years remaining term to maturity or at variable rates.

10% Discount: Other bills, certificates of deposit and FRNs with less than five years remaining term to maturity.
Other Government, Government guaranteed and local authority marketable debt with more than five years remaining term to maturity.

Discount to be determined: All other marketable assets.

Similar discounts will pertain to comparable foreign currency assets. Assets not covered will be a matter for agreement, on a common basis, arising out of discussions with individual banks. Assets known to be of doubtful value are excluded from the measurement, or treated on a case-by-case basis. Contractual irrevocable standby facilities made available to the bank by other banks provide support which should be recognised, and they may be included as equivalent to a sight asset. Due regard, however, will be paid to their remaining term and the possibility that they may not be renewed. Standby facilities provided by a bank to other banks are treated in the same way as commitments to lend at some uncertain future date. Where items in course of transmission or collection are material, credits in course of transmission are deducted from debits in course of collection and the balance added to assets at the start of the maturity ladder. Items in suspense are normally treated on a gross basis.

The Bank will also wish to discuss with individual banks how far into the future it is desirable to measure liquidity profiles which depend very much on the circumstances of each bank. The point of maximum excess of liabilities over assets normally occurs within the first six months, although it can be later and it is therefore proposed that the profile should be measured up to 12 months. The Bank recognises, however, that in analysis and discussion it may be appropriate to concentrate more on the earlier maturities.

As a separate matter, the Bank will also wish to continue to monitor the overall maturity transformation undertaken: for the further ahead a bank's assets mature, the more difficult it is to estimate confidently the credit and other risks which will attach to them until they mature, or to forecast the circumstances in which the bank will then be trading.

The Bank's aim is to relate its measurement to the realities of the circumstances of each bank, and to achieve this, discussions with each bank are needed. For example, the proper treatment of parental responsibilities for the liquidity of branches, subsidiaries and affiliates may require special considerations. If these operate mainly in the UK, the Bank may seek additional information from individual banks in order to monitor on a consolidated basis. This may be less appropriate if the branches, subsidiaries and affiliates operate abroad for, even if the UK parent bank has ultimate responsibility, local conditions and regulatory requirements may mean that the liquidity needs of the parent and the operation abroad are so different that consolidation of the two would be unhelpful. In these cases, the Bank needs to satisfy its prudential objectives in some other way: for example, by examination of the internal arrangements of the parent bank for monitoring and controlling its worldwide liquidity needs.

The Bank had not in the past closely monitored the overall liquidity of UK branches of foreign banks, but had taken steps to ascertain that this is done by the head offices of these banks. The Bank has indicated that it will wish to do so in the future, taking account of the relationship between the branch and its head office, and will have particular regard to positions in sterling.

In the 1983/84 annual report of its activities in the exercise of the functions conferred on it by the 1979 Banking Act the Bank of England commented that during the year the Bank held discussions with a large number of institutions on the management of their liquidity and it was confirmed that individual institutions' needs for liquidity vary considerably, depending on the nature of their activities and their role in the markets. Informed by these discussions, the Bank will now be seeking to form and agree guidelines for liquidity appropriate to individual institutions or groups of institutions.

CHAPTER SIX

The Offshore Currency Deposit Markets and Offshore Banking Centres

Part 1

The Offshore Currency Market

It may appear incongruous to incorporate the subject of the offshore currency market in a section of this publication dealing with Regulation and Control. However, as the development of this market is essentially resultant from anomalies which exist between the application of regulatory, monetary and fiscal policies by individual countries, it seems appropriate to consider it in that context.

The so-called "Euro" and "Asian" currency deposit markets are International markets in which freely convertible currencies are deposited and lent outside of the regulations, restrictions and constraints that may normally apply within the national boundaries of the country of issue of those currencies. These are markets in which the right of ownership to currencies – euro-dollars, asian-dollars, euro-marks, euro-swiss, euro-yen, euro-sterling and euro-ECU to name a few – are held and transferred either permanently or temporarily. These currencies have no separate existence from currencies without the Euro or Asian prefix, they are simply ordinary deposits the right to which is vested and retained in external hands until such time as they might be transferred to official or resident ownership within their country of issue. The terms "Euro" and "Asian" have no special significance other than to identify the geographical regions in which the banks, which transact business in these external funds, are domiciled.

The "Euro" and "Asian" currency markets are effectively part of one substantial International Offshore Currency Deposit market through which banks domiciled in several countries around the world take and make foreign currency deposits and which creates chains of financial transactions. Only the net impact of these transactions is reflected as part of each bank's nostro or other accounts maintained with banks domiciled within the domestic deposit market of the respective countries of issue of the currency (e.g. a U.S. dollar nostro account in New York).

The concept of banks in various parts of the world accepting foreign currency deposits is not a new phenomenon but prior to the 1950s these funds were more commonly employed within their respective domestic currency markets for funding nostro accounts or converted through the foreign exchange markets into the domestic currency of the deposit holding bank. The origin of these international markets in their present form is normally attributed to a preference of various Eastern European governments, for political reasons during the early 1950s, to maintain their substantial claims in US dollars outside of the US by placing US dollar deposits – euro-dollars – with banks domiciled throughout Western Europe but in particular London and Paris. Thereafter it was those deposit holding banks' appreciation that if these funds were deployed outside of the US banking system, at a time when there was a substantial external demand for US dollar finance, the effective overall cost of funding would be reduced as they would not be subject to non-interest bearing reserves which were imposed on deposit liabilities by the Federal Reserve under Regulation D of the US Banking Act of 1933. Non-interest bearing reserve requirements were applied at a level of 10% of reservable liabilities but have subsequently been reduced to 3% on reservable time and savings deposits.

Furthermore by accepting finer net margins banks were not only able to lend US dollars more competitively than banks domiciled in the US but also able to pay interest on a more competitive basis. Section 19 of the Federal Reserve Act prohibited banks within the US from paying interest on deposits with an original maturity of less than 30 days (this period has subsequently been reduced to 7 days) and also under implementation of Regulation Q, relatively low interest rate ceilings were imposed in regard to the payment of interest on other deposits. Regulation Q of the US Banking Act of 1933 provided the Federal Reserve with authority to apply limits on the rates of interest payable on deposits. At the date of this publication Regulation Q is only applied in respect of certain defined savings and time deposits of less than US$2,500.

In summary, apart from country risk and political considerations, the main two incentives for the development of an external deposit market in US dollars were:
- non-interest bearing statutory deposit requirements,   and
- the imposition of interest rate ceilings on domestic deposits.

The success of any market is dependent upon adequate liquidity – both supply and demand. Several factors added to the liquidity of US dollars in the International Currency Deposit Market. These included US monetary and fiscal guidelines imposed during the 1950s and 1960s, through the Voluntary Foreign Credit Restraint programme, the Foreign Direct Investment Programme and the Interest Equalization Tax. Collectively these guidelines were designed to discourage the outflow of capital from the US domestic markets and respectively requested that banks domiciled in the US restrict foreign loans, limited overseas capital investment by US residents from domestic sources and taxed income on foreign securities. During 1967 the UK authorities imposed restrictions on the use of sterling as a source of funding for third country trade which was replaced to a large extent by externally generated US$ funds. Each of these measures increased demand for "offshore" finance.

In the absence of any exchange control restrictions on residents of the United States, the offshore market was not only able to attract substantial externally held deposits at more competitive rates of return, but also to draw sizeable deposits from the domestic market. Additionally, US official policy in 1979, which resulted in the freezing of Iranian funds, precipitated the transfer of many large foreign controlled investments within the US to the international currency deposit and capital markets.

Albeit that the impact of Regulation Q, Section 19, and lending constraint requirements, have to all intents and purposes disappeared, non-interest bearing statutory reserves are still required to be provided.

The euro-currency Deposits market is now the largest deposit and funding market in the world. According to statistics available to the Bank for International Settlements of the currency breakdown of external liabilities of reporting banks (excluding liabilities in domestic currency), industrial reporting countries, excluding USA, as at the end of June 1985 total deposits amounted to the equivalent of US$1,217 billion. The US dollar remains the predominant currency with 73.60% followed by Deutschemarks 10.00%, Swiss francs 5.00%, Yen 2.10%, Sterling 1.80%, ECU 2.0% and other currencies 5.50%.

The presence in the euromarkets of these other major currencies is also influenced by either similar controls and directives, as referred to above, or in some instances the imposition of withholding taxes.

In West Germany banks are required to place non-interest bearing mandatory reserve requirements with the Bundesbank and the authorities have on occasions imposed ceilings on non-resident DM deposits to discourage the impact of these funds on the Domestic markets.

In Switzerland mandatory reserve requirements are not a normal feature of the banking system. However, the Swiss authorities do apply a 35% withholding tax on interest paid on Swiss Franc bank deposits inclusive of those emanating from non-residents, but exclusive of inter-bank deposits with an original maturity of under one year; a requirement which on return criteria alone makes Switzerland unattractive to non-resident depositors of Swiss Francs. A further incentive for the development of the Swiss Franc as an offshore currency is the imposition, from time to time of minimal or negative interest rate ceilings upon non-resident Swiss Franc deposits placed with banks in Switzerland. The purpose of this monetary control is, as in West Germany, to protect the domestic economy against the impact of the flow of external funds. In passing it is pertinent to mention that Swiss Banks are authorised to accept funds in Swiss Francs and foreign currencies on a Fiduciary (held in trust) basis. Such funds are off-balance sheet items, and whilst being subject to specific regulations under Swiss laws, they are exempted from other regulatory, monetary and fiscal influences, in particular those relating to withholding taxes, interest rate constraints, capital adequacy, liquidity and any reserve requirements that may be imposed from time to time. These deposits provide a substantial source of funds to the international currency deposit market.

The Japanese authorities apply non-interest bearing reserve requirements on eligible deposits, withholding taxes on private non-resident deposits, and they regulate domestic interest rates. They also impose extensive exchange control regulations which have restricted non-resident access for funding purposes to the domestic yen market.

Although sterling continues to be an active offshore currency its importance has declined within this market since the abolition of exchange control regulations in October 1979 since that time coupled with its general weakness against other major traded currencies. Both resident and non-resident sterling is now freely convertible. Since August 1981 the Bank of England's system of monetary control centres around the mandatory liquid asset requirement (MLA) for eligible banks. The MLA costs incurred by banks operating in the UK are not suffered by those overseas dealing in euro-sterling transactions, but these costs, inclusive of a one half percent non-interest bearing mandatory deposit of eligible liabilities with the Bank of England, are marginal. Non-resident funds are exempt from the composite rate tax on interest structure which was introduced with effect from April 1985.

The subject of composite currencies, Special Drawing Rights (SDR) and the European Currency Unit (ECU) – are developed in further detail in Chapter 15, however as they are designed to provide common international units of account and are not subject to the control of any individual country the ECU's prominence within the offshore international markets is a natural development rather than one associated with any particular regulatory implications. However, where these units are funded from or utilised in their component currencies, those components will, if domiciled in domestic markets, be subject to the monetary and fiscal regulations related thereto.

From a regulatory viewpoint this "offshore market" operates outside of the supervisory processes of any single authority and does not, therefore, formally have available to it any specific lender of last resort facilities.

Although offshore currencies function outside of the regulatory controls applicable to those currencies' country of issue, the banks which operate within this market are subject to the regulations of their respective country of operation, be it host or parent authority. Therefore a bank's ability to be competitively active in this market will be dependent upon that country's policy as to whether it wishes to discourage, encourage or be indifferent to the development of euro-currency activity. This policy will be reflected through each countries' regulatory, monetary and fiscal policies and will in the main involve similar matters to those already discussed, but applied to each individual country's treatment of banks foreign currency assets and liabilities, rather than those imposed on their domestic currency unit. The following matters constitute three key factors which have contributed to the development of euro-currency centres:

- the ability to maintain foreign currency accounts on a freely convertible basis

- the treatment of foreign currency deposits for mandatory reserve purposes

- withholding tax on foreign currency deposits

An examination of the above factors as applied by some of the countries in which the world's major financial centres are situated, clearly indicates why London and, to a lesser extent, Paris have developed, and why London continues to be the largest financial centre upon which the international currency deposit market is based.

Although the UK and France impose mandatory reserve requirements on domestic Eligible Liabilities (MLAs) these requirements do not extend to a bank's holding of foreign currency deposits. The United States, West Germany and Japan each apply mandatory non-interest bearing requirements on a bank's total holdings of both domestic and foreign currency Eligible Liabilities (Reservable Assets). Although Hong Kong applies rules in regard to minimum holdings of specified liquid assets to both Hong Kong dollars and

112

foreign currency deposits, there are no mandatory non-interest bearing requirements, and reserves may comprise assets priced at market-related rates. The Swiss authorities do not normally apply reserve requirements to either swiss franc or foreign currency deposits. However, under Swiss fiscal legislation standard rate withholding tax is applied to interest on both resident and non-resident deposits of any denomination of currency, except for domestic and foreign bank balances with an original maturity of under one year.

Similarly, up until its abolition in 1982, Hong Kong imposed a 15% withholding tax on all deposits inclusive of non-resident foreign currency deposits (other than banks), and Japan a 20% withholding tax on private non-resident deposits. Although France and the UK impose withholding tax requirements, in France non-resident foreign currency deposits and in the UK all non-resident deposits, both sterling and foreign currency, may be exempted from these requirements. The US authorities require withholding tax to be applied to all US resident and non-resident deposits, in both US dollars and foreign currency, unless the paying bank is in possession of a resident tax identification number or certificate of domicile for non-residents. In addition, as US banks are required to apply withholding tax to other interest income which may pass through them, unless the aforementioned criteria are complied with, similar rules relate to their Nassau operations conducted in the United States. In this latter case the US bank is acting in its role as paying agent and not as the Nassau operation. In West Germany interest continues to be paid gross on all deposits.

Exchange control regulations may also prohibit banks from accepting foreign currency deposits from residents and/or non-residents. However, of the major financial centres discussed only Japan and France have formally imposed exchange control regulations. French residents are not permitted to hold foreign currency accounts and non-residents are discouraged from holding French franc deposits through the imposition of withholding taxes. A similar situation exists in Japan. In the UK and West Germany there are no current exchange restrictions in force. However, in both countries there exists the legal basis for the swift re-imposition of controls, in the Exchange Control Act 1947 and the Aussenwirtschaftsgesetz 1961 respectively.

Encouraged by these regulatory anomalies banks in ever increasing numbers expanded their operations by establishing "off shore" branches, subsidiary and associated companies to gain access to the euro-currency market. Within this development, other features emerged which included the establishment of consortia banks and syndicated lending through which banks were able to share the credit and country risks, as increased demands were made for substantial facilities by individual companies and countries. American and Japanese banks were quick to enter this market. A particular advantage to US banks was the existence of a further regulatory anomaly whereby US$ funds deposited with US domiciled banks by their foreign branches were, until 1969, exempted from the reserve requirements imposed through Regulation D. Therefore, many US banks used the international currency market as a substantial funding source for their domestic operations, an activity which has also been encouraged through constraints imposed upon the development of more conventional funding bases, by restriction on interstate domestic banking and some individual States' control over the branching activities of banks. For Japanese banks the euro-markets provide a funding source for both Japanese trade finance and overseas investment, the largest proportion of which is arranged in US dollars.

Those regulatory monetary and fiscal differences already discussed have not been the only incentives for the developments of "offshore" operations. Neither are Paris and London the only centres upon which these were established. Other traditional financial centres of lesser importance had regulations conducive to euro-currency activities whilst other countries were not so ambivalent to these developments. Opportunity existed for tax havens such as those found in the Channel Islands and Carribean, which had become substantial deposit centres, to extend their banking industry and encourage the establishment of offshore banks. Several countries, for a variety of different reasons, introduced specific legislation to licence and encourage their development as "Offshore Banking Centres". These included Singapore, the Philippines, Bahrain, Cayman Islands, Panama, the Bahamas and the International Banking facilities (IBFs) within the United States. These particular areas and their regulation are discussed specifically in Part 2 of this Chapter. To increase and retain a market share of commercial business it was frequently considered necessary for many international banks to establish and maintain a presence in most, if not all, of these areas.

Additionally, with the development of instant electronic communication systems which are now available, some countries encouraged the growth of "brass plate" or "shell" booking centres, whereby banks arrange and transact business in one country but record and book it with another. Consequently, international banks not only have the opportunity to develop activities within the international currency deposit market in one or several countries, but are also able to attract certain transactions towards a particular domicile. These decisions will be dictated by each individual bank's perceived policy objectives and fiscal considerations. For example, where a bank's gearing or lending capabilities are constrained in one centre, the level of business carried out in its offshore subsidiaries may be developed in those countries which permit higher levels of activity. A bank's own taxation position may make some of the traditional financial centres or "Offshore Banking Centres" particularly attractive. Benefits may be derived through bilateral tax agreements or a fiscal authority's treatment of particular types of transaction. The imposition of stamp duty on certain transactions in one country may lead to a bank booking its business in another country.

Part 2
Offshore Banking Centres
The Singapore Government encouraged the establishment of Singapore as the centre of the Asian Currency Market since 1968.

"Offshore" banking in Singapore is normally conducted through a bank's Asian Currency Unit (ACU). An ACU is an integral part of a licensed banking operation conducted in Singapore. Other than the separation of its activities for accounting, fiscal and reporting purposes, together with the exemption of certain of its activities for regulatory and fiscal requirements, an ACU has no separate identity from the bank within which it is situated.

Except for acting as issuer of the currency, the Monetary Authority of Singapore (MAS) is vested with the usual responsibilities associated with the role of Central Banker, Regulator and Supervisor. The MAS issues three types of licence to banks – full, restricted and offshore. Any of these three licence holders may apply to the MAS for authority to operate an ACU. All of these licences require a full physical banking presence in Singapore. Each bank must be adequately capitalised and is subject to the same supervisory process. The essential differences between the full and other types of licence are:

- That only those banks issued with full licences may offer a full range of retail banking services for both residents and non-residents.

- Both restricted and offshore licensed banks are only allowed one branch, and are precluded from undertaking specific types of deposit and other transactions with non-bank residents of Singapore.

Despite the absence of exchange control regulations, the government of Singapore does not wish to encourage the growth of the Singapore dollar as an international currency in the development of its offshore banking activities. Consequently ACUs are only permitted to undertake limited business with residents or non-residents in Singapore dollars. The MAS apply stringent criteria when considering applications for each type of licence, including economic need issues, and will only accept those banks which they consider will contribute to the economy, standing and reputation of Singapore as a highly regulated and controlled international financial centre. The MAS will consider and, if appropriate, authorise foreign controlled branch banking operations, but the head office of such banks is required to retain net funds of at least S$3 million in Singapore at all times, and provide an undertaking in respect of the total of its branch obligations in Singapore (inclusive of any ACU operations). Subsidiary and associate companies require to be incorporated in accordance with Singapore commercial laws and must be capitalised to a level deemed appropriate by the MAS, but in any event this will not be less than S$3 million. The MAS holds authority to withdraw licences should it be dissatisfied with the activities or conduct of specific banks.

ACU transactions are exempt from statutory reserve and liquidity requirements. Corporate taxation is applied on ACU profits at a reduced rate of 10% and several transaction types are provided with tax holidays including all offshore syndicated credit facilities arranged in Singapore and futures business undertaken through the Singapore International Monetary Exchange (SIMEX). Deposit interest paid to non-residents by approved banks in Singapore is generally exempted from Singapore withholding tax. Although ACUs are not separately capitalised, the MAS control their growth by imposing individual limits on balance sheet size. In addition to the submission of a full range of specified and detailed periodical returns inclusive of a monthly statement of Assets and Liabilities to the MAS, on site inspections are undertaken and the MAS requires external auditors to confirm during their annual audit that each bank is complying with the directives of both the MAS and requirements of the Banking Act.

In the Philippines the formal supervisory and regulatory body for banks is the Monetary Board but much of the supervisory process is undertaken by the Central Bank. Offshore banking facilities within the Philippines are provided through two types of authority:

- Offshore Banking Units (OBUs)

- Foreign Currency Deposit Units (FCDUs)

OBUs are authorised under presidential decree number 1034 and FCDU's under presidential decree number 1035 issued in September 1976. Decree number 1034 facilitates the establishment of foreign currency operating units by branches, subsidiaries or affiliates of foreign banks without any other presence in the Philippines. Decree number 1035 provides for banks, both local and foreign with domestic operations within the Philippines, to obtain authority to accept foreign currency deposits and undertake similar activities as OBUs. Both operations require a full banking presence within the Philippines and are subject to the full supervisory requirements and arrangements of the Central Bank of the Philippines.

In considering applications for an OBU the Central Bank will review a foreign bank's capital structure, liquidity and managerial capabilities together with applying economic need criteria. Irrespective of its status as a branch, affiliate or associate, the authorities will also call for an undertaking that the parent will support all of an OBUs liabilities and hold at least the equivalent of US$ 1 million as deposits with the Central Bank or in other defined assets within the Philippines. FCDUs are an integral part of the domestic banking operation and are not therefore subject to separate capital considerations or liquidity requirement. Frequent returns are required from all banks including statements of assets and liabilities and foreign exchange transactions, on a monthly basis. In addition, annual inspection examinations are undertaken by the Central Bank.

OBUs and FCDUs are only authorised to transact business in foreign currencies and these are limited to those in which the international reserves of the Philippines are authorised to be held, which include all the major international currencies. For the purpose of corporation tax a bank's profits are separated between those accruing from business with non-residents (including other OBUs and FCDUs) and those with residents. The former is subject to preferential treatment for corporation tax which is currently zero- rated with the latter being taxed at the appropriate standard corporate rate.

Both OBUs and FCDUs are required to maintain 100% foreign currency cover against deposit liabilities. OBUs must maintain 15% of this amount as deposits with the Central Bank of the Philippines, but FCDUs are exempted from this requirement. At least 70% of the foreign currency cover provided must be maintained in the applicable base foreign currency of the liabilities, with up to a maximum 30% comprising other permitted foreign currencies. The Peso equivalent of any swaps undertaken with the Central Bank qualifies as foreign currency cover. Interest on foreign currency deposits maintained with OBUs and FCDUs is specifically exempted from the mandatory withholding tax requirements applicable to deposits with commercial banks.

In Bahrain, the Bahrain Monetary Agency (BMA) exercises control over the banking industry and since 1975 has provided for Offshore Banking Units (OBUs) to be established in Bahrain through a branch, subsidiary or associate company structure. Commercial banks established in Bahrain may also apply for OBU licences and must provide separate accounting arrangements to cover offshore operations. Foreign banks' associate and subsidiary companies require to be incorporated and established in accordance with Bahrani commercial law and defined capital requirements. In considering applications from foreign banks for the establishment of a branch operation the BMA will wish to satisfy itself of the parent's commitment to that operation.

Apart from Bahrani dinar current accounts OBUs are able to offer a full range of banking services to non-residents. OBUs are not permitted to deal with companies or individuals resident in Bahrain except with the specific consent of the BMA. OBU liabilities are exempted from the mandatory reserve requirements imposed on commercial banks and all profits are tax free, albeit an annual licence fee of Bahrani dinar 10,000 is payable. Withholding taxes are not imposed on interest payments within Bahrain. All OBUs are subject to the regulatory and supervisory processes of the BMA including the submission of regular returns, audited accounts and inspection reviews. Returns required to be submitted to the BMA include an analysis of assets and liabilities by currency, class of customer, country analysis and maturity profile.

Panama does not have a Central Bank and control of the banking sector is vested in the National Banking Commission. The Commission includes the Minister of Planning and Economic Policy, the Finance and Treasury Minister, the General Manager of the Banco Nacional di Panama, three representatives from private banks nominated by the Panama Banking Association and one banking representative appointed by the government.

The Commission issues general and international licences. The former type of licence authorises banks to engage in banking business both within or outside Panama whereas the latter provides for foreign banks to conduct offshore banking activities from an office established in Panama. Although all licensed banks must have fully paid in or assigned capital of not less than Bilbaos 1 million, only general licensed banks must retain the total of this minimum capital requirement in defined assets within the Republic of Panama. International licensed banks are required to retain at least Bilbaos 500,000 in this form.

International licensed banks are exempted from the statutory reserve, and amongst other things contingency credit and liquidity requirements which are imposed upon general licensed banks. The National Banking Commission requires all banks to submit various periodic reports to its Secretariat and in addition banks are required to provide copies of any internal audit inspections and annual independently audited accounts. Returns submitted include monthly statements showing the bank's asset and liabilities position, an analysis of credit facilities and other assets, on a quarterly basis.

The centre of the banking industry in the Bahamas is Nassau, the name usually associated with these offshore banking operations. Unlike those centres already discussed, the Bahamas facilitates banks operating on either a direct or indirect representative basis. In the case of the former a physical presence is established as an operating unit, in the latter a bank does not have any physical presence within the Bahamas, except a registered place of business and a list of named appointed officials which can be provided through a resident trust company or other body.

The Minister of Finance issues two types of banking licence – restricted and unrestricted; the former limits operations only to those parties specified in the licence with the latter providing for full banking operations to be undertaken. A distinction between domestic banking and offshore operations is provided through the exchange control regulations under which banks may apply to be designated either resident or non-resident. Resident and non-resident applies to the type of business a bank undertakes and not to the domicile of its business activities. Non-resident banks are only permitted to deal in foreign currencies and otherwise in general operate outside of local exchange control requirements, inclusive of profit and dividend remittances. Resident banks may transact business with residents in Bahamian dollars. Banks wishing to partake in both domestic and foreign currency business are, within the context of the exchange control regulations, required to be appointed authorised dealers.

Although the Minister of Finance issues licences, the authority for processing applications and subsequent supervision is the Central Bank of the Bahamas. Operations can be established as branches, subsidiaries or affiliates and on application references are required and the Central Bank will wish to ensure that a foreign bank's head office supervisory authority supports the application for a licence in Nassau. There are no specific capital requirements for branch operations, but the Central Bank require locally incorporated companies to have a minimum paid up capital of at least Bah$1 million. Licences are issued on the basis of an annual licence fee which at the date of this publication was Bah$10,000 for a resident and non-resident licence and Bah$45,000 for an authorised dealer. The Bahamas provide a tax free environment within which to conduct "offshore" banking operations and upon approval the only formal regulatory and reporting requirement imposed is the submission on an annual basis of audited financial statements to the Central Bank within four months of the end of the licensed bank's financial year.

Nassau operations have provided an attractive point of entry into the International Currency Markets for many US domiciled banks subject to the constraints imposed through Regulations D, Q and 19. The US authorities have accepted the principle of US banks establishing "Brass plate" operations in Nassau and running Nassau desks within their US branch operations. In this context it is pertinent to mention that where US banks use liabilities generated through Nassau desks to fund domestic lending, non-interest bearing reserves have to be provided on an equivalent amount of 3% of liabilities and a bank's taxable income from this type of operation is not exempt from US fiscal regulation. With the development of these US bank operations together with Nassau's general attraction as a booking centre for other banks, the Bahamas has developed as the centre of one of the largest Euro-dollar based operations outside of London.

Similar facilities to those described for the Bahamas also exist in the Cayman Islands. The major difference between the Bahamas and the Cayman Islands is that the Cayman Authorities distinguish between domestic and offshore banking operations through licensing procedures, and not from exchange control designations. Category 'A' licences permit domestic and offshore operations with category

'B' licences limited to offshore operations. As with the Bahamas a physical presence is not required; Cayman Island operations may be used as 'shell' booking centres, and the only practical reporting requirement is the annual submission of audited financial statements.

Although the United States has not been prepared to amend the domestic regulatory requirements which are responsible for the development of the US dollar as the major offshore currency, the Federal Authorities did in 1981 accede to New York State's request to exempt defined International Banking Facilities (IBF) deposits from Regulation D & Q requirements. These exemptions made it practicable for banks domiciled within New York State to introduce from 3rd December 1981 "offshore" banking units under state legislation passed in 1978 which authorised the establishment of IBF's in that state and exempted their operations from New York State and City taxes. IBF's have no separate identity from the banks within which they are established other than the segregation of IBF transactions within their accounting records and a requirement to maintain specified documentation related thereto. Banks, inclusive of Edge Act branches, domiciled in, and wishing to establish IBF's in New York State are required to advise/apply to the superintendent of banks, State of New York Banking Department and in the case of Federal licensed banks to the Federal Reserve.

The term "international banking facility" is defined as a set of asset and liability accounts for international banking facility time deposits and international banking facility extensions of credit and any related . accounts segregated in the books of a banking institution in New York State this authority is in accordance with the provisions of Section 19.3 of the General Regulations of the New York State Banking Board. In general, an IBF is authorised to undertake banking business in US dollars and other currencies with non-residents and other IBF's. IBF's may not accept individual deposits below the equivalent of US$100,000, accept any deposits other than interbank funds repayable on less than 2 days demand, raise deposits through the issue of bearer instruments, or lend to non-residents to finance operations within the US. IBF's may, however, operate in specified secondary transactions. As an integral part of a banking operation

IBF transactions are subject to the appropriate official supervisory processes applicable to each bank.

As a result of the development of IBFs in New York State it is usual to find individual banks simultaneously undertaking activities related to domestic, Nassau and IBF operations, and the three being segregated for accounting and recording purposes. The major difference between IBF and Nassau activities being that the former may only transact business with non-residents whereas the latter may undertake business with US residents.

The foregoing is by no means an exhaustive description of the many offshore banking centres which have established themselves throughout the world. It is merely intended to illustrate the varying nature of the different types of offshore banking centres. Other centres include the Channel Islands, the Isle of Man, Taiwan, Sri Lanka, the Netherlands Antilles, and the British Virgin Islands.

CHAPTER SEVEN

Principles of Exchange Control

Introduction

Controls are restrictive and any form of exchange control, by its very nature, will not only tend to have an inhibiting effect on free international trade but also upon a bank's access to international markets. Controls, however, are often considered necessary in order to maintain economic and/or exchange rate stability, although such measures will often prohibit new markets from developing or artificially restrict growth and development of international business and investment. During periods of contracting imports, weak export markets, substantial increase in debt servicing costs and a general development of adverse terms of trade, many developing countries adopt, or intensify, restrictive exchange and trade practices. Such was the situation in the early 1980s when rising unemployment in industrial countries stimulated protective policies in selective industries and these included the placing of limits on imports of certain goods from the more competitive countries and accordingly led to a general tightening of bilateral and multilateral agreements. Exchange control in the United Kingdom was suspended in October 1979, although the Act remains on the Statute Book and can be re-introduced should it be considered necessary without a great deal of legislation. The fact that the administrative machinery in the UK has been disbanded would be no reason for not re-introducing exchange control if the government of the day considered it to be necessary. Banking operations conducted in an environment governed by exchange control regulations are, of course, quite different from those in an exchange control free environment. Bankers in the UK who experienced the post 1979 changes were confronted with new business opportunities when the long established regulations were swept away. As new markets and international banking operations and services developed in London there was a greater awareness by bankers of other types of control and regulations, in particular fiscal and accounting matters.

Exchange control may be described as the limitation of free dealings in the exchanges or of free transfers of funds into other currencies and other countries. The effect of exchange controls on an international business is a restriction on the free movement of funds between subsidiaries and between currencies. As a result funds may accumulate at a profit centre where they are not required or reinvestment opportunities are strictly limited, and from which it is impossible to transfer them. On the other hand, it may be impossible to make additional investments in a particular subsidiary, because the country's exchange controls prevent capital inflows. Constraints may also be imposed on the provision of additional funding to branch operations from external sources. For example, in some countries, inclusive of Japan, Canada and South Korea, the regulatory authorities place constraints upon the element of funding in domestic currencies which can be sourced from foreign currency deposits. The usual modus operandi for implementing this requirement is to place swap limits upon individual banks or specify a percentage of total liabilities that may be funded from external sources.

The treasurer of a multinational bank needs to monitor the distribution of funds so that imposition of foreign exchange controls will have a minimum effect on its operations.

In an environment of exchange control regulations many countries distinguish between "resident" and "non-resident" funds with the latter being freely convertible. Such regulations will define the forms of permitted transactions. These invariably include accounts with banks authorised by the exchange control regulations. It is usual that only funds emanating from external sources, approved investments or other non-resident accounts in the normal course of business can be credited to non-resident accounts. Any funds which are required to be transferred from any other domestic source to non-resident accounts must comply with or be approved by the authorised institution(s) established for this purpose. This usually applies equally even where such funds originally emanated from a non-resident source. Both France and Spain are typical of countries which, in May 1985, had such regulations.

In Spain peseta ordinary accounts (interior/blocked accounts) are the normal accounts held by Spanish residents for use within Spanish territory and are not convertible or transferable abroad. Non-residents may only hold such accounts when designated "tourist ordinary peseta accounts". Convertible peseta accounts may be held by non-residents (and emigrants savings accounts), but once funds are transferred from a convertible account or a foreign currency account into a resident account then the process may not be reversed without prior approval.

The impact on domestic economies of "non-resident" funds, whether recognised through exchange control regulations or emanating from a freely convertible source, has in the past made it necessary for separate controls to be introduced. For example, in the 1970s specific controls were imposed to guard strong currencies such as Swiss Francs and Deutschemarks against unwanted inflows of non-resident domestic funds resultant from the sale of foreign currencies, particularly dollars. Such controls typically are forerunners of currency revaluations and devaluations; they are often used by governments attempting to alleviate the need for currency re-alignment. In addition they may be used to strengthen the effects of a parity change. The economic and other factors which indicate the need for parity changes, also indicate the possible imposition of exchange controls.

Exchange control regulations exist in the majority of countries in the world as an important tool in regulating the monetary affairs of a country with balance of payments problems. Whilst the regulations are generally designed to contain the potential outflow of investment funds without adversely impeding the country's trading capabilities or foreign exchange earning capabilities, controls tend to restrict world trade and restrict access to the international capital market.

The central bank is normally charged with the management of exchange control regulations but usually delegates much of the administration to the commercial banks of its country.

It is not intended within the scope of this book to cover specifically, even in outline, the various systems in force throughout the world. The changes in this field are fairly frequent and to be comprehensive on the subject many loose leaf volumes would be needed.

The areas which may be addressed specifically or generally by such regulations relate to:

- Matters of administration regarding authorised banks' depositories, and methods of applying for permissions.

- The import and export of financial paper such as bank notes, bills of exchange, securities and insurance policies.

- Loans to resident companies controlled by non-residents.

- Requirements for certificates of deposit.

- Permissions needed for transactions in foreign currency securities.

- Permissions needed for securities denominated in the home currency.

- Disposal of estates, wills, trusts and other settlements.

- The issue and recording of securities by registrars, payments of interest, dividend and capital repayments on securities.

- Travel and education facilities including:
  - allowances for travellers
  - emergency funds
  - various other payments related to travel,
  - accounts abroad for travellers
    and
  - study grants and correspondent courses

- Outward direct investment

- Inward direct investment

- Disinvestment

- The way in which residential status must be determined and the action to be taken when a person changes status.

- Emigration of residents and treatment of assets, which may be restricted.

- Banking transactions on behalf of non-residents in particular the types of accounts which may be maintained.

- Residents holding foreign currency, accounts held abroad (retained accounts), foreign currency accounts with local banks, and blocked funds.

- Requirements concerning payment for exports.

- Dealing in foreign notes and coin.

- Imports and the requirements, if any, to be met before payment can be made.

- Requirements for both spot and forward foreign currency dealing.

- Permissions for futures and options contracts and requirements for dealing in these markets.

- Gold transactions.

- Requirements to be met for residents to obtain permission to borrow foreign currency.

- Permissions for documentary credits, contract guarantees, loans and overdrafts to non-residents.

- Arrangements in respect of countries with whom a regional arrangement exists such as LAIA (Latin American Integration Association).

- Local currency payments by non-residents.

- Types of insurance and freight payments.

- Commodities.

- Cash gifts to non-residents.

- Payments to non-resident dependants.

- Payments due for various services by residents to non-residents and to residents temporarily employed abroad.

- Transactions concerning countries with whom major political disputes or differences exist.

- Property owned by residents abroad for private use.

- Control of inflows.

The restrictive nature of exchange and trade controls is widely accepted as fact and, in recognition, the International Monetary Fund (IMF) was established in 1945 as an independent organisation whose headquarters are based in Washington D.C. Its functions embrace the promotion of the following six criteria for its 144 member countries, and it should be noted that the abolition of exchange restrictions was by no means the paramount *raison d'être* for the IMF.

- Exchange rate stability
- Removal of exchange restrictions
- International monetary co-operation
- Growth and acceleration of world trade
- High levels of employment and improving
    standards of living
- Development of national productive resources

The IMF's Articles of Agreement *inter alia* prohibit member countries engaging in (directly or indirectly) multiple currency practices or any discriminatory currency arrangements without the Fund's approval.

130

Consequently exchange controls cannot be considered in isolation from other controls which each individual country or group of countries which may be part of a trading block may impose.

Quantitative Control Techniques

Quantitative controls imposed on imports physically limit goods/services which a country may import from abroad. These controls are usually imposed in order to protect local industry from severe competition from one or more foreign countries. This is an area of extreme national sensitivity, and protectionist pressures on governments have multipled since the Tokyo Round, a GATT (General Agreement on Tariffs and Trade) meeting at ministerial level in 1973. The ministers met again in 1982 and agreed to make a determined effort to ensure that GATT principles were adhered to, and to avoid taking measures which would restrict or distort international trade. The relatively high unemployment levels in industrial countries at a time of world recession did not make their task easy. Relaxation of quantitative controls is often achieved by degrees in the form of the negotiation of bilateral agreements (between two countries) on a country-by-country basis, rather than by the country imposing the control abolishing it altogether for the industry or product involved. The quantitative import controls may also take the form of anti-dumping legislation imposed by certain countries on imports from countries with whom they have not entered into any bilateral trade agreement for a particular product sold at prices below a basic price level set by the importing country. Another form of quantitative control is the negotiation of a "restraint agreement" whereby the importing country is able to avoid imposing formal import quotas but nevertheless persuades a supplier country(s) to limit the volume of imports of a product to an agreed level. Quantitative controls in the form of total prohibition occur from time to time as a result of a view taken by the importing country in the interests of its own national security or barriers based on technical standards which are often designed to favour a home producer. A mechanism of quantitative control is import licensing whereby licence requirements may be introduced on specific products which previously could be imported freely, or conversely relax licensing requirements on items previously subject to regulation.

Quantitative controls may also be applied to exports particularly where they are considered essential products for home consumption or industry and sometimes as a result of national defence strategy or policy.

Fiscal Controls

Import surcharges, import duty and taxation also place economic/commercial barriers to the free movement of goods/services across frontiers. Measures adopted include the imposition of an extra ad valorem duty on all goods imported subject to VAT; stamp duty on imports and financial services; import surcharges on all goods or specific classes of product; and selective import and excise taxes. Fiscal measures are also adopted in order to stimulate exports from a particular industry or specific products. Examples include tax rebate schemes for exports, export tax credit arrangements, reduced level income/corporation taxes for profits arising from export sales and specific types of financial and banking services. Some countries employ such fiscal levies merely to increase government revenue rather than for domestic supply purposes.

Fiscal/Payment Controls

Advance import deposit schemes act as a very severe disincentive to trade, particularly if the percentage of the value of the goods to be imported, which is required to be deposited, is high. In some countries an advance exchange licence deposit is also required which necessarily means that the importer has to submit up to 100% of the local currency required for payment of the import, in advance of the foreign exchange permit or licence being issued, which is needed to enable him to buy the foreign currency for remittance abroad in settlement.

Controls by Mandatory Payment Terms

Mandatory deferred payment terms may be imposed for the settlement of goods imported. Documentary credits may be required specifically by the authorities in the buyer's country. Forward purchases of foreign currencies may be prohibited or limited to within a few days prior to the due payment date. Official and unofficial protracted delays may be experienced at various times.

On the export side of the coin, preferential finance schemes and credit terms which reduce the final cost of goods exported act as inducements to overseas buyers to prefer the products so subsidised. Various export credit guarantee schemes in the form of insurance cover and/or financial support arrangements are modified from time to time and tend to stimulate trade rather than the converse. Retention of foreign currency earnings is often prohibited under exchange control regulations and these have to be surrendered either at the official rate to the central bank or at the market rate. There exist variations of the percentages to be surrendered at each rate, and likewise the periods which exporters may retain foreign currency receipts before surrender is sometimes adjusted according to the perceived national economic requirements of the country.

With a view to expanding exports the number of counter purchase and barter transactions has increased significantly over the past five years (1981-85). Such transactions are more frequently seen when exchange restrictions and other restrictive trade practices are intensified.

Convertibility and Multiple Currency Practices
A currency is said to be convertible if the holder (irrespective of his own domicile) may exchange it freely into the currencies of other countries. Certain currencies are fully convertible where there exists no restriction in respect of the nature of the transaction giving rise to the required exchange, or of the resident qualification of the holder. Examples of freely convertible currencies include the US Dollar, Sterling, Swiss Franc and Deutschemark. A large number of countries apply exchange restrictions to their own residents and therefore recognise external (non-resident) convertibility only. Perhaps one of the most common approaches to exchange control is the creation of two tier, or even multiple tier, exchange rates for a currency as a result of drawing a distinction between the types of transaction involved. Financial transfers as opposed to commercial transfers in respect of goods and services is the most common division. A third

tier rate is sometimes created by a special rate for foreign tourists. Other dual systems exist in some countries for exports on the one hand and imports on the other, the former usually being at the market or commercial rate and the latter at a separate official exchange rate. The only major West European country to operate a dual currency system is Belgium and the system applies to non-residents only. A resident of Belgium will just have an ordinary Belgian Franc bank account but a non-resident's Belgian Franc bank account will be designated either a "financial" or a "convertible" account. There are, therefore, two foreign exchange markets for the Belgian Franc. They are the official market and the free market:

- The **official market** which caters for the following transactions: imports and exports of goods; freight costs and customs duties; manufacturing, assembly, maintenance and repair charges; commissions and brokerage; insurance premiums and indemnities (excluding those relating to life cover); payments to travel agencies; salaries, wages, pensions and fees; royalties and related expenses; Belgian and Luxembourg taxes and penalties; administrative expenses incurred by foreign companies on behalf of their resident branches or subsidiaries; payments of dividends, interest and transfer of branch profits.

- Exchange control permission is required for any of the above transactions where transfers of more than BFcs.25 million are concerned. All official market transactions must be supported with documentary evidence of the transaction. **For non-residents** Belgian Francs bought or sold on the official market are called "convertible francs".

- The **free market** applies to transactions including: securities, bank notes and capital investment in Belgium. **For non-residents** Belgian Francs bought or sold on the free market are called "financial francs".

- There is freedom of exchange control between Belgium and Luxembourg for all purposes; the exchange and currency regulations apply equally to both countries. The Belgian Franc is legal tender in Luxembourg and has equal value in both countries.

- Both the financial and the convertible francs float freely, except that the central bank intervenes to maintain the value of the convertible franc against the other EMS currencies to within the specified limits.

The Belgian approach is particularly important as an illustration of a dual currency system. An interesting feature of this type of dual currency system is that it will work well provided that the two rates remain relatively close (as is the case with the Belgian Franc). However, to make this happen demands central bank intervention in some form to maintain the "financial" rate close to the commercial or "official" rate at times when they would normally diverge as a result of free market pressures.

CHAPTER EIGHT

Control of Dealing

Chapter 2 discusses the responsibilities of senior management in formulating exposure limits, policy directives and strategy particularly in relation to a bank's treasury and dealing functions. Thereafter it is equally important for management to establish a suitable control system to ensure compliance with these directives and safeguard against operational risks. Within a dealing environment it is generally recognised that a specialist audit function is required to undertake this role and this chapter considers the fundamental requirements of such a unit to ensure that adequate internal controls over dealing operations exist. The UK auditing standards and guidelines define an internal control system as:

> "the whole system of controls, financial and otherwise established by management in order to carry on the business of the enterprise in an orderly and efficient manner, ensure adherence to management policies, safeguard the assets and secure as far as possible the completeness and accuracy of the records".

The necessity for heightened controls, particularly to cover foreign exchange dealing operations of banks falling under the supervisory authority of the Bank of England, was stressed as early as 1974.

During December 1974 the Governor of the Bank of England addressed a letter to all UK authorised banks on the subject of the control of foreign exchange operations. It was indicated that following from the "undertakings of ultimate responsibility" which the Bank of England seeks from banks which are shareholders in banks registered in the UK, that British banks must be expected to accept similar responsibility for their branches and banks overseas in which they have a shareholding. Therefore it is incumbent on such parent or shareholding banks to satisfy themselves, in their own interests, that the foreign exchange activities of their relevant overseas operations are conducted to high standards.

Losses suffered during 1974 by banks in a number of countries resulted from imprudent, often unauthorised foreign exchange operations which naturally had a serious adverse impact upon the banks concerned, confidence in the markets, and indirectly on some countries' foreign exchange reserves. The Bank suggested that each bank should undertake a rigorous review of its internal regulations governing procedures for all foreign exchange dealings at home and abroad. In conducting this review the following points were identified for consideration for a prudent change of policy. Where applicable:

- Some general managements seem to have placed their dealers in an exposed position by looking well beyond the service element of the dealing function and imposing ambitious profit targets upon them.

- In some overseas offices, managements do not appear to have paid sufficient attention to the relations between dealers and brokers; in London the Foreign Exchange and Currency Deposit Brokers Association has exercised a beneficial influence in this area.

- Dealers should never write their own outgoing confirmations or receive incoming confirmations.

- Forward deals should always be confirmed at once; in particular, confirmations should not be delayed until instructions are passed just prior to maturity.

- There should be unannounced snap checks of dealing activities between regular internal audits or inspections.

- Central management should from time to time, on a random basis, seek from correspondent banks independent second confirmations of outstanding forward contracts.

- A bank should check with its correspondent's Head Office or main dealing office, if it notices that a branch of that bank has suddenly or unaccountably significantly expanded its operations in the forward market.

In 1974 the foreign exchange positions of branches and wholly-owned subsidiaries overseas were not included in the regular foreign exchange returns made to the Bank. Nevertheless the Bank wished to be informed about the foreign exchange limits applied or authorities granted by banks registered in the United Kingdom to their overseas branches and wholly-owned subdiaries abroad, and of the frequency such branches or subsidiaries reported their positions to their Head Office or parent. The Bank also asked to be kept informed of any changes made in these arrangements.

Within a dealing environment the prime control objectives must be to safeguard the assets of a bank and at the same time ensure adherence to management policies.

Many of the international and domestic financial markets are not sited in one building as formal exchanges; they are dealer to dealer telephone markets. During trading there is no independent supervisor or arbitrator available, a dealer does not have to substantiate the existence of his authority to trade and therefore can commit the bank to unlimited risk if not properly controlled. Many of the large losses which have been sustained by banks have arisen from dealers acting either without or outside of delegated authority. Inadequate controls and lack of suitable division of responsibility have enabled adverse positions to be maintained without management knowledge or detection. Such situations do not always involve an abuse of position for personal gain but are often the consequence of misplaced zeal and judgment, and subsequently a desire to conceal from management the true extent of a loss.

Within the structure of any dealing environment it is essential to provide for appropriate divisions of responsibility between dealing, processing and accounting staff, with the senior officer responsible for each area reporting independently to senior management. Thereafter responsibilities and as appropriate, authorities or limits must be formally and precisely communicated and acknowledged by each member of staff. This is particularly relevant to dealing staff and the following should be considered:

Trading Limits:
- Each dealer's maximum outright position limit must be clearly defined, differentiating between intra-day (or daylight) exposure, and end of day positions.

- Each dealer's authority to operate within mis-matched limits for each dealing book, e.g. currency deposits, foreign exchange, or other portfolios, must be defined.

- Stop-loss limits or the necessity to report adverse dealing positions at a particular level of loss, must also be clearly defined and established.

- Predefined bank and other counterparty limits must be established.

- Where other forms of control over trading exposure are imposed these must be clearly communicated.

Senior management will normally approve overall limits by type, period and currency, and where appropriate indicate maximum aggregate positions for each dealing centre, or a group where positions are transferred from centre to centre. These authorities will be vested in a specified person, usually the treasury manager or chief dealer who, whilst retaining responsibility for ensuring compliance therewith, will, within the overall authority delegated to him, provide specific sub-limits to each dealer dependent upon his experience and object traded. Thereafter each dealer should be solely responsible and accountable for positions maintained.

Trading Policy:
- Outright open positions for day-time trading must at all times be contained within the limit specifically delegated in writing to each individual dealer.

- Dealers may be allowed, through specific authority delegated to them, to maintain close of business outright open positions. However, in the absence of such authority square (to near square) positions should be achieved.

- Mis-matched positions by period for both loans/deposits, foreign exchange and all other trading must be contained within the specific authority delegated in writing.

140

- Dealers may only undertake transactions with other market participants within approved counterparty limits and/or credit limits for the principal name.

- Where transactions are undertaken in respect of a customer it is the responsibility of the dealer concerned to ensure that an appropriate limit is available to accommodate such business.

- Each dealer must ensure profitable utilisation/covering of surplus/deficit overnight cash balances as projected (based on deals transacted and past experience) on the actual nostro account balance(s) in the currencies or commodities under his control.

- Under no circumstances should a dealer enter into a swap transaction where the spot rate to be applied bears no relationship to the current spot rate.

- If a forward contract is to be extended, the maturing contract must first be liquidated by applying the current market spot rate and any difference between the maturing forward contract price and the liquidated spot rate is for account of the customer concerned. The extended forward contract is then established at a new forward rate based on the close-out rate.

- No other deals may be written or extended at artificial, manufactured or blended rates or rates other than those within the spread currently prevailing in the market.

- Customer or corporate dealers must only base quotations upon rates obtained from the market dealers; such quotations and rates applied must not be finer than those quoted by the market dealers. This practice is not necessarily observed by all banks. In the authors' opinion any policy which permits quotations to be made outside of market rates must pass careful screening and be justifiable in terms of return to the bank, acceptable market practice, and adequate monitoring and control procedures being in place. Indeed, if such practices are permitted close management scrutiny is essential.

- In undertaking trading activity dealers must act prudently at all times and in particular be aware of structuring positions and portfolios where extraneous circumstances i.e. the introduction of penal, restrictive or exchange control regulations, could adversely impact upon their trading decisions.

- "Put through" business to accommodate a particular bank name at the behest of brokers, jobbers or other parties must not be arranged.

Any deviation from the above policy must receive the specific approval of the manager responsible for the dealing operation or other appropriately delegated officers on a deal by deal basis.

Operational Policy:
- Within the authority delegated to him each dealer is solely responsible and accountable for positions maintained by him. In this connection, all deals transacted must be properly recorded in the dealer's own position record and subsequently agreed at the close of business each day with the settlement records and/or, if appropriate, any other position record maintained. During the day or after business has been concluded, all deals transacted must be checked with the broker, jobber, bank telex backing sheets or Reuters' printouts, etc. by the dealer responsible unless another officer has specific responsibility for so doing thus ensuring that all trades undertaken during the day have been positioned and passed to the processing and accounting areas. It is also the responsibility of each dealer to ensure that all transactions are, as appropriate, properly recorded on dealing slips or other initial record of trade and submitted to the operations areas for further processing at the time the deal is concluded. Some dealing systems automatically update on a real time basis the dealer's position and process confirmations without the necessity of raising dealing slips. Where

dealing slips are raised a system of time recording and numbering each deal should be used as it will assist in ensuring all deals are promptly recorded and undertaken within the market spread.

- Although still said to be illegal in some countries, it is increasingly common for a dealing environment to record all telephone lines utilised in the dealing and immediate back-up function, i.e. exchange of delivery instructions or settlements department. Whilst this facility does provide a control technique it is normally only used to resolve subsequent discrepancies and misunderstandings of trades undertaken. When installing recording equipment both brokers and banks should take steps to inform other market participants that conversations will thereafter be recorded. Access to such recording equipment should be controlled closely. To avoid any implication of invasion of privacy, wherever possible, both parties to a conversation are invited to be present when it is necessary to resort to this facility to resolve a problem.

- The accuracy of all information recorded on dealing slips and the legibility thereof, are important factors to ensure misunderstandings do not occur in the processing and accounting area. Where unusual or complicated deals are concerned a brief note providing an audit trail to the transaction should be attached.

- Dealers must take care to annotate on dealing slips the correct rates at which the deals were concluded. Fictitious rates must not be recorded on dealing slips for any reason. A graphical display on some dealing systems will automatically show any deal written outside the market spread and be available during the day for senior management perusal. Additionally many banks have programmed their computers which process the deals to ensure that there is a daily tolerance for spot movements based upon anticipated movements during the day. The computer will reject any transaction which is outside the tolerance.

To avoid any misunderstanding it is important that dealers are made aware of the code of moral and ethical conduct a bank desires them to follow and in this connection the following issues should also receive consideration.

Moral and Ethical Policy:

- Dealers are expected to act prudently and in the best interests of their bank at all times. In addition to internal requirements they must be conscious of and work within the requirements of any local statutory regulations, exchange control or other regulations imposed by central monetary authorities and codes of conduct issued by local regulatory market or exchange bodies.

- The highest level of confidentiality must be maintained and the anonymity of the markets respected at all times.

- Should a dealer receive a request to transact a deal outside of current market rates, notice a willingness by dealers in other banks to deal outside current market rates, or consider that another bank or counterparty is trading at an unusually large volume, the matter should be brought to the attention of management immediately.

- Similarly, if a dealer hears through the market any suggestion of a problem in relation to any counterparty, management should be informed immediately.

- Whilst the necessity of personal contact with counterparties, customers, banks, brokers and other market participants is recognised, dealers must act prudently in accepting entertainment. Prior approval should be obtained from the agreed authority within the bank to any entertainment offered outside of the individual dealer's normal working hours. Gifts or favours must not be accepted without similar prior approval.

It is also necessary to place the following restrictions within a dealer's terms of reference:

- Under no circumstances should dealers become involved either directly or indirectly in processing and accounting issues, in particular confirmations, brokers notes and pay and receive procedures. Any computer facilities made available to dealers must be on a restricted access basis.

- Dealers should normally only be permitted to transact business with brokers, jobbers, banks or counterparties from their (the dealers) place of work. A principal's dealer shall at no time deal from within the offices of a broker or vice versa. The transacting of business by dealers from locations outside the office or exchange where appropriate, should require the specific authority of senior management which should only be accorded in exceptional circumstances. Dealing from the office outside customary business hours should be discouraged.

- In the author's opinion under no circumstances should a dealer be allowed to conduct own account trading on a direct basis within the markets. Specific written permission must be obtained from the agreed authority for own account trading in any of the financial markets within which the bank operates. Such authority should only be granted exceptionally and clearly define the parameters of such trading as dealers should be discouraged from operating in these markets for their own account. All transactions undertaken should be executed on a formal basis through another dealer.

Although it is accepted that close relationships will develop between dealers and brokers, the following guidelines should be clearly communicated:

- A principal's dealers and brokers have a common interest in preserving the anonymity of the market and are equally responsible for the maintenance of confidentiality. The standing of the market and the mutual trust which is its corner-stone outweighs any transient gain to which a breach of confidentiality might give rise and the exchange of confidential information in respect of third parties in any setting whatsoever and in whatever direction it flows is forbidden. Bank dealers must not press a broker for information which would be improper for him to pass. When installing open voice communication systems both brokers and banks must exercise care in the siting of speakers to prevent the occurrences of breaches of confidentiality and to take such other steps as may preserve individual bank's anonymity in the market.

- Dealers should wherever possible give brokers prior indication of those categories of principal with whom they would be unwilling to do business, in order that the smooth operation of markets be facilitated and frustrations on all sides be minimised.

- Dealers should not place any orders with brokers with the intention of asserting the name of a counterparty who can be immediately contacted direct with a view to concluding such deals for a further amount.

- Brokers should pass details and banks be prepared to receive them as soon as practicable after deals have been concluded.

- A principal's dealer shall visit the offices of a broker only upon the express invitation of the management of the broker concerned and with the prior knowledge and approval of the person responsible for money market operations of the relevant principal. Such visits shall be carefully supervised so as to protect confidentiality.

- Dealers must act prudently in accepting entertainment from brokers. It shall be the responsibility of management in both principals and brokers to ensure that entertainment offered in the course of business does not exceed reasonable limits.

With regard to evening entertainment, which by its nature is more difficult to control, a formal invitation should be made to the appropriate manager of a bank if a broker wishes to entertain a bank dealer in the evening. Evening entertainment should be carefully monitored by brokers' senior management with particular reference to its frequency, cost and style.

- No broker, including management, employees and persons acting in concert with such parties, shall offer or give inducement to dealing room personnel of a principal. No gifts or favours whatsoever shall be so given unless the broker is satisfied that the person responsible for money market operations in the principal concerned has been informed of the nature of the gift or favour. Employees of principals or persons acting in concert therewith shall not solicit inducements from brokers nor shall receive unsolicited gifts or favours from brokers without informing the person responsible for money market operations in the principal concerned of the nature of such gifts and favours.

- The making or arranging of bets between brokers and principals is unacceptable.

It is the responsibility of brokers to ensure that:

- Their customers understand fully the limitations of the brokers' responsibilities for business conducted.

- All their principals understand that they are required to conform, where appropriate, to the code of conduct and market practice.

- Their staff carrying out transactions on behalf of principals are adequately trained in the practices of the market place, in the firm's responsibilities to principals and in the need to adhere to the code of conduct and other guidelines that may be issued from time to time.

- Their principals understand that the ultimate responsibility for assessing the creditworthiness of a counterparty must rest with the principals themselves.

In the process of establishing the authority and responsibilities delegated to dealers it must be mentioned that whilst ultimately they will be judged upon performance and in particular profitability, it is considered prudent to ensure that no undue pressure in relation to profit motivation is placed on them as this could impact adversely upon their judgments and activities. Neither overt nor covert pressure to make profits should be applied either by senior dealing control management or by local branch management where dealing is conducted. It is also pertinent to mention that in some markets dealers must be licensed in which event a bank must obtain and retain on file the appropriate licence.

The subject of segregation of duties must not be overlooked when defining the authority and responsibilities of the processing and accounting areas and in this direction it is equally important to ensure that staff other than dealers do not have access to the dealer's equipment, i.e. direct lines, telex machines, Reuters dealing facilities, etc. It is normal practice for the dealing room to be a secure and restricted area at all times. Additionally the following operational "back-up" functions require close attention.

Confirmations :
Within the context of the telephone markets, the importance of confirmations (and brokers' notes) and verification thereof, cannot be over-stressed, as they are normally the first formal notification of a trade undertaken. This is particularly so where forward value dates are concerned. Same day, one day and spot value transactions will frequently be settled prior to a confirmation being received. It is however essential that confirmations for all deals are despatched immediately the deal is concluded, and that all details are verified on incoming confirmations. In the event of delay in the receipt of confirmations from counterparties prompt remedial action should be taken to obtain the necessary confirmation. Similarly immediate attention must be given to confirmations received which cannot be

148

identified with a recorded transaction. In the case of "in value deals", it is the authors' opinion that it is sufficient to verify the exchange of the underlying currencies or commodities in accordance with the terms of the contract as recorded within a bank's records, and thereafter no follow-up action is required. Further information on this topic and "out of value" transactions may be found in Section 4.

Where differences are noted between inward confirmations and the detail as recorded, management should be advised and immediate steps should be taken by the manager or a responsible officer outside of the dealing room to establish reasons for the discrepancies. If they are of significance or should a confirmation be received for which a deal cannot be traced, management must be advised immediately. Whilst discouraged in some areas of the world, it is the authors' opinion that signature verification of incoming confirmations is an essential element of control and at the discretion of management, either full or random sampling should be undertaken. Where unsigned computer-produced confirmations are accepted, a suitable indemnity should be obtained or held from the counterparty concerned. Special care should be taken to ensure that inward confirmations do not contain any qualifying clause which may prohibit the fulfilment of the underlying contract on the value or maturity dates. Where such clauses are in evidence they should be immediately brought to the attention of senior management for prompt remedial action to be taken if considered appropriate.

All confirmation procedures and controls must be undertaken by staff who are not connected with or have access to the dealers or dealing room. Under no circumstances should dealers be involved in procedures relating to incoming and outgoing confirmations.

Brokers and jobbers notes:
The same regulations for dealing staff's non-involvement in confirmations should equally apply to brokers notes. All detail on incoming brokers notes must be reconciled with the bank's records of the transaction and should any discrepancies be apparent these should be reported to the appropriate designated senior officer and taken up directly with the broker concerned by staff not involved in dealing.

After verification of detail, brokerage or commission rates and the individual charges should be checked. In due course when the relative statements are received, commissions and charges are agreed prior to payment.

All brokerage and commission payments should be analysed on a monthly basis and special attention paid to the scrutinisation of these accounts for evidence of any excessive operations, large fluctuations in charges or particular partiality towards an individual broker or jobber. Whilst the markets normally establish ethical codes of conduct for the relationship between brokers, jobbers and dealers, instances are still reported of these relationships being abused to the benefit of the individuals concerned and often to the detriment of a bank.

Nostro/correspondent bank reconciliations:

It is essential that the correspondent statements of account in both currency and commodity are efficiently reconciled on a regular basis to ensure that all outstandings are identified, investigated and agreed. Accounts should be reconciled whenever the account has worked and at least monthly. Large accounts, e.g. main US dollar accounts, must be balanced on a daily basis due to the number and size of entries which undoubtedly will be generated over them. However, more importantly, upon receipt of statements it is essential that items are immediately 'marked off' against the in-house nostro record, thereby identifying any large outstandings which can then be immediately investigated.

In many cases particularly same day, one day and spot value transactions, discrepancies can be highlighted before a confirmation has been received. The receipt of unanticipated amounts will be identified, investigated and, as appropriate, corrected. If the possibility exists of funds being paid/received with incorrect value or in an incorrect amount, the error can be rectified quickly and with a minimum of cost. If funds are not received on the value date a claim for compensating value will need to be submitted to the counterparty.

Revaluation "mark to market" and profit calculations:

Procedures for revaluation and/or mark to market exercises must be established with attention being focused on where precisely the rates used for this purpose originate. The rates used for revaluation calculations must be checked or provided independently of the dealing room. If undertaken properly revaluation will highlight any substantial underlying trading losses which have not been reported or identified. It is normal practice for dealers to maintain a running position of the profits as they estimate them to be. These should be compared with the result as reflected from a revaluation of the accounting records, and any significant discrepancies investigated and monitored.

All accounting and memorandum records must be properly and accurately maintained to ensure the accurate and timely reporting of all profit and loss figures at the desired frequencies and in accordance with each bank's accepted accounting principles.

Other aspects of security which must be considered in the context of a dealing environment, bearing in mind the very high value of the transactions and documents which are handled are:

- There is a need to create a clearly defined authority for authenticating and authorising incoming payment or release/delivery instructions, together with authority to originate and approve outward payment instructions. Extreme care should be taken to control all outward payments especially those in favour of third parties. Delivery procedures for securities, commodities and bullion should ensure that delivery only takes place when good value funds have been credited to the bank's account, unless an approved delivery risk limit exists within which the transaction may be effected.

- Procedures and responsibilities for the control of items of security and other items of value including test key data and equipment should be clearly defined. Under no circumstances should dealing staff be allowed access to such items.

- Procedures to ensure appropriate documentation and mandates for customers should be established especially when unsigned instructions by telex, telephone and customer terminals, are received. Within the interbank market it is common practice to establish trades without any formal documentation apart from confirmations and a list of authorised signatories; this is normally considered to be an acceptable practice. However, in all other cases the bank's full account opening facilities must be completed for the type of account involved, e.g. individual, joint, company, etc. Signing authorities must be established and verified. As appropriate, Memorandum and Articles, board resolutions, powers of attorney or joint and several mandates must be obtained. Where necessary any security formalities should be completed prior to business being undertaken and records of any liens or other charges against deposits properly recorded.

- Security arrangements for computer and communication systems should also be established and defined. Dealing areas are generally dependent upon the degree of sophistication of their communications and computerised systems. The necessity for dealing rooms to be secure areas has already been mentioned. Levels of access to computerised facilities need to be considered, and systems so designed as to ensure that audit trails are available and appropriate levels of computer security are maintained with adequate back-up arrangements. It is an increasingly common practice within banks to have a specialised unit to consider issues related to computer security risk, and where this is so the unit should also embrace the computer facilities of a dealing operation. The heightened security features provided by SWIFT and encryption as against the continued use of tested telex must be considered.

Errors made in processing, reconciliations, payment, receipt or delivery procedures can be costly in terms of subsequent claims and the value dating process, and therefore concise procedural manuals should exist to cover every aspect of the support functions related to a dealing operation.

The authors are aware that there is often an unfortunate tendency for some specialised areas to believe that they operate outside of a bank's normal control procedures. This should not be the case unless specific senior managerial authority preferably in writing has been obtained for dispensation from such requirements. It is also essential that banks do not become involved in trading new instruments until adequate control, recording and reporting systems are in place.

Finally, formal arrangements must be established for the production of accurate and timely accounting records to conform with the bank's accounting policy and local legislation on the subject. Information must be prepared to meet dealer, management, audit and external reporting requirements. Inter alia such information will include:

- Outright positions updating, reporting and agreement
- Forward maturity profiles
- Clearing and cash control
- The settlement of deals at maturity
- Facilities to monitor utilisation against extant counterparty limits

All deals transacted on any particular day must, in the normal course of events, be properly accounted for or recorded in the formal records of the bank on the same day. Where for any reason this is not possible, approval to defer must be obtained from the manager responsible for the dealing centre. Irrespective of any ancillary detail of positions or other information maintained, the accounted records are the prime record of account to which all other information must be related and agreed.

A bank will wish to control all of its dealing activities wherever they are undertaken. It is therefore necessary to disseminate control requirements to each area involved in dealing. Where a policy of centralised dealing activities has been introduced, it is important that the mandate of other areas are clearly defined so that within a limited authority they also conform to the same desired principles and level of control. Any delegated authority for outright or mis-matched positions being run by such units will require specific central approval for all excesses, (whether over established limits or created as one-off situations). All positions must be reported in order to enable the parent to monitor total group exposures.

All of the above topics are prerequisite to establishing and maintaining effective control of a dealing operation. Additionally, formally established policies, procedures and systems provide the necessary environment within which an effective audit control function can operate. This latter activity will comprise both preventative and detective action, i.e. prevention of errors and irregularities and also the detection of irregularities which have occurred. This will be achieved through the implementation of formal audit programmes which will be fully documented with formal reports being prepared and submitted to management on the auditor's findings. These programmes will ensure inter alia that:

- Appropriate divisions of responsibility are maintained between dealing, processing, accounting and control functions.

- Counterparty limits are established, and the system caters for the judicious management of apportionment of such limits to different dealing rooms within the group. If systems provide for limits to be temporarily borrowed/reallocated between different sections of a dealing room or bank, then there must be a clearly defined procedure for arranging, approving and recording such allocation.

- Dealing positions are maintained within established limits and that all other regulations imposed on trading are complied with.

- Line dealing management assesses or reviews positions throughout the day.

- Any excesses created, either counterparty or dealing position limits, are reported to senior management.

- Dealing is only transacted by persons authorised to do so within the authority delegated to them individually, and in the interests of the bank, in accordance with its dealing policy.

- All deals undertaken are promptly and accurately recorded.

- Confirmations are exchanged and agreed.

- Brokers and jobbers notes are received, examined and verified and the charges are closely monitored and analysed.

- Revaluations are properly undertaken, at appropriate current market rates, and accounting and profit figures are correctly compiled and reported.

- Nostro and other reconciliations are performed accurately and all unrecorded items are under prompt investigation.

- Returns reflect an accurate and true representation of the actual transactions/positions etc.

- Position records are accurately maintained and agreed.

- Regular reviews of limits are undertaken.

- Periodic reviews of systems and procedures are undertaken.

- Dealing policy documents are regularly reviewed and updated in the context of any changes in the market requirements and developments in market practice (good and bad).

- Any losses, problems or operating difficulties are thoroughly and promptly investigated and resolved.

- Settlement procedures are being complied with.

- Payment, receipt and delivery procedures are being complied with.

- Security arrangements are being complied with.

- Staff are properly trained.

- The relationship between dealing staff and management is such that the former can freely own up to making mistakes and are positively disuaded from concealing them.

The frequency and depth of audit projects will be established and regularly reviewed in the light of these findings. Where weaknesses are identified, frequencies and depth of testing should be increased. Conversely, where areas are operating efficiently, it may be prudent to decrease the frequency and depth of examination to devote more time to other areas. The audit programme should be supplemented by regular studies of specific areas and should cover all aspects of operation, including work-flow efficiency, identifying and subsequently making recommendation for the necessary correction in any areas of risk or potential risk. The way in which audit control is implemented is all important. A "no tick no check" approach, i.e. an audit function based merely upon the numerical verification of data, serves little purpose. A full appreciation of the underlying nature of all transactions, particularly new products and the risk implications related thereto, are absolutely essential, together with an awareness of potential risk situations, e.g. the examination should be undertaken of accounts being maintained by other banks or counterparty dealers or their relatives with a vested interest in the market.

Normally the audit control function also will have responsibility for preparing, developing or, as appropriate, scrutinising exposure, excesses, budgets, profit performance, management accounts, dealing limit reviews, dealing policy issues and other management information relating to dealing activities.

The method by which these responsibilities are discharged will be dependent upon the dealing structure of each particular bank. For example, for excess reporting a bank with a small number of dealing centres and an effective communication and reporting system, may operate from centralised limits with any excesses being reported to the controlling centre. Alternatively, where a larger network is concerned, control will be achieved through exception reporting, i.e. each individual centre will be provided with maximum exposure limits for both trading and counterparty purposes, with any excesses over these limits being reported immediately. Within this latter procedure the parent's control unit will be aware of its total potential exposure, and can quickly avail itself of actual positions.

Where a bank has several dealing operations the parent institution's control unit will also have overall responsibility for these other

156

operations. It is important therefore that reporting lines recognise and reflect this, even if by a "dotted line" responsibility. This subject not only relates to audit but frequently extends to other specified senior executives who have a line responsibility for specialised dealing activities, albeit that various dealing centres are part of a regional area for which direct responsibility rests elsewhere.

In these situations the parent control unit will ensure that an effective internal audit capability is established within each area incorporating all the criteria already discussed within this chapter. Thereafter it will:

- Establish and maintain a regular reporting system of selected data to facilitate continued parental surveillance, monitoring and control, together with providing a base of information from which management reports may be prepared, for example:

  > Telex advice of all excesses over every limit established
  > Details of outright positions
  > Outstanding forward purchase and sales together with loans/deposits
  > Forward mis-matched positions
  > Profit and loss
  > Brokerage and commission
  > Various detail related to balance sheet considerations, i.e. liquidity, size and mix of assets and liabilities, margins attained, etc.

- Obtain local management confirmation that specific controls and dealing policies are being complied with.

Additionally, the central control function will undertake both regular and surprise audit inspections of these operations with the frequency and depth of such visits being determined by the apparent operating efficiencies or deficiencies of the areas concerned. During such visits they will ensure that acceptable levels of technically competent senior staff and management are available to safeguard the interests of the bank. Surprise visits are also frequently carried out by senior ex-dealers from Head Office who spend a considerable time in the dealing room sniffing the atmosphere and seeing how their dealing colleagues behave generally.

It is essential that internal control functions retain at all times their independence and integrity and therefore must be responsible to a member of senior management who is not involved within day to day trading activities or other areas which they examine.

The subjects of the control of dealing operations and risk exposure would be incomplete without reference to fraud, the instances of which are unfortunately increasing. Whilst the diligent implementation of control procedures will afford an element of protection against this risk it is also essential that all members of staff are fully aware of potential fraudulent approaches.

Fraud in its variety of forms tends to keep pace with technical developments in banking and commerce and regrettably these activities are not accompanied by any recognisable physical attribute of the practioners. In law, fraud means dishonesty and is defined in Derry v Peek (1889) as "being proven" when it is shown that false representation has been made:

    i)   knowingly, or
    ii)   without belief in its truth, or
    iii) recklessly or carelessly whether it be true or false

There is no doubt that a banker must exercise reasonable care and he is legally bound to follow up any suspicion of fraud to satisfy himself that it is unfounded before developing a proposition. It is essential, therefore, for bankers to be able to identify whether a proposition is spurious or not and the best way of achieving this is with a working knowledge of the international markets and how transactions are structured. Many potentially fraudulent approaches are naive, patently obvious and, therefore, quite easy to identify. These include proposals which are quite unrealistic in terms of the market, the bank or customer's balance sheet by way of amount. Some transactions are often referred to as mega-deals and involve tons of gold, vast quantities of oil, or huge deposits of money. Frequently such proposals are introduced by a friend of a friend and the real source of wealth is kept at arms length on the pretext of required confidentiality. However, in practice it may not always be easy to discover if a fraud has been perpetrated or is being attempted as a grey area exists between a bad banking proposition and fraud.

There has undoubtedly been a development in the sophistication of fraudulent propositions as well as the variety and skill of confidence tricksters in approaching bankers, lawyers, accountants and corporate treasurers, as well as the public at large. Many bankers on hearing a proposition which they do not understand will immediately recall that "they do not know everything", and wrongly assume that because the proposition does not make any sense to them it is due to their own lack of technical knowledge. In the authors' experience, bankers, accountants and lawyers generally know a lot more than they will admit to themselves, and certainly have the ability to recognise most propositions of a spurious nature on the basis of common sense and a working knowledge of their own discipline. Naturally, bankers are properly trained to be polite and helpful, otherwise there is little business that they could expect to generate. A legacy of this excellent training is that the individual is usually inhibited when challenged with a proposition he does not understand, and even when he recognises that there is something decidedly "wrong with it", he will be as helpful as possible in explaining why the proposition does not work, suggesting alternative ideas, or providing introductions to other people who may be able to help. This can be an extremely dangerous practice as it trains the opposition. As a basic rule when a potential fraud is suspected, the bank should:

i)   immediately terminate all discussions on the subject
ii) convey nothing in writing or on a telex, and
iii) consider severing any banking connection or connections it may have with the individual or individuals concerned.

As a result of becoming involved, even unwittingly, a bank may lose its money and reputation, both with its customers and possibly with the authorities in one or more countries. The more sophisticated approaches involve propositions introduced via a highly respected and reputable source. Introductions through bankers, lawyers, accountants, major corporate entities and one's own board of directors naturally lend credibility to an approach and are generally sufficient to ensure that the bankers at least listen carefully to the proposition. In some cases names of reputable organisations and individuals have been used without their authority, adequate but false proof of representation having been made. It is essential that potentially fraudulent propositions are not passed round. Bankers should not, on receiving such an approach, introduce the parties concerned to anyone else, as by so doing they will be giving unwarranted credibility to the proposition by adding the bank's name in the form of an informal reference. Even a letter or communication formally refusing a proposition can be used to good advantage by the fraudster if it has the right bank's name at the top!

The successful practitioner of the spurious deal is said to be gifted with an instinctive understanding of human psychology. He will, for example, be unlikely to introduce himself as a principal and in his alleged role of representative or agent he will not disclose the identity of his principals except in the most general terms. One American lawyer, when describing the approaches made by these professional confidence tricksters, said that "aside from love, no human emotion is so useful in unseating sound judgment as greed". Whenever someone is offering something for nothing, suspect it at once and remember that no one gives away money. Indeed, great care should be exercised when any of the following features occur in a proposition being offered:

- If the transaction involves amounts which are substantially larger than are normally experienced for a particular customer or market for the transaction concerned, especially if the client has no previous experience of the industry or commodity involved.

- If there is any undue haste to complete a transaction, particularly a complicated one, where large amounts of money are involved.

- If there is any over-emphasis on maintaining secrecy. Remember that it should be quite unnecessary for anyone to request a banker to keep confidential any matters of a financial nature brought to him professionally. Only in the most exceptional circumstances should a bank disclose information to third parties and such circumstances might, of course, include those when it is

160

deemed to be in the bank's interest to do so. If additional assurance that the proposition will be kept confidential is demanded, this should be suspected. There may be good reason to be careful.

Beware of any technical double talk, particularly if it comes out with total confidence and the propositioner, whom you may be meeting for the first time, is clearly at ease with large figures. This is often accompanied by impressive name dropping (companies, directors, etc.).

Avoid the temptation to pass messages which have no banking significance, particularly if the content is not understood. Banks do not run a postal service nor are they a telex bureau. The passing of messages through a bank may be designed to create an apparent and totally unmerited involvement of the bank in the proposition itself. Such messages have been known, in the past, to have been forged and correspondence with such individuals is undesirable. The authors have seen one telex, the original of which was sent by the bank to the proposer and stated that "the bank was not interested in the proposition". The copy had the word "not" deleted. People who are involved in fraud may also be involved in other forms of crime.

Resist the temptation to let bank premises for a "few hours" unless the individuals are well known to the bank, and the precise reason for such an unusual request is fully understood and acceptable.

The newspapers often bear stories of substantial transactions or events happening somewhere in the world. News of the Iranian hostage money and the break up of ATT among others, were closely followed by a number of approaches being made allegedly referring to the huge sums involved. These "look alike" propositions should be treated with great care, particularly where requests for fiduciary or trust services have been requested. Experience has shown that such events have been taken as a relatively plausible excuse to obtain correspondence from banks, lawyers and accountants which is then used to defraud gullible investors, usually in some other country, of fees paid in advance for loans which never materialise.

In April 1983, the Bank of England issued a Notice to Institutions authorised under the Banking Act of 1979 which, amongst other things, concerned the risk of "fraudulent invitations". Recognised banks and licensed deposit-takers were reminded by this Notice of approaches by persons unknown to them suggesting participation in substantial business out of all proportion to their normal scale of activities. Banks were reminded that often such propositions are made with the object of committing a fraud. The Bank of England has asked to be informed of all offers which are considered dubious so that appropriate warnings may be given to other institutions, and advises that the greatest care would be taken to respect any necessary confidences. When fraud is suspected in a bank it is imperative that the appropriate designated senior management be advised immediately and that the bank's internal rules regarding communication to anyone be strictly observed.

Whilst retaining an awareness of spurious propositions it is essential that an appropriate perspective is maintained towards new business offered to the bank. There is no doubt that there has been a growth, both in volume and sophistication of potential fraudulent approaches, but this should not colour a banker's judgment to the extent that worthwhile and profitable business is turned aside. The most important things to remember are the need to understand exactly what the client requires, why he is doing it, how it works and to ensure that it is in accordance with legal and statutory requirements, and established market practices, principles and terms.

CHAPTER NINE

Introduction to Money Market Instruments and Money Market Calculations

The Treasury functions of a bank engaged in international and domestic banking operations, and some functions as conducted within the departmental structures of branches of banks operating abroad, are discussed in Chapter 1. A prime function identified in that Chapter was "the funding of the bank's or branch's banking business". Funding is defined as "the acquisition of liabilities". It refers in general to various techniques of attracting money for different periods of time, for a variety of bank purposes such as lending, investing, acquisitions, capital or liquidity, from a variety of sources. To achieve their funding objectives banks must be able to offer investors an appropriately broad choice of investment instruments if they wish to be able to tap the widest range of investment liquidity. Strategically, this is often considered to be a sound policy, in case one source of funds "dries up" alternative sources may be tapped. In addition, arbitrage opportunities can occur when sourcing in one market and placing, lending or investing in another.

Chapter 2 deals with exposure management and cites liquidity as a major risk consideration, a subject which is expanded upon in Chapter 3 and discussed from the view-point of supervisory authorities in Chapter 5. It was established that liquefiable assets provide an essential ingredient to successful cash flow management by providing a potential source of funds for a bank's short term obligations both to repay depositors and meet its commitments to lend.

Banks and other deposit-taking instititions are not unique in their consideration of funding sources. These issues are equally important, to a greater or lesser extent, to governments, quasi government entities, state and municipal bodies as well as private sector institutions and corporate entities. Liquidity requirements have to be met and there are many factors which will affect the supply of, or demand for, suitable funds.

By reference in particular to the US, UK and Eurocurrency markets this section deals with the source, nature and market mechanisms related to short-term money market; Government and other non-commercial bank, money market, and capital debt instruments. Several of these instruments provide important alternative funding sources for short-term funds without recourse to conventional loans and deposits. They provide attractive sources of funds to the issuer, as they secure access to funding requirements through the primary markets at predetermined fixed rates of interest which, in the case of short-dated instruments, are normally only slightly below money market rates. To the investor they either provide acceptable collateral security and/or desired/essential liquidity through the activities of secondary markets which have developed in these instruments, at higher returns than might otherwise have been available for the right of immediate conversion into cash. Speculative trading activities can take place by using some of these instruments, without placing undue pressure on balance sheet footings, the profit or loss being immediately realisable through subsequent sales within the secondary markets. In those countries where banks are required to maintain MLAs, several of these instruments are classified as qualifying assets. The particular instruments discussed in this section are:

• Certificates of Deposit	• US Treasury Bonds
• Bank Bills	• UK Gilt-edged Stock
• Trade Bills	• UK Local Authority Bills
• Commercial Paper	• UK Local Authority Bonds
• Repurchase Agreements	• UK Local Authority Stocks
• Broker and Dealer Loans	• US Federal Agency Securities
• UK Treasury Bills	• US Municipal Bonds
• US Treasury Bills	

The marketability and therefore the realisable value of liquifiable assets are determined first by their negotiability, and secondly by the availability and depth of a secondary market in which each type of instrument is traded. It will be noted throughout this section that this differs from instrument to instrument and from country to country.

Different types of investor have widely differing investment parameters and, whilst it is quite impossible to quantify all the types of instrument which may be of interest to each classification of investor, it may be useful to identify some types of investor and their likely investment criteria before discussing the individual instruments.

- *Wealthy individuals* who may be resident anywhere in the world. They often seek bearer investments which provide anonymity, liquidity and no liability to withholding taxes on their investment. The quality of the asset is usually of high importance to this group of investor which generally seeks investment opportunities in currencies that have potential relative strength. Also the financial strength or credit rating of the borrower is normally of prime significance, as indeed is the perceived relative economic and political strength of the borrower's country. No investor would be overjoyed if fiscal or monetary regulations were to be imposed which could adversely offset the value of the investment. Often the private investor lacks financial expertise or, more commonly, the time to devote to the management of his resources, and as there exists a wide variety of alternative opportunities for outright speculation or gambling – the true private investor tends to be somewhat conservative in his investment objectives, however ill-defined they may be. The demand for the investment services offered by the institutions, as described below, is a natural development and substantial funds are being lodged by private investors with a variety of managed funds and trusts.

- *Managed funds* are invariably established to attract a particular sector of investor requirements and the continued ability to attract funds often depends upon the manager's proven and published performance compared with competitors and the market as a whole. The level of achieved success is as varied as the specialised composition of the various funds. Portfolio specialisation can range from eurocurrency deposits to property and

165

mining, from bullion and precious metals to "soft" commodities, from growth of capital to high income portfolios, from fixed interest debt instruments to equity, from highest quality government securities and AAA rated debt to lower quality higher risk investments – and, of course, any mix of these. Geographical specialisation is also commonplace such as Japanese funds and US Dollar funds. Some funds are specifically structured to attract the small retail investor, for example, unit trusts, whilst others are designed for the major institutional investor such as pension funds. Clearly widely differing portfolio strategies are adopted by the fund managers but from time to time they will all have the need to maintain higher or lower levels of liquidity and flexibility.

- *Insurance companies'* investment requirements range from the life, marine and product underwriters who tend to seek long-term investments to the life, motor, accident and general underwriters whose need for liquid assets is higher and who therefore often seek shorter maturities. Insurance companies and banks also act as trustees for trust funds which are maintained under entirely independent management from the trustee. They also manage substantial individual discretionary portfolios for private and corporate clients who frequently require flexibility and liquidity.

- *Bank trustee* operations are subject to statutory trust legislation in the country in which the trust is managed. This invariably has the effect of limiting the range of investments permissible for trust portfolios. Trustees are required therefore to seek high quality low-risk instruments generally with a limited geographical spread.

- *Government agencies and municipalities* are usually major borrowers within the financial markets. However they frequently have substantial but irregular surplus cash flows which give rise to a cautious approach to investments. They generally tend to keep a relatively liquid portfolio of short-term funds and securities with a maturities spread of up to five years.

- *Central Banks* and their equivalents are providers to the indigenous banking system of short-term funding, directly in some cases, or indirectly in others. Rediscount facilities, a principal function of central banks, is to supply liquidity to the banking system.

- Other major sources of funds include the wide range of *Corporations* and the *Supranational Institutions*.

- Last, and indeed one of the most important sectors is *commercial banks*. Commercial banks are required to retain adequate liquidity and therefore need a portfolio of short-term money market assets. These include various forms of short-term government paper, CDs issued by other banks, and bank bills accepted by other banks. Some of the floating rate notes, as described in Chapter 24, which tend to be traded as money market instruments are also held by banks. Since the publication in November 1984 of the Bank of England paper on qualifying capital for banks, the appetite of banks for holding other bank's FRNs has diminished – the same principles have been adopted by a number of countries and the banks with operations in any of them will be affected.

In every institution the amount of liquidity which is available for investment purposes is liable to fluctuate over a given period of time, and often specifically depends on the investor's business climate as well as the prevailing general economic and political scenarios in which he operates. What we are saying is that an investor's appetite for any given asset (be it a certificate of deposit, a long-term bond or debenture, a bank deposit, or whatever else), will depend upon whether the potential investor has sufficient liquidity to make a new investment, how long he perceives such liquidity to exist and what influences him so far as "risk versus return on the investment" is concerned.

To compare various money market instruments with say, market deposits, it is important to distinguish the relationship between rates of interest and discounts. It is particularly important to understand the calculations and criteria relating to those instruments which are priced on different formulae in the primary and secondary markets. The examples which follow may be helpful to illustrate the difference between primary and secondary market functions and pricing structures.

In the London Certificate of Deposit market the primary market exists between the issuing bank and the original depositor. A new CD may be issued either direct to a depositor or indirectly through a secondary market dealer. It follows that if a CD is not negotiated to a third party prior to its maturity then the transaction is confined to the primary market. The secondary market's function is to provide the depositor with liquidity. Traders in the secondary market quote two way prices (sell and buy) for first-class bank CDs, which enables the depositor to obtain cash for all or part of a CD holding prior to maturity.

In the secondary market, CDs are traded at a premium or a discount to par plus accrued interest. The premium or discount, if any, will be calculated on the basis of differential of interest yields on the CD and the money market, ruling at the time of negotiation, for the remaining period of the CD. The mechanics are illustrated as follows:

The depositor buys a 100,000 Sterling CD on 12th April 1984 to mature in three months' time on 12th July 1984 (91 days) at $8\frac{7}{8}\%$ per annum. Let us assume that the depositor wishes to realise the proceeds of his CD on 22nd May 1984 (40 days later) and that a secondary market dealer was quoting

$$\text{(i)} \quad 8\tfrac{13}{16}\% - 8\tfrac{7}{8}\%$$
$$\text{or} \quad \text{(ii)} \ 8\tfrac{1}{2}\% - 8\tfrac{9}{16}\%$$
$$\text{or} \quad \text{(iii)} \ 9\tfrac{1}{4}\% - 9\tfrac{5}{16}\%$$

Taking example (i)

$$£100,000 \times \frac{(365 \times 100) + (8\tfrac{7}{8} \times 91)}{(365 \times 100) + (8\tfrac{7}{8} \times 51)} = £100,960.69$$

The depositor was able to buy and sell his CD at the same rate ($8\frac{7}{8}\%$ per annum) perhaps owing to hardening (rising) interest rates or a flattening yield curve, or the structure of the buyer's CD portfolio.

If we compare the actual return to the depositor in this example (£960.68) with the interest he would have received on a fixed deposit account at the same rate for the same period of 40 days, there is a shortfall of £11.91.

Assume alternative investment

$$£100,000 + \frac{8\frac{7}{8} \times 40}{100 \times 365} \times £100,000 = £100,972.60$$

The reason for this is because the secondary market dealer is paying the accrued interest on 40 days (£960.68) 51 days earlier than if the CD had been held until maturity. The cost to the dealer of being "short" of this sum is deducted from the proceeds paid to the depositor, and is calculated on a discount to yield basis @ $8\frac{7}{8}\%$.

$$\text{e.g. } £960.68 \times \frac{8.875}{100} \times \frac{51}{365} = £11.91$$

The proceeds formula applied to Sterling CDs with a maturity of less than one year is therefore :

$$A \times \frac{(365 \times 100) + (R \times T)}{(365 \times 100) + (Y \times D)} = P$$

Where A = the principal amount
R = interest rate stated on the CD
T = total tenor (in days) of the CD
Y = yield to maturity at which the CD is purchased
D = remaining days from date of purchase to maturity
P = proceeds received by the depositor

It is not normal practice to charge buyers any commission in the primary market or to charge sellers commission in the secondary market so in examples (i) – (iii) the proceeds are actual.

Looking at example (ii) and applying the secondary market discount formula to the market rate of $8\frac{9}{16}\%$ we get:

$$£100,000 \times \frac{(365 \times 100) + (8.875 \times 91)}{(365 \times 100) + (8.5625 \times 51)} = £101,004.25$$

Here the depositor has held a fixed interest security while interest rates were falling and by selling it after 40 days has obtained a cash benefit having foregone the higher yield on the CD for the remaining period.

The actual yield the depositor obtained on the CD may be calculated as follows:

$$Y = 100 \frac{\left(I \right)}{\left(A \times \frac{D}{365} \right)}$$

Where Y = the yield to the depositor
I = the actual income
A = face amount of the CD
and D = number of days the depositor held the CD

$$Y = 100 \frac{\left(1{,}004.25 \right)}{\left(100{,}000 \times \frac{40}{365} \right)} = 9.1638\%$$

The investor has improved the return on his investment by 0.2888% for the first 40 days which he would have been unable to do if he had placed his funds in a fixed period deposit account at the outset.

In example (iii) the market rates have hardened in the meantime and the secondary market dealer will buy the CD at $9\frac{5}{16}\%$.

Once again by applying the discount formula the return to the depositor is as follows:

$$£100{,}000 \times \frac{(365 \times 100) + (8\frac{7}{8} \times 91)}{(365 \times 100) + (9\frac{5}{16} \times 51)} = £100{,}899.76$$

This represents a return on his investment of:

$$100 \times \frac{\left(899.76 \right)}{\left(100{,}000 \times \frac{40}{365} \right)} = 8.2103\% \text{ or a loss of } 0.665\%$$

Sales of Sterling CDs are for cash settlement on the same day in the London market against delivery of the CDs sold. Transactions are

170

normally completed by 2.00 p.m. on the dealing day. The depositor may decide to retain his CD until maturity or until an improvement in currency short-term interest rates.

The above examples illustrate the flexibility of a CD from the holder's view-point. A further example might be appropriate to demonstrate the gearing potential such investments have.

Assume a depositor buys a £100,000 CD for 3 months maturity at $8\frac{7}{8}\%$ and current interest rates fall by $\frac{3}{4}\%$ as a result of a cut in base rates the next week, after 5 days, so that the secondary market is bidding at $8\frac{1}{4}\%$. The return on the investment would be as calculated below if the depositor decided to sell.

$$\pounds100,000 \times \frac{(365 \times 100) + (8\frac{7}{8} \times 91)}{(365 \times 100) + (8\frac{1}{4} \times 87)} = \pounds100,241.48$$

$$100 \times \frac{\left(\begin{array}{c}241.48\end{array}\right)}{\left(100,000 \times \frac{4}{365}\right)} = 22.04\%,$$

an improvement on yield of 13.16% or almost $2\frac{1}{2}$ times better return than the original CD was yielding. If the interest rate yield curve over the life period of the CD was to U-turn then higher yields may be achieved by astute fund managers who, if they gauge the market correctly, could place proceeds in shorter, say, overnight funds as the market rates move up. Indeed the shape of the yield curve of the Sterling CD market frequently acts as an indicator of the dealer's perception of the 3 months and 12 months interest rate movements. The secondary market dealer will quote his rates on the basis of the following:

- the London interbank market less $\frac{1}{16}\%$ to $\frac{1}{8}\%$

- the dealer's perception of future interest rate movements

- the dealer's funding policy and liquidity position

- the dealer's appetite for increased or reduced exposure in/of the issuing bank's name and the level of utilisation of credit limits established for the dealer's own internal prudential controls

Medium-term Sterling CDs with final maturities in excess of one year have interest paid annually. The calculation of proceeds of a CD sold in the secondary market with more than a year to run is illustrated as follows:

Assume a CD for £100,000 is issued on 12th April 1984 having a total life of three years and bearing interest at $10\frac{3}{4}\%$ per annum, is sold to a secondary market trader 120 days later at $9\frac{1}{4}\%$ with two years and 245 days to run to maturity.

On 12th April 1987 – Principal sum due   £100,000
Interest due April 1987   £ 10,750
£110,750

Discount for 1 year

$$\frac{110{,}750}{1 + \left(\dfrac{9.25}{100} \times \dfrac{365}{365}\right)} = £101{,}373.00$$

Interest due April 1986   £ 10,750.00
£112,123.00

Discount for 1 year

$$\frac{112{,}123}{1 + \left(\dfrac{9.25}{100} \times \dfrac{365}{365}\right)} = £102{,}629.75$$

Interest due April 1985   £ 10,750.00
£113,379.75

Discount for 245 days

$$\frac{113{,}379.75}{1 + \left(\dfrac{9.25}{100} \times \dfrac{245}{365}\right)} = £106{,}751.64$$

Proceeds received for 120 days holding

This represents a return of 20.54% per annum.

Floating rate CDs (FRCDs) sometimes known as variable rate Sterling CDs, were introduced into the London market in March 1978. These are traded on a sterling price rather than on a yield to maturity basis. Interest on Sterling FRCDs may be paid every three or six months according to the terms shown on the CD itself.

The proceed's calculation of a Sterling FRCD:

Assume a five year Sterling FRCD for £100,000 has been issued and is to be sold with one year and 21 days to run to maturity. The last interest date was 21 days before the value date, the three monthly coupon is currently 9% and the agreed sterling price is $99\frac{3}{4}$.

$$\text{Proceeds} = \frac{\pounds 100,000 \times 99.75}{100} = \pounds 99,750.00$$

$$\text{Interest accrued} = \frac{\pounds 100,000 \times 9 \times 21}{100 \times 365} = \underline{\pounds \quad 517.81}$$

$$\begin{array}{ll} \text{Total received} & \underline{\pounds 100,267.81} \\ \text{by the seller} & \end{array}$$

The interest has been paid to the original holder(s) for the first 12 payments at the end of each three monthly period when due, and will be re-calculated for the final seven payments in due course for payment to the new holder(s). Only the thirteenth interest period of the life of the CD illustrated above requires to be adjusted between buyer and seller so far as interest accrued is concerned. The sterling price will take into account, however, the discount on the early payment of interest accrued, e.g. £517.81 paid by the secondary market dealer 70 days before the latter receives reimbursement from the issuing bank. When interest payments or repayment of the principal sum are made it is essential that the CD is presented for such payment(s) through a recognised bank and the payments are made and recorded on the back of the certificate itself. This will provide added protection to both issuer and holder against fraud. Returning to the above illustration, the discount of $\frac{1}{4}$% taken by the secondary market trader will reflect, inter alia, the interest rate differential between the current coupon of 9% and that ruling for a 70 day (almost two months) period at the time the CD is sold. By establishing what the interbank rate (Y) was likely to be , we can illustrate how the secondary market trader may have set his price at 99.75 on the CD offered to him. The proceeds formula for Sterling CDs with a maturity of less than one year may be used as follows:

$$£100,000 \times \frac{(365 \times 100) + (9 \times 91)}{(365 \times 100) + (Y \times 70)} = £100,267.81$$

$$\frac{37319}{(36500 + 70Y)} = \frac{100,267.81}{100,000}$$

$$Y = \frac{\left(\dfrac{100,000 \times 37,319}{100,267.81}\right) - 36500}{70} = 10.28\%$$

In the illustration above, the interbank market at the time of the sale was, say, $10\frac{1}{4}\%$ to $10\frac{9}{32}\%$ range for 70 day term deposits.

The calculation of the sterling price can, therefore, be made as follows by applying the proceeds formula:

$$A \times \frac{(365 \times 100) + (R \times T)}{(365 \times 100) + (Y \times D)} = P \text{ where :}$$

A = principal sum
R = the current interest coupon on the FRCD
T = the tenor of the current interest period, in days
Y = the interbank reinvestment yield ruling on the disposal date
D = the number of days to the next interest payment date
P = the proceeds paid to the FRCD vendor

We can see above that P = £100,267.81 of which interest accrued amounting to £517.81 must be deducted to establish a sterling price *exclusive* of accrued interest of £99,750 (net proceeds). Therefore, the sterling price =

$$\frac{\text{Net proceeds} \times 100}{\text{The principal sum}} = 99.75$$

The worked examples which follow illustrate the methods of calculating the dollar prices and, therefore, the proceeds payable of eurodollar CDs sold on the secondary market in London before maturity, for:

    i)   CDs with a year or less to run to maturity
    ii) CDs with over a year to run to maturity
    iii) FRCDs

i)   Face value of the CD US$1,000,000
    Fixed rate of interest applicable is $11\frac{5}{8}\%$ p.a. on a 360 day base
    Initial period from issue to maturity 1 year
    Period to run from date of sale to maturity is 91 days
    The agreed sale is on a yield basis at $10\frac{3}{4}\%$ p.a.

First calculate the full value of the CD at maturity:

$$\$1,000,000 \times \frac{11.625}{100} \times \frac{365}{360} + 1,000,000 = \$1,117,864.58$$

Now calculate the amount of interest accrued due to the seller: 274 days interest at 11.625% on $1 million is:

$$\$1,000,000 \times \frac{11.625}{100} \times \frac{274}{360} = \$88,479.17$$

Then calculate the discount factor, being the cost to the buyer of paying the principal sum plus interest accrued to the seller 91 days before it is recoverable at maturity. (Assume that the market rate for 3 months eurodollars is approximately $10\frac{3}{4}\%$.)

$$1 + \frac{(10.75}{(100} \times \frac{91\,)}{360)} = 1.027174$$

Next calculate the actual sales proceeds paid to the seller. This is the value of the CD at maturity ($1,117,864.58) divided by the cost (discount) factor above (1.027174)

$$= \frac{1,117,864.58}{1.027174} = \$1,088,291.35$$

Although secondary market quotations are normally on a yield basis as shown above for US dollar London CDs, it is possible to price such transactions in terms of a dollar price per US$100.

So the calculation of the principal dollar amount and secondary market price at the time of sale is as follows:
The actual sales proceeds paid ($1,088,291.35) less the accrued interest due to the seller ($88,479.17) is the principal dollar amount per $1 million

$$\$1,088,291.35 - 88,479.17 = \$999,812.18$$

To obtain the dollar price per $100, divide by 10,000 to give *$99.981218* per $100.

Now for the second example of a CD with more than a year to run to initial maturity.

ii) Face value of the CD US$1,000,000
Fixed interest payable annually at $12\frac{3}{4}\%$
Original life of the CD 3 years including a leap year.
The CD is sold with 2 years 251 days to run.
The CD is purchased at a yield of $11\frac{1}{4}\%$ as interest rates had fallen during the first four months.

First calculate interest payable each year:
Years 1 and 2

$$\$1,000,000 \times \frac{12.75}{100} \times \frac{365}{360} = \$129,270.83$$

Year 3 (Leap Year)

$$\$1,000,000 \times \frac{12.75}{100} \times \frac{366}{360} = \$129,625.00$$

Then calculate the amount receivable at maturity including interest. Take the last year first and work backwards as follows:

The principal sum	US$1,000,000
The last year's interest thereon	US$ 129,625
(leap year 366 day year)	US$1,129,625

The discount for 365 days at $11\frac{1}{4}\%$ for the 365 days penultimate year on US$1,129,625 is:

$$\frac{1,129,625}{1 + \left(\frac{11.25}{100} \times \frac{365}{360} \right)} = \text{US\$}1,013,969.14$$

The penultimate year's interest (365 days) is added

US$1,013,969.14 + US$129,270.83 = US$1,143,239.97

The discount for 365 days @ $11\frac{1}{4}\%$ on US$1,143,239.97 is

$$\frac{1,143,239.97}{1 + \left(\frac{11.25}{100} \times \frac{365}{360}\right)} = \text{US\$1,026,190.16}$$

US$ 129,270.83   add the first year's interest (365 day year)

US$1,155,460.99

The discount for 251 days @ $11\frac{1}{4}\%$ on $1,155,460.99 for 365 day year is:

$$\frac{1,155,460.99}{1 + \left(\frac{11.25}{100} \times \frac{365}{360} \times \frac{251}{365}\right)} = \$1,071,421.38,$$

being the total proceeds payable to the seller

The interest accrued for the 114 day investment period is

$$\text{US\$1,000,000} \times \frac{12.75}{100} \times \frac{114}{360} = \text{US\$40,375.00}$$

Once again the normal method of secondary market quotation is on a yield basis, but it may be expressed as a dollar price. To express the sale price per US$100 – first deduct the interest accrued to the seller ($40,375.00) from the total amount he will receive ($1,071,421.38) and then divide by 10,000 = 103.1046. Owing to the fall in US dollar interest rates the higher yielding dollar CD is now priced over par.

iii) FRCDs in US dollars are normally priced in the secondary market on a dollar price rather than a yield to maturity. In the primary market they are priced on a 3 or 6 month coupon basis at a mark-up over LIBOR. Assume a US$1 million FRCD with semi-annual coupons and a 4 year maturity is to be discounted with 17 months to run. The current coupon is 11%, the dollar purchase price is $99\frac{1}{4}$ and the last interest date 35 days from the sale value date.

Where A = the principal sum
R = the current interest coupon on the FRCD
D = the number of days from the last interest payment date
Q = the dollar price per US$100
P = the proceeds payable to the seller

The formula below may be applied:

$$P = \frac{(A \times Q)}{100} + \frac{(A \times R \times D)}{360 \times 100}$$

$$\text{So } P = \frac{1{,}000{,}000 \times 99.25}{100} + \frac{1{,}000{,}000 \times 11 \times 35}{100 \times 360} = \$1{,}003{,}194.44$$

Where T = the tenor of the current interest period in days
N = the number of days to the next interest payment date
Y = the approximate interbank reinvestment yield ruling on the disposal date.

The formula

$$Y = \left(\frac{A \times [(360 \times 100) + (R \times T)]}{\dfrac{P}{N}} \right) - (360 \times 100)$$

may be applied to determine the equivalent yield price

$$Y = \left(\frac{(1{,}000{,}000 \times (36{,}000 + 2{,}002))}{\dfrac{1{,}003{,}194.44}{147}} \right) - 36{,}000 = 12.79586\%$$

The proof may be calculated:

Principal plus interest for the current interest
period ($1 million + 182 days at 11% p.a.) US$1,055,611.11
Less total proceeds paid to the seller   US$1,003,194.44
                                              US$ 52,416,67

The number of days left to run to the next maturity day is 147

So $52,416.67 \times \dfrac{360}{147} = \$128,367.35$

$$\dfrac{\$128,367.35 \times 100}{\$1,003,194.44} = 12.79586\%$$

An illustrated example of the net proceeds calculation of a medium-term (over one year) fixed interest CD may be helpful since the interest payments are made semi-annually. All the other facilities described may be calculated as illustrated above under the London Eurodollar CD market.

Assume a US$1,000,000 CD is to be sold on the secondary market after two years and 90 days have elapsed from its original maturity of four years. It has a fixed interest coupon of $13\frac{1}{2}\%$ and is being sold on a yield basis of $12\frac{3}{4}\%$. In order to calculate accurately the proceeds payable to the seller, the remaining interest periods for the current and subsequent interest periods must first be determined.

The current interest period is the fifth and the remaining periods, the sixth, seventh and eighth. Interest due will be:

5th period 92 days + 90 days	Interest due = US$68,250
6th period 183 days	Interest due = US$68,625
7th period 182 days	Interest due = US$68,250
8th period 183 days	Interest due = US$68,625

Assume that there is no leap year occurring during the periods 5-8, and that all these periods end and commence on good value days, e.g. not weekends or bank holidays, otherwise the number of days and cashflow would differ from the example.

$$1,000,000 \times \dfrac{13.5}{100} \times \dfrac{183}{360} = 68,625$$

$$1,000,000 \times \dfrac{13.5}{100} \times \dfrac{182}{360} = 68,250$$

Next calculate the amount available to the purchaser at maturity. US$1,000,000 (principal sum) + US$68,625 (the last interest coupon) US$1,068,625 is payable at maturity.

Finally, working backwards from the last (8th) interest period calculate the discount maturity proceeds by applying the following formula:

DP_1 = discounted proceeds taken from subsequent interest period plus interest due on period being calculated
Y = secondary market purchase yield
T = number of days
DP_2 = discounted proceeds for the interest period being calculated.

$$DP_2 = \cfrac{DP_1}{\left(1 + \cfrac{Y \times T}{100 \times 360}\right)}$$

Note the first DP_1 = the amount available to the purchaser at maturity
and the last DP_2 = net proceeds actually received by the seller

Discount calculation for the 8th interest period:

$$DP_2 = \cfrac{1{,}068{,}625}{\left(1 + \cfrac{(12.75 \times 183)}{(100 \times 360)}\right)} = 1{,}003{,}580.44$$

Add interest for 7th period $\underline{\quad 68{,}250 \quad}$

$$1{,}071{,}830.44$$

Discount calculation for the 7th interest period:

$$DP_2 = \cfrac{1{,}071{,}830.44}{\left(1 + \cfrac{(12.75 \times 182)}{(100 \times 360)}\right)} = 1{,}006{,}925.69$$

Add interest for 6th period $\underline{\quad 68{,}625 \quad}$

$$1{,}075{,}550.69$$

180

Discount calculation for the 6th interest period:

$$DP_2 = \frac{1,075,550.69}{\left(1 + \frac{(12.75 \times 183)}{(100 \times 360)}\right)} = 1,010,084.58$$

$$\begin{array}{lr} \text{Add interest for 5th period} & 68,250 \\ \hline & 1,078,334.58 \end{array}$$

Discount calculation for the 5th interest period where $DP_2 =$ the discounted proceeds actually received by the seller –

$$DP_2 = \frac{1,078,334.58}{\left(1 + \frac{(12.75 \times 92)}{(100 \times 360)}\right)} = US\$1,044,307.56$$

In the bill market the discount rates quoted may *appear* cheaper than interbank money market interest rates for corresponding periods and it is essential to compare the true cost or yield on a like for like basis. The discount rate is always lower than the corresponding yield and taking *sterling bills* as an example, can be calculated as follows:

$$\begin{array}{lll} \text{When: Discount rate} & = & R \\ \text{Principal} & = & P \\ \text{Number of Days} & = & \dfrac{D}{365} \\ \text{True Yield} & = & Y \\ \text{Cost of Discount} & = & C \end{array} \qquad C = P \times \frac{R}{100} \times \frac{D}{365}$$

A three month (91 day) bill for £100,000 nominal discounted at $8\frac{7}{8}\%$ per annum would cost the vendor 9.075% per annum true yield.

Since:

$$100,000 \times \frac{8.875}{100} \times \frac{91}{365} = £2,212.67 \qquad £97,787.33 = \text{Proceeds}$$

$$Y = \frac{R \times P}{\text{Proceeds}} \qquad \text{True Yield} = \frac{8.875 \times 100,000}{97,787.33} = 9.075\% \text{ p.a.}$$

In other words the discount to yield differential for this three month bill works out to be 20 basis points, (0.20% p.a.). At that time the cost of three month interbank sterling was $9\frac{3}{8}$% ie 30 basis points over the true yield of the discounted bill. However, in order to compare the total costs to the customer it is necessary to make a further comparison of the respective rates taking into account the relative mark-up charged by a bank for a loan and the rate of acceptance commission.

Using the rates quoted above the total cost of a LIBOR linked loan would be:

3 month LIBOR	9.375% p.a.
Assume and add MLA costs	0.15% p.a.
Assume and add mark-up (spread)	1.00% p.a.
Total Cost	10.525%

It has already been shown that at a discount rate of $8\frac{7}{8}$% p.a. a £100,000 91 day bill would produce net proceeds of £97,787.33. However, from this sum acceptance commission must also be deducted, assuming a 1% p.a. rate this amounts to £249.32 ie

$$£100,000 \times \frac{1}{100} \times \frac{91}{365} = £249.32$$

thereby reducing net proceeds received to £97,538.01.

Using the formula $\dfrac{Y = R \times P}{\text{Proceeds}}$ the true cost can be calculated:

$$\frac{8.875 + 1.00 \times 100,000}{97,538.01} = \underline{\underline{10.124\%}}$$

In this example the comparative advantage of using the acceptance credit route is therefore 40 basis points (0.40% p.a.). It should, however, be noted that there is no *consistent* relationship between the bill market rate and the interbank rates. Over the years 1976–1983 the differential between the three month eligible bill rate and three month sterling LIBOR on a fully adjusted basis for comparison, ranged between a $\frac{5}{8}$% higher LIBOR to a $\frac{3}{4}$% higher bill rate.

The comparison is one which is of importance to the customer who is often given an option to draw on a loan basis under an "either or" facility. These options are often found in large acceptance facilities which are provided by a syndication of banks.

The spread between eligible and ineligible bank bills will vary but is usually to the order of 5 to 20 basis points. The dealing spread between bid and offered rates is normally $\frac{1}{8}\%$.

US dollar banker's acceptances transactions are calculated on the basis of a 360 day year as per the following example:

Establish the dollar price of a US$100,000 banker's acceptance maturing in 114 days discounted at a straight discount rate of 9%:

Where: P = the dollar price
        R = the straight discount rate
        T = the time (in days) to maturity
        D = the discount amount per $100 face value

Apply the following formulae:

$$D = \frac{T}{360} \times R \text{ and } P = \$100 - D$$

$$\text{So } D = \frac{114}{360} \times 9 = 2.85\% \qquad P = 100 - 2.85 = \$97.15$$

The dollar price is expressed per US$100 and is, therefore, US$97.15 in the above example. To obtain the amount of dollar proceeds received from the discount, multiply the price by the face value of the bill and divide by 100:

$$\text{US\$} \frac{97.15 \times 100,000}{100} = \text{US\$97,150} = \text{proceeds received}$$

It may be necessary for investors to compare the yield on a banker's acceptance with an interest bearing security. In order to convert the discount to an equivalent yield basis the following formula may be applied:

Where: Y = the equivalent yield on the interest bearing security

$$Y = \frac{D}{P} \times \frac{365}{T} \times 100$$

$$\text{So, } Y = \frac{2.85}{97.15} \times \frac{365}{114} \times 100 = 9.3927\%$$

The same result may be obtained by applying the formula:

$$Y = \frac{R \times 365}{P \times 360} \times 100$$

$$\text{So, } Y = \frac{9 \times 365}{97.15 \times 360} \times 100 = 9.3927\%$$

The US Treasury Bill discount calculation is based on a 360 day year. The price of a T Bill expressed as a percentage, may be determined by the following formula:

$$US\$100 - \frac{\text{Number of days to maturity}}{360} \times \text{the discount rate } (\%)$$

A 91 day T Bill discounted at 7.73% would be priced

$$US\$100 - \frac{91}{360} \times 7.73 = 98.046$$

Competitive bids are made on a *price basis* e.g. 98.046 with up to 3 places of decimals.

From the investor's viewpoint it may be necessary to compare the yield on a T Bill with other types of investment such as a bond, the latter being calculated on a 365 day year. The following formula may be applied where no interim coupon income is due from the bond during the maturity period of the comparison:

$$\frac{365 \times 100 \times \text{Discount Rate}}{(360 \times 100) - (\text{Discount rate} \times \text{number of days})} = \text{Yield}$$

184

Applying figures from the example above:

$$\frac{36500 \times 7.73}{36000 - (7.73 \times 91)} = 7.9936\% \text{ compared with the straight discount rate of } 7.73\%$$

Various US Treasury certificates, bonds and notes are issued from time to time by auction. These are often coupon bearing instruments and tenders are made for such paper on a yield basis, rather than the price basis adopted for T Bill auctions. The interest receivable on coupon issues tends to complicate the calculation of a true comparison of yields with T Bills having an outstanding maturity of more than six months.

The annual investment return on T Bills can be calculated with the following formula where:

$Y = $ Yield
$D = $ Days, being the duration of the investment
$A = $ Purchase price
$B = $ Sale price

$$Y = 100 \times \frac{B - A}{B} \times \frac{365}{D}$$

Assume that the 91 days T Bill illustrated above was purchased at a discount rate of 7.73% and sold after 24 days @ 6.5% discount. The purchase price would have been 98.046 (as shown above) and the sale price would need to be calculated as follows:

$$\text{US\$100} - \frac{(91 - 24)}{360} \times 6.5 = 98.790$$

Applying the yield formula above:

$$Y = 100 \times \frac{98.79 - 98.046}{98.79} \times \frac{365}{24}$$

So the annual investment return was 11.454% p.a.

If an investment manager wishes to obtain a specific yield and ascertain what discount rate or investment period might be applied to achieve this objective, then the above formula may also be used.

185

Chapters 10 and 11 of this section deal respectively with Certificates of Deposit and Bank Bills. These are money market instruments which are originated by banks either directly or indirectly for funding purposes and also provide liquidity to the monetary system through both the primary and secondary markets. Chapter 12 considers Commercial Paper, Repurchase Agreement and Broker and Dealer Loans, instruments which are usually subject to specific negotiation involving both the borrower and lender either directly or indirectly. Finally Chapter 13 examines those negotiable short-term money market instruments which are issued outside of the banking system, normally by government, quasi government, state and municipal bodies.

CHAPTER TEN

Certificates of Deposit

Introduction

Certificates of deposit often referred to as "CDs" are negotiable interest bearing certificates evidencing a time deposit with a bank. Since 1961 US commercial banks have issued negotiable bearer CDs and five years later negotiable bearer dollar CDs were launched in London thereby heralding the international CD market. Before 1961 the US banks issued registered non-negotiable certificates of deposit for which there was limited appeal. CDs are issued by banks in the following 12 countries in the currency of these countries:

UK in Sterling	Kuwait in Kuwaiti Dinars
USA in US Dollars	Bahrain in Bahraini Dinars
Canada in Canadian Dollars	Hong Kong in Hong Kong Dollars
Japan in Yen	Singapore in Singapore Dollars
South Africa in Rand	Malaysia in Ringgits
Australia in Australian Dollars	France in French Francs

International markets have developed from US Dollar denominated CDs in the following places:

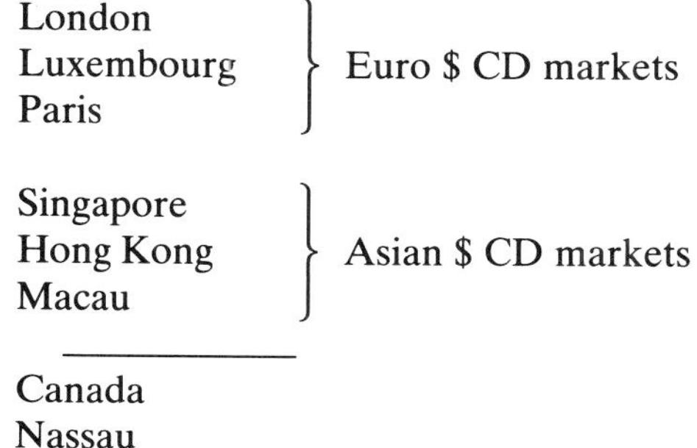

Finally, some London banks also issue CDs in SDRs, and in ECUs, Euro-Yen, Euro-Australian dollars, and Euro-Canadian dollars.

The London CD Market

Provision was made for the issue of sterling denominated CDs in the United Kingdom domestic market in the 1968 Finance Act. Sterling CDs may be issued in amounts from the minimum of £50,000 in increasing multiples of £10,000 to £1,000,000. Should the holder of a CD wish to sell part of a single CD it may be split into multiples of £10,000 provided that there remains a minimum of £50,000. There existed already established primary and secondary markets in US Dollar CDs in London so when the sterling market opened in October 1968 there were some 50 bank issuers in the primary market. As already mentioned in Chapter 9 the primary market exists between the issuing bank and the original depositor. The secondary market comprises members of the London Discount Market Association (LDMA) and members of the International CD Market Association (ICDMA). Sterling CDs are issued at par on an interest to maturity basis for periods which may range from 28 days to five years, but sterling CDs may now be issued for as little as seven days to compete with the sterling commercial paper market and various government securities. Interest is paid at maturity on issues of one year or less, and is paid annually on fixed rate issues of over one year to the maximum maturity of five years. There is no withholding tax payable on the interest which is, therefore, paid gross.

Sterling CDs normally yield about $\frac{1}{8}\%$ under the bid side of the interbank deposit market. The market spread varies from $\frac{1}{16}\% - \frac{1}{8}\%$ and normal settlement would take place on the same day if the deal was transacted before 12 noon, otherwise it will be settled on the following working day.

A specimen sterling certificate of deposit is shown opposite:

EURODOLLAR CDs were first introduced in London in 1966, and the market grew rapidly to become the world's largest CD market in 1983, even outstripping the US domestic CD market in terms of volumes outstanding. US dollar CDs are issued in London in amounts being multiples of US$1,000 with a minimum of US$25,000. The professional market, however, quotes the finest rates for wholesale amounts of, say, US$1,000,000 or more. The maximum maturity is five years with interest payable annually on CDs with an initial maturity in excess of one year and at maturity for maturities up to one year. Interest is calculated on the basis of actual days over a

Negotiable Certificate of Deposit
Standard Chartered
Standard Chartered Bank
37 Gracechurch Street London EC3V 0BX
Certificate No.
C000000
£500 000
Maturity Date
19
Fixed
SPECIMEN
Standard Chartered Bank
certifies that the sum of FIVE HUNDRED THOUSAND Pounds Sterling has been deposited upon terms
that it is payable to bearer on surrender of this certificate, through a Recognised Bank, at 37 Gracechurch Street,
London EC3V 0BX, on the fixed, with interest at
the rate of per cent.
per annum calculated on a 365 day year basis from the date hereof to the date of maturity only, payable at maturity if one
year or less from the date hereof, and otherwise annually on the anniversary of the date hereof and at maturity.
For and on behalf of Standard Chartered Bank
Authorised Signature
Authorised Signature
BRADBURY, WILKINSON & Co Lᵈ NEW MALDEN, SURREY, ENGLAND.

360 day year. London US dollar CDs are usually issued at par on an interest bearing basis and occasionally they are issued at a discount.

A specimen US dollar certificate of deposit is shown opposite:

The first discount eurodollar CDs were issued in May 1981 followed by an issue the next month of discount Floating Rate Certificates of Deposit (FRCDs). The discount CDs issues are initially bought at a price below par and redeemed at maturity at par, and therefore do not bear interest. The mechanics of interest calculation on discount CDs is very similar to that applied to treasury bills and to bankers acceptances for which worked examples have been provided in Chapter 9. It remains to be seen whether this type of instrument proves to be as popular or even more popular than the normal interest bearing CDs in years to come.

The secondary markets for London dollar CDs exist in both London and New York. The markets are over-the-counter markets and are not quoted/listed on any stock exchange, for although they are negotiable securities they are also important money market instruments. The average daily turnover of eurodollar CDs during 1983 reported by dealers to the Federal Reserve Bank was well in excess of US$1,000 million equivalent. The secondary market is very active and CDs are usually deliverable in London on the second working day following the deal with payment normally being made in New York in immediately available funds for value the second working day after the deal. Delivery and settlement may take place on a same day value basis if specifically required by the depositor. If the holder of a eurodollar CD wishes to sell part of a single CD, then it may be split into multiples of US$1,000 provided there is a minimum of US$25,000.

Two American banks in London operate a clearing system for US dollar CDs, and Euro-clear and Cedel which are discussed in Chapter 25 will accept longer term CDs.

Other London CDs are issued in SDR and ECU denominations. The SDR CDs were first introduced in June 1980. These CDs were issued in multiples of US$250,000 and for tenors of three to six

Negotiable Certificate of Deposit
Standard Chartered
Standard Chartered Bank
37 Gracechurch Street London EC3V 0BX
Certificate No.
London 19
D 000000
THIS CERTIFIES that there has been deposited with this Bank the sum of ONE MILLION U.S. Dollars
(U.S. $1,000,000) repayable or greater on together with interest thereon
at the rate of per cent. per annum (calculated on actual days on a
360-day-year basis) from the date hereof to maturity only upon surrender of this Certificate through the
medium of a bank to this office. Repayment will be made at this office by draft or telegraphic transfer on
New York.
All rights and obligations hereunder shall be determined by English Law.
For and on behalf of Standard Chartered Bank
Authorised Signature
Authorised Signature
BRADBURY, WILKINSON & CO LD NEW MALDEN, SURREY, ENGLAND.

months; the earlier issues were based upon the market rates of the then existing basket of 16 currencies which made up the IMF Special Drawing Right. Since January 1981 the composition of the SDR was changed to the following five currencies – US dollars (42%), Deutschemarks (19%), Yen, French Francs and Sterling (each 13%) and the SDR CDs issued from 1981 onwards have been based on this smaller basket. The SDR CD is issued, negotiated, traded, settled and repaid in a manner similar to the London US dollar CD. The first London FRCD in SDRs was issued in January 1981.

London ECU issues were first introduced in 1983 and were based on the market rates of the nine currencies which then constituted the ECU. Since Greece joined the EMS in 1984 the Greek drachma has been included in the ECU making it a basket of 10 currencies. The first instrument denominated in ECUs was a eurobond issue launched in 1981. Since then the ECU has become a currency in its own right as, by 1985, it was used for invoicing, travellers cheques, CDs, FRNs, RUFs (Revolving Underwriting Facilities), Foreign Exchange (spot and forward), Bank accounts, Loans, Deposits, Treasury certificates, Leasing contracts, Participating debentures with warrants, as well as straight eurobonds.

A specimen SDR certificate of deposit is shown opposite

Towards the end of 1984 euro-yen CDs were introduced into the London market. Euro-yen CDs are issued in denominations of Yen 250 million, Yen 100 million, Yen 50 million and Yen 25 million. Banks wishing to issue such instruments are required to conform to the BBA (British Bankers' Association) CD Guidelines and obtain prior approval from the Japanese Ministry of Finance (MOF). The maturity may not exceed six months and sales of such CDs may not be made to Japanese residents.

Tap, tranche and "roly-poly" CDs describe the ways in which CDs are issued. A "tap CD" sometimes referred to as a "straight CD" is issued by the borrowing bank itself when it wishes to tap the market without the intermediation of a securities house. By issuing tap CDs the bank can meet depositor demand on an individual requirement basis, without the need of such investors seeking the bank's paper on

Negotiable Certificate of Deposit
Standard Chartered
Standard Chartered Bank
37 Gracechurch Street London EC3V 0BX
Certificate No.
Maturity Date
Fixed
A000000
London
19
THIS CERTIFIES that there has been deposited with this bank the sum of TWO HUNDRED AND FIFTY THOUSAND SDRs (SDR 250,000) (as defined overleaf) on terms that it is payable to bearer on surrender of this Certificate, through the medium of a Recognised Bank, to this office on the maturity date of this Certificate, together with
Interest at the rate of ....per cent. per annum, calculated on actual days on a 360 day year basis from the date hereof to the maturity date hereof only, payable at maturity.
Payment of the deposit and interest will only be made in U.S. Dollars by draft or telegraphic transfer on a bank in New York designated by us in the amount calculated as stated on the reverse hereof.
All rights and obligations in relation to this Certificate shall be governed by English Law.
For and on behalf of Standard Chartered Bank
Authorised Signature
Authorised Signature
BRADBURY, WILKINSON & Cº Lº NEW MALDEN, SURREY, ENGLAND.

the secondary market. Single taps frequently exceed US$250,000 and are placed with institutional investors. Tranche CDs are block issues of fixed interest CDs or of FRCDs which are privately placed by a securities house or houses in syndicate with investors rather than a direct offering by the issuing bank to the public in the market. The issuing bank normally has a programme for its nominated securities house(s) to place up to a stated limit (from US$10 million to over US$500 million) for tranche issues. A roly-poly CD is very similar in structure to a managed FRCD tranche issue. The main difference is that FRCDs normally have maturities in excess of one year and usually three to five years, roly-polys have a maturity matching the coupon period (usually three months) but there exists a commitment by the manager or underwriter of the original CD to buy all subsequent CDs at each maturity. Fixed rate roly-polys may be issued with a coupon for every issue, alternatively, floating rate roly-polys assume a new interest rate, if applicable, for each issue. Such commitments are usually for three to five year periods. The original purchaser of the roly-poly CD may sell it before maturity in the secondary market if he chooses – after all it is a negotiable CD, but should he choose to do so he will still be liable to take up all semi-annual or quarterly subsequent issues under the commitment until the facility expires perhaps in, say, four years' time. FRCD coupons are based on a one, three or six month rollover period and similar maturities/rate fixings apply to roly-polys. There are some 50 security and investment houses which offer management and underwriting services to high quality issuing banks for FRCDs, roly-poly CDs, tranche fixed interest CDs and discount CDs. Managed CD issues will incur structured fees of about $\frac{1}{4}\%$ – $\frac{1}{2}\%$ of the issue amount payable front-end and, perhaps, issue fees of $\frac{1}{2}\%$ annually.

An indication of the size and structure of the London CD market can be obtained monthly by reference to the Bank of England Quarterly Bulletin. The figures outstanding on the monthly reporting day of CDs issued in pounds million are given under two headings "sterling liabilities" and "other currency liabilities". The totals of balance sheets of banks in the UK is followed by statistics of retail banks, accepting houses, other British banks, American banks, Japanese banks, other overseas banks, consortium banks and, under another heading, the balance sheet statistics of the discount market.

What volume of CDs is held in the reporting institution's portfolios is recorded in the sterling and other currency assets. On 14th December 1983, the reporting day, £80,249 million were issued by the reporting banks and outstanding, of which £15,595 million were held by other reporting banks, and a further £2,044 million held by the discount houses, the balance of £62,610 million being held by other institutions and individuals. The monthly variations in these volumes can be significant (up to 10%) and depending on market conditions and anticipation of rate changes the maturing paper might not necessarily be replaced straight-away, or the depositor's appetite for CDs may have altered over the period. On the above reporting day £9,792 million of the £80,249 million issued CDs were denominated in sterling and £70,457 million in other currencies of which well over £70 billion were US dollar CDs. The statistics reveal the volumes issued by each sector of banks in the UK listed above. The American banks US dollar CDs account for the largest individual segment of this market and on 14th December 1983 their reported outstanding US dollar CDs issued was £32,436 million.

On 30th June 1983 the Bank of England issued a notice on certificates of deposit to all recognised banks, licensed deposit taking institutions and other interested parties, in which it describes its attitude to the issue of CDs as follows:

- London CDs may only be issued by institutions authorised to accept deposits under the Banking Act 1979 or specifically exempted under Schedule 1 of that Act, and must be issued and payable in the UK.

- Before any financial institution makes its first issue of CDs in London it is asked to inform the Bank of England.

- Before any CDs are denominated in a new currency for the London market, the Bank of England would wish to be satisfied that the authorities in the country of the currency concerned are in agreement with such a development and that a genuine market for such CDs was likely to develop.

- CDs are short-term market instruments and, therefore, their life should be limited to a maximum of five years. A few extra days of grace may be granted in this connection if the maturity date does not fall on a business day.

- For sterling CDs the minimum denomination should not be less than 50,000, the minimum term to maturity not less than 28 days and the calculation of interest on an actual day basis.

- Whilst CDs may carry interest at a fixed or variable rate, the instrument when issued must clearly indicate when payment of interest or repayment of principal will be effected should the maturity date fall on a non-business day. This is not, however, necessary where there is a clearly established market practice.

- CDs may incorporate an early redemption option provided such option lies with the holder. If it is intended to issue CDs with an option for the issuer to repay early on a specific date, the following points must be observed:
  i) the terms of the option should be clear to the original purchaser and subsequent holder, and the method of advising the holder, should the issuer intend to exercise such an option, must be very clearly established

  ii) issues of such instruments by foreign institutions should not run counter to the wishes of their own parent country's supervisory authority. Foreign institutions are expected to inform the Bank of England of their intention to issue such instruments before they do so in order that the Bank can consult the relevant authorities abroad.

- Zero coupon CDs may be issued at a discount so long as the instrument itself clearly indicates to all interested parties that it is a zero coupon CD, and in cases where the CD has been issued with an original maturity of more than a year there exists some means of periodic verification and authentication of such instruments which is incorporated in the terms of the issue. (The authors note the reason for this precaution stems from the forgery in 1983 of zero rated bearer bonds issued by J.C. Penney Global Finance N.V.)

- Although it is not normal market practice for an issuer to purchase its own CDs in the secondary market prior to maturity, the

Bank of England accepts that such activities can assist in certain circumstances in the maintenance of an orderly market. However, they would expect issuing institutions intending to do this to advise the Bank of England.

- The Bank of England would not normally expect institutions to take as collateral CDs issued by themselves or by companies within their own group. However, on occasions they might be included in a parcel of CDs lodged as security by a discount house and the authors are given to understand that the Bank may be prepared to make an exception in such a case. The Bank of England does not deal in CDs nor are they eligible at the Bank as security or margin for advances to the discount market.

- Outstanding CDs, both issued and held, must be reported by monetary sector institutions to the Financial Statistics Division at the Bank of England on the appropriate forms. If a reporting institution holds CDs which it has itself issued, these must be excluded from both sides of its balance sheet.

The subject of a bank's liquidity position in connection with CDs is worthy of mention. On the liabilities side, the issuing bank in seeking support funding for its lending commitments can rely on successfully accessing the CD market only so long as the market remains in existence and there remains an investor demand for the issuing bank's paper. If, for instance, other rated debt issued by the bank is significantly down-graded by the rating agencies, investor demand could evaporate or be reduced. Even for managed issues the underwriters can, in certain extreme circumstances, withdraw their commitment, so when the issuing bank might really need this form of short-term funding it might not be available. In the authors' view such facilities cannot, therefore, be considered *guaranteed* standby arrangements. On the assets side of a bank's balance sheet, investments or trading portfolios of other bank's CDs may be held or traded. There is a school of thought to which the authors do not subscribe, that such holdings could *always* be melted (discounted in the secondary market) in the event of short-term liquidity being required. In all normal circumstances CDs issued by top quality banks will be liquefiable in the secondary market, but it is considered very questionable whether, should a doomsday euromarket holocaust situation arise, *any* leading bank's obligations would find favour with investors. Holdings of short-term government securities provide more certain liquid assets for banks' standby purposes. It is also important that banks consider CD issues when reviewing their overall exposure to the interbank markets for funding purposes. Holdings of other banks' CDs will utilise available limits and through the secondary market process issuing banks must consider CDs as potential exposure within the interbank markets unless CDs issued are in their possession.

Illustration of the time-table for a managed FRCD issue

For the week preceding launch: The issuer and lead bank prepare the following documents:

> The invitation and allotment telexes; the issue agreement; the interest determination agreement and draft certificate of deposit. The security printer should be asked to proceed with the manufacture of any new engraved plate which may be required as soon as possible and they should also be brought into discussions on the forms of protection needed for the certificates as early as possible.

> Appointment of the reference banks and board resolutions of the issuing bank for authority to issue, if required.

Launch date: The lead bank despatches invitation telexes.

First week after launch date: Final indications of interest are received by the lead bank.

Approximately nine days after launch: The issue and interest determination agreements are signed, and allotment telexes despatched by lead manager to the investors.

Two days before close and receipt of funds: The interest rates are quoted by the reference banks for the first interest determination period. Acceptances of allotment are received from investors and the security printer delivers the definitive certificates to the lead bank.

Two days later: The FRCD issue is closed by the issuer receiving same day settlement funds (if a US dollar issue) from the lead bank's subscription account in New York to the credit of the issuer's account in New York nominated for this purpose. The bearer CDs are simultaneously made available to the order of the lead bank who will arrange for them to be delivered as appropriate to investors in accordance with the allotments made and accepted.

Later: An advertisement of the issue will appear in newspapers and magazines as may be agreed between lead managers and issuing bank. This is often referred to as a "tombstone".

A final word on the London CD market – CDs which are issued in amounts of less than £50,000 (or equivalent) or have an original tenor of less than 28 days are subject to withholding tax, otherwise all CDs are free from withholding taxes.

The US CD Market

Until 1961 only non-negotiable certificates were issued, but thereafter the leading New York commercial banks, and then banks all over the USA, developed the negotiable US dollar CD into the important money market instrument it is today. The minimum denomination is US$100,000, with a minimum maturity of 14 days, although there is no statutory restriction on the upper end of the maturity range which has been as long as 10 years. By far the majority of domestic US dollar CDs are issued with a final maturity of less than one year – the most popular period being for three months. Unlike the medium-term London US dollar CDs, the domestic US dollar CD has interest payment periodicity of six months if the initial final maturity is in excess of one year. The issuing bank will not redeem its CD prior to maturity nor will US banks normally take their own CDs as acceptable loan collateral since in the event of default, early redemption of the paper without applicable penalty would automatically ensue. The secondary market comprises the leading securities houses and some of these dealer firms specialise in trading CDs with less than 14 days to run. There is no equivalent in New York to the London call money markets and the dealer firms trading short-date CDs, usually in round lots of $1 million or more, provide investors with short-term liquidity. These firms are also very active in the re-purchase agreement market explained later in Chapter 12.

In addition to the fixed interest CDs, the leading banks in the USA also issue variable rate CDs. Unlike the FRCDs which are priced on a LIBOR plus interest basis, variable rate CDs are priced on an agreed premium over the composite rate compiled and published by the Federal Reserve Bank for secondary market leading bank CDs. This rate is usually re-fixed every 30 or 90 days.

Normal US domestic CD settlement terms are for delivery and value the next working day with payment being made in cleared funds. In the US market roly-poly CDs are normally issued for six month periods with commitments of two years or longer.

There exists in the USA substantial primary and secondary markets for eurodollar CDs. This is due to the high demand from US investors in the public sector as well as individuals, corporates and financial institutions in the private sector.

The US domestic market differentiates between CDs issued by indigenous banks and those issued by US branches and agencies of banks outside the USA. These latter instruments are sometimes referred to as "Yankee CDs" and in most respects, so far as the technical aspects are concerned, they are virtually the same, but the market *will* differentiate between the level of return in favour of the domestic CD, the yield differential being anything from 10 to 80 basis points for a three month maturity. Yankee CDs which have a maturity in excess of one year may only be issued in registered form in order to comply with US tax legislation introduced at the end of 1982. Otherwise, Yankee CDs may be issued in bearer or registered form, either on a par plus interest basis or on a discount basis. Issuers of Yankee CDs are required to file a notice with the New York Banking Authorities before issuing CDs and are not permitted to issue them direct to individuals but arrange for them to be placed direct with institutions or issued through one or more investment houses.

Other CD Markets
Canada

The Canadian chartered banks issue bearer deposit notes (BDNs) which are Canadian dollar denominated CDs issued for maturities of seven days to one year but normally on a 30,60 or 90 day basis, in amounts in excess of Can.$100,000 up to Can.$25 million per BDN, although the usual denomination is Can.$250,000. The secondary market is active for BDNs as well as for guaranteed investment certificates which are similar to CDs but issued by the Canadian trust companies. US dollar and sterling CDs are also traded on the Canadian secondary CD market. BDNs are normally issued at a discount, although some have been issued in interest bearing form. BDNs are subject to Canadian withholding tax at 25%, reduced to 15% for investors resident in certain tax treaty countries and is free from withholding tax as far as foreign charities and certain government bodies are concerned.

Interest is calculated on a true yield basis of a 360 day year, and normal settlement is same day up to 12 noon and thereafter to be settled on the next business day unless there is an agreement from both parties for deferred settlement arrangements.

A specimen Canadian bearer deposit note is shown overleaf:

The Asian Markets

In Japan tap Yen CDs are issued for three to six month periods in amounts in excess of Yen 25 million. Japanese CDs are issued in registered form not bearer and are, therefore, not bearer documents. It is normal procedure for the issuing bank to act as custodian, although it is possible to arrange for CDs to be delivered to another bank. As these CDs are deposits rather than securities, any secondary market transactions require the issuer's agreement which is given as a matter of routine. The secondary market, however, is greatly restricted as a result. Interest is calculated on a true yield basis of a 365 day year and is payable at maturity. Yen CD yields are normally slightly over those of the Gensaki (i.e. short-term broker loan market) yields. Withholding tax is levied on all interest payments at a basic rate of 20%. For foreign central banks and other

Canadian Bearer Deposit Note

National Westminster Bank of Canada
Banque National Westminster du Canada

No. CD 00394

Certificate of Deposit
Certificat de Dépôt

SPECIMEN

Principal/Capital ....

Date/Date ....

In consideration of a deposit received, National Westminster Bank of Canada promises
En considération d'un dépôt reçu, Banque National Westminster du Canada promet

to pay at the principal office of the Bank in the City of
de payer au principal bureau de la Banque dans la ville de ....

the principal amount of
le montant en capital de ....

in lawful money of   on
en monnaie légale de ....   le ....

against presentation and surrender of this certificate plus
contre présentation et remise de ce certificat plus ....

interest payment(s)   at a rate of   percent
paiement(s) d'intérêt le ....   au taux de .... pourcent

per annum, to or to the order of
l'an, à ou à l'ordre de ....

....

National Westminster Bank of Canada
Banque National Westminster du Canada

by/par ....   by/par ....
NOT NEGOTIABLE   NOT NEGOTIABLE
Authorised Officer/Dirigeant autorisé   Authorised Officer/Dirigeant autorisé

This certificate is not redeemable prior to maturity but is transferable prior to maturity at the principal office of the
Bank by execution of the form of transfer on the reverse hereof.
Ce certificat n'est pas remboursable avant échéance; il est toutefois cessible avant échéance au principal bureau
de la Banque en signant la formule de transfert à l'endos de la présente.

foreign government entities, there is no withholding tax. The market is regulated by the Japanese Ministry of Finance and there are limitations on the amount of Yen CDs that foreign and domestic banks may issue. The market was first established in 1979, the same year the Malaysian ringgit market started. Ringgit CDs may be issued in amounts between M$100,000 and M$1 million for periods of between six months and three years, the interest being calculated on a 365 day year. The Hong Kong dollar CD market began in 1977. The secondary market is very thin for the tap issues made, in both fixed and floating rate CDs. The latter are now bearing coupons which are calculated on the average 30 day HIBOR (Hong Kong Interbank Offered Rate) determined monthly but paid quarterly in arrears. Banks in Hong Kong also issue US dollar CDs for which there exists a more active secondary market owing to the absence of withholding tax on them.

In 1970 the Singapore CD market started and has maintained its role as the principal centre in the Asian US dollar CD market as well as issuing CDs in Singapore dollars. CDs are issued in the domestic Singapore market in a minimum of S$100,000 and multiples of S$50,000 upwards to a maximum of S$1 million and may be either on a fixed or floating rate basis, the majority of which are FRCDs based on $\frac{1}{4}$% over SIBOR (Singapore Interbank Offered Rate) and rollover every three months. The US dollar CDs issued in Singapore are usually referred to as the Asian dollar CD market. The issues are in minimum amounts of US$50,000, and multiples of US$50,000 upwards. Next to London Singapore is the most important offshore CD market.

Other CD Markets
Italian savings banks today issue 18, 24 and 36 month CDs in Lire, and whilst these are transferable they are in registered form and the secondary market for such instruments is decidedly thin.

It is very important for banks to be aware of the probable extent of investor demand for each asset offered in a variety of likely economic and political situations. For example, a bank decides to issue a certificate of deposit in a financial centre in local currency where previously no established CD operations existed. An assessment would take place to identify to whom such CDs would have an appeal and whether any regulatory prohibitions existed or cost coefficient constraints (such as reserve assets or MLAs) would apply. During 1982/83 some half a dozen branches of foreign banks in Spain decided on such a course of action. Later, new regulations and mandatory coefficients were announced by the Central Bank (Bank of Spain) which tended to contract the available funding alternatives and make customers deposits for six and 12 month periods more expensive to attract on rates of interest competitive with official higher yielding alternative investments in the form of discounted pagares del tesoro (treasury bills). Whether the authorities of the host country are satisfied or not with new developments in money market or funding schemes naturally depends upon their traditional methods of considering such innovations as well as whether they are considered appropriate in the current economic climate. The Spanish CD market in pagares bancarios in the latter part of 1983 and 1984 was not prohibited by the authorities, although by controlling the yield on the financial paper offered through the Madrid Stock Exchange, the return to the investor on the new bank CDs was made uncompetitive.

Risk of Fraud

The bearer nature of the majority of certificates of deposits renders them particularly prone to risks of forgery and fraud. Indeed, during the early 1980s there were a number of cases where bank CDs had been forged with a considerable degree of expertise. Until the abolition of UK exchange control in 1979, US dollar CDs were classified as foreign currency securities and as such were required to be retained by an authorised depository, so far as UK residents were concerned. Since then that practice is no longer mandatory, although banks generally offer custodian services when tap CDs are requested. The further development of issues of tranche CDs, which grew up during the 1970s, increased the number of certificates in circulation. All CDs are security printed and these bearer certificates generally are retained by depositories such as CEDEL and Euroclear and various banks in safe custody but, nevertheless, a small proportion of such instruments will inevitably find its way into the hands of private individuals. It would not be advisable for a book of this nature to contain any details of the precautions that need to be taken.

CHAPTER ELEVEN

Bank Bills

Introduction

Bank bills comprise those bills which are either accepted or endorsed by a bank. The banker's acceptance is evidenced by a bank adding its undertaking of payment of a bill of exchange by signing the bill on the face of it and clearly indicating the place at, and date on, which it will be paid. Bills of exchange may be drawn on a bank for the purpose of the bank adding its acceptance thereto for a wide variety of financial reasons. The banker's acceptance markets, however, tend to be solely or principally concerned with transactions which are trade-related rather than with those business transactions which are not.

The bill of exchange must be a term bill or, as Americans describe it, a time draft, payable at a fixed or future determinable date later than the date of drawing. The purpose of drawing such a bill on a bank is to obtain finance by creating an instrument (the accepted bill) which is usually readily marketable and which may be simply converted into cash by selling it on a discounted basis. The quality of the bank's name on the bill will determine the degree of its marketability and often the relative discount rate applied. In some cases the discount price and marketability of the instrument also depends on the nature of the transaction being financed with the banker's acceptance.

There are two basic underlying facilities which generate bankers' acceptances; documentary credits and clean acceptance credits. Any form of payment, or of finance, provided under a documentary credit is conditional upon the terms of the credit being met by the beneficiary, unless the applicant is prepared to take up the documents tendered despite the discrepancies noted. A sight documentary credit enables the exporter to obtain payment from, say, the UK advising bank shortly after presentation of documents to that bank locally. This is subject, of course, to the caveat of compliance with the credit terms. This payment (under a sight credit) may be –

i)   with recourse – if the credit is negotiable in London and payable abroad,

or

ii)   an outright payment if the credit is payable in London.

In either event the exporter is receiving funds sooner than he would on a collection or on an open account basis. A documentary acceptance credit gives rise to one type of banker's acceptance. Whenever a commercial contract has been arranged, the contracting parties will agree on a mutually acceptable method of settlement of indebtedness whether the nature of the underlying contract involves the movement of goods, the provision of services or discharge of any other form of debt or obligation. Whilst the documentary credit as a settlement and financial vehicle is normally established for international trade related contracts, this is by no means always the case.

Clean acceptance facilities may be used inter alia to provide finance for either an importer of goods or an exporter where the chosen settlement arrangement is either on a "collection" basis or on an "open account" basis. In addition to the London Accepting Houses Committee which comprises 16 of the leading merchant banks, other major banks in London also provide this type of finance. An agreed amount with a revolving limit is established often with the underlying trade bills acting as collateral security if they are being collected by the financing bank. The customer lodges with the bank a tenor bill of exchange drawn on the bank which is accepted and usually discounted by the latter although it may be discounted elsewhere. At maturity a new bill is often drawn on the bank, the discount proceeds of which will cover most of the amount due on the maturing bill. In other words, the customer only needs to pay the discount charges on each new drawing as the facility rolls on, plus acceptance commissions.

Apart from the varying costs incurred in the underlying methods of settlement, both facilities are subject to acceptance commission and the discount charges. Acceptance commissions usually vary between $\frac{1}{16}\%$ per annum to $1\frac{3}{4}\%$ per annum ($1\frac{0}{00}$ per month or 1.2% per annum is a quite common charge made for a banker's acceptance under a documentary acceptance credit arrangement) but some banks are prepared to accept even lower commissions.

The accepting bank charges an acceptance commission for providing its irrevocable primary obligation in the acceptance. The accepted bill is, therefore, the liability of the accepting bank rather than the company drawing it, although it nevertheless still represents a contingent obligation of the drawer and all subsequent endorsees, if any.

The London Bankers' Acceptance Market
On the reporting date, 15th February 1984, £16,285 million acceptances were outstanding of which £1,541 million were in currencies other than sterling and the balance of £14,744 million in sterling. The outstanding discounted sterling bills amounted to £5,424 million principally split between the retail banks and discount houses and £9,320 million had been rediscounted with the Bank of England or retained by the drawer undiscounted. From the table below it can also be seen that of acceptances totalling £1,541 million equivalent in other currencies, £1,400 million equivalent was outstanding in the market and £141 million equivalent was either held by the drawer or had been financed on other markets (notably New York).

Source	*Sterling Assets held*		*Bills held in other currencies*	*Total Acceptances*
	Eligible bills	*Non-Eligible bills†*		
Retail banks	2,547	72	58	2,302
Accepting houses	29	8	84	3,357
Other British banks	167	49	26	2,220
US banks	51	9	29	3,035
Japanese banks	—	—	156	1,894
Other overseas banks	58	89	908	3,323
Consortia banks	—	7	97	154
Total reporting banks	2,853	234	1,359	£14,744† and in currency £1,541
Discount market		2,337	41	

Notes: totals may differ due to rounding – Source Bank of England
Quarterly Bulletin, March 1984
†these figures include local authority bills, promissory notes and other ineligible paper including bills of exchange.

The nine discount houses which form the London Discount Market Association (LDMA) obtain most of their funds from banks in the UK on a very short-term basis (nearly 90% of which are call or overnight deposits). They employ between 35% – 50% of their total footings in the higher yielding bank bills with maturities not in excess of 187 days. The majority of these LDMA assets are in eligible form which gives the discount houses immediate liquidity as such paper is rediscountable with the Bank of England. Indeed, it is through this mechanism of the discount houses operations that the Bank of England acts as lender of last resort to the UK banking system. Although the Bank of England does not impose any direct limit for monetary control purposes on the volume of acceptances written by eligible banks, it has its unpublished internal limits on its own portfolio holding of each acceptor's paper. These limits are notional and related to the acceptor's capitalisation and volume of business done in sterling; moreover if these holdings were to approach an individual's limit the Bank of England would discuss the situation with the particular acceptor. The initial discount facility is usually provided by a bank, but may also be provided direct by one of the London discount houses. Costs naturally depend on the nature of the facility – the clean acceptance facility is usually established to finance outstanding bills sent for collection and/or items pending open account remittances – whereas under the documentary acceptance credit each bill drawn represents a particular shipment as a rule. Both can provide export finance as well as import finance, although the costs incurred with documentary credits (which offer a relatively safer method of settlement) are somewhat greater.

The London banker's acceptance market comprises, as the table on the previous page illustrates, bills in sterling and those in foreign currency - the sterling paper being sub-divided into bills which are eligible and those which are not. The discount rate applied depends on whether the paper is eligible for discount by the Bank of England. Eligible paper is discountable at the finest rates and to qualify must meet the following criteria:

- It must be drawn in sterling, although the invoice may be drawn in foreign currency.

- It must be accepted by one of the 138 recognised banks (as at 1st July 1985) whose bills are eligible for discount by the Bank of England.

- It must be a properly executed bill of exchange, payable in the UK and claused in a manner which clearly indicates the underlying purpose for which it was drawn.

- It must have a tenor not in excess of 187 days.

- The underlying transaction must be self-liquidating, may be trade-related, and evidence of the cross frontier (not necessarily involving the UK) movement of goods, may be required. Services already provided, for which an unconditional obligation to pay has been established, and, in certain cases, the finance of stock in a warehouse may also be considered as eligible transactions.

The Bank of England does not lay down a precise definition of the transactions in respect of which it is prepared to purchase bills accepted by eligible banks, but as a guide the types of transactions which would *not* qualify for the fine eligible bill discount rates include:

- Bills drawn for a tenor longer than 187 days.

- Bills whose drawer and acceptor have a shareholder link – these are often described as "pig on pork" bills.

- Bills drawn by one bank on another bank, although there are exceptions in the case of licensed deposit takers drawing bills on eligible banks for specific reasons such as the provision of hire purchase or leasing credit where bills are being drawn against identifiable receivables.

- Bills payable outside the UK, although it is not necessary for bills to be payable in London alone. If they are payable elsewhere within the United Kingdom, they must show the address of the paying bank or branch.

- Bills drawn for the purpose of foreign inland finance or hire purchase (although certain exceptions may sometimes be made where sovereign risk is involved for periods of up to six months only pending the launch of a bulldog issue by the sovereign borrower).

- Bills drawn for services not yet provided, such as insurance, freight and shipping costs, or air tickets.

- Bills drawn in respect of capital goods transactions - only the last six months instalment can be financed as an eligible bill.

- Bills which have not been drawn on and accepted by an eligible bank.

Ineligible bank paper may be discounted for transactions which do not meet the above criteria or which have been drawn on and accepted by ineligible banks. The market differential of such paper depends on the perceived quality of the acceptor in the market. The differential might typically be $\frac{1}{8}\%$ to $\frac{1}{4}\%$ more than bills of corresponding size and tenor which are eligible.

The Bank of England expects eligible banks only to generate for rediscount purposes paper with eligible characteristics as described above. Ineligible banks may, however, have access to the rediscount market for any bills since whatever they offer will only be treated by the discount houses as ineligible because of the acceptor's designation and be priced accordingly. Eligible banks may, if they wish, add their acceptance to bills which cannot fulfil the criteria of eligibility, and then discount such paper for their customers. They may *not*, however, re-discount such paper and will have to hold it in their own portfolios until maturity. The rate quoted by the eligible bank for such ineligible transactions should be based on the ineligible rate in order to reflect the MLA (Mandatory Liquid Asset) cost to the eligible bank for maintaining such assets in its portfolio until maturity.

Bearing in mind that the Bank of England criteria for eligibility require the need for the drawer to describe on the bill itself the underlying nature of the commercial transaction, there may be an understandable reluctance by some drawers to have such information communicated to third parties. If the bill is discounted such divulgence of information occurs per se. Accordingly, it would be prudent for bankers to ensure that their customer's confidentiality is respected particularly when it is of material importance to the drawer and hold such bills as portfolio investments. As a bank's own acceptances do not constitute MLAs mandatory requirements will result in an additional funding cost to the bank as a lender or holder of such discounted paper.

A final point on the required London market practice for eligible paper concerns the need to maintain *two* good names on all bills rediscounted. If the drawer's future viability is uncertain then the accepting bank is expected to withdraw all outstanding bills with that name and do so by buying them back at rates reflecting current market conditions.

Customers will expect the discount quotation to be at market rates for the type of paper, currency and size of bill offered. Banks generally recognise the need for competitive quotations and in practice there are rarely meaningful differences. Shopping around for better rates can be speculative and costly for a customer as quotations may harden if market rates rise during the "shopping period", but, of course, the customers may be lucky if market rates should fall in the meantime. It is true to say that, historically, discount rates have not experienced the same degree of short-term volatility as foreign exchange rates.

London banker's acceptances in foreign currencies are calculated as above but on the basis of a 360 day year and the yields tend to be based on eurocurrency interbank rates for the currency and period concerned.

The US Banker's Acceptance Market
It is not too surprising that there are many similarities between the UK and the US banker's acceptance practice and market. Only banks in the USA may create banker's acceptances traded in the market.

211

The banker's options with acceptance transactions are the same, namely:

i) to complete only the first stage of the transactions, e.g. to accept the bill. It advances no funds but merely guarantees payment at maturity for a commission. The acceptance by itself is not a receivable liability. The holder of the bill can still obtain funds prior to maturity by discounting it with a dealer firm in the secondary market.

ii) to discount the accepted bill and hold it in portfolio as an investment, and

iii) to accept a bill, discount it and then rediscount it. The proceeds of the rediscounted paper are not subject to reserve requirements so long as the bill conforms to the type described in Section 13(7) of the Federal Reserve Act and keeps within the applicable aggregate limits shown in the Federal Reserve Bank chart below:

Synopsis of Major Rules and Regulations Governing Bankers' Acceptances

Category	Member Banks	Nonmember Banks	Edge Act Corporations	State-chartered foreign branches and agencies
Customer limitations:				
Bankers' acceptances eligible for discount	10% of capital unless secured	Governed by state loan limitations*	10% of capital unless secured†	Governed by state loan limitations*
Bankers' acceptances ineligible for discount	For national banks, 10% of capital; state members governed by state loan limitations*	Governed by state loan limitations*	10% of capital	Governed by state loan limitations*

Category	Member Banks	Nonmember Banks	Edge Act Corporations	State-chartered foreign branches and agencies
Reservability of bankers' acceptances sold into the market: Bankers' acceptances described in Section 13(7) of the Federal Reserve Act‡	Not reservable; the total outstanding must not exceed 50% of capital (100% with prior approval of the Board of Governors)§	Not reservable; aggregate limits set by state laws¶	Not reservable; but bankers' acceptances in excess of 200% of capital must be secured	Not reservable; aggregate limits set by state laws¶
Other bankers' acceptances	Reservable; no aggregate limits#	Reservable; aggregate limits set by state laws¶	Reservable; no aggregate limit	Reservable; aggregate limits set by state laws¶
Acceptability of bank name for purchase by Federal Reserve and as collateral for advances	Acceptable in principle**	Acceptable in principle**	Acceptable in principle**	Acceptable in principle**

* The customer limit on the sum of eligible and ineligible acceptances for New York State-chartered banks and branches and agencies of foreign banks is apparently 10 percent of the bank's overall capital. Those chartered in Illinois are subject to 15 percent of capital for ineligible acceptances (except dollar exchange) unless secured, in which case the limit is 50 percent. In California, eligible acceptances (except dollar exchange) are limited to 10 percent of shareholders equity and capital notes unless secured, in which case the limit is 50 percent. The total of secured and unsecured ineligible acceptances is limited to 20 percent of shareholders' equity and capital notes.

† Unless (i) the excess represents the international shipment of *goods* and the Edge corporation is fully covered by primary obligations to reimburse it for that portion which is guaranteed by banks or bankers, or (ii) the Edge corporation is covered by participating agreements from other banks.

213

‡ The revised Regulation D effective 13th November 1980 slightly expanded the category of acceptances which were exempt from reserve requirements (provided the aggregate limit was satisfied); previously acceptances described in Section 13(7) and eligible for discount were exempt.

§ In addition, domestic acceptances are limited to 50 percent of such capital. According to the Published Interpretations of the Board of Governors (paragraph 1700), when a member bank purchases its own acceptance the acceptance is not included in the aggregate limit. However, when the acceptance is sold, it is included in the limit.

¶ New York State and Illinois State-chartered banks and United States branches and agencies of foreign banks have no aggregate acceptance limit. In California eligible acceptances are subject to 50 percent of shareholders' equity, capital and notes and with permission of the Superintendent of Banking to 100 percent. Ineligible acceptances have no aggregate limit.

One exception is that dollar exchange acceptances are limited to a separate and distinct 50 percent of capital and are not included in the limits imposed by Section 13(7) of the Federal Reserve Act.

** Individual banks must satisfy requirements set by the Federal Open Market Committee.

Source: Federal Reserve Bank New York Quarterly Review

Under Section 13(7) of the Federal Reserve Act, a member bank cannot create acceptances in amounts in excess of its own capital. In practice, however, the paper held by the accepting bank in its own portfolio is not included in this figure which, therefore, only applies to the volume of paper each member bank sells or re-discounts. The underlying nature of the transaction is also important to identify whether the transaction is subject to or exempt from reserve requirements and whether the acceptance is eligible. Eligibility refers to paper which may be purchased by a Federal Reserve Bank (FRB) either by way of discount or by way of collateral for repurchase agreements (Repos). There are approximately 250 bank names which are eligible as acceptors of bills which are lodged as collateral for Repos and in practice the FRB now only conducts its open market operations in banker's acceptances through Repos. Therefore, column I in the following chart has more practical significance than column II.

Bankers' Acceptances: Eligibility and Reservability

Type of bankers' acceptance	I Eligible for purchase* (Repos)	II Eligible for discount†	III Exempt from reserve requirements if sold#
Export-Import, including shipments between foreign countries:			
Tenor – 6 months or less	Yes	Yes°	Yes
6 months to 9 months	Yes	No	No
Domestic shipment, with documents conveying title attached at the time of acceptance:			
Tenor – 6 months or less	Yes	Yes°	Yes
6 months to 9 months	Yes	No	No
Domestic shipment, without documents conveying title:			
Tenor – 6 months or less	Yes	No	No
6 months to 9 months	Yes	No	No
Shipment within foreign countries:			
Tenor – any maturity	No	No	No
Foreign storage, readily marketable staples secured by warehouse receipt:			
Tenor – 6 months or less	No	Yes°	Yes
6 months to 9 months	No	No	No
Domestic storage, readily marketable staples secured by warehouse receipt:			
Tenor – 6 months or less	Yes	Yes°	Yes
6 months to 9 months	Yes	No	No
Domestic storage, any goods in the United States under contract of sale or going into channels of trade and secured throughout its life by warehouse receipt:			
Tenor – 6 months or less	Yes	No	No
6 months to 9 months	Yes	No	No

Type of bankers' acceptance	I Eligible for purchase* (Repos)	II Eligible for discount†	III Exempt from reserve requirements if sold#
Dollar exchange, required by usages of trade, only in approved countries:			
Tenor – 3 months or less	No	Yes	No**
3 months to 9 months	No	No	No
Finance or working capital, not related to any specific transaction:			
Tenor – any maturity	No	No	No

Tenor refers to the full length of time of the acceptance from date of inception to maturity. To be eligible for discount, a bankers' acceptance must be endorsed by at least one member bank, as provided in Section 13(6) of the Federal Reserve Act.

* Authorisation announced by the Federal Open Market Committee on 1st April 1974.

† In accordance with Regulation A of the Federal Reserve Act.

In accordance with Regulation D of the Federal Reserve Act.

° Providing that the maturity of non agricultural bills at the time of discount is not more than 90 days.

** According to revised Regulation D, these acceptances are reservable, but the Federal Reserve Board's legal staff have expressed an opinion that the exemption from reserve requirements is also applicable to dollar exchange acceptances.

Source: Federal Reserve Bank New York Quarterly Review

To be eligible for financing in the US market, banker's acceptances must be drawn in US dollars. Whilst there is no minimum amount, they are usually traded in round lots of $100,000, $200,000, $\frac{1}{4}$ million, $\frac{1}{2}$ million and $1 million.

The paper must have a tenor of less than six months at the time of discounting; but bills with maturities of 270 days or less which have been accepted by a member bank of the FRB system and which meet the other requirements of eligibility, provide eligible security for borrowing by way of Repos from the FRBs. Secondary market dealer firms differentiate between eligible banker's acceptances issued by:

i) the major money centre banks (the larger commercial banks)
ii) well known US regional banks and US branches of major foreign banks, and,
iii) less well known banks

This is reflected in the rates they are prepared to quote, and follows the same pattern as the rate differentials quoted by dealer firms for CDs. Funds raised by banks from the sale of banker's acceptances, which are exempt from reserve requirements, can be cheaper than funds raised through CDs.

An example of a US Bankers Acceptance is shown overleaf:

Banker's Acceptances in other Countries
In Italy three types of "acceptances", issued by authorised banks, are traded in the secondary market: however, they are all subject to withholding tax. Historically, Italy is the home of the bill of exchange and it is not surprising that the Italian bill market is well developed. The paper is priced on a true yield basis of actual days over a 365 day year. The secondary market will trade promissory notes and non-trade-related accommodation paper as well as bills of exchange with maturities of up to six months.

Despite withholding tax, the Canadian banker's acceptance market is well established and available to non-residents. The acceptances held by the banks in their own portfolios do not contribute towards meeting their mandatory reserve requirements and, therefore, the majority are either rediscounted or sold to other investors in the market. The maximum permitted maturity is 90 days, the minimum size is Can.$100,000 per bill and there are no regulations limiting the volume that may be issued by a company or accepted by a bank. Quotations and calculations are based on a true yield of actual days over a 365 day year.

US Bankers Acceptance

SPECIMEN   DUE 9.2.84

BILL   OF   EXCHANGE

NO: NWT-101-002   DATE: March 7, 1983   US$ 1,000,000.00   DOLLARS U.S. CURRENCY

this Bill of Exchange (Letra de Cambio)   79 days after sight

pay to the order of   NATIONAL WESTMINSTER BANK LIMITED

for value received.

NATIONAL WESTMINSTER BANK LIMITED
NEW YORK BRANCH
100 WALL   STREET
NEW YORK, NEW YORK 10005

ABC OIL INC.

NO 48389

Authorised Signature(s)/Title

An example of a Canadian banker's acceptance is shown overleaf:

In many countries there is no secondary market for banker's acceptances which, therefore, must be held by the accepting bank in portfolio. In other countries the market is restricted for various reasons, for example, in West Germany and the Netherlands the paper is not available to non-resident investors, and in Germany there is stamp duty on the obligations as well.

Trade Bills

Trade bills are bills of exchange drawn by one non-banking commercial entity and accepted by another. Banks often refinance such paper by buying it at a discount and normally hold it until maturity. The secondary market for rediscounting trade paper is relatively thin and largely depends on the quality/standing of the two names on the paper. Trade bills do not, as a rule, attract so fine a discount rate as bank bills.

Canadian Bankers Acceptance

National Westminster Bank of Canada
Banque National Westminster du Canada

BA0003

**BANKERS' ACCEPTANCE
ACCEPTATION DE BANQUE**

SPECIMEN

19___ Due Date/Date d'échéance

On/Le ___ 19___

without grace, for value received, pay
sans délai, contre valeur reçue, veuillez

to or to the order of the undersigned drawer the sum of
payer au tireur soussigné ou à son ordre, la somme de $

Dollars

Currency and Amount/Devise et montant

Drawn by/Tiré par:

Name of Drawer/Nom du tireur

To/À:
National Westminster Bank of Canada
Banque National Westminster du Canada

Branch/Succursale

By/par:

Authorized Officer/Dirigeant autorisé

Authorized Officer/Dirigeant autorisé

ACCEPTED/ACCEPTÉ

Date/Le ___ 19___

Payable at/Payable à
National Westminster Bank of Canada
Banque National Westminster du Canada

Branch/Succursale

By/par:

Authorized Officer/Dirigeant autorisé

Authorized Officer/Dirigeant autorisé

CHAPTER TWELVE

Commercial Paper, Repurchase Agreements, Broker and Dealer Loans

Introduction

Commercial paper is a money market instrument and is the market name used to describe short-term promissory notes issued by various industrial, financial and insurance companies in the USA and elsewhere, and by utilities and sovereign borrowers as well. The most important market is in the USA; markets also exist in Australia, Canada, Japan, and from March 1986 in the UK; and offshore US dollar commercial paper in the UK and Singapore. The commercial paper market is a logical development of the inter-company loan market. There is no active secondary market in commercial paper (including the USA), the notes being placed directly with the investor or with investors through dealer firms.

In Australia, promissory notes issued by major companies are treated as money market instruments, have maturities of 90 or 180 days and have higher yields than bank CDs of similar maturities.

In Canada, notes are normally issued in denominations of Can.$100,000 or more for maturities from overnight to a year. The issuers include the Canadian subsidiaries of foreign companies and banks and notes may be held by either Canadian or foreign investors, although they are subject to Canadian withholding tax. Some paper is secured, most issues are unsecured but nevertheless are supported by a parent company guarantee or by standby bank lines of credit. It is normal procedure for the issuer to enter into two agreements:

    i)   an agency agreement with a bank for the latter to pay interest and handle delivery of notes sold,
           and

    ii)   a placing agreement with the dealer(s) who markets the notes.

An issuing circular is prepared which gives all material details of the notes for investors. Interest is paid on the basis of a true yield over a 365 day year.

In Japan, commercial paper is issued for maturities of 90 and 120 days often on a roll-over basis. The paper may be either secured or unsecured and, as the investors are other companies and banks who generally hold the notes in their portfolios until maturity, there is little scope for secondary market operations. The development of Asian dollar commercial paper began in 1980 in Singapore with managed issues priced over either three months or six months SIBOR, plus a margin, and principally placed with financial institutions. Also in 1980 euro-commercial paper (ECP) was first launched in London and priced at a mark-up over LIBOR – maturities generally range from 30 to 180 days and the issues are managed with the notes being placed direct with investors, principally banks. There is virtually no secondary market for such paper. The notes are usually sold at a discount on a yield equivalent to a LIBOR rate determined by three or four reference banks plus a margin. The notes are usually issued in bearer form in minimum denominations of US$100,000 or more.

ECP issues may be underwritten or not underwritten depending on the corporate borrowing objectives, and they may have tender panels or nominated dealers to place the issue. From the earlier days of Note Issuing Facilities (NIFs) and Revolving Underwriting Facilities (RUFs) the ECP market has developed rapidly during the period 1980–1986.

US Commercial Paper
The issuers may borrow in their own names directly from investors or through dealers. Of the 1,200 or so institutions in 1984 issuing such paper the principal borrowers were financial institutions being subsidiaries of major industrial companies, as well as banks and bank holding companies. Major non-resident institutions can raise funds through issues of yankee commercial paper and the market procedures for such issues are identical to those for a domestic issue apart from a 20-60 basis point differential in yield for similarly rated issuers

Euro-commercial note (front)

Front of Note

ISSUE DATE: FEB 21, 1984
NOTE NO.

CHRYSLER
FINANCIAL CORPORATION

ON ____AUG 20, 1984____________ , Chrysler Financial Corporation promises to pay

THE SUM OF ________________________________

(includes discount of $ ______________)

to the order of ____BEARER___________________

at the office of (a) European Banking Company Limited at 150 Leadenhall Street, London, EC3V 4PP England or (b) European American Bank & Trust Company at 10 Hanover Square, New York, New York 10015, or its designated agent in New York City.

Countersigned for purposes of
Authentication Only.
European Banking Company Limited,
Issuing Agent

By ________________________________
AUTHORISED SIGNATURE

CHRYSLER FINANCIAL CORPORATION

________________________   ________________________
VICE PRESIDENT & TREASURER   VICE PRESIDENT—FINANCE

SPECIMEN

Euro-commercial note (back)

Reverse Side of Note

Chrysler Financial Corporation (the "Company") agrees with the holder of the Note printed on the reverse hereof, effective upon the authentication of such Note, that the Company will pay as additional interest such amounts as are necessary in order that the net payment of the principal of this Note to a holder who, as to the United States, the Commonwealth of Puerto Rico, and each territory and possession of the United States and place subject to its jurisdiction, is a nonresident alien individual, a nonresident alien fiduciary of a foreign estate or trust, a foreign corporation, or a foreign partnership one or more of the members of which is, as to the United States, the Commonwealth of Puerto Rico, and each territory and possession of the United States and place subject to its jurisdiction, a nonresident alien individual, a nonresident alien fiduciary of a foreign estate or trust, or a foreign corporation, after deduction for any tax, assessment or governmental charge (including any hereafter enacted) of the United States or any political subdivision or taxing authority thereof or therein, imposed by withholding with respect to such payment, will not be less than the amount provided in this Note when due and payable; *provided, however,* that the foregoing obligation to pay additional interest shall not apply to any tax, assessment or governmental charge which is imposed by reason of one or more of the following: (a) such holder (or a fiduciary, settlor, beneficiary, shareholder or member of a holder, if such holder is an estate, trust, corporation or partnership, or a person holding a power over an estate or trust administered by a fiduciary holder) being considered as (i) being or having been engaged in trade or business, or being or having been physically present, in the United States, the Commonwealth of Puerto Rico, or any territory or possession of the United States or place subject to its jurisdiction; (ii) having a relationship or former relationship with the United States, the Commonwealth of Puerto Rico, or any territory or possession of the United States or place subject to its jurisdiction, including, without limitation, such person's current or former relationship as a citizen or resident thereof; or (iii) a personal holding company or foreign personal holding company with respect to the United States; or (b) a change in the law which becomes effective more than 15 days after such payment becomes due or is duly provided for, whichever occurs later.

In addition, the Company shall not be obligated to make any payment of additional interest (i) to any holder who is not the beneficial owner of this Note if such beneficial owner would not have been entitled to the payment of the additional interest provided for had such beneficial owner received such payment directly or (ii) to any holder whose failure to provide proper documentation evidencing that such holder is not a United States person, citizen or resident results in the withholding of United States tax.

The foregoing agreement and the Note printed on the reverse hereof are governed by and are to be construed in accordance with the laws of the State of New York.

CHRYSLER FINANCIAL CORPORATION

VICE PRESIDENT & TREASURER   VICE PRESIDENT–FINANCE

in favour of the domestic borrower. The paper is issued at a discount from its face value and the rate is determined by the maturity of the note and the general level of short-term rates. The notes are drawn payable to bearer and are fully negotiable although the secondary market may be somewhat limited perhaps just to the dealers handling a given issuer's paper. The degree of liquidity of bank yankee commercial paper issued to non-US banks is, however, satisfactory. The stated maturity may range from one day to a maximum of 270 days, although most maturities are concentrated in the 15 – 45 day area. The denominations can be as small as US$25,000 although the usual minimum round lot is US$100,000 and the normal denomination in multiples of US$1 million. The notes are payable in same day value funds on the maturity date and the majority of issuers have designated a New York bank or banks as paying agents. Normal trading is for delivery and settlement in New York, although arrangements can be made for this to be effected elsewhere.

Unlike US public equity or bond issues, commercial paper is exempt from registration with the Securities and Exchange Commission (SEC) under either Section 3(a)3 or Section 4(2) of the Securities Act of 1933.

1. **Section 3(a)3** – Current Transaction Exemption
This exemption applies to notes which are issued for a maturity of less than 270 days and used to finance current transactions. This most widely used form of commercial paper is generally to fund working capital, but it does not have to be allocated to specific transactions.

2. **Section 4(2)** – Private Offering Exemption
Privately placed notes are sold to a limited number of "sophisticated investors" (usually 20 – 200). These notes may have maturities from a few days to many years. When maturities are longer than 270 days, such obligations are called "private placements" rather than commercial paper. Proceeds of these notes may be used, on an interim basis, to fund non-current long-term construction projects as well as non-current short-term transactions.

Over the years the US commercial paper market has tended to be a less expensive source of short-term funds than, say, bank lending based on eurodollar market rates or on US domestic market rates and much cheaper than long-term debt because of the positive shape of the yield curve. Establishing and maintaining a US commercial paper programme is not expensive, although the costs of the normally required unused back-up credit facilities and commercial paper rating must be considered. For most borrowers it is the practice to arrange alternative credit to support all outstanding commercial paper. Standby lines of credit or revolving credit agreements with the world's major commercial banks are normal. Another form of support of particular value to smaller institutions is a first-class bank guarantee. This is usually structured by way of a letter of credit issued by the bank for a period of between one and three years. A major bank will probably already have been accredited the highest rating by the rating agencies for its own commercial paper and by guaranteeing the smaller company's commercial paper enables the latter to gain access to the market and on the best possible terms. Compared to the longer-term debt market the US formalities and legal requirements are not too onerous. The required documentation includes a memorandum describing the borrower's activities (not a prospectus), an up-to-date balance sheet and income statement (report and accounts) and ratings. Almost all commercial paper issued through dealer firms is rated by at least one, and usually two, of the following independent rating agencies: Moody's Investors Services Inc, Standard & Poors Corp., or Fitch Investors Services.

As a bank liability commercial paper has proved to be a flexible and reliable short-term funding instrument at relatively low borrowing costs and available even in terms of tight credit. As a bank asset, other institution's commercial paper, having an original life to maturity of not more than 90 days can, depending on the use of proceeds, be treated as eligible collateral for borrowing by member banks from the Federal Reserve Bank.

Repurchase Agreements (Repos)
Anyone with a portfolio of acceptable securities can use them as collateral for short-term funding. What constitutes "acceptable securities" depends upon the market practice in the centre concerned. In Italy, for instance, the market is limited to Ente Nazionale par

l'Energia Elettrica bonds. Other markets exist in Canada, Australia (buy-backs), West Germany (pensionsgeschäft), Japan (gensaki), a very small market in the UK, and the principal market in the USA.

A Repo, sometimes called "RP", is a combination of two simultaneous transactions in a single contract – the sale of securities for immediate payment and the commitment by the seller to repurchase the securities at a later date. The sale and repurchase are often executed at the same price or at prices calculated to yield the agreed rate of return on the actual amount invested. The Repo is a money market instrument in its own right and provides the investor with a tailor-made facility to suit his precise maturity needs from overnight to up to one year, the most common period being for one business day. Repos may be issued for fixed terms from one day to one year, or as "on demand" Repos which either the borrower or the lender may choose to cancel. Member banks of the Federal Reserve System may acquire liquidity by Repos of US Government or Federal Agency securities, without incurring any reserve requirements.

A reverse Repo is a Repo as viewed from the stand-point of the lender of funds. He will receive the securities and enter into a sale agreement for a given maturity.

In the US, Repo market transactions are in minimum amounts of US$1 million and normally US$5 million with interest calculated on an actual day basis for a 360 day year on the dollar amount invested. In the UK, the Bank of England enters into Repos with the discount houses from time to time as one of three open market operations to relieve a shortage of funds in the banking system. The other two being outright purchases of paper, and brokers loans from overnight to seven days. The Bank of England buys treasury bills, eligible bank bills, and corporation bills for eventual resale on fixed maturities. The discount rates are based on specific maturity bands; band 1 is up to 14 days, band 2 between 15 and 33 days, band 3 between 34 and 63 days, and band 4 between 64 and 91 days. Whilst most major banks and discount houses in the UK will provide specific Repo or reverse Repo facilities for corporate treasurers, the latter have adequate access to place funds to earn interest from overnight and short term; as a result the corporate demand for Repos in the UK is very limited. In the USA however, Repos are the principal method of short term corporate investment (under 14 days).

In Australia, buy-backs and reverse buy-backs of eligible paper, including government securities, are carried out between the Reserve Banks and secondary market dealers for open market operations to control liquidity in the banking system. The commercial market in buy-backs is quite well established, normally for periods of up to three months and in amounts of A$½ million or more.

The West German pensionsgeschäft is a Repo of fixed interest anleihen (loans or bonds) or schuldscheindarlehen (note loans) which is quite popular with insurance companies and other institutional investors for short term liquidity purposes.

The Japanese gensaki agreements are a major source of call money and the market is very well established for maturities from overnight to six months. The Bank of Japan is active in the market which also comprises major companies, banks and securities houses and a wide spectrum of investors.

The Canadian Repo and reverse Repo market operates in a very similar way to that in the USA but on a substantially reduced scale.

Transactions are usually only arranged between institutions enjoying a high degree of confidence in one another and the contracts are normally of very short duration so risks are generally considered small. In 1981, a US government securities firm, Lombard-Wall Inc., collapsed and in 1984 Lion Capital Group, another US government securities firm, did likewise. In both instances legal questions arose concerning the treatment of a Repo as a "loan" or as a "purchase and a sale of securities". In the case of Lombard-Wall Inc. outstanding Repos were treated as a loan and the securities being used as collateral were frozen temporarily when the borrower went into liquidation. The investors were concerned that the bonds could lose their value before being freed by the bankruptcy judge. Despite the fact that a Repo implies that entitlement to securities is physically transferred from the seller (borrower) to the buyer (lender) the US courts action has caused investors to become unsure whether they can cash their collateral securities held in the event of a borrower's bankruptcy.

Broker and dealer loans

The brokers and dealers referred to in the heading embrace those conducting business on the New York Stock Exchange, the American Exchange and other securities markets in the United States. On the New York Stock Exchange (NYSE) for example members may be categorised as:

- floor brokers who act for other Stock Exchange members and can handle a wide range of stocks and substantial volumes

- commission brokers who act for their clients

- traders who are registered by the Securities & Exchange Commission to transact business for their own account

- specialists who are brokers and dealers in particular stocks and are subject to SEC and NYSE registration and regulation as they can also transact business for their own account.

The brokers and dealers are investment bankers and in order to fund their various portfolios of securities they resort, inter alia, to borrowing from the commercial banks. The loans are made on fine terms and are secured (collateralised) by marketable securities. They are short-term loans with normal maturities ranging from call to 30 days. Clients of the investment banks frequently retain cash and margin accounts with them and the balances on such accounts enjoy interest based on broker loan rates. The broker/dealer loans provided by banks are strictly controlled and may only be arranged by member banks of the Federal Reserve System and those which otherwise comply with the SEC Act requirements relating to securities loans. Where collateralised margin accounts are concerned, clients running debit (or overdrawn) balances will be charged interest on the basis of the broker loan rate. This rate is generally pitched at up to $1\frac{1}{2}\%$ under the New York prime loan rate (NYPLR). Movements of the interest rate quoted for US dollar brokers loans is often an indicator of impending movement of other short-term US dollar interest rates, and NYPLR movements generally react swiftly to broker loan rate trends.

CHAPTER THIRTEEN

Government and other Non-Commercial Bank Money and Capital Market Instruments

Probably by far the most common form of short-term fund raising employed by government is by way of Treasury Bill tender and issue.

A UK Treasury Bill is a bearer instrument drawn by the Bank of England out of the National Loans Fund in denominations of £5,000, £10,000, £25,000, £50,000, £100,000, £250,000 or £1 million. Treasury bills are issued on a discounted basis through tender to the Bank of England, and are redeemed at their face value at maturity. The normal tenor of the bills is 91 days although on occasions bills with shorter maturities are issued. There exists a substantial secondary market provided by the discount houses to enable holders to sell (rediscount) their bills, even though the Bank of England's obligation to repay is confined to the maturity of the bill. Tenders of a minimum of £50,000 are invited through a discount house, bank or moneybroker each Friday for a volume of bills announced the previous Friday, for delivery on any selected business day the following week, with same day settlement in cash or draft drawn on the Bank of England. The London Discount Market Association (LDMA) comprises nine firms which ensure that the tender is taken up by underwriting it at the minimum accepted tender price. All tenders received in excess of this price will be allotted in full.

US Treasury Bills often referred to as "T Bills", are also bearer instruments issued at a discount by auction through the Federal Reserve Bank of New York, and are redeemed at their face (or par) value at maturity. Three month and six month T Bills are issued regularly by the US Treasury each Monday (unless the Monday is a Bank Holiday and then on the preceding Friday) – with settlement on the following Thursday when the 3 and 6 month T Bills (issued earlier) mature. T Bills have maximum liquidity as they are primary obligations of the US Government and are issued more frequently than any other instrument and in very substantial volumes. This gives rise to a secondary market with significant depth. In addition to the 3 and 6 month T Bills, a Thursday auction occurs every four weeks (with settlement on the following Thursday) of one year T Bills. The size of each auction varies according to the US Treasury's funding requirements and current economic policy, the amounts offered may be the same, greater than, or less than the volume of maturing T Bills. Subscriptions for new issues of T Bills in the primary market are made on either a competitive, or a non-competitive basis. Bids on a competitive basis are submitted in minimum sums of US$10,000 and are awarded according to the bid price – the highest prices being satisfied first. Buyers on a non-competitive basis agree to take up a specified amount at a price which is the average of the accepted bids and they will be allotted the full amount of their tender. The amounts to be auctioned are announced before the auction – in the case of Monday auctions on the preceding Tuesday afternoon, and for Thursday auction on the previous Friday. The US Treasury generally announces its likely liquidity requirements for each quarter beforehand, and indicates the types of funding which are being considered.

Longer-term government funding is primarily achieved through government securities which in the US mainly comprise Treasury Bonds and which, in the UK, are commonly referred to as "Gilts" or more properly gilt-edged stock.

US Treasury Bonds are registered securities which may carry a fixed or floating rate of interest and are normally issued with maturities of between 10 and 30 years but may be issued for shorter maturities. Those with floating coupons normally have the rate of interest accruing changed weekly on a formula of $\frac{1}{2}\%$ over the weekly tender rate for Treasury Bills. The term "Treasury Bond" includes those securities which are marketable in denominations ranging from US$1,000 to US$1,000,000 for which a large and active secondary market exists, and a whole range of non-marketable securities with no secondary market at all. This second category includes various issues of US Savings Bonds; individual retirement and retirement plan bonds; current income bonds; bonds sold directly to government agencies (called 'Government Account Series'); State and Local

Government Bonds; bonds sold directly to foreign governments and central banks (called 'Foreign Series'), and bonds denominated in foreign currency and sold to non-residents – called 'Foreign Currency Series' or 'Carter Bonds'. US Treasury Bonds are issued through some 37 primary dealers in Government Securities which comprise a mix of banks and Securities and Investment houses. Issues are made by tender at a premium or discount against the face value with application being submitted through primary dealers and the latter underwriting, within predefined percentages, each issue at the lowest accepted tender price. Physical deliveries of US Treasury Bonds are not available and beneficial ownership is registered either directly or indirectly on central accounts maintained with the Federal Reserve Board. Subsequent purchases and sales are settled by wire transfer within the central system.

Traditionally within the **UK**, primary issues of government securities were made by application to the Bank of England for purchase at a fixed offered price. However, due to the vagaries and volatility of interest rate movements, this system was amended to a tender procedure at or above a minimum specified tender price. UK issues of government securities are not underwritten but any under-subscribed amount is taken up by various government departments and subsequently offered for sale on a tap basis through the appointed Government Broker. There is a substantial secondary market in government securities which historically was the prerogative of a small number of specialised Stock Exchange jobbers with access thereto being through the medium of registered brokers working on a commission basis. During 1986 this market-making function will be broadened to include some 29 (or more) companies representing the interests of banks, security houses, brokers and other financial service groups functioning as market makers in government securities.

UK Gilts are registered securities for which physical documentation is made available. Initially registration usually takes place within four weeks of a new stock being issued but where partly-paid stocks are concerned beneficial ownership is represented by allotment letters in bearer form and registration will be deferred to coincide with the final payment being made. Gilts are usually issued with a fixed redemption date for various periods up to 30 years or with redemption on pre-determined dates at the option of the Government. Some un-dated stocks are also in existence. On most stocks interest is paid net of the UK basic standard rate of taxation; however, approximately 30 stocks exist which may be issued in bearer form and interest paid gross to non-UK residents. Within the secondary markets, stocks with a life of over five years are quoted as a composite price on the basis of ex-interest and cum-interest but those with a remaining life of five years or less require the separate settlement of interest accrued between buyer and seller. Settlement is normally made on the next business day following the transaction. Gilts comprise both fixed and floating rate coupons. In the latter case, interest rates are usually quoted as a margin over the average of the weekly Treasury bill tender price for the interest period.

Other important sources of funding instruments comprise govern-ment agencies and local (municipal authorities). Within the UK **Local Authority Bills** may be issued to supplement funds raised by the rates or other paper described below. Under the Local Government Act 1982, Schedule 13 enables local authorities to issue corporation bills, which are Local Government Promissory Notes. These instruments, which form part of the London Money Market have several names, being described as revenue bills or money bills as well. Normally such paper is issued by tender with a tenor of 91 days although 6 month bills are also issued sometimes. All issues are made with Bank of England prior approval and the tender procedure is similar to UK Treasury Bills with the Discount Houses and Clearing Banks taking up most of the paper. This short term borrowing by Local Authorities is made on an irregular basis to meet cash flow requirements and the denomination of bills issued are £5,000, £10,000, £25,000, £50,000 and £100,000.

The medium-term debt requirements of UK local authorities are largely met by issuing **Local Authority Bonds**. These registered secur-ities are quoted on The Stock Exchange and normally have a maturity of 1 year and 6 days (yearlings) although some are issued for longer periods of up to 5 years. The new bonds are brought to market by investment merchant banks, stockbrokers or discount houses who manage underwriting syndicates to take them up in initial tranches of between £$\frac{1}{4}$ million and £2 million. Applications are made on Tuesdays for next day settlement on Wednesday. The secondary market operates on minimum amounts of £1,000; interest is paid in arrears semi-annually after tax, on a LIBOR related basis.

Local authority stocks provide longer-term funding with maturities of up to 30 years and, indeed, undated and irredeemable stocks are issued occasionally. These registered securities are made infrequently and are issued directly through The Stock Exchange either on an underwritten basis by a merchant bank or as a private placement. Although the transaction size is in multiples of one penny the volume of deals on the secondary market is normally very low and the market thin.

Variable-rate coupon local authority bonds and stocks are a floating rate version of the fixed interest or coupon securities described above. Local authority variable-rate bonds and stocks are frequently priced on a margin over the 6 month LIBOR as determined by a number of named reference banks on the basis of a formula appearing on the bonds or stocks. Such rates are changed six-monthly. Price fluctuations of variable-rate securities are less than that of fixed-rate securities in volatile market conditions.

US Federal Agency securities are issued by some 20 different agencies, some of which are federally sponsored but under private sector ownership, others such as Eximbank are federally owned by the US Treasury, or are securities issued by executive government departments such as the US postal service. The various debt instruments issued include: secured and unsecured bonds, loans, participation certificates, notes, debentures guaranteed or otherwise, and mortgage-backed bonds. The most important in terms of the volume of securities issued are the Federal National Mortgage Association (FNMA or Fannie Maes) short term debenture, discount notes or mortgage-backed bonds.

The FNMA securities range from short-term money market instruments to long-term mortgage-backed bonds. The short-term discount notes with initial maturities from 30 days to one year, are sold on a discount basis redeemable at par on maturity. The medium-term funding is achieved by issuing debentures which bear coupons with semi-annual maturities in minimum denominations of US$10,000. The FNMA is a Federally sponsored privately owned agency which purchases mortgages in the house mortgage market. Other privately owned Federally sponsored debt-raising agencies include: The Student Loan Marketing Association (sometimes called "Sallie Maes"); The Federal Home Loan Mortgage Corporation (sometimes called "Freddie Macs"); Federal Home Loan Banks; Federal Land Banks; Farm Credit Banks; Federal Intermediate Credit Banks; and Banks for Co-operatives.

The Government National Mortgage Association Securities (GNMA – sometimes called "Ginnie Maes") are participation certificates with initial maturities of between 25 and 30 years. Quoted yields are on the average life basis of generally 12 years, rather than on a yield to maturity basis. The GNMA is owned by the US Treasury and the securities issued bear an indirect federal guarantee.

US Municipal Bonds are issued by state and local governments to supplement income raised by taxation and specifically to finance major construction projects, education, pollution control, hospitals and utilities. The municipal bonds can be issued in registered or coupon form and may be the general obligations of a state or of a large city. In addition a number of non-guaranteed revenue bonds are issued, most of which have been rated by the leading rating agencies.

CHAPTER FOURTEEN

Introduction to the Financial Markets

As identified in Chapter 1, a prime responsibility of the Treasury Function of an international bank is the control and development of dealing operations incorporating cash, forwards, futures and options contracts, interest rate and currency liability swaps, and forward rate agreements in some or all of the following: foreign exchange, deposits, negotiable instruments, securities, gold and commodities.

The subject of internal control over these operations is discussed in Chapter 4, and in considering funding instruments section 3 develops the subject of various primary and secondary markets in which negotiable instruments and securities are traded. This section of the publication now considers the structure and nature of other specific markets, the types of transactions traded and a bank's involvement therein, their relationship to each other, and the other activities of a bank; the mechanics of contracting a transaction together with the confirmation, settlement and delivery procedures related thereto. In particular, Chapter 15 examines the international and domestic currency deposit and money markets, with particular emphasis on the interbank deposit markets; Chapter 16 – The Foreign Exchange Markets; Chapter 17 – The Futures Markets; Chapter 18 – The Option Markets; Chapter 19 – The Interest Rate and Currency Liability Swap Markets; and Chapter 20 – The Forward Rate Agreement Markets. Finally Chapter 21 examines in more general terms the various markets in which gold is traded. Within the terms of reference for this publication it is considered that the gold markets are sufficiently representative of commodity markets in general and therefore this latter subject is not developed.

Markets are meeting places for the purpose of buying and selling goods and the markets discussed in this publication perform a similar function. However, the underlying transactions not only relate to buying and selling but also include markets for investing and borrowing, swapping and establishing future and forward prices for buying and selling and investing and borrowing. All contracts within the foreign exchange market and many gold and commodity markets are contracts of sale with the title to, and possession of, the subject matter being transferred to the buyer on the appropriate value date. Within the deposit markets the contracts traded are substantive contracts of loan or deposit with interest being the price payable for the use of the capital sum – the principal. The basis upon which interest is calculated often varies from market to market and instrument to instrument. For example within the interbank deposit markets the interest rate period is normally calculated on the actual number of days of the underlying contract over a 365 day base for sterling and 360 day base for most other currencies. However within the euro-capital note markets interest on currency instruments, inclusive of sterling, is normally quoted on the basis of a 360 day year with 12 months of 30 days and 4 quarters of 90 days over a 360 day base. Several futures contracts also use this latter formula.

Although markets are meeting places, they need not necessarily be physical meeting places. The dispersed markets of foreign exchange, interbank deposit, interest rate liability swap, foreign currency liability swap, forward rate agreements and the eurobond securities markets, are telephone/telex markets. Each comprises many principals, investors and borrowers throughout the world being represented by many hundreds of dealers and brokers who are linked through a network of telephone lines, telex machines and a variety of automated dealing services. Conversely, futures and most domestic securities markets are central meeting places with transactions being undertaken on the floor of an exchange and in many cases off-floor trading is strictly prohibited.

Within the context of these markets, each transaction is an individual deal and each deal constitutes a specific contract. There are usually two principals to each contract – the buyer and the seller, the borrower and lender or the swappers. Each principal refers to each other as his counterparty; together they are the counterparties to the contract. A contract is established immediately two counterparties

238

agree the terms of a transaction. This may be orally by telephone or on the floor of an exchange, by telex or through any other form of communication or dealing system. The contract terms may be either implied by market custom and practice, governed by rules and regulations, or be the subject of unique detailed terms agreed between the counterparties for each transaction. Thereafter the counterparties are normally required to exchange expeditiously and verify with each other in writing. the details of the contract and its terms. This may comprise the exchange of a relatively simple confirmation or be the subject of a specific and detailed agreement document. Although these confirmation and documentation procedures are an integral and important procedural part of such transactions, they only record the detail of already binding contracts, and failure to comply with (or complete) these procedures does not affect otherwise the legal obligations of the counterparties concerned.

Dealers and traders in any market should be placed in a position so they may safely assume that the persons executing trades with them have the necessary mandates and authorities, and do not require any formal evidence thereof. Conversely, each dealer and trader will be aware of the mandates and authorities governing his activities, and of the counterparties with whom he is authorised to transact business.

Some of the instruments discussed in this section are relatively recent innovations which have not been subject to legal precedent, custom or practice. In particular, as interest rate swaps and forward rate agreements are not contracts of loan or deposit, questions remain outstanding, at the time of publication, as to their legal standing. Within the legislation of many countries, gaming and wagering transactions are not legally enforceable and due to the lack of any underlying contract of loan/deposit in support of a transaction it is possible, in the absence of any identifiable commercial reason for its existence, that the contract could be ruled to be a gaming or wagering transaction and therefore rendered voidable, or illegal to consummate.

In considering financial and other forms of market it is essential to distinguish clearly between the transactions traded therein. Cash, forward, futures and option contracts, together with interest rate and currency liability swap and forward rate agreements are all different types of transactions. Each transaction type has its own characteristics and may form the basis of separate and distinct, but closely related, markets in the same underlying subject matter. For example foreign exchange, deposits, securities, gold and commodities may be traded as cash, forward, future or option contracts. Additionally one instrument may be based upon another, for example options on futures contracts.

Cash transactions refer to those transactions which are due for settlement and/or delivery on the day the transaction is completed, i.e. same day settlement. Although they are short dated forward contracts, it is also usual to include within the definition of cash transactions both one day and spot value transactions. One day value transactions are due for settlement the following business day and spot value transactions the second business day following the consummation of a trade.

This definition of spot is always used in the international markets. However, until April 1984 when it moved in line with international convention, spot Yen (Yen against the US dollar) as traded within the Tokyo market was for same day value, albeit that at the same time spot Yen was being traded within other markets as two day value. In Hong Kong the principal area of trading is, in terms of the US/Hong Kong dollar, the telegraphic transfer rate which is for one day value.

Forward contracts (which are contingent assets and liabilities) relate to transactions which are due for settlement on an agreed date or within an agreed period in the future. Both cash and forward contracts require settlement to be made in full between the counterparties for the contracted amount on the value date and in the case of substantive contracts of loan and deposit, repayment as at the maturity date. Cash and forward contracts may only be cancelled or amended with the mutual consent of the counterparties concerned and this will usually involve settlement of any financial differential. Although the cash and forward markets usually have accepted trade quantities and trade periods, they do also provide for contract amounts and value dates to be individually agreed and established between the counterparties.

240

The futures markets are markets in which the traded object is a standardised contract approved by a futures exchange. Futures contracts are contracts to deliver a specified quantity of the underlying product on, or between, agreed future settlement dates; in the case of commodities the quantity of the product is also specified in the contract terms. These contracts are individual to the futures exchange upon which they are traded and neither the size nor the terms and conditions of the contract may be changed other than by the exchange. Trading in futures is usually restricted to the floor of the exchange of their origin. The futures markets exchange and allied clearing house procedures facilitate contracts being unilaterally closed out, by either counterparty undertaking further transactions on the exchange. Thereafter settlement is only made between those principals with contracts outstanding as at the last trading date.

Option contracts are unilateral contracts and are only binding upon the grantor of an option. They provide the purchaser of an option with the right, but not the obligation, to take delivery under the terms of the contract. Option markets comprise both "exchange traded" options and "over the counter" options. Exchange traded options are standardized option contracts which are traded on an exchange. Over the counter options are non-exchange option contracts which are negotiated between the grantor and purchaser of an option. Each option contract requires the payment of a premium by the option purchaser to the option grantor. Exchange traded options may either be exercised, left to expire unused or, as with futures contracts, closed out by simply undertaking further transactions on the exchange. Over the counter options may be exercised (or surrendered for a cash settlement) or left to expire unused. Where an option is exercised either a net cash payment of the difference between the current rate and the exercise rate or full settlement of the underlying contract amounts may take place.

Interest rate and currency swap agreements are contracts whereby the counterparties undertake to swap cash flows related to agreed quantities of their respective liability obligations and make settlement for these cash flows at predetermined intervals either on the basis of gross payments or settlement of the net difference due between the counterparties concerned. Within the terms of these agreements, each counterparty retains his primary obligation for the underlying liability. Interest rate liability swap agreements do not require the principal amount of the contract to change hands. Currency swap agreements may or may not require the counterparties to exchange the underlying currencies at the commencement of the contract but always require the counterparties to exchange the underlying principal sums in the underlying currencies at the expiration of the swap agreement.

Forward rate agreements which are effectively over the counter futures, are contracts in which the counterparties indemnify each other against the impact of any change in interest rate on the notional principal amount of a deposit for a fixed period of time in the future. Within the terms of forward rate agreements principal amounts do not change hands and settlement is made by a payment representing the difference between the contracted rate and the settlement rate.

In each market all settlements and payments are normally required to be made in the appropriate immediately available form with good title, be freely transferable and be made without deduction. Settlement can only be made on a business day in the place where settlement is due to be made. When a value date is agreed which is not a business day, market custom and practice, specific agreement, or more formalised rules and regulations will determine the business day on which settlement is to be effected. Where settlement or delivery crosses international borders good value dates will require to be business days in each of the centres where settlement or delivery is required to take place. Although a bank in London may desire to settle in US dollars with a bank in Zurich and it is a business day in both of these centres, settlement can only be made if it is also a business day in the United States.

As explained above, cash, forward, futures, options, interest rate liability swaps, currency liability swaps and forward rate agreements are quite distinct types of transaction. In practice, it is quite common for the terms "cash price", "cash markets", "physical price" and "physical markets" to be used when referring to both cash and forward markets to differentiate from "futures prices", "futures markets" and also "option prices" and "option markets". The practice has also developed of referring to interest rate and currency liability swaps simply as "swaps". This can be misleading as many other forms of swap are traded in various markets, for example gold swaps, deposit swaps, foreign exchange swaps, etc.

Foreign exchange, deposit, forward, future, options, interest rate and currency liability swaps together with forward rate agreement markets, are generic terms which relate to five large classes of market by instrument. Each of these classes contains many distinct and separate markets that require further identification by currency, commodity or other subject matter traded and by place of domicile and whether traded on an exchange or over the counter.

The currency deposit markets are a segment of the "financial markets". The financial markets include both the short- term money markets and longer-term capital debt markets with the currency deposit markets being part of the former. The subject of capital debt markets is developed in more detail in sections 5, 6 and 7. Each of these markets may be sub-divided into domestic and international. Domestic markets refer to local financial markets which exist within the national boundaries of individual countries and their activities are normally confined to the currency of issue of that country. Domestic financial markets are subject to the regulations, restrictions, and constraints of individual countries and therefore the extent to which each individual market is accessible by foreign participants may be restricted. Several countries place regulatory boundaries around their domestic financial markets which often make it impossible, or prohibitive, for non-residents or foreign controlled companies and banks to gain access thereto. However, many countries do permit limited access for transactions related to underlying trade, whilst others actively encourage both residents and non-residents to borrow and invest in all or many selected areas of their domestic financial markets, thereby introducing a foreign sector to those domestic markets. These latter countries include the United Kingdom, United States, West Germany and Switzerland.

The international financial markets comprise those "offshore" currency markets described in Chapter 6 and include separate markets in US Dollars, Deutschemarks, Swiss Francs, Yen, Sterling, ECUs and several other currencies. These markets operate outside of the regulations, restrictions and constraints that may normally apply within the national boundaries of the countries of issue of those currencies. The international markets are in themselves freely accessible for both investment and funding purposes. However, an individual bank's ability to access these markets remains subject to any local regulation, restriction or constraint which may be imposed by regulations imposed by its own country of domicile.

Whilst it is often implied in the broadest context, that foreign exchange rates are floating and that the currencies are freely tradable, this is not true for many currencies. Exchange control regulations, two tier financial systems, constraints on capital flows, negative interest rates, withholding tax together with official exchange rate policy, alignment with another currency or basket of currencies and similar constraints all limit, to a greater or lesser extent, the impact of market forces upon individual nations' foreign exchange rates. Some countries impose rigid control over foreign currency transactions with all foreign exchange receipts and payments being effected or even managed through official channels and many countries require to be provided with some evidence of underlying commercial business in support of any foreign exchange transaction undertaken. Consequent upon these restrictions, world currencies consist of a broad spectrum from those of the Eastern block, in which activity is completely restricted, through to those, like Sterling and the US dollar, which, subject to official market intervention mechanisms, float quite freely. The various levels of constraints imposed by individual countries impact upon the markets which may, or may not, have developed in each currency. Whilst buying and selling rates may be provided and transactions undertaken in most individual currencies, major foreign exchange markets are limited to Deutschemarks, Sterling, Yen, Swiss Francs and the US Dollar. Lesser markets are available in other currencies including the Canadian and Australian Dollar, French Franc, Italian Lire, Belgian Franc, Spanish Peseta, Norwegian and Swedish Kroner and Dutch Guilder, together with the so called "exotic markets" which include, for example, the Hong Kong and Singapore Dollars, the Malaysian Ringgit, the South African Rand and the Kenyan Shilling.

Domestic financial and foreign exchange markets are established in most of the major financial centres of the world, and one or more types of market may exist within any particular country. For example, in the United Kingdom all of the financial markets are centred on London but in the United States foreign exchange markets exist in New York, Chicago and Los Angeles, with money markets operating within the 12 regions in which Federal Reserve banks are established, and there are stock exchanges in several cities.

Futures exchanges are established in several places including New York, Chicago, London, Toronto, Winnipeg, Amsterdam, Sydney, Singapore and Tokyo and permission to operate in most of these markets is granted to both residents and non-residents alike. Collectively these exchanges include futures markets in deposits in various currencies, Treasury Bills, Treasury Bonds, Gilts, individual stocks and bonds, stock indices, gold and other commodities and provide for contracts in Deutschemark, Sterling, Yen, Swiss Francs and other foreign currencies against the US dollar. The largest financial futures market is situated in the International Monetary Market in Chicago. Many of these futures exchanges, together with several stock exchanges, including those in London and Philadelphia, provide markets in traded options.

The major international (eurocurrency) markets are based upon London, New York and Singapore, together with Paris which is the main centre for the euro-sterling market. London and Zurich are the major international centres of the physical gold markets and although several futures markets provide contracts for gold trading, the major futures market is situated within the Commodity Exchange (COMEX) in New York.

Although the techniques used in interest and currency liability swaps and forward rate agreements may be applied to, or as appropriate, between any currency or currencies, the major markets for trading each of these instruments initially has been established in London.

Each of the markets mentioned above has its own separate identity and in many cases its own market customs, practice, systems, procedures, rules and regulations and code of conduct. However, irrespective of these separate identities, in many cases modern communication systems have, to all intents and purposes, both nationalised and internationalised them. For example it is not unusual for a domestic US dollar transaction to be arranged between member banks of different Federal Reserve banks or for a foreign exchange or eurocurrency deposit dealer in London to transact business with counterparties in Tokyo, Hong Kong, Singapore, New York, Chicago and Los Angeles during any particular business day.

Collectively these various markets provide the mechanism for:

- the transfer of funds, domestic and foreign currencies, bullion and commodities between the original supplier and ultimate user.

- the transference of risks between those who require protection and those who are prepared to accept them.

- current, forward and future price determination through a process of bid and offered prices.

Each market comprises a mix of principals and brokers. Principals will include and represent the interests of, traders, dealers, investors, hedgers, abitragers and speculators. As defined in this publication, traders are defined as commercial users and suppliers, with the exception of "floor traders" in a futures exchange. Dealers are "market-makers". "Dealers" quote concurrently bid and offered prices at which they are prepared to buy and sell. Dealers provide a service to other market members and endeavour to take advantage, for profit, of the spread between buying and selling prices. An investor seeks a return on a capital investment and enters the markets for income generation and security of capital. "Hedgers" are transferers of risk. They enter the market to cover perceived risk exposure and will undertake contracts with a view to: offsetting possible changes in the value, return on, or cost of underlying assets and liabilities; protecting the cost or proceeds of anticipated purchases or sales of assets and liabilities at some future date; hedging underlying structural positions, or net investment exposure. An "arbitrager" takes advantage

246

of any rate or pricing differential which he perceives to exist between markets. The activities of arbitragers add efficiency to each market by closing price distortions which become apparent. "Speculators" are the risk takers within a market. A speculator is prepared to assume the capital risk associated with maintaining "open" positions. As discussed in Chapter 2, open positions result from being net "long" or "short" of respectively assets or liabilities (inclusive of contingent assets and liabilities). It is normally accepted that banks do not speculate.

There is a conception that within a market environment there is a winner and loser to each transaction. This is totally incorrect. Each participant enters these markets for a perceived objective and specific purpose, the achievement of which represents success. Other than a speculator, the fact that a price, exchange rate or interest rate subsequently increases or decreases is of no concern to that participant, albeit perhaps representing a lost opportunity. Speculation is also frequently confused with gambling. There is a subtle and important difference. Speculation is the assumption of an already existent risk for its perceived profit potential. Gambling is the creation of chances on which to place wagers. Winners, losers and gamblers belong in casinos and on the race tracks. Their place is not in the financial markets.

Direct access as principal to various markets is frequently restricted or selective. The domestic and international currency deposit and foreign exchange markets are the preserve of banks. Also large interbank markets are developing in over-the-counter options and forward rate agreements. Interest rate and currency liability swaps have developed two distinct segments. The first is a specific interbank market, the second a corporate market which comprises a wide range of interests including both banks and other corporate entities. On futures exchanges direct access is restricted to members.

Brokers are an integral and essential part of many markets. Within dispersed markets they provide, as intermediaries, a common market place in which "buyers" and "sellers" are brought together on a principal to principal basis. On futures exchanges floor brokers are frequently the only medium of access to the markets by non-members of an exchange. The role of brokers also differs from market to market. In the interbank deposit and foreign exchange markets a deposit and foreign exchange broker's role is entirely one of an intermediary, but in the futures markets floor brokers frequently have direct responsibility as a principal. Brokers charge fees for their services. Although the fundamental purposes behind the activities of traders, dealers, investors, hedgers, arbitragers, speculators and brokers are entirely different, they are complementary in that the presence of all provides liquidity to the market. Liquidity is an essential ingredient to the success and effectiveness of a market as it facilitates business being executed expeditiously and in substantial quantities.

Each market can be measured in terms of both its size and its depth. The size of a market is measured in terms of turnover. The depth, or more properly, the liquidity of a market is related to supply and demand. Liquidity impacts upon the ease with which business may be transacted and this can only be ascertained from current market experience. The difference between size and liquidity may be illustrated by reference to the foreign exchange markets in London and New York. There is usually substantial liquidity in the London foreign exchange markets throughout the day for the major traded currencies. London is operational at the same time as the other major European centres and opens before the Far East markets close. Activity increases as New York opens for business and the markets in New York are active until London and the other European centres close. Thereafter, other than a flurry of activity as the IMM futures market closes in Chicago, the New York markets have very little liquidity and difficulty can be experienced in transacting business. Similarly when New York closes the American west coast foreign exchange market effectively stops trading. Consequently although in turnover terms, New York is a large foreign exchange market, there is little depth to this market in the afternoon. Liquidity is affected by several factors other than supply and demand and even the larger markets can have liquidity problems. This is particularly so in periods of highly volatile conditions or when sizeable increases or decreases in the direction of either foreign exchange rates, interest rates or commodity prices are anticipated or experienced. In situations of high volatility, i.e. when the market is moving erratically in both

248

directions, both supply and demand often evaporate as dealers widen spreads to protect their positions. During periods of a large anticipated movement in direction either supply or demand will disappear according to the anticipated direction.

Markets function on bid and offered prices. A bid price is the price at which participants are prepared to borrow or purchase and the offered price is the price at which they are willing to sell, lend or grant. There are many factors which influence these prices which often involve both fundamental and technical analysis. The concept of supply and demand is as important to the determination of foreign exchange and interest rate levels and futures and options prices as it is to commodity prices. Monetary policy, economic theory, statistics, chart points and information; political considerations and events; a country's stability, balance of payments and economic development; future expectations and capital flows will all play their part to a greater or lesser extent in influencing the price determination process.

The reasons for, and extent of, each individual bank's participation in these various markets will differ from bank to bank according to its spread, and the depth, of underlying commercial business together with its perceived trading and dealing objectives. A bank's ability to access these various markets will be subject not only to the regulations of each market, but also to the controls and regulations of the country of the bank's domicile. Subject to these considerations, a bank may enter these markets merely to cover underlying commercial transactions, to cover its own internal funding or utilisation requirements, to hedge perceived exposure or net investment positions, as an investor or a broker, or to participate as a dealer, trader, arbitrager or speculator for its own account. Although an individual bank may undertake any one, a number, or all of these roles it is important to distinguish between them as each has a separate and distinct function and involves different risk/reward relationships and require different monitoring and control procedures.

In covering underlying commercial transactions a bank is responding to its clients' demands for money, foreign exchange, bullion and/ or commodities in the markets, either on a gross or net basis. These cover transactions are resultant from the services a bank provides to its customers. The bank will represent the interests of those of its clients who are the depositors (suppliers) and borrowers (users) of funds; the users and providers of foreign exchange, and the producers and users of bullion and commodities. The motives behind each individual client's transactions will be different. These may be derived from cash flows related to its client's domestic business transactions; be resultant from the finance of foreign trade; the desire to hedge; fund a foreign investment; consequent upon a dealing function; or, although most banks discourage clients entertaining such activity, be purely of a speculative nature. These clients may also include some correspondent banks who do not enter the markets themselves and therefore their transactions not only represent the interest of that bank, but also those of its clients.

As a commercial enterprise an international bank, like any other multinational corporation, generates cash flows and has structural and investment positions in a variety of currencies. These require funding, realisation, investing and hedging. In addition, liquidity is required to be maintained, reserves and MLAs established and inherent exposure risks which are created as a result of a variety of underlying commercial transactions, for example interest rate mismatches, all require to be covered.

Many major banks are prepared to be market-makers and quote two way prices within the interbank markets. However, many other banks are not market-makers but merely participants. Such banks may undertake transactions through deposit and foreign exchange brokers or on a direct basis with the market-making banks. Brokers provide facilities for any individual bank to support either side of the market, with the broker making prices, on the basis of a mix of individual quotations from several different principal banks. Although there are two segments to the various interbank markets, i.e. the market-making banks and the broker market, they are complementary and supportive of each other with market-making banks frequently buying and selling through, and supporting prices in, the broker market. In a highly liquid and volatile market, time is of the essence in conducting business and it is time-consuming for dealers to contact several different banks to endeavour to obtain the best rates available. Within this environment the intermediation of brokers is an essential ingredient to the success of dispersed markets by providing a central market place for price determination and in which principals can negotiate and arrange to transact business.

As will be appreciated from reading this chapter there are many hundred individual financial markets throughout the world. Each market has its own customs and practices, rules and regulations, and codes of conduct which may, or may not, be formally documented. It would be impossible for the authors to comment upon each individual market, but equally in considering these markets generalities would be of little value. Consequently, within the following chapters, the authors have based their comments on the custom and practice and rules and regulations which exist in specific countries.

London is the major international financial centre of the world, with more than 260 domestic and 335 foreign licensed banks and deposit taking institutions, authorised by the Bank of England to operate within the UK. Most of these entities have a presence in the City and its various markets. Among other things London is the major centre for international currency deposit and foreign exchange markets. Therefore, in considering both the interbank domestic and international currency deposit and foreign exchange markets the authors have been guided by the custom and practice of the London markets.

The interbank markets which have developed in London in over the counter options, forward rate agreements, interest rate and currency liability swaps are all relatively new. These markets have not been the subject of either legal precedent or previous custom and practice. In October, 1984 the British Bankers' Association (BBA) established, through its Foreign Exchange Committee, three working parties to liaise with market interests, including the Foreign Exchange and Currency Deposit Brokers Association, with a view to drawing up recommended terms and conditions for transactions in these markets. During the course of 1985 the BBA has published recommended terms and conditions for dealing in the London interbank markets in each of these instruments. These documents and their terms and conditions now constitute established custom and practice for the London interbank markets and have, as appropriate, been considered by the authors in developing these topics.

Futures and exchange traded currency option markets in financial instruments are also relatively recent innovations. However, in commodities these instruments do have long established antecedents in the United States. Therefore, in considering these markets, attention has been focused upon market custom, practice and regulation which appertain within the United States.

CHAPTER FIFTEEN

Euro and Domestic Interbank and Customer Deposit Operations and Procedures

Customer Deposit Operations

In the context of pricing structures, a bank's funding base has four major components:

- equity and capital debt.

- so called "free funds" which comprise current, impersonal and other non-interest bearing accounts, where the cost of funds is related to operating expenses.

- retail deposits taken at "counter" or "advertised" rates which may include interest bearing current account balances, call, notice, savings and fixed rate deposits.

- market related deposits which comprise all of those deposits taken at money market rates and at rates related thereto.

This latter class of deposit is frequently referred to as "market related", "market bid" or "wholesale" deposits. These funds, which may emanate from private clients, commercial entities, banks or other financial institutions, are usually the direct responsibility of a bank's treasury operations. Each deposit transaction is in itself a substantive contract for loan and deposit between two counterparties whereby one agrees to pay the other a sum of money – interest – in consideration for the use of an agreed amount of money – the principal. Increased volatility and high levels of interest rates related to many currencies in recent years have resulted in a substantial shift of funds from bank "free" and advertised rate deposits, to deposits at market related rates and other forms of direct investment. Consequently, market related deposits now often comprise the largest proportion of many individual banks' overall liability base. In considering market related transactions, it is important to distinguish between the "bank deposit" market, the "bank credit" market and the "interbank markets", which may exist in each country.

For competitive reasons, many banks are prepared to pay the finest interbank market rates to private and commercial clients for deposits, and also provide facilities at fine margins over interbank market rates. Although the practice is not always supported by the authors, it is also true that some banks often take client deposits above market rates and lend below market rates in the anticipation of receiving additional ancillary benefits; the point being that, when examined closely, in practice very few of these anticipated ancillary benefits appear to come to fruition. These activities between a bank and its clients are defined as the "bank deposit market" and the "bank credit market" respectively. These markets comprise normal bank/customer relationships in which substantive contracts of loan and deposit are arranged between banks and their clients. In the bank credit markets the bank is the lender and the customer the borrower and in the bank deposit market the bank is the borrower and the customer is the lender. The only difference between these contracts of deposit and other deposits which a bank may obtain or provide to its clients is the pricing structure upon which each transaction is based and often the method of access to the bank. Access may be directly into the treasury, through a bank's retail operations or through the intermediary services of a money broker. Where deposits of this nature are accepted, or placed, through or at a bank's retail outlets the treasury area usually provides a fine rate of interest linked to current market rates to the bank operating area. Thereafter it is left to the retail area concerned to take a margin on the deposit or loan by paying a finer, or charging a higher rate of interest in accordance with the client's status and the size of transaction. In pricing these transactions in retail outlets it should be remembered that the market rates quoted by a treasury are for "marketable amounts" as quoted within the interbank market. These are, for example, rates which are normally applied to deposits for a minimum amount of one million dollars or 500,000 sterling.

254

Although resistance may be felt it is expected, when dealing with customers in the bank credit and deposit markets, that formal documentation, mandates and, as appropriate, lending limits etc. will be obtained prior to transacting business. Where transactions emanate at, or through, other areas of a bank's operations it is often the responsibility of the originating area to care for these requirements. Thereafter, business will be conducted on a similar basis to transactions in the markets which are discussed later in this chapter.

To continue to attract corporate and private funds banks require to provide a wide choice for investors' needs in order to meet their particular investment criteria. Assuming the fundamental point that the investor is "comfortable" with obligations issued by the bank seeking funds in addition to the bank deposit market in which he may place deposits at call, on notice or on fixed terms, the investor might also be able to choose from the following list of investment instruments the most suitable for his particular investment criteria.

- Certificates of deposit – tap or tranche
  and bearer deposit notes – fixed rate or floating rate

- Bankers acceptances

- Commercial paper

- Repurchase agreements (REPOS) – fixed term
  – demand
  – day-to-day

- Eurobonds – fixed rate
  – floating rate
  – zero coupon
  – droplock

- Foreign bonds – fixed or floating rate

- Domestic debentures

- Equity

Introduction to the Euro and Domestic Currency Deposit Markets
As discussed in section 3 and Chapter 14, short-term money markets comprise a wide variety by both deposit type and investment instruments. The composition and depth of each country's domestic money markets differ considerably. Whilst the financial markets in many developing countries simply consist of a bank credit and bank deposit market together with an often restricted equity market, other countries have extensive, highly sophisticated and liquid short-term money markets and longer-term capital debt markets.

Within the large financial centres, particularly those of the major industrialised countries, domestic short-term money markets may typically include several secured and unsecured markets in both deposits and instruments. For example, they may include the bank credit market, the bank deposit market, commercial paper market, bankers acceptance market, sale and repurchase markets, broker loans market and the interbank deposit market. Secondary markets may also exist and include a certificates of deposit market, commercial paper market, bankers acceptance market, treasury bill market and local or municipal authority bond market. The foreign segments of short-term domestic markets may apply to all of these instruments or be more restrictive and limited to principal to principal transactions of a non-negotiable nature.

The various types and depths of market which are available in each country also differ. For example, in the UK short-term interbank sterling deposit market, funds are available for various periods of up to six months in a highly liquid and active market. Large amounts and volumes of business can also be undertaken in periods from six months to one year. However, within the United States the domestic US dollar interbank deposit market is primarily related to a substantial overnight federal fund market. There is a preference, in other periods, for the various paper and secured money markets which exist in that country. When compared with other financial markets the interbank market in deposits for longer periods is relatively small. Although Switzerland is a highly developed and sophisticated financial centre, the domestic Swiss Franc interbank market is negligible,

256

due to the excess liquidity which normally exists within the banking system in that country.

The short term euro-markets principally comprise currency deposit markets, with a large certificate of deposit market in US dollars and a small element of commercial paper. As at the 31st December 1984 the external assets and liabilities (euro-currencies) of reporting banks in industrial reporting countries, as published by the Bank for International Settlements (BIS) indicate the following size and currency comparison of these markets. These figures are expressed in the equivalent of billions of US dollars.

	Assets	Liabilities
US Dollars	778.20	892.70
Deutschemarks	117.00	113.80
Swiss Francs	51.80	56.20
Yen	22.10	21.70
Sterling	14.50	15.90
French Francs	9.20	10.30
Guilders	9.20	10.40
Others	37.90	35.00
	1,039.90	1,156.00

The Sterling Inter-Bank Deposit Market
The following provides an illustration of London interbank money market rates and discount houses deposit and bill rates at a time when they reflected a negative yield curve.

(Tables are shown overleaf)

	Interbank Sterling Certificate of Deposit	Interbank Deposits	Company Deposits	Market Deposits	Treasury (Buy)	Treasury (Sell)
Overnight	—	$12\frac{5}{8}$–$12\frac{1}{4}$	—	$12\frac{5}{8}$–$12\frac{1}{8}$	—	—
2 days notice	—	$12\frac{5}{8}$–$12\frac{1}{4}$	—	—	—	—
7 days notice	—	$12\frac{7}{8}$–$12\frac{5}{8}$	$12\frac{15}{16}$	$12\frac{5}{8}$	—	—
One month	$12\frac{3}{4}$–$12\frac{5}{8}$	$12\frac{13}{16}$–$12\frac{5}{8}$	$12\frac{7}{8}$	$12\frac{3}{8}$	$12\frac{5}{16}$	$12\frac{1}{4}$
Two months	$12\frac{9}{16}$–$12\frac{7}{16}$	$12\frac{5}{8}$–$12\frac{7}{16}$	$12\frac{3}{4}$	$12\frac{1}{4}$	$12\frac{1}{8}$	12
Three months	$12\frac{7}{16}$–$12\frac{5}{16}$	$12\frac{5}{8}$–$12\frac{7}{16}$	12	12	12	$11\frac{7}{8}$
Six months	12.00–$11\frac{7}{8}$	$12\frac{3}{8}$–$12\frac{3}{16}$	—	—	—	—
Nine months	$11\frac{15}{16}$–$11\frac{13}{16}$	$12\frac{3}{16}$–12.00	—	—	—	—
One year	$11\frac{13}{16}$–$11\frac{11}{16}$	$12\frac{1}{8}$–$11\frac{15}{16}$	—	—	—	—

	Eligible Bank (Buy)	(Sell)	Fine Trade (Buy)	Local Auth. negotiable bonds	Local Authority Deposits	Finance House Deposits
Overnight	—	—	—	—	$12\frac{3}{4}$	—
2 days notice	—	—	—	—	$12\frac{3}{4}$	—
7 days or	—	—	—	—	—	—
7 days notice	—	—	—	—	$12\frac{3}{4}$	—
One month	$12\frac{5}{16}$	$12\frac{1}{4}$	$13\frac{5}{16}$	$13\frac{1}{4}$–13	$12\frac{11}{16}$	$12\frac{3}{4}$
Two months	$12\frac{1}{8}$	$12\frac{3}{32}$	$12\frac{3}{4}$	$12\frac{7}{8}$-$12\frac{5}{8}$	$12\frac{9}{16}$	$12\frac{5}{8}$
Three months	12	$11\frac{31}{32}$	$12\frac{5}{8}$	$12\frac{3}{4}$–$12\frac{1}{2}$	$12\frac{1}{2}$	$12\frac{9}{16}$
Six months	$11\frac{1}{2}$	$11\frac{7}{16}$	$12\frac{1}{8}$	$12\frac{5}{8}$–$12\frac{3}{8}$	$12\frac{5}{16}$	$12\frac{5}{16}$
Nine months	—	—	—	$12\frac{3}{8}$–$12\frac{1}{8}$	—	$12\frac{3}{16}$
One year	—	—	—	$12\frac{1}{4}$–12	$11\frac{7}{8}$	$12\frac{1}{8}$
Two years	—	—	—	—	$11\frac{11}{16}$	—
Three years	—	—	—	—	$11\frac{5}{8}$	—
Four years	—	—	—	—	$11\frac{1}{2}$	—
Five years	—	—	—	—	$11\frac{1}{2}$	—

It is practice in both the sterling money markets and the eurocurrency markets for interest rates to be expressed as whole numbers, and fractions derivative from a sixty fourth, and they represent simple rates of interest per annum for a principal amount of loan and deposit.

The first two columns in the table illustrated, i.e. sterling certificates of deposit and interbank respectively, represent the rates of interest in the London interbank sterling certificate of deposit market and the London interbank sterling deposit market. Each of these columns provides two prices which are respectively the offered and bid prices. The offered price is the rate of interest at which the quoting bank is prepared to buy or lend, and bid is the rate at which it is prepared to issue or borrow. The offered price is higher than the bid price. In the London sterling and currency interbank markets the offered price is usually quoted first. If a banker is able and willing to deal simultaneously for the same amount and period at both of these rates the spread, i.e. difference between the two rates, will be his gross profit margin. In this context it is useful to note that if the loan or purchase of a CD is from an eligible bank name it would be nettable against a UK recognised bank's eligible liabilities for the purpose of calculating MLA requirements. These rates provide banks which require to borrow or lend funds with an indication of the interest rate they may be required to pay to cover the position by either issuing CDs or borrowing funds, i.e. the offered rate, and rate of return they may expect to receive from investing these funds either by buying a certificate of deposit or lending in the interbank market. It will be noted that the CD rates are lower than the deposit rates, for example the three month CD rate is quoted as $12\frac{7}{16} - 12\frac{5}{16}\%$ p.a. and the deposit rate at $12\frac{5}{8} - 12\frac{7}{16}\%$ p.a. This reflects the lower return a buying bank is willing to accept for the privilege of negotiability. This provides the purchasing/investing bank with available liquidity and capital profit opportunity which may be taken from future downward movements in interest rate levels. It is also relevant to note the difference in spread between the comparative offered and bid prices for CDs and for deposits, e.g. 1 month CDs $= \frac{1}{8} (12\frac{3}{4} - 12\frac{5}{8})$ compared with $\frac{3}{16} (12\frac{13}{16} - 12\frac{5}{8})$. This is indicative of the fact that a wider margin is required on deposits placed due to their permanent impact on balance sheet footings during their life. As CDs have the flexibility of resale to the buying bank and represent cheaper funds to the issuing bank, banks are prepared to trade them on finer margins. It is unlikely, these days, that many banks will be satisfied with a gross profit margin of only $\frac{3}{16}$% p.a. between loans and deposits and a dealer's expertise will be needed to manage his positions within authorised mis-matched exposure limits to achieve higher returns. The interbank overnight deposit market, call, 2 and 7 day notice funds do trade in normal circumstances on a $\frac{1}{8}$% margin due to their short-term impact on balance sheet footings.

Within the London markets the key interest rate is normally taken to be the three month interbank offered rate which should reasonably reflect the appropriate levels of minimum lending rate (MLR), i.e. banks monitor MLR against the 3 month interbank rate. Should these two rates move out of line, customers will arbitrage the banks by either drawing funds on their MLR related accounts and placing these funds in the interbank market when the interbank rates are higher than MLR, or borrowing funds in the interbank market to fund their borrowing requirements and repaying overdrafts when interbank rates are lower than MLR.

The level of local authority deposits, company deposits and market deposits generally dictates the interest rate that discount houses bid for deposits. These deposits and bank call and short notice money are required to fund their various instrument portfolios. The prices for market deposits refer to deposits which the discount houses take from banks on a secured basis. These deposits comprise the secured money that banks in the UK are required to maintain as part of their MLAs, a subject which was developed in Chapter 5. As banks must provide MLAs and are therefore a captive market together with the fact that these loans are secured, the bid price of $12\frac{1}{8}$% for market deposits is $\frac{1}{8}$% lower than the comparative rate of $12\frac{1}{4}$% in the interbank overnight deposit market.

It will also be noted that the prices quoted by discount houses for overnight sterling deposits indicate an offered and bid rate. Although discount houses primarily utilise the interbank market as a funding source for the inventory of money market instruments and investments which they carry, they do frequently have funds to lend due to their own trading activities, but more importantly they are the conduit between the Bank of England (the Bank) and the UK banking sector through which the Bank conducts its day-to-day discount window operations.

During periods of day-to-day money shortages within the banking system, or when the Bank wishes to influence interest rate levels downwards, the Bank may choose to provide funds to the system by discounting (buying) eligible assets from, or undertaking sale and repurchase agreements for eligible assets with, members of the LDMA who in turn on-lend these funds to the banking system. Conversely, in periods of surplus liquidity within the banking system, or if the Bank wishes to place upward pressure on rates, the Bank may choose to sell assets to the discount houses. Through this latter process, the Bank takes funds from the system and replaces them with assets which the discount houses have to fund by increasing their borrowing from the banking system. This places upward pressure on interest rates within the market. Eligible assets are those money market and treasury instruments which the Bank defines as being eligible for rediscount. With the exception of trade bills, all of the assets quoted above by the discount houses comprise eligible assets. The arrangements which the Bank of England imposes upon the discount houses are concerned with the general liquidity of the banking system and not with the distribution of surpluses and shortfalls of funds between banks. The distribution and re-cycling of surpluses and shortfalls between individual banks is the primary function of the sterling interbank deposit market and in particular the overnight segment of this market.

Treasury (buy) treasury (sell), eligible bank bills (buy) and eligible bank bills (sell), fine trade bills (buy) and local authority negotiable bonds reflect the closing bid and offered prices at which the discount houses, the market-makers in these instruments, are prepared to buy and sell. The primary and secondary markets which exist for sterling certificates of deposit, treasury bills, eligible bank bills (bankers acceptances), fine trade bills and local authority negotiable bonds and their pricing structures are discussed in section 3.

Domestic US Dollar Money Market Rates

The following are representative of key domestic money market rates as they may be quoted to banks in New York:

Federal Funds	Treasury Bills	Government Repos
Ask $7\frac{7}{8}$	3m 6.99–6.95	o/n 7.80–7.75
Bid $7\frac{3}{4}$	6m 7.12–7.08	1wk 7.70–7.50
Last $7\frac{7}{8}$	yr 7.15–7.11	2wk 7.55–7.37
		1mo 7.40–7.35

Dealer commercial paper bid	CDs bid	Bankers acceptances bank rates	Prime broker loans
30 7.50	Aug. 7.52	Aug. 7.45	
60 7.45	Sep. 7.52	Sep. 7.35	
90 7.40	Oct. 7.52	Oct. 7.35	
120 7.35	Nov. 7.54	Nov. 7.35	8.50–8.75
180 7.35	Dec. 7.55	Dec. 7.35	

The Federal fund rates are like the sterling rates quoted as fractions derivative from a sixty-fourth. The other rates are expressed in terms of percentages per annum in whole numbers and basis points. When examining other rate quotations in the US care should be exercised to establish if "decimal style" quotations are basis points. For example, within the bond market rates are expressed in this format when in fact the number to the right of the decimal point is the numerator of a fraction with a denominator of a sixty fourth.

The Federal fund rates comprise an overnight offered and bid price of $7\frac{7}{8} - 7\frac{3}{4}$ and inform us that the last trade was reported as executed at $7\frac{7}{8}$. Within the United States, individual banks deal directly with the Federal Reserve System and statutory reserves have historically comprised non-interest bearing deposits placed by banks with one of the 12 Federal Reserve Banks. "Federal Funds" is the term used to describe those funds which comprise the cleared balances of banks with the various Federal Reserve banks. The Federal fund market, which is principally an overnight market, is the market in which the banking sector adjusts reserve positions between those banks with excess requirements and those with shortfalls. It is effectively the equivalent of the overnight element of the London sterling interbank deposit market.

In the United States the Federal Reserve system conducts its day-to-day discount window operations on a direct basis with member banks and not through a selected area of the market. Discount window facilities are usually provided by sale and repurchase agreements covering eligible paper. Eligible paper comprises those instruments defined by the Federal Reserve Board as being acceptable for rediscount with Federal Reserve banks. Within the Federal Reserve rules, Federal fund transactions between banks are classified as non-deposit borrowings and as such are not subject to the requirements of Regulation D or Regulation Q. Also The Comptroller of the Currency has excluded these transactions from lending limits which are imposed on banks within the United States.

Substantial markets have developed in trading federal funds and many major US banks quote bid and offered prices for them irrespective of their own underlying position. Reserves are measured over reserve periods and banks frequently will be short of reserves during periods of high day-to-day Federal Fund rates with a view to "making up" their requirements during periods of excess liquidity and lower rates. The federal fund market is a bank-to-bank market with transactions being arranged either directly or through the services of an intermediary broker. Settlement is made through the Federal Reserve wire transfer system which provides facilities to transfer the funds between the counterparties' respective reserve accounts. Interbank transactions in federal funds may be undertaken on a secured or unsecured basis but the latter is the more common practice.

Only bid prices are quoted for commercial paper, CDs and bankers acceptances with the other side of the market being the brokers' and investment banks' clients with whom these instruments are placed.

The key indicator to prime rate levels in the US is usually taken to be the broker loan rate with any persistent increase or decrease in the perceived relationship between these two rates indicating a possible rise or fall in prime rates. Within the New York money markets, it will be noted that these key rates do not make reference to the interbank deposit market for periods other than overnight. All of the other prices indicated above comprise those funding instruments discussed in Section 3.

Other Domestic Market Rates

As indicated, both the nature and structure of the short-term money markets and in particular the interbank deposit markets, differ between London and New York. As illustrated by the following extract from the *Financial Times* of selected money rates. Similar disparities also exist with and between other interbank markets. It will be noted that the *Financial Times* does not follow London market convention and reports rates with the bid side first.

Money Rates

	Frankfurt	Paris	Zurich	Amsterdam
Overnight	5.45–5.55	$10\frac{1}{4}$	$1\frac{7}{8}$–$2\frac{1}{8}$	$6\frac{5}{8}$–$6\frac{3}{4}$
One month	5.45–5.60	$10\frac{3}{16}$–$10\frac{5}{16}$	$5\frac{1}{8}$–$5\frac{1}{4}$	$6\frac{5}{8}$–$6\frac{3}{4}$
Two months	5.45–5.60	$10\frac{1}{4}$–$10\frac{3}{8}$	—	—
Three months	5.50–5.65	$10\frac{1}{4}$–$10\frac{3}{8}$	$5\frac{3}{16}$–$5\frac{5}{16}$	$6\frac{5}{8}$–$6\frac{11}{16}$
Six months	5.55–5.70	$10\frac{3}{8}$–$10\frac{1}{2}$	—	$6\frac{5}{8}$–$6\frac{11}{16}$
Lombard	6.0	—	—	—
Intervention	—	$10\frac{1}{8}$	—	$6\frac{5}{8}$

	Tokyo	Milan	Brussels	Dublin
Overnight	6.09375	$14\frac{3}{8}$–$15\frac{1}{8}$	8.35	$11\frac{3}{4}$–12
One month	6.21875	$14\frac{1}{4}$–$14\frac{5}{8}$	$8\frac{5}{8}$–$8\frac{3}{4}$	$11\frac{3}{4}$–12
Two months	—	—	—	$11\frac{3}{4}$–12
Three months	6.28125	$14\frac{5}{8}$–15	$8\frac{3}{4}$–$8\frac{7}{8}$	$11\frac{3}{4}$–12
Six months	—	—	$8\frac{3}{4}$–9	$11\frac{3}{4}$–12

Both Frankfurt, Paris and Dublin are indicative of relatively liquid markets up to the six-month period. Zurich, Amsterdam, Tokyo, Milan and Brussels each reflect quotations for short-dated money together with quotations for overnight and one month together with a market in three-month money. However, of these centres only Amsterdam and Brussels quote rates for six-month money. The Lombard rate and intervention rates for Frankfurt, Paris and Amsterdam respectively, reflect the official upper limit at which the central bank of those countries may, if it so chooses, open its discount window. The fact that the bid side of the rate in Amsterdam is holding at this level, is a clear sign that the window is being activated. Money markets in Frankfurt are trading below the intervention level and within Paris rates have moved above the intervention level indicating that the central bank is not making funds available.

Euro-Currency Deposit Rates
The following is an extract from the table of interbank eurocurrency interest rates as shown in the *Financial Times*.

EURO-CURRENCY INTEREST RATES
(Market closing rates)

	Sterling	U.S. Dollar	Canadian Dollar	Dutch Guilder	Swiss Franc	D-Mark
Short-term	$12\frac{1}{4}$–$12\frac{5}{8}$	$7\frac{7}{8}$–8	$8\frac{3}{4}$–$9\frac{1}{4}$	$6\frac{5}{8}$–$6\frac{7}{8}$	$2\frac{1}{4}$–$2\frac{3}{4}$	$5\frac{3}{8}$–$5\frac{1}{2}$
7 days' notice	$12\frac{9}{16}$–$12\frac{11}{16}$	$7\frac{11}{16}$–$7\frac{13}{16}$	$8\frac{7}{8}$–$9\frac{1}{8}$	$6\frac{5}{8}$–$6\frac{7}{8}$	$3\frac{1}{8}$–$3\frac{3}{8}$	$5\frac{3}{8}$–$5\frac{1}{2}$
Month	$12\frac{5}{8}$–$12\frac{3}{4}$	$7\frac{5}{8}$–$7\frac{3}{4}$	9–$9\frac{1}{4}$	$6\frac{5}{8}$–$6\frac{3}{4}$	$5\frac{1}{8}$–$5\frac{1}{4}$	$5\frac{7}{16}$–$5\frac{9}{16}$
Three months	$12\frac{3}{8}$–$12\frac{1}{2}$	$7\frac{5}{8}$–$7\frac{3}{4}$	$9\frac{5}{16}$–$9\frac{9}{16}$	$6\frac{5}{8}$–$6\frac{3}{4}$	$5\frac{3}{16}$–$5.\frac{6}{16}$	$5\frac{7}{16}$–$5\frac{9}{16}$
Six months	$12\frac{1}{8}$–$12\frac{1}{4}$	$7\frac{13}{16}$–$7\frac{15}{16}$	$9\frac{5}{16}$–$9\frac{9}{16}$	$6\frac{9}{16}$–$6\frac{11}{16}$	$5\frac{1}{4}$–$5\frac{3}{8}$	$5\frac{1}{2}$–$5\frac{5}{8}$
One year	$11\frac{7}{8}$–12	$8\frac{3}{16}$–$8\frac{5}{16}$	$9\frac{7}{16}$–$9\frac{11}{16}$	$6\frac{9}{16}$–$6\frac{11}{16}$	$5\frac{1}{4}$–$5\frac{3}{8}$	$5\frac{9}{16}$–$5\frac{11}{16}$

	French Franc	Italian Lire	Belgian Franc Conv.	Fin.	Yen	Danish Krone
Short-term	$10\frac{1}{8}$–$10\frac{1}{4}$	$13\frac{1}{4}$–$14\frac{1}{4}$	$8\frac{3}{4}$–9	$8\frac{5}{8}$–$8\frac{7}{8}$	$6\frac{3}{16}$–$6\frac{5}{16}$	$9\frac{3}{4}$–$10\frac{1}{4}$
7 days' notice	$10\frac{1}{8}$–$10\frac{1}{4}$	$13\frac{1}{8}$–$14\frac{1}{8}$	$8\frac{3}{4}$–9	$8\frac{5}{8}$–$8\frac{7}{8}$	$6\frac{3}{16}$–$6\frac{5}{16}$	$10\frac{1}{4}$–$10\frac{3}{4}$
Month	$10\frac{5}{16}$–$10\frac{7}{16}$	$13\frac{5}{8}$–$14\frac{1}{8}$	$8\frac{3}{4}$–9	$8\frac{5}{8}$–$8\frac{7}{8}$	$6\frac{3}{16}$–$6\frac{5}{16}$	$9\frac{3}{4}$–$10\frac{1}{4}$
Three months	$10\frac{1}{2}$–$10\frac{5}{8}$	$13\frac{5}{8}$–14	$8\frac{3}{4}$–9	$8\frac{11}{16}$–$8\frac{15}{16}$	$6\frac{1}{4}$–$6\frac{3}{8}$	$9\frac{3}{4}$–$10\frac{1}{4}$
Six months	$10\frac{11}{16}$–$10\frac{13}{16}$	14–$14\frac{3}{8}$	$8\frac{3}{4}$–9	$8\frac{3}{4}$–9	$6\frac{1}{4}$–$6\frac{3}{8}$	$9\frac{5}{8}$–$10\frac{1}{8}$
One year	$11\frac{1}{8}$–$11\frac{3}{8}$	$14\frac{1}{4}$–$14\frac{3}{4}$	$9\frac{1}{8}$–$9\frac{3}{8}$	$9\frac{1}{8}$–$9\frac{3}{8}$	$6\frac{5}{16}$–$6\frac{7}{16}$	$9\frac{5}{8}$–$10\frac{1}{8}$

The principal eurocurrency markets comprise short-term interbank deposit markets. The interest rates quoted now require little explanation. Rates throughout indicate bid and offered prices respectively for each period in each currency. If we consider the rate structures of euro-sterling, with rates from one month to one year declining on the offered side from $12\frac{3}{4}$ through $12\frac{1}{4}$, $12\frac{1}{4}$ to 12, sterling has an inverted rate structure i.e. a reverse rate curve. This rate structure is indicative of, and reflects, the sentiment of the market at that time, anticipating a further decline in interest rate levels. In a flat market one would expect the euro-sterling and domestic sterling rates to be compatible as there is insufficient differential created through regulatory requirements to impact upon the rates. However, the euro-sterling markets are the major money markets in which external views are taken on the future of UK interest rates. The fact that the euro-sterling rates quoted above are below those previously discussed for the domestic sterling market indicates that euro rates are anticipating further declines within the domestic sterling rates. Conversely, if market sentiment was such as to indicate an underlying increase in UK rates, the euro rates would tend to lead the domestic rates to higher levels. Although the period interest rates within the Federal fund market have not been shown, one would normally expect to see the Federal fund rate $\frac{1}{16}\%$ lower than comparative rates within the euro markets thus reflecting the impact of the 3% non-interest bearing reserve requirements imposed within the US on interbank deposits taken from outside of the United States. The US dollar is flat up to three months and thereafter has a rising or positive interest rate curve from a three month rate of $7\frac{3}{4}$ through $7\frac{15}{16}$ at six months and $8\frac{5}{16}$ for one year. This reflects the sentiment that rates have levelled, for the time being, but the longer-term outlook may be upward.

US\$ CDs, SDRs and ECUs
The following represents prices for the London interbank market in US\$ certificates of deposits which were discussed in Chapter 10, together with SDRs and ECUs.

	$ Cert of Deposits	SDR Linked Deposits	ECU Linked Deposits
1 month	7.55–7.45	$8.00-7\frac{3}{4}$	$9\frac{1}{2}-9\frac{3}{8}$
2 months	7.55–7.45	$8.00-7\frac{3}{4}$	$9\frac{1}{2}-9\frac{3}{8}$
3 months	7.60–7.50	$8\frac{1}{16}-7\frac{13}{16}$	$9\frac{1}{2}-9\frac{3}{8}$
4 months	7.70–7.60	$8\frac{1}{8}-7\frac{7}{8}$	$9\frac{1}{2}-9\frac{3}{8}$
5 months	8.05–7.95	—	—
6 months	8.20–8.10	$8\frac{3}{8}-8\frac{1}{8}$	$9\frac{1}{2}-9\frac{3}{8}$

The SDR

The SDR (Special Drawing Right) is a liability of the IMF (International Monetary Fund) to its members and other specified international bodies, introduced in 1970 as an additional source of international liquidity. Its value was originally defined in terms of gold ($\frac{1}{35}$th of an ounce, equivalent to US$1 at the then prevailing rate). In 1974 it was linked to a basket of sixteen currencies, reduced at the beginning of 1981 to five. The SDR has also been used to denominate contracts in private markets, but its use has been considerably less widespread than that of the ECU.

With effect from 1st January 1981 the SDRs composition is defined as the sum of the following (in brackets: the percentage weightings as at 1st January, 1981):

US Dollars	0.54	(42)
Deutschemarks	0.46	(19)
British Pounds	0.071	(13)
Japanese Yen	34.00	(13)
French Francs	0.74	(13)

The ECU

Created by the European Economic Community (EEC) in 1978, to come into operation early the following year, the ECU is defined, like the EEC's earlier European Unit of Account (EUA), as the sum of fixed amounts of the currencies of EEC member states. The amounts are chosen to reflect the relative economic importance of the currencies concerned. The ECU's composition is reviewed every five years, but may be reviewed more frequently in certain circumstances.

Its main official uses are as the European Community's unit of account and in the European Monetary System (EMS), where central rates and margins against the ECU are set for all the currencies participating in the system. One of the most striking features of the ECU has been its growing use for pricing contracts in private markets, a process encouraged both by the European Commission and by some EEC member states.

With effect from 17th September 1984, the ECU's composition is defined as the sum of the following (in brackets: the percentage weightings as at 17th September 1984):

Deutschemarks	0.719	(32.00)
French Francs	1.31	(19.00)
British Pounds	0.0878	(15.00)
Italian Lire	140.00	(10.20)
Dutch Guilder	0.256	(10.10)
Belgium Francs	3.71	(8.20)
Danish Kroner	0.219	(2.70)
Greek Drachma	1.15	(1.30)
Irish Pounds	0.00871	(1.20)
Luxembourg Francs	0.14	(0.30)

Banks buy and sell, accept deposits, extend facilities, issue CDs in either or both SDRs and ECUs, and more recently issue travellers cheques denominated in ECUs.

As neither of these currencies has an individual country of domicile and therefore a natural clearing house, it was usual until recently to establish a common unit of account in which these deposits were received and paid (normally in US dollars) to avoid the necessity of receiving and paying each of their component parts. However, clearing facilities for ECUs are available in Brussels, London, Paris and Luxembourg, with the BIS in Basle planning to introduce similar facilities during 1986. Through cross currency calculations discussed in Chapter 16, it is relatively easy to establish an exchange rate for these units against any individual currency. Provided a dealer is aware, at the outset of a transaction, which major currency he will receive and is subsequently required to repay, appropriate interest rate levels and exchange rates for dealing in these units can be determined accurately through eurocurrency swap deposit techniques which are also discussed in detail in Chapter 16.

Finally, in considering all of the interbank rates above, it is worth mentioning that there is an element of tiering within these markets. Prime bank names are often able to attract funds below the offered price at any point in time, whereas lesser names or names associated with adverse country risk implications are often required to pay a premium.

The Interbank Markets
The interbank markets are, as the name implies, bank-to-bank markets. The interbank deposit markets are dispersed markets with business being transacted by dealers, usually situated in their own bank's dealing room conducting business with each other as principals.

The primary and historical purpose for which the interbank deposit market exists is to enable banks with negative cash flows to borrow from banks with positive cash flows on a day-to-day basis; thereby providing a conduit between the primary suppliers of funds and the ultimate users of funds. However, times have changed and the market has developed into a market place to which individual banks may resort for a variety of purposes. These may include the generation of funding requirements, utilisation of surplus deposits or internal resources, liquidity requirements, protection against interest rate sensitivity, the establishment of positions, taking views on future interest rate movements or simply acquiring interbank assets and liabilities for dealing purposes or balance sheet growth. In the market there is a chain of financial transactions which links the initial supplier and ultimate user of funds as maturity transformations take place and they pass from bank to bank. There exists an inter-relationship of country risk and credit risk considerations between banks in the market as a result, and a substantial amount of double accounting is called for if one wishes to assess the actual size of the market itself.

Interbank markets do not create additional funds, they merely redistribute funds which are already in the system between the supplier and user. The only factor which will affect the supply of funds is the official movement of funds between the private and public sector of an economy. This may result from central bank discount window activities, official monetary policy requiring more reserves, through fixed requirements or substantial flotations of public issues within the private sector. However, large amounts of money do move between the domestic and international markets, and also between the short-dated money markets and capital investment markets.

Major banks in the market quote two-way prices for interbank deposits and trade thereon. Other banks are more selective and will quote competitive two-way prices but otherwise are not market makers, but merely participants within the markets functioning through money brokers or on a direct basis with a market-making bank. Brokers provide facilities for any individual bank to support either side of the market with the broker making the prices on the basis of a mix of individual quotations from several different participating banks. Although there are two segments to the interbank deposit markets – the market-making banks and the broker market – they are integrated markets with market-making banks continuously using and supporting prices in the broker market. In both markets banks trade on a principal to principal basis.

Many individual banks and brokers communicate their rates by contributing to Reuters, Telerate or other similar automated media. However, these rates can only be taken as indication rates, and firm prices can only be obtained by contacting the quoting bank or broker either by telephone, telex or through other forms of communication or dealing service. Although automated media is an important source of data, a dealer's primary forms of communication for keeping in touch with markets are direct telephone lines to brokers, banks, internal Group dealing centres and other major users and suppliers of money. Most major dealing rooms have loud-speaker systems which are fed from brokers' offices and facilitate an instant awareness of prices as communicated internally within those offices. As already, discussed business is conducted through two-way prices comprising offered and bid rates.

It may be helpful to outline briefly the mechanism of price determination through the process of bid and offered prices in the deposit markets. As discussed elsewhere in this publication there are many factors which influence the general direction of prices and interest rate levels. It is therefore imperative for dealers to be aware instantly of all events that may impact upon rates immediately they happen or as soon as the information becomes available. Each dealing room is normally equipped with the latest automated and electronic technology to facilitate such communication and a constant flow of data and key monetary indicators are provided to dealers through these facilities. Where the market in general anticipates a rising rate trend, the majority of players within that market will wish to contain the placement of funds in short-dated periods. Conversely the borrowers will be endeavouring to take deposits for as long a period as possible. Within this scenario it is usual for interest rates for short-dated periods to decline further whereas the longer-dated periods increase disproportionately. Where the market anticipates declining rates, emphasis will be placed upon placing funds for as long a period as possible and borrowing in the short-dated funds with a view to locking in profits after the expected rate movements have taken place. This increases the cost of short-dated funds but places increased downward pressure on rates for longer-dated funds. In general, a dealer's success and expertise can be measured by his ability to anticipate these events and their results rather than simply being reactive to them. Within the deposit markets the primary consideration, on a day-to-day basis, is supply and demand and this is particularly relevant to day-to-day money as each bank must balance its cash positions. Supply and demand will determine who controls the market. Where there is a shortage in the market the lenders will control the movement of rates in an upward direction by their supply of money to the market and the market will work in the opposite way when the supply of funds exceeds the demand. Although it was previously stated that in normal conditions a $\frac{1}{8}\%$ p.a. spread between overnight sterling offered and bid prices was usual, in times of substantial shortages the bid rate has moved up to hundreds of percent per annum with no offers forthcoming.

The London Interbank Sterling and Currency Deposit Markets – Practice and Procedure

The contracts of loan and deposit arranged within the interbank market are little different from any other form of deposit except that they are transacted between two banks. The salient features are:

- Principal amount
- Interest rate
- Period
- Value Date

- Principal amount –
  Through market practice there are minimum quotation quantities established within each market and in each currency – often referred to as "marketable sums". These vary from market to market. The minimum quote quantity is the minimum principal amount that one counterparty would expect the other to agree, immediately the type of transaction and interest rate had been established. Within the London sterling and currency deposit markets, the standard quote quantities may be illustrated by the following:

	Amount
Sterling	500,000
US Dollars	1,000,000
Deutschemarks	5,000,000
Yen	500,000,000
Swiss Francs	5,000,000

These are minimum quotation amounts and counterparties are free to deal in larger amounts. Within a market environment this would be achieved by asking for an indication of the amount prior to indicating whether the bank asking for a firm quotation was a borrower or lender. The phraseology would be "in what size" or "to what amount". The response may be specific or general as the quoting bank will not wish to disclose its position to the other participant in the market. The response may be, for example in the case of sterling, up to 5 million or a more general "in size" response indicating a much larger amount. When dealing through a broker the enquiring bank may ask specifically for an indication of size on either the offered or bid rate in the knowledge that its position will not be divulged indiscriminately by the broker.

- Interest Rates –
The interest rates quoted are expressed as simple interest per annum on the principal amounts for the period of fixed rate contracts of loan and deposit. Interest rate changes on call or short notice accounts are subject to agreement between the counterparties to the transactions. Interest rate changes may be originated by either the borrowing or lending bank and, for notice in respect of call, one and two days notice must be given before twelve noon on the date of such notice and for notice periods of longer duration before 4.30 p.m. Where deals are concluded through a broker, arrangements for rate changes would also normally be made through that broker. On fixed term deposits for periods up to one year, interest is payable at maturity. On deposits in excess of one year interest would be paid annually and at maturity, subject to any special arrangements. Within the interbank markets sterling is quoted on the basis of a 365 day year, whereas all other major currencies are quoted on the basis of a 360 day year.

- Periods –
Unless otherwise agreed, rates are quoted on the basis of straight dates for the periods concerned irrespective of the number of days. For example a three month deposit with a start date of 25th July would have a maturity date of the 25th October. If the 25th of October were a weekend or a holiday, the maturity date would be the following working day. Consequently a three month deposit may be for an underlying period of anything from 89 days through to 97. Notice in respect of call, one and two days notice money must be given before twelve noon on the date of

such notice and for notice periods of longer duration before 4.30 p.m.

- Value dates –
  The value date of a transaction is determined by the currency traded. As the primary purpose of domestic markets is to redistribute surpluses and shortfalls within the system between banks, domestic sterling (as in all other domestic markets) is traded on a same day value basis, i.e. for settlement today. In the London interbank currency market, the normal quotation is for two day spot value, i.e. the second business day following the trade date although the same day, and one day value, transactions may be undertaken. Funds are, of course, repayable with interest on their maturity date with good value.

A fundamental prerequisite for dealing with any particular name in these markets is to know of the existence of a credit limit being available for that purpose. When dealing through a broker the name of the lender will only be disclosed after the borrower's name has been accepted by the lender. The borrower does have the right to refuse to take funds from any particular lender or buyer with whom he does not wish to do business, provided that he is prepared to accept at that time sums up to the same amount and at the same price from an alternative acceptable name immediately shown to him by the broker.

The modus operandi for negotiating, and subsequently processing, a deposit transaction is indicated below. These procedures are common to all types of traded instruments and therefore they will not be repeated in full in subsequent chapters.

Within the parameters explained above, a dealer will negotiate and transact a deal either by telephone, telex, Reuters, or other similar dealing services. During these negotiations and prior to agreeing a transaction, a dealer will ensure that, as appropriate, all necessary credit control approvals are available and also that any trade undertaken will not exceed agreed dealing limits.

Let us assume that on the 29th July a bank – the "lending bank" has an interest to enter the market to lend US\$1 million for six months, value the 31st July, and the US\$ interest rates are $8\frac{5}{16} - 8\frac{3}{16}$. There is a surplus in the market and prices are only firm on the bid side. The dealer may decide to place these funds at the bid price of $8\frac{3}{16}$ for six months. He would enter the market through a broker to enquire of the rates and would be quoted $\frac{5}{16} - \frac{3}{16}$ but only firm at $\frac{3}{16}$, the broker and dealer both being aware that the whole number at that time is 8. As the response was firm at $\frac{3}{16}$ the dealer "gives" at $\frac{3}{16}$ and the deal is done for one million dollars. The broker is at this point committed. Otherwise he would have to find a borrower at the price and will come back to the lending bank with a principal bank name (which normally he knows is acceptable to that bank). Subject to verifying that a credit limit is available for the borrowing bank to cover this transaction, the lending bank agrees to the transaction and, if the name provided is not acceptable, the broker must provide another name. The value date of the transaction is 31st July (spot value) and the period six months; therefore a maturity date of 31st January (a period of 184 days) is automatically agreed.

Interest would be calculated on the transaction as:

$$\frac{\text{PRT}}{\text{basis days} \times 100} = \text{Interest}$$

i.e. $\dfrac{1{,}000{,}000 \times 8.1875 \times 184}{100 \times 360} = \text{US\$41{,}847.22}$

Immediately upon transacting the trade, each dealer will enter the transaction in his position records and record the necessary details for recording and processing purposes. This will be achieved either manually through the preparation of a dealing slip or as increasingly practised, by direct input to a computer system. For purposes of illustration dealing slips are utilised:

Examples of deal slips raised by the borrowing bank and the lending bank respectively are on the following pages.

Example of a deal slip raised by the borrowing bank

TREASURY DIVISION

DATE 29.7.85

DEPOSIT

DEAL TYPE **4**

BROKER A A A   LIEN

CUSTOMER NAME: LENDING BANK

VALUE DATE: 31.7.85

ULT RISK DATE

MATURITY DATE: 31.1.86

CURRENCY	AMOUNT	INTEREST RATE	360	365	INTEREST AMOUNT
USD	1,000,000.00	8.1875%	X		USD 41,847.22

SPECIAL INSTRUCTIONS

INTEREST FREQUENCY   INTEREST DATE

CALL/CCA   NUMBER

RAISED BY

CUSTOMER'S CORRESPONDENT

FM 8580 (2/85)

The dealers may also exchange payment (settlement) instructions, through the broker. This latter information may not of necessity be recorded at the time of a transaction and may be the function of subsequent conversations between support areas in the respective banks. Where the counterparty bank is in another country this will normally be achieved through the broker, and where the counterparty bank is in the same country, directly with the bank concerned.

The relative dealing slips, copies related thereto, or computer data will immediately pass to the processing area of the bank, where duplicate position records will be maintained with which to agree the dealer's positions (in this instance the US dollar cash positions). The position records will detail all maturing and new deals and will also anticipate/diarise for their appropriate dates all maturing deals. During the course of each business day confirmations will be produced and despatched by each principal to each principal with whom trades have been undertaken. As this trade was undertaken through a broker, the broker will also confirm the deal to both principals. Examples of these certificates are shown on the following three pages.

Example of a deal slip raised by the lending bank

TREASURY DIVISION   DATE 29.7.85

ADVANCE

CUSTOMER NAME	VALUE DATE
BORROWING BANK	31.7.85

DEAL TYPE

1 LOANS
2 INVESTMENTS
3 BILLS & CERTIFICATES

`1`

BROKER | A | A | A |

ULT RISK DATE	MATURITY DATE
–	31.1.86

CURRENCY	AMOUNT	INTEREST RATE	360	365	INTEREST AMOUNT
USD	1,000,000.00	8.1875%	X		USD 41,847.22

SPECIAL INSTRUCTIONS

BORROWING BANK'S PAYMENT INSTRUCTIONS

INTEREST FREQUENCY   INTEREST DATE

CALL/CCA   NUMBER

RAISED BY

NEW CUSTOMER'S CORRESPONDENT

MATURING CUSTOMER'S CORRESPONDENT

Example confirmation to the borrowing bank from the lending bank

Confirmation

LENDING BANK

To.

BORROWING BANK

DATE 29.7.85

OUR CONTRACT No. 100000

VALUE 31.7.85

MATURITY DATE   31.1.86

WE CONFIRM HAVING ADVANCED TO YOU

CURRENCY	AMOUNT	RATE	INTEREST AMOUNT
USD	1,000,000.00	8.1875%	USD 41,847.22

360/~~365~~ DAY YEAR

TO BE PAID TO:

BORROWING BANK
NEW YORK CORRESPONDENT

BY

LENDING BANK
NEW YORK CORRESPONDENT

BROKER NAME: BROKER

THIS CONFIRMATION REQUIRES AN AUTHORISED SIGNATURE   ______________________________

Upon receipt of each other's confirmation and that of the broker, each bank will immediately verify the details with their own accounting records. If terms and conditions differ from normal market custom, the dealer should annotate such information on the deal slip and this should be recorded in the support areas. Thereafter it should be ensured that the inward confirmation from the counterparty bank does not incorporate any clauses in the agreement which are contrary

Example confirmation to the lending bank from the borrowing bank

Confirmation

BORROWING BANK

To.

LENDING BANK

DATE   29.7.85

OUR CONTRACT No.   100000

VALUE   31.7.85

MATURITY DATE   31.1.86

WE CONFIRM HAVING TAKEN FROM YOU A DEPOSIT

CURRENCY	AMOUNT	RATE	INTEREST AMOUNT
USD	1,000,000.00	8.1875%	USD 41,847.22

360/~~365~~ DAY YEAR

TO BE PAID TO

BORROWING BANK
NEW YORK CORRESPONDENT

BY

LENDING BANK
NEW YORK CORRESPONDENT

BROKER NAME: BROKER

THIS CONFIRMATION REQUIRES AN AUTHORISED SIGNATURE

to common market practice. Subsequently the transactions will be accounted and recorded and interest accruals recorded in accordance with the accounting practices discussed in Chapter 32. Upon maturity the above settlement and confirmation procedures will be reversed for principal plus interest. It is pertinent to mention that there is an increasing tendency within the markets for unsigned computer produced confirmations to be utilised; unsigned confirmations are, of

281

Example of brokers confirmation to the lending bank

BROKERS NOTE

BROKERS NAME	TYPE OF DEAL:- CURRENCY ADVANCE
	DATE:- 29.7.85 REF:-
LENDING BANK NAME	BORROWING BANK NAME
AMOUNT:- US$1,000,000.00	FROM:- 31.7.85 - 31.1.86
INTEREST RATE:- 8.1875%	
PAYMENT INSTRUCTIONS:-	BORROWING BANK NEW YORK CORRESPONDENT
BROKERAGE:- US$102.22	

Example of brokers confirmation to the borrowing bank

BROKERS NOTE

BROKERS NAME	TYPE OF DEAL:- CURRENCY DEPOSIT
	DATE:- 29.7.85 REF:-
BORROWING BANK NAME	LENDING BANK NAME
AMOUNT:- US$1,000,000.00	FROM:- 31.7.85 - 31.1.86
INTEREST RATE:- 8.1875%	
PAYMENT INSTRUCTIONS:-	BORROWING BANK NEW YORK CORRESPONDENT
BROKERAGE:- US$102.22	

---

course, binding. In these instances it is customary to obtain a suitable indemnity from the issuing bank re errors, omissions etc. Where discrepancies are noted it is essential that they are immediately clarified and corrected.

At the end of each day each dealer will verify that all transactions undertaken have been processed correctly. This will be achieved either by telephone confirmation, from telex backing sheets or hard copies taken from a computerised dealing system (Reuters). Assuming all deals have been recorded and the day's cash position covered within perceived criteria, a dealer should have no further involvement with a transaction.

Where the transaction is for a foreign currency (as in the example) on or prior to the value date, payment instructions will be despatched by the lending bank to its correspondent bank to effect payment to the borrowing bank's correspondent bank with good value on the value date, alternatively where a transaction is in local currency arrangements will be made to pay either directly or indirectly on the value date. In London this is normally achieved by bankers payments being despatched between relative counterparties or, through the Clearing House Automated Payment System. Within New York, overseas banks will normally make US dollar payments through the Clearing House Interbank Payment System (CHIPS). On the transaction each of the parties will be required to pay brokerage and under arrangements extant at the time of this publication this would be calculated at a rate of .02% p.a., an amount of US$102.22. Both parties would be required to settle the brokerage upon receipt of the brokers statement as at the end of July.

Forward/Forward Transactions
Although with the introduction of forward rate agreements, which are discussed in Chapter 20, they are now less common, it was quite common for dealers to arrange forward forward deposit transactions in the interbank markets. This expression refers to transactions arranged for value some time in the future. For example a dealer may have made a six-month loan and obtained a three-month deposit which he desires to hold as funding for the first three months and

establish a rate now for funding the second three-month period of the loan. The pricing mechanism for this type of transaction constitutes the base of the formula for pricing forward rate agreements and futures and therefore requires consideration. The formulae are:

Where Rff = Forward forward interest rate
     R1 = Rate first period
     R2 = Rate second period
     T1 = Time first period
     T2 = Time second period
     B = Period basis i.e. 360 day or 365 days

given R1, R2, T1, T2

$$Rff = \frac{(R2 \times T2) - (R1 \times T1)}{\left[1 + \left(\frac{R1 \times T1}{100 \times B}\right)\right] \times (T2 - T1)}$$

given Rff, R1, T1, T2   using Tff = (T2 - T1)

$$R2 = \left(\frac{Rff \times Tff}{T2}\right) \times \left[1 + \left(\frac{R1 \times T1}{100 \times B}\right)\right] + \frac{R1 \times T1}{T2}$$

given Rff, R2, T1, T2   using Tff = (T2 - T1)

$$R1 = \frac{(R2 \times T2) - (Rff \times Tff)}{T1 \times \left[1 + \left(\frac{Rff \times Tff}{100 \times B}\right)\right]}$$

Swap Deposits

A common dealing technique within a bank's dealing and trading operation is the swap deposit which is often referred to as "currency swap" and "currency switch". The purpose of this technique is to fund a lending in one currency from deposits in another currency, by

284

covering the exchange rate risk through the foreign exchange market. This technique is discussed in greater detail in Chapter 16 but the principles can be illustrated by a simple example.

Let us assume a dealer quoted a price of $5\frac{5}{16} - 5\frac{3}{16}$ to a customer and received a DM10 million deposit for 6 months. The dealer did not have a requirement for DM and could only lend them in the market at the same rate of $5\frac{3}{16}$. There would be no profit in the transaction and processing costs would be incurred. If the dealer placed the funds in the market through a broker, brokerage charges would also be incurred. In addition the transaction would adversely affect the return on asset figures and impact upon balance sheet ratios. Consequently the dealer may consider alternative strategies for utilising these funds and may find that the dollar dealer requires to fund a eurodollar loan for the same period with market rates quoted at $8\frac{5}{16} - 8\frac{3}{16}$. The dealers may examine the possibility of swapping the DMs into US$ by selling spot and buying forward. Let us assume a spot middle rate of US$/DM of 2.8875 and a forward rate of 2.8455. (The basis for calculating forward rates is also discussed in detail in Chapter 16.) From the above we can calculate that:

Cost of DM 10 million for 180 days @ $5\frac{3}{16}$

$$\frac{PRT}{100 \times 360} = \text{Interest}$$

$$\frac{DM\ 10\ \text{million} \times 5.1875 \times 180}{100 \times 360} = \text{DM } 259,375.00$$

Therefore, principal plus interest at maturity = DM 10,259,375.

Based on the current spot market rate of 2.8875, the dealer could sell DM10 million for US$3,463,203.46.

Based on the forward rate for 180 days, he could simultaneously buy DM10,259,375 @ 2.8455 against US$ = 3,605,473.55 to realise his DM principal plus interest at maturity.

Therefore, the interest the dealer requires to break even on his DM deposit is

$$
\begin{array}{ll}
& \text{US\$3,605,473.55} \\
\text{Less} & \underline{\text{US\$3,463,203.46}} \\
& \text{US\$ \ 142,270.09}
\end{array}
$$

From the simple interest formula

$$
R = \frac{I \times 100 \times 360}{PT}
$$

$$
R = \frac{142,270.09 \times 100 \times 360}{3,463,203.46 \times 180} = 8.216\%
$$

Therefore the DM dealer can lend US\$ to the US dollar dealer at 8.216% which is better than $8\frac{5}{16}\%$ (8.3125) which the dollar dealer would require to pay for dollars in the market. A net improvement between them of .09625% p.a.

The above calculations may be expressed as the following arbitrage formula which is explained in Chapter 16.

$$
\text{Interest Difference} = \frac{\text{Swap} \times 36000}{\text{No. days} \times \text{Spot}} + \frac{\text{Euro \$} \times \text{Swap}}{\text{Spot}}
$$

Codes of Conduct and Market Practice
The code of conduct and market practice for trading in the London interbank sterling and currency deposit markets are considered in conjunction with those relating to the interbank foreign exchange market in Chapter 16.

CHAPTER SIXTEEN

Foreign Exchange Markets – Practices and Procedures

Foreign Exchange Markets

Collectively the interbank foreign exchange markets probably constitute in turnover value the largest market in the world. Apart from official holidays and week-ends the markets operate 24 hours a day. They comprise hundreds of foreign exchange dealers throughout the world, turning over in total the equivalent of billions of dollars in foreign exchange each day through a network of brokers, telephone lines, telexes and dealing services. With modern technology and communications networks it is possible, but not often practised, for a dealing room to trade actively around the clock. In theory, from the close of the European markets business can be transacted in New York, the West Coast of America, New Zealand, Australia, Tokyo, the Far and Middle East markets and back into Europe.

Exchange rates move continuously and one financial centre interacts with the next. Some are more active and liquid than others – the European markets and in particular London, still maintain their lead in this regard. Whilst the media in each financial centre will quote closing prices, these are merely a reflection of exchange rates at a point in time and these prices will instantly change as centres in a different time zone merge at the start, during and at the end of each centre's working day. The somewhat erratic and subsequent explosive development of the foreign exchange markets during the last decade; the structure of the markets; the speed at which trades are transacted; the value of business undertaken; the terminology which has evolved, together with dealing jargon utilised, have all combined to surround the foreign exchange market with an aura of mystique.

The purpose of, and a bank's operations in, these markets are relatively simple to understand. However, the risks which are inherent in conducting business therein must, as explained in Chapter 2, be carefully assessed, monitored and controlled. An inherent risk of dealing and transacting any form of business in these markets is the elapse of time between the opening and closing of positions. Substantial losses have been incurred resultant from activities in these markets by some banks. For example Bankhaus Herstatt, the Lugano branch of Lloyds International and Franklin National each take their place in the annals of the foreign exchange markets.

The foreign exchange markets are interbank markets in which banks trade with each other to cover and anticipate the foreign exchange requirements of their customers and also to trade for their own account. As with the interbank deposit markets discussed in the previous chapter, banks transact business on a principal to principal basis. These transactions may be arranged directly on a bank to bank basis or by using the intermediary services of a foreign exchange broker. Most major banks function as market-makers in various financial centres of the world and are continuously prepared to make two way prices for the major traded currencies. However, within each financial centre the main currency traded is usually the currency of domicile of that country against the US dollar. For example, in London sterling/dollar and in Frankfurt dollar/deutschemark.

Almost all trade and capital movements which cross international borders give rise to the right to a foreign currency asset or create a foreign currency liability. Subject to regulatory constraint these currencies may be retained in that currency and placed or borrowed in the eurocurrency or domestic markets for that currency or, alternatively, as is the most common practice, such currencies are bought and sold for the home currency of the beneficial owner.

Value Dates
Foreign exchange comprises both cash and forward transactions. The date upon which a foreign exchange transaction is agreed is referred to as the deal or dealing date and the date upon which settlement is to be effected is the value date. A good value date must be a day upon which banks are open for business in both countries of the underlying currencies. Within the international foreign exchange markets it is accepted practice that settlement will be by way of good value cleared funds.

288

Within the context of the international foreign exchange markets the principal rate of exchange for any currency in terms of another is the *spot rate*. The spot rate relates to deals transacted with a value date two business days after the deal date. Forward rates (i.e. transactions with a value date after the spot value date), same day rates (i.e. the value and deal dates are the same) and one day value rates (i.e. value day following deal date) are a function of interest rate differentials upon the spot rate. One day value or "Tom Next" (tomorrow/next day) as they are commonly referred to and spot value transactions are effectively short dated forward deals.

A past-value foreign exchange transaction does not create an asset or liability; it merely exchanges an asset or liability in one currency for an asset or liability in another currency at an agreed rate of exchange. However, until they come into value forward foreign exchange contracts are contingent assets and liabilities.

Foreign Exchange Exposure

A bank's outright foreign exchange exposure or, as it is more commonly referred to, outright foreign exchange position, in any specific currency is represented by the net difference between both in-value and not-in-value assets and liabilities in that currency irrespective of the value date of each transaction. Where assets exceed liabilities, a bank is said to hold a long position in that currency and conversely where liabilities exceed assets, a short position. Where assets equal liabilities the position is said to be square. As a long currency position will, in accounting terms, represent a short base currency position and a short currency position a long base currency position, it is normal practice for overall foreign exchange exposure in all currencies to be measured in terms of the base currency unit. Although the method of measurement of overall exposure differs from bank to bank, it is the authors' opinion that this exposure should for internal control purposes be measured as the aggregate of the base currency equivalent of all foreign currency positions, irrespective of whether they are long or short. However, it is recognised that in many banks this measurement is based on the net base currency equivalent of long and short currency positions, with cross currency positions being perceived to compensate each other.

As discussed in Chapter 2 and developed in more detail in Chapter 32, the composition of a bank's total foreign exchange position frequently comprises transactions established for several different purposes and it is therefore necessary for both management and control purposes to segregate a bank's dealing positions from those relating to its internal structural or hedging requirements with each being subject to separate measurement and accounting procedures.

Forward Exchange Positions

Although a bank may maintain a square or near square foreign exchange position in each currency traded and thereby be protected against subsequent movements in foreign exchange rates, care must also be exercised to properly manage, and control the forward maturity ladder of not-in-value deals. Where not-in-value currency purchases and sales do not equate to each other on a daily basis a bank's dealer will at maturity be required to fund or utilise shortfall/surplus currency funds either through the currency deposit or foreign exchange swap market at the then prevailing rates of interest. As a consequence each forward mis-matched position represents a potential interest rate risk which must be controlled and monitored in a similar manner as mis-matched deposit positions. In considering any form of market related activity it is important to distinguish between an interest rate risk and a capital risk. The former is based upon a return per annum, the latter on price movement and there is not an effective hedging correlation between the two.

Foreign Exchange Rates

Whilst the terms "buy" and "sell" are used within the foreign exchange markets, they are to some extent an anachronism and can be misleading. Every foreign exchange transaction is in itself the purchase of one currency and the sale of another. For example, in simple terms if one buys US dollars against sterling, one has simultaneously sold sterling.

A foreign exchange rate is an expression, as a ratio, of the value of one currency in terms of another currency and it is important to be punctilious in the manner in which these terms are communicated. The first currency of a quotation comprises the subject currency and the second is its value expressed in terms of the second currency. For example a rate for one pound sterling expressed in terms of US dollars is written £/US$1.40 conversely a rate for US$/£ is a rate for one US dollar expressed in sterling and would read US$/£0.7143 (1/1.40).

The significance of the United States dollar in terms of foreign exchange rates since 1944 was mentioned in the opening chapter and it is common practice within the international foreign exchange markets to relate the rate of exchange for all major currencies to or against United States dollars. The most common format is to express a currency as a ratio to one United States dollar unit. However, historically sterling has been quoted in terms of United States dollars to a one pound sterling unit and this practice continues. Similarly, through their previous association with the Scheduled Territories, this format of quotation against the US dollar has been extended to some other currencies. The Australian dollar, New Zealand dollar, South African rand and Irish pound are all quoted in this manner, with the Indian rupee being quoted in the same way but from a subject currency unit of 100 rupees. There are also many currencies which through traditional and historic links continue to be quoted in terms of one unit of sterling or other currency, for example, Malawi kwacha, Kenya shilling, Seychelle rupee, Zimbabwe dollar, Ghana cedi, Gambian dalasi, Botswana pula. The Tanzanian shilling and Zambia kwacha are however often quoted against one unit of either the pound sterling or the United States dollar. Whilst it is relatively easy to recognise and remember the basis of quotations in the major currencies, care must be exercised when dealing with an unfamiliar currency quotation. As explained in Chapter 14 the major international foreign exchange markets are limited to Deutschemarks, Sterling, Yen, Swiss Francs and the US Dollar and discussion within this chapter will be principally concerned with those currencies. Subject to any official support or intervention the rates of exchange between these five currencies are determined by market forces without any official lower or upper ceilings. Although each of the major currencies is quoted to or against the US dollar it is a mistake within the environment of a floating rate structure to measure the strength or weakness of a currency against the US dollar or indeed any other single currency unit.

Between the date of the Bretton Woods agreement in 1944 and the Smithsonian Agreement in 1971, the US dollar provided a reasonable bench-mark against which changes in the value of other currencies could be evaluated. However, since 1971 the markets have been subjected to an increasing range of often localised influences and larger movements in individual rates have been the norm. Consequently, in order to assess the overall relative strength of any individual currency, increasing use is now made of comparisons with a basket of currencies, each of which is weighted to reflect its relative importance.

The Sterling Exchange Rate Index, published daily in the Financial Times, is based on a basket of 17 currencies and was first published in its present form in 1981, the index being based upon an average of daily closing rates in 1975. The index is calculated by the Bank of England nine times each day. A similar index exists to evidence the movement of sterling against those eight currencies participating in the EMS exchange rate system.

Foreign exchange rate levels are subject to many monetary, economic and political factors. Historically a country's balance of payments and capital flows have been key influences upon exchange rate levels. However, with the abolition of exchange control and a freedom in most major industrial countries for its residents and non-residents to freely borrow or lend in, and buy or sell both domestic and foreign currencies, speculative influences are now undoubtedly a dominant factor in the determination of exchange rates.

Spot Rates
In the foreign exchange markets a full quotation, or a two way price, as it is often referred to, has a bid and offered side. On the basis of the quotations made the bid side is the rate of exchange at which the maker of the quotation will buy the subject currency, the offered side is the rate at which he will sell the subject currency. The difference between the bid and offered side is the "spread". This can be illus-

trated by the following examples of a bank's spot rate quotations between the US dollar and Sterling, Deutschemark, Yen and Swiss Franc.

	Quotation	*Bid*	*Offered*	*Spread*
£St/US$	1.4440–45	1.4440	1.4445	5 points
US$/DM	2.6750–60	2.6750	2.6760	10 points
US$/SF	2.1900–10	2.1900	2.1910	10 points
US$/Yen	232.65–75	232.65	232.75	10 points

In considering the implication of the above rates it must be remembered that:

i) Sterling (the subject currency) is quoted in terms of the US dollar, whereas the others are in currency amounts in terms of one US dollar (the subject currency).

ii) Every rate of exchange whether bid or offered is in itself the "price" for the purchase of one currency against the sale of another.

Therefore at the rates quoted the bank would:

i) Buy sterling (sell US dollars) @ 1.4440

ii) Sell sterling (buy US dollars) @ 1.4445

iii) Buy US dollars (sell Deutschemarks) @ 2.6750

iv) Sell US dollars (buy Deutschemarks) @ 2.6760

v) Buy US dollars (sell Swiss Francs) @ 2.1900

vi) Sell US dollars (buy Swiss Francs) @ 2.1910

vii) Buy US dollars (sell Yen) @ 232.65

viii) Sell US dollars (buy Yen) @ 232.75

293

When considered in the context of the maxim "buy high" "sell low", the style of quotation in the international markets often leads to considerable confusion and it may be helpful to briefly expand on this subject. As sterling is quoted as the subject currency in terms of so many US dollars in the international market, the bid rate is the rate at which the quoting bank will buy sterling (sell US dollars), the offered rate is the rate at which they would sell sterling (or buy US dollars). A domestic branch operation normally quotes buying and selling rates for a currency – not sterling. Therefore they would buy US dollars (sell sterling) at the offered rate and sell US dollars (buy sterling) at the bid rate. The two transactions at the same price levels are identical.

Spreads quoted within the markets are normally, in real terms relatively small. As is illustrated in the above example the value of each spread is different. In the sterling quotation each point (or pip) represents one hundredth of one US cent, in Deutschemarks one hundredth of one pfennig, in Swiss Francs one hundredth of one cent, and in Yen one hundredth of one Yen. A spread of five points in cable – market terminology for spot Sterling/US dollar – is indicative of a normal market quotation. However, spreads frequently widen as market volatility increases and liquidity diminishes. In a highly volatile, but thin market, spreads of 15, 20, 30, 50 or even 200 points in cable are not unknown. With the exception of Yen, exchange rates for the major currencies are quoted and calculated to four decimal places.

It is a misnomer to consider that in the world of foreign exchange markets the spread represents the profit margin. This is only the case if a dealer is able to simultaneously trade for like amounts on his bid and offered side. In the real world a dealer is continually trading in the market by opening, closing, building and unwinding positions. Rates of exchange are constantly moving – and the bid and offered sides may move to a new trading range by five points or more at a time. Although a dealer may improve prices in relationship to the market at any point in time his ultimate success will largely depend upon his ability to anticipate market movements correctly and to be able to run with, rather than against, the market trend over a period.

If one were to listen to a bank's dealer making prices in the market it would bear little resemblance to the quotations as previously illustrated. Asked for a sterling/dollar price by another bank's dealer he would merely quote "40-45". In response to a request for dollar/deutschemarks – "50-60". He assumes the counterparty is aware, first which is his bid and which his offered side, and second what his "big figure" is, i.e. sterling/dollar 4 of 1.44 and dollar/deutschemarks 7 of 2.67. In a very volatile market he may add reference to this number by indicating it is "on the figure" 4 or 7 respectively. Similarly, when quoting dollar/swiss francs he would simply say "the figure to 10" implying a "big figure" 9 of 2.19. In response to his sterling/dollar quotations the dealer may get the reply "5 yours", and to his dollar/deutschemark quotation "5 mine". It would be quite reasonable for anyone to be puzzled as to what business had actually been transacted. The amount 5 normally implies millions for Sterling, US dollars, Swiss francs and Deutschemarks, but in yen it would imply 5 billion. Therefore two questions remain. At which rate of exchange has each transaction been concluded; and in what currencies are the 5 millions denominated. Within the London market the response from the counterparty would be taken to imply they had sold the quoting bank £5 million @ 1.4440 i.e. the subject currency. The deutschemark counterparty bought the subject currency from the quoting dealer i.e. US$5 million @ 2.6760. It is important to note that one dealer should not deal on another dealer's price when it is clear that the price has been made on the wrong big figure.

As far as a dealer is concerned he quotes the rates and therefore he stipulates his bid and offered quotations to the enquirer on the basis of the subject currency. As previously illustrated all his prices are graded in the international markets against US dollars. However, rates of exchange as quoted in the international markets are of little value to a corporate customer or a branch operation which is servicing customer requirements. Their primary interest is normally in relation to foreign exchange rates expressed in or against their own domestic currency unit. Where domestic exchange rates are quoted with the foreign currency being expressed as the subject currency in terms of the domestic currency they are referred to as direct quotations. Exchange rates with the domestic currency being the subject currency expressed in terms of the foreign currency are indirect quotations.

The bases of these rates are a derivative of the market rates through "cross-rate" calculations, for example, to calculate a mid-market deutschemark/swiss franc rate we know from the rates previously illustrated that:

$$1 \text{ US\$} = \text{SwFcs } 2.1905$$
$$1 \text{ US\$} = \text{DM } 2.6755$$

therefore 1 DM $= \dfrac{2.1905}{2.6755} = \text{SwFcs } .8187 \text{(i.e. DM/SwF rate} = .8187)$

similarly 1 SwFc $= \dfrac{2.6755}{2.1905} = \text{DM } 1.2214 \text{(i.e. SwFc/DM rate} = 1.2214)$

As sterling is quoted in terms of US dollars the derivation is different. To calculate a mid-market rate sterling/deutschemark we know that:

$$\text{£1 sterling} = \text{US\$ } 1.44425$$
$$\text{DM } 2.6755 = \text{US\$1}$$

therefore £1 sterling $= 1.44425 \times 2.6755 = \text{DM } 3.8641 \text{ (i.e. £/DM rate} = 3.8641)$

These examples are based on mid-market rates whereas full quotations have a bid and offered side, which require to be determined and defined as to what is being bid and what is offered and by whom. Let us assume a bank in Frankfurt was required to buy swiss francs from a customer for deutschemarks. As the international markets do not quote deutschemark/swiss francs the dealer would upon completing the proposed deal require to enter the market and sell swiss francs/ buy US dollars, sell US dollars/buy deutschemarks at another bank(s) quotation rates to square his position.

Consequently the bases of the derivation to establish the buying and, as appropriate, selling rates are the market rates at which cover could be obtained. Therefore on the assumption that the market is quoting:

US$/SwFc @ 2.1900 (other bank's bid for dollars)
          2.1910 (other banks offered for dollars)

US$/DM   @ 2.6750 (other bank's bid for dollars)
          2.6760 (other banks offered for dollars)

the Frankfurt dealer could
  Buy US$/sell SwFcs @ 2.1910 (other banks offered for dollars)
  Sell US$/buy DM   @ 2.6750 (other banks bid for dollars)

therefore the Frankfurt dealer's buying rate for swiss francs in terms
of 1 deutschemark is calculated as

$$1DM = \frac{2.1910}{2.6750} = \text{SwFcs .8191 Frankfurt dealer's offered rate for DM}$$
$$\text{– Sell DM buy SwFcs}$$

Similarly the Frankfurt dealer could
  Sell US$/buy SwFcs @ 2.1900 (other banks bid for dollars)
  Buy US$/sell DM   @ 2.6760 (other banks offered for dollars)

therefore the Frankfurt dealer's selling rate for swiss francs in terms
of 1 deutschemark is calculated as:

$$1DM = \frac{2.1900}{2.6760} = \text{SwFcs .8184 Frankfurt dealer's bid rate}$$
$$\text{for DM – buy DM sell SwFcs}$$

Conversely if the above rates were expressed in terms of 1 swiss franc
as they may be if quoted by a Zurich dealer:
$$1 SwFc = \frac{2.6750}{2.1910} = \text{DM 1.2209 Zurich dealer's bid rate}$$
$$\text{for SwFcs – Buy SwFcs sell DM}$$

$$1 SwFc = \frac{2.6760}{2.1900} = \text{DM 1.2219 Zurich dealer's offered rate}$$
$$\text{for SwFcs – sell SwFcs buy DM}$$

If a dealer in London was asked for a quotation sterling/deutsche-marks and the market rates were:

Sterling/US$ 1.4440 (other bank's bid for sterling)
               1.4445 (other bank's offered for sterling)
US$/DM   2.6750 (other bank's bid for dollars)
               2.6760 (other bank's offered for dollars)

Should the dealer be asked to sell deutschemarks he would be required to:
  Buy DM/sell US$ @ 2.6750 (other bank's bid for dollars)
  Sell Sterling/buy US$ @ 1.4440 (other bank's bid for sterling)

therefore, the sterling/DM selling rate is the multiple of the two bid rates:

2.6750 × 1.4440 = DM 3.8627 London dealer's bid rate for sterling – buy sterling sell DM

Similarly if the dealer bought deutschemarks he would be required to:

Sell DM/buy US$ @ 2.6760 (other bank's offered for dollars)
Sell US$/buy sterling @ 1.4445 (other bank's offered for sterling)

therefore, the sterling/deutschemark buying rate is the multiple of the two offered rates:

2.6760 × 1.4445 = DM 3.8655 London dealer's offered rate for sterling – sell sterling buy DM

We will now consider a situation in which two currencies are both quoted in the market in US dollar terms per currency unit, e.g. sterling and Australian dollars. Let us assume an Australian dollar/US dollar rate of .9442–47 and continue with a sterling/US dollar quotation of 1.4440–45. At .9442 a second bank is prepared to buy Australian dollars (sell US dollars) and at .9447 sell Australian dollars (buy US dollars). The derivation is similar to that used in two dollar unit based currencies and at mid-market rates:

298

$$\text{Aus.}\$1 = \text{US}\$ \ .94445$$
$$\text{£St.}1 = \text{US}\$ \ 1.44425$$

therefore, $\quad \text{£St.}1 = \dfrac{1.44425}{.94445} = \text{Aus.}\$ \ 1.5292$

or conversely Aus.$1 $\quad = \dfrac{.94445}{1.44425} = \text{£St.}6539$

In the market a first bank could:

Sell A\$/buy US\$ @ .9442 (other bank's bid for A\$)
Buy A\$/sell US\$ @ .9447 (other bank's offered for A\$)
Sell sterling/buy US\$ @ 1.4440 (other bank's bid for sterling)
Buy sterling/sell US\$ @ 1.4445 (other bank's offered for sterling)

therefore, first bank's bid rate for sterling is:
$$\dfrac{1.4440}{.9447} = 1.5285$$

offered rate for sterling is:
$$\dfrac{1.4445}{.9442} = 1.5299$$

i.e. buy sterling (sell Australian dollars) @ 1.5285
sell sterling (buy Australian dollars) @ 1.5299

The following reflects cross rates as they would be quoted by banks in New York, London, Frankfurt, Zurich and Tokyo.

	New York	London	Frankfurt DM	Zurich SwFcs	Tokyo Yen
Sterling	1.4440–45	—	3.8627–55	3.1624–49	335.95–21
US dollar	—	1.4440–45	2.6750–60	2.1900–10	232.65–75
Deutschemarks	2.6750.60	3.8627–55	—	81.84–81.91	86.94–01
Swiss Franc	2.1900–10	3.1624–49	122.09–19	—	106.18–28
Yen	232.65–75	335.95–21	1.1495–545	.9409–18	—

New York quotes sterling in terms of US dollars (direct quotation) and the other currencies in currency terms per one US dollar (indirect quotation), i.e. the international rates. London quotes all rates against one unit sterling (indirect quotations) whilst the other three centres reflect direct quotations. It will also be noted that banks in Germany quote Deustchemarks to 100 units Swiss Francs and 100 units yen. Banks in Switzerland similarly quote Swiss francs to 100 units Deutschemarks and 100 units yen.

It is often implied that arbitrage opportunities frequently exist between exchange rates quoted in various centres, i.e. it may be possible to buy Swiss Francs against sterling at a more advantageous rate by going through Yen or Deutschemarks. Prior to the development of the international markets and modern communication systems this was possible. However, as illustrated above all rates are calculated effectively from the same prices – those of the international markets – and this type of arbitrage opportunity is no longer available or if it does temporarily exist market forces lead banks to adjust prices quickly.

Forward Rates
An outright forward exchange contract is simply a contract to buy or sell foreign exchange on a specified date or during a specified time in the future at an exchange rate agreed on the deal date. Although there is a substantial commercial demand for outright forward foreign exchange transactions which provide the opportunity for clients to hedge and cover against the future vagaries of exchange rate movements, the international foreign exchange markets do not trade outright forward transactions. Apart from outright spot rates the other principal foreign exchange rate quotations readily available to a dealer within the foreign exchange markets are "swap prices". A swap price is quoted in points, a swap transaction being the simultaneous purchase and sale of two currencies for spot delivery and an opposite sale and purchase of the same currencies at a future value date. Therefore if a dealer sold a currency forward on an outright basis to a client he would buy the equivalent of the currency spot and thereafter swap the transaction (i.e. sell spot and buy forward) to the date the currency was required to meet the future obligation to the client.

As with spot prices there are offered and bid sides to swap prices. However, unlike spot rates which, within the major currencies, are floating without upper or lower limits, there is a natural upper and lower limit within which swap prices normally move.

These upper and lower limits are established by interest rate differentials and if these limits are exceeded, deposit swap arbitrage opportunity will be available. Deposit swap arbitrage is the physical movement of funds from one currency to another in order to obtain an improved rate of return, and, if available, the opportunity will be exploited until the swap moves back within the arbitrage limits. Therefore, prior to examining swap prices and how they are traded it would be appropriate to consider again briefly the principles of swap deposit arbitrage discussed in Chapter 15 which also provides the basis upon which outright forward sales and purchases are priced.

In calculating an outright forward price for a client a dealer will assume that he has to borrow funds at current market rates to pay the counter-value of the spot purchase of currency for the period of the forward trade and also assume that he will lend the currency funds generated into the market until they are required to meet his future obligations. The costs or benefits derived from undertaking these transactions are reflected as an adjustment to the relative spot rates by way of a premium (cost) or discount (benefit). Where currencies (the quoted currencies) are expressed in currency terms against a unit of one US dollar (the subject currency) and US dollar interest rates are higher than the respective currency rate it will reflect as a premium on the other currency (which is also a discount on the US$) and will be deducted from the spot rate. If US dollar rates are lower than the currency interest rate it will reflect as a discount on the other currency (which is also a premium on the US$) which must be added to the spot rates. The currency with the *lower* interest rate has its own currency quoted at a premium on the forward. For example, with US$/DM with deutschemark rates being lower than US dollar rates the deutschemarks are at a premium on the forward and the US dollars are at a discount on forward – this is the same thing. The margins (premiums or discounts) will be added or deducted as follows: $ margins, $ at a premium, $ per £1, therefore dollars are dearer forward than spot, there are fewer of them, the US$ premium (Sterling discount) is deducted. Also, if DM margins, DM at a premium, DM per $1, therefore deutschemarks are dearer forward than spot, the deutschemark premium (which is also a US$ discount) is deducted from the spot rate. When the subject currency of a quotation is at a discount the points are deducted from the spot rate and when the subject currency is at a premium they are added to the spot rate.

As previously indicated the only true value of one currency in terms of another is as reflected in the market by the spot rates. Therefore to establish a forward rate of exchange the dealer will consider the true opportunity cost of hedging or covering the transactions at other banks' rates in a similar manner to cross rate calculations. However in dealing for a future date, interest rate differentials must be considered and reflected as an adjustment to the appropriate spot rate. The calculation of outright forward exchange prices, discounts and premiums is entirely a mathematical function of the current spot exchange and interest rate differentials, and the resultant rates are not as many people believe an indication of where the market thinks spot rates of exchange will be in the various forward periods. Nevertheless a movement of interest rates can affect the spot exchange rate.

If we were to assume that within the euro-market the six month rates for US dollars are $10\frac{3}{16}$–$10\frac{1}{8}$ and for Deutschemarks 6–$5\frac{15}{16}\%$ and a spot rate of exchange US\$/DM 2.6750–60 the six months outright forward prices can be calculated as follows:

A dealer can borrow US dollars @ $10\frac{3}{16}\%$ p.a. for six months (offered), let us assume US\$1 million, sell these dollars @ 2.6750 (other bank's bid for dollars) and lend Deutschemarks @ $5\frac{15}{16}$ (bid) through the market. Therefore at maturity:

$$
\begin{array}{llr}
\text{Receive: DM Principal} & & 2,675,000 \\
\text{plus interest} \quad \dfrac{2,675,000 \times 182 \times 5.9375}{360 \times 100} & = & \underline{80,296.44} \\
& & \text{DM}2,755,296.44
\end{array}
$$

Pay: US$ Principal   1,000,000

plus interest $\dfrac{1{,}000{,}000 \times 182 \times 10.1875}{360 \times 100} = \underline{51{,}503.47}$

US$1,051,503.47

The cross rate of the above is $\dfrac{2{,}755{,}296.44}{1{,}051{,}503.47} = 2.6203$

Therefore the 6 months
forward outright rate 1US$ = DM2.6203 (bid for dollars)

Spot rate   = DM 2.6750

Forward rate   = DM 2.6203

Forward discount
on the US$ i.e.
premium on the
DM   = 547 points

A dealer can borrow DM @ 6% p.a. (offered) for six months, let us assume DM2,676,000, sell these for US dollars at 2.6760 (offered) and lend US dollars at $10\frac{1}{8}$ (bid) through the market. Therefore at maturity:

Pay: DM Principal   2,676,000

plus interest $\dfrac{2{,}676{,}000 \times 182 \times 6}{360 \times 100} = \underline{81{,}172}$

DM2,757,172

Cross rate $= \dfrac{2{,}757{,}172}{1{,}051{,}187.50} = $ DM   2.6229

Therefore the 6 months
forward outright rate 1US$ = DM2.6229 (offered for dollars)

Spot rate   = DM 2.6760

Forward rate   = DM 2.6229

Forward discount
on the US$
i.e. premium
on the DM   = 531 points

To obtain a perfect hedge the dealer is required to buy or sell forward the gross interest element of one side of the transaction thereby bringing everything back to a single currency at maturity. In the above example the dealer would usually sell the US dollar interest for deutschemarks, the quoted currency.

The above calculations can be translated into the following mathematical formula:

$$\frac{\text{Interest Rate Differential} \times \text{Spot} \times \text{Days}}{360 \times 100 + [\text{Days} \times \$ \text{ Deposit Rate}]} = \begin{array}{l} \text{Outright Forward} \\ \text{Discount/Premium} \\ \text{(Swap price)} \end{array}$$

Therefore outright forward bid for dollars =
$$\frac{4.25 \times 2.6750 \times 182}{360 \times 100 + [182 \times 10.1875]} = 547 \text{ points discount on the US\$}$$

and outright forward offer =
$$\frac{4.125 \times 2.6760 \times 182}{360 \times 100 + [182 \times 10.125]} = 531 \text{ points discount on the US\$}$$

The discount points equate with the differential between the relative spot and forward rates.

i.e. Spot	2.6750	2.6760
less Discount		
on the US$	547	531
Forward	2.6203	2.6229

The above formulae can be re-structured to achieve different objectives, for example to calculate the interest rate differentials reflected by outright forward discounts and premiums:

Interest rate differential
$$(\% \text{ p.a.}) = \frac{\text{Swap} \times 360 \times 100}{\text{spot} \times \text{days}} + \frac{\text{Swap} \times \text{US\$ interest rate}}{\text{spot}}$$

Therefore based on the previous example

$$\% \text{ p.a.} = \frac{.0547 \times 360 \times 100}{2.6750 \times 182} + \frac{.0547 \times 10.1875}{2.6750}$$

$$= \quad 4.0447 \quad + \quad .2083 \quad = 4.25\% \text{ p.a.}$$

and

$$\% \text{ p.a.} = \frac{.0531 \times 360 \times 100}{2.6760 \times 182} + \frac{.0531 \times 10.125}{2.6760}$$

$$= \quad 3.9250 \quad + \quad .2009 \quad = 4.125\% \text{ p.a.}$$

Foreign Exchange Market Swaps
From the above formulae calculations, and on an assumption that a dealer has to enter the market through US dollars to buy and sell and borrow and lend, the spread between the bid and offered prices is inherent in these rates. In the examples quoted above an interest rate spread of $\frac{1}{16}\%$ per annum has been utilised for each currency. However, as the minimum spread between bid and offered interest rates for these periods is normally $\frac{1}{8}\%$ per annum, this results in the premium/discount points as calculated above incorporating the equivalent of at least $\frac{1}{4}\%$ p.a in addition to the spread between the bid and offered rate of exchange.

The substantial commercial demand for both swap deposit transactions and outright forward sales and purchases of currency resulted in a substantial interbank market being established in swaps to facilitate banks adjusting their respective positions with each other without the necessity of physically borrowing and lending currencies to cover these transactions.

However as a margin of $\frac{1}{4}\%$ or more is unacceptably high for an interbank market for this purpose, a much finer margin developed to facilitate banks' requirements. Bid and offered prices within the swap markets are determined by supply and demand, together with interest rate expectations, but they are contained within the outer parameters of the arbitrage opportunities which would be available if swap prices move outside of the swap deposit prices as calculated previously, i.e. the currency swap deposit formula establishes the limits within which swap prices can fluctuate without triggering an arbitrage opportunity.

An analogy can be drawn between swap deposit arbitrage and a triangle – let us call it the swap deposit arbitrage triangle. In all triangles the angles must total 180°. Let us assume angles A and B represent the two deposit rates, angle C the swap price. If any of the three angles are varied one or both of the other angles or the swap price must move to compensate. If they do not, a triangle is not formed and arbitrage opportunity will be available until the triangle is re-established. The six month US$/DM swap in the example quoted above is on arbitrage if the offered side reaches 531 or the bid side 547 of the swap deposit (note the offered side of the swap can go through the offered side of the deposit swap and the bid through the bid without triggering arbitrage). If the offered side goes to 530 or the bid side to 548 arbitrage is available for a marginal return; as the offered price diminishes and the bid price increases the arbitrage margin increases to the point that the arbitrager will enter the market.

If the spot rate moved to 2.6670-80 and the interest rates remained the same the swap deposit arbitrage point would be:

$$\text{Bid (for US\$)} \quad \frac{4.25 \times 2.6670 \times 182}{360 \times 100 + [182 \times 10.1875]} = \text{545 points discount for dollars (premium for DM)}$$

$$\text{Offered (for US\$)} \quad \frac{4.125 \times 2.6680 \times 182}{360 \times 100 + [182 \times 10.125]} = \text{529 points discount for dollars (premium for DM)}$$

Assume US$ interest rates moved to $10\frac{1}{8}-\frac{1}{16}$, DM interest rates and spot remained the same then the swap deposit arbitrage point would re-establish at 531 offered, 523 bid –

$$\text{Bid (for US\$)} \quad \frac{4.125 \times 2.6750 \times 182}{360 \times 100 + [182 \times 10.1250]} = \text{531 points discount for dollars (premium for DM)}$$

Offered (for US$)

$$\frac{4.0625 \times 2.6760 \times 182}{360 \times 100 + [182 \times 10.0625]} = 523 \text{ points discount for dollars (premium for DM)}$$

Conversely if DM interest rates moved to $6\frac{3}{8}$ offered, $6\frac{1}{4}$ bid –

Bid (for US$)

$$\frac{3.9375 \times 2.6750 \times 182}{360 \times 100 + [182 \times 10.1875]} = 507 \text{ points discount for dollars (premium for DM)}$$

Offered (for US$)

$$\frac{3.75 \times 2.6760 \times 182}{360 \times 100 + [182 \times 10.125]} = 483 \text{ points discount for dollars (premium for DM)}$$

Whenever the subject currency of a quotation is at a discount the adjustment to the bid side of the rate is higher than the adjustment to the offered side; when it is at a premium the adjustment to the bid side is less than the adjustment to the offered side. Let us assume that DM interest rates were $10\frac{3}{16}$ offered – $10\frac{1}{8}$ bid, and US$ were 6% offered and $5\frac{5}{16}$ bid.

A dealer can borrow US dollars at 6%, sell these at 2.6570 and lend Deutschemarks at $10\frac{1}{8}$ bid = interest rate differential 4.125% or borrow DM at $10\frac{3}{16}$ offered, sell these at 2.6760, lend US$ at $5\frac{15}{16}$ bid – interest rate differential 4.25%. Therefore

Outright forward bid (for US Dollars) =

$$\frac{4.125 \times 2.6750 \times 182}{360 \times 100 + [182 \times 6]} = 541 \text{ points premium for dollars (discount for DM)}$$

Outright forward offer (for US Dollars) =

$$\frac{4.25 \times 2.6760 \times 182}{360 \times 100 + [182 \times 5.9375]} = 558 \text{ points premium for dollars (discount for DM)}$$

Swaps are tools of the interbank market and are quoted and traded therein in terms of points of discount or premium and not outright forward bid and offered rates of exchange. Within the market there is no indication of whether the quotations are premiums or discounts. This is implied by the manner of quotation. Where the subject currency of the underlying exchange rate quotation is at a discount (the quoted currency at a premium) the bid side of the rate for the subject currency (offered for the quoted currency) is higher than the offered side and when the subject currency of the underlying exchange rate quotation is at a premium (the quoted currency at a discount) the bid side of the rate for the subject currency is lower than the offered side. In practice quotations of bid and offered swap prices are made in terms of the quoted currency and not the subject currency and therefore the bid points against the subject currency are referred to as offered and the offered points against the subject currency bid. When transacting a deal offered and bid points are not applied to the respective bid and offered spot rates of exchange but to an "effective" spot rate as agreed between the principals (either directly or indirectly through a broker). This rate must be within the range of current spot rates and is usually established at around mid market levels.

Swaps have developed for the convenience of dealers to avoid them having to access the deposit markets to cover outright forward or deposit swap transactions. A "swap" transaction effectively simulates the process of simultaneously buying or selling one currency for another currency spot against an equal but opposite forward trade. This facility also provides a vehicle through which views can be taken on interest rate movements in various currencies, through the impact of interest rate differentials on these prices.

Swaps are normally quoted within the market as tomorrow next (tom next) being the day after deal date into spot or from spot overnight, one week, two weeks, three weeks, one, two, three, four, five and six months, nine months and one year.

As with deposit trading in covering commercial business undertaken to specific "odd" dates for clients within the interbank swap market which trades for standard periods, maturity mis-matches will

308

be created. As previously discussed these mis-matches will be subject to the vagaries of future interest rate differentials and therefore cover will be arranged short or long on the basis of a dealer's perception of the likely trend. Thereafter subsequent short dated swaps are arranged as the gaps reach or approach their value dates.

Chart 1 on the following page illustrates a series of premiums and discounts based upon deposit arbitrage (outright forward) calculations at the spot rates of exchange and resultant interest rate differentials against the rates indicated. Chart 2 on the next page provides selected examples of inter-bank foreign exchange swap prices as they may be traded within the parameters of the arbitrage calculations reflected in Chart 1. It will be noted that points discount and premium are quoted in decimals of one point and not to the nearest point as reflected in the earlier examples used with this chapter.

Chart 1

CHART I

PERIOD	US DOLLARS % P.A.	£ ST/US$	£ STG % P.A.	US$/DM	DM % P.A.	US$/YEN	YEN % P.A.	US$/SF	SF % P.A.
SPOT		1.4050		2.6780		218		2.20	
TN	7.5/8–7.3/8	1.79–1.59	12.1/8–11.7/8	2.18–1.90	4.13/16–4.11/16	.76–.53	6.1/2–6.3/8	3.13–2.82	2.3/4–2.1/2
SN	7.15/16–7.13/16	1.61–1.47	12.1/8–11.7/8	2.42–2.23	4.13/16–4.11/16	.95–.79	6.1/2–6.3/8	3.32–3.09	2.3/4–2.1/2
WEEK	7.15/16–7.13/16	11.30–10.29	12.1/8–11.7/8	17.87–16.57	4.5/8–4.1/2	6.61–5.55	6.1/2–6.3/8	23.22–21.62	2.3/4–2.1/2
1	8.3/16–8.1/16	42.24–40.01	11.3/4–11.11/16	87.30–81.58	4.1/2–4.3/8	34.95–30.29	6.7/16–6.5/16	71.72–67.02	4.1/2–4.3/8
2	8.1/16–8	83.69–79.30	11.11/16–11.9/16	167.74–159.23	4.1/2–4.3/8	64.80–57.86	6.7/16–6.5/16	137.80–130.81	4.1/2–4.3/8
3	8.3/16–8.1/8	115.61–109.09	11.9/16–11.7/16	254.06–241.39	4.9/16–4.7/16	103.41–93.08	6.7/16–6.5/16	205.23–194.83	4.5/8–4.1/2
4	8.1/4–8.3/16	145.21–136.55	11.7/16–11.5/16	338.99–322.10	4.5/8–4.1/2	142.57–128.80	6.7/16–6.5/16	269.20–255.33	4.3/4–4.5/8
5	8.1/4–8.1/8	176.35–162.28	11.3/8–11.1/4	405.47–378.18	4.11/16–4.9/16	173.42–151.13	6.7/16–6.5/16	327.46–305.03	4.3/4–4.5/8
6	8.5/16–8.3/16	195.61–179.01	11.1/4–11.1/8	479.10–446.89	4.3/4–4.5/8	204.92–178.59	6.1/2–6.3/8	393.59–367.09	4.3/4–4.5/8
9	8.7/16–8.3/8	255.50–237.43	11.1/8–11	715.76–680.27	4.13/16–4.11/16	330.17–301.17	6.7/16–6.5/16	597.80–568.65	4.3/4–4.5/8
12	8.5/8–8.1/2	309.23–277.70	11.1/16–10.15/16	967.53–906.16	4.7/8–4.3/4	470.02–419.70	6.7/16–6.5/16	820.47–770.09	4.3/4–4.5/8

Chart 2

CHART II

	STERLING SWAPS		DEUTSCHEMARK SWAPS		YEN SWAPS		SWISS FRANC SWAPS	
SPOT	1.4050		2.6780		218		2.20	
1 MONTH	42.25 -41	40.50 -40	87.25 -87	82-81.50	35-34	31-30.25	71.75-71	67.50-67
2 MONTHS	83.50 -83	80-79.25	167.25 -167	160.25 -159.25	65-64	58-57.75	138-137.50	131-130.75
3 MONTHS	115.50 -115	110-109	254-253	243-241.50	103.50 -103	94-93	205.25 -205	196-194.75
6 MONTHS	196.50 -196	180-179	479-478	449-447	205-204	179.50 -178.50	393.75 -393	338-337
12 MONTHS	309-305	280-277	967.50 -965	910-906	470-468	420-419.75	820.50 -819	771-770
	These market quotations imply that there is pressure for either sterling rates to rise or dollar rates to fall	These market quotations imply that there is pressure for either sterling rates to fall or dollar rates to rise	These market quotations imply that there is pressure for either dollar rates to rise or deutschemark rates to fall	These market quotations imply that there is pressure for either dollar rates to fall or deutschemark rates to rise	These market quotations imply that there is pressure for either dollar rates to rise or yen rates to fall	These market quotations imply that there is pressure for either dollar rates to fall or yen rates to rise	These market quotations imply that there is pressure for either dollar rates to rise or SFC rates to fall	These market quotations imply that there is pressure for either dollar rates to fall or SFC rates to rise

The recording, processing and confirmation of swap transactions are effected as two separate deals for each of the value dates at the actual rates of exchange based upon the "effective" spot rate as agreed at the time of the contract. Based upon a spot rate of US$/DM of 2.7375 and discount points of 475 against the US$ the dealing slips, confirmations and brokers notes illustrative of this type of transaction are shown on the following pages.

Example of spot buying bank's deal slip

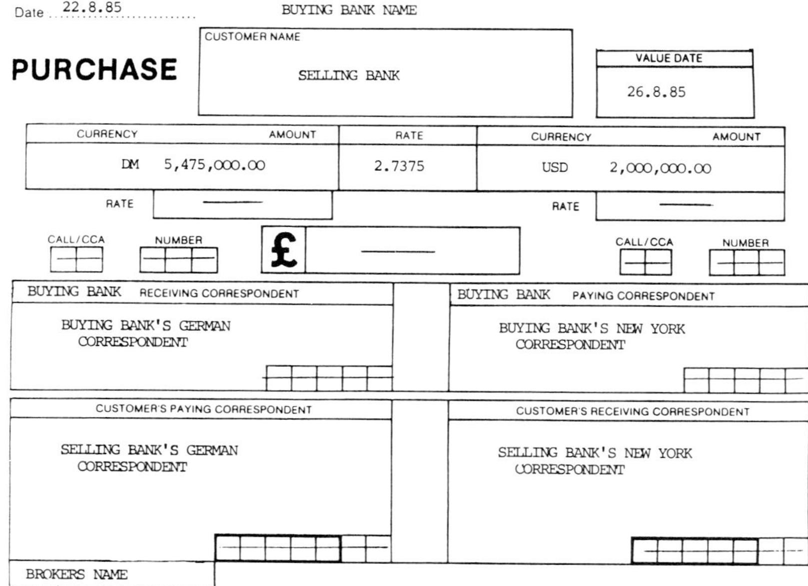

Example of spot buying bank's confirmation

Confirmation

<u>BUYING BANK NAME</u>

SELLING BANK NAME AND
ADDRESS

DATE   22.8.85

OUR CONTRACT No.   100003

VALUE   26.8.85

WE CONFIRM HAVING PURCHASED FROM YOU

CURRENCY	AMOUNT	RATE	CURRENCY	AMOUNT
DEM	5,475,000.00	2.7375	USD	2,000,000.00

RECEIVE INSTRUCTIONS

PAY INSTRUCTIONS

AT
BUYING BANK'S GERMAN
CORRESPONDENT

BY
BUYING BANK'S NEW YORK
CORRESPONDENT

FROM
SELLING BANK'S GERMAN
CORRESPONDENT

TO
SELLING BANK'S NEW YORK
CORRESPONDENT

TRANSACTED THROUGH BROKER – BROKERS NAME

THIS CONFIRMATION REQUIRES AN AUTHORISED SIGNATURE

Example of spot buying bank's brokers confirmation received

BROKERS NOTE

BROKERS NAME   BUYER CONFIRMATION

TO: BUYING BANK

WE CONFIRM HAVING NEGOTIATED THE FOLLOWING ON YOUR BEHALF:

PURCHASE	:	DM 5,475,000.00
EQUIV.	:	USD 2,000,000.00
RATE	:	2.7375
VALUE DATE	:	26.8.85
SETTLEMENT INSTRUCTIONS	:	DM FROM: SELLING BANK GERMAN CORRESPONDENT USD TO: SELLING BANK NEW YORK CORRESPONDENT
SELLER	:	SELLING BANK NAME
BROKERAGE AMOUNT	:	STG ____________

Example of spot selling bank's deal slip

Date 22.8.85 — SELLING BANK NAME

SALE

CUSTOMER NAME
BUYING BANK NAME

VALUE DATE
26.8.85

CURRENCY	AMOUNT	RATE	CURRENCY	AMOUNT
DEM	5,475,000.00	2.7375	USD	2,000,000.00

RATE — RATE —

CALL/CCA   NUMBER   £ —   CALL/CCA   NUMBER

SELLING BANK'S PAYING CORRESPONDENT

SELLING BANK'S GERMAN
CORRESPONDENT

SELLING BANK'S RECEIVING CORRESPONDENT

SELLING BANK'S NEW YORK
CORRESPONDENT

CUSTOMER'S RECEIVING CORRESPONDENT

BUYING BANK'S GERMAN
CORRESPONDENT

CUSTOMER'S PAYING CORRESPONDENT

BUYING BANK'S NEW YORK
CORRESPONDENT

BROKERS NAME

FM 8574 (10/84)

Example of spot selling bank's confirmation

SELLING BANK NAME

Confirmation

BUYING BANK NAME AND ADDRESS

DATE 22.8.85

OUR CONTRACT No. 100001

VALUE 26.8.85

WE CONFIRM HAVING SOLD TO YOU

CURRENCY	AMOUNT	RATE	CURRENCY	AMOUNT
DEM	5,475,000.00	2.7375	USD	2,000,000.00

PAYMENT INSTRUCTIONS

RECEIVE INSTRUCTIONS

BY
SELLING BANK'S GERMAN
CORRESPONDENT

AT
SELLING BANK'S NEW YORK
CORRESPONDENT

TO
BUYING BANK'S GERMAN
CORRESPONDENT

FROM
BUYING BANK'S NEW YORK
CORRESPONDENT

TRANSACTED THROUGH BROKER — BROKERS NAME

THIS CONFIRMATION REQUIRES AN AUTHORISED SIGNATURE

Example of spot selling bank's brokers confirmation received

BROKERS NOTE

<u>BROKERS NAME</u>   SELLER CONFIRMATION

TO: SELLING BANK

WE CONFIRM HAVING NEGOTIATED THE FOLLOWING ON YOUR BEHALF:

SALE   :   DM 5,475,000.00

EQUIV.   :   USD 2,000,000.00

RATE   :   2.7375

VALUE DATE   :   26.8.85

SETTLEMENT INSTRUCTIONS   :   DM TO: BUYING BANK GERMAN CORRESPONDENT
                              USD FROM: BUYING BANK NEW YORK
                              CORRESPONDENT

BUYER   :   BUYING BANK NAME

BROKERAGE AMOUNT   :   STG _______________

Example of forward selling bank's deal slip

Date ....22.8.85........ SELLING BANK NAME

SALE

CUSTOMER NAME

BUYING BANK NAME

VALUE DATE

26.2.86

CURRENCY	AMOUNT	RATE	CURRENCY	AMOUNT
DEM	5,380,000.00	2.69	USD	2,000,000.00

RATE ———   RATE ———

CALL/CCA   NUMBER   £ ———   CALL/CCA   NUMBER

SELLING BANK PAYING CORRESPONDENT

SELLING BANK'S GERMAN
CORRESPONDENT

SELLING BANK RECEIVING CORRESPONDENT

SELLING BANK'S NEW YORK
CORRESPONDENT

CUSTOMER'S RECEIVING CORRESPONDENT

BUYING BANK'S GERMAN
CORRESPONPONDENT

CUSTOMER'S PAYING CORRESPONDENT

BUYING BANK'S NEW YORK
CORRESPONDENT

BROKERS NAME

FM 8574 (10/84)

Example of forward selling bank's confirmation

SELLING BANK NAME

Confirmation

BUYING BANK NAME AND ADDRESS	DATE 22.8.85
	OUR CONTRACT No. 100004
	VALUE 26.2.86

WE CONFIRM HAVING SOLD TO YOU

CURRENCY	AMOUNT	RATE	CURRENCY	AMOUNT
DEM	5,380,000.00	2.69	USD	2,000,000.00

PAYMENT INSTRUCTIONS

BY
   SELLING BANK'S GERMAN
   CORRESPONDENT

TO
   BUYING BANK'S GERMAN
   CORRESPONDENT

RECEIVE INSTRUCTIONS

AT
   SELLING BANK'S NEW YORK
   CORRESPONDENT

FROM
   BUYING BANK'S NEW YORK
   CORRESPONDENT

TRANSACTED THROUGH BROKER – BROKERS NAME

THIS CONFIRMATION REQUIRES AN AUTHORISED SIGNATURE

Example of forward selling bank's brokers confirmation received

BROKERS NOTE

BROKERS NAME   SELLER CONFIRMATION

TO: SELLING BANK

WE CONFIRM HAVING NEGOTIATED THE FOLLOWING ON YOUR BEHALF:

SALE	:	DM 5,380,000.00
EQUIV.	:	USD 2,000,000.00
RATE	:	2.69
VALUE DATE	:	26.2.86
SETTLEMENT INSTRUCTIONS	:	DM TO: BUYING BANK GERMAN CORRESPONDENT USD FROM: BUYING BANK NEW YORK CORRESPONDENT
BUYER	:	BUYING BANK NAME
BROKERAGE AMOUNT	:	STG _____________

Example of forward buying bank's deal slip

Date ....22.8.85........

PURCHASE

BUYING BANK NAME

CUSTOMER NAME

SELLING BANK NAME

VALUE DATE

26.2.86

CURRENCY	AMOUNT	RATE	CURRENCY	AMOUNT
DEM	5,380,000.00	2.69	USD	2,000,000.00

RATE — — — — —

RATE — — — — —

CALL/CCA NUMBER £ — — — — CALL/CCA NUMBER

BUYING BANK RECEIVING CORRESPONDENT

BUYING BANK'S GERMAN
CORRESPONDENT

BUYING BANK PAYING CORRESPONDENT

BUYING BANK'S NEW YORK
CORRESPONDENT

CUSTOMER'S PAYING CORRESPONDENT

SELLING BANK'S GERMAN
CORRESPONDENT

CUSTOMER'S RECEIVING CORRESPONDENT

SELLING BANK'S NEW YORK
CORRESPONDENT

BROKERS NAME

FM 8574 (10/84)

Example of forward buying bank's confirmation

Confirmation

BUYING BANK NAME

DATE	22.8.85
OUR CONTRACT No.	100002
VALUE	26.2.86

SELLING BANK NAME AND
ADDRESS

WE CONFIRM HAVING PURCHASED FROM YOU

CURRENCY	AMOUNT	RATE	CURRENCY	AMOUNT
DEM	5,380,000.00	2.69	USD	2,000,000.00

RECEIVE INSTRUCTIONS

PAY INSTRUCTIONS

AT
BUYING BANK'S GERMAN
CORRESPONDENT

BY
BUYING BANK'S NEW YORK
CORRESPONDENT

FROM
SELLING BANK'S GERMAN
CORRESPONDENT

TO
SELLING BANK'S NEW YORK
CORRESPONDENT

TRANSACTED THROUGH BROKER – BROKERS NAME

THIS CONFIRMATION REQUIRES AN AUTHORISED SIGNATURE ________________________

Example of forward buying bank's brokers confirmation received

BROKERS NOTE

BROKERS NAME   BUYER CONFIRMATION

TO: BUYING BANK

WE CONFIRM HAVING NEGOTIATED THE FOLLOWING ON YOUR BEHALF:

PURCHASE   :   DM 5,380,000.00

EQUIV.   :   USD 2,000,000.00

RATE   :   2.69

VALUE DATE   :   26.2.86

SETTLEMENT INSTRUCTIONS   :   DM FROM: SELLING BANK GERMAN CORRESPONDENT
                               USD TO: SELLING BANK NEW YORK CORRESPONDENT

SELLER   :   SELLING BANK NAME

BROKERAGE AMOUNT   :   STG ______________

The London interbank Sterling, Currency Deposit and Foreign Exchange markets – Code of Conduct and Market Practice

The Bank of England has over the years maintained close surveillance over the London inter-bank sterling, currency deposit and foreign exchange markets. Chapter 5 considers the regulation and supervision of banks and in particular, mentions the licensing and authorising procedures to which they are subject. As mentioned in the previous chapter, as at the time of this publication there are in excess of 600 licensed banks and deposit taking institutions authorised to operate within the UK. Within the London currency deposit and foreign exchange markets, brokers are also subject to central bank authorisation. The Bank has established procedures for according, suspending or withdrawing recognition to brokers. Within this authority various criteria are established in regard to applications to establish a broking operation and these require sponsorship from at least six banks who, inter alia, must testify as to the proposed broker's technical expertise, indicate that they know of nothing to the detriment of the applicant, including its propriety and its actual and proposed broking principals, and should indicate their willingness to accept a line from, and use the services of, the applicant. At the time of this publication there were 14 "recognised brokers" operating in the currency deposit market and 8 in the foreign exchange markets. They are:

Foreign Exchange and Currency Deposits

Guy Butler (International) Ltd.
Charles Fulton & Co. Ltd.
Godsell Astley & Pearce (Foreign Exchange) Ltd.
Harlow Meyer Savage Ltd.
Kirkland-Whittaker Group Ltd.
Marshall Woellwarth & Co. Ltd.
R.P. Martin PLC
Tullett & Tokyo Forex International Ltd.

Currency Deposits only

Astley & Pearce
Currency Brokers International
Godsell & Co. Ltd.

Meridian Deposit Brokers Ltd.
Shortloan International Ltd.
Tradition (London Brokers) Ltd.

"Recognised" brokers are able to operate only within the framework of the arrangement with the Bank and the provision of services outside these arrangements can only be undertaken from separate establishments. The Bank maintains a list of recognised brokers which is available on request at all times during business hours. Although this formal authorisation from the Bank of England does not extend to brokers operating in the sterling interbank markets, they are required to be members of the Sterling Brokers Association and this latter body defines similar qualifying criteria. Within each market, principal banks are free to choose whether they deal direct with each other or use the services of a broker who is a "recognised broker". Banks must not use or deal through the United Kingdom office of a broker not recognised by either the Bank of England or the Sterling Brokers Association. Brokers are free to pass commercial names, but they must be fully equipped to give information to banks upon the latest published financial statements of such principals.

In these markets brokers are purely intermediaries and receive commission usually referred to as "brokerage fees" for their services. Until the 31st December 1985 banks in the United Kingdom may accept brokerage charges only within the minimum and maximum scales laid down by the Bank or, in the case of sterling, the Sterling Brokers Association. After that date rates of "brokerage" including any negotiable discount are to be agreed individually between brokers and banks. In future these commissions are to be negotiated in advance by directors or senior managers on each side and in no event by dealers themselves. Thereafter in no circumstances may an agreed rate be varied during the course of transacting a deal and in any case in which there is no agreed rate, no deal shall be transacted until a rate has been agreed. It is expected that agreed rates on brokerage and any negotiable discounts will remain in force initially for a minimum period of one year. Brokerage is normally payable at the end of the month in which the deal is done or otherwise by special arrangement.

325

The Bank of England's promulgations on the subject of a code of conduct for the currency deposit and foreign exchange markets were initially embodied in the Stilling letter of 1967 but more recently in a letter of the 30th July 1975 (the O'Brien letter) conveyed through the President of the British Bankers Association (BBA) to all authorised banks. The Bank made further recommendations to amend the O'Brien letter and these amendments were principally embodied in five letters from the BBA. The first dated 15th December 1978 and addressed to all authorised banks (the second O'Brien letter); the second dated 19th December 1979 (the third O'Brien letter); the third dated 17th November 1981 (the Faulkener letter) and replaced by the fourth dated 20th January 1984 (the Bevan letter) and the fifth dated 18th September 1984 (the Atherton letter).

Among other matters these amendments set out procedures for the recognition by the Bank of England of brokers authorised to offer a service in foreign exchange and/or currency deposits referred to previously. On the 10th May 1985 the Bank of England issued a resume of the current situation together with the Bank of England code of practice for the regulation of recognised brokers. The code of conduct for principals and brokers in the sterling deposit market was originally produced in 1979 and a subsequent revised version was provided by the Bank of England in March 1985. The purpose of these letters and codes is to ensure the good order of the markets concerned and that all those who use them are aware of the arrangements and are prepared to adhere to them. To assist the Bank in monitoring the observance of the code of conduct for principals and brokers in the sterling deposit market, it established a joint standing committee – the joint standing committee for principals and brokers in the sterling deposit market – on which both principals and brokers are represented. The function of this committee is to advise the Bank, and membership is at the invitation of the Bank.

Similarly the Bank has also established a joint standing committee – the joint standing committee for principals and brokers in the foreign exchange and currency deposit markets – to be the machinery for regular and smooth communication within the United Kingdom markets. Membership of this joint standing committee is, for banks, at the invitation of the Foreign Exchange Committee of the British

Bankers' Association and, for brokers, at the invitation of the Foreign Exchange and Currency Deposit Brokers Association. As a part of this task, and with the approval of the Foreign Exchange Committee of the British Bankers Association and Foreign Exchange and Currency Deposit Brokers Association, the joint standing committee issues guidelines on the proper practices to be adopted in the market. A paper on this subject was first issued in 1975 and up-dated last in 1984. Banks are required to assist the Bank in supervising the conduct of the foreign exchange and deposit markets in the United Kingdom.

Although there are two distinct documents covering the code of conduct and market practice for firstly the interbank foreign exchange and currency deposit markets and secondly, the sterling interbank deposit markets, they are similar. Generally, as appropriate, their requirements extend to the certificates of deposit markets and any other instruments which are dealt within these markets. Inter alia, the codes of practice and conduct:

- require that all deals with London counterparties are to be conducted on the basis of these codes. Any deals with overseas counterparties made on the basis of standard practice in other centres must be qualified to this effect and the terms specified.

- emphasise that both principals and brokers have a common interest in preserving the anonymity of the market and are equally responsible for the maintenance of confidentiality. The standing of the market and the mutual trust which is its corner stone outweighs any transient gain to which a breach of confidentiality might give rise and the exchange of confidential information in respect of third parties in any setting whatsoever and in whatever direction it flows is forbidden.

- specify that interest on a deposit or loan is paid at maturity, or annually and at maturity, unless special arrangements are made at the time a deal is concluded. On secured loans the members of the LDMA do not pay interest at intervals of less than 28 days. The current general practice is to calculate at close of business on the penultimate working day interest outstanding on secured loans to the last working day of each calendar month and to pay the interest thereon on the last working day of the month. Notice in respect of call, one and two day notice money or changes in interest rate in respect of such money shall be given before noon unless previously arranged. Notice in respect of any other notice money and of changes in rates in respect of such money shall be given before 4.30 p.m. unless previously arranged.

- require brokers to pass details, and banks be prepared to receive them, as soon as practicable after deals have been concluded. The cost and likelihood of errors and misunderstandings is much increased by delay and the consequent need to pass details in batches. In this connection, however, brokers should not normally pass payment instructions where a transaction has been arranged between United Kingdom banks. In these instances, the counterparty banks themselves have a responsibility to give and receive instructions with minimum delay.

- require that brokers should issue confirmations with the minimum of delay at the latest by the value date to a designated place in the bank for such deliveries.

- require banks to check confirmations carefully and immediately (particularly those arriving for value today) in order that discrepancies may be revealed quickly and differences minimised and that they should make enquiries of brokers about particular confirmations which are not received within a reasonable time of the the deal being concluded. The handling of confirmations must take account of the desire of brokers to have a realistic time limit placed on the liability for differences by imposing an obligation upon recipients to check such confirmations. Brokers confirmations constitute an important check upon the detail of deals arranged by brokers and must be sent out without delay. As the majority of differences payable by brokers arise from errors occurring in the quotation of interest rates or the passing of payment instructions, the principals must check confirmations carefully upon receipt so that discrepancies should be quickly revealed and differences minimised. Principals shall also make enquiries of the brokers about particular confirmations which have not been received within a reasonable time of a deal being concluded or about any changes in contract terms, e.g. calls, rate changes, rate fixings etc.

- require that when a principal has informed a broker of his requirement at a rate the principal shall deal in a marketable amount and at the quoted rate with acceptable names and shall remain bound so to deal unless either the broker was informed otherwise at the time of the acceptance or a time limit was placed upon the principal's interest (for example, "firm for one minute only"). At the same time brokers are expected to make it clear whether the prices quoted are firm or merely for guidance and to give an indication of the amount involved; they are also expected to confirm with banks at reasonable intervals that their interest is still firm. A broker who quotes a firm rate without qualification shall be committed to deal at that rate in a marketable amount. Where a broker is quoting only on the basis of one or two names he shall qualify his quotation, e.g. "one small offerer" or "only two names" paying. The amount required to validate normal quotations in the spot and forward markets for different currencies varies. The minimum marketable amount is generally familiar to those involved in particular markets, but it is recommended that banks proposing to deal in unfamiliar markets ask brokers what amounts are sufficient to validate normal market quotations. If the amount to be dealt with is lower than this amount then the proposed amount should be specified by the bank when it initially requests the price.

- require that the name of a borrower or issuer shall be disclosed only when the broker has ascertained that the potential lender or buyer seriously intends to do business. Once a lender or buyer has asked the key question of who pays or whose paper is it, he is considered committed to do business at the price quoted with the name acceptable to him and if not the particular borrower or issuer in question, then with an alternative acceptable name provided the alternative name shall be immediately shown to him by the broker. In negotiating foreign exchange transactions bank names should never be disclosed until the deal is being closed and brokers may make it clear when asked when an overseas name is being offered and banks have the right to ask for that name before concluding deals. Where a London bank's name proves unacceptable to another London name and the broker quite properly refuses to say by whom it was refused the bank may sometimes feel that the broker has in fact quoted a price which cannot be substantiated. In such cases, which will hopefully remain rare, the principals of the broking firm concerned may ask the Bank of England to obtain the reluctant counterparty's confirmation that he did have business to do at the quoted price and to assure the aggrieved party that this was so without of course revealing the reluctant bank's name.

- require that the name of a lender or buyer shall be disclosed only after the borrower's or issuer's name has been accepted by the lender or buyer, and the borrower or issuer shall have the right to refuse the particular lender or buyer, provided that he be prepared to accept at that time sums up to the same amount and at the same price from an alternative acceptable name immediately shown to the broker.

- recognise the right of a bank to turn down a name which includes the taking of deposits and could therefore require predisclosure of the name before closing the deal. However, in dealing with brokers, principals should whenever possible give brokers prior indication of those categories of principals with whom they would be unwilling to do business in order that the smooth operation of the markets be facilitated and frustration on all sides be minimised.

- require that a bank's management should issue clear guidelines to their staff as to the nature and extent of dealing after hours and they should make specific arrangements to ensure that all such deals are properly authorised and confirmed by telex direct to the counterparty's dealing room. The foreign exchange market has been used to dealing almost round the clock. Dealing after hours in other centres must therefore form an integral part of the operations of many international banks both in London and elsewhere. However, there are additional hazards involved in such dealing. For example, when dealing continues during the evening either in London or in any other centre, from premises other than the bank's dealing rooms, one of the banks involved might subsequently deny or simply forget having done a deal. Brokers, too, could find themselves involved or might run the risk of a claim from a bank whose counterparty denies having dealt.

- establish dispute procedures. Differences may result either from errors in payment or repayment instructions, or from a broker having in good faith indicated a firm rate being unable to substantiate his quotation, whilst there is a moral responsibility so to do. If both parties to any dispute about a difference agree, they may invite the respective joint standing committee to arbitrate. All unresolved disputes between principals and brokers concerning the application of the code of conduct or of market practice may, subject to the agreement of both parties, be referred for arbitration to the respective joint standing committees. In such cases, the decision of the joint standing committee shall be final. Serious breaches of these codes of conduct should be reported to the Joint Standing Committee which will investigate them and report its findings as appropriate to the Foreign Exchange Committee, and the British Bankers Association or the Foreign Exchange and Currency Deposit Brokers Association. Persistent difficulties experienced by a broker in collecting brokerage may also be reported to the joint standing committee.

- require that all principals and brokers participating in these markets adhere to the spirit as well as to the letter of the code of conduct, shall uphold it at all times and shall ensure that all parties acting in concert therewith shall act in a manner in keeping with the maintenance of a high reputation for the London markets.

These documents also establish those codes of conduct related to personal relationships between broker and principals highlighted in Chapter 8.

These codes of conduct and market practice are of more than academic interest to those directly involved in financial markets other than the interbank sterling and foreign currency deposit and foreign exchange markets both within and outside of the United Kingdom. Most UK based foreign exchange and currency deposit brokers have internationalised themselves and they comprise the major broking force in the international foreign exchange and currency deposit markets together with several domestic markets. Additionally all major UK banks operate in most, if not all, of the major financial centres and financial markets of the world. These facts together with the number of foreign banks that operate within the London markets have resulted in these codes of market practice and conduct effectively establishing themselves as the basis of accepted international standards; and also as applicable and appropriate custom and practice in many other domestic interbank deposit and foreign exchange markets, the direct bank to bank market and several other related financial markets in other forms of instruments.

CHAPTER SEVENTEEN

Futures Markets – Practice and Procedures

Introduction

Futures refer to all standard contracts traded on a futures exchange. Financial futures trading in currencies commenced with the opening of the International Monetary Market (IMM), a subsidiary of the Chicago Mercantile Exchange (CME) on 16th May 1972. Gold futures developed immediately residents of the United States were authorised to buy and hold gold on the 2nd January 1975. Futures in financial instruments were first traded on the Chicago Board of Trade Exchange (CBOT) on the 24th October 1975. Both financial futures and futures in currencies were introduced in London with the opening of the London International Financial Futures Exchange (LIFFE) during September 1982. Similar instruments are now also available on exchanges in Australia, Canada, Holland and Singapore. A London Gold Futures Market (LGFM) was established in April 1982, but anticipated business levels did not materialise and this exchange subsequently closed during 1985.

Although the concepts of trading this type of instrument are in many countries relatively new, they have been a major part of the United States commodity sector for well in excess of 100 years and now constitute a multi-million dollar retail and wholesale business. Consequently futures exchanges, and businesses associated therewith, have become a highly regulated industry in the United States. This has resulted in several aspects of the industry within that country being different from the more recently established futures markets in other countries. Additionally practices and procedures are not consistent between exchanges either inside or outside of the United States. Therefore, in this chapter the subject of futures is not developed in its entirety as common market practice but in many instances explains the different standards which may be applied.

A futures exchange is a central meeting place that provides facilities for its authorised trading members to buy and sell futures contracts by "open outcry" auction. "Open outcry" is exactly what it implies. These are face to face exchanges on which trading takes place by word of mouth, with all prices instantly available to all participants in the market. Futures contracts are binding agreements to buy or to sell standard quantities of specific commodities at a currently determined price for delivery at a specified time in the future.

The Futures Contract

The contracts traded on futures exchanges are standardized contracts, the specifications of which are established by each exchange and therefore specifications for the same underlying object may differ from exchange to exchange. Futures contracts are not tangible objects or negotiable instruments which physically pass from buyer to seller, they comprise legally binding contracts based upon the specifications which are formulated by an exchange in a format that facilitates them being readily bought and sold on that exchange in contract unit sizes. The buyer and seller know exactly what the underlying commodity is and only require to indicate the number of contracts, referred to as "lots", bought or sold; the trading price and month of delivery of the transaction, and the floor member with whom the trade was executed.

The main characteristics of standardised contracts are provided below. These characteristics are illustrated by reference, in sequence, to the specifications of the 90 day US Treasury Bill contract of the IMM, and sterling currency contract of LIFFE as at the date of this publication:

- Contract type:
  - 90 day US treasury bill
  - sterling

- Contract size or contract unit of trading:
  - US$1 million
  - £25,000

334

- Contract grade or standard: The specific commodity or instrument type which may be offered when making delivery,
  - US Treasury Bills with 91 days to maturity
  - Sterling currency in London

- Delivery months: the predetermined months of expiration in each year during which delivery is to be made,
  - March, June, September and December,
  - March, June, September and December,

The number of delivery months which are traded at any one time will be determined at the discretion of each exchange.

- Delivery time: the time of delivery within the delivery month on which the underlying contract is to be settled,
  - begins on the first day of the spot month on which a 13-week treasury bill is issued and a one-year treasury bill has 13 weeks remaining to maturity
  - second Wednesday of the delivery month

- Last trading day: the last day for trading in each contract during the delivery month. This day will be defined and will also normally include a specified time during that day when business will cease,
  - 10.00 a.m. on the business day preceding the first day of the spot month
  - 10.31 a.m. on the second business day prior to the delivery day

- Quotation Size: the units of the total contract size and manner in which price quotations are made,
  - US$100 minus the rate of interest
  - US Dollars and cents per one pound sterling unit

- Minimum price fluctuation: defines the smallest "tick" or point increment of movement per quotation size,
  - one basis point per quotation size
  - one hundreth of a basis point of the rate

Therefore, the minimum price movement on these examples would be:
- 90 day US Treasury Bills – US$25 i.e.

$$\frac{(.01 \times 1,000,000 \times 90)}{360 \times 100}$$

Where .01 = minimum price fluctuation
1,000,000 = contract size (US$1 million)
90 = period of underlying treasury bill
360 = basis number of days
100 = percentage conversion

Sterling – US$2.50 i.e. (25,000 × .0001)
Where 25,000 = contract size
.0001 = minimum price fluctuation

The Futures Exchange
A futures exchange is a self regulated, non-profit making institution in which its members play an active role in voting and serving as officers. Each has its own trading, organisational and membership rules with which its members, and as appropriate, their employees, are expected to comply. Although these rules differ from exchange to exchange, they have the common objective of maintaining financially sound, orderly, competitive and supervised markets. To cover expenses, overheads, etc. each exchange imposes levies and charges on its members, including exchange fees or transaction charges for each contract concluded on the exchange. Exchanges do, on occasions, formalise links with other exchanges to facilitate their respective members being able to trade on the other exchange. This is of particular importance within the international context, when members may wish to trade outside of normal fixed trading times of one exchange. The first major international link of this nature was between the Singapore Monetary Exchange and Chicago Mercantile Exchange, where a full mutual offset system exists.

Whilst the daily supervision of each exchange rests with the board of that exchange, exchanges are normally also subject to surveillance

336

by official bodies. In the United States of America futures contracts may only be traded on a Board of Trade exchange designated for that purpose by the Commodities Futures Trading Commission (CFTC). The CFTC was established in 1974 to supervise and regulate all the futures markets operating within the United States. Prior to the formation of the CFTC this responsibility was vested in the Commodity Exchange Authority (CEA), but the latter's mandate was restricted to regulating futures in specifically listed agricultural commodities. All exchanges designated by the CFTC are subject to the continued supervision and regulation of the CFTC, with each new type of contract requiring their prior approval. In the United Kingdom the Bank of England watches over LIFFE.

Each exchange and/or its supervisory body will, inter alia:

- establish trading, accounting and recording standards, procedures and practices with which all or specific members are expected to comply.

- regularly review the financial integrity and status of each member.

- have audit and investigation departments, together with other supervisory committees to examine members activities and records.

- hold authority to introduce stringent disciplinary procedures, including the right to suspend, expel and withdraw membership, should market members abuse the privileged position afforded to them, disrupt the orderly conduct of the markets, fail to comply with accounting and other rules of the exchange or fail to meet the financial criteria of the exchange, its clearing house or its supervisory body. (The role of a clearing house is developed later in this chapter).

- establish confirmation procedures –
  confirmation requirements for executed trades differ from exchange to exchange. In the United States the CFTC requires all exchange members to confirm trades with each other. In prac-

tice, some exchanges allow this to be by verbal communication, others require more formal procedures. On the LIFFE floor, members are not required fully to exchange contracts between themselves and it is left to the matching and clearing function to identify any discrepancies.

Membership of an exchange is achieved by the purchase of a "seat", or the purchase of a licence to a seat on that exchange. Although the number of "seats" on any one exchange is limited, they are transferable and may be leased on some exchanges from non-trading members. However, the purchase or lease of a seat will be subject to the purchaser or lessee satisfying the qualification requirements and financial criteria of the membership rules of the exchange which will require proof of adequate ability and financial integrity. Some exchanges will only accept individuals as members although in most cases these exchanges will extend some membership rights to a company with whom the individual member is associated. In particular, the clearing house will normally provide clearing membership and also, upon the receipt of notice, the exchange will recognise an institution's interest in the beneficial ownership of a seat. Where exchanges accept corporate membership, a nominated floor member together with their alternates will require to be registered with, and acceptable to, the exchange.

Membership does not always automatically provide trading authority and members may be required to apply specifically for floor membership to be able to undertake business on the floor of an exchange. A demonstration of expertise including a period of assessment or other form of examination by the exchange is also common practice for all floor personnel. Bonding requirements for individual floor members are not unusual within the United States. Some exchanges also provide restricted trading membership, which only facilitates trading in one particular – or a limited number of – specified contract types on the exchange. One seat on an exchange will only permit the deployment of one floor member. Floor members are the only persons authorised to trade on the floor of an exchange and they will include brokers and hedgers.

There are two types of broker that operate exclusively within an

338

exchange; they are "floor brokers" and "pit brokers". Floor brokers will execute orders on the floor of the exchange as agent for other members of that exchange, who may or may not have a presence on the floor of the exchange. "Pit brokers" will execute orders on the floor of the exchange as agent for members who also have a presence on the floor but prefer, for one reason or another, not to execute particular transactions themselves. Both of these brokers charge fees for the services they provide. Floor traders are the speculators within these markets who buy and sell contracts on an exchange with a view to profiting from subsequent price movements. Hedgers represent dealers, producers or commercial users, and their activities on the exchange relate to covering positions in the underlying subject matter of each contract. Dealers do not feature on the floor of an exchange as the market making process comprises all interests on the floor.

The trading rules of each exchange will clearly define the manner of trading on that exchange. Access to the trading floor is normally tightly controlled, being restricted to floor members and exchange officials, together with their respective, but often limited number, of employees.

On the floor of an exchange the trading of each separate contract is undertaken in a designated "pit", "ring" or such other place, as directed by the exchange for that purpose. Trading can only take place within the area designated and only during such trading periods for that contract as defined by the exchange. The contract specifications will include details of the times during which contracts are traded on the exchange. The "opening" and the "close" of each period of trading is normally signified by the sounding of a bell. The purpose of these requirements is to ensure that:

- A common market place exists for all orders in that contract

- The competitive determination of prices in each futures contract

- All trades are focused into the market place

- Access is allowed to the market for all orders

On the floor of an exchange business is conducted on the basis of bid and offered prices. However, the format of prices quoted on a futures exchange may or may not be similar to those used in the corresponding cash and forward markets and care requires to be exercised when using futures as a hedge against, or arbitraging with, the physical markets. For example Euro Dollar and Sterling deposit contracts are normally quoted as a discounted price for a nominal 100 US$ or pounds sterling respectively on a ninety day quarter over a 360 day base whereas the corresponding cash markets make quotations as simple rates of interest, for the actual number of days over respectively a 360 and 365 day base. Futures Bond and Gilt prices are usually quoted on a similar basis to the corresponding cash markets i.e. a discounted basis on a nominal 100 units. Currency contracts may comprise either direct or indirect quotations and do not always follow the international standards. Each exchange will provide for a continuous flow of price information to be made available to interested parties outside of the exchange, although when formally communicated this normally comprises a single price at which the last trade was undertaken.

Most futures exchanges prohibit the posting of any "kerb-traded" contracts on the exchange. "Kerb-trading" refers to trading which takes place outside of the designated trading area or outside of the trading periods for that contract. There are, however, exceptions to this rule. For example some exchanges accept the posting of 'exchange for physical' transactions. Exchange for physicals enables participants to exchange futures contracts for commodities in other locations or markets. The prime requirement for an exchange for physical transactions is the existence of a physical position either spot or forward in the cash markets. This position is bought or sold against an equal but opposite spot or forward transaction with a similar spot and forward position being established on the exchange. The cash market transactions can then be reversed leaving a square position and either the spot or deferred delivery month on the exchange liquidated.

The Clearing House
An integral, but separate function to the operations of a futures exchange, is that of the clearing house. Each exchange appoints a

340

clearing house through which all contracts traded on that exchange are cleared and registered. Clearing houses may be independent bodies, comprise subsidiary or associate companies of an exchange or be owned by all or some of the clearing members of an exchange. However, irrespective of their ownership, for the purpose of their function, they are completely independent of the exchange and are profit making organisations. Members of the exchange who wish to become clearing members must make separate application for membership of the clearing house and in addition to any specific fees associated with membership will be required to pay a registration fee on each contract cleared and registered on their behalf.

The clearing house will only clear trades and have a direct relationship with its members and therefore those members of an exchange who are not clearing members must make arrangements to be in account with a clearing member, or members, prior to being able to commence trading on the exchange. Clearing members will charge other members clearing fees for this facility.

Whilst documentation and procedural requirements will differ from clearing house to clearing house (and indeed exchange to exchange) the functions, obligations and activities of a clearing house in regard to futures contracts are fundamentally the same throughout the world. During a business day trade tickets or other reports are submitted to the clearing house by both the buyer and seller of each contract traded. The details required by the clearing house are:

- The contract and contract month

- The number of lots, that have been bought and sold

- The contract price per lot

- Identity of the buyer and seller and, as appropriate, the clearing member through whom the trade is to be cleared

The clearing house or exchange will "match", i.e. agree the detail on corresponding purchase and sale tickets, and thereafter those which are matched and are acceptable to the clearing house will be processed. The clearing house will have the authority to accept or reject, after consultation with the board of the exchange, the registration of any contract and also, without assigning any reason, make the registration of any contract subject to any condition stipulated by them.

Any trades reported by buyers and sellers which are not matched or differ in detail, i.e. trade size or trade price, will be rejected by the clearing house. It is then the responsibility of the floor members who executed the transaction to investigate and correct the trade and arrange for its re-submission to the clearing system. Rejected items will comprise those which are simply in error and can be readily resolved and re-submitted, together with those which are in dispute between floor members. In this latter case, if the floor members are unable to resolve the issue, it will be referred through the disputes procedures to an exchange official who will, if necessary, normally have the authority to instruct either one or both of the parties to close the deal in the pit for clearance and registration through the clearing house pending the resolution of the dispute.

At the end of each business day the clearing house will provide each clearing member with a trading statement giving details of all accepted contracts which it has received in that member's name, together with a list of any outstanding rejected items. The clearing member is required to verify this detail and confirm within a stipulated time period its acceptance of those cleared contracts or advise the exchange of any contracts which are to be transferred to the clearing account of another clearing member. The clearing member may also correct any rejected items for acceptance by the exchange for that day's trading. In practice the correction of rejected items and the re-allocation of trades normally takes place during the day and will not be outstanding on these statements.

On receipt of the clearing member's acceptance of daily trades, the clearing house will register contracts and issue a registration statement to each member. Up to the point of registration floor members have direct contractual relationships as principals with each other. However, once a contract is registered the clearing house will, subject to any restrictive clauses incorporated in its rules or other conditions stipulated by it from time to time, guarantee the fulfilment of all

342

contracts by their clearing members and, from the point of registration, the clearing house becomes the seller of the contract to each buyer and the buyer of the contract to each seller as principal to principal.

As every registered contract involves a matched purchase and sale the clearing house is in balance at all times with the open long positions of clearing members being equal to the open short positions of other clearing members. Open contracts are those which have been bought or sold without the transaction having been offset or "liquidated" by a subsequent sale or purchase. These procedures facilitate participants in the market to open, and subsequently to liquidate positions merely by executing orders and without the necessity of seeking out the original contracting party. In futures trading each contract month is treated in isolation. The purchase of one long March contract and the sale of one short June contract within the same contract type will create a "long March open position" and a "short June open position" - a straddle position – within that contract. To "liquidate" these positions a market participant would merely require to sell one March contract and buy one June contract.

Within the United States, clearing members are required to segregate the positions of their clients from their own positions with the clearing house. Most clearing houses will allow one account to be maintained for all clients, an "omnibus" account, although one or two exchanges do require gross client positions to be maintained. Similar requirements do not exist as far as the International Commodities Clearing House (ICCH), the clearing house for LIFFE is concerned, and these clearing members may maintain one position representing the aggregate of its own and of its clients positions.

From the time of registration of a contract with the clearing house, each participant within the futures markets is released from credit control considerations related to each other and thereafter has a credit risk with the clearing house until such time as a position is subsequently closed or delivery takes place. The credit risk for the period from consummation of a trade to registration is normally accepted by clearing members on the basis of the exchange's frequent vetting of the financial integrity of its members together with the other controls implemented to ensure performance.

Margins

To secure the performance of each outstanding contract registered in the name of clearing members, the clearing house will require its members to place "initial" ("opening" or "original") margin with, or to the order of, the clearing house. These margins will be required on each open position as reflected in the accounts of the clearing house. In the United States a clearing member's client's net, or where appropriate, gross positions, and their own open positions must each be separately margined.

The levels at which these margins are established will be determined by the clearing house, in conjunction with the exchange and will be based upon the assessed maximum movement which may be expected in the market on any one day. Initial margins/levels only constitute a relatively small percentage of the underlying contract value and are effectively collateral against day to day price movements rather than a deposit covering the contractual liability.

Initial margin requirements are usually calculated on the basis of each day's closing positions and collected from, or any excesses re-paid to, clearing members on the subsequent business day. Initial margin levels are normally the same for "nearby" and "deferred" month positions, "nearby" being the next delivery month and "deferred" being the more distant months. Some exchanges do however require higher levels of margin for "spot month" contracts. The "spot month" is the current delivery month for each contract. The definition of when a contract is treated as spot month varies. It may for example be the business day upon which the nearest month contract expires; the first day of the delivery month of the nearest month contract, or a specified number of days before the last day of trading of the nearest month contract. Each clearing house will have the right to increase or decrease original margin requirements and at its discretion it may charge individual clearing members higher or lower levels of original margin, and some clearing houses introduce scale levels relative to the absolute size of clearing members open positions.

Reduced levels of original margin requirements are frequently allowed for specific trades which a clearing house recognises as being acceptable as compensating positions against each other. These may include:

- Inter-delivery month spreads –
  these comprise straddle positions where long positions in one month are compensated by short positions in another month of the same contract. In considering inter-delivery month spreads exchanges may
  - have higher levels of reduced margin for spreads involving spot month contracts
  - not differentiate between spot and other months, or
  - require that spot month contracts are ignored for the purpose of calculating spreads.

- Inter commodity spreads –
  This will provide for long positions in one contract to be offset by short positions in another contract traded on that exchange where it is perceived that a close correlation exists between the price movements of various types of contract traded.

- Hedge margins –
  These are available to recognised hedgers of cash market positions. Clearing members who require to take advantage of this facility for themselves or their clients must apply for the appropriate registration as a hedger to the clearing house. Registered hedgers will be subject to random inspection to ensure they are trading for this purpose.

Additionally, some exchanges permit positions in the same type of, or correlating contracts established on one exchange to be offset by positions in similar or related types of contract on other exchanges. To qualify for this set-off a clearing member may be required to be a clearing member of both exchanges on which offsetting contracts are traded. Where the contracts are for different contract unit sizes, pro-rata adjustments are made.

Initial margin requirements for the IMM 90 day US Treasury Bill contract and the LIFFE sterling contract are:

	Near and Deferred Months	*Delivery Month*
US$1,000,000 US Treasury Bill Contract:		
Initial margin	US$2,000	US$2,000
Hedge margin	not available	not available
Inter-delivery month spread	US$400	US$400
Inter-commodity spread*	US$500	US$500
Inter-exchange spread	not available	not available

*Available against US domestic certificates of deposits and eurodollar time deposits

£25,000 Sterling contract:		
Initial margin	US$1,000	US$1,000
Hedge margin	not available	not available
Inter-delivery month spread	US$100	not available
Inter-commodity spread	not available	not available
Inter-exchange spread	not available	not available

Using the above, the calculation of initial margin requirements is illustrated by the following examples.

	Number of Contracts bought and sold		
	Short	*Long*	*Open Positions*
Spot delivery month (March)	17	12	5 Short
June	52	36	16 Short
September	19	28	9 Long
December	7	15	8 Long

Initial margin:

US Treasury bills = *17 straddle positions
  @ US$400 each = US$6,800
  ** 4 open contracts
  @ US$2,000 each = US$8,000
  Total initial margin = US$14,800

  * Calculated as 17 open long positions (9 September
  + 8 December) against 17 of the 21 open short positions
  (5 spot + 16 June).
** The difference between the 21 short and 17 long positions

Sterling = *5 spot month contracts
  @ US$1,000 = US$5,000
  ** 16 straddle positions
  @ US$100 = US$1,600
  *** 1 open contract
  @ US$1,000 = US$1,000
  Total initial margin = US$7,600

   * Spread margins are not available for spot month contracts.
  ** Calculated as 16 June short positions offset against 17
  long positions (9 September plus 8 December).
*** The difference between the 17 long positions (September and
  December) and 16 short positions (June).

Assuming a clearing member on the IMM also had the following
positions in certificates of deposit, with CDs having the same initial
and inter-delivery month spread as treasury bills, the initial margin
requirement would be:

	Number of CD and *Treasury Bill contracts*		
	Short	*Long*	*Open Positions*
June	11	7	4 Short
September	3	14	11 Long
December	–	2	2 Long

Initial margin:

US treasury bills   * 17 inter-delivery spread
positions @ US$400=   US$6,800

Certificates of deposit
     **   4 inter-delivery spread
positions @ US$400=   US$1,600

US treasury bills–CD
     ***   4 inter-commodity spreads
@ US$500   =   US$2,000

CDs   ****   5 open contracts
@ US$2,000   =   US$10,000

Total initial margin   =   US$20,400

    * 17 open long positions (9 September 8 December) against
17 of the 21 open short positions (5 spot + 16 June)
   ** 4 open short June positions against 4 of the 13 long
positions (11 September + 2 December)
  *** Balance of 4 short Treasury Bill contracts against 4 of
the remaining certificate of deposit positions
**** The remaining 5 long Certificate of Deposit contracts.

Each clearing house will prescribe the methods by which initial margin requirements can be satisfied. In the United States these will normally provide for cash deposits, the deposit of defined securities with a specified percentage of the current market value acceptable as margin, or utilisations under bankers letters of credit issued in favour of, and acceptable to, the clearing house. At the time of this publication all initial margin requirements imposed for LIFFE contracts, have to be satisfied with cash deposits.

In addition to initial margins each clearing house will require that all profits and losses are settled between its clearing members on a daily basis. As the clearing house is the buyer or the seller of each registered contract to each clearing member, this means that the clearing house 'marks-to-market' each member's daily activities and open positions.

A mark-to-market exercise is the valuation of the contract price of each outstanding contract against the current day's settlement price for that contract month. Within this process the previous day's closing position, at the previous day's settlement price, together with all purchases and sales during each day at their contract price, are revalued at the closing settlement price for each contract month. Effectively this means that all profits and losses on each day's trading are realised with outstanding open positions being marked to market against the current day's settlement price. This can be illustrated by the following examples.

If we assume a clearing member has a long open position in gold of 10 February contracts at a contract price equal to the previous day's settlement price of 320 and the following business day he sells these contracts at 322 his profit will be:

$(322 - 320) \times 10 \times 100 = \text{US\$2,000}$
where   10 = the number of contracts
       100 = ounces per contract.

In a mark to market exercise with a February settlement price of US$327 this transaction would reflect as:

March Bought 10 @ 320 Settlement 327 +$7,000 (327–320 × 10 × 100)
March Sold   10 @ 322 Settlement 327 −$5,000 (327–322 × 10 × 100)

                Daily profit   +$2,000

If the same position holder had undertaken a series of contracts which opened and liquidated positions in the same contract month, the same principle is applied:

			Settlement		
March B	10 @ 320		327	+	US$7,000
B	1 @ 322		327	+	5,000
B	3 @ 323		327	+	4,000
S	5 @ 325		327	−	2,000
S	1 @ 321		327	−	6,000
		Daily profit			US$8,000

Total bought   14
Total sold   6

Open position   8 contracts long @ 327, which would be carried forward as an open position for that contract month

Those members reflecting an overall loss are required to pay such losses to the clearing house, and those reflecting overall profits receive these profits. These payments are referred to as variation margin.

The daily settlement price for each contract date is established by each exchange or clearing house. This price may be the last price traded, the average of a range of prices, or where it is considered closing prices were not reflective of the market, it may be based upon the judgment of exchange officials. For the purpose of establishing variation margin calls each contract type is initially treated in isolation. However, some exchanges do allow profits and losses in various related contract types to be settled on a net basis.

Whilst as a general principle all futures clearing houses mark to market on a daily basis, LIFFE formally closes all contracts to market and opens new contracts the following day at the previous day's settlement price. This subtle but important difference is due to legal considerations related to United Kingdom gaming legislation.

The mark-to-market exercise is completed as at the close of business each day and the clearing house will require all variation margins to be settled by its members the following business day. Variation margin requirements will normally have to be settled with the clearing house in cash although some will accept variation margin calls being satisfied by the the deposit of defined marketable securities. Utilisations under letters of credit are not normally accepted to satisfy variation margin between the clearing house and clearing members. If a clearing member does not satisfy margin calls expeditiously the clearing house will liquidate the positions through "buying in" to close short positions and "selling out" to close long positions. The clearing house is, within its guarantee, liable for the full obligations of a defaulting clearing member.

In addition to clearing house requirements in respect of original and variation margins, each exchange imposes rules upon its clearing members (and as discussed, separately its non-clearing members) to collect from non-clearing members minimum levels of initial and variation margin requirements as established by the exchange. This is part of the procedure an exchange uses to secure the obligation of its non-clearing members. The basis upon which initial margin requirements are calculated will be similar to those which have been discussed in relation to the clearing house and its members. The minimum levels will usually be the same as those applied to clearing members, although this need not necessarily be the case. They are minimum levels and each clearing member may at his discretion impose higher requirements on individual non-clearing members. Most exchanges will require that clearing members are in possession of sufficient initial margin prior to accepting trades from non-clearing members whilst others are prepared to rely on the clearing member being satisfied that they will collect margin within a reasonable period of time. In addition to initial margin, each exchange will also require clearing members to calculate variation margin due to or from non-clearing members on a daily basis, with all resultant profits and losses not necessarily settled, but debited or credited to the non-clearing member's account with the clearing member.

Within the United States futures markets, the necessity to collect variation margin for resultant losses is normally related to initial margin maintenance levels as established by each exchange. These requirements provide that any losses as reflected by the daily mark to market process, may be set against initial margins provided the net level of initial margin does not fall below the defined minimum maintenance level for that contract. If the minimum maintenance margin level is reached the exchange will require that clearing members collect sufficient funds to reinstate margins at their full required initial margin level. These arrangements must not circumvent initial margin requirements and all new contracts require full initial margin to be separately provided. These will usually comprise one, or more, of cash, securities or letters of credit. On LIFFE, maintenance levels are not used and all shortfalls resultant from closing to market must be collected immediately in cash.

A clearing member is responsible to the clearing house at all times for the full margin contributions of all its clients, both original and variation. Should a non-clearing member default on a margin call the clearing member will be required to liquidate that member's position and meet if necessary any resultant shortfall between the close out price and the equity held in the customer's accounts or from his own resources.

Commission Brokers

The previous pages have focused upon the relationships between the exchange, the clearing house and their respective members. The participation of non-exchange members, which will also include brokers, traders, hedgers, speculators and dealers, now follows:

In the same way that the clearing house will only act as principal with its clearing members, each exchange will only allow its members to act as principals to each other on any contract undertaken on that exchange. Consequently, all other participants in these markets must, either directly or indirectly, be the client of, and undertake contracts through, members of that exchange on a principal to principal relationship. Exchange members, both clearing and non-clearing, who enable non-exchange members to participate on the exchange are "commission brokers".

Within the context of the futures markets a "commission broker's" liability extends beyond the role of agent which is normally implied in a broker/principal relationship. Each "commission broker" and their respective clients are principals to each other on all contracts arranged between them. Thereafter it is the "commission broker's" responsibility to execute a client's order, as principal directly on the exchange.

We previously examined the roles of members who operate exclusively on the exchange which included "pit brokers", "floor brokers", "traders" and "hedgers". This fifth type of member – the "commission broker" is probably the most important within the futures industry next to the exchange and the clearing house. In practice many of these functions are interchangeable with any one member from time to time undertaking one or more roles. However, it is important to distinguish clearly between each role as they have very different liabilities and responsibilities. A "commission broker" need not necessarily execute the orders of its clients on the floor of the exchange and will frequently use the services provided by "floor brokers".

As a consequence of the privileged position extended to "commission brokers" each exchange's rules will include specific provisions designed to protect their clients interests. Inter alia these will usually:

- Establish procedures and systems to ensure that adequate accounting and other records are maintained

- Provide for the production of timely and accurate reports and positions for each client

- Require the segregation of clients positions within the records of the "exchange commission broker"

- Provide clients with confirmations of each transaction

- Specify a procedure for the allocation of trades between clients, and between clients and "broker"/"trader"

- Restrict withholding orders from the market place

- Disallow the crossing of trades between clients, without first offering them in the market place

- Prohibit taking the other side of clients orders without them being offered in the market

- Specify procedures for discretionary orders placed by clients

- Prohibit the disclosure of customer orders held

- Require all orders to be time stamped

- Arrange for the time recording of orders executed

Conversely, to protect the financial integrity of the exchange, its members and the clearing house, all "commission brokers" who are exchange members will be required by the exchange to collect from their clients at least the minimum levels of initial margin established by the exchange and as appropriate, maintain adequate maintenance margin levels for, or collect variation margins on, all losses resultant from a daily mark-to-market of clients positions. The minimum requirements are normally on the same basis, and provide similar reduced levels, as those already described for the relationship between clearing and non-clearing members. Each "commission broker" is responsible to the exchange to make good any shortfalls or losses resultant from its clients activities and is required to close out any positions on which margin calls are not made promptly.

The above comments specifically refer to "commission brokers" who are exchange members. However, within the futures industry "commission brokers" are not always members of the exchange on which they buy and sell contracts for clients and it is therefore necessary to distinguish further between "exchange commission brokers" and "non-exchange commission brokers". The "non-exchange commission broker" acts as a principal for contracts with their clients, and also as a principal and a client of an "exchange commission broker", with the latter subsequently executing orders as principal on the exchange. The protection afforded to clients of "exchange commission brokers" by the exchange rules will only apply to clients of its members, and does not extend to the clients of "non-exchange commission brokers".

354

Within the United States all "commission brokers", whether exchange or non-exchange, are Futures Commission Merchants (FCMs) and must be registered with and approved by the CFTC. Each FCM is subject to the regulatory control and supervision of that body. FCMs are the only bodies in the United States authorised to accept orders for the purchase or sale of futures contracts from non-exchange members.

The regulatory requirements imposed upon FCMs in the United States are often more specific, detailed, and require higher financial criteria than those which may be imposed by individual exchanges upon their members. Consequently, each exchange is required to apply CTFC standards to all members who are FCMs. Each "exchange FCM" is required to maintain its own positions separately from those of its clients not only in its internal records, but also with the clearing house or, as appropriate, with its clearing member. Additionally, the CFTC stipulate procedures for "exchange FCMs" to follow when dealing with "non-exchange FCMs" and "overseas commission brokers". In particular these require each "exchange FCM" to ensure that its "non-exchange FCM" and "overseas commission broker" clients not only similarly segregate their clients positions with the member FCM but also provide gross initial margin on each individual clients's open position.

Separately from the specific requirements that an exchange places upon member FCMs, the CFTC require all exchange and non-exchange FCMs to comply with recording, reporting and accounting practices as defined by them. Inter alia, these provide for:

- Client Protection in Trading
  – including risk disclosure relating to futures trading. Confirmation of all trades. The manner in which customers orders are treated, for example time stamping orders and execution of trades, allocation of trades between customers, not crossing trades or taking the other side of orders, etc.

- The Protection of Clients Funds and Property
  – segregation of client funds, restricted investment criteria for funds held, restrictions on collateral security which may be

accepted as margin or to cover losses and the provision of loans and guarantees by FCMs.

Similar regulation of "non-exchange commission brokers" is not applied outside of the United States and therefore clients dealing with such brokers are not afforded any additional protection other than that which is available through normal commercial enquiry and legal processes. However, it is worth mentioning that within the UK an association styled "The Association of Futures Brokers and Dealers" has been formed as an investor protection agency for the commodity and financial futures markets.

There are two further brokers/commission agents that provide services in futures contracts. These are traditional "money brokers" who act as intermediaries between clients and their commission brokers, and within the United States, the "Introducing Broker" who plays a specific role as a commission agent to FCMs. In these roles neither party is a "commission broker" and they do not act as principals.

Having described the various participants and their manner of access to the futures markets it may be helpful to reflect briefly upon the practical implications of exchange and clearing house margin procedures previously discussed.

A clearing member's position with the clearing house will represent not only his own open position and total outstanding contracts but may also include those of his clients including non-clearing members. Similarly each individual non-clearing member's position will comprise its own open position and total outstanding contracts together with those of its clients. The clearing house requires its members to place minimum initial margins with the clearing house on all open positions. In turn, by the rules of the exchange, each member of the exchange is also required to obtain at least minimum initial margin requirements, as defined by the exchange, from all of its clients either exchange or non-exchange. Therefore, through this mechanism all open contracts entered into directly with or by exchange members in the market place is margined, albeit the gross margin received by non-clearing members may not equate with the margins they place

356

with their clearing member(s). Similarly the margins placed by clearing members with the clearing house may not equate with those it receives from its exchange and non exchange clients.

Resultant from variation margin procedures, all profits and losses on both closed and open contracts are calculated and settled between the clearing house and its members each day. Additionally all exchange members are required to have sufficient funds from their clients to cover all losses on open contracts either by way of equity, variation margin requirements or initial margin maintenance levels. Through this mechanism all losses, both due and accrued, are provided for each day. Within the United States similar procedures extend to "non-exchange commission brokers". Outside of the United States this is not necessarily so.

Consequently, not only do the exchange and clearing house procedures facilitate the buying and selling of contracts, they also encourage positions to be opened and subsequently liquidated with the variation margin procedure realising profits and collecting losses immediately. This procedure provides the opportunity to trade on a highly leveraged basis in the underlying subject matter without the financial commitment of delivery that exists within the cash markets.

As may be appreciated from the above, the levels of original and initial margin requirement are integral elements to the overall security of these markets, and are based on the anticipated level of daily price movements. However, it is a fact that at times price volatility exceeds these anticipated levels. Therefore, as a further step to secure the performance of obligation, exchanges impose daily price limits on contracts, to provide for the re-calculation and re-establishment of margin levels. These limits are expressed as a price above or below the previous day's daily settlement prices and should the market price exceed this level – referred to as "limit up" or "limit down", – trading is suspended at that level for that day or a period of time, unless cash market prices return to levels which would facilitate trading to recommence within the range established. Although this modus operandi has merit in the context of market integrity it does impose problems, as it creates artificial distortions between futures and cash market prices, and also precludes participants from liquidating positions on the exchange.

This was a major problem during the "silver crisis" of 1979/80 when both silver and gold futures prices went "limit up" immediately the market opened on an escalating market and subsequently "limit down" on a collapsing market. The problems associated with this situation are:

- The financial ability of a short position holder on a rising market, or, on a falling market a long position holder, to meet a continuing daily variation margin requirement to the extent of the price limit for any sustained period of time.

- The ability of position holders to provide the necessary funds to purchase and deliver the contract(s) if forced into delivery.

- The ability of the exchange members and/or, more particularly the clearing house to honour their respective obligations should one, or a number, of the major participants in the market fail due to these circumstances.

To avoid these problems and to allow both spot and deferred futures prices to converge with cash market prices, it is frequently the practice for exchanges not to impose any daily price limit on the then current spot delivery month contract and similarly some exchanges also have limit free periods for a specified period on all, or some contracts, towards the end of each day's trading. This is usually restricted to the last hour. A number of exchanges provide for increased scaled price limits which will be introduced if a contract goes limit up or limit down on a specified number of successive trading days. Exchanges may also establish flexibility in these circumstances to amend daily settlement prices to reflect cash prices more properly, for the purpose of calculating and collecting variation margin.

Arrangements between clearing members and non-clearing members, together with arrangements between their respective clients regarding the payment of accrued profits or any initial/maintenance margin levels higher than the minimum established by the exchange, are subject to individual negotiation. However it should be noted that the responsibility that a clearing member accepts in clearing for a non-clearing member is an onerous one and should not be treated lightly. The non-clearing member is operating on the exchange "unfettered", but all his deals are being guaranteed by a clearing member.

Daily price limits, margin and contract specifications are published by each exchange. However they are subject to amendment and it is advisable to verify such detail with the exchange or a commission broker prior to trading in a particular contract.

The functions and activities which a bank may undertake within the futures markets is determined by:

- The banking legislation within which it operates

- The rules of an exchange or its regulatory body

- Any exchange control imposed limitations on its activities outside of its country of operation

- Any exchange control or other regulatory limitations of the country in which a futures exchange is domiciled

- Internal policy considerations of the bank itself

Within the United Kingdom, banking legislation does not restrict either the type of activity or the role a "recognised bank" can undertake in financial futures markets, although any exposure positions created thereby, would have to be measured within appropriate guideline limits imposed by the Bank of England from time to time. Most major banks have seats on LIFFE and operate as traders, hedgers and exchange commission brokers within that market. Additionally, banks operating in the UK have access to futures markets within the United States and other countries either through FCMs or other commission or introductory brokers. Within the United States the FDIC, FRB and the Comptroller of Currency have authorised banks to undertake financial futures transactions and several banks have FCM subsidiaries.

Delivery Procedures on Financial Futures Contracts

In practice only a very small percentage of futures contracts which are traded, ultimately result in delivery. However, delivery procedures are an important part of a contract, the completion of which is normally a responsibility of the clearing house.

Clearing houses will either stand at the centre of all delivered contracts with each long and short position holder settling with the clearing house, or remove themselves as the buyer of each sale contract and seller of each purchase contract and re-establish a direct contractual relationship between clearing members requiring delivery. It would be unusual if these members were the same contracting parties that registered an original purchase and sale. The requirements covering the time of delivery, notice to deliver, and the nature of the delivered subject matter will vary by contract type. The invoice price of delivered contracts is the exchange delivery settlement price (EDSP) which will be established by designated officials of the exchange and will be based upon, or assessed at, a price or prices close to the delivery date or on the last day of trading. As at the last day of trading outstanding contracts will, for variation margin purposes, be closed out at the EDSP and all profits and losses will have been paid or received through the process of variation margin.

Depending on the contract, delivery may be made at the following times:

- on any business day in the delivery month, either before, on, or after the last date of trading; or

- on the last day of trading; or
- on or within a specific date or period after the last day of trading.

Delivery procedures will require notice to be provided to the clearing house. Where the time of delivery provides flexibility, notice will normally be initiated at the seller's option when delivery may be implemented prior to the last day of trading and at the buyer's option when delivery may only take place subsequent to the last trading date. Where delivery is a fixed date both buyers and sellers will be involved in initiating delivery procedures. When delivery is made prior to the last day of trading it will be based upon an established EDSP one or two days prior to delivery being effected.

Where delivery is at the seller's option, the seller will be required to provide a notice to deliver to the clearing house. Upon the receipt of such notice the clearing house may at its discretion or within defined criteria assign a long position holder (previously a buyer) to take direct delivery from the short position holder. Alternatively, the short position holder may be required to tender delivery of the contract standard to the clearing house and the clearing house will provide notice and make delivery to a long position holder. Therefore, under the terms of these arrangements any long delivery month position holder during the delivery period may be required, and must be prepared, to take delivery.

Where delivery is at the buyer's option, the buyer (long position holder) will initiate a request to take delivery and the clearing house will either assign a notice to a short position holder (previously a seller) to make direct delivery or alternatively the clearing house will take delivery from the assigned short position holder and make delivery to the long position holder.

In the case where contracts call for delivery on a fixed date all short and long position holders will be required, on or prior to the delivery date, to provide notice to the clearing house of their intention to deliver or take delivery respectively. The clearing house will then, as appropriate, either match long and short position holders and notify each of the other's identity, or require short position holders to tender the required settlement to the clearing house and the clearing house will allocate settlement to long position holders.

Clearing members who do not wish to take or make deliveries have to close their positions on or before the last day of trading or as appropriate, the commencement of a delivery period.

Delivery takes many forms and may involve a cash settlement, the physical commodity, defined documents of title to a commodity or a deposit facility to be established. In some cases adjustments may be required to cover differences between the value of the delivered con-

361

tract standard and the settlement price related thereto. In conjunction with the examination of various financial futures contracts in the following pages some of these differences are demonstrated.

It is normal for clearing houses to require clearing members to ensure that their clients with open positions near to the last trading date or upon commencement of a delivery month are prepared to accept, or make delivery, of the underlying object otherwise such positions must be liquidated. Where delivery is required by a client each clearing member is responsible for settlement with the clearing house or, where applicable, another clearing member. All exchange members are thereafter responsible for settlement to, or from, their clients, with non-clearing commission brokers similarly liable to their clients.

Futures Markets
Futures exchanges on which financial, currency and gold futures are traded include:

The United States of America
- The International Monetary Market (IMM) – with contracts in Sterling, Canadian Dollars, Dutch Guilders, Deutschemarks, Japanese Yen, Mexican Peso, Swiss Franc and French Franc against the US Dollar; Gold; 90 day US Treasury bills; Domestic Certificates of Deposit; and Eurodollar Time Deposits.

- The Chicago Board of Trade (CBOT) – with contracts in Kilo Gold; US Treasury Bonds; $8\frac{1}{2}$ to 10 year US Treasury Notes; Government National Mortgage Certificates (GNMAs) and the Major Mint Index.

- The Index and Option Market (IOM) which is a division of the Chicago Mercantile Exchange – Standard and Poors (S & P) 500 Stock Index and the S & P 100 Stock Index.

- Mid-American Commodity Exchange (MIDAM) – US Treasury Bonds; US Treasury Bills; and Gold.

362

- Kansas City Board of Trade (KCBT) – Value Line Average Index.

- Philadelphia Stock Exchange (PHLX) – index of US Gold and Silver shares; Index of US Gaming and Hotel shares.

- Chicago Board of Options Exchange (CBOE) – New York Stock Exchange (NYSE) Double Index.

- American Stock Exchange (ASE) – Computer Technology Index; Oil and Gas Index; Transportation Index.

- New York Futures Exchange (NYFE) – NYSE Composite Index.

- New York Commodity Exchange (COMEX) – Gold.

- Pacific Stock Exchange – Technology Index (the 'Silicon Valley' shares index).

United Kingdom
- The London International Financial Futures Exchange (LIFFE) – with contracts in 20 year Gilt Interest Rate; 3 month Sterling Interest Rate; US Treasury Bond; 3 months Eurodollar Interest Rate, Sterling, Deutschemark, Swiss Franc and Japanese Yen against the US Dollar; and the FT-SE 100 Index.

Canada
- Winnipeg Commodities Exchange – Gold.

- Toronto Futures Exchange – Leading Canadian Stock Index, Canadian Treasury Bonds.

Singapore
- Singapore Mercantile Exchange (SIMEX) – Eurodollar, Gold and Yen currency contracts.

Australia
- Sydney Futures Exchange (SFE) – Gold, 2 year Australian Treasury Bonds; Australian Stock Exchange, Australian Stock Exchanges All Ordinaries Share price index; 90 day Bank Accepted Bills of Exchange; Eurodollar Interest Rate Contracts; US Dollar, Sterling and Japanese Yen against the Australian Dollar.

Japan
- Tokyo Gold Exchange – Gold.

The four most actively traded futures are the:

- CBOT   – Treasury Bond
- CME   – S & P 500 Index
- COMEX – Gold
- NYFE   – NYSE Composite Index

These contracts together with the various LIFFE contracts the S.F.E. Australian Stock Exchanges Ordinaries Share price index and the IMM Deutschemark contract are described below:

CBOT – US Treasury Bond Contract
The CBOT US Treasury Bond contract with contracts traded during 1984 totalling nearly 30 million, which represents a daily turnover of approximately 125,000 contracts – the equivalent of US$12.5 billion per day, is around 10% of the total average US treasury bond debt outstanding during the whole of that year – is the most actively traded futures contract in the world.

The contract size is US$100,000 nominal value of a notional 15 year US Treasury Bond at a coupon rate of 8%.

Price quotations are expressed as a percentage of the nominal value of US$100 with minimum increments of one thirty second of a point, or US$31.25 (1,000 × .03125) per "tick" (one thirty second point) size per contract. A quotation of US$67.10 = US$67,100.00 per contract (1,000 × US$67.10).

364

Delivery months are March, June, September and December, with the last trading day for the spot month contract being seven business days prior to the last day of the month, and the next spot month commencing on the first business day of the delivery month. As reflected by the following extract from the Financial Times of the 20th June, 1985, the current spot month (June) is still quoted as the last trading date has not yet been reached. A total of 10 contract months are quoted. The first column reflects the latest price traded as at the time these figures went to press. The high and low related to that day's trading and the prev(previous) the previous day's closing price. New contracts are introduced at the discretion of the CBOT.

US Treasury Bonds
8% US$100,000 32nds of 100%

	Close	*High*	*Low*	*Prev.*
June	79–21	79–25	79–14	80–03
September	78–11	78–14	78–06	78–28
December	77–09	77–11	77–03	77–25
March	76–09	76–09	76–04	76–24
June	75–11	75–12	75–04	75–25
September	74–15	74–15	74–08	74–29
December	73–21	73–21	73–21	74–02
March	–	–	–	73–09
June	72–08	72–09	72–08	72–17
December	71–02	71–02	71–02	71–06

A maximum price limit for a day is established at $\frac{64}{32}$nds or US$2,000 (1,000 × US$2) per contract and if the price limit is reached then trading ceases for the day unless prices return to within that day's limit. If price limits are reached on successive days a progressive scale of increased limits is applied. There are no price limits for spot month contracts.

The clearing house for the CBOT is the Chicago Board of Trade Clearing Corporation (CBOTCC) which is an independent corporation. In common with most United States clearing houses for the purposes of delivery the clearing house re-establishes direct contact between long and short position holders.

365

Delivery may be made on any business day during the delivery month at the seller's option. The last delivery day is the last business day of the month. As the contract is a notional US treasury bond, delivery is made with any US Treasury Bonds maturing at least 15 years from delivery date if not redeemable; and if redeemable, not so for at least 15 years from the delivery day. As these bonds will have various maturity dates beyond 15 years and various coupon rates, the invoice price on delivery is adjusted by a "conversion factor" system to adjust for coupon rates apart from 8% and for varying maturity or call dates. The conversion factor is obtained by reference to a par value multiplier at which bonds of various outstanding maturities and coupons would have a bond equivalent yield of 8% p.a. This procedure does allow the seller or short position holder to deliver the cheapest (most advantageous) stock available at the time of delivery. As prices and yields vary by stock a calculation can be made between the cash market prices and the futures settlement price to determine equivalent prices. This relationship between the two markets is referred to as the basis price and is considered later in this chapter. The maturity date of delivered bonds is taken to be the period from the first delivery day of the relevant contract month to the redemption date (or earliest redeemable date), reduced to the nearest lower three months which coincides with the delivery month. In addition to the invoiced settlement price all accrued interest on delivered bonds will be invoiced and paid. Settlement is through the Federal wire transfer system.

Registration for hedge status may be applied for on this contract. Original/initial and maintenance margins are established with reduced levels for inter-delivery months together with inter-commodity spreads with the CBOT, GNMA, 10 year treasury notes and treasury bond futures option contract.

CME – S & P 500 Index Contract

The Standard & Poors (S & P 500 index) comprises 500 blue chip stocks most of which are quoted on the Big Board (NYSE). Its base value was originally 10, and as the following extract from the *Financial Times* illustrates, the index value on 18th September 1985 was 187.34 and it has a daily volume of approximately 70,000 contracts:

366

Standard and Poors

	18 June	17 June	14 June	13 June	12 June	1985 High	Low	Since Compilation High	Low
Composite	187.34	186.53	187.10	185.33	187.61	191.06	163.68	191.06	4.40
						(6/6)	(4/1)	(6/6/85)	(1/6/32)

S & P 500 Futures Index (CME) 500 Times Index

	Open	High	Low	Settle	Change	Lifetime High	Low	Open Interest
June	187.60	188.10	186.55	186.75	−.80	191.95	155.70	28,916
September	190.60	191.20	189.50	189.70	−.90	195.60	158.10	50,367
December	193.60	194.20	192.50	192.75	−.95	199.10	175.40	867
March 86	197.00	197.70	196.00	196.45	−.95	202.25	188.80	113

The contract size of the CME S & P 500 index is the index value × US\$500 which, given an index value as at the 18th June of US\$187.34, is the equivalent of US\$93,670 and approximately 12,500,000 contracts were traded during 1984.

As reflected in the second quotation above, which is from the Wall Street Journal of the 19th June 1985, the futures contract quotation quantity is one unit of the index value with a settlement price of US\$186.75 for the June contract – a contract price of US\$93,375. The minimum price fluctuation per unit of contract is US\$.05 giving a minimum price movement per contract unit of US\$25 (US\$.05 × 500). There is no daily price limit established on this contract. Delivery months are March, June, September and December, with the delivery day being the last day of trading, which is the third Friday of the delivery month. As a stock index is not readily available in a tangible form, delivery comprises a cash settlement based on the delivery settlement price as quoted by the exchange. Different levels of margin are applied for speculative and hedge transactions, with both initial and maintenance levels established. Reduced spread margins are available for inter-delivery months, including spot, and intra-commodity spread margins are available for positions in the S & P 100 Index and the KCBT value line index. The clearing house for the CME contracts is the Chicago Mercantile Exchange Clearing Corporation, a wholly owned subsidiary of Chicago Mercantile Exchange.

367

COMEX – 100 ounce Gold Contract

This contract had an annual turnover of just over 9 million contracts during 1984. The contract size is 100 ounces with a contract grade of 100 long ounces (5% more or less) of refined gold assuming not less than 995 fineness, cast either in one bar or in three one kilogram bars by a refiner approved by the exchange. Delivery months are February, April, June, August, October and December with the current spot month. Where a spot month is not resultant from a maturing deferred delivery month a spot month contract is introduced. This procedure is not applicable to financial futures. The number of delivery months which are traded at any one time will be determined at the discretion of the exchange. Delivery may be made on any business day between the first notice day and the last delivery day (this period is approximately one month) at the seller's option. Trading takes place up to the close of trading on the business day preceding the first day upon which notice to deliver can be made. The quotation size is US dollars and cents per fine troy ounce and the minimum price fluctuation 10 cents per troy ounce i.e. US$10 per contract. As indicated by the following extract from the Financial Times as at the 20th June 1985 there were 12 months quoted together with the spot month – June.

Gold 100 troy oz. US$/troy oz.

	Close	*High*	*Low*	*Previous*
June	322.3	326.7	322.5	327.7
July	323.0	–	–	328.6
August	324.8	329.4	324.5	330.5
October	328.3	332.8	328.2	334.0
December	332.2	337.0	331.5	337.8
February	336.2	340.0	338.0	341.8
April	340.3	343.0	343.0	345.8
June	344.9	348.4	347.0	350.4
August	349.7	354.5	354.5	355.1
October	354.7	–	–	360.0
December	359.7	–	–	364.9
February	364.8	–	–	370.1
April	370.1	–	–	375.4

In common with most commodity options a spot month is always quoted to facilitate access to, or disposal of, physical stock through the futures exchange.

A daily price limit of US$30 per ounce is placed on deferred month contracts but the spot month trades without limit. In volatile markets Comex have authority to mark to market deferred month contracts at prices related to the spot month contract to ensure variation margins are settled on a realistic basis. Notice of delivery can be initiated at any time during the spot month at the seller's (short position holder's) option and requires two days prior notice to be given to the clearing house – Comex Clearing Association Incorporated – which is owned by its clearing members. Upon receipt of a notice to delivery the clearing house allocates long position holders, in accordance with those members holding the longest dated contracts, to take direct delivery from the short position holder.

NYFE – New York Stock Exchange Composite Index Contract

The NYFE, New York Stock Exchange Composite Index comprises all the shares listed on the New York Stock Exchange. The daily turnover is approximately 14,000 contracts. In 1965 its face value was US$50 and its value on the 18th June 1985 was US$108.75.

NYSE All Common

18 June	17 June	14 June	13 June	1985 High	Low
108.75	108.28	108.56	107.69	110.69	94.60
				(6/6)	(4/1)

As with the S & P 500 index this contract is quoted in terms of US$500 × the index value giving it a contract value of US$54,375 as at that date. The minimum price movement is US$.05 or US$25 per contract. Its delivery months are March, June, September and December with the last day of trading being the business day prior to the last business day of the delivery month. Delivery is by cash settlement made on the last business day of the delivery month. Margin requirements provide for both speculative and hedged positions and incorporate initial and maintenance levels.

Summary of LIFFE Futures Contracts – June 1985

FUTURES

CONTRACT	TWENTY YEAR GILT INTEREST RATE	THREE MONTH STERLING INTEREST RATE	US TREASURY BOND
UNIT OF TRADING	£50,000 nominal value notional gilt with 12% coupon	£500,000	US$100,000 par value notional US Treasury bond with 8% coupon
CONTRACT STANDARD	Any Gilt Stock with a life of between 15–25 years, as listed by LIFFE	A 3-month Sterling deposit facility at a designated bank in London, or cash settlement (at buyer's option); from December 1985 delivery month onwards, cash settlement only	Any US Treasury bond with a life of at least 15 years
DELIVERY MONTHS	March, June September, December	March, June September, December	March, June September, December
DELIVERY DAY	Any business day in delivery month (at seller's choice)	Second Wednesday of delivery month; from December 1985 onwards, first business day after the last trading day	Any business day in delivery month (at seller's choice)
LAST TRADING DAY	11.00 Two business days prior to last business day in delivery month	11.00 One business day prior to delivery; from December 1985 onwards, third Wednesday of delivery month	09.00 US CST (usually 15.00 London time) Seven business days prior to last business day in delivery month
QUOTATION	Per £100 nominal	100.00 minus rate of interest	Per $100 par value
MINIMUM PRICE MOVEMENT (Tick size & Value)	£1/32 (£15.625)	0.01 (£12.50)	$1/32 ($31.25)
INITIAL MARGIN (Straddle Margin)	£1,000 (£250)	£1,000 (£500)	$1,250 (zero)
TRADING HOURS	09.30–16.15	08.20–16.02	08.15–16.10

THREE MONTH EURODOLLAR INTEREST RATE	FT-SE 100	STERLING	DEUTSCHE MARK	SWISS FRANC	JAPANESE YEN
US$1,000,000	Valued at £25 per full index point (e.g. value £25,000 at 1000.0)	£25,000	All Currencies are traded against US$: DM125,000 SF125,000 Y12,500,000		
A 3-month Eurodollar deposit facility at a designated bank in London, or cash settlement (at buyer's option); from December 1985 delivery month onwards, cash settlement only	Cash settlement	Currencies will be deliverable in the principal financial centres in the country of issue			
March, June September, December	March, June September, December	March, June, September, December			
Second Wednesday of delivery month; from December 1985 onwards, first business day after the last trading day	First business day after the last trading day	Second Wednesday of delivery month. Third Wednesday from December 1985 delivery month onwards.			
11.00 Second business day prior to delivery; from December 1985 onwards, two business days prior to the third Wednesday of delivery month	11.20 The last business day in the delivery month	10.31 10.32 10.33 10.30 Two business days prior to delivery			
100.00 minus rate of interest	FT-SE 100 Index ÷ 10 (e.g. 100.00)	US$ per £	US$ per DM	US$ per SFr.	US$ per 100 Yen
0.01 ($25.00)	0.05 (£12.50)	0.01 cents per £ ($2.50)	0.01 cents per DM ($12.50)	0.01 cents per SFr. ($12.50)	0.01 cents per 100 Yen ($12.50)
$1,000 (zero)	£750 (£250)	$1,000 ($100)			
08.30–16.00	09.35–15.30	08.32–16.02	08.34–16.04	08.36–16.06	08.30–16.00

LIFFE Contracts

The specifications for LIFFE contracts as at June 1985 as issued by LIFFE are detailed on pages 370–71.

As at the date of this publication all LIFFE contracts have delivery months of March, June, September and December. No daily price limits are applicable to spot month contracts or for any contract during the last one hour of each day's trading. The spot period for the currency, 3 month eurodollar and 3 month sterling contracts begins on the first day of the delivery month, with that of the 20 year gilt and US treasury bond commencing seven business days before the delivery month and the FT-SE 100 index contract five business days before the last trading day. Initial and variation margins are required from all participants in the market with reduced margins available for inter-delivery month straddle positions within contracts, exclusive of spot positions. Differentials are not drawn between speculators and hedgers for margin purposes. The clearing house for all LIFFE contracts is the International Commodities Clearing House (ICCH), the shareholding of which is held by Barclays, Lloyds, Midland, National Westminster, Standard Chartered and Royal Bank of Scotland. ICCH stands between buyers and sellers of all delivered contracts.

The contract standard for the 20 Year Gilt requires delivery to be made of any gilt with 15/25 years to maturity as listed by LIFFE. Stocks with an option or redemption date will be considered to have an outstanding term to the first redemption date. Stocks must be delivered in multiples of £50,000 nominal value. No variable rate, index-linked, convertible or partly paid gilts may be delivered. Stocks are not deliverable within the period of three weeks and one day before the ex-dividend date and interest on delivered stocks must be payable half-yearly. As with the CBOT and LIFFE US treasury bond contract settlement is based on a conversion price factor system.

Quotation prices fluctuate in terms of premiums and discounts per 100 nominal stock in the same manner as the cash markets. The minimum price movement represents one thirty-second or £15.625 per contract (500 × .03125). Prices are quoted on the exchange in terms of points rather than fractions with each point representing one thirty-second.

The three month sterling interest rate contract is quoted on a discounted basis of £100 less the annual rate of interest on a 360 day (not 365) base in basis points divided equally into four 90 day periods. The minimum price movement per £100 is 1 basis point, or £12.50 on a contract size of £500,000. The daily price limit is 100 basis points which is equivalent to £1,250 on a £500,000 contract. Delivery may be taken at the buyer's option in a three month sterling deposit facility at a designated bank in London or as a cash settlement. Where a deposit is required any difference between the actual rate at which the deposit is established and the exchange delivery settlement price (EDSP) will be settled by the buyer and seller with ICCH.

Although the contract specifications for the LIFFE US Treasury Bond are fundamentally the same as those already described for the CBOT contract, they do differ in regard to margin requirements, price limit applications and delivery procedures, including the manner in which the EDSP is established. Margins and price limits have already been explained. The EDSP for LIFFE is based on the weighted average of the price of contracts traded in the minute preceding 09.00 US Central Standard Time (CST). If no contracts are traded during this time it will be by reference to the lowest offer and highest bid or, if none, to the price of contracts at that time on the CBOT and in the cash markets. The CBOT EDSP is the last price before close at 14.00 CST or, if the pit committee decide this is artificial, the previous price or average of the two is established at their discretion. The ICCH stands at the centre of all cleared contracts whereas the CBOT clearing corporation re-establishes contractual liability between its clearing members. ICCH allocates deliveries on a pro rata basis to long position holders and CBOTCC allocates in order of the longest dated contracts.

Three month eurodollar interest rate contracts are quoted in the same manner as the sterling contract except that the contract size is US$1,000,000. Therefore 1 basis point movement is the equivalent of US$25 per contract and the daily price limit US$2,500. Delivery requirements are the same with the buyer having the option to take a deposit or a cash settlement. It is mentioned that in contrast the Eurodollar contract traded on the IMM only facilitates cash settlement.

373

The Sterling, Deutschemarks and Swiss Franc currency contracts are quoted in terms of one currency unit against US dollars. The Yen contract is quoted in terms of 100 currency units against the US$. The minimum price movement is US$12.50 on each currency contract except sterling which is US$2.50. Daily price limits are established at a level equivalent to US$1,250 for each contract which equates to 5 cents for sterling and 1 cent for the other three contracts. Delivery procedures require that currencies are delivered in the principal financial centres in the country of the currency of issue against the receipt of payment in US dollars.

The FT-SE 100 share index was launched in 1984 and comprises the top 100 shares quoted on the Stock Exchange London (measured by capitalisation) which accounted for nearly 70% of the total market value of all UK equities. The base value of the index was set at 1,000 on 1st January 1984, and as the following extract from the Financial Times indicates, was 1284.1 on 19th June 1985:

FT-SE Share Index

Index No.	Days Change	Day's High	Day's Low	18.6.85	17.6.85	14.6.85	13.6.85	12.6.85	Year Ago
1284.1	+ 0.1	1287.7	1282.5	1284.0	1284.4	1275.5	1278.9	1291.4	1035.6

FT-SE 100 Index

£25 per full index point

	Close	High	Low	Prev.
June	128.70	129.30	128.45	128.25
September	129.00	129.50	128.90	128.65

The quotation size of the LIFFE contract as reflected by the quotations of LIFFE prices from the Financial Times as at the same date is the index value divided by 10. The contract size is the index value multiplied by £25, i.e. £25 per full index point. Therefore the contract value of the September contract as at the 19th June 1985 was £32,250 (1290 × 25). Unlike the other index contracts already considered there is a price limit of 100 points or £1,250 per contract. Delivery is effected by a cash settlement at the EDSP.

Australian Stock Exchanges Ordinaries Share Price Index

The Australian Stock Exchanges All Ordinaries Share Price Index comprises over 250 Australian companies listed on the Sydney and Melbourne stock exchanges, the market value of which is approximately 90% of the value of all listed shares. The index had an original base of 500 and as illustrated by the following extract from the Financial Times was A$851.30 on the 19th June 1985:

	19	18	17	14	1985	
	June	*June*	*June*	*June*	*High*	*Low*
Australia						
All.Ord.						
(1/1/80)	851.3	840.2	841.5	840.4	904.5	715.3
					(20/5)	(7/1)

The SFE Australian Stock Exchanges All Ordinaries Share Price Index contract is the index value × 100 – A$85,130 as at the 19th June, and has a daily turnover of approximately 3,000 contracts per day.

Prices are quoted in the same form as the ASE Ordinaries Price Index expressed to one decimal place and there is no daily price limit established on this contract. The delivery months are March, June, September and December with the last day of trading being the second last business day of the delivery month with settlement in cash. The clearing house is the ICCH.

IMM – Deutschemark Contract

The IMM Deutschemark currency contract is based on a contract size of DM.125,000. Delivery months are January, March, April, June, July, September, October and December. The last day of trading is two business days before the third Wednesday of the delivery month and the delivery day is the third Wednesday of the delivery month. The minimum price movement per currency unit is US$.0001 giving a minimum price movement per contract of US$12.50 (.0001 × 125,000). The daily price limit is established at US$.01, in contract terms US$1,250. Daily price limits do not apply to the current spot month. As indicated by the following extract from the Wall Street Journal of the 20th June 1985, the September contract at a settlement price of .3304 had a value of US$41,300 (125,000 × .3304).

West German Mark (IMM) – 125,000 marks; $per mark

	Open	High	Low	Settle	Change	Lifetime High	Lifetime Low	Open Interest
September	.3343	.3346	.3296	.3304	−.0034	.3560	.2925	47,986
December	.3363	.3366	.3317	.3324	−.0033	.3610	.2971	1,687

Minimum original/initial and maintenance levels of margin are established with higher levels for delivery months. Reduced margin levels are available for inter-delivery month and inter-commodity spreads with Sterling, Canadian Dollar, Japanese Yen, Swiss Franc and French Franc contracts.

Delivery requires the delivery of Deutschemarks by the short position holder against the receipt of US Dollars.

Hedging, Trading and Speculating in Financial Futures

Financial futures contracts provide many opportunities to trade, speculate and hedge in, and between, different types of risk and instrument. This can be achieved on a high leverage basis and without the necessity of having to deliver, buy or hold any of the underlying instruments and currencies or be involved in the implications related thereto. However, the possible impact of immediate and future margin requirements must be considered.

Foreign currency futures contracts provide a vehicle to trade, hedge or speculate in foreign exchange rate risk; the US$ 90 day Treasury Bill, US Domestic Certificate of Deposit, 3 month Eurodollar Deposit, 3 month Sterling Deposit and the Australian Dollar 90 day Bankers Acceptance Contracts provide for short-term interest rate risk in those currencies; US Treasury Bonds, US Treasury Notes, GNMAs, Sterling 20 year Gilt Contract, Canadian and Australian Treasury Bond Contracts provide for longer term interest rate risk. Stock indices provide opportunities to trade, hedge or speculate in the general price performance of the major part, or specific sectors of, several stock markets and gold contracts, in the future price of gold. Immediately the underlying objective has been achieved, or subsequent events give rise to a desire to change direction or restructure positions, access is available to markets in which contracts can be easily liquidated, with profits and losses realised immediately.

376

Other than dealing for their own account on the exchanges the most beneficial opportunities provided to banks by the financial futures markets is the ability to hedge underlying interest rate and investment risk without inflating balance sheet footings. Similar attractions do not apply to currency contracts as they do not provide any advantage over the forward market and have the disadvantage of margin requirements.

In practice a perfect hedge does not exist between the futures and cash markets. First, financial futures contracts are standardised contracts which are traded on a discounted basis. As such, they have specific and restricted delivery dates which do not often coincide with normal trading periods in the cash markets, and make it difficult to match them within the normal contract sizes of each market transaction. Secondly, futures require initial but, more importantly, also have variation margin implications, the effect of which cannot be established with any accuracy at the outset of a contract. Cash market transactions do not normally have margin implications, therefore any adverse margin payable to an exchange will not be compensated by an inflow of funds. Thirdly, although the major considerations are the same, different factors affect the size and liquidity of cash and futures markets. Chapter 16 discusses the factors which may influence swap prices and the arbitrage triangle which is based on the current spot prices and interest rate differentials between two currencies. Given a market environment which is free of any intervention, control or restrictions, there is a triangle within which the foreign exchange swap prices would be contained through the activities of arbitragers. The basis of future currency contracts is established in a similar manner. The basis for short dated interest rate contracts is calculated through an equivalent cash market forward/forward price; this is covered in Chapter 15. Thereafter these prices are adjusted for any known factors which affect the futures market but do not affect the spot and forward markets. These will include:

- perceived adjustments for margin costs

- different interest periods

- different interest basis, i.e. 360 or 365 days

- differences in contract amounts

- differences between the relationship of perceived movement between the basis of futures prices and those of forward prices.

The difference between the spot price and future contract price is referred to as the basis. The spot price is the zero point at which the prices of all futures contracts will, assuming the delivery of a tangible subject matter, ultimately converge with the cash market price. Where contracts are based on intangible, i.e. notional subjects, e.g. gilt and treasury bond contracts, this convergence is assessed in establishing the delivery price and is not perfect.

Consequently when looking at futures as a hedge the major consideration of a bank is the perceived differentials which should exist between the futures and cash market prices. This subject is considered in the context of the following examples.

Let us assume a corporate treasurer has a borrowing requirement of US$50 million with a 6 month roll-over next due on 1st June. In April he considers rates will rise substantially above current levels of $11\frac{1}{4}\%$. The price for the June futures contract is currently 88.95 reflecting a yield of 11.05%.

Action Sell 100 June 3 month eurodollar interest rate contracts. As the eurodollar contract is based on a three month deposit of US$1 million, double the capital value is needed to lock into a rate for the 6 months until next roll-over, i.e. $2 \times 50 = 100$ contracts.

Outcome At 1st June the price of the June 3 month eurodollar contract is 87.75 (12.25% yield) and the interest rate on the roll-over that day is $12\frac{1}{2}\%$ for the 6 months money. On 1st June he buys 100 June contracts to close out his futures position.

378

Summary

Cash market	*Futures*
16th April	

Cash market	Futures
Current market interest rate $11\frac{1}{4}\%$ for loan roll-over at 1st June Interest cost for 6 months US$2,312,500	Sell 100 June eurodollar contracts
1st June	
Roll-over loan at $12\frac{1}{2}\%$ Interest cost for 6 months US$3,125,000	Buy 100 June eurodollar contracts at 87.75. Price movement from 88.95 to 87.75 = 120 ticks at \$25 per tick on 100 contracts
Additional cost of borrowing *US$312,500*	Profit on futures *US$300,000*

The tick value is fixed by the contract terms at a constant value of US\$25 or $0.01\% \times \frac{1}{4}$ ignoring the fact that the number of days in the quarter will not be one quarter of 360.

The example demonstrates how the treasurer has been able to offset US\$300,000 of the increase in interest cost of US\$312,500. Thus the hedge was 96% effective and the treasurer obtained an interest rate cost of 11.30% compared to $11\frac{1}{4}\%$ in April and $12\frac{1}{2}\%$ in June.

The failure of the hedge to be 100% effective is due to the so-called change in basis, which represents the shortfall of US\$12,500 or 5 basis points on 100 contracts. The basis narrowing over the period in this case would have been mainly as a result of the approach of the delivery date, by which stage the basis will be zero.

Assume a bank has a well diversified investment portfolio and anticipates that a decline in stock values is imminent. The bank does not wish to switch its holdings into interest bearing stocks because of the cost and work involved as well as uncertainty overhanging the direction of interest rates. In the meantime, they decide on a short hedge to cover them during the next six months on LIFFE. This means in effect that they will sell futures contracts. Let us assume that the FT-SE 100 was 1113 on 17th May, and the December 1985 contract was 110.90. Assuming the holder sells 10 × December contracts on 17th May, he will put up an initial margin of 15,000 and the contracts will be valued at 25 × 1091 (27,275 × 10 contracts = 272,750 total). If in four month's time the market index is, say, 660 and the December contract 65.30, the holder may decide to close out his contracts at 65.30, particularly if he considers that his share portfolio's performance will be likely to improve over the immediate future. He will realise a profit by closing out as follows:- 10 contracts × (65.30 × 10) × £25 = (£163,250) – a profit of £109,500 to compensate for a substantially reduced value share portfolio. If the decision to close out also proves to be correct then the portfolio value will benefit from the market's improvement. The total value of the portfolio will then possibly increase from its value as at 17th May, particularly if the portfolio being hedged responds to the same degree to market movements as tracked by the particular index employed. This responsiveness of an investment portfolio to overall market fluctuations is referred to as the "Beta Factor" - with a perfect hedge the beta factor will be 1.00. The following advantages may be achieved by initiating a short hedge position, they are:-

- Saving time in selling individual stocks
- Elimination of stock selection for sale
- Lower total costs as no sales brokerage is incurred
- Investment portfolio structure is left undisturbed
- Income yield is maintained from the portfolio
- Flexibility to unwind or reverse the position quickly
- Risks of selling wrong stocks is eliminated
- Depending on market and the participant's tax domicile, there may be an advantage.

A long hedge involves the purchase of stock index futures contracts, which is a strategy adopted by some investors to protect themselves against rising share prices when new investment is anticipated which cannot be made immediately. The advantages of a long hedge are:-

- Saving time in buying individual shares
- Elimination of stock selection for purchase
- Flexibility to unwind or reverse the position quickly
- Lower total costs as low purchase brokerage is incurred
- Ability to fix current prices for future purchases.

Banks, fund managers and other professional institutions who run investment and/or trading portfolios in securities will use the equity futures contract as an important hedging tool. A final advantage for them which should be recorded is the absence of liquidity in the contract which might be the case with deals in individual stocks. Substantial positions can be hedged without upsetting the market price of individual shares, which would happen if big blocks of shares were bid or offered on a physical Stock Exchange. The general market risk can be hedged leaving the fund manager, if he wishes, exposed selectively to specific risks in individual shares which produce an identified and acceptable Beta mismatch.

CHAPTER EIGHTEEN

Option Markets – Practice and Procedures

Introduction to Option Contracts

Although foreign currency, interest rate and stock options are among some of London's more recent financial instruments the antecedents of this type of contract, can, within various other markets, be traced back many years – a similar contract referred to as "Privileges" was first traded on the Chicago Board of Trade in the 1860's.

Option contracts are unilateral contracts which are only binding upon the seller of the option. They provide the buyer with the right, but not the obligation, to buy or sell an agreed quantity of a particular currency, stock, financial instrument, futures contract, commodity or other quantifiable subject matter at an agreed price, at the expiry of, or during a specified period of time. Call options provide the purchaser with the right to buy the underlying subject matter. Put options provide the right to sell the underlying subject matter. These unique characteristics provide the buyer with a high leverage position in which to deal for a quantifiable cost.

The buyer of an option is normally referred to as the option "holder" or "owner", the seller of an option the option "grantor", "writer" or "issuer". The price at which the option holder has the right to put or call the underlying subject matter is referred to as the "strike", "striking" or "exercise" price. The striking price of an option is said to be "at-the-market" or "at-the-money" when the current market price of the commodity is the same as the striking price of the option. A call option is "in-the-money" when the striking price is lower than the commodity's current market price and it is "out-of-the-money" when its striking price is higher than the current market value. Conversely, a put option is "in-the-money" when the striking price is higher than the current value of the commodity and "out-of-the-money" when the striking price is lower than the current market value.

The option purchaser makes a payment – "the premium" – to the option grantor for the right to put or call the commodity at an agreed striking price and subsequently, whatever the price of the commodity, the option holder can never lose more than that premium together with, as appropriate, any additional brokerage, commission or other fees that may be charged in establishing the contract. These principles can be illustrated by the following simple examples.

Example I
An investor purchases a call option on £1,000,000 for three months at a striking price of US$1.30 and a premium of US$0.029 per pound. The total premium paid is US$29,000 (1,000,000 × 0.029) and no other fees are payable. Within the terms of this contract the purchaser has the right, but not the obligation, to call, i.e. buy, £1,000,000 at an exchange rate of 1.30 US dollars to the pound at any time during the life of the option. If he exercises the option he will be required to pay to the grantor of the option US$1,300,000 for which he will receive £1,000,000.
Let us consider:

The spot price sterling/US dollar subsequently moves to 1.40 and the investor exercises the option:

Market value of £1,000,000 @ 1.40	= US$ 1,400,000
Cost of £1,000,000 under option @ 1.30	= US$ 1,300,000
Cost of option (premium only)	= US$ 29,000
Net profit	= US$ 71,000

Looked at from a different perspective the purchaser has been able to buy £1,000,000 for which he has paid US$1,300,000. He could now sell the sterling for US$1,400,000. For this privilege he has paid a premium of US$29,000.

The spot price sterling/US dollar continues at the 1.30 level throughout the life of the contract and therefore the current market price is the same as the strike price. The option holder may or may not exercise the option but in any event has lost his premium:

Market value of £1,000,000 @ 1.30	= US$ 1,300,000
Cost of £1,000,000 under option @ 1.30	= US$ 1,300,000
Cost of option	= US$ 29,000
Net loss	= US$ 29,000

The market price of sterling/US dollar is below 1.30, say 1.20, the option will be abandoned as the option holder could, if he required the sterling, purchase £1 million at the current market price for US$1,200,000 as against US$1,300,000 under the contract. The resultant loss on the option is limited to the premium, i.e. US$29,000.

It should however be noted that if the investor was hedging against an underlying requirement to buy sterling the option would have provided him with protection against loss while the eventual downward price movement enabled him to purchase sterling at 1.30 theoretically giving him a net profit of US$71,000.

Example II

An investor purchases a put option on £1,000,000 for three months at a striking price of 1.30 and a premium of US$0.025 per pound. The purchaser has the right to put, i.e. sell, to the grantor of the option £1,000,000 at an exchange rate of 1.30 US dollars to the pound at any time during the life of the option. If he exercises the put option he will be required to pay £1,000,000 and will receive US$1,300,000. The possible scenarios may be:

Spot price sterling/US dollar 1.20

Market value of £1,000,000	= US$ 1,200,000
Sale of £1,000,000 under option	= US$ 1,300,000
Cost of option	= US$ 25,000
Net profit	= US$ 75,000

Again looked at a different way he has received US$1,300,000 for £1,000,000. If he were to immediately sell the US dollars at 1.20 he would receive back £1,083,333.33 sterling.

Spot price sterling/US dollar 1.30

Market value of £1,000,000	= US$ 1,300,000
Sale of £1,000,000 under option	= US$ 1,300,000
Cost of option	= US$ 25,000
Net loss	= US$ 25,000

If the market price of sterling/US dollar is above 1.30 the option will be abandoned with the resultant loss limited to US$25,000.

Again, as in the first example, as a hedge against an underlying requirement the investor would have in this instance benefited from the increase in the value of sterling.

All the call options granted on a specific subject matter are referred to as a "class" of option and similarly all the put options written on a specific subject matter are a "class" of option. Within a class all contracts whether put or call which have the same striking price and expiration date are referred to as a "series" of options.

To put or call the underlying subject matter at the striking price the option holder must "exercise" the option on or prior to the "expiration date". A call option holder is said to exercise when he notifies the grantor ("notice of exercise") that he will make settlement in return for the underlying subject matter at the striking price and take "delivery" in accordance with the terms of the contract. Conversely, a put option holder exercises when he notifies the grantor that he will deliver the underlying subject matter and requires settlement in accordance with the contract terms. The period during which an option holder may exercise is the "exercise period". The exercise period will be dependent upon the terms of the underlying contract. Some options may be exercised and delivery take place at any time during the life of the contract whilst others may only facilitate delivery within a stipulated period, usually on the expiration date or upon a specified day or number of days retrospective from the expiration date. An option written on "American terms", often referred to as an "American option", denotes that it can be exercised and delivery take place at any time during the life of the contract. However, the first settlement date is usually specifically stated as the premium payment date or otherwise defined. Those options written on "European terms" are exercisable at any time during the life of the option but delivery can only take place on the value date therefore European options are generally only exercised at maturity. "American terms" and "European terms" are purely generic in nature – options are quoted under both terms in both Europe and America. The "expiration date" is the last date upon which exercise may be effected and the terms will usually incorporate a specific time of expiration, the "expiration time" which is the latest time on the exercise date that the grantor will accept notice of exercise. If an option contract is not exercised during the exercise period the option will be considered abandoned and the grantor is under no further obligation. It is important to note that the onus of exercising an in-the-money option lies with the holder.

After notice of exercise has been given the option holder must comply with the payment, delivery or settlement requirements related to the particular contract. For example, if the subject matter of a call option is gold, the option holder will pay the grantor the full contract price to obtain the gold. A put holder would deliver the required quantity of gold to the option grantor and receive payment. The premium is the cost of the option and is not adjusted against the settlement price if an option is exercised. In practice, for reasons developed later in this chapter, only a very small percentage of options result in exercise and delivery.

Although the option holder can lose no more than the premium he pays together with any brokerage, commissions or other agreed fees, he has the potential to benefit from all favourable net movements between the underlying market and striking price. The purchaser of a call option will benefit by the amount the market price of the commodity rises above the striking price in excess of the premium plus any other fees. The purchaser of a put by the amount the market price falls below the striking price less the premium and any other fees.

Conversely, a grantor's maximum profit potential is limited to the amount of premium, together with any other fees he receives. Options may be granted on a covered or uncovered basis. A covered option is one where the option is granted against a position held by the grantor in the underlying subject matter of the option. An uncovered option is one where the grantor has no position in the underlying subject matter. Writers of both covered and uncovered options are subject to unlimited risk in the following situations:

Covered call   – underlying price falls
Covered put   – underlying price rises
Uncovered call – underlying price rises
Uncovered put – underlying price falls

Option premiums comprise two component parts, the "intrinsic value" and the "time value". The intrinsic value is effectively the amount by which an option is in-the-money. The difference between the intrinsic value and the total premium is the time value and if there is no intrinsic value, as will be the case with an out-of-the-money or at-the-money option, the total premium will consist of time value. Assessment of the time value of an option is covered later in this chapter.

As an example a call option on £1,000,000 has a striking price of 1.25 dollars to £1 and the premium is US$62,500 with the current spot price £/US$1.30. The intrinsic value is US$50,000 [(1.30 – 1.25) × 1,000,000] and therefore the time value US$12,500 (62,500 – 50,000).

As premiums comprise both intrinsic and time value very few options are exercised. The early exercise of an in-the-money option will be settled at the striking price and only the intrinsic value realised. However, if an option was covered by selling an equal and opposite option or surrendering the option, the premium received would include both intrinsic and time value.

There are two fundamental types of option :

- Exchange Traded Options
- Over the Counter Options (OTCs).

Exchange Traded Options
Exchange traded options, which are generally based upon American terms, are standardized and are quoted and traded on an exchange in

388

a similar manner to futures contracts examined in Chapter 17. Exchange traded options in a variety of instruments, currencies and commodities, together with options on futures contracts, are traded on several futures, options, stock and commodity exchanges. However, procedures related thereto are very similar, with the exchange clearing house providing the same facilities as with futures whereby after registration they become the purchaser or grantor of each contract thus facilitating the easy liquidation of long and short positions and relieving participants within the market of credit risk upon each other. Although margin requirements comprise an integral part of the procedures of exchange traded options, these do differ from futures contracts and take cognizance of the unilateral nature of options in applying these procedures. Margin requirements and procedures together with the treatment of covered and uncovered grantors and compensating trading positions differ from exchange to exchange.

As with futures the payment of fees and the satisfaction of margin in particular can adversely impact upon the economics of option trading, and therefore these requirements should be carefully considered prior to trading. Premiums are quoted separately for puts and calls in terms of bid and offered prices. To understand option quotations it is easier to think of the bid and offered prices in terms of their representing the prices at which a market participant is prepared, at a point in time, to purchase (bid) or the price at which a participant is prepared to grant (offered). As already explained the rights and obligations together with the associated potential profit/risk profiles related to purchasing or granting these instruments are completely different. Prices are usually quoted in terms of one unit of the subject matter of the contract.

On an exchange the buyer of an option, either put or call, is the purchaser and the seller is the grantor or writer of an option. Upon acceptance and registration the exchange clearing house is the counterparty to each clearing member for each contract. Consequent upon this latter procedure exchange traded option contracts may be opened and subsequently liquidated or exercised without the necessity of contact with the original grantor of an option. The purchase of a call or a put will result in either the opening of a long position or the closing of a previous short position in that class and series. As discussed later in this Chapter similar procedures do not apply to over-the-counter options. The sale of a call or put will open a short position or close a previous long position in the same class and series. Conversely the purchase of a call or put will either open a long position or close a previous short position in that class and series, i.e. options on the same subject matter and with the same striking price and expiration date.

It is emphasised that a March purchase of a call contract with a striking price of US$130 would not close a June sale of a call contract with a striking price of US$130. Similarly, the purchase of a March put contract at a strike price of US$150 would not close the sale of a March put at a strike price of US$155. Puts and calls are different instruments; the sale of a call can never be closed by the purchase of a put or conversely the purchase of a call with the sale of a put. However the purchase and sale of put and call options of varying strike prices and periods may be used to adjust the risk profile of an option portfolio.

Exchanges normally facilitate the trading of options on American terms thus providing the holder with the right to exercise and take delivery at any time during the life of the contract. Where a purchaser does exercise, the exchange clearing house assigns, at its discretion, notice of exercise to a clearing member with a short position in the same series and class as the option exercised. Consequently any short position holder must be prepared to accept an assignment of exercise and make delivery at any time during the period for which the short position is held.

In examining exchange traded options in the context of this publication there are four quite distinct types of option which require consideration. They are:

- Traded currency options
- Traded share, stock and bond options
- Traded stock index options
- Traded futures option contracts

Traded Currency Options

Exchange traded currency options are at the time of this publication undertaken on seven exchanges – Philadelphia Stock Exchange (PHLX), Chicago Board Options Exchange (CBOE), European Options Exchange (EOE) in Amsterdam, Montreal Exchange (ME), Vancouver Stock Exchange (VSE), London Stock Exchange (LSE) and London International Financial Futures Exchange (LIFFE). The contract size, terms and conditions and regulations of each exchange differ and therefore as with futures when considering exchange traded contracts of whatever nature it is necessary to examine each individual exchange's requirements. For the purpose of this publication the currency contracts of the PHLX are developed in some detail with those traded on the LSE and LIFFE briefly outlined.

PHLX – Traded Currency Options

As at the end of August 1984 the PHLX, which falls under the supervisory authority of the Securities and Exchange Commission (SEC) of the United States, had introduced trading in foreign currency options. Contracts against US Dollars are available in:

Currency	Contract Size
Sterling	ST 12,500
Canadian Dollar	CAD 50,000
Swiss Francs	CHF 62,500
Deutschemarks	DM 62,500
Japanese Yen	JPY 6,250,000
French Franc	FFR 125,000

The range of striking prices quoted is in intervals of US$0.05 for Sterling, US$0.02 for Deutschemarks, Swiss and French Francs and Canadian Dollars, and US$0.0002 for Japanese Yen. At the commencement of a new contract being introduced the exchange will normally establish three striking prices, one which reflects as near as possible the current spot price and one either side. Additional strike prices are added in relationship to spot price movements. Premiums for Sterling, Deutschemarks, Swiss Francs and Canadian Dollars are quoted in US cents per unit of the underlying currency, whilst those for Japanese Yen are quoted in hundredths of a cent per currency unit. It is therefore necessary to multiply the premium quotation by the contract size to obtain the premium per currency contract unit in US Dollar terms. The minimum price fluctuation is US cents 0.01 for Deutschemarks, Swiss Francs and Canadian Dollars, US cents 0.05 for Sterling and US cents 0.0001 for Japanese Yen. Therefore the minimum premium movement per contract is US$6.25 for Deutschemarks (62,500 × .01), Swiss Francs (62,500 × 0.01), Sterling (12,500 × 0.05) and Japanese Yen (6,250,000 × 0.0001), and US$5 for Canadian Dollars (50,000 × 0.01). Daily price limits are not imposed.

The expiration months are March, June, September and December, with a maximum of four contracts being quoted for each class of option at any one time giving maximum life cycles of three, six, nine and 12 months. Expiration dates are the Saturday before the third Wednesday of the appropriate expiration month. As the expiration date is a Saturday, customers are required to notify their brokers of their intention to exercise by at least the last trading day prior to the expiration date. This will ordinarily be the Friday preceding the expiration Saturday. The final exercise settlement date is the third Wednesday of the expiration month. The clearing house issuing and guaranteeing contracts is the Options Clearing Corporation (OCC) who stand at the centre of all exercised options. Exercise procedures require that the purchaser who exercises, delivers US dollars to the OCC bank account within two business days after the notice to exercise. The grantor or seller of the call option – as assigned by the clearing house – is required to deliver similarly the currency amount of the contract within two business days to the designated OCC account in the country of the underlying currency. Conversely the exercisor of a put is required to deliver the foreign currency amount and the assigned grantor of a put the US dollar amount to the designated accounts of the OCC within two business days subsequent to exercise. To avoid delivery risk exposure the OCC will not pay away the foreign currency amount of a call option to the purchaser until four business days following exercise although the grantor will receive the US Dollar amount after two business days. In the case of a put option neither the US Dollar or foreign currency amount is paid to the ultimate beneficiary until four business days after exercise. However, guarantee arrangements may be made which facilitate payments to and from the clearing house being effected on the settlement date.

392

As indicated by the following based upon an extract from the Wall Street Journal, the strike prices for British pounds ranges from .105 to .135 against a current market price of 129.24 cents. Call premiums for the September contracts between strike prices of .105 and .125 reflect the impact of intrinsic value. For example, the September contract at .110 has an intrinsic value of 19.24 cents (129.24 − 110) and time value of 1.56 (20.80 − 19.24) cents per £1, i.e. US$2,405 (12,500 × .1924) and US$195 (12,500 × .0156) per contract respectively.

Currency Options – Philadelphia Exchange

Option	Strike Price	Calls – Last			Puts – Last		
		Jun.	Sept.	Dec.	Jun.	Sept.	Dec.
12,500 British Pounds – cents per unit							
B.Pound	.105	s	25.50	25.60	s	0.10	r
129.24	.110	s	20.80	21.00	s	r	r
129.24	.115	s	16.00	16.30	s	r	2.25
129.24	.120	s	10.50	r	s	1.90	3.70
129.24	.125	s	6.60	r	s	3.75	5.50
129.24	.130	s	4.25	5.80	s	6.50	r
129.24	.135	s	2.50	4.70	s	r	r
50,000 Canadian Dollars – cents per unit							
C.Dollar	.71	s	r	r	s	r	0.60
73.23	.72	s	1.39	r	s	r	r
73.23	.73	s	0.75	r	s	0.75	1.30
73.23	.74	s	r	r	s	1.43	r
62,500 West German Marks – cents per unit							
D.Mark	.30	s	3.30	r	s	r	0.37
32.86	.31	s	2.48	r	s	0.33	r
32.86	.32	s	1.64	2.25	s	0.56	r
32.86	.33	s	1.06	1.65	s	0.94	r
32.86	.34	s	0.70	1.30	s	r	r
32.86	.35	s	0.41	0.84	s	r	r
125,000 French Francs – 10ths of a cent per unit							
F.Franc	.105	s	4.40	5.30	s	2.05	r

Option	Strike Price	Calls – Last			Puts – Last		
		Jun.	Sept.	Dec.	Jun.	Sept.	Dec.

6,250,000 Japanese Yen – 100ths of a cent per unit

Option	Strike Price	Jun.	Sept.	Dec.	Jun.	Sept.	Dec.
J.Yen	.38	s	2.66	r	s	0.12	r
40.36	.39	s	r	r	s	0.27	r
40.36	.40	s	1.09	r	s	0.57	r
40.36	.41	s	0.64	1.09	s	1.09	r
40.36	.42	s	0.37	0.70	s	r	r
40.36	.43	s	0.21	0.45	s	r	r

62,500 Swiss Francs – cents per unit

Option	Strike Price	Jun.	Sept.	Dec.	Jun.	Sept.	Dec.
S.Franc	.35	s	4.73	r	s	r	r
39.24	.36	s	3.76	3.98	s	0.21	0.47
39.24	.37	s	r	r	s	0.35	r
39.24	.38	s	2.28	r	s	0.67	0.95
39.24	.39	s	1.65	2.20	s	1.07	1.40
39.24	.40	s	1.01	1.78	s	r	r
39.24	.41	s	r	r	s	r	r

r = not traded
s = no option offered
Last is premium (purchase price)

Margin requirements on PHLX differentiate between long position holders (buyers), short position holders (grantors) and in the latter case, covered and uncovered option grantors. The purchaser is required to pay the full amount of the agreed premium. Fully covered option grantors are not subject to margin requirements and immediately obtain premiums in full if for short call options they deliver to a PHLX member organisation either:

- The number of units of foreign currency underlying the short call option position, or

- A "call option guarantee letter" issued by an exchange or options clearing corporation approved custodian certifying that the custodian holds for the account of the customer foreign currency in an amount greater than or equal to the number of units of foreign currency underlying the short call position.

A short put option position holder delivers to a PHLX member organisation either:

- US dollars in amount greater than or equal to the aggregate exercise price of the put option position, or the following instruments which may be considered substitutes for US dollars provided that the market value of these instruments equals or exceeds the aggregate exercise price of the short put option position when written and the instrument matures in one year or less:

  - securities issued and guaranteed by the United States or its agencies;
  - negotiable bank certificates of deposit; or
  - banker's acceptances issued by banking institutions in the United States and payable in the United States; or

A "put option guarantee letter" issued by an exchange or options clearing corporation approved custodian certifying that the custodian holds for the account of the customer US dollars in an amount greater than or equal to the aggregate exercise price of the put option position(s).

Uncovered short call and uncovered short put option grantors are required to provide initial margin which is subsequently subject to maintenance levels being maintained. Premiums held by the clearing house may be utilised to meet both initial and maintenance margin requirements. PHLX require initial margins to be calculated on the following basis:

- In-the-money option:
  130% of the option premium plus US$750 per option contract, not to exceed an amount equal to 100% of the option premium plus US$2,500 per option contract.

- Out-of-the-money option:
  130% of the option premium plus US$750 less the out-of-the-money amount per option contract, to an amount no less than 130% of the option premium plus US$250 per option contract.

The upper limit of 100% of option premiums plus US$2,500 for an in-the-money option would only trigger when 130% of the option premium plus US$750 exceeded US$834 per contract, i.e. a premium value of US$5,834. The lower limit for out-of-the-money options triggers when the out-of-the-money value exceeds US$500.

Example:
  Let us assume a member granted on uncovered March sterling contract at a unit cost strike price of 139 and a unit premium of 5.50 cents.

The initial premium = 12,500 × .055	US$ 687.50
Initial margin = 130% of premium	US$ 893.75
Plus	US$ 750.00
	US$ 1,643.75

Thereafter maintenance levels are required to be provided. These are calculated on the same basis as the above by reference to either:

- the exchange daily settlement price, or
- the last bid and offered price in the market.

The PHLX provide members with the choice but do require that members are consistent. The daily settlement price is calculated on a formula which utilises the day's closing or last sale price for each contract period and the closing spot foreign exchange rate within the cash markets.

Example:
  Continuing the example above let us assume the position remained open and the member had elected to settle on the daily settlement price which was established the following day at 6.50 cents. For that contract margin maintenance would be calculated as:

Premium = 12,500 × .065 =	US$ 812.50
Initial margin = 130% of premium	US$ 1,056.25
Plus	US$ 750.00
	US$ 1,806.25
Less previous day	US$ 1,643.75
Maintenance margin required	US$ 162.50

Assuming the member elected the last prices quoted which were bid 6.35, offered 6.65, the basis of the calculation would be the offered price as he is short the option. Therefore:

Premium = 12,500 × .0635	US$ 793.75
Initial margin = 130% of premium	US$ 1,031.88
Plus	US$ 750.00
	US$ 1,781.88
Less previous day	US$ 1,643.75
Maintenance margin required	US$ 138.13

Upon close out of a transaction all margins together with the relative premiums are paid by the clearing house. Each long position holder receives any profit which may be due on open positions on a daily basis.

Reduced initial margins are available for call spreads, put spreads and short straddle positions within contracts. The spread positions referred to are more specifically inter-delivery spreads both by months and within months. These are available where a long call position in one series of an option class expires on or after a short call position in a different series of the same class. In these circumstances the margin will be the lesser of the margin required on the short position in isolation as an uncovered short position or the amount by which the striking price of the long call (or short put) exceeds the striking price of the short call (or long put) plus the full amount of the premium on the long position.

A straddle position results from the sale (grant) of both a short put and short call position in the same class. The margin required for straddle positions is the greater of the margin required on the short call or the short put positions calculated separately as uncovered short positions plus any unrealised loss on the other position.

Initial margin requirements may be satisfied by the deposit of cash or securities, alternatively, by utilisations under an approved irrevocable letter of credit. Maintenance requirements must be satisfied by a deposit of cash or securities of sufficient value to meet the margin call. Utilisations of letters of credit may not be used to satisfy maintenance requirements. It is the responsibility of member or participant organisations to collect initial and maintenance margins promptly from their clients and in no event should these be collected later than seven business days following the day the margin call is made.

LSE – Traded Currency Options

The LSE commenced trading options on the 16th May 1985. As indicated from the following extract from the Financial Times of the 17th July, there are two contracts traded on the LSE, £/US$ and US$/DM.

		Calls			*Puts*		
		June	Sept.	Dec.	June	Sept.	Dec.
£/US$	120	19.00	19.00	19.60	0.30	1.60	2.90
*138.96	125	14.00	14.70	15.60	0.65	2.70	4.30
cts)	130	9.60	11.35	12.40	1.70	4.20	6.30
	135	6.20	8.30	9.80	3.30	6.40	8.70
	140	3.70	6.00	7.40	5.90	9.10	11.30
US$/DM	32	3.00	3.40	3.90	0.20	0.45	0.70
(*34.75	33	2.25	2.70	3.25	0.32	0.70	1.00
cts)	34	1.42	2.10	2.60	0.62	1.10	1.30
	35	0.95	1.50	2.00	1.10	1.55	1.90

The contract sizes are respectively £12,500 and DM62,500. Strike prices are quoted as US dollars and cents per £1 sterling, therefore the first strike price equates to an exchange rate £/US$1.20 and the second a US$/DM rate of .32. The premiums are quoted in cents per £1 sterling and DM1 unit respectively with minimum movement of 5 cents for sterling and 1 cent for DM which equates to a contract quotation size of US$6.25 for both contracts. Premiums are payable in full one business day following the purchase of the option. The expiration months are March, June, September and December with an expiration time established at 6.00 p.m. on the Friday before the third Wednesday of those months. The contracts are on American terms and delivery takes place on the third business day following notice of exercise. The clearing house is the London Options Clearing House (LOCH), a wholly owned subsidiary of the LSE. However, LOCH is managed, and contracts are guaranteed, by ICCH. Delivery procedures require the delivery of sterling and deutschemarks against the payment of US dollars. Margins are required to be provided on all short positions and is calculated as 10% of the US dollar value of the contract plus or minus the amount by which the contract is in or out-of-the money but are subject to a minimum margin of £250. Reductions may be claimed for inter-currency straddle positions and are available for any long positions held. Initial margins may be provided in cash or by the provision of security acceptable to the clearing house. Contracts are marked to market on a daily basis and shortfalls must be settled by 10.30 a.m. on the following business day. There is a position limit of 10,000 contracts in any one class of options, client commission fees are negotiable and there is an exercise fee of £20 per transaction plus 30p per contract up to a maximum of £240 per day.

LIFFE – Traded Currency Options
LIFFE introduced American type currency options with a US$/£ contract on the 27th June 1985. The contract size is £25,000 with expiration months of March, June, September and December. Quotations are in US cents per £ with a minimum price movement of 0.01 or US$2.50 per contract.

LIFFE has been rather unique in its approach to initial margins, variation margins and premiums. Initial margins are based on the perceived hedge ratio calculated as a percentage of the initial margin requirements for the US$/£ futures contract. The subject of the perceived hedge ratio, or delta factor as it is more frequently called is discussed later in this chapter with regard to option pricing and hedging. Within these requirements the percentage is calculated by reference to the relationship between the strike price and current underlying market price. Initial margins are required to be maintained by both buyers and sellers of options. Consequently, buyers are not required to pay premiums until the contract is either exercised or closed. In addition, the daily variation margin is based for new contracts on the difference between the initial trading price and the closing settlement price and for old contracts the previous day's settlement price and the current closing settlement price. Reduced margins are available for various strategic trading positions both within this option and between the option and the US$/£ futures contract.

Traded Share, Stock and Bond Options

Contracts for traded share, stock or bond options are based on individual physical shares of companies, corporations and governments. The largest exchange for the trading of these options is the Chicago Board Options Exchange (CBOE) which trades several hundred listed options, most of which are quoted shares on the New York Stock Exchange (NYSE). The CBOE also provides for option trading in treasury bond futures contracts. Other traded option markets in the USA include the American Stock Exchange and the New York Stock Exchange. The European Option Exchange facilitates trading in some 12 stocks and six Dutch bonds. The London Stock Exchange (LSE) trades some two dozen or so listed shares. Exchange traded stock option markets also exist in Australia and South Africa.

LSE Stock Options

Within the LSE options are quoted in one of the three monthly expiry cycles available within the year:

- January, April, July, October
- February, May, August, November
- March, June, September December

The specific date within the month on which a contract expires will be announced by the LSE when the contract is introduced. Three expiration months will be quoted at any one time, providing maximum life cycles of three, six and nine months. A contract unit normally represents 1,000 shares but where the face value of shares stands at a much higher face value than the norm a contract unit may represent 100 shares.

400

In recognition of the wide range of underlying market prices, the intervals between strike prices quoted at any one time are determined by the LSE in accordance with the following scale:

50 – 140p	10p intervals
140 – 300p	20p intervals
300 – 420p	30p intervals
420 – 500p	40p intervals
500 – 1,000p	50p intervals
1,000p and above	100p intervals

At the time of introducing new contracts two prices will be quoted for puts and two for calls, representing the appropriate scale either side of the current market price. Premiums are quoted in pence per share unit of the underlying share with a minimum price movement of £0.01 per share unit which represents £10 minimum per 1,000 share contract. Clearing members only comprise Stock Exchange members and as is customary within the Stock Exchange, investors trade, and as appropriate, provide notice of exercise, etc. through brokers.

The basic principle of margin requirements from short position holders on LSE traded options is 20% of the market price of the underlying security plus or minus respectively the in-the-money or out-of-the-money value of short positions. Margins required are calculated on a daily basis and may be satisfied by the deposit of cash or a limited range of specified securities.

The following extract from the Financial Times "London Traded Options" shows the prices of three London Stock Exchange traded options as at 19th June 1985.

Option		Calls			Puts		
		July	*Oct.*	*Jan.*	*July*	*Oct.*	*Jan.*
British	460	73	88	–	3	10	–
Petroleum	500	35	53	67	6	15	22
(*526)	550	10	23	38	30	33	42
	600	1½	11	20	80	82	87

		Calls			*Puts*		
		June	*Sep.*	*Dec.*	*June*	*Sep.*	*Dec.*
Beecham	330	12	28	35	3	9	12
(*338)	360	2	12	20	25	28	33
	390	1	5	11	55	55	57

		Calls			*Puts*		
		Aug.	*Nov.*	*Feb.*	*Aug.*	*Nov.*	*Feb.*
Barclays	335	57	67	–	3	5	–
(*382)	360	–	–	57	–	–	12
	385	23	32	–	17	23	–
	390	–	–	37	–	–	32
	435	6	12	–	60	65	–

The asterisked figures in brackets represent the closing market prices of the underlying stock. The second column indicates the various strike prices which are currently available and the remaining columns are premium quotations for calls and separately puts. Within the markets the premium quotations have bid and offered sides but the premiums indicated for the purpose of publication only include the last offered prices within the market on the previous day.

If during the life of a contract there is a bonus issue and the number of new shares created is an exact multiple of the number of old shares in issue the LSE and LOCH will proportionately increase the number of open contracts. Where it is not a multiple of the number of old shares the contract unit size will be increased proportionately.

Traded Stock Index Options
Exchange traded markets in stock index options include:

- The Index and Option Market with the Standard & Poors (S & P) 100 and 500 indexes and NYSE double index
- The Chicago Board Option Exchange also with the S & P 100 and 500 indexes
- The American Stock Exchange with five separate indices:
- The Amex Margin Market Index
- The Amex Market Value Index
- The Amex Oil and Gas Index

- The Amex Computer Technology Index
- The Amex Transportation Index
- The New York Futures Exchange with the NYSE composite index
- The London Stock Exchange with the FT-SE100 index
- The Kansas City Board of Trade with the Value Line Index

LSE – FT/SE100 Index Options

The LSE FT/SE100 Index option contract represents a notional value of £5 multiplied by the index value which is also quoted in pound sterling terms. From the prices indicated below this would value each contract at £6,420 (1,284 × 5). Strike price intervals are of 50 index points. Expiration dates are the last business day of March, June, September and December with three contracts trading at any one time providing maximum life cycles of three, six and nine months. The option premium is quoted in pence per unit of 1p of the notional value of £5 (i.e. 500 units per contract) multiplied by the market value of the index. From the prices below, a June call option contract at a strike of 1,250 would be granted at a premium of £190 (38p × 500), the underlying contract value being £6,250. In this example the premium would represent intrinsic value of £170 (500 × (1,284 – 1,250)) and a time value of £20. Contracts are written on American terms and if exercised the intrinsic value settled in cash by the assigned grantor of the option.

		Calls			*Puts*		
		June	Sept.	Dec.	June	Sept.	Dec.
FT–SE	1200	88	105	–	$1\frac{1}{2}$	13	–
Index	1250	38	62	77	2	20	32
(*1284)	1300	7	35	47	20	44	57
	1350	2	18	32	70	82	90

The basis of initial and daily maintenance margin requirements is $12\frac{1}{2}\%$ of the current index value of the contract plus or minus respectively the in-the-money or out-of-the-money amount. Therefore in the example above premiums would be:

$12\frac{1}{2}\%$ of £6,420	=	£815.00
Plus in-the-money element	=	£170.00
Total premium	=	£985.00

Traded Futures Option Contracts

Traded option markets in different types of futures contract exist in various exchanges. These include the IMM using its sterling, deutschemark, swiss franc and eurodollar contracts; COMEX with its gold contract; NYFE using the NYSE composite share index; IOM with its S & P 500 share index and more recently LIFFE with its eurodollar contract.

IMM Deutschemark Futures Option

The following extract from the Wall Street Journal reflects the various futures option contracts traded on the IMM. The strike prices and premium quotation are in similar format to those described in previous pages.

Chicago Mercantile Exchange

Eurodollar (CME) $ million; pts. of 100%

Strike Price	Calls–Settle			Puts–Settle		
	Sep–C	Dec–C	Mar–C	Sep–P	Dec–P	Mar–P
9100	1.20	0.99	0.77	0.08	0.33	0.56
9150	0.81	0.70	–	0.17	0.50	–
9200	0.49	0.43	0.35	0.34	0.73	–
9250	0.26	0.25	–	0.59	–	–
9300	0.11	0.13	–	–	–	–
9350	0.05	–	–	–	–	–

British Pound (CME) 25,000 pounds; cents per pound sterling.

Strike Price	Calls–Settle			Puts–Settle		
	Sep–C	Dec–C	Mar–C	Sep–P	Dec–P	Mar–P
1225	7.70	–	–	2.35	4.90	–
1250	6.20	7.65	–	3.35	5.90	–
1275	4.90	6.45	–	4.55	–	–
1300	3.80	5.45	–	5.95	–	–
1325	2.90	4.60	–	–	–	–
1350	2.20	–	–	–	–	–

W.German Mark (CME) 125,000 marks, cents per mark

Strike	Calls–Settle		Puts–Settle	
Price	Sep–C	Dec–C	Sep–P	Dec–P
31	2.27	2.73	0.29	0.59
32	1.59	2.10	0.58	0.91
33	1.02	1.55	0.99	1.32
34	0.62	1.14	1.56	1.87
35	0.35	0.80	2.28	2.50
36	0.19	0.58	3.09	3.23

Swiss Franc (CMC) 125,000 francs; cents per franc

Strike	Calls–Settle			Puts–Settle		
Price	Sep–C	Dec–C	Mar–C	Sep–P	Dec–P	Mar–P
37	2.74	3.26	–	0.35	0.67	0.87
38	2.03	2.61	3.03	0.62	0.98	1.18
39	1.43	2.05	3.50	0.99	1.38	–
40	0.98	1.59	2.02	1.51	1.87	–
41	0.64	1.20	–	2.15	–	–
42	0.40	0.88	–	–	3.08	–

The IMM Deutschemark futures contract is discussed in Chapter 17. The contract size of the DM option contract is one DM futures contract. Contract months are March, June, September and December with three contract months normally trading at any one time. These four months coincide with four of the eight months for which the IMM futures contract is traded. Striking prices are quoted in US Dollars at one cent intervals and at the commencement of a new contract month there are five striking prices each for puts and calls, one to the nearest whole cent of the Deutschemark futures contract with two prices either side of this figure.

Additional strike prices are listed when the Deutschemark futures price touches within 50 basis points of either the second highest or second lowest strike prices. No new strike prices will be listed within less than 20 calendar days of the expiration date of the underlying contract. Premiums are quoted in cents per currency unit with a minimum price fluctuation of US$.01c. representing US$12.50 per contract. There is no price limit as to premium movements during a trading session, albeit there is a limit of 100 points move on the underlying futures contract.

As described in Chapter 17, it is normal practice with DM futures contracts for sellers intending to make delivery of the physical commodity to tender notice of delivery prior to the cessation of trading in that contract. Therefore the DM option contract ceases trading, and has an expiration time of 5.00 p.m., two Fridays before the third Wednesday of the contract month.

NYSE Composite Index Futures Option Contracts
The New York Stock Exchange contract comprises one NYSE composite index futures contract. Premiums are quoted in terms of NYSE composite index futures contract in basis points. The option premium dollar amount is equal to the number of basis points multiplied by five. Therefore a premium of 1.00 (100 basis points) is equal to US$500. The minimum price fluctuation is .05 or 5 basis points equal to US$25 per contract. The contract months are March, June, September and December with three option months traded at any one time. Strike price intervals are evenly divisible by two and a minimum of four prices are quoted at all times, one in-the-money, one at-the-money and two out-of-the-money. The last trading day is the same as the NYSE composite index futures contract which is the business day prior to the last business day in the contract month. Options may be exercised on any NYSE business day during the life of the contract. A long call option holder that exercises, is delivered a long position in the underlying futures contract. If the assigned grantor is a covered writer his long position is liquidated. If he is an uncovered writer a short position in the underlying futures contract will be assigned. The futures position will be established at the strike price of the option contract. Conversely, a long put position when exercised receives a short position and the assigned short position holder a long position in the underlying futures contract. Exercises made on the final day of trading result in a cash settlement rather than the assignment of a futures position and at the close of business

on the last trading day all in-the-money options will be automatically exercised.

A long option position holder only requires to pay the full premium in cash but short position holders require to provide both initial and variation margins which are applied through maintenance levels.

COMEX Gold Futures Option Contract

The Comex contract is traded for three of the corresponding months to the underlying Comex gold futures contract, i.e. April, August and December. Four consecutive option contract months are traded at any one time providing maximum life cycles of four, eight, 12 and 16 months. Increments between strike prices are determined by the underlying gold price within the following scale:

Under US$300	US$10
US$300 – 500	US$20
US$500 – 800	US$30
US$800 and above	US$40

Five initial strike prices are posted for each series of option and further strike prices are added when the price of the underlying futures contract moves half-way between the third highest and the second highest strike price or the third lowest and second lowest strike price. Trading ceases at 2.30 p.m. New York time on the second Friday of the month prior to the expiration of the underlying futures contract. Long position holders must notify brokers of their intention to exercise by 3.00 p.m. New York time on any business day on which the option is traded including the expiration date. The option will expire on the last trading date. There are no daily restrictions on price movements.

LIFFE Eurodollar Futures Option

The contract size of the LIFFE eurodollar futures option is one three month eurodollar interest rate futures contract which has a value of of US$1 million. It is on American terms with expiration months of March, June, September and December. Margins are calculated on a

407

similar basis to those described for the LIFFE US$/£ currency contract and are related to delta factor based upon the futures initial margin requirement of US$1,000. Reduced margins are available for offsetting positions in options and between the underlying futures contract.

Over the Counter Options (OTCs)

OTCs refer to option contracts which are established between the purchaser and grantor of an option, either directly or through a broker or other agent with the terms and conditions of the option being negotiated and agreed between the parties involved. These latter options may be tailor-made to a purchaser's requirements or, if regularly quoted by the grantor, have many similar standardized characteristics of an exchange traded option.

OTCs have a long and chequered history within the United States and it may be of interest to reflect briefly upon these markets in that country as there may well be lessons to be learnt from their experience.

As mentioned at the beginning of this Chapter, a form of commodity option styled 'privileges' was traded on the Chicago Board of Trade Exchange during the 1860s. These options were primarily in wheat and, following pressure from producers, the Illinois State Legislature prohibited this type of trading on the CBT although these contracts continued to trade off the exchange. In the 1930s Congress prohibited trading on privileges and subsequently in 1936 the Commodity Exchange Authority (CEA) was established which was the regulatory body responsible for supervising futures trading in specified agricultural commodities. The CEA banned option trading in all commodities covered by its mandate. However, other commodities began to be traded on exchanges outside of the mandate of the CEA and new option markets developed based upon these commodities. In addition, a substantial business developed in "London options" purporting to be based on the contracts of the London Commodity and Metal Exchanges. In reality many of these options were written on a naked (uncovered) basis, i.e. the grantors did not cover them with either option or futures contracts or physical inventory, alternatively the grantors had covered their obligations within the London markets but failed to meet margin calls and were subsequently closed out. Thereafter following dramatic price increases in the underlying commodities, the grantors were unable to meet their obligations and investors lost millions of dollars in both premiums and potential profit.

Concurrent with the development of the "naked" and "London option" schemes a further form of option emerged styled "dealer" options which were the origins of "OTC" options within the United States. These options were granted by reputable dealers in the physical commodity against inventories, futures contracts or otherwise hedged by the dealers in sufficient quantity to cover their open option positions. Dealer options were not subject to the abuses and fraud which surrounded the "naked" and "London option" business.

The authority of the CFTC, which was established in 1974, also extended to the supervision of options traded both on and off the Board of Trade exchanges. Following various unsuccessful attempts by the CFTC to contain the fraudulent activities surrounding options, they adopted in November 1976 interim regulations governing off exchange commodity option transactions which stipulated registration, disclosure, segregation and book-keeping requirements for option grantors. The CFTC also proposed implementing test programmes that would ultimately require all options to be purchased and sold on or through the facilities of CFTC designated boards of trade. Despite these interim measures, fraud and malpractices continued until April 1978 when the CFTC suspended trading of all commodity options except "trade" options. "Trade" options are basically "hedger options" and comprise options offered to a producer, processor or commercial user, who enters into a commodity option transaction for purposes related to its business as such.

Subsequently in June 1978 the CFTC also adopted a "dealer option" exemption regulation which enabled them to authorise certain dealers to continue offering "dealer" options. To qualify for exemption dealers were required to be:

- domiciled in the United States,

- in the business of granting options on the physical commodity on 1st May 1978,

- in the business of buying, selling, producing or otherwise utilising that commodity.

In addition, several other conditions were established with which dealers had to comply. Inter alia these requirements included:

- Daily segregation of funds by the dealer to cover any equity accruing to option customers through a mark to market exercise

- No person other than a Futures Commission Merchant (FCM as discussed in Chapter 17) could solicit or accept orders for the purchase or sale of a commodity option

- Only FCMs were authorised to accept funds or other property (or extend credit in lieu) as payment for the purchase price in connection with a commodity option transaction

- 90% of the purchase price of a commodity option must be held by the FCM in a segregated client account and treated as the customer's funds until the option either expires or, if the customer exercises the option, until all rights of the customer in the option have been fulfilled

- Risk disclosure requirements

Dealer and trade options differ only in the context of how they are traded between the principals involved, i.e trade options do not necessitate the interface of a FCM or require to be subject to the other statutory CFCC requirements applied to dealer options. Financial options offered by a bank to its clients or other banks within the USA are primarily trade options and fall outside of the requirements imposed by the CFTC on "dealer options".

410

Initially five companies, Mocatta Metals Corporation (MMC), The Mocatta Corporation, Dowdex, Comark and Valeur First Boston Corporation received exemption to sell "dealer" options through appointed FCMs and following the relaxation of these previous restrictions more recently other dealers have been authorised to write "dealer" options.

The foregoing resume not only explains the origins of the terms "trade" and "dealer" options within the OTC markets of the USA, but also illustrates the frauds and malpractices which can develop in an unregulated environment and emphasises the high risks involved in this type of trading. The traded option markets within the United States including those mentioned in this chapter, for example the CBT, CME, CBIE, AMEX, IMM and Comex are all part of a pilot scheme for exchange quoted options proposed by the CFTC in 1976. The experience of option markets in general within the United States formed the case study upon which the more recent financial option markets outside of that country have developed.

Although within the UK, share, stock and bond options primarily remain exclusively exchange traded options, an increasing number of banks now not only deal in exchange traded currency options, but also grant, purchase and make markets in OTC currency options, and a market is developing in interest rate options (interest rate guarantees). Whilst this development has, to some extent, taken place without consideration being given to the standardization of practices, uniformity of contracts and terms and conditions, the underlying principles of option trading are the same. Several banks quote separate bid and offered prices for call and put contracts. Whereas exchange quotations comprise a mixture of purchasers and grantors interests, a market-making bank is prepared to re-purchase an option upon the basis of bid and offered quotations for premium price both puts and calls. Some banks will only create a two way activity by granting options with a facility of subsequent re-purchase and settlement rather than purchase a separate contract from a client. This practice has an advantage in regard to credit risk considerations. The net settlement amount shall represent the price difference in the holder's favour between the original strike price and the settlement price.

411

A market-making bank will normally issue the terms and conditions upon which it is prepared to trade in options and, unless otherwise agreed, a counterparty trading upon that bank's quotations. either purchasing or granting, will be bound by such terms and conditions.

It may be helpful to consider briefly the differences between OTCs and traded options through a comparison of the advantages and disadvantages of OTC options against exchange traded options.

The main advantages of OTC options over exchange traded options include:

- Their flexibility - individual market makers will be prepared to grant or purchase options in contract sizes and premium bases which are required.

- Quotations available for a broader spread of major currencies.

- Initial and maintenance margins are not mandatory.

- When trading directly with the grantor, brokerage commissions and other front end fees including exercise and delivery fees are not normally charged.

- Quotations may be obtained and deals transacted outside of the limited trading periods and strike prices of an exchange.

- Subject to counterparty limits being available interbank market participation is available to all banks.

- Corporate customers frequently prefer to trade directly with their bank on a principal to principal relationship and access to prices is readily available to them.

The main disadvantages of OTC options against exchange traded options are:

- Liquidity – the lack of two way liquidity may impact adversely upon an individual bank's premium quotations faster than those of an exchange.

- Exercise and close out procedure are readily available for exchange traded options merely by undertaking further trades – although an investor can open a long or short position with an individual counterparty and subsequently close his position either with another counterparty or exchange, exercise, margin, close out and re-purchase procedures will be required to liquidate both positions.

- Re-purchase procedures require acceptance of the original grantors current price quotations which may not be competitive.

- An option purchaser accepts a direct credit exposure on the grantor.

- Standardized options are less likely to be the subject of error in negotiation and their terms and conditions are subject to exchange regulation.

The London Interbank Options Markets

Following from the developments of the OTC market the BBA issued during August 1985 terms and conditions, known as London Interbank Currency Option Market (LICOM) terms, which are to be treated as normal market practice for the interbank OTC option market in London. Banks are free to deal on other terms if they wish but should consider themselves under an obligation to make clear to any counterparty in what way their terms for such transactions would differ from the LICOM terms. In the absence of such clarifications, banks and brokers in the London interbank market are expected to follow what is now established market practice for trading these instruments.

Within the options markets, contract terms are negotiated and agreed either orally or by telephone, and subsequently confirmed in writing. Within the LICOM terms this is effected by a simple exchange of confirmation.

413

Although without any agreement to the contrary all options are assumed to be on American terms, these terms also establish market practice for European options. LICOM terms and conditions require that quotations are based on strike prices which are quoted as "direct", "indirect" or "cross currency quotations". In this context direct and indirect quotations are used in reference to the US dollar with a direct quotation being a currency expressed in terms of the dollar, i.e. DM/US$3.26 and an indirect quotation being where the dollar is expressed in terms of one unit of the other currency, e.g. US$/£1.39. Cross currency rates are applicable where the dollar is not a currency to the transaction, e.g. DM/£4.5314. The form of quotation indicated here is different from the more common foreign exchange notation. There are of course DM3.26 to US$1, US$1.39 to £1 and DM4.5314 to £1. LICOM terms also requires that wherever the US dollar is a currency to the transactions it is the counter currency to the contract and that the other currency is the underlying currency of the option contract. In the case of cross currency transactions the first currency of the quotation, i.e. in the case above deutschemarks, is the underlying currency of the contract. Consequently, in the case of the three rates quoted, deutschemarks, sterling and deutschemarks would be the underlying currency on which the option contract is based. If a bank wishes to provide US dollars and receive deutschemarks within the option terms and the dollar is a currency to the transaction it will either buy a call or sell a put. Where it wishes to receive dollars and provide deutschemarks it will sell a call or buy a put. Within the markets standard quotation sizes, the quotation amount, are determined by the unit upon which the strike price is related, i.e. US$/£ the quotation amount would be for sterling, DM/US$ for US dollars, and £/DM for sterling. Premiums on direct and indirect quotations are in dollars and respectively quoted as a percentage of the US dollar amount.

All premiums are payable to the nominated account of the granting bank in good value funds on the premium payment date, which is defined as the spot value date. Premiums payable in US dollars are made through the New York clearing house interbank payments system and in the case of a cross currency transaction in the country of domicile of the premium currency amount.

414

Within the London markets banks may agree at inception of an option trade that settlement, if any, will be on either a principal or net cash basis. For counterparty risk considerations, the BBA recommend settlement on a net cash basis. As a means for establishing cash settlement amounts the BBA provide daily currency settlement prices for selected currencies. The settlement price is fixed by reference to the middle market spot foreign exchange prices in the interbank market. These fixings are made at 3.00 p.m. London time each business day on the basis of eight quotations provided by eight of 12 reference banks. The middle four of these prices are averaged and the result rounded to nearest conventional foreign exchange market point. This settlement price is known as "LICOM settlement price". Initially daily fixings are made available for pounds sterling, deutschemarks, Japanese yen and Swiss francs against US dollars. These currencies together with any currencies subsequently added thereto, are known as the "LICOM currencies". Where net cash settlement is required but a surrender premium cannot be agreed by the counterparties, then the holder retains the right to exercise the option. The net settlement amount is paid in the same currency as that in which the original premium was paid to the grantor.

The expiration time for any option to be settled on a principal settlement basis is 3.00 p.m. London time on the expiration date. Expiration time for any option to be settled on a net settlement basis is 2.30 p.m. London time on the expiration date. The settlement amount will then be based on that day's 3.00 p.m. LICOM fixing.

Options may only be exercised in whole and not in part. Arrangements for surrender or exercise may be made by telex or telephone and a subsequently written confirmation is provided in sufficient detail by the option holder to the grantor so that the option can be positively identified. This will require:

- date of original contract
- grantor's reference number
- underlying currency and amount
- strike price
- counter currency and amount

- whether call or put
- expiration date
- settlement instructions for surrender premium

The grantor shall not be required to notify or pre-notify the holder of expiration of an option and failing surrender or exercise, an option will be deemed to have expired.

Following surrender or exercise, the net cash settlement or as appropriate the exchange of principal amounts is made with good value on the settlement date. For a European option the settlement date is the second business day immediately following the expiration date which (together with the preceding business day) is a business day in New York and the countries of the respective underlying and counter currencies of the option concerned. For an American option the settlement date may be specified by the holder as the earliest of the first settlement date or if later the second business day immediately following the notice of exercise which (together with the preceding business day) is a business day in New York and the countries of the respective underlying and counter currencies of the option concerned. At the latest the second business day immediately following the expiration date which (together with the preceding business day) is a business day in London, New York and the countries of the respective underlying and counter currencies of the option. Where dollars are to be paid or received settlement is made through the New York clearing house interbank payments system.

The BBA have provided recommended standards of confirmation. Based on the following example of a sale and purchase between two banks these are exhibited on the following pages. It will be noted that these confirmations also provide for surrender (re-sale) of an option.

Example: Sale Ticket

ABC BANK LIMITED

Broker

Customer name

XYZ BANK LTD.

SALE

Deal type: **S**

Commodity code: D E M

Customer number: 0 0 0 1

Contract date: 26 / 07 / 85

Underlying currency: DEM 2,800,000

Strike price: 2.80

Counter value: USD 1,000,000

Quantity in lots:

Value date: 29 / 01 / 86

Option: **C** x   Type: **P**   Call   Put

Declaration date: 27 / 01 / 86

Declaration time: 15.00

Declaration location: LONDON

Actual price: 3.70

Premium required: $37,000

Premium payment date: 30.07.85

Deal number: 0 0 0 0 0 1

Instructions
Receive premium from

ABC NEW YORK

Raised by

Example: Purchase Ticket

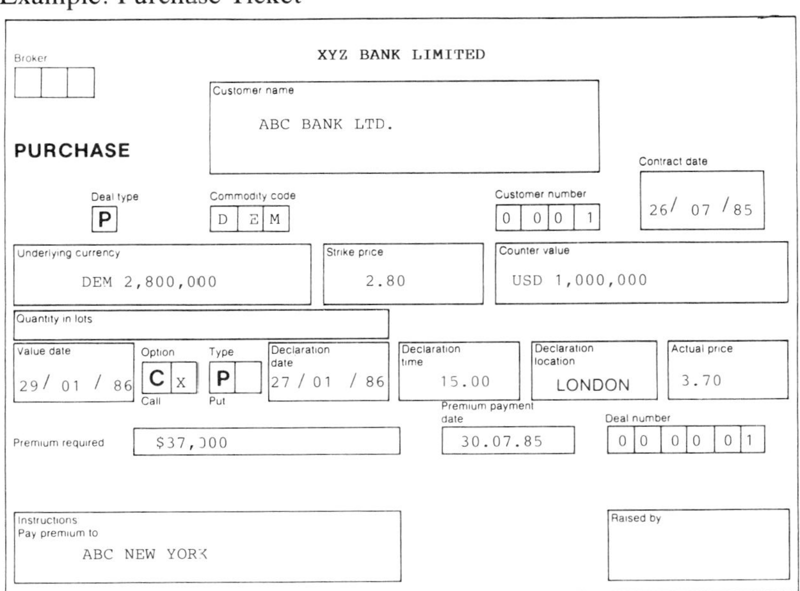

Example: Confirmation originated by grantor

F. 1   <u>EXAMPLES OF CONFIRMATIONS</u>

ABC BANK LTD.

Main Street, London E.C.2.

To: Foreign Exchange Options
        Confirmation Section,
      XYZ Bank Ltd,
      Moorgate,
      London, E.C.2.

<u>CONFIRMATION OF FOREIGN CURRENCY OPTION GRANTED</u>

We confirm that we have GRANTED/~~RESOLD~~* TO YOU the following currency option:

Our Original Reference No:**   via PHONE/~~TELEX~~/~~BROKER~~*

Option Reference No: 0001	Date of Transaction: 26.07.1985
Settlement: NET CASH/~~PRINCIPAL~~*	Type: AMERICAN/~~EUROPEAN~~*
CALL/~~PUT~~* on Underlying Currency and Amount:	DEM 2,800,000
At Strike Price:	2.80
Against Counter Currency and Amount:	US$ 1,000,000
First Settlement Date:***	
Expiration Date:	27 JAN 1986
Option Price:	3.70
Our Premium Due:	US$ 37,000
Premium Payment Date:	30 JULY 1986
Premium Settlement Instructions:	ABC BANK, NEW YORK

*   delete as appropriate
**   if relevant
***   if different from premium payment date

<u>London Interbank Foreign Exchange Market Practice</u>

Options entered into under the above arrangements shall be subject to the normal conditions of business for transactions in the London interbank foreign exchange markets and also to the specific conditions of the London Interbank Currency Options Market Standard Terms and Conditions, "LICOM TERMS", as published by the B.B.A. in August, 1985.

Signed:

For and on behalf of
ABC Bank Ltd.

Example: Confirmation originated by purchaser

F. 2 <u>EXAMPLES OF CONFIRMATIONS</u>

XYZ BANK LTD.

Moorgate, London E.C.2.

To: Foreign Exchange Options
      Confirmation Section,
      ABC Bank Ltd,
      Main Street,
      London, E.C.2.

<u>CONFIRMATION OF FOREIGN CURRENCY OPTION PURCHASED</u>

We confirm that we have PURCHASED/~~REPURCHASED~~* FROM YOU the following currency option:

Our Original Reference No:**   via PHONE/~~TELEX/BROKER~~*

Option Reference No: 0001	Date of Transaction: 26.07.1985
Settlement: NET CASH/~~PRINCIPAL~~*	Type: AMERICAN/~~EUROPEAN~~*
CALL/~~PUT~~* on Underlying Currency and Amount:	DEM 2,800,000
At Strike Price:	2.80
Against Counter Currency and Amount:	US$ 1,000,000
First Settlement Date:***	
Expiration Date:	27 JAN 1986
Option Price:	3.70
Our Premium Due:	US$ 37,000
Premium Payment Date:	30 JULY 1985
Premium Settlement Instructions:	ABC BANK, NEW YORK

*   delete as appropriate
**   if relevant
***   if different from premium payment date

<u>London Interbank Foreign Exchange Market Practice</u>

The above transaction is subject to the normal conditions of business for transactions in the London interbank foreign exchange markets and also to the specific conditions of the London Interbank Currency Options Market Standard Terms and Conditions, "LICOM TERMS", as published by the B.B.A. in August, 1985.

Signed:

For and on behalf of
XYZ Bank Ltd.

Banks' Activities in Options

Banks may use options as speculative instruments providing opportunity for immediate profit, for trading purposes to cover underlying commercial requirements, as hedging instruments to protect underlying exposures or anticipated requirements, or as a dealer (market-maker) in these instruments.

However, in considering their use for any of these purposes the underlying difference in the nature of puts and calls, the rights and obligations conferred in the granting or the purchasing of these instruments, together with the risks involved must be related to the specific objectives which are to be accomplished. For example, this is particularly true in foreign exchange where two monetary values are involved. Let us assume a bank has a US dollar long position against sterling at 1.30 that it wishes to protect against a weakening dollar. It may either buy a call on sterling or grant a put on sterling. At face value either course may appear to achieve the objective. However,* the purchase of a call option guarantees the bank against the weakening dollar but if the dollar strengthens provides the bank with the opportunity to abandon the option and take advantage of the dollar's improvement. Conversely, while the grant of a put option protects the bank in theory against a weakening dollar it would leave the bank exposed in practice as the option would not be exercised. If the dollar strengthened the put would be exercised.

The prime consideration in purchasing options relates to perceived price movement of the underlying subject matter relative to a quantified premium cost. Those related to option granting are concerned with premiums as a source of additional income or profit potential against the perceived risk of underlying price movement. Alternative strategies involving different risk reward ratios are often available to achieve the desired object and it must be remembered that whenever a bank grants a call option it must be prepared to make delivery of the subject matter, or where it grants a put, to take delivery.

The choice of option that a bank writes will determine the premium it receives but in general the higher the premium the greater the risk of exercise. In terms of time value an at-the-money option will attract the highest premium.

420

Naked or uncovered put or call options will normally only be written for speculative purposes when the bank has a strong view that the market value of the underlying object will either move in a direction that means the option will expire worthless (grant call – underlying price movement is down or grant put – underlying price rises) or that the adverse movement will be such that any loss in relation to the eventual in-the-money element will be at least covered by the premium received. A bank may also look at granting options when it feels that the premium quoted is somewhat higher than normally may be anticipated and look to profit from a decrease in the option premium to enable a profitable close out to be made.

Short dated out-of-the-money call options would be most suitable for this purpose but an at-the-money option may be considered as it would generate a higher premium. The shorter the period of an option the less is the likelihood of large price fluctuations. The downside risk to the call grantor is unlimited beyond the break-even point which is the exercise price of the call plus the premium received. If the market does not move as anticipated, and rises beyond the break-even point, risks are high; the bank can only contain its exposure by closing or otherwise covering its position at a loss.

Covered call options may be written with a view to generating income from an anticipated decline in the market price. In deciding which option to write, the bank will consider the size and manner of movement anticipated and whether or not it wishes exercise to take place. The bank may have a view that the underlying exchange rate may weaken but requires to retain the long position for other commercial reasons, for example an overseas capital investment. The granting of a call option would generate premium income which, if the view is correct, could be offset in part to reserves against the decline in the value of the net asset value. However, if the view is incorrect and the price rises the grantor will have the benefit of the improvement in the net asset value. Where it is considered a price will rise a bank with a long investment position which it wishes to sell at current levels may write a call option to generate additional income with the intention of exercise taking place. However, it does run the risk that if the price declines the option will not be taken up and the bank may lose on the price movement. Conversely, if a margin can be

421

made, simultaneously the bank may be able to buy a put option as a hedge against this eventuality.

As speculative instruments the purchase of calls and puts provide opportunity to benefit from an anticipated rise or fall respectively in the price of the underlying subject matter. They provide unlimited profit potential for limited loss risk and greater leverage than is available in either the cash or futures markets. The choice of option for speculative purposes will depend upon the expected nature of the anticipated movement. A gradual and unspectacular increase or decrease will probably require a near or at-the-money option with sufficient time available to achieve the anticipated increase or decrease, a deep out-of-the-money or short term option is unlikely to be attractive. If a large rise or fall in the short term is anticipated a slightly out or even deeper out-of-the-money call or put respectively may be considered.

The purchase of calls and puts may also be used as a hedge to establish a maximum possible price of an anticipated requirement, or receipt of the underlying currency. If we were to assume a bank had a short position in its base currency due to an overseas investment and, whilst it was comfortable with the long term risk, it wished to protect against the impact of a possible short term fall on its reserves, it could purchase a call option thereby protecting the bank against an adverse movement.

The purchase of a call option in the base currency of a bank for future known requirements such as foreign currency profit remittances will secure a price against a strengthening of the base currency against the remittable currency. Should the exchange rate subsequently improve as anticipated the call will be exercised but if the price decreases the option will be abandoned and the profits sold at current market prices.

Should a dealer wish to open a short position in anticipation of a price decline, he could establish a hedge to quantify his potential downside risk should prices rise. The purchase of a call option could achieve this objective. If the dealer's view is correct and the market price declines, the cost of this protection will reduce the profit on the cash position. However, if the market price increases he can either exercise the option to close his position or sell the option and close the short position in the market thus realising both the intrinsic and any remaining time value of the option to offset against the loss on the cash position.

The following provides a practical illustration of using options:

Situation –
UK bank has to fund US dollar investment from 21st July 1984 to 19th December 1984 equivalent £1,000,000
Relevant – market prices

US$/£ spot		1.3980
Swap	21.5.84 – 19.12.84	+0.0220
US$ LIBOR	21.5.84 – 19.12.84	12.375
£ LIBOR	21.5.84 – 19.12.84	9.8125

Possible action –
   Borrow US$1,398,000 from 21.5.84 to 19.12.84 at 12.375
   Interest US$101,879.25
   Covered forward at 1.4200 (1.3980 + 0.0220)
   Total Cost £71,745.95

   Borrow £1,000,000 from 21.5.84 to 19.12.84 at 9.8125
   Interest £56,993.15
   Convert £1,000,000 to US dollars at 1.3980 = US$1,398,000
   Purchase December 1.42 sterling call at cost of US$44,530 (3.13%) = £31,852.65 at 1.3980

Possible outcome at expiration date –
   Assuming US$/£ spot price 1.3000
   Action: 1.   abandon option
           2.   purchase £1,000,000 at 1.3000 =
                US$1,300,000
   Total cost of transaction:

Interest cost	£56,993.15	Dr
Option premium	£31,852.65	Dr
Exchange rate profit US$98,000		
at 1.3000	£75,384.61	Cr
	£13,461.19	

   Therefore performance against US dollar borrowing
   = saving £58,284.76

Assuming US$/£ spot price 1.5000
Action: 1.   exercise option
therefore you buy £1,000,000 at 1.4200
Cost US$1,420,000
US$ shortfall = 22,000

Total cost of transaction:

Interest cost	£56,993.15	Dr
Option premium	£31,852.65	Dr
Cover of US$ shortfall 22,000		
at 1.5000	£14,666.67	Dr
	£103,512.47	

Therefore performance against US dollar borrowing
= additional cost £31,766.52
Performance against unhedged exchange position
Action: 1.   buy £1,000,000 at 1.5000
Cost US$1,500,000
US$ shortfall = 102,000
Total cost of transaction:

Interest cost	£56,993.15	Dr
Cover of US$ shortfall 102,000		
at 1.5000	£68,000.00	Dr
	£124,993.15	

Therefore the total saving by purchase of option as opposed to not hedging is £124,993.15 – £103,512.47 = £21,480.68.

Alternatively –
The bank may borrow £1,000,000 at $9\frac{13}{16}$ from 21.5.84 to 19.12.84 at $9\frac{13}{16}$ = £56,993.15
Convert £1,000,000 to US dollars at 1.3980 = US$1,398,000
Purchase December 1.4200 sterling call option to the value of £1,000,000 at cost of US$44,530.00 = £31,852.65 at 1.3980.
Grant* December 1.3400 sterling put option to the value of £1,000,000 to receive US$11,520.00 = £8,240.34 at 1.3980.

*granting an option gives the counterparty the right but not the obligation to exercise.

Possible outcome at expiration date –
Assume US\$/£ spot price 1.3000
Action: 1.   abandon option purchase
        2.   counterparty exercises option to
            sell sterling
            therefore you buy £1,000,000 at 1.3400
            cost US\$1,340,000
            US\$ profit 58,000

Total cost of transaction:

Interest cost	£56,993.15	Dr
Option premium paid	£31,852.65	Dr
Option premium received	£ 8,240.34	Cr
Exchange rate profit US\$58,000		
at 1.3000	£44,615.38	Cr
	£35,990.08	

Therefore performance against US dollar borrowing
+ saving £35,755.87

Assume US\$/£ price 1.5000
Action: 1.   exercise option
            therefore you buy £1,000,000 at 1.4200
            cost US\$1,420,000
            US\$ shortfall 22,000
        2.   counterparty abandons option purchased from you

Total cost of transaction:

Interest cost	£56,993.15	Dr
Option premium paid	£31,852.65	Dr
Option premium received	£ 8,240.34	Cr
Cover of US\$ shortfall 22,000		
at 1.5000	£14,666.67	Dr
	£95,272.13	

Therefore performance against US dollar borrowing
= additional cost £23,526.18
Performance against unhedged exchange position
Action: 1.   buy £1,000,000 at 1.5000
            cost US\$1,500,000
            US\$ short fall 102,000

Total cost of transaction:

Interest cost	£56,993.15	Dr
Cover of US$ shortfall 102,000		
at 1.5000	£68,000.00	Dr
	£124,993.15	

Therefore total saving by purchase and grant of options as opposed to not hedging = £124,993.15 − £95,272.13 = £29,721.02.

Hedging Strategies –	
Cost of US dollar deposit cover	£71,745.95
Purchase of option	
1.30 saving	£58,284.76
1.50 additional cost	£31,766.52
However saving against no hedge	£21,480.68
Purchase and grant of option	
1.3000 saving	£35,990.08
1.5000 additional cost	£23,526.18
However saving against no hedge	£29,721.02

Option Pricing and Hedging

No one within any market can determine accurately the actual price for currencies, stocks, bonds, gold or other commodities in the future. The only factors that can be established with certainty are current prices and historical trends. Consequently a large element of the expertise used in pricing both the premium value and hedging strategy for options is based upon assumptions and probability factors determined by current and historical data. The objective being to establish the correct delta factor, which is the rate at which the price of an option and the hedge ratio changes in relation to the price change of the underlying subject matter. As previously discussed, option premiums comprise both intrinsic value and time value. For most options time value is a function of four factors:

- Period –
- Current market price v strike price
- Interest rates
- Volatility

- Period –

  The longer the period an option has to run increases the probability that the option will at some point during its life move into-the-money or, if already in-the-money, increase in intrinsic value. Therefore longer dated options are generally more expensive than shorter-dated options. If we say a one month option costs US$1,000 then it would be logical to assume that a four month option costs US$4,000 and say a nine month option costs US$9,000. These are logical assumptions but in the case of options quite wrong. The two main reasons for buying an option are first to provide protection against a risk that the buyer would otherwise be unwilling to accept, and second to give the buyer the profit potential that otherwise he would have by owning the subject matter. So when selling an option the grantor is effectively leasing profit potential and as with leasing agreements the monthly cost is less for a longer lease. Experience has told option grantors that the relationship of cost to time for options works on a square root relationship. So if we look at our original assumption knowing that a one month option costs US$1,000 then the four month option would not cost US$4,000 but US$2,000, two being the square root of four, and a nine month option would not cost US$9,000 but US$3,000, three being the square root of nine.

In option pricing it is also necessary to consider the impact of the decreasing period of an option during its life. Accounting convention and logic would tell us that this should be amortised on a straight line basis. However, again this is not the case, and experience shows option grantors that the actual movement of time value is very small until the last 30 or so days of an option's life. The time value decay curve is in fact a square root curve.

- Current market price v striking price –

  Generally speaking the nearer the striking price is to current market levels the higher is the probability that the option will move into-the-money. Therefore the nearer the striking price is to the market price the higher the premium time value. Deep out-of-the-money options and deep in-the-money options command very little time value. Maximum time value is for an at-the-money option. As an option moves into-the-money it obviously becomes more expensive as it commands both time value and intrinsic value. As the buyer has to pay more for the option to control the same amount of currency it has less leverage. Consequently, as leverage is one of the main advantages for using options, it becomes less attractive to a buyer and for that reason the option price does not move initially at the same speed as the price of the underlying currency, but at about half the speed. The deeper into-the-money that the option goes, the greater the speed of price movement as the more its price movements equate with that of the underlying currency. However, on the basis that eventually the option price will move at the same speed as the underlying price, the movement will be made up of intrinsic value only with no time value. Conversely, as the option moves out-of-the-money it is obviously cheaper and commands greater leverage and is therefore a more attractive instrument. However, as it moves further out-of-the-money the speed of price change becomes less and less until the point where no possibility of exercise exists and the option becomes worthless.

- Interest rates –
  The effect of forward premiums and discounts on the option value require to be considered separately in regard to European and American style options. European type options may only be exercised for delivery on the expiration of the option and for that reason when pricing the option most attention is given to the forward outright price of the underlying currency as this is where the hedge against the risk of exercise will be taken. American type options may be exercised for delivery value spot or at any time up to the expiration date of the option, so grantors must consider the likelihood of early take up. Early exercise would be expected on an option that is deep in-the-money, as the option would not only command its intrinsic value but also time value. Therefore, with American type options the likelihood of early exercise is considered when pricing the option and both the spot and forward prices are taken into the calculation of option value.

The premium for an option is often paid immediately. Therefore the premium has earning potential to the option grantor and

428

represents a loss of potential income to the option holder. This is reflected as a discount in the option premium calculation and will be based upon current levels of interest rates – the higher the interest rate the larger the discount.

- Volatility –
With the exception of the possible exercise dates, and in the case of American options the delivery date, each of the factors discussed above are determinable. Future volatility is not, and the assumptions calculations and probability factors used in measuring its expected course, are the secret of option pricing. This is achieved on the basis of what the option writer does know and that is the price history of the underlying subject matter in relation to the counter currency. Volatility is certainly the most arbitrary figure that goes into an option calculation and can vary quite widely from one writer to another depending upon what assumptions that grantor uses to calculate volatility. The calculation would normally treat the more recent prices as having greater significance as these will be perceived to be of more importance than movements of some months ago. Having established the criteria for measurement it is then necessary for the grantor to consider its implications. For example, if perceived volatility is calculated and reflects that sterling has moved by about 3% over the last three months then for a three month option the premium would take into account the possible repetition of that movement and provide for the fact that the movement may be greater. What is obvious in these calculations is that in times of high volatility option premiums are higher than during periods of low volatility.

Different levels of volatility will affect the speed at which an option price will move. During periods of perceived normal volatility the option price will initially move at about 50% of the movement of the underlying currency price with that movement becoming greater as the option moves into-the-money, eventually getting to the point of a one for one movement when the likelihood of exercise is 100%. In periods of high volatility the option price tends to move far more quickly but takes longer to move on a one-for-one basis as the market is so volatile that the option has to move deeper into-the-money before likelihood of exercise is 100%. In periods of low volatility the opposite happens. The price tends to move more slowly but the point at which it is perceived that it should be on a one for one basis, as 100% likelihood of exercise is reached, will be much sooner.

With stock options the impact of dividend payments upon premiums will also be considered. When a stock goes ex-dividend its underlying market price immediately discounts this payment and therefore where appropriate, adjustments will be made to premiums to reflect this element.

The above factors are primarily based upon a view that prices should be developed on the basis of granting and not buying. This is obviously correct in relation to the risk/reward potential. However, current levels of supply and demand will also impact upon option prices. For example, if there were many purchasers of options but few grantors the latter's risk potential would increase as the opportunity to hedge sales with purchases would diminish. Premiums will therefore be lower in highly liquid markets. Supply and demand work very much as in any other market but probably in a more pronounced way in the early stages of a developing market and the larger the size of a deal, the greater it will impact on current premium prices.

A bank's market-making role in OTC options, as with other forms of dealing, will be directed towards making profits on spreads. In this role the ultimate objective will be to match purchases and grants by class and by series of option thus taking profits from premium spreads. In practice the attainment of this objective is rarely attainable simultaneously in other than very liquid markets.

Consequently banks endeavour to cover potential risk exposure through hedging strategies. Within option trading such strategies are individual and complicated; they are continually up-dated and amended as a result of each opening and closing transaction, current exposure positions, including the correlation of straddles, etc. Recent and current market prices together with all the other factors which comprise option premium value are considered. Most of these hedging programmes are computer systems based on a mass of mathematic algorithms being activated by a mix of pre-determined constant assumptions and criteria which are continually up-dated with variable factors, e.g. current prices, interest rates, perceived volatility, etc. The most common hedging programmes currently in use were initially based upon the Black-Scholes formula for calculating theoretical option prices which provides pricing parameters and, by application, a formula for calculating a desired hedge ratio within the parameters of the variable factors required. Details of this formula and comment thereon may be found in most academic publications on Investment or Options trading and hedging techniques. Whilst the detailed development of this subject is outside the scope of this publication, the following simple example illustrates the basic assumption of hedging strategy. This example constitutes only a part of the overall philosophy of a option hedging theory. *It is not suggested or recommended for use in isolation from other factors including all of those already mentioned.*

Let us assume a dealer grants a three month at-the-money call option on £1 million against US dollars at a strike price of 1.3000 for a premium of US$50,000. The option is on American terms and can be exercised with delivery taking place at any time. On a £1 million contract a 100 point move in the market price (i.e. 1.3000 to 1.3100 or 1.3000 to 1.2900) represents US$10,000 in contract terms. We know that the market price can only do one of three things. It can stay as it is, it can move up, or it can move down. If the market price moves above 1.3000 the call option will be in-the-money, if it moves down the option will be out-of-the-money.

If the grantor does nothing and merely writes the option on a "naked" basis and the underlying price rises, he would lose US$10,000 for every 100 point move. If the price stayed the same or fell he would retain the total profit as premium. Therefore his profit/risk profile would be :

Market price	*Profit Potential*
1.3000	US$ 50,000
1.3100	US$ 40,000
1.3200	US$ 30,000
1.3300	US$ 20,000
1.3400	US$ 10,000
1.3500	US$ Nil
1.3600	US$ 10,000 loss

Plus US$10,000 additional loss of each 100 point increase until exercised

If the grantor were to immediately enter the cash market and take 100% cover he would require to sell dollars and buy sterling at 1.3000 thereby being short US$1,300,000 and long £1,000,000 this would protect him against a rising market. However, should the market subsequently fall the option would not be exercised but the value of his hedge would depreciate and his profit/risk profile would be:

Market price	*Profit Potential*
1.3000	US$ 50,000
1.2900	US$ 40,000
1.2800	US$ 30,000
1.2700	US$ 20,000
1.2600	US$ 10,000
1.2500	US$ Nil
1.2400	US$ 10,000 loss

Plus US$10,000 additional loss for each 100 point decrease until he unwound the hedge

Let us assume a third alternative. The trader adopts a middle course, and in the knowledge that the market can only subsequently stay the same or move either way he hedges 50% and does nothing else. If the underlying price moves consistently down, for every basis point move the value of the hedge will decrease by US$5,000 but this can be absorbed against the premium receipt of US$50,000. Therefore the dealer will be able to absorb a 1000 point decrease before the impact of falling prices on his hedge value results in losses. If the underlying price increases and is exercised at any time up to 1.4000 the value of his hedge will increase to offset 50% of his loss on providing cover on exercise. If the price rises above 1.4000 the dealer will lose US$5,000 for every basis point up until exercise. However, what he has achieved is to widen in underlying price terms the range in which he will make a profit.

The profit risk profile may now be illustrated by the following:

Market Price	Premium Received	Loss on Exercise	Initial Hedge	Net profit/ Loss
Plus US$5,000 loss for each additional 100 point decrease until option expires				
1.1900	50,000		−55,000	−5,000
1.2000	50,000		−50,000	Nil
1.2100	50,000		−45,000	5,000
1.2200	50,000		−40,000	14,000
1.2300	50,000		−35,000	15,000
1.2400	50,000		−30,000	20,000
1.2500	50,000		−25,000	25,000
1.2600	50,000		−20,000	30,000
1.2700	50,000		−15,000	35,000
1.2800	50,000		−10,000	40,000
1.2900	50,000		− 5,000	45,000
1.3000	50,000		Nil	50,000
1.3100	50,000	−10,000	+ 5,000	45,000
1.3200	50,000	−20,000	+10,000	40,000
1.3300	50,000	−30,000	+15,000	35,000
1.3400	50,000	−40,000	+20,000	30,000
1.3500	50,000	−50,000	+25,000	25,000
1.3600	50,000	−60,000	+30,000	20,000
1.3700	50,000	−70,000	+35,000	15,000
1.3800	50,000	−80,000	+40,000	10,000
1.3900	50,000	−90,000	+45,000	5,000
1.4000	50,000	−100,000	+50,000	Nil
1.4100	50,000	−110,000	+55,000	− 5,000
Plus US$5,000 loss for each addition 100 point increase until exercised				

Following from the above it is logical that a hedge position may be adjusted as the option moves in or out of the money. Using our 2,200 point range (i.e. $1.4100 - 1.1900 = 2,200$ points) the grantor may reduce his hedge by 5% for each 100 point fall or increase by 5% for each 100 point rise. At 1.2000 he would be 100% uncovered but the option is deeply out-of-the-money and it is assumed will not recover. At 1.4000 he is fully hedged as exercise is now assumed to be 100% certain. Each change in hedge ratio will move the top and bottom of the profit and loss scale. This would effectively mean that at 1.4000 or 1.2000 the grantor would not be showing Nil profit but a profit of US$22,500 having taken into account his loss on reducing his hedge position as the price falls, or the loss on the average price of his hedge against the strike price as the price rises.

The extension of the above strategy is that upon granting an in-the-money option at a strike of 1.3500 hedge 75%; or on issuing an out-of-the-money option at 1.2500 only hedge 25%. By adopting this strategy the trader has endeavoured to contain both his upside and downside risk potential but to achieve this objective he is prepared to utilise the total premium received and limit any profit potential in a range of within 1000 points either side of the current market price of the underlying currency However, more importantly, within the example he is prepared to be an uncovered option grantor at 1.2000.

However, as it has been explained above, it is assumed that the market moves uniformly in one direction or the other throughout the life of the option and does not consider the costs of hedging. In reality markets do not behave in a rational manner nor do they move consistently up or down; periods of high volatility frequently occur and deep out of-the-money options can revert to being substantially in the money. A perfect hedge is rarely available and even the most sophisticated programmes are often unable to provide against all eventualities and large losses may result from unanticipated events and additional hedging costs. The real risk within an option programme is not where you are now, but where you might be tomorrow should the unanticipated happen. For example what is the position if exchange rates suddenly and unexpectedly move within seconds 5 or even 10% in response to a world event or concerted Government intervention. It is important that these risks are not overlooked and they should be continuously quantified and controlled within the context of "what if" scenarios.

434

CHAPTER NINETEEN

Interest Rate and Currency Liability Swap Agreements

Introduction to Interest Rate and Currency Liability Swap Agreements

Like financial futures interest rate and foreign currency options, interest rate liability swap agreements (interest rate swaps) and cross currency liability swap agreements (currency swaps) – for the purpose of this Chapter collectively called "swaps" – are relatively new innovations to the financial markets. Currency swaps as described in this chapter should not be confused with the spot against forward "foreign exchange swap" discussed in Chapter 16.

Swaps are not future contracts of sale or substantive contracts of loan and deposit and do not confer an obligation or right to "buy" or "sell" an underlying subject matter. Swaps simply comprise contracts to exchange (swap) cash flows related to the characteristics of two counterparties' debt obligations. They involve the payment of amounts determined by reference to a notional principal amount although, as discussed below, in the case of currency liability swap agreements, they may require an exchange of the principal sums involved at the commencement of a contract and, in any event, do require an exchange of principal at the end of the contract. Although swaps are bilateral contracts between the parties thereto, it is important at the outset to make it clear that these contracts do not in any way alter, amend or invalidate the direct responsibilities that each counterparty has to his principals for the underlying debt obligations.

Swap techniques and their purpose are relatively easy to understand. However, the range of agreements which are written; their lack of standardization; risks of non-performance; lack of clarity on the fiscal implications of swaps; the possibility of infringing anti-gaming and betting legislation that exists in many countries, and consequently the detailed terms and subsequent documentation

435

which are required to negotiate and formulate them, do add to their mystique. Albeit that an interbank market has developed in swaps, this market is also somewhat different from the other types of market discussed in Sections 3 and 4 due to the terms which are required to be established prior to a contract being agreed.

Through an exchange of payments, interest rate liability swaps provide two counterparties with a mechanism through which each may effectively assume the characteristics of the other's debt obligations in the same currency. The basis for an interest rate swap is a notional underlying principal amount of loan and deposit, between two counterparties, whereby one counterparty agrees to pay to the other agreed sums referred to as "interest payments". These sums are calculated as though they were interest on the principal amount of the notional loan and deposit, in a specified currency, during the life of the contract through the application of predetermined formulae, based upon the interest rate pricing structure of each other's underlying liabilities. Interest rate swap agreements may be based upon fixed to floating or floating to floating interest rate structures.

Example of a fixed to floating interest rate liability swap:

FIXED/FLOATING

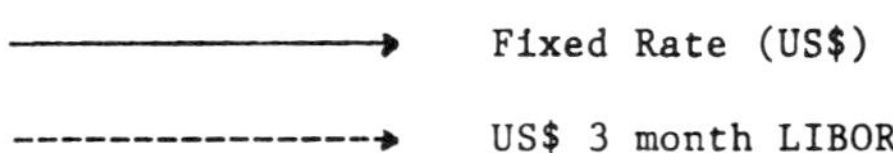

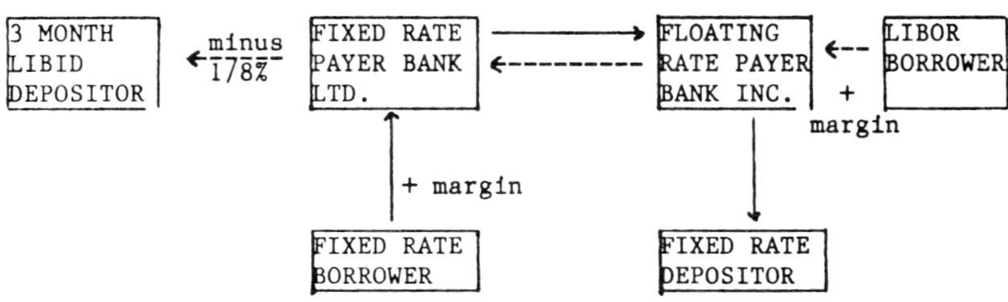

Example of a floating to floating interest rate liability swap:

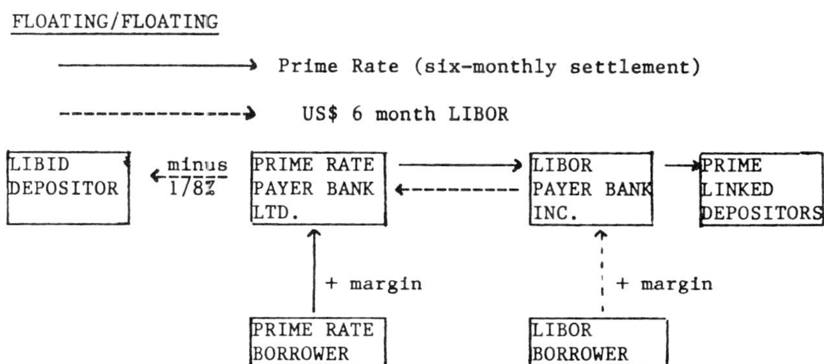

A currency swap agreement is a contract between two counterparties to exchange (swap) both the principal amounts of, and payments related to, the interest rate flows on their respective debt obligations in two different currencies. Although in theory, the techniques of a currency swap agreement require that the full principal amount of a currency swap should be exchanged at the commencement of the agreement and subsequently reversed, at the expiry of an agreement, at the same rate of exchange, in practice this does not always happen. As both of the counterparties are able, and one or both may, prefer to establish independently at current spot rates, any necessary immediate adjustments to their respective currency positions necessitated by the currency swap, these agreements may not always require an initial exchange of principal. However, the terms of currency swap agreements do always require that the full principal currency amounts of each currency in terms of the other is exchanged at the maturity of the contract at a predetermined rate of exchange. Whichever course is taken this is normally achieved by recording one currency as the fixed principal amount and the agreed rate of exchange for calculating the principal amount in the second currency.

Albeit that the primary objective of a currency swap is usually to re-structure effectively the currency base of a liability it will also involve cash flows of interest which may be related to either similar or different interest rate pricing structures. Consequently currency

437

swaps are more specifically defined as cross currency fixed to floating interest rate liability swaps; cross currency fixed to fixed interest rate liability swaps, and cross currency floating to floating interest rate liability swaps, and an example of each follows:

Example of a fixed to floating currency liability swap:

CURRENCY SWAPS

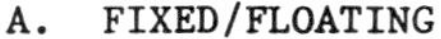

A. FIXED/FLOATING

1. Initial Exchange of Principal

——→ SF equivalent of US$10 million
- - - - → US$10 million

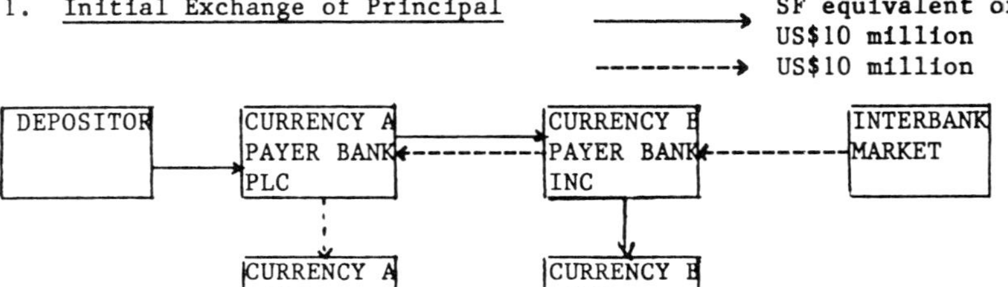

2. Interest Flows (ignoring margins)

——→ SF @ 5.90% annually
- - - - → US$ @ 6 month LIBOR

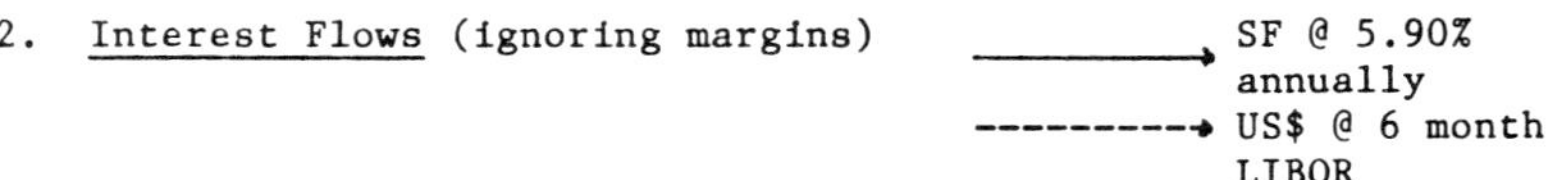

3. Final Exchange of Principal (ignoring final interest payment)

——→ SF equivalent of US$ 10 million
- - - - → US$ 10 million

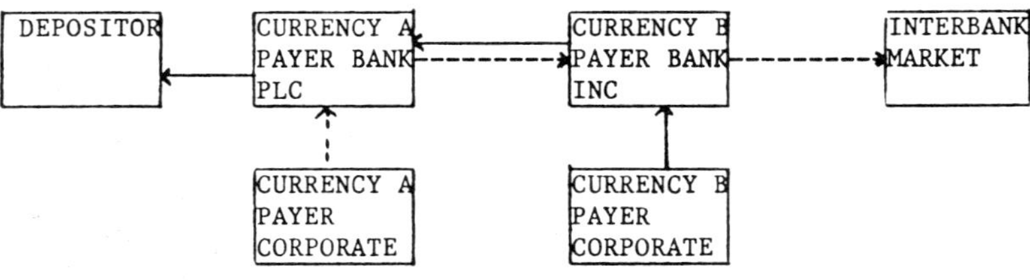

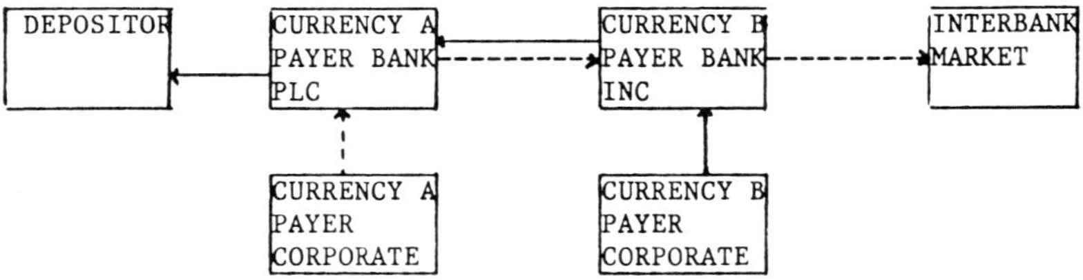

Example of a fixed to fixed currency liability swap:

<u>CURRENCY SWAPS</u>

B. <u>FIXED/FIXED</u>

1. <u>Initial Exchange of Principal</u>

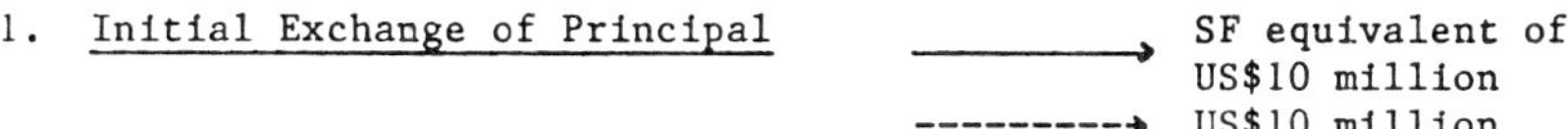

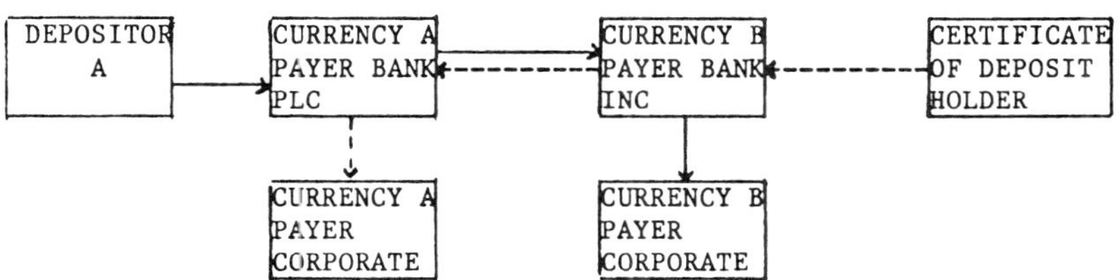

2. <u>Interest Flows</u> (ignoring margins)

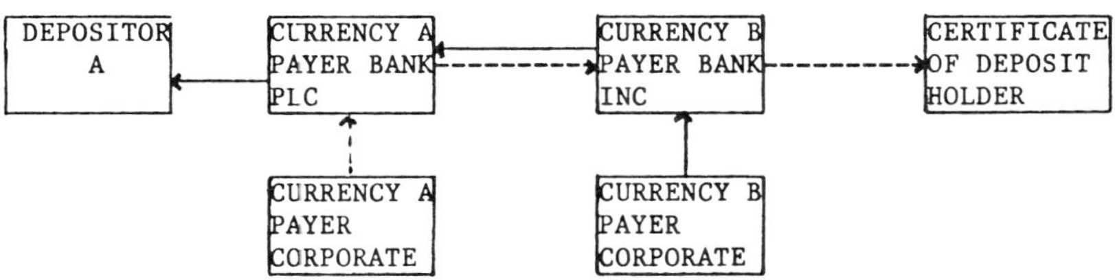

3. <u>Final Exchange of Principal</u> (ignoring final interest payment)

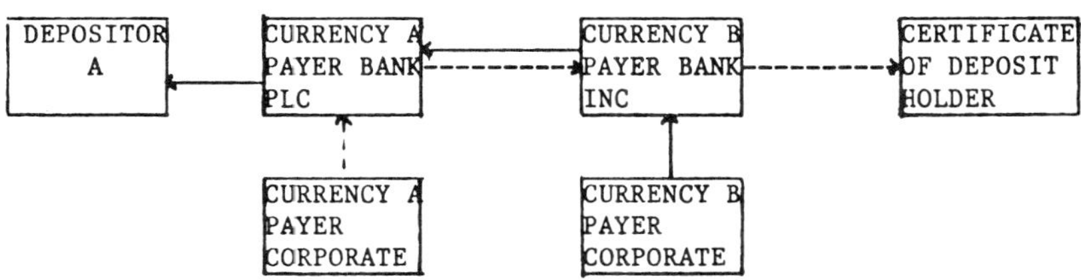

Example of a floating to floating currency liability swap:

CURRENCY SWAPS

C. FLOATING/FLOATING

1. Initial Exchange of Principal

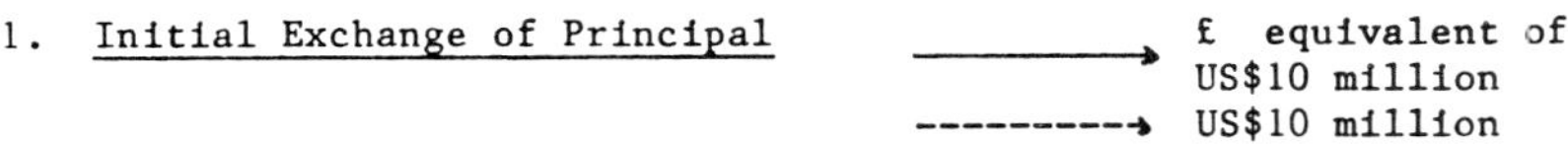

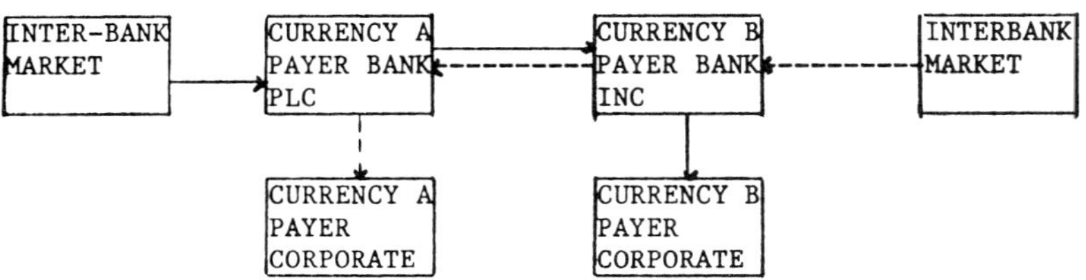

2. Interest Flows (ignoring margins)

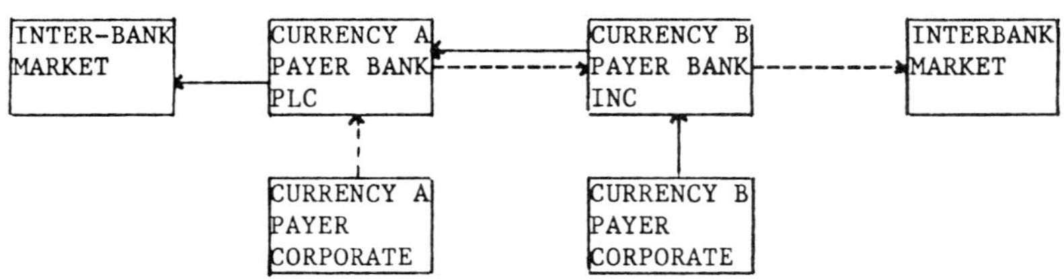

3. Final Exchange of Principal (ignoring final interest payment)

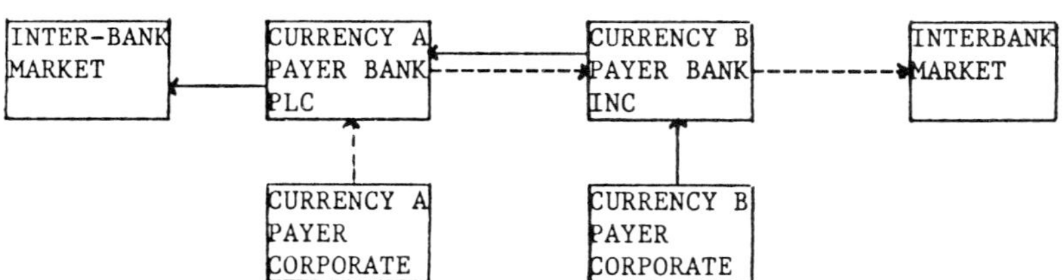

Reasons for Swapping

High levels of volatility in both exchange and interest rate levels, and the risks associated with exposure related thereto have resulted in increased attention being given to both asset and liability management. Through its internal liability and cash flow management processes each corporation, both bank and non-bank, will continually establish, review, plan and amend its desired funding structure and implement various strategies to protect its income, cash flows and structural positions. The success of many commercial businesses largely depends upon successful "sourcing", and the success of financial institutions upon their funding policy. Conversely the failure of both types of institution has frequently been caused by a lack of attention to the protection of structural and funding positions and their related cash flows.

Funding and sourcing policies will invariably include, to a greater or lesser extent, a mix of requirements for fixed and floating rate liabilities in short-, medium- and long-term debt in a variety of currencies. For example, many commercial, industrial, construction and other businesses continually have substantial requirements for medium- and long-dated fixed rate funds in a mix of domestic and foreign currencies to secure the pricing base for specific contracts, projects or investments. These same entities also often follow a strategic preference to maintain a high level of their external funding sources for non-specific purposes in the form of fixed term debt provided this can be achieved within the parameters of a predetermined economic cost. In the achievement of this latter objective, funding is frequently carried as short-term floating rate debt, pending a switch into longer-dated fixed rate debt as the opportunities and interest rate levels present themselves. It is also true that perceived views on future movements in interest rates and foreign currency values frequently make it desirable to change direction by reversing previously arranged fixed funding to a floating rate basis or vice versa. However, in implementing these strategies corporate entities must not only ensure that adequate and suitable funds are available to meet all current operational needs, but also protect their capability of future access to external sources and therefore it is often desirable to contain the necessity for excessive market entry to re-structure current liabilities.

441

Conversely, as already discussed in this publication, many financial institutions, in particular banks, have a preference for a high level of floating rate funds which are compatible with the pricing structures applied to the major proportion of their asset base. As discussed in Chapters 2 and 3, it is also important that banks secure access to a mix of liabilities from a broad spectrum of sources and provide adequate levels of capital to maintain acceptable gearing ratios. The achievement of this latter objective also frequently requires banks to access the capital debt markets.

However, in practice, irrespective of the extent to which sourcing, funding and fiscal objectives are planned and desired objectives established, it is often the case that these objectives may not always be attainable. This may be either due to the markets perception of the credit risk (and thereby the pricing structure) related to a particular company, country risk issues, or that funds in a desired currency, period or interest rate level are not obtainable or available:

- There is a wide range in, and between respectively, banks' and investors', perception of credit risk. Several names which are readily accepted in the short-term money markets may not be so attractive to the longer-term capital debt markets. Consequently there are different constraints on market access placed on each corporation. Although many individual entities may be readily able to raise floating rate debt in one or more short-term money markets, their perceived long-term credit risk may be such that they are denied access to fixed or floating rate funds in the longer-term capital debt markets.

- Anomalies also exist between an individual corporation's ability to raise funds in different financial centres. For example, although a triple A rated US corporation may have little difficulty in raising fixed rate funds from the US capital markets, similar funds may not be so readily available from capital markets outside of the US where their name may not be so well known.

- Sizeable differentials also frequently exist between the bank credit markets and the capital debt markets in margin pricing. Bank floating rate funds may, according to the perceived credit risk of a company, be available within a range of $\frac{1}{8}\%$ to $\frac{3}{4}\%$ p.a. over LIBOR, whereas differentials based upon perceived credit risk for floating rate funds, for similar companies, in the capital debt markets may discriminate by up to 2%.

- Pricing differentials can also be created in the capital markets because of the investor's appetite for a particular type of debt instrument. For example, although a bank may desire to obtain floating rate funds in the capital debt market it could find that it is required to pay a slight premium over LIBOR but, at the same time, it may be able to attract fixed rate capital funds at a substantial discount to which similar funds would be available to other organisations.

- Country risk issues related to both the country of domicile and residence of a borrower are also important factors both in the determination of the availability of funds and price structure related thereto. For example, where a particular name, or group of names, from the same country, tap a foreign or international capital market, the market's appetite for that country may quickly dry up and premiums be placed upon future issues due to country risk considerations.

- Credit risk issues related to a particular name are also important and the capital debt markets may become saturated with and turn aside any particular name which persistently enters the market.

- Although there may be a supply and demand for fixed and floating rate funds in a variety of currencies and across a broad time spectrum, these may not always be readily available within the financial markets due to a lack of liquidity or activity within a particular sector of the time or currency spectrum.

The composition of domestic, foreign and international financial markets and their division between the short-dated money markets and longer-term capital debt markets is explained in Chapter 14. Traditionally, the bank credit market and interbank deposit markets have provided highly liquid sources for short-term floating rate debt and short-term fixed rate debt with the latter usually restricted to a maximum period of 12 months. However, since the 1950s the bank credit market in particular has developed, through the process of maturity transformations, as a substantial provider of medium-term commitments for floating rate funds. Following from these activities and due to interest rate risk considerations, banks have a preference for floating rate liabilities and often have not accepted fixed rate medium-term deposits for periods of over one year. Conversely, the longer-term capital debt markets have traditionally provided fixed rate debt requirements for periods in excess of seven years but have also more recently supported substantial quantities of debt priced on a floating rate basis. Consequent upon this division of function, there is a lack of any highly liquid debt market between the types of finance provided by these two segments of the financial market.

There has also been an absence of highly liquid secondary markets for amending or re-structuring various forms of liabilities without refinancing through further market entry. Some flexibility may be provided by floating convertible issues or issues with warrants attached thereto, conveying to the investor a separate tradeable right to buy additional debt on given terms, or various other forms of put or call options, but these are often not particularly attractive to investors or sufficiently flexible to effectively re-structure perceived funding requirements on a regular basis.

Similarly, whilst there is a highly liquid spot and short-dated foreign exchange market in many currencies, this is often restricted and a comparable market in which to cover longer-term exchange rate exposure does not exist. Among other things, Chapters 15 and 16 considers the subject of deposit swap techniques which, by using the foreign exchange markets, enable liabilities in one currency to be used to fund assets in another currency. Usually to avoid exposure these techniques require that the exchange and interest rate risk is hedged and therefore are dependent upon the availability of an active foreign exchange spot and forward or swap market in those currencies. In practice the level of liquidity of forward markets in many currencies is strictly limited and often only available for forward periods up to three, six or exceptionally 12 months. Only the major traded curren-

444

cies and a small number of second tier currencies are available for longer periods.

Swaps have developed from the existence of these anomalies, weaknesses and lack of equity in and between various segments of the financial and foreign exchange markets. Swap techniques can act as an effective substitute for the functions required from certain markets which may be inactive. This is achieved by a mechanism through which any two counterparties may obtain mutual benefit by exchanging the cash flows related to new or existing debt to reach different perceived funding objectives. These benefits may simply comprise an ability to obtain funds in currencies or at fixed or floating rates of interest which might not otherwise be available to them. They may open additional funding sources, for example, by enabling banks to take fixed rate medium-term deposits and effectively change their characteristics to preferred floating rate liabilities. Alternatively, they may be used to achieve mutually beneficial funding on more favourable terms by arbitraging between, or otherwise taking mutual advantage of, any one or a mix of disparities and anomalies which may exist between their respective internal and external debt structure, financial positions, future requirements and quality of access to different financial markets.

Other factors may influence one's choice of an interest rate or currency swap transaction. Due to exchange control or other regulations, foreign branches, subsidiaries and associates may frequently accumulate local currency resources which may not be remittable. These funds may provide the basis of a currency swap which in addition to protecting the funds from exchange rate volatility during the period of the swap, will also generate funding in another currency. Tax advantages may be available when highly priced fixed or floating rate debt is raised in fiscal regions where tax sparing capabilities are available or, conversely, when high interest rate differentials between two currencies are converted into future foreign exchange gains in countries where they may be tax deferrable until realisation.

The techniques used in liability swaps could, if required, be equally applied to re-structuring assets. However, the development so far has centred upon segments of liabilities.

Swap Documentation

Interest rate liability swap documentation closely resembles, in some respects, an interest make-up agreement. Due to the requirements to exchange currencies, currency liability swap documentation is more complex than interest rate liability swap documentation. However, both sets of documentation are similar to a loan agreement with, for example, clauses on warranties, covenants and conditions, events of default and termination and prevailing law. Swap documentation can at times run up to 20 pages or more. The documentation incorporates in detail both the financial and legal aspects of the transaction.

From a treasury view-point the financial and in particular, the payments and exchange section is the most important. This section will specifically define and establish the methods and basis of calculation of interest payment amounts, interest rate periods, the payer and receiver and the payment dates. It will include:

- fixed rate or rates of interest

- calculation date

- calculation period

- fixed rate payment date

- fixed rate payer or, in the case of fixed to fixed, the payers.

- the basis and formula upon which the floating rate, or rates, are to be established and calculated

- rate fix date

- floating rate payment date, or dates

- floating rate payer or payers.

- for currency swaps the value date or dates and rate of exchange

Interest rate swaps frequently facilitate the netting off of amounts with a single differential being paid provided interest payment dates are co-terminous. For fiscal reasons usually they call for payments to be made through the intermediary of a bank. Within the UK the revenue authorities have confirmed that these payments need not be subject to withholding taxes when a bank acts as intermediary. The floating interest rate may be related to any one of several definitive interest rates. It may be LIBOR, LIBID, Prime, Treasury Bill or Treasury Bond or other specified rate and may be constructed on a fixed or floating rate basis within each interest rate period. For example, the average of a monthly LIBOR rate of a six-monthly interest rate period. Reference rates or a reference bank or banks will also be included and the time at which rates are to be fixed on the rate determination date. Although it would be an unusual feature, swaps may on occasions provide for one or both counterparties to have the option to vary within a specified range, future interest rate periods, as the agreement progresses: for example, anyone of a one, three, six or 12 month interest rate period.

Interest payments may be co-terminous or may require settlement on different dates and be for different interest rate periods determined by each counterparty's underlying liability obligations, but the final maturity will always be matched.

From a legal aspect it is important, particularly when dealing with a non-bank counterparty, that the documentation incorporates recitals of the parties to the agreement and the reasons for their entering into the agreement. These recitals, and in particular the reasons for the transaction, have added importance in that they satisfy a perceived need to ensure that the swap agreement entered into does not violate any gaming act. For example, either English Gaming Law or the New York Gaming Statute, which would render the agreement void. German law also has a Gaming Act and it is normal for swap contracts involving deutschemarks, or where German banks are concerned, to be written through offshore affiliates. When dealing with bank counterparties it does appear reasonable to assume swaps are required for underlying commercial purposes.

It is usual for payments to be required to be made free of any deductions including withholding taxes, and special attention is focused upon procedures that will apply if, for any reason, circumstances should change throughout the period of the agreement which may change the achievement of this objective.

Of necessity swap documentation incorporates more lengthy definitions than usual and these are illustrated by the definitions to be found in the BBA terms and conditions for the London interbank swap market which are exhibited as Appendix III of this publication.

Credit Risk Considerations

Although interest rate swaps do not involve an exchange of principal amounts, and currency swaps normally require funds being simultaneously exchanged at predetermined rates of exchange, there are important credit risk issues related to these instruments. These risks relate to:

- the failure of either party to meet their obligations within the terms of the agreement. Should one counterparty default, the other would be left with an open interest rate risk and also in the case of a currency swap an exchange risk exposure.

- delivery risk on coincident payment dates where net settlement is not called for.

- risk of non-receipt where payment dates are not coincident.

The credit risk exposure for an interest rate swap is not, at first glance, a particularly easy thing to assess and it will certainly depend on whether the interest flows are co-terminous or not. If the interest flows are payable on the same day, e.g. both six monthly or both annually, and a netting arrangement is incorporated the risk exposure will be lower than if the bank were to pay interest semi-annually on a company's floating rate debt and the company were to pay annually on the bank's fixed rate debt or coincident gross interest payments are required. Each type of agreement has been written. If the company should default or in any way refuse or be unable to honour its obligations to pay the interest flow, then the agreement would fall away and, as no principal sum has been lent or borrowed by either party, the principal amount is not at risk.

448

The immediate cost of a default by the company, assuming co-terminous or gross payments, would be any net or gross amount owed by the company to the bank for the current period; it will be appreciated that the bank may be owing the company on a net basis. However, and usually more significantly, the bank would be exposed as regards interest rates for the remaining period of the swap, since a company default deprives the bank of its hedge, replacement of which may prove costly. Banks take many different approaches to quantifying this latter exposure, which is in fact an amalgam of credit risk (on the company) and interest rate risk.

However, banks would normally take into account a view of the likely future variation of the fixed rate at which another swap could be found, and also the number of years to the maturity of the swap. An example of a typical calculation along these lines would be as follows:

> An interest rate swap of US$25 million for 10 years, with the company paying 12% fixed semi-annually to, and receiving 6 month LIBOR from, the bank. The bank assumes that the minimum rate at which a replacement swap could be found during the next 10 years would be 7% p.a.

> Thus, maximum risk = US$25 million × 10 years @ (12%–7%) = US$12.5 million

It will be appreciated that this risk will decline throughout the period of the swap (i.e. with six months left, it will be only US$0.625 million), in a manner similar to a loan with semi-annual repayments, so that the average risk throughout the swap term will be US$6.25 million.

The Swap Markets
Currency swaps initially in the form of parallel loans and currency exchange agreements were developed during the mid 1970s and evolved in their present form subsequent to relaxations which took place in the exchange control regulations of major countries, in particular the UK. It was not until 1982 that interest rate swaps made

their impact, when they received wide publicity as they were first used by banks and other multinational corporations as a vehicle to arbitrage their prime names in selected capital debt markets for fixed term debt and swap floating rate cash flows for fixed rate cash flows with lesser rated names in those markets. Through these arrangements floating rate funds at all-in costs substantially below LIBOR were being generated. Let us consider:

In the event that a bank is seeking long-term debt for balance sheet purposes and the funds arising therefrom are not required for any specific purpose, then consideration should be given to ways in which such monies might be profitably employed. The cost of capital funding is inevitably more expensive than, say, interbank sources and even if these are obtainable in smaller amounts for similar maturities, corporate treasurers of major companies and institutions will invariably seek long-term borrowing for capital or other purposes at a price which they consider to be acceptably low, bearing in mind factors such as the currency, period, and the market's perception of the borrower's quality. If banks and other advisers in the market have indicated that rates may continue to fall, most corporate treasurers would prefer to defer raising long-term fixed interest debt until such a prophecy appears to have been fulfilled. If rates are likely to rise and it is thought that over a period they may stay high, then the demand for long-term fixed debt tends to increase. The very high interest rates for US dollars and many other currencies experienced from 1978 through the early 1980s drove a number of corporate treasurers to raise medium- or long-term debt on a floating rate basis. When rates fell in 1982/83 and fixed debt was again being raised in the capital markets by major names, interest swaps developed as they enabled corporate entities to adjust their liabilities from exposure to floating rates to a fixed rate funding *without* incurring any additional borrowing. This saved them using up bank lines and it also enabled certain companies who would not have been able to tap the capital markets in their own names to obtain medium- and long-term liabilities at fixed rates of interest which would have otherwise been denied to them. Coincidentally with this development, banks were able to obtain long-term fixed rate capital debt and change this debt structure to floating rate by entering into an interest rate swap. The bank, acting as principal, may cover the total cost of raising the capital debt

450

by entering into an agreement with a company for the company to pay the fixed interest payments plus a margin sufficient to cover the costs of the issue. At the same time the bank agrees to pay part of the company's interest on its floating rate funds.

Example of an interest rate swap with a bank
acting as principal:

INTEREST FLOWS

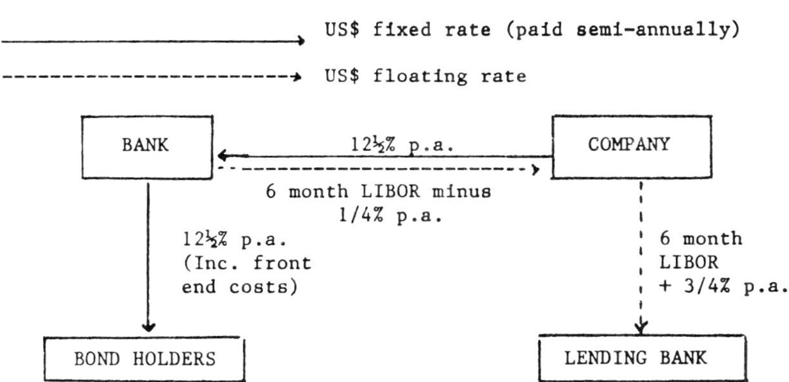

The bank, as a high-quality borrower, is able to raise a 10 year bond of US$25 million at $12\frac{1}{4}$% p.a., with front end costs which equate to 0.25% p.a., payable semi-annually. However, the bank really needs LIBOR-linked money to fund its floating rate loans to customers.

The company, as a lesser credit, would need to pay $13\frac{3}{4}$% p.a. to raise a 10 year bond of US$25 million, but perceives a need for fixed rate money, perhaps to fund fixed assets.

By swapping, the bank achieves funding at $\frac{1}{4}$% below LIBOR (i.e. $\frac{1}{4}$% below the rate it would normally obtain from the interbank market); the company effectively borrows its required fixed rate money at $13\frac{1}{2}$% p.a. (i.e. $12\frac{1}{2}$% + $\frac{1}{4}$% + $\frac{3}{4}$%), which is $\frac{1}{4}$% below the rate it would have to pay by issuing bonds in its own name. The costs indicated here being made up from $12\frac{1}{2}$% payment to the bank for funds raised by the latter on the capital markets; $\frac{1}{4}$% being the amount under LIBOR payable to the bank; and $\frac{3}{4}\%$ being the estimated mark-up payable by the company over LIBOR on their existing bank facilities.

The compatibility of the needs of the corporate counterparty with the capital fixed rate funds raised by the bank bears examination. The counterparty's needs are often smaller than the amount raised by the bank. Normally a major name such as a leading bank may not consider going to the market for piecemeal smaller amounts and this means that substantial sums of US$100–500 million would normally be raised by the bank. This would clearly be too large for the majority of lesser rated counterparties. The illustration shows a US$25 million transaction which is a fairly typical amount for a counterparty to take and it is not unusual for a bank to do several swaps for one of their fund raising transactions. The terms of the swaps can also be mismatched. Sterling, US dollars and deutschemark fixed interest capital funds have been raised for periods of 15 years or more. The majority of corporate counterparties do not have an appetite for swaps for periods of more than, say, five to seven years or, perhaps, 10 at the most. Any swap entered into by a bank with a counterparty for a period less than the maturity of the capital liability will create a potential interest rate exposure for the unhedged period when the swap agreement expires. For the initial five years or so the bank's position may be hedged but, depending on interest rate levels when the swap agreement terminates, a bank may experience a severe interest rate exposure at that time.

The corporate counterparty may require a currency other than that raised on a fixed rate basis by the bank and the bank may then consider a currency swap. Fixed rate sterling may have been raised by the bank in the form of a bulldog, euro-sterling or domestic issue, depending on the bank's domicile. The counterparty may wish to pay fixed rate interest flows to the bank and have the bank pay their LIBOR linked floating rate US dollar obligations. With a currency swap there exists an additional risk of loss in the event of default, or the unwinding of the swap agreement, as the bank would be left with a fixed rate liability in sterling and a floating rate asset in US dollars. Therefore, the potential foreign exchange exposure should be estimated and included in the calculation of the total risk.

Euro-bond issues are now a daily occurrence and it is estimated that up to 80 percent of all issues are the subject of subsequent swap arrangements. Concurrent with these developments a substantive market also emerged in which the participants are concerned with swapping cash flows related to extant liabilities as their perceived funding strategies and objectives change.

The swap market has therefore developed into two distinct markets with banks playing a leading role in each, first swaps related to the short and medium dated market and secondly those related to the longer dated capital debt markets.

The successful completion of a swap transaction is to a large extent dependent upon either directly or indirectly identifying and thereafter negotiating mutually acceptable terms with a suitable counterparty. Consequently, the availability of opportunity to utilise this technique is somewhat restrictive and the markets comprise a corporate market with many participants from different sectors of commerce and industry together with banks.

A bank's function may take the form of simply acting as the arranger of a swap undertaken directly between two counter-parties; as intermediary principal to both sides of a swap agreement between two or more customers as a dealer in swaps, or, as already discussed, as principal for its own requirements.

In its role as arranger a bank will effectively act as a broker and will usually be involved in initiating the transaction, mediating mutually acceptable terms and conditions between the counterparties concerned, together with drafting and arranging the completion of the necessary documentation. For these services the bank will have no other responsibilities other than ensuring due care and attention in discharging its responsibilities. The bank will normally in these circumstances charge a front end arrangement fee for its services.

Swaps may be contracted directly between the two counterparties but usually, where two non-bank counterparties are concerned, there is a preference for using an intermediary bank for several reasons. These include:

- Confidentiality –
Within a swap transaction there is not a necessity for the under-lying swappers to know the identify of the other. Indeed it is usually the case that both parties have a preference for a bank to act as intermediary to preserve confidentiality and identity.

- Withholding tax –
In the UK the revenue authorities have rules that, although it is not interest, swap payments may be treated as such when a bank acts as principal, and withholding tax is not applicable to such payment.

- Credit risk considerations –
Corporates have a preference to replace the credit risks of the counterparties with each other for that of a bank. This function is usually undertaken by the bank establishing itself as a principal counter-party to both sides of the swap transaction by the completion of separate back-to-back agreements with each party to the transaction. Through this procedure the bank normally also establishes itself as the conduit through which all payments related to the agreement will flow. For these services the bank will generate annual off balance sheet income but will create contingent liabilities. Invariably, by implication, one of the parties is usually a greater credit risk than the other. It must only be a matter of time before these contingent liabilities are required to be included within mandatory calculations for liquidity and/or capital adequacy purposes. As an alternative to these arrangements, a bank may on occasions be requested to provide performance guarantees to one of the counterparties covering the other's performance within the terms and conditions of the agreement which is contracted directly between them. In any event, as is usual with all credit risk incurred by a bank, it will be necessary for the intermediary bank to establish, through its normal internal credit approval processes, appropriate credit limits for each of the counterparties concerned to cover the perceived credit risk related to each transaction.

Several banks have established themselves as market-makers in these instruments and are prepared to quote firm prices. An increasing number of banks are also prepared to take on fixed rate obligations without an immediate outlet and hedge the inherent risk of carrying these funds. Various alternatives are available to hedge these risks through cash, futures and option markets, as a short-term expediency, pending swaps being arranged. For example, for fixed rate obligations US dollar treasury bonds or gilts may be considered a suitable vehicle to hedge either in the cash or futures markets.

In addition to the two markets already mentioned, a large interbank market has also developed in swaps particularly for switching from fixed rates up to two years. Within this short-dated market banks quote prices either on a bank to bank basis or through the intermediary services of brokers for various types of currency and interest rate swaps. Some banks act as market-makers therein and others merely participate. However, the prices quoted are in many cases only indication rates and trades are not conducted with the same velocity as they are in the other markets previously discussed in this section.

The development of these various markets has added attractions as it provides increased opportunity for banks to extend their deposit taking activities into longer dated fixed rate funds and find outlets to swap these funds into the characteristics of floating rate debt in both the interbank and corporate markets.

Due to increased activity in the interbank market the BBA have issued recommended terms and conditions for operations within the London interbank market referred to as "BBAIRS terms" for defined swaps initially up to a maximum maturity of two years. These terms and conditions are of necessity lengthy, and are reproduced in Appendix III which shows the standardized terms and conditions upon which contracts can be agreed, and subsequently evidenced by a relatively simple exchange of confirmations. However, due to the complexities and variations of these instruments, dealers in the interbank markets are required to take care in negotiating their terms and the BBA provides the following schedule of matters recommended for special attention in negotiating terms of proposed swap transactions:

Dealers must:

- Identify themselves and the capacity in which they are acting, i.e. as principal or as broker.

- Identify which side of a swap they are on in terms of what they wish to pay and receive as cash flows throughout the life of the swap, e.g. payer of fixed rate dollars against floating rate dollars; payer of fixed rate swiss francs against floating rate dollars. Discussing positions in terms of providers/takers or bid/offer side can cause misunderstanding in some sectors of the market.

- Specify the maturity of the proposed transaction, giving details of any date matching requirements and how "stump" periods will be handled.

- Identify the principal amounts in which they wish to deal and, in the case of cross currency swaps, how the principal amounts will be determined and whether there will be an initial exchange.

- Specify, in respect of pricing:

  - the fixed rate at which they pay/receive and the basis on which the rate is calculated and paid, e.g. actual/360; actual/365; 360/360: paid annually/semi-annually/quarterly;

  - what period floating rate they wish to pay/receive, frequency of reset and frequency of payment;

  - the extent of their commitment (i.e. whether "indicative" or "firm") and if a firm price is being shown, the period during which this is open for acceptance. If a party is to place reliance on a firm price as a basis for proceeding with an associated transaction, this should be stated. It is always advisable to re-confirm that a price is "firm" before entering into related deals;

  - if pricing in terms of a spread over a US treasury bill/note yield, which side of the market is being used to determine the basis yield;

456

- whether rates quoted in respect of a brokered deal are gross or net of any commissions payable.

- Specify in whose name the contract will be concluded and whether guarantees will be given/required.

- State clearly the conditions to which the swap is subject prior to being "done", e.g.:

  - obtaining credit approval;

  - availability of counterparty for matching deal;

  - ability to execute an associated transaction.

- Specify one of the currencies as the currency of the contract (referred to as currency A) and the other currency (referred to as currency B) which will be identified as a currency equivalent at the agreed rate of exchange.

- Specify any required terms which are not in accordance with BBAIRS terms.

BBAIRS terms are treated as normal market practice for interbank transactions falling within the categories covered. Banks continue to be free to deal on other terms if they wish, but should consider themselves under an obligation to make clear to any would-be counterparty in which way their terms for such transactions would differ from BBAIRS. In the absence of such clarification banks and brokers in the London interbank market are expected to quote on the basis of BBAIRS terms.

The BBAIRS terms distinguish between three separate types of swap. These are:

- **Single Currency Fixed/Floating Swaps** in which one party exchanges payments determined by reference to a fixed rate of interest in return for payments from the other determined by reference to market deposit rates.

Cross Currency Swaps in which either:
- the two parties exchange payments determined by reference to fixed rates of interest in two different currencies; or

- one party makes payments by reference to a fixed rate of interest in currency and the other in US dollars by reference to market deposit rates.

Cross Currency Floating Rate Swaps in which the two parties exchange payments in two different currencies with both amounts being determined by reference to market deposit rates.

Once the terms of a proposed transaction have been agreed and a deal contracted, the contracting parties should promptly exchange written confirmations of the particulars of the swap concluded. Any discrepancies in the parties' understanding of the transaction can thus be identified at an early stage and steps taken to rectify the situation. This is particularly important in circumstances where negotiations have taken place through a broker, in which case the broker should send written confirmation to each of the contracting parties. The BBA have issued suggested formats for confirmations and these are included in Appendix III.

The BBA have also made arrangements to establish and publish daily interest rate settlement rates to be known as "BBA settlement rates" for specified currencies and periods which may be utilised as rate fixes for swaps. Initially, the rates are restricted to each monthly period up to 12 months for US dollars, pounds sterling, deutsche-marks, swiss francs and yen (the BBAIRS currencies). These fixings are made at 11.00 a.m. each day on the basis of quotations provided by eight out of a panel of 12 banks designated by the BBA as refer-ence banks. Within these arrangements the middle four quotations from the reference banks are averaged and the result rounded up, if necessary, to the nearest five decimal places of 1% to determine the BBA daily settlement price, the bottom two and top two quotations being ignored.

458

CHAPTER TWENTY

The Forward Rate Agreement Market

Forward Rate Agreements (FRAs) or, as they are sometimes referred to, Futures Rate Agreements, provide a mechanism through which two counterparties may obtain protection from future interest rate movements. FRAs are effectively off balance sheet forward-forward transactions as were discussed in Chapter 15. They also simulate, without an underlying obligation to deliver, the characteristics of futures contracts in respect of currency deposits, which were discussed in Chapter 17.

The basis of an FRA is a notional contract of loan and deposit between two counterparties, whereby one counterparty agrees to pay to the other a sum, calculated as though it were a fixed rate of interest on a specified principal amount, in a specified currency, for an agreed fixed period of time in the future. In the context of FRAs the agreed fixed rate of interest is referred to as the "contract rate"; the currency as the "contract currency"; the principal as the "contract amount", and the period of deposit as the "contract period". An FRA contract does not imply an obligation to lend or deposit and therefore neither the contract amount or interest thereon change hands.

Within the terms of an FRA contract, the counterparties agree that they will indemnify each other against the impact of any change in interest rates on the notional loan and deposit. This is achieved by making a cash settlement between the contract rate and a pre-defined reference rate "the settlement rate" which is agreed on the "fixing date" for payment on the value date of the underlying notional contract of loan and deposit. Where the settlement rate is higher than the contract rate the seller of the contract, the notional lender, agrees to pay to the buyer of the contract, the notional borrower, a cash settlement, as calculated within the parameters of a predetermined formula. This cash settlement represents the value of the interest rate differential between the contract rate and the settlement rate as applied to the amount and period of the notional deposit. Conversely, where the settlement rate is lower than the contract rate the buyer of the contract, the notional borrower, agrees to pay to the seller of the contract, the notional lender, a cash settlement as calculated on a similar basis.

The cash settlement, which is referred to as the "settlement sum" or "fee" is payable on the the settlement date. The settlement date is normally defined as the value date of the underlying notional contract of loan and deposit. As the settlement sum is payable on the value date and not the maturity date of the notional deposit, it is calculated on a discounted basis.

The basis for establishing the settlement rate and the formula by which the settlement sum is calculated will be clearly defined and agreed within the terms and conditions of each FRA contract. The basis of establishing the settlement rate may comprise, or be related to, the selling or buying bank's interbank offered rate, a reference bank's offered rate, the average of two or more reference banks' offered rates, or some other interest rate formula as established at a specific time on an agreed date, the "fixing date", in the future. Where the settlement rate is higher than the contract rate, the settle-ment sum is calculated by applying the following formula, which is a derivation of that used to calculate forward/forward prices which was explained in Chapter 15:

$$
\begin{aligned}
\text{Where} \quad &CR = \text{Contract Rate} \\
&SR = \text{Settlement Rate} \\
&CA = \text{Contract Amount} \\
&D = \text{Days of Contract Period} \\
&IB = \text{Interest Base, i.e. 360 or 365 days}
\end{aligned}
$$

$$
\frac{(SR - CR) \times CA \times D}{IB \times 100} \times \frac{1}{1 + \dfrac{(SR \times D)}{(IB \times 100)}} =
$$

Settlement sum – Payable by the seller of the contract to the buyer of the contract

Conversely where the settlement rate is lower than the contract rate

$$\frac{(CR - SR) \times CA \times D}{IB \times 100} \times \frac{1}{1 + \dfrac{(SR \times D)}{(IB \times 100)}} = \text{Settlement sum} -$$

Payable by the buyer of the contract to the seller of the contract

As a base for pricing these transactions a dealer will utilise a forward/forward pricing formula.

Transactions may be arranged through oral negotiation, by telex or other form of communications network or in writing and thereafter be supported by an exchange of confirmations of contract details. As with options and interest rate liability swaps, questions remain outstanding as to the legal implications of FRAs. Although it is generally thought that in practice it is unlikely that bank's activities in FRAs could be ruled to be anything other than related to underlying commercial considerations, a similar view might not equally apply to its customers' activities in these instruments. Consequently after entering into an FRA contract with a non-bank counterparty, it is imperative that the contract be fully documented. This can be by way of detailed documentation (which typically may include definitions of terms used, recitals of purpose and reasons for the contract, indemnity re settlement sum, basis of determination and calculation of the settlement sum, requirements for notification of settlement rate, notices, payment form and requirements, payments on a non-business day and governing law) or, by the incorporation within the confirmation of a statement of commercial use. If this latter course is taken, legal opinion should be obtained on the wording used.

With the exception of those contracts issued in terms of FRAB-BA terms, which are discussed in this chapter, the practice has developed within the interbank market of incorporating within confirmations a simpler statement of commercial use similar to the following example.

"The seller bank understands that the buyer bank confirms that it has entered into this FRA in the ordinary course of its banking business with a view to protecting its position in relation to specific future interest rate obligations which the counterparty now has. The terms of such obligations could and would be identified but for commercial and competitive reasons are not being disclosed as part of this FRA".

Although FRAs were first reported as being traded in the London markets during 1983, no formal figures have been published upon which to base an indication of market size. FRA techniques provide the seller of a contract with the opportunity to obtain protection against a future fall in interest rates, and the buyer of a contract protection against a future rise in interest rates. Consequently FRAs may be used for a variety of purposes which may include either the hedging of extant interest rate mis-matches or the establishment of an interest rate for a known future commitment or requirement. For example:

Let us assume on the 1st September 1985 two banks established an FRA through a London broker on the basis of:

Contract Currency	– Pounds Sterling
Contract Amount	– 1 million
Contract Rate	– $10\frac{1}{2}\%$
Period	– 1st June–1st September 1986
Fixing Date	– 1st June 1985
Settlement Date	– 1st June 1986

The underlying reason for this contract being established is that the buyer bank has negotiated a fixed period loan for the 1st June–1st September at $10\frac{3}{4}\%$ and he wishes to protect his margin of $\frac{1}{4}\%$ against rising funding costs. Conversely, the seller of the contract has a mismatched position in his asset/liability portfolio whereby he is £1 million long for the same period which he wishes to protect against a falling market.

Example 1

Let us now assume a settlement rate of $12\frac{1}{2}\%$. The settlement sum payable by the seller of the contract to the buyer would be calculated as:

462

$$\frac{(SR - CR) \times CA \times D}{IB \times 100} \times \frac{1}{1 + \dfrac{(SR \times D)}{(IB \times 100)}} = \text{Settlement sum}$$

Therefore

$$\frac{(12.5 - 10.5) \times £1,000,000 \times 92}{365 \times 100} \times \frac{1}{1 + \dfrac{(12.5 \times 92)}{(365 \times 100)}} = £4,887.12$$

Example 2

Let us now assume that rates had moved downwards and the settlement rate was established at $9\frac{1}{2}\%$. The settlement sum payable by the buyer of the contract to the seller of the contract would be calculated as:

$$\frac{(CR - SR) \times CA \times D}{IB \times 100} \times \frac{1}{1 + \dfrac{(SR \times D)}{(IB \times 100)}} = \text{Settlement sum}$$

Therefore

$$\frac{(10.5 - 9.5) \times £1,000,000 \times 92}{365 \times 100} \times \frac{1}{1 + \dfrac{(9.5 \times 92)}{(365 \times 100)}} = £2,461.60$$

Let us now consider the position of the buyer bank and the seller bank separately in relation to the first example. The buyer bank has a loan 1st June – 1st September at $10\frac{3}{4}\%$ upon which he will receive interest value 1st September of:

$$\frac{P \times R \times T}{IB \times 100} = \frac{£1,000,000 \quad 10.75 \times 92}{365 \times 100} = £27,095.89$$

As at settlement date he can take a 3 month deposit in the interbank market at LIBOR of $12\frac{1}{2}\%$ which would cost:

$$\frac{£1,000,000 \times 12.50 \times 92}{365 \times 100} = \underline{£31,506.85}$$

Net Loss $\qquad\qquad\qquad £\ 4,410.96$

However, he receives a cash settlement sum of £4,887.12 from the seller bank which he can now invest, let us assume also at LIBOR of $12\frac{1}{2}\%$ which will provide interest of:

$$\frac{£4,887.12 \times 12.50 \times 92}{365 \times 100} = £153.98$$

Therefore value 1st September he will receive
  principal plus interest of   £ 5,041.10

Therefore net profit   =   £630.14

His objective had been to lock in a profit of $\frac{1}{4}\%$
which can be calculated as $\dfrac{1,000,000 \times .25 \times 92}{365 \times 100} = $ £630.14

On a similar basis we can determine the position of the seller bank. His anticipation of a fall in market rates did not materialise. As at 1st June, rates for the subject period have improved by 2% and he can therefore lend his long position at an improved margin of 2%, i.e.

$$\frac{1,000,000 \times 2 \times 92}{365 \times 100} = £5,041.10$$

However, within the terms of the FRA he is required to pay the buyer bank the settlement sum on the 1st June the cost of which he must set against the apparent profit. Hence:
The amount paid to the seller   £4,887.12
Interest loss as calculated above   £153.98

Total cost of hedge   = £5,041.10

In addition each party will have paid brokerage on the transaction which at the time of this publication would have been charged at a rate of $\frac{1}{64}\%$ p.a. i.e. £39.38 each.

The Interbank Markets

Interbank markets in FRA contracts are established in London for various eurocurrencies and domestic sterling. Within these markets contracts are arranged directly between banks and indirectly through the intermediary services of brokers.

Quotations are made as bid and offered prices expressed as a percentage per annum and not on a discounted basis. Irrespective of which bank's price is the contract rate the buyer of the contract is always the bank seeking to protect against rising rates and the seller the bank seeking to protect against falling rates. Quotations are, unless otherwise agreed, for the conventional value dates and periods applicable to each month for the currency concerned.

In addition to the initial exchange of confirmation each counterparty is required to provide the other with a "Notice of Settlement" on the fixing date. The notice of settlement will include details of the contract and notional deposit, settlement rate, settlement sum and settlement instructions.

Terms and conditions for the London interbank forward rate agreement market as recommended by the forward rate agreements working party of the British Bankers Association, and endorsed by the Foreign Exchange Committee and approved by the Executive Committee of that association were introduced during September 1985. These terms and conditions are reproduced in their entiety as Appendix 4 of this publication. The application of these recommended terms and conditions referred to as the "FRABBA Terms" are confined to the London interbank market initially for transactions with maturities up to and including two years. These terms do not address the subject of terms and conditions which individual banks may elect to quote to their customers. Banks are free to deal with each other on other terms as they wish but they must make clear to any would-be counterparty in what way(s) their terms differ from FRABBA terms and any variation thereto must be specified in the documentation. In the absence of such clarification banks and brokers in the London interbank market are expected to follow what is normal market practice by quoting on the basis of FRABBA terms.

Within FRABBA terms, banks are expected to calculate the settlement sum due under conventional value date transactions on the basis of the appropriate BBA settlement rate, referred to in Chapter 19. Where banks undertake transactions for broken dates, for which BBA settlement rates are not available it is the responsibility of the counterparties to the transaction to agree both the basis for establishing an alternative rate and the reference banks to be used for this purpose.

The BBA have designed and provided specimen FRA confirmations and settlement confirmation notices which they recommend be used for FRAs contracted under FRABBA terms and conditions. These are reproduced on the following four pages in completed form for the example transaction previously used in this chapter on the basis of a $12\frac{1}{2}\%$ settlement rate.

CONFIRMATION
To Be Used on the Agreement Date

CONTRACT
0001
CONFIRMATION NOTICE

AGREEMENT DATE
1st September 1985

TO:- Buyer Bank

FROM:- Seller Bank

We are pleased to confirm the following Forward Rate Agreement ('F.R.A.') made between ourselves as per FRABBA Recommended Terms and Conditions dated September 1985. (~~Direct~~/Broker .. London.... Brokers......)

CONTRACT CURRENCY & AMOUNT ..... Sterling Pounds 1 Million ....

SETTLEMENT DATE ..1st June 1986. MATURITY DATE ..1st September 1986.

CONTRACT PERIOD (DAYS)........ 92 ....

CONTRACT RATE .... 10.5.... % per annum on an actual over
~~360~~/365 basis

SELLER'S NAME .... SELLER BANK ....

BUYER'S NAME .... BUYER BANK ....

NON-STANDARD TERMS & CONDITIONS (IF ANY) ....N/A........................

Any payment to be made to us under the F.R.A. hereby confirmed should be credited to our Account Number .... 7832471 ....
at .... XYZ BANK ....

Please advise by telex, or cable us immediately, should the particulars of this confirmation not be in accordance with your understanding.

Either:-   Or:-

SIGNED: .... TESTED TELEX CONFO
FOR AND ON BEHALF OF

..... SELLER BANK..............

NOTICE OF SETTLEMENT
To Be Used on the Settlement Date

CONTRACT   *AGREEMENT DATE*
0001   1st September 1985
SETTLEMENT
1st June 1986
CONFIRMATION NOTICE

TO:- BUYER BANK
FROM:- SELLER BANK

We are pleased to confirm the following Forward Rate Agreement ('F.R.A.') made between ourselves as per FRABBA Recommended Terms and Conditions dated 1st September 1985. (~~Direct~~/Broker ..London..... Brokers.......)

CONTRACT CURRENCY & AMOUNT ..STERLING POUNDS 1 MILLION.......

SETTLEMENT DATE .1ST JUNE 1986. MATURITY DATE ..1ST SEPTEMBER 1986.

CONTRACT PERIOD (DAYS) ...92 ....

CONTRACT RATE .... 10.5 ..... % per annum on an actual over
~~360~~/365 basis

SELLER'S NAME .... SELLER BANK ....

BUYER'S NAME .... BUYER BANK...

NON-STANDARD TERMS & CONDITIONS (IF ANY) ..... N/A.......................

SETTLEMENT RATE ...... 12.5.............. % per annum
SETTLEMENT SUM ...... £4887.12........... ($/£ etc.)
SETTLEMENT INSTRUCTIONS:-

WE PAY THE SETTLEMENT SUM ON THE SETTLEMENT DATE TO YOUR ACCOUNT NO. .... 841723......... AT .... ABC BANK..............................

WE RECEIVE THE SETTLEMENT SUM ON THE SETTLEMENT DATE AT OUR ACCOUNT NO. .... AT ....

Either:-   Or:-

SIGNED: .... TESTED TELEX CONFO
FOR AND ON BEHALF OF

....

CONFIRMATION
To Be Used on the Agreement Date

CONTRACT
1004

AGREEMENT DATE
1st September 1985

CONFIRMATION NOTICE

TO:- Seller Bank

FROM:- Buyer Bank

We are pleased to confirm the following Forward Rate Agreement ('F.R.A.') made between ourselves as per FRABBA Recommended Terms and Conditions dated 1st September 1985. (~~Direct~~/Broker .. London.... Brokers........)

CONTRACT CURRENCY & AMOUNT ..Sterling Pounds 1 Million.....................

SETTLEMENT DATE .1st June 1986. MATURITY DATE ..1st September 1986

CONTRACT PERIOD (DAYS) .... 92...

CONTRACT RATE ..... 10.5............................. % per annum on an actual over
~~360~~/365 basis

SELLER'S NAME .... Seller Bank ....

BUYER'S NAME .... Buyer Bank..

NON-STANDARD TERMS & CONDITIONS (IF ANY) .... N/A........................

Any payment to be made to us under the F.R.A. hereby confirmed should be credited to our Account Number ...... 841723...
at .... ABC Bank...

Please advise by telex, or cable us immediately, should the particulars of this confirmation not be in accordance with your understanding.

Either:-   Or:-

SIGNED: .... TESTED TELEX CONFO
FOR AND ON BEHALF OF

.... SELLER BANK...............
:

NOTICE OF SETTLEMENT
To Be Used on the Settlement Date

CONTRACT
1004
SETTLEMENT
1st June 1986
CONFIRMATION NOTICE

AGREEMENT DATE
1st September 1985

TO:- Seller Bank

FROM:- Buyer Bank

We are pleased to confirm the following Forward Rate Agreement ('F.R.A.') made between ourselves as per FRABBA Recommended Terms and Conditions dated 1st September 1985. (Direct/Broker .London..... Brokers........)

CONTRACT CURRENCY & AMOUNT ..Sterling Pounds 1 Million ....

SETTLEMENT DATE .1st June 1986. MATURITY DATE .1st September 1986.

CONTRACT PERIOD (DAYS) ....92 ....

CONTRACT RATE ....10.5.......... % per annum on an actual over
360/365 basis

SELLER'S NAME .... Seller Bank ....

BUYER'S NAME ....Buyer Bank ....

NON-STANDARD TERMS & CONDITIONS (IF ANY) .... N/A ....

SETTLEMENT RATE .... 12.5............. % per annum

SETTLEMENT SUM ...... £4887.12........... ($/£ etc.)

SETTLEMENT INSTRUCTIONS:-

WE PAY THE SETTLEMENT SUM ON THE SETTLEMENT DATE TO YOUR ACCOUNT NO. .... AT ....

WE RECEIVE THE SETTLEMENT SUM ON THE SETTLEMENT DATE AT OUR ACCOUNT NO. ... 841723.......... AT .... ABC Bank ....

Either:-   Or:-

SIGNED: .... TESTED TELEX CONFO
FOR AND ON BEHALF OF

....

470

CHAPTER TWENTY ONE

The Gold Markets

To a greater or lesser extent gold was the common unit of account in which both domestic and international trade was measured in many countries for in excess of three thousand years. Consequently gold, albeit not in its present form, has been the subject matter of dealing for that length of time. Although the gold standard finally came to an end as a result of the Bretton Woods agreement in 1944, gold continues to comprise a major part of many countries' reserves and is the subject of substantial private investment. Additionally, following the removal of previous restrictions on the ability of private individuals to hold gold bullion within the United States at the beginning of 1974 and in the United Kingdom with the suspension of the exchange control regulations during 1979, substantial markets have developed and several banks continue to play a leading role as market-makers in these markets.

There are two distinct segments of the gold markets. First the traditional physical gold markets which are dominated by the London Gold Market and to a lesser extent, the Zurich Gold Market. Second, what may be described as the "paper markets", which comprise both futures and option markets and are to be found in substantial depth within the United States. In addition, large gold markets exist in Hong Kong and India, albeit the latter is very much a domestic market, with both the import and export of gold being strictly prohibited. The cash and forward markets are very similar to the activities of the deposit markets, as explained in Chapter 15 and foreign exchange markets, as explained in Chapter 16.

The activities and functions of futures markets and exchanges were explained in detail in Chapter 17 and those of options in Chapter 18. The largest markets in the world for gold trading are now established on futures exchanges, and in particular that of Comex in New York. It is of interest to compare the annual turnover on Comex with that of the annual production of gold. It is estimated that the total world annual production of gold outside of the Comecon countries during

1984 was approximately 41.2 million fine ounces. Comex had an annual turnover of nine million futures contracts of 100 oz each which is the equivalent of 900 million fine ounces. The subject of dealer and traded options were discussed in Chapter 18, and a substantial market exists within the United States for these options in gold. The pricing mechanisms and hedging parameters are similar to those developed and discussed in regard to foreign currency options. The variety of over-the-counter options in gold is of interest in that it may provide an indication of where the over-the-counter option markets in foreign currency may develop. For example, they include such interesting concepts as look-back options which provide the investor with the opportunity in the future to purchase gold at the best price over the underlying period of the contract. Obviously the hedging techniques utilised in pricing these options are sophisticated and they do, of necessity, demand a high premium.

The London Gold market comprises five members. These are Mocatta & Goldsmid Limited, Sharps, Pixley Limited, N.M. Rothschild & Sons Limited, Johnson Matthey Bankers Limited, Samuel Montagu & Company Limited. Each of these companies is or has a close association with a bank. Mocatta & Goldsmid is a subsidiary of Standard Chartered; Sharps, Pixley Limited is a wholly owned subsidiary of Kleinwort Benson; Samuel Montagu is a wholly owned subsidiary of Midland Bank; N.M. Rothschild & Sons Limited are bankers and members of the gold market in their own right; following the collapse of Johnson Matthey Bankers, Johnson Matthey is now controlled by the Bank of England. Banks also comprise the centre of the Zurich gold market with Union Bank of Switzerland, Swiss Banking Corporation and Swiss Credit Bank being major participants within this market. In addition to purchases and sales in various forms, services provided through a bank's gold business may also include:

- insured storage facilities
- delivery orders
- bullion clearing services
- pricing and price protection programmes for miners

The unit of weight measurement for gold is usually expressed as ounces troy or metric units. The purity of gold content of different forms of gold is expressed as a measure of fineness as parts of 1,000 or carats. The following table may be helpful.

Weight:
1 oz troy	= 31.10 grams
32.15 oz troy	= 1 kilo
32,150 oz troy	= 1 metric ton

Purity:
1000 parts (pure)	= 24 carats
916.6 parts	= 22 carats
750 parts	= 18 carats
583.3 parts	= 14 carats
375 parts	= 9 carats

Having established the weight and purity of the underlying gold, the gold content is calculated by multiplying the gross weight by the purity. This is illustrated by the following figures:

Gross Weight	Agreed fine gold content in ounces troy		
	Bars of 995.0 assay	Bars of 999.0 assay	Bars of 999.9 assay
1 kilo	31.990	32.119	32.148
$\frac{1}{2}$ kilo	15.995	16.059	16.074
$\frac{1}{4}$ kilo	7.998	8.030	8.037
200 grammes	6.398	6.424	6.430
100 grammes	3.199	3.212	3.215
50 grammes	1.600	1.607	1.608
20 grammes	0.640	0.643	0.643
10 grammes	0.321	0.322	0.322
5 grammes	0.161	0.161	0.161
100 ounces	99.500	99.900	99.990
50 ounces	49.750	49.950	49.995
25 ounces	24.875	24.975	24.998
10 ounces	9.950	9.990	9.999
5 ounces	4.975	4.995	5.000
1 ounce	0.995	0.999	1.000
10 tolas	3.731	3.746	3.750
5 taels	5.987	6.011	6.017

Coins	*Fine Gold Content in Ounces Troy*
Krugerrand	1.0000
$\frac{1}{2}$ Krugerrand	0.5000
$\frac{1}{4}$ Krugerrand	0.2500
$\frac{1}{10}$ Krugerrand	0.1000
Mapleleaf	1.0000
$\frac{1}{2}$ Mapleleaf	0.5000
$\frac{1}{4}$ Mapleleaf	0.2500
$\frac{1}{10}$ Mapleleaf	0.1000
Sovereign	0.2355
$\frac{1}{2}$ Sovereign	0.11755

Physical gold is available and deliverable in many different shapes and sizes ranging from bars of 1 kilo to $\frac{1}{4}$ kilo, 200 grammes down to 5 grammes, 100 ounces down to 1 ounce, 5 taels and 10 tolas. Taels are a Chinese unit of weight and tolas an Indian unit of weight. Five taels is equal to 6 ounces troy and 10 tolas 3.75 ounces troy. To this list must be added the many gold coins which are still produced and bought and sold by bullion and coin dealers. These include Krugerrands, Austrian 100 Kroner, UK Sovereign, Mexico Peso, US Double Eagles, Eagles and the Canadian Maple Leaf, to name a few. Each kilo bar of gold has an individual identification number. As each of these forms of gold has a different intrinsic gold content, the price will initially be based upon the value of their underlying gold content and secondly upon the cost of their production and rarity value. However, to a gold dealer the former is the important consideration.

To facilitate gold trading in, and between, these various forms of gold, it is necessary to establish a common unit of measurement, as gold purchased in one form may be required in another. This would involve further melting, refining and processing and subsequent assaying. Unlike foreign exchange and currency deposits for which the title to the underlying subject matter can only ultimately be transferred from one person to another in the country of domicile of those currencies, the title to gold, subject to local regulations, may be made anywhere in the world. Consequently gold bullion available for delivery from a supplier in Johannesburg has a different value to a dealer than gold bullion available in Tokyo if the dealer has sold that gold to a user in Tokyo.

Consequent upon the above factors it is necessary that gold bullion traded within the international gold markets has clear contract and delivery standards in a similar manner to futures contracts so that each participant in the market knows exactly what he is buying and selling. The common unit of dealing is a bar with a London location conforming to London delivery standards within the following specification:

- Weight — minimum gold content 350 fine ounces, maximum gold content 430 fine ounces. The weight of each bar shall be expressed in ounces troy in multiples of .025 of an ounce and must turn the scale at the weight indicated.

- Fineness – minimum 995 parts per 1,000 fine gold.

- Marks – serial number, stamp of acceptable melter and assayer.

Each bar, if not marked with the fineness and stamp of an acceptable assayer, must be accompanied by a certificate issued by an acceptable assayer stating the serial number of the bar and the fineness. If a bar bears more than one assay stamp, preference shall be given to the British assay. Where a bar bears no British assay the lowest figure will be taken. Gold said to be 1,000 fine will be marked down to 999.9 fine. Bars should be of good appearance, free from surface cavities or other irregularities, layering and excessive shrinkage, and must be easy to handle and convenient to stack. The appearance of any bar tendered will not constitute a reason for rejection and a buyer may not stipulate any particular brand of bar. If a bar included in the specification is tendered and it does not suit the buyer's requirements, the cost of melting and/or refining will be at his charge. Bars not confirming to the specification may be sold on the market, but the seller will be charged with the cost of making them good delivery.

At the time of this publication there were 56 smelters and assayers resident in 19 countries which are acceptable to the London market.

Gold may also be bought and sold in any currency. Therefore for international trading a common unit of currency is also required and, like the foreign exchange markets, this is based upon the US dollar.

Internationally, and in London, quotation prices are expressed in US dollars per fine ounce for delivery with spot value in the above format to a location in London. Bullion dealers will provide quotations in any currency through an interaction of the US dollar spot price and the relevant exchange rate with the currency concerned. Each participant in the markets is not required to buy and sell gold in contract sizes which equate to bar sizes and even if they were, the spectrum of bar weights and fineness would make it impossible for the market to operate. Gold may be bought and sold in the markets and thereafter may be held on an allocated or unallocated basis with the dealer. Allocated gold implies that specified bars (or other form of gold) are individually identified and are segregated as such, within the vaults of the custodian. Unallocated gold is recorded as balances of account, which are represented by part of the gold stocks or dealing positions of a gold dealer. The accounts on which these balances are held may be closed out or adjusted by further purchases and sales or subsequently claimed and delivered. Where gold bullion is allocated or subsequently delivered it is usual for a small adjusting purchase or sale to be required as it is unlikely that the fine gold content of the bars delivered will equate exactly with the amount bought or sold. Where purchases and sales do not equate with bar sizes, or gold is required in a different form, similar adjustment may be made to reflect the difference in price between the traded and the delivered form.

Forward market prices, as in the forward exchange markets, are based upon interest rate differentials based on the spot price and related to the cost of carrying the metal until the forward delivery date. The format of the calculation of these prices is exactly the same as that used in the foreign exchange markets. As with foreign exchange trading, where a cross currency transaction is required, cover will be negotiated immediately in the spot market and as appropriate, subsequently reversed out in the swap market. Gold provides a further dimension to arbitrage activity in that the presence of gold in so many different forms and centres against a variety of currencies provides for increased opportunities. However, as in the foreign exchange markets, modern communications and the development of computerised dealer aids are increasingly negating such opportunities for arbitrage.

As an alternative to dealing at current market prices, clients of members of the London gold market may buy or sell bullion at the organised London fixing. The London fix takes place at 10.30 in the morning and 3.00 p.m. on each business day. At the fix the five members of the bullion market meet and agree a price at which all sales and purchases within the fix are established. Thereafter both buyers and sellers pay or receive the actual fix rate but buyers only are required to pay a commission. Similar to Libor rates the London fix is often taken as the basis of financial arrangements involving gold prices.

Trading and operational procedures are essentially the same as those discussed for the other markets, with contracts being established by telephone, telex, and other forms of communication and subsequently confirmed in the form of an exchange of confirmations. Dealing limits are similar to those imposed on bank foreign exchange dealers, i.e. outright dealing limits for both intra-day and overnight positions in gold within which the dealers are to operate. Counterparty credit limits are a major feature of control and the dealers will ensure that all exposures are contained within the confines of these limits, with the only major difference related to delivery procedures.

Physical gold is an inconvenient commodity to move and transport around the world, and therefore dealers and other recognised depositories provide storage facilities in the major international financial centres. Transfers of gold are effected between participants' accounts. Physical deliveries can be made to reduce credit risks or where stocks exceed acceptable levels with a depository, or are insufficient to meet the requirements to support a deficit cash balance on an account/account relationship. The major dealing houses and banks are normally in account with each other and other participants are normally in account with these dealers.

Account/account trading implies that a client has both currency and gold accounts and buys and sells within pre-determined limits; the underlying accounts being respectively debited or credited with the bullion and/or the currency amounts. Where an account holder requires the currency to be domiciled in a currency other than US dollars, the bullion house will arrange the necessary foreign exchange to accommodate these requirements. Where an investor is either long or short of bullion, it will be subject to a daily mark-to-market to ensure that sufficient funds are available to cover short positions or, conversely, sufficient metal available to meet the value of the debit balances. These accounts are usually subject to margin calls and margin calls must be met expeditiously or the right is reserved to close out the positions, with any differences being claimed from the counter-party concerned. Account/account relationships should be distinguished from holding accounts related to allocated gold. On these accounts, bullion houses merely act as custodian for clients' requirements, for which service fees are charged to cover storage, insurance, etc. When trading, these clients are expected to make or take cash settlements on the applicable value date.

Gold certificates are frequently issued representing the right of ownership to gold. These may take the form of negotiable instruments or be restricted to a named beneficiary and require any assignment thereof to be recorded with, and advised to, the issuer of the certificate. In passing it is mentioned that silver and several other commodities are traded on the basis of warrants, whereby the silver or other subject matter is held with recognised depositories and ownership transferred in the form of bearer warrants.

Within the gold markets it is market practice to make or take deliveries and make cash settlements for net quantities or amounts of all transactions on each value date. As a consequence of this practice, forward trading positions for forward value dates are measured in credit control terms on a net basis of purchases and sales. It is also normal practice to revalue all client current and forward positions on a mark to market basis and as appropriate require margins to be paid where excesses are evident over extant position limits. If these margins are not provided bullion dealers will have established, through documentation procedures, the ability to close out all positions and claim any resultant shortfall from their client.

Liquidity within the gold markets is subject to substantial flows and ebbs. During periods of low volatility within the underlying gold price there is very little business undertaken. As volatility increases, substantial liquidity is in evidence. Interest rates also have an important bearing upon the activities of the gold market, insofar as gold is, to all intents and purposes, a non-income yielding investment. Consequently, in periods of high interest rate levels investors are reluctant to participate in these markets unless sufficient capital growth is perceived to be available from underlying price movements, or a hedge is perceived to be required against underlying inflationary trends. However, gold activities are not confined to dealing. As a commodity gold may be used to establish different financial transactions on the basis of producer and user requirements with different facilities being made available in accordance with interest rate structures.

As previously stated, gold stocks have very little earning capability if they are held in a vault. Consequently, it is a common practice for bullion houses to find outlets for inventory. For example, gold leasing arrangements may be provided to users of the underlying commodity, with charges and pricing being related to current interest rate structures. Forward gold prices and indeed other commodity prices are frequently referred to as being in backwardation. 'Backwardation' implies that the price for forward delivery is less than the current market price. This reflects the impact of an inverted rate structure within the cash markets and may be a determining factor as to when to negotiate purchases and sales of stocks. Conversely, the term 'contango' relates to the situation where the price for forward delivery is greater than the current market price.

Cash and carry opportunities often arise in gold and other commodities. This refers to situations which exist in the market, whereby it is possible to buy or sell spot metals and simultaneously sell or buy forward thereby creating a profit from the underlying funding implications of the transaction. When these opportunities arise, the activities of arbitragers again come into play, and these distortions are reversed. Several banks arrange swap facilities against bullion whereby gold is bought spot from, and sold forward to, a client, with costs being related to the underlying carry of the metal during the period of the facility being extended, thus providing funds to the holders of bullion. Within these arrangements, it is usual to request for an excess margin to be made available in the event that the value of the underlying gold falls. This may be made available as a cash or gold margin.

CHAPTER TWENTY TWO

Introduction to Domestic, Foreign and International Capital Debt Markets

The term "Capital" may be applied quite properly to a number of different classes of liability ranging from money market instruments and bank borrowing to equity. This chapter, however, describes a narrower definition of "capital" which generally excludes money market instruments and bank borrowings, but which is often recorded in the "capital base" of the issuer's balance sheet as a bond, note or debenture debt. Equity and other qualifying capital base items such as reserves are not addressed in this Section. Chapter 29 differentiates between Public and Private placements and deals with the latter specifically, focusing on the borrower's view-point. This chapter concentrates on the types of public debt, whether listed on a stock exchange or not.

Another word in this chapter which requires initial defining is "markets". Compared with the foreign exchange and interbank money markets, the markets for specific securities are much smaller. In the first place there are two markets, the primary market and the secondary market. The primary market is the market for new issues during the syndication or the placing period and has only a temporary existence for each issue until the paper has been placed or allotted by the lead manager. The secondary market takes over from this point when the initial distribution period is over. The existence of a primary market naturally depends on the investor's demand for the paper being offered at the time a new issue is being considered. A secondary market can really only be considered to exist if a number of participants are prepared to quote two-way prices for the security traded and be prepared to deal on them. Furthermore, the distribution of the traded security should be sufficiently widespread or a market cannot develop effectively. Imagine, for example, the difficulties a lead manager would have as a market-maker if the distribution was restricted to, say, half a dozen banks which had no intention of making a market in the paper or placing it with investors. The paper would probably be dumped on to the market and the lead manager could end up virtually holding the entire issue!

The lead manager of any issue takes great care to ensure that the principal allotments are given to institutions which can perform an effective distribution to interested investors. The ability of such investment houses to place paper is called their "placing power". The banks and investment houses involved in the managing and placing of new issues generally do have substantial placing power. Distribution, and therefore the market size, can be affected by many factors. The quality of the issuer, for example, might not come up to the very high requirements of trusts' investment portfolios. Exchange control regulations in some countries prohibit their residents investing in overseas securities, or through monetary controls can make it uneconomic for potential resident investors in their country to do so. The fiscal regulations in the issuer's country can substantially limit the distribution by imposing a withholding tax on income due to the investor irrespective of the investor's own tax domicile. Indeed it is largely as a result of the legal, fiscal and monetary controls and regulations prevailing in various countries that there is a segmentation of the markets into "domestic", "foreign" and "international" as described in the next section of this chapter.

Domestic, Foreign and International Markets
The domicile of a debt issuer and the currency of that issue are generally sufficient criteria to categorise the nature of an issue.

A domestic debt issue is one which the issuer may raise within his own country and is denominated in his own country's currency. For example, a Swiss company raising Swiss Franc debt in Switzerland is a totally "domestic" operation. Domestic issues invariably have a greater attraction to resident investors than those elsewhere as most securities are subject to withholding tax and foreign investors may not be willing or able to take advantage of any double taxation agreement that might exist between their own country and the issuer's. The

482

yield on investments subject to withholding tax, even where an effective treaty exists, may not prove attractive to a foreign investor because of the delay in reimbursement of the amount of income withheld. Domestic issues, therefore, are placed largely (but by no means exclusively) with residents of the issuers country. In many countries the authorities exempt certain foreign government investors from withholding taxes and this tax-exempt category generally includes certain government agencies and usually the central bank. Another feature of most domestic markets is that the debt instruments are normally issued in "registered" form rather than "bearer". Local stock exchange regulations and fiscal considerations in certain countries require that debt issues may only be made in registered form. To many investors, the form of security (whether registered or bearer), is of little or no importance, but to others who seek the anonymity of bearer investments, registered securities are not likely to be widely distributed.

A foreign debt issue is one which a foreign borrower may raise on a domestic capital market of another country with the paper denominated in the currency of the market. For example, a Dutch company raising US dollar debt in the USA may be described as a foreign debt issue and the market jargon for a foreign issue on the US domestic market is a "Yankee bond". Issues of yen securities in Japan by foreign borrowers are called "Samurai issues"; issues of sterling securities in London by foreign borrowers for sale principally to UK resident investors are called "Bulldog issues". Only in a few countries with well developed securities markets and relaxed or no exchange control regulations, do the authorities permit non-residents direct access to long-term funding on the domestic capital market. In addition to the Yankee, Samurai and Bulldog markets, there are foreign bond markets in Switzerland, West Germany, the Netherlands and, to a smaller extent, Canada. Exchange and monetary control regulations can and do close foreign bond primary market operations, often as a result of internal political or economic necessity. The availability of long-term French Francs, for example, was somewhat limited during the period when the international capital markets were developing (1960s – 70s – 80s). In fact the availability to French domestic borrowers over the period was also limited partly as a result of a relatively high interest rate scenario. The "windows" for long-term

French Franc debt have so far been open to non-residents for very short periods and restricted to a few of the highest quality borrowers. A feature of most domestic and foreign debt issues is the requirement by the central bank in some countries to submit to a queue procedure so that a new issue calendar may be created to ensure the volume of new issues brought to market each month can be controlled by the monetary authorities. In January 1984, the queuing requirement for new issues in Switzerland was abolished. The Japanese market is subject to the approval of the Ministry of Finance and a queue system regulates the number of Samurai issues permitted. Bank of England permission is required on the timing of new Bulldog issues and the Government Broker must be informed of potential new issues. The Dutch National Bank must approve all new Guilder foreign bonds, and as the number of new issues is closely regulated, a long queue is not unusual and liberalisation of this market is anticipated in 1986. Canadian foreign debt issues are rare owing to the substantial cost-saving and administrative advantages to foreign borrowers issuing Euro-Canadian dollar bonds which are free from withholding tax and do not require registration with any Canadian securities commission. There is no effective differentiation made between a foreign issuer and a domestic issuer on the Canadian domestic capital debt market. Yankee bond issues must be registered with the US Securities and Exchange Commission (SEC). Although the SEC does not control the number of issues made, the lengthy administrative requirements for such issues and attendant legal and accounting costs involved, tend to make the Yankee bond less attractive to foreign borrowers than eurobonds. The West German foreign debt issues are virtually homogenous with the international debt issues for all practical purposes. The main difference perhaps lies in the composition of the syndicate of banks which bring the issues to the primary market. If German banks alone are launching a Deutschemark debt issue for a foreign borower the issue may technically be classified as a foreign debt issue. If non-German banks are included in the managing syndicate it may be classified as an "international" or "euro" issue. The Bundesbank does not make any such distinction and requires that all potential new issues are regulated by the Foreign Issues Sub-Committee of the German Central Capital Market Committee and take their place in the queue. All Deutschemark issues must be lead managed by a bank with an operation in Germany. This may be either a German bank or a foreign owned bank with legal status domiciled in the Federal Republic. The Italian lire bond market opened in September, 1985 for the first time in many years, issues being strictly controlled by the authorities.

The international debt markets may be described as eurobond or note markets in which issues usually in bearer form are underwritten or bought by an international syndicate of investment houses and/or banks. The securities are placed with investors internationally but sometimes will specifically exclude nationals of the currency in which the securities are denominated. For example, there are strict prohibitions on the sale of US dollar eurobonds to US citizens. This is described in more detail in Section 6. There are no official queuing requirements for timing consents for eurobonds with the exception of Deutschemark and Euro Sterling denominated issues which do not technically recognise a Euro-issue. An unofficial queue exists for those ECU issues which are lead managed by the leading Belgian banks, for the sake of an orderly market.

An important feature of eurobond issues is the absence of withholding taxes. Although in some countries the fiscal authorities *will* exempt foreign investors in foreign debt issues raised on the indigenous capital market from withholding tax, with eurobonds there is no withholding tax. Indeed, if withholding tax was applied to such instruments and introduced as a new measure, then it would effectively terminate any meaningful eurobond activity within that country. The eurobond markets, therefore, exist in countries which maintain a favourable fiscal environment. They also require a well developed infrastructure of financial institutions and as a result the centres which have established such activity are London, Luxembourg and Singapore, with London being pre-eminent. Eurobonds have been issued in the following currencies although some currencies are very limited.

US dollars	Deutschemarks	Australian dollars
Sterling	Guilders	Hong Kong dollars
Yen	Canadian dollars	Kuwaiti dinars
Luxembourg Francs	Bahrain dinars	Lire
French Francs	Norwegian Krone	SDRs
		ECUs

Notably there is no euro-market for Swiss Francs owing to Swiss central bank opposition to the development of an offshore Swiss Franc capital market.

The boundaries between the euro issues and foreign debt issues can be indistinct in some cases, and give rise to no cost differential, as with the Deutschemark markets. The difference between the euro sterling and the bulldog issues is also marginal but as there does exist a cost differential between the two, a comparison is important. Bulldog yields are calculated on a true yield basis of actual days divided by 365 day year, whereas euro sterling issue yields are worked on the basis of a 360 day year. In practice, however, this gives rise to a differential of only 0.0025%, and although it is important to be aware of the difference in techniques applied to each, one must look elsewhere for the reason for comparable price differentials. Bulldogs generally bear interest payable semi-annually – euros on the other hand are issued on an annual interest periodicity. Most euro sterling issues are made for shorter maturities whereas the bulldogs tend to have longer final maturities, and this makes it difficult to obtain an effective comparison from a common base. Bulldogs are subject to withholding tax at the UK standard rate of income tax and this can only be avoided by non-residents disclosing details. Furthermore, bulldogs are usually issued in registered form and there is, perhaps, a degree of premium for lack of confidentiality which contributes to the relatively higher price investors are prepared to pay for euros. This is further evidenced by the relative liquidity in the two markets – the bulldog being the smaller and less liquid. Commissions on bulldogs are higher than euros and so are all the market spreads from time to time, both factors tend to make bulldogs less attractive to the discerning investor and so create a price differential in favour of the euro sterling issue. Although still subject to withholding tax, a UK resident's holdings of bulldogs is not subject to capital gains tax. This concession was introduced in 1984 and caused the yield differential between the bulldog and domestic markets to close by a few points, yet it created a clearer division between the two markets. UK resident investors tend to show even greater preference for bulldogs with the marginal absence of capital gains tax benefit; at the same time the international investor shows a greater preference for euro sterling paper as the price of bulldogs hardens in relation to the euro sterling paper, as increased demand from UK investors builds up for bull-dogs.

A UK company raising funds through a Dutch financing vehicle by means of a euro sterling issue will have to pay the extra cost involved for administration and the portion of Dutch taxation which is not recoverable even under the favourable double taxation agreements. A domestic issue would attract a slightly higher coupon (tax deductable) but have the following material benefit. The coupon interest is subject to withholding tax and this may be retained by the issuer for up to three months as the payment of such tax is made quarterly. Issuers of bulldogs would also benefit from such cash retentions to the extent that the issue was placed with residents or non-UK residents who have failed to declare their domicile.

In addition to the subjects discussed above an issuer's ability to access both foreign and international capital debt markets and an investor's ability to invest in overseas domestic, foreign and interntional capital debt markets will also be subject to any exchange control or other similar regulation imposed in his country of domicile.

CHAPTER TWENTY THREE

Types of Debt Instrument

Bearer and Registered Securities
Bearer securities have a particular appeal to investors who wish to retain absolute anonymity. There is no holder's register and the security does not mention the name of the investor. Ownership of bearer stock passes on delivery to the purchaser. Because of the market practice it is unusual:

i)   to find bearer bonds which are subject to withholding tax on coupon interest paid, although there are a few bearer share issues for UK companies, and

ii) for bearer bonds to attract any form of stamp duty or transfer tax on negotiation

The holder is responsible to ensure he arranges collection of his income from the bearer securities by having the coupons cut and collected from the nominated paying agent. Failure to do so or to present the bond or note for redemption when due as a result of the security being lost, stolen or destroyed, will not mean that the investor automatically forfeits all his rights to payment of capital or income provided that they are found, returned or replaced and are presented for payment before prescription. Presciption in this context means the limitation of time within which action must be taken.

Bearer shares are commonplace in Switzerland and the norm in Germany, and in both countries non-residents are permitted to own them. Holders of bearer shares and long-dated or perpetual bearer loan stocks will, after a while, run out of coupons. So that the holder may continue to claim his income there is a talon attached to the coupons which may be presented when due to the paying agent, usually with the final coupon, in exchange for a new sheet of coupons for the next few years income plus, of course, another talon. It is quite common for the certificate, bond or note to be replaced at that time as well, so the issuer may have to arrange for a reprint of the securities after, say, 22 or perhaps 44 years have elapsed from the initial issue date. This is because coupons are usually attached to the certificate and the printers have limitations to the physical number of coupons which can be produced in one document.

Following US tax changes introduced in January 1984 all capital debt issues in the USA, yankee and domestic, are likely to be issued in registered rather than in bearer form. Most domestic debt issues and nearly all equities in the UK are issued in registered form. The issuer of registered securities is responsible to ensure a register is kept which records the names and address of all holders of the stocks or shares and the amount held. Some UK companies prefer to keep their own register, particularly if the company is small and there are only a few shareholders. However, over half the total of UK shareholder accounts are handled by the registrar services provided by the UK clearing banks and half a dozen others, and these handle the companies whose shares are heavily traded. In addition to retaining the shares/stock registers, the registrar will prepare new share or stock certificates, pay dividends and interest when due, provide data for the statutory returns required of the issuers, and generally deal with numerous enquiries from holders and brokers.

US and Canadian registered certificates can be converted into quasi-bearer documents in the UK as a consequence of them being registered in a "good marking name". Each certificate contains a blank form of transfer printed on the back as follows:

FOR VALUE RECEIVED .... hereby sell, assign and transfer unto ....
....
      Please print or typewrite name and address including
         postal zip code of assignee.
the within Bond of
and do hereby irrevocably constitute and appoint ....
....Attorney
to transfer the said Bond on the books of said Bank with full power of substitution in the instrument.

Dated ....

The name of the registered holder will be printed on the face of the certificate and if the transfer form on the reverse is completed by the registered holder, then the certificate can be transferred to another holder. The Stock Exchange, London, has published a list of brokers whose names are considered good for marking names, which means in effect they may have such certificates registered and endorsed in their name and act as collection agents for the coupon or dividends thereon. The advantage to holders of US and Canadian registered securities being in marking names, lies in the cost. Administrative delays in transfer, and problems relating to probate in respect of deceased holder's investments, are substantially reduced by a reputable UK broker acting as a nominee. Because of these advantages marking name securities in London will command a better price than identical North American securities in other names, and while it is quite possible for an investor/holder to have such securities registered in his own name there is generally no commercial or administrative advantage for him to do so.

Straight Debt

Straight debt may be described as fixed interest bonds or debentures which do not convey any option for the investor to convert into equity. A debenture is an acknowledgment of indebtedness usually given by an incorporated company either under seal or under hand. In many cases debentures include a charge on the assets of the company – this class of debenture includes the all-moneys, mortgage, secured, and sandwich variety of "domestic UK market" debt instruments which are not generally issued for distribution to international investors on the international capital markets. Simple and naked debentures which are unsecured or not accompanied by any security, are the forms of debentures which are discussed in this book and in the context of the international markets, and the only security they convey are the unpledged assets and the creditworthiness of the issuer.

Investors in fixed coupon securities may well find the secondary market for their holdings illiquid if interest rates and yields harden – indeed if they do decide to dispose of them in such circumstances they will naturally incur a capital loss, if, as one assumes, trading is carried

491

out at market rates. If interest rates fall capital gain opportunities will arise. Funding and fiscal considerations and investment management philosophy will determine the various postures adopted by different investors when yields change. During rising rate scenarios some will be concerned with loss of gain. In terms of current yields, many investors who have borrowed to finance their portfolio will be concerned at narrowing yields or funding losses unless fixed rate funding has previously been obtained. With falling rates some investors are concerned about reinvestment of the proceeds in lower yielding securities even if an immediate capital gain may be obtained.

The majority of bonds and notes issued are in "bullet" form with repayment being made in one lump sum at a stated maturity. Staggered redemption is, however, often written into capital loan stock agreements in the form of either a sinking fund or a note purchase arrangement. With a sinking fund the issuer makes a repayment of his debt at stated regular intervals either through purchasing bonds or notes in the open market, or arranging for an agent to do this on his behalf, or for regular drawings by lot to take place. These drawings are sometimes done by random numbers being selected by the paying agent and sometimes by a series being drawn. The series method is preferred in the Deutschemark issues to the random number system. "Purchase" funds involve the mandatory purchase by the issuer in the market of a determined number of bonds or notes if they trade in the market below a stated price at certain specified times. So far as the investor is concerned, such an arrangement helps to stabilize the price of the investment so that its value is maintained at or near to par.

An example of a straight eurobond is shown opposite:

Partly Paid Issues
It is quite a normal procedure for UK domestic loan stock to be issued on a partly paid basis with, say, 20% or 25% payable initially and the balance usually in one subsequent instalment within, say, six months. Eurobonds and notes have also been issued on a deferred purchase basis. The issue proceeds will not be received in one lump sum and it may be easier to employ the proceeds, if smaller amounts

Straight Eurobond

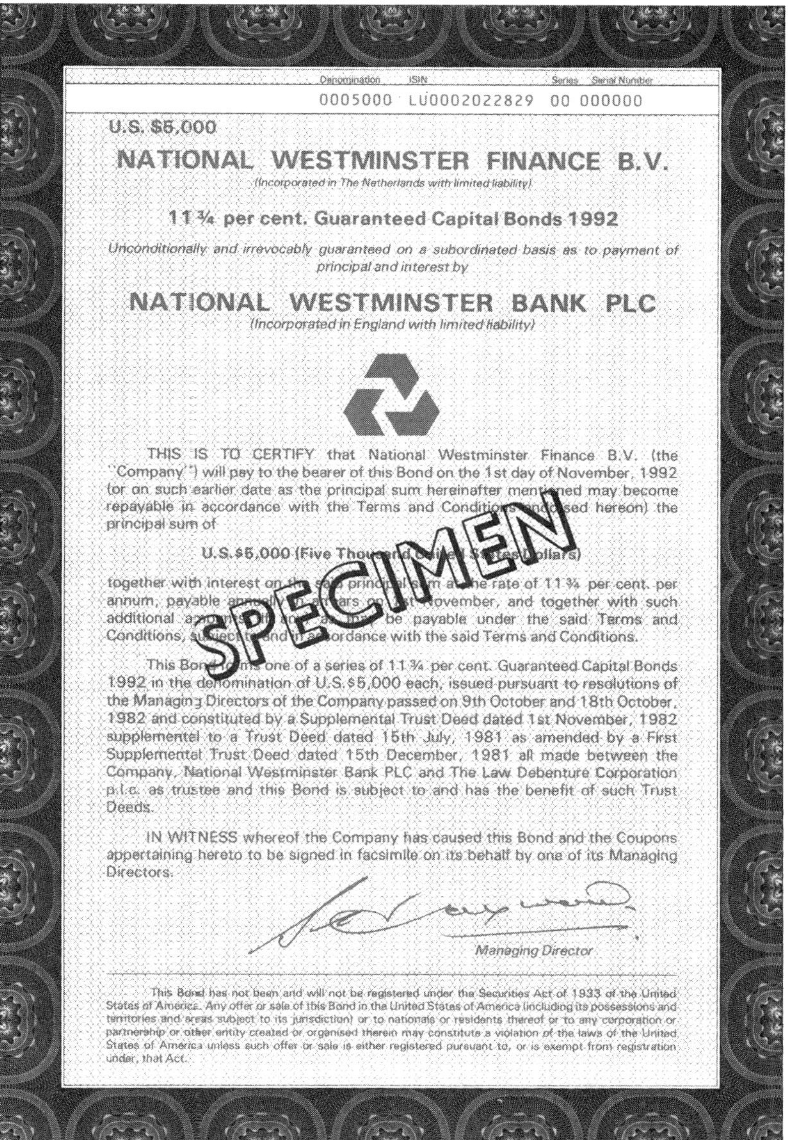

are received, in one or more instalments. The investor may derive a gearing benefit as he will only initially be required to pay, say 20% on the value of his partly paid investment. The price volatility of partly paids is proportionally greater than fully paid bonds and there is therefore a more speculative element with the initial holdings. If the investor fails to honour any subsequent calls then his holding will be forfeit.

Zero Coupon and Deep Discount Issues
Sometimes known as "streakers" the bonds are issued at a deep discount which is generally calculated to give a slightly lower equivalent annual yield to maturity than conventional interest bearing paper. For investors who have a high tax exposure to coupon interest income and are domiciled in a country whose fiscal authority treats any profit arising from zero coupon issues as a capital gain at a lower tax incidence, they have a significant attraction. They also offer the investor protection against falling interest rates so far as the reinvestment of coupon interest received is concerned, as the yield to maturity calculated at the time of purchase is locked in straight away. Deep discount bonds and zeros are fixed interest securities, although they are subject to greater price volatility than comparable conventional interest bearing issues and, therefore, attractive to the more speculative investor. These three advantages to the investor are usually weighed against a lower cost to the issuer and lower yield to the investor. Tax and accounting procedures need to be closely examined by the issuer and investor before involvement in zero coupon stocks – requirements differ substantially between different countries.

An example of a zero coupon note is shown opposite:

Convertible stocks
Fixed interest securities that are exchangeable at a later date into ordinary shares on predetermined terms are called "convertibles". They have been popular in the USA for a long time, but it is only in the 1970s that currency convertibles have come into common use in the London markets.

494

Citicorp Overseas Finance Corporation N.V.

(Incorporated with limited liability in the Netherlands Antilles)

Guaranteed Zero Coupon Note Due August 18, 1984

Unconditionally guaranteed by

CITICORP

U.S.$1,000   No.000000

CITICORP OVERSEAS FINANCE CORPORATION N.V., a company established in Aruba, Netherlands Antilles (the "Company"), for value received, hereby promises to pay to bearer on presentation and surrender of this Note the principal sum of One Thousand United States Dollars (U.S.$1,000) on August 18, 1984. The principal of this Note shall not bear interest, except in the case of default in payment of principal, and in such case the amount in default shall bear interest at the rate of 14.4238 per cent per annum (to the extent permitted by applicable law) from the date of default in payment to the date such payment has been made or duly provided for. The principal of the Notes (as hereinafter defined) will be payable in lawful money of the United States only against surrender of the Notes either (a) at the corporate trust office of Citibank, N.A. in New York City, or its successor as Paying Agent, or (b) at the option of the holder, subject to applicable laws and regulations and subject to the right of the Company to discontinue or to terminate the appointment of any such offices or agencies, at the main offices of Citibank, N.A. in London, Paris, Frankfurt am Main, Amsterdam, Zurich and Brussels and at the main office of Citibank (Luxembourg) S.A. in Luxembourg, or at any other paying agency maintained at the time by the Company for such purposes. Payments at the offices referred to in (b) above will be made by check or bank draft drawn on, or by transfer to a United States dollar account maintained by the payee with, a bank in New York City, subject in each case to any laws or regulations applicable thereto. The Company covenants that until the principal of this Note shall have been paid or moneys therefor made available to the Paying Agent and repaid to the Company or Citicorp as provided in Paragraph 5, the Company shall at all times maintain an office or agency in New York City for the payment of such principal as herein provided.

GUARANTEE OF CITICORP

FOR VALUE RECEIVED, CITICORP, a corporation duly organized and existing under the laws of the State of Delaware, hereby unconditionally guarantees to the holder of the Note upon which this Guarantee is endorsed the due and punctual payment of any and all amounts required to be paid on said Note according to the terms of said Note, when and as the same shall become due and payable, whether at maturity, upon redemption or otherwise, according to the terms thereof and of the payment agreement referred to therein. In case of the failure of Citicorp Overseas Finance Corporation N.V. or any company which may have assumed the obligations of Citicorp Overseas Finance Corporation N.V. under said Note pursuant to the provisions thereof, in either case as said Note (Citicorp Overseas Finance Corporation N.V. or such other company, as the case may be, being the "Company") principally to pay any such amount, Citicorp hereby agrees to cause any such payment to be made as and when the same shall become due and payable, whether at maturity, upon redemption or otherwise, and as if such payment were made by the Company.

Citicorp hereby agrees that its obligations hereunder shall be unconditional, irrespective of the identity of the Company, the validity, regularity or enforceability of said Note or the Fiscal Agency Agreement, the absence of any action to enforce the same, any waiver or consent by the holder of said Note with respect to any provisions thereof, the recovery of any judgment against the Company or any action to enforce the same, or any other circumstances which might otherwise constitute a legal or equitable discharge or defense of a guarantor. Citicorp hereby waives diligence, presentment, demand of payment, filing of claims with a court in the event of insolvency or bankruptcy of the Company, any right to require a proceeding first against the Company, protest, notice and all demands whatsoever and covenants that this Guarantee will not be discharged except by complete performance of the obligations contained in said Note and in this Guarantee.

Citicorp shall be subrogated to all rights of the holder of said Note against the Company in respect of any amounts paid by Citicorp pursuant to the provisions of this Guarantee; provided, however, that Citicorp shall not be entitled to enforce or to receive any payments arising out of, or based upon such right of subrogation until none of the Notes of the Company known as "Guaranteed Zero Coupon Notes Due August 18, 1984" shall remain Outstanding (as defined in said Note).

The obligation of Citicorp hereunder shall rank pari passu with all other unsecured and unsubordinated indebtedness of Citicorp.

This Guarantee shall be governed by, and construed in accordance with, the laws of the State of New York.

Subject to the next following paragraph, Citicorp hereby certifies and warrants that all acts, conditions and things required to be done and performed and to have happened precedent to the creation and issuance of this Guarantee and to constitute the same the valid obligation of Citicorp have been done and performed and have happened in due compliance with all applicable laws.

This Guarantee shall not be valid or become obligatory for any purpose until the certificate of authentication on the Note upon which this Guarantee is endorsed has been signed by the Fiscal Agent under the Fiscal Agency Agreement referred to in said Note.

IN WITNESS WHEREOF, CITICORP has caused this Guarantee to be executed in its corporate name by one of its officers thereunto duly authorized by a facsimile of his signature, and a facsimile of its corporate seal to be impressed, imprinted or engraved hereon, attested by its Secretary or any Assistant Secretary by a facsimile of his signature.

Dated as of November 23, 1982.

Attest:

Secretary

CITICORP

By

Executive Vice President

IN WITNESS WHEREOF, CITICORP OVERSEAS FINANCE CORPORATION N.V. has caused this Note to be executed in its corporate name by one of its Managing Directors, by facsimile of his signature, and a facsimile of its corporate seal to be impressed, imprinted or engraved hereon.

Dated as of November 23, 1982.

CITICORP OVERSEAS FINANCE CORPORATION N.V.

By Wallace A. Campbell

Managing Director

This is one of the Notes described in the within-mentioned Fiscal Agency Agreement.

CITIBANK, N.A.,
as Fiscal Agent

By

Authorized Officer

Convertibles must be judged both as fixed interest stocks and as potential equities. The cost of buying what is, in effect, an equity option is measured by the difference between the yield on the convertible and the yield on an alternative fixed interest investment that has no such option, or in other words the income forfeited by choosing a convertible instead of a straight bond, debenture or preference share.

In addition to measuring the "option cost" it is necessary for the issuer and for the investor to determine the market price of the existing equity and the effective price at which the convertible can be exchanged into ordinary shares later on.

Normally, the holder of a convertible receives less income than he would on a straight debenture and (if he immediately exercises his right to convert) fewer shares than he could have got for the same money, had he invested outright in the equity. He may think it worthwhile to invest in a convertible if he wishes to avoid an equity commitment but at the same time "keep his foot in the equity door". Such a two-way hedge is not available free, and the investor should be sure to evaluate the total cost before deciding on a convertible. In addition to the option cost and the conversion premium he must try to assess the price that would be obtainable for his convertible, if the price of the ordinary shares does not rise sufficiently to encourage holders to convert. In such a situation, the convertible will be valued in the market as a straight fixed interest stock.

Convertible loan stocks have two attractions for the issuer. They may enable him to raise loan capital when the market conditions are difficult and, therefore, offer the conversion incentive to the investors who might not have been interested without it. The second advantage lies in the lower than usual coupon normally achievable as the investors may cede immediate yield benefits in order to gain the conversion option. The more attractive and apparently obtainable the conversion pricing is, the lower will be the coupon the issuer can attach to the loan stock. If the conversion price is set too low and exercised very soon afterwards, the issuer gains little or no advantage from the low stock coupon and may have just as well made a rights issue.

496

An example may be helpful to illustrate the operational features and calculations of convertible bonds:

UK Plc issues a convertible bond in denominations of US$10,000 at a time that the market price of its shares were £5 each, and the dollar/sterling exchange rate $2.00. The conversion price is set at £5.60 per share and for the purpose of calculating the number of shares to be issued on conversion the exchange rate of US$2.00 shall be used throughout the life of the issue. The number of shares into which each bond may be converted is therefore 892. This figure is sometimes referred to as the conversion ratio and is found by taking the amount of each bond ($10,000) dividing it by the exchange rate in the terms of the issue ($2.00) and dividing the result (£5,000) by the determined conversion price £5.60 = 892.86 or (892 whole shares). The conversion price was set at a 12% premium over the current market price. To obtain this figure the following formula should be applied:

$$
\begin{aligned}
\text{Where} \quad CP &= \text{Conversion premium} \\
Bp &= \text{Price \% of the bond (100\% or par)} \\
P &= \text{Conversion price (£5.60)} \\
Sp &= \text{Share price in the market (£5.00)}
\end{aligned}
$$

$$
CP = \frac{(P \times Bp)}{(Sp \times 100)} - 1 \times 100 = 12\%
$$

Now this may seem a complicated way of arriving at a simple answer. However if the issue was launched at a premium or discount to par the result would not have been 12% in the example.

If the bonds were issued at a discount at, say 98.5%, and the share price moved to £5.07 the effective conversion premium would be reduced on both counts as follows:

$$
\begin{aligned}
Bp &= 98.5 \\
P &= 5.60 \\
Sp &= 5.07
\end{aligned}
$$

$$
CP = \frac{(5.60 \times 98.5)}{(5.07 \times 100)} - 1 \times 100 = 8.80\%
$$

The variable factors which must be assessed by investors before exercising a conversion option include:

- The current market price of the bond itself – changes of interest rate will affect the value of fixed interest securities.

- The current market price of the shares.

- Changes in exchange rates between the currencies of the bonds and shares.

- The timing of interest payments and dividends – it is possible to lose accrued interest on bonds converted on dates other than interest payment dates and it is possible to obtain the dividend income on the shares perhaps having held them for a relatively short period. The share dividend may be paid in one currency and the bond coupon in another (as is the case with the example) and the exchange rate on coupon interest paid (or accrued and forgone).

Returning to the example – assume that the US dollar had weakened to US$2.20 in the meantime, the premium would be eliminated altogether and the discount on conversion would be 1.09% since:

$$\frac{P \times Bp \times R_1}{Sp \times 100 \times R_2} \qquad \text{where } R_1 = \text{the exchange rate in the loan terms}$$
$$\text{and } R_2 = \text{the exchange rate at conversion date}$$

$$\frac{(5.60 \times 98.5 \times 2.00)}{(5.07 \times 100 \times 2.20)} - 1 \times 100 = 1.09\% \text{ (discount on conversion)}$$

Whether it is profitable for the investor to exercise such a conversion to take advantage of the 1.09% conversion discount in his favour will depend on the coupon v dividend flow position at the material time.

Assume that the eurobond has a 10% coupon payable semi-annually and conversion was considered 120 days from the last interest payment date, and 40 days before the next dividend payment date.

The cost expressed as a percentage per annum of "lost income" of accrued coupon interest which the investor must forego is the coupon amount times the actual number of days interest has accrued, over 360, so:

$$10\% \times \frac{120}{360} = 3.33\% \quad \text{adjusted for exchange differences}$$

$$3.33 \times \frac{2.00}{2.20} = 3.03\%$$

Assume the net dividend declared was 28p per £1 share with advance corporation tax of 30%, the grossed up net dividend =

$$28 + \frac{(28 \times 30)}{(\quad 70)} = 40\text{p per share}$$

The gross yield is the gross dividend as a percentage of the market price which, when applied to the example, is:

$$\frac{0.40}{5.07} \times 100 = 7.89\% \, Note - \qquad \text{This measures the current cash return on the investment.}$$

The dividend payment will be received 20 days before the due date of payment of the next coupon on the bond.

Collating all the factors in the example, the investor started with a conversion *premium* of 8.80% adjusting this for exchange rate movement in his favour it became a conversion *discount* of 1.09%. Adjusting for the net loss of accrued coupon interest the conversion factor reverted to a *premium* of 1.94%. The dividend benefit to the investor of 7.89% returns the conversion factor to a *discount* of 5.95%. Finally, the fact that the income from the dividend could be invested some 20 days earlier than the coupon interest adds to the total profitability of the conversion for the investor. Of course, whether the investor decided to convert at this point depends on his views as to the potential for even more favourable changes in the variable factors indicated above.

If the exchange rate moved to $1.38 the net conversion *premium* as calculated above with all other factors being the same would be 54.61% making it quite unprofitable to convert the dollar stock into the sterling equity on such terms. Indeed, a share price increase of some £3.16 would be needed to compensate for such a foreign exchange difference.

Warrants

Bonds may be issued with debt warrants or with equity warrants which in most cases may be detached and traded separately or traded with the bond. Warrant issues may also be made without bonds. A warrant conveys the right for the holder to subscribe for a specified type and quantity of security at a stated price and within a given period. The types of securities may be fixed interest or floating rate loan stock/debentures or perhaps shares which may or may not convey voting rights. A borrower may choose to issue warrants rather than make a convertible issue for either additional debt or for more equity. If the warrant expires without the holder having exercised his rights then it becomes valueless. Indeed, the majority of debt warrants issued in the eurobond market were not exercised. The exercise period for equity warrants often commences shortly after the issue date and terminates at maturity of the issue or perhaps a year earlier, although there have been a number of equity warrant issues with the much shorter exercise option period; shorter exercise periods are normal with debt warrant issues. Until exercised, the issuer does not obtain any additional debt or equity capital. However, he may arrange for the sale of debt warrants separately and derive additional income thereon at prices which have ranged from nil to $40 per warrant. When sold with a bond attached, a much lower coupon is usually negotiated by the issuer to compensate for the potential benefits conveyed in the warrant.

The ratio between the warrant and bond price is called its gearing or leverage. Since the bond price exceeds its warrant's value considerably, a relatively small change in the value of the bond has a geared-up greater change on the value of its warrant. In fact this ratio may be increased still further if more than one warrant is issued per bond – many have two and, where the denomination of the underlying security is higher, up to 10 warrants per bond have been known. Taking a debt warrant issue as an example to illustrate the impact of gearing, let us assume that the warrants are priced at $2\frac{1}{2}\%$ of the nominal bond value and each warrant is initially sold at $25 conveying the option for the holder to convert it into a US$1,000 bond at par. If the bond price rose by 1% the corresponding increase in the underlying warrant value would be 40%. This may be more clearly illustrated with the following chart:

Debt Warrant Value		*Bond Value*	*Gearing % Calculation*
On Issue	$25	$1,000	$\dfrac{1000}{25} \times 40$
After 1% increase in bond price	$25 + (40% of $25) = $35	$1,010	$\dfrac{1010}{35} = 28.86$
After another 1% increase in bond price	$35 + (28.86% of $35) = $45.10	$1,021	$\dfrac{1021}{45.10} = 22.64$
Assuming a fall in bond value after issue of 1%	$25 − (40% of $25) = $15	$990	$\dfrac{990}{15} = 66$
After another 1% fall in bond price	$15 (66% of $15) = $5.10	$980.10	$\dfrac{980.10}{5.10} = 192.18$

The investor's downside risk is limited to $25 on $2\frac{1}{2}\%$ of the bond value. Note the drag effect on the gearing ratio as the warrant increases in value. Investors clearly benefit from a relatively lower initial value not merely to the issuer's detriment in cash terms but also because of the gearing impact shown above. Issuers must pitch the level of the debt warrant just right to achieve maximum cash to reduce the overall cost of the issue (savings ranging from $\frac{1}{8}\%$ to $2\frac{1}{2}\%$ on the coupon amount of the issue have been achieved by this technique). The issuer also has the benefit of a possible increase in the amount of outstanding debt if the warrant option is exercised without incurring any additional new issue expenses.

Now turning to international bonds with equity warrants attached which were first introduced in 1968 (12 years before bonds with debt warrants were introduced), there are three important variables to consider which differentiate between equity and debt warrant issues. The share price is one, and the foreign exchange factor the next and the size and timing of dividend income, the third. Share prices are often much more volatile in price movements than fixed interest debt instruments. The shares are most likely to be denominated in the currency of the country in which the issuer is domiciled and the bond is generally denominated in US dollars, although issues have been made in sterling and Swiss Franc denominated debt. It is normal practice to denominate the warrant amount which the holder is required to subscribe for shares in the same currency as the shares. In the example given below the warrant specifies a figure of Yen 1,178,500 which must be subscribed for shares in the company. This figure is calculated at the exchange rate of Yen 235.70 per US dollar on the bond value of US$5,000. The share price at which the warrant option may be exercised (the exercise price) is Yen 550 but this is subject to anti-dilution adjustments, if relevant. If no adjustments are necessary to the exercise price the number of shares that may be purchased for Yen 1,178,500 is 2,142. The anti-dilution provision is designed to protect the warrant holder if the value of the shares is reduced, for example, by the declaration of a dividend, bonus or rights issues or if there are further issues of stocks with either equity warrants or convertible into equity.

Taking a simple illustration – assume the current market share price is $153; that the warrant exercise price of shares is $126, and the warrants are initially sold at $40. The "nominal" value of the warrant is only $153 – $126 = $27, although they are being sold at a premium of $13 more. The conversion premium would be $ $\dfrac{13}{153} \times 100 =$ 8.50% over the current share price. The current total purchase consideration is $166 which is $13 more than the current market value.

502

An example of a low coupon fixed rate bond with equity warrant attached is shown overleaf:

American Depositary Receipts (ADR)

An ADR is a negotiable receipt for foreign securities. Its purpose is to simplify the procedures and practices for US resident investors relating to their purchase, holding and sale of investments denominated in foreign currencies. They are treated for ownership and transfer purposes in the same way as US share certificates.

An ADR certificate will show the depositary bank in the USA and indicate the liability of that bank to pay dividends declared, as well as matters relating to proxies, rights issues and fees relating to the underlying shares. The nominated ADR depositary will certify that the ordinary shares have been deposited and will be held during the life of the ADR, indeed an ADR holder has the right to obtain delivery of the actual shares should he so desire, although in practice, he would not normally wish to lose the facility of the ADR for his foreign share investment. The majority of ADRs are "sponsored" or initiated by the non-US company which is an appropriate arrangement for an acquisition by way of a share exchange. Sponsored ADR programmes involve the voluntary entry by the issuing company into the US domestic market, it is therefore mandatory to file with the SEC. Such issues are normally listed on a national exchange or NASDAQ, and a depositary agreement is established between the shareholders, the depositary bank and the non-US issuing company. NASDAQ is a communication system used by securities dealers in the USA (National Association of Securities Dealers Automated Quotation System). The NASD regulates the over-the-counter securities market. The depositary bank charges a fee for the following services:

- Issuing the ADR

- Transferring ownership

- Payment of dividends

- Stock distributions (rights or bonus issues)

- Any proxy work

- Cancellation of the ADR

Low coupon fixed rate bond with equity warrant attached

Denomination	ISIN	Series	Serial Number

0005000 US606769AB36 00 000000

U.S.$5,000

Mitsubishi Corporation

(Mitsubishi Shoji Kabushiki Kaisha)

(Incorporated with limited liability under the Commercial Code of Japan)

U.S. $100,000,000
5 3/4% Notes due 1988

THIS IS TO CERTIFY that MITSUBISHI CORPORATION (the "Company") will pay to the bearer of this Note on 21st November, 1988 (or on such earlier date as such sum may become payable in accordance with the Terms and Conditions endorsed hereon (the "Conditions")) upon presentation and surrender of this Note the principal sum of

U.S.$5,000 (Five thousand United States dollars)

together with such additional amounts (if any) as may be payable under the Conditions, and will pay interest on the said principal sum at the rate of 5 3/4 per cent. per annum from and including 21st November, 1983 payable annually in arrears on 21st November in each year (the first payment being made on 21st November, 1984), upon presentation and surrender of the Coupons appertaining hereto as the same shall severally become due and/or upon presentation of this Note where so required, all in accordance with the Conditions.

This Note forms one of a series of Notes either issued as Bearer Notes in the denomination of U.S.$5,000 each or as Registered Notes in the denomination of U.S.$5,000 each or an integral multiple thereof in an aggregate principal amount of U.S.$100,000,000. The Notes are issued pursuant to resolutions of the Board of Directors of the Company passed on 26th October and 4th November, 1983 and subject to and with the benefit of the provisions of a Fiscal Agency Agreement dated 21st November, 1983 and made between the Company, The Bank of Tokyo Trust Company and the paying agents therein named.

The Notes have been issued in conjunction with an issue of bearer warrants conferring upon the holders thereof stock subscription rights pursuant to Article 341-8 *et seq.* of the Commercial Code of Japan.

IN WITNESS WHEREOF the Company has caused this Note and the Coupons appertaining hereto to be signed in facsimile on its behalf by its President.

Mitsubishi Corporation

By

President

ISSUED in London as of 21st November, 1983.

Any United States person who holds this obligation will be subject to limitations under the United States income tax laws, including the limitations provided in sections 165(j) and 1232(c) of the Internal Revenue Code.

THOMAS DE LA RUE AND COMPANY LIMITED

Denomination	ISIN		Series	Serial Number
0005000	US6067691153		00	000000

WARRANT

to subscribe for Shares of Common Stock of

Mitsubishi Corporation

(Mitsubishi Shoji Kabushiki Kaisha)

MITSUBISHI CORPORATION (Mitsubishi Shoji Kabushiki Kaisha) HEREBY CERTIFIES that the Bearer of this Warrant is entitled, on and subject to the terms and conditions set out below and on the reverse hereof, at any time on or after 1st March, 1984 until the expiry of the Lodgement Period (as defined in Condition 5, being in any event not later than 7th November, 1988) to lodge this Warrant and subscribe ¥1,178,500 for Shares of the Common Stock of Mitsubishi Corporation (the "Company").

The Warrants (as defined below) are issued subject to and with the benefit of a Deed Poll dated 21st November, 1983 and executed by the Company (the "Deed Poll", which expression includes any deed executed in accordance with the provisions thereof and expressed to be supplemental thereto, as such Deed Poll and any such supplemental deed may from time to time be modified in accordance with the provisions thereof) and are constituted and enforceable severally by each Warrantholder (as defined in the Deed Poll) against the Company insofar as each such Warrantholder's Warrant is concerned. The Deed Poll has been deposited with, and will be held by or to the order of the Fiscal Agent (as so defined) with a specified office in London and copies thereof and of the Fiscal Agency Agreement (as so defined), including the form of the Notes (as so defined) and of the Warrant Agency Agreement (as so defined) are and will be available for inspection by Warrantholders at the registered head office for the time being of the Company and at the specified offices of each of the other Warrant Agents (as so defined), in each case for so long as any Warrant remains unexercised (as so defined) and for so long thereafter as any claim against the Company by any Warrantholder in relation to the Warrants or the Deed Poll shall not have been finally adjudicated, settled or discharged. The Company hereby acknowledges the right of every Warrantholder to the production of the Deed Poll. Warrantholders will be deemed to have notice of all the provisions contained in the Deed Poll, the Fiscal Agency Agreement and the Notes, which shall be binding on the Warrantholders in so far as they affect the rights or interests of the Warrantholders, and may obtain copies thereof upon request to any Warrant Agent.

This Warrant forms one of an issue of 20,000 Warrants to subscribe in aggregate ¥23,570,000,000 for Shares of the Common Stock of the Company (the "Warrants"), issued pursuant to resolutions of the Board of Directors of the Company passed on 26th October and 4th November, 1983 in conjunction with an issue by the Company of US$100,000,000 5 3/4 per cent. Notes due 1988 (the "Notes") pursuant to Article 341-8 *et seq.* of the Commercial Code of Japan.

IN WITNESS WHEREOF the Company has caused this Warrant to be signed in facsimile on its behalf by its President.

Mitsubishi Corporation

By *Yohei Uimura*

President

ISSUED in London as of 21st November, 1983.

Unsponsored ADRs are those which are issued by the depositary bank when the company is considered to be entering the market involuntarily; this can happen where the company's paper is already traded in the USA. Involuntary entry does not require the company to file with the SEC although the SEC may require additional information to be submitted, particularly relevant notices relating to the issue distributed to shareholders. Unsponsored ADRs are normally traded on the over-the-counter market. The mechanics of a depository agreement are:

(i)   The issuer selects a bank to serve as depositary

(ii) The agreement between the company and depositary is prepared and will include:

- The form of the ADR
- The number of shares to be represented by each ADR
- The deposit of shares by the company
- The transfer of ownership
- Surrender of ADRs and withdrawal of underlying securities
- Lost, stolen, damaged or destroyed ADRs
- Dividends, distribution in cash or further securities
- Voting rights and proxies
- Currency conversion
- Rights issues
- Removal or resignation, and substitution of depositary
- Publications and reports to ADR holders, stock exchanges and others
- Renumeration and expenses

(iii) Completion of SEC requirements and formalities relating to the issue.

(iv) Prepare and submit documentation to support a listing on a national stock exchange or on an over-the-counter secondary market trading operation.

(v)   Finalise the agreement with the depositary to act as transfer agent and to fulfil the obligations listed above.

506

CHAPTER TWENTY FOUR

Floating Rate Notes

Floating rate notes (FRNs) are normally negotiable bearer notes with coupon interest being set periodically according to a predetermined formula. US dollar FRNs were first introduced on the international eurobond market in 1970 and over the following 15 years have proved to be an extremely popular source of funds. Over this period almost US$180 billion has been raised in some 500 issues in the eurobond market accounting for approximately one quarter of the total amount raised in that market. The foreign bond market (yankees) for FRNs commenced in 1974 but its development has been much slower than the euro FRN, partly because of the more onerous regulatory requirements and lack of flexibility in launching a yankee compared with a euro, and partly on cost grounds. For significant periods it has proved cheaper to raise euro finance than funding with a yankee issue as the latter have been in direct competition with higher yielding short-term money market instruments and, therefore, to be attractive to investors, the yankee yields have been pitched marginally higher than equivalent euros.

The yankee bonds are issued in registered form. Denominations of US dollar FRNs were traditionally in amounts of US$1,000. However, partly as a result of inflation, they are often issued in larger denominations of US$5,000, US$10,000 or up to US$500,000.

Corporate borrowers who seek a long-term commitment of funds yet feel that interest rates are too high for a fixed interest coupon over the entire period of the borrowing, may consider raising a floating rate note issue. The advantage to them is that the interest rate payable on the borrowing will be brought into line with current market rates applicable usually to the three or, more commonly, the six month London Inter-Bank Offered Rate (LIBOR) for the currency concerned. From the investors' view-point a floating rate note issued by, say, a bank provides them with a higher rate of return than they could expect to receive from a deposit with that bank over the same period. In addition to sovereign credit borrowers, municipalities and other major corporate entities, many banks have resorted to raising debt in this manner frequently "subordinated" for capital purposes. In November 1984 the Bank of England issued guidelines on the holding by banks of other bank's or banking group's subordinated paper. Primary market-makers, being those financial institutions which can satisfy the Bank of England that they act as lead managers or underwriters for new issues of bank capital, may hold (as a concession) other bank's subordinated paper for up to three months (subject to the Bank of England's overview). After this time a full deduction will be made from the primary market-maker's own capital base. Such institutions may trade in issues which it has managed or underwritten within the scope of the three month concession.

Secondary market-makers, being those financial institutions which can demonstrate to the Bank of England that they undertake a committed and regular function as market-makers in bank capital issues, will agree a concession with the Bank of England which will vary from institution to institution according to the scale and nature of its business. The guidelines indicate that the concession will allow an amount of bank capital paper to be held up to 20% of an institution's adjusted capital base (as defined in the Bank of England's paper, the Measurement of Capital), to be held free of deduction. Calculation of concessions takes place at the close of business daily and is applied to all long positions held overnight.

For both primary and secondary market-makers all holdings of debt under a concession will be weighted, as appropriate, as quoted or as unquoted securities, in the risk asset ratio calculation. Any holdings of bank capital paper which fall outside these concessions will be deducted in full from the holder's capital base. The purpose behind this logical development was to prevent banking institutions from artificially creating capital debt.

The calculation of the interest rate on a floating rate note is invariably the responsibility of a nominated "agent" bank. The responsibilities of the agent bank include obtaining interest rate quotations from the specified reference banks immediately following the precise time of quotation on each interest determination date as set out in the terms and conditions of the floating rate note. There are usually four or five reference banks and the normal fixing is at 11 a.m. London time for LIBOR related quotations. Some notes have been written for interest to be determined at 3 p.m. London time, although this is relatively unusual. The Financial Times also quotes the arithmetic mean of five reference banks' quotations at 11.00 a.m. each day and there are some floating rate notes which use this formula for the basis of assessing the applicable rate for the next interest period. The borrower should consider choosing first-class banks which have a substantial interbank presence in euro-currencies in order to obtain the best possible (lowest) rate applicable. Banks which are not in the first tier may find that cost of funds to them is slightly higher and, therefore, the rate at which they are prepared to offer funds will also tend to be higher. Borrowers should always, therefore, consider retaining the services of prime banks in the field. The terms of the notes invariably make it possible for the reference banks to resign or be changed at the option of the borrower. Usually the trustee, if there is one, will have to agree to any changes made. However if any reference bank found itself consequently having to pay more for its funds there would be a good reason for the borrower to change that bank for another. Reference banks' services are normally provided free of charge and, although formal letters of agreement to quote rates to the agent bank are exchanged with the borrower, any reference bank has the right, if it chooses, to resign from this role. The interest rate is calculated by the agent bank on the basis of the arithmetic mean of the three or four reference banks required to submit their quotation. Frequently this gives rise to an "unusual" figure and it is, therefore, market practice for the rate determination on floating rate notes to be rounded upwards, if necessary, to the nearest $\frac{1}{16}$% above the arithmetic mean. Market practice for floating rate notes is to quote rates in steps of $\frac{1}{16}$% (0.0625%). The word arithmetic mean is normally applied in the documentation to avoid the ambiguity of the word "average" which can have several meanings. The interest determination day for floating rate notes in the euromarkets is normally two business days before the next interest period commences. The definition of the business day is all important to the documentation and essentially is one in which the banks in both London and the principal financial centre of the currency of the note, are open for business. For example, if notes are denominated in US dollars then the business day may be defined as one in which banks are open for business in both London and New York. The majority of floating rate notes specify a minimum interest rate payable. If the interest rate when determined by the agent bank (being the arithmetic mean of the quotations given by the reference banks, plus the set margin, if any, over LIBOR) comes to less than the minimum rate stated in the documentation, then the minimum rate will apply. From an investors' view-point this would have significant benefits if interest rates were to fall substantially. It is normal for borrowers, however, to negotiate for as low a minimum rate as they can obtain and some issues have been made with no minimum rate at all. A call feature is very important so far as the borrower is concerned in a floating rate note issue. This will give him the opportunity of redeeming the issue normally on an interest payment date but prior to the stated final maturity. Sinking funds and note purchase funds are unusual for a floating rate debt and it is normal for the issue to be repaid as a "bullet" in one sum at maturity. Should interest rates fall significantly during the life of the issue and the borrower wishes to substitute the floating rate note (which might well be subject to the minimum at that time) for a new (low coupon) fixed rate issue, then a call option would give him the opportunity of redeeming the FRN early.

Returning to the interest rate structure of floating rate note (FRN) issues, interest is payable in arrears on the interest payment date. Some borrowers, however, may be required to arrange for funds to be available one day before this although such is not normally the case where the issuer is a bank. The interest is payable in arrears and calculated on the number of days in each interest period on the basis of a 360 day year. The interest on euro-floating rate note issues is payable free from all withholding taxes. The majority of FRNs have their interest formula structured over a LIBOR rate. Issues have been known to be priced over the bid side, although this is rarer and many issues have been priced over the mean of the bid and offered rates. So that the agent bank is able to calculate the latter arrangement, reference banks naturally have to quote both the offered and the bid side of their rates at the agreed stated times.

From an investor's point of view, FRNs are usually considered to be less speculative as an investment than straight issues. At the same time it is recognised that, with a falling interest rate scenario, investors will not derive the same degree of capital gain on a floating rate issue than they would on a straight issue. The market price on top quality floating rate paper is likely to remain at or near par. The issuer will be acquiring floating rate liabilities which may prove to be more expensive to him than floating rate funds acquired on a committed bank line. The structured front-end fees inherent in all managed issues, coupled with the running costs of servicing the debt, must be calculated by the issuer in order that he may assess the actual cost of the money. Chapter 26 gives an example of such costing in the case of debt raised by a bank. It may prove necessary for the issuer to hedge his floating rate liabilities if his overall "book" in that currency reveals an unacceptable exposure to maturity mis-match. In Chapter 19 interest rate swaps are explained and this is one device that can be used to improve the structure of the issuer's balance sheet.

The most common currency in which FRNs are issued is undoubtedly the US dollar. Since 1980 FRNs have been issued in currencies other than the US dollar. FRN issues have been made in Swiss Francs, Sterling, Deutschemarks, SDRs, ECUs and even in Kuwaiti Dinars. While some of these issues are priced on the basis of LIBOR plus a margin, others are geared to the indigenous short-term deposit rates plus a margin, or to the average yield of outstanding medium-term government bonds plus a margin. Sterling debenture and bulldog issues have been priced over the domestic LIBOR rate and the yields calculated on the basis of a 365 day year, all euro notes being calculated on a 360 day year. ECU and most SDR issues are priced over LIBOR for ECUs and SDRs respectively.

Occasionally issues are priced over London Inter-Bank Bid (LIBID) rates.

An example of an FRN convertible into 10% capital bonds is shown overleaf:

During periods of relatively high interest rates when floating rate notes have been issued, some borrowers have included a conversion option to convert the debt from floating rate to fixed rate. This is an option which the investor may exercise and normally is geared to take effect from any interest payment date during the first five years of a

No.000000   U.S. $5,000

National Westminster Finance B.V.

(Incorporated in The Netherlands with limited liability)

U.S. $100,000,000 Guaranteed Floating Rate Capital Notes 1992

Convertible until 1986 into 10 per cent. Guaranteed Capital Bonds 1992

Unconditionally and irrevocably guaranteed on a subordinated basis as to payment of principal and interest by

National Westminster Bank Limited

(Incorporated in England with limited liability)

THIS IS TO CERTIFY that National Westminster Finance B.V. (the "Company") will pay to the bearer of this Note the principal sum of

U.S. $5,000 (Five Thousand United States Dollars)

on the Interest Payment Date (as defined in Condition (5) endorsed hereon) falling in October, 1992 (or on such earlier date as the said principal sum may become repayable in accordance with the Terms and Conditions endorsed hereon) together with interest on the said principal sum at rates determined in accordance with the provisions of Condition 3 endorsed hereon from 23rd October, 1980, payable in arrears on each Interest Payment Date and, should the bearer hereof elect to convert this Note into a Bond pursuant to Condition 5 endorsed hereon, on the Conversion Date (as described in the said Condition 5), and together with such additional amounts (if any) as may be payable under Condition 7 endorsed hereon, subject to and in accordance with the said Terms and Conditions.

This Note forms one of a series of 20,000 Notes of U.S. $5,000 each, in the aggregate principal amount of U.S. $100,000,000, issued pursuant to resolutions of the Managing Directors of the Company passed on 26th September, 1980 and 7th October, 1980 and constituted by a Trust Deed dated 23rd October, 1980 made between the Company, National Westminster Bank Limited and The Law Debenture Corporation, Limited as trustee and is subject to and has the benefit of such Trust Deed.

This Note is convertible at the option of the bearer hereof on 30th April and 31st October in each of the years 1981 to 1986 (inclusive) into an equal principal amount of 10 per cent. Guaranteed Capital Bonds 1992 of the Company in accordance with Condition 5 endorsed hereon.

IN WITNESS whereof the Company has caused this Note and the Coupons appertaining hereto to be signed in facsimile on its behalf by one of its Managing Directors.

Managing Director

Issued in London as of 23rd October, 1980.

                                   FRN convertible into 10% capital bonds

life of the issue. Otherwise it would not prove to be of much attraction to the investor. The issuer would be likely to include such a feature if the fixed interest rate was pitched at an acceptable level for his own long-term fixed funding and, at the same time, he was advised the feature would be helpful to launching the issue in relatively tight market conditions and, therefore, couched in terms attractive to the investor. Whilst it is normal for FRN issues with a conversion to fixed interest feature also to have a call feature, the call feature would only apply to the FRN and not to any subsequent fixed interest bonds which may be issued at the investor's option. This would enable the issuer to redeem any part of the outstanding floating rate issue early and yet protect any investors who had exercised their option and taken up the fixed interest paper.

Another feature which has been introduced is the "drop-lock" issue. This is similar to the conversion option from floating to fixed rates as described above, except that at any interest determination date should the coupon, as calculated for the FRN purposes, be less than a specified fixed rate in the issue, then the fixed rate will automatically lock and the entire issue would become a fixed rate issue at the specified rate for the rest of its life, irrespective of where market rates move thereafter.

Another variation of the "drop-lock" locking procedure was based on the level of medium-term US treasury bond rates. If this rate reached or fell below the stated fixed interest rate on the security on two consecutive rate determination dates, then the whole issue would automatically lock in at the fixed interest rate for the remainder of its life. Drop-locks do not need to have minimum rates as the rate for automatic conversion to a fixed interest security serves the same purpose and is generally found to be pitched at a much higher rate than the usual minimum rates found in the more conventional FRN issues. Very special features like "drop-locks" are sometimes referred to as issues with "bells and whistles" attached. This market jargon sometimes aptly describes the more unusual, imaginative and generally innovatory issues that are often brought to market when the conditions for new straight-forward new issues are difficult. A "plain vanilla" issue is a description of a straight-forward issue without any special features. Generally investors prefer the vanilla flavour issues to those with "bells and whistles" but on occasions a new idea, such as the "drop-lock", can enable an issue to be launched in market conditions which would otherwise make it difficult or impossible for a issue to take place on the terms achieved without the special feature. The secondary market is noticeably weak so far as issues with special features are concerned; the same applies where the issuer is a lesser known "credit" or situated in a country which subsequently experiences economic or political difficulties. The price for such securities can be calculated on a yield basis and can appear to be at or near par like any other FRN for which there is a healthy secondary market. However, if an investor was to offer paper which might have acquired some greater element of credit risk than was apparent at the time of issue, the price would almost certainly be marked down before buyers could be found.

Investors taking any FRN paper into their portfolio at or near par price which is not of the highest quality, should be prepared to surrender a discount to any buyer of the securities at a later date should they wish to dispose of them prior to maturity. Indeed, some lower quality credits may well be treated as private placements, bearing in mind the virtual absence of a secondary market for lower quality paper.

Some FRN issues have been made on a "tap" or "multiple tranche" basis. The initial tranche will be placed like any other new issue and the amount left on tap can be taken up as and when favourable market conditions occur. There is generally a stated tap period during which time the issuer has the option to obtain up to the stated maximum amount of the issue. This technique saves the borrower from making, say, two separate issues with all the documentation and negotiation that this normally entails. It also enables the borrower to take up the funds piecemeal and perhaps facilitate the employment of proceeds. The method adopted by the lead manager in approaching the market to place the tap tranches will make a difference to the documentation that needs to be produced. For example, immediately any invitation telexes are sent out to a selling or underwriting group of banks, they will require that the issuer also produces a prospectus or, in its absence, an extel card, and a lot of the documentation which would be needed for a new issue will be required for the tap approached in such a manner.

At the time of publication FRNs have been issued in amounts ranging from US$10 million to nearly US$2 billion and the range of maturities has been from three years to infinity. No doubt inflation will change these statistics however. The final maturities in order of popularity are seven years, five years, 10 years, 12 years and 20 years for issues made up to 1985. Another form of tap issue was developed in 1981 when FRNs were issued with detachable or separate warrants. Each FRN is accompanied by one or more warrants giving the right to the investor to subscribe to more of the issuer's debt within a given period of time. The warrant is, therefore, similar in effect to a stock option. The warrants have a life of their own which is always shorter than the life of the relevant FRN, and is usually referred to as the "warrant exercise period". The FRN warrant exercise period does not vary so widely as the exercise period for straight warrant issues, the range for FRN issues made between 1981 – 1984 being from six months to 16 months. The longer the exercise period the better, so far as the investor is concerned, as there is a greater chance that it can be exercised profitably. Most FRN warrants convey the option for investors to purchase at par within the option period a fixed interest bond or debenture at a specified interest rate.

A "call option" has featured in very nearly all FRN issues. This gives the issuer the right to redeem the note prior to maturity at a stated time from issue. The non-call periods vary according to the normal maturity of the issue but can range from "immediate call" to "12 years to first call". However, three or four year non-call periods are the most common.

A "put option" has featured in about 14% of all FRN issues. This gives the investor the option to obtain repayment at par or at the issue price prior to the normal maturity of the issue. Although the range of periods over which the option may not be exercised is similar to that of call options, described above, the most common non-put periods have been ten years or more and seven years respectively.

Two types of perpetual FRN have been issued. The first has an investor's option to redeem, and the second only the issuer's call option for the otherwise irredeemable or undated notes. Neither have a final maturity. The Bank of England's criteria for qualifying

515

bank capital for issuers of perpetual subordinated debt and for other subordinated debt is discussed in Chapter 28.

The first SDR denominated FRN was launched in 1981 after the SDR basket was reduced from the original 16 currencies to five currencies. The pricing formula for reference banks to quote to the agent bank is related to the interbank offered rates for SDRs.

An example of a eurodollar FRN is shown opposite:

Quasi-FRNs
Some straight debt issues with put options, also referred to as Retractables, sometimes include an option for the issuer to adjust the coupon. Such issues enable the investor at certain stipulated dates during the life of the issue to redeem his holdings at par. The issuer may also exercise a call option to redeem at par, or continue to pay interest at the existing rate, or pay interest at a new determined fixed rate to the next option date, or pay interest on an FRN basis or a rate which can only be determined shortly before the new interest period commences. The obvious flexibility of such an instrument also has its disadvantages. The borrower will not be sure of the amount of capital outstanding throughout the issue nor be sure of its cost, and there may be administration and accounting disadvantages as well. A real "bells and whistles" issue is an adjustable coupon retractable eurobond with debt warrants attached!

A recent (1984) innovation is a straight eurobond for the first seven years of a 12 year bullet maturity and an FRN for the last five years – the reverse of the drop lock.

No. 000000

U.S.$5,000

National Westminster Finance B.V.

(Incorporated in The Netherlands with limited liability)

U.S. $175,000,000 Guaranteed Floating Rate Capital Notes 1991

Unconditionally and irrevocably guaranteed on a subordinated basis as to payment of principal and interest by

National Westminster Bank Limited

(Incorporated in England with limited liability)

THIS IS TO CERTIFY that National Westminster Finance B.V. (the "Company") will pay to the bearer of this Note the principal sum of

U.S. $5,000 (Five Thousand United States Dollars)

on the Interest Payment Date (as defined in Condition 3(b) endorsed hereon) falling in July, 1991 (or on such earlier date as the said principal sum may become repayable in accordance with the Terms and Conditions endorsed hereon) together with interest on the said principal sum at rates determined in accordance with the provisions of Condition 3 endorsed hereon from 15th July, 1981 payable in arrears on each Interest Payment Date, and together with such additional amounts (if any) as may be payable under Condition 6 endorsed hereon, subject to and in accordance with the said Terms and Conditions.

This Note forms one of a series of 35,000 Notes of U.S. $5,000 each, in the aggregate principal amount of U.S. $175,000,000, issued pursuant to resolutions of the Managing Directors of the Company passed on 19th and 26th June, 1981 and constituted by a Trust Deed dated 15th July, 1981 made between the Company, National Westminster Bank Limited and The Law Debenture Corporation, Limited as trustee and is subject to and has the benefit of such Trust Deed.

IN WITNESS whereof the Company has caused this Note and the Coupons appertaining hereto to be signed in facsimile on its behalf by one of its Managing Directors.

Managing Director

Issued in London as of 15th July, 1981.

BRADBURY, WILKINSON & C? L? NEW MALDEN, SURREY, ENGLAND.

Eurodollar FRN

CHAPTER TWENTY FIVE

Eurobond Operations

This Chapter describes certain operations in the Eurobond secondary market, which is the market for issues after the initial distribution has ended and allotments have been made by the lead manager.

Markets exist in the principal financial centres, with London being the most important. Whilst banks are the predominant institutions in the market, participants also include investment houses. Dealing takes place primarily on a principal to principal basis, generally without the intermediary of brokers. Whilst very large proportions of the securities traded are listed on a stock exchange, eurobonds are rarely dealt over the exchange, but in an over-the-counter (OTC) market. Some of the essential features of secondary market transactions are as follows:

- Settlement takes place on the seventh calendar day after the dealing day. N.B. the seven days include week-ends and national holidays.

- Prices are quoted as a percent of par.

- Accrued interest is calculated on the basis of the value day and assumes a year of 360 days, and this will be added to the purchase price quoted, for the period since the last interest payment date.
  Example:
  On 1st October 10 bonds nominal value US$5,000 are sold at a price of 98.
  The issue has a fixed interest coupon of 10% payable annually on 1st April.

Value date is 8th October

Principal ($50,000) × Price (98) = $49,000

ADD

Accrued interest for 187 days

$$\$50,000 \times \frac{10}{100} \times \frac{187}{360} \quad = \quad \$2,597.22$$

Amount paid to seller $\quad = \quad \underline{\$51,597.22}$

- Principally an "over-the-counter" market – purchases and sales of eurobonds not being exercised over a stock exchange.

- There are two clearing houses, Euro-clear and Cedel which have depositories in most financial centres where bonds are held and delivery may be made. Most settlement is through these clearing houses where buyer *and* seller have an account – cash balances must be retained with the clearing house or associated bank.

Secondary Market Settlement and Delivery Periods from Dealing Date

Market	*Period*
Eurodollar bonds	7 calendar days or longer as may be agreed
Yankee	5 working days in New York
Deutschemark foreign and euro	7 calendar days or longer as may be agreed
Euro Guilder notes	7 calendar days or as agreed
Samurai	As agreed
Euro sterling	7 calendar days
Swiss Franc	1 or 2 days or later for foreign investors
Guilder foreign bonds	1 or 2 days or later for foreign investors
Bulldog	1 day

NOTE – Primary market eurobond settlement is the longer of seven calendar days or the closing date of the issue normally without the bonds being delivered on the same day. Secondary market delivery is usually arranged to coincide with payment and the clearing house will arrange for the instructions from buyer and seller to be matched and effect the transfer. Most transactions in the euro-capital markets are over-the-counter (not made through a stock exchange) even although the securities are usually listed.

Cedel

Cedel is one of the two major independent organisations created to effect the clearing, physical exchange, and settlement of securities, also storage of bearer securities and precious metals. In 1970 Cedel (Centrale de Livraison de Valeurs Mobiliers) SA, was established in Luxembourg and is always referred to as Cedel. There are 93 shareholders situated in 16 different countries and over 1,150 participants. Cedel and Euro-clear together hold some 60% of all bond clearing.

Its stated aims are "to assist all professional organisations in the international securities market". The system offers the following advantages:

- Elimination of physical deliveries of securities

- Centralised depository system

- Settlement of transactions effected

- Guarantee of safety and observance of banking secrecy

- Solutions to problems related to safe custody of securities and the settlement of transactions

Cedel operates through a network of agents in different countries and participants can access the system merely by giving brief instructions to Cedel using their standard form or telex. Following a new issue when Cedel is used as the depository, the securities are physically deposited with one bank, usually the paying agent to the issue.

Deposits of securities can be made on a fungible or non-fungible account and the certificate numbers of all securities are recorded. A fungible account is one in which the certificate numbers are not available to the participant and a non-fungible account is one where the certificate numbers are available to the participant. In addition to the securities account, a participant will require a cash account with Cedel for settlement purposes. The credit balances of the participant's cash accounts are kept with first-class banks and the interest earned thereon is distributed to the participants on a monthly basis.

Apart from receipts and deliveries of securities and the safe custody thereof, Cedel provides coupon collection, bond drawing and redemption services. On settlement day all statements and advices are mailed to the participant and they will also receive daily money statements showing the day's movements. Annual inventory statements of all securities deposited are sent to the participant showing the market price, nominal value of each security and the total value of the portfolio in US dollars. Indeed, this statement is available on a monthly, quarterly or semi-annual basis if required. Cedel is a depository which can handle closing operations and distribution of allotments in the primary market and assist the lead manager to centralise payments.

Cedel operates a securities lending facility whereby investors who have their securities deposited with them may earn additional interest on those securities which Cedel are able to match with a borrower's requirement. Cedel does not disclose the identification of the borrower and lender to each other except where the borrower has defaulted. In the event of default by the borrower there exists an underlying guarantee issued by a syndicate of banks lead-managed by Citibank N.A. Loans may be made of either straight or convertible bonds in the Cedel system for a fixed period not in excess of six months. The lenders may specify other participants to whom they do not wish loans to be made and they may also be selective as to the bonds that are available for lending. Confirmations are despatched to both borrower and lender by Cedel. Borrowers are required to put up cash or other bonds acceptable to the guarantor as collateral for any borrowing from the system. Cash collateral will receive interest at the same rate as the cash balances with Cedel, although it is more usual for borrowers to use as collateral securities that they, themselves, already have in the system. Straight bonds lodged as collateral must retain a market value of 110% of the amount of the value of the bonds borrowed and convertible bonds lodged as collateral 125% of the amount of the bonds borrowed. The rules and regulations laid down by Cedel are in accordance with the Law of the Grand Duchy of Luxembourg, and the City of Luxembourg is the non-exclusive place of jurisdiction in the event of any legal action taken.

Euro-clear

The Euro-clear system provides buyers and sellers of internationally traded securities with a method of settling their transactions as well as a variety of custody services. Created in 1968 by Morgan Guaranty Trust Company of New York, which operates the system from its Euro-clear operations centre in Brussels, it was acquired by Euro-clear Clearance System PLC in 1972. The system is owned by 120 banks, brokers and investment institutions and operated under contract by Morgan Guaranty Trust Company. There are over 1,300 participants, and Euro-clear and Cedel between them have accepted some 13,000 issues into their systems. The principal functions of the system include:

- automated settling of securities transactions

- safe custody service for internationally traded securities

- service for the closing and initial distribution of new issues

- securities borrowing and lending service

Coupled with the above functions, Morgan Guaranty, Brussels, provides, on behalf of participants, the following facilities:

- securities clearance accounts

- cash accounts in various currencies required for settlement

- a comprehensive reporting and statement service, and facilities to handle the receipts and deliveries of securities into and from the Euro-clear system

The types of securities accepted into the system include bonds, notes and debentures in bearer or registered form, straight, floating, zero and convertible, and denominated in some 24 different currencies including composite units. Tranche certificates of deposit, depository receipts, warrants and equity shares in fungible form are also accepted.

Participants wishing to lend or borrow securities may do so in two ways. They may be automatic borrowers or lenders, or opportunity borrowers or lenders. Automatic borrowers authorise Morgan Guaranty, Brussels, to identify their needs as opposed to the opportunity borrowers who identify their own needs and ask Euro-clear to fulfil their requests. Automatic lenders agree to make available for lending all or specified securities held in their security clearance accounts, whereas the opportunity lenders may be asked, from time to time, when the securities available from automatic lenders are not sufficient to fill specific borrowing needs. Lenders of securities may expect to receive 3% per annum on the market value of the securities plus accrued interest at the time of lending. Borrowers will pay on the same basis between 4% and $4\frac{3}{4}$% depending on the market value of outstanding borrowings. Additional services provided by the Euro-clear system includes paying agency (principal or sub-paying agent), fiscal agency and trustee services. A comprehensive range of advices, statements and confirmations are available often on a daily basis whenever there is activity over the participant's account or when requested.

In order to streamline new issue procedures new guidelines were introduced in 1985 for delivery of global notes to be made to a "common depositary" for the transfer of payment to the issuer of the holding of the global security(s) in common for both Euro-clear and Cedel systems. There are four named banks in the UK and two on the Continent which are the only banks which may be used for this purpose. The common depositary is only responsible for taking the temporary global security, signing a receipt, making payment for the amount due to the issuer, and confirming the payment made – it has no other role or responsibility.

Listing Considerations

Consideration should be given by a prospective issuer as to whether the debt should be listed or not and if so on which stock exchange. The principal advantage of listing from the issuer's view-point is that it gives the issue a degree of prestige quality and from the investor's point of view enables him to obtain a published market quotation. Listed eurobonds are not normally traded on the stock exchanges to any great extent, but are traded over the telephone in the secondary market which is comprised of stockbrokers, investment houses and banks. It follows that the listing procedures and regulations of the chosen stock exchange must be observed. On The Stock Exchange, London, applications for listing may only be made through a member firm of stockbrokers. This broker will handle all the documents and deal with the Stock Exchange as instructed by the lead manager of the issue. It is common practice to have more than one broker and then the issuer must nominate the broker which will handle the transaction and documentation so far as the Stock Exchange is concerned.

On the 1st January 1985 new listing regulations of The Stock Exchange were brought into effect and are contained in the up-dated "Yellow Book". The administrative framework was established under statutory instrument in compliance with an EC directive, and places duties on The Stock Exchange as the competent authority to treat all cases alike.

Listing prerequisites include inter alia:

- Pre-submission of documents for approval by The Stock Exchange – in particular 4 copies of the listing particulars circular incorporating the previous five years's balance sheets.

- A completed personal questionnaire from all directors.

- Two copies of relevant board resolutions relating to the issue.

- Two copies of the trust deed or fiscal agency agreement.

- The bond or note. If the definitive bonds or notes will not be ready by closing date, a global bond or script certificate will be required. The normal procedure is for a global bond to be held by the common depository being one of five banks acting as fiscal agent pending the completion of the closing. The global notes are then lodged with either Cedel or Euro-clear pending exchange for definitive paper in due course.

- An Extel card containing full terms and conditions of the issue. Details of the borrower and guarantor will also be required on an Extel card, although this information is frequently already held by Extel Statistical Services Limited and a duplication is not necessary.

- The formal notice which used to be called the "box advert", illustrated overleaf, must appear in at least one leading daily newspaper.

- It is normal for a draft timetable of the issue to be submitted with the above documentation.

- The application form for admission of securities to listing is re-produced below. This will need to be accompanied by payment of the listing fees, a certified copy of a board resolution of the borrower giving authority to the issue, and a declaration by each director of the borrower and guarantor (this is only required on the first occasion the company issues or guarantees a loan stock listed on The Stock Exchange, London).

- Powers of Attorney of each of the directors.

- The Stock Exchange is also interested in the number of bonds to be subscribed through the broker, stock exchange members and the selling group. Before any dealing commences on the Stock Exchange a signed copy of the listing particulars must be lodged with the Exchange.

526

In due course, after listing has been granted, the following definitive documentation is required by The Stock Exchange, London.

- At least four certified copies of the Extel cards

- A newspaper containing the formal notice

- A specimen copy of the definitive bond

- A certified copy of the subscription agreement

- An engrossment of the trust deed or fiscal agency agreement

The Stock Exchange requires that the definitive bond or note must contain the terms and conditions of the issue, the authority under which the issuer is constituted and the authority under which the bond or note is issued; dates of interest payment must appear with a straight issue; and authenticating signature(s) (which may be in facsimile). So far as the terms and conditions are concerned, there must, at all times, be a paying agent in London or such other place as The Stock Exchange may agree. All notices which relate to the issue must be published in at least one leading daily London newspaper and, finally, prescription is normally from a minimum period of twelve years in respect of the principal sum and twelve years in respect of the interest. Prescription is the period of time which may elapse from the respective due dates for payment after which the holders will no longer be entitled to repayment should a claim subsequently be made.

National Westminster Finance B.V.

(Incorporated in The Netherlands with limited liability)

U.S. $150,000,000

11¾ per cent. Guaranteed Capital Bonds 1992

Guaranteed on a subordinated basis as to payment of principal and interest by

National Westminster Bank PLC

(Incorporated in England with limited liability)

The issue price of the Bonds is 100 per cent. of their principal amount.

The following have agreed to subscribe or procure subscribers for the Bonds:

County Bank
Limited

Credit Suisse First Boston
Limited

Morgan Stanley International

Orion Royal Bank
Limited

Arab Banking Corporation (ABC)

Bank of Tokyo International
Limited

Banque Nationale de Paris

Banque Paribas

Crédit Lyonnais

Deutsche Bank Aktiengesellschaft

Girozentrale und Bank der österreichischen Sparkassen
Aktiengesellschaft

Handelsbank N.W. (Overseas) Ltd.

Morgan Guaranty Ltd

Salomon Brothers International

Swiss Bank Corporation International
Limited

Union Bank of Switzerland (Securities)
Limited

S.G. Warburg & Co. Ltd.

Westdeutsche Landesbank Girozentrale

The Bonds have been admitted to the Official List by the Council of The Stock Exchange subject only to the issue of the Bonds.

Interest is paid annually in arrears on 1st November, the first payment being made on 1st November, 1983.

Particulars of National Westminster Finance B.V. and the Bonds are available from Extel Statistical Services Limited, and may be obtained during usual business hours up to and including 3rd November, 1982 from:-

County Bank Limited,
11 Old Broad Street,
London EC2N 1BB.

Strauss, Turnbull & Co.,
3 Moorgate Place,
London EC2R 6HR.

Cazenove & Co.,
12 Tokenhouse Yard,
London EC2R 7AN.

20th October, 1982

Formal notice of bond issue

APPLICATION FOR ADMISSION OF SECURITIES TO LISTING

.... 19....

To: The Secretary
Quotations Department,
The Stock Exchange

We .... (Public Limited Company) hereby apply for the undermentioned securities to be admitted to the Official List of The Stock Exchange subject to the requirements from time to time of the Council of The Stock Exchange, and published in "Admission of Securities to Listing".

SHARE CAPITAL

Authorised	Issued (and paid up) inclusive of present issue
....................in	....
....................in	....
....................in	....
....................in	....
£	£

Amounts and descriptions of securities for which application is now made (include distinctive numbers if any)

....

....

....

The securities for which application is now made
(a) are/are not identical in all respects and

....

....

(b) are/are not identical in all respects with an existing class of security

....

....

(c) either have been in the previous six months, or will be the subject of an application for listing in another member state of the European Economic Community.
stating when ....
and on what stock exchange(s) ....
(Delete as appropriate)

We declare that
(1) all the conditions listed in Chapter 2 of Section 1 of "Admission of Securities to Listing", insofar as applicable and required to be fulfilled prior to application, have been fulfilled in relation to the company and the securities for the admission of which application is now made, and
(2) all information required to be included in the listing particulars has been included therein, or, if the final version has not yet been submitted (or approved), will be included therein before it is so submitted.

Details of renounceable document (where applicable):
(a) Type of document ....(which must comply with Chapter 3 of Section 9 of Admission of Securities to Listing).
(b) Proposed date of issue ....
(c) Last day for splitting:
(i) nil paid ....
(ii) partly paid ....
(iii) fully paid ....

(d) Last day for renunciation ....

Definitive certificates (in respect of the class of security/securities for which listing is sought) have already been issued for ....
stock/shares and will be ready on .... for ....
stock/shares.

We undertake to lodge with you the required declaration in due course.

Signed ....
Director or Secretary
or other duly authorised officer
for and on behalf of

....
public limited company.

CHAPTER TWENTY SIX

Yankee Bonds

**Reporting and Registration Requirements in
the United States, and Applicable Securities Law**

Non-US resident issuers contemplating a public financing in the United States must be aware of the Federal Securities Laws and mandatory Registration and Reporting procedures before a debt is offered to the public. The exception for certain types of securities and certain types of security transactions are covered elsewhere in the book under Private Placements, Certificates of Deposit and Commercial Paper.

The SEC, The Securities and Exchange Commission, "Guide 61" is issued for the purpose of assisting banks and bank holding companies in the preparation and filing of their registration statements for a new issue. The Guide specifies certain items which the SEC normally expects to be disclosed. The following information is normally required over the issuer's and guarantor's (where applicable) last five financial years:

- Balance sheet

- Loan portfolio sub-divided into geographical areas

- Category of borrower

- Fixed rate and floating rate loans, and a maturity analysis

- Non-performing loans including allowances, adjustments to reserves and right-offs

- Investment portfolio details categorised as to size, quality and structure

- Return on equity and assets

- Details of average deposits sub-divided into domestic and international

- Interest rates and interest differentials in respect of average interest earning assets and average interest bearing obligations, average yields, average cost of funds and changes in interest income and interest payments for the last two financial years.

- Details of all international business

It is recognised that the SEC requirements for disclosure by non-US banks and bank holding companies present considerable difficulties where management information is not readily available and where accounting practices materially differ from American domestic banks' practice. Accordingly, SEC staff are available for discussion with borrowers who are interested in raising capital on the US domestic market, where the impracticability or impossibility of full compliance in certain areas can be discussed.

At the centre of the Federal regulations is the 1933 Securities Act which has two basic objectives, namely, to provide investors with financial and other information concerning securities offered to the US public and to prohibit misrepresentation, deceit and other fraudulent acts and practices in the sale of securities generally. Investors may obtain data given in a registration statement which includes a prospectus that has to be filed with the SEC. Securities intended to be offered to the US public may not be sold until the SEC has declared that the registration statement is "effective". The SEC does not make any judgments on the merits of any offering, it merely ensures that full and fair disclosure is made. The Securities Act 1933 contains provisions for investors who suffer loss due to violations of registration disclosures, or other requirements of the Act, to benefit from civil remedies against the participants in the offering.

The Securities Act contains quite stringent disclosure requirements which are designed to enable the public to make informed decisions about investing in securities. This leads to considerable differences in the procedures and strategy between a yankee or other US domestic issue and a eurobond.

534

The yankee issue will be exposed in the market from the time the registration statement is filed with the SEC. During the next three to eight weeks which may elapse before final comments are received from the SEC, the underwriters will seek to establish the level of investor interest in the issue. In due course the coupon rate and issue price are agreed and then the underwriting contract is signed and the notes/bonds issued. The much shorter procedures in the euromarket 10–12 days between launch and signing of the subscription agreement, means that the borrower in a yankee issue is exposed to adverse changes in market conditions over a much longer period. In the US domestic market the underwriters may not offer paper to investors at a discount, which includes any part of their underwriting or selling commissions, as is the practice in the euromarkets. This means that the pricing of a yankee issue is more critical to its success than a euro-issue pricing as there is no room for manoeuvre thereafter. Furthermore, in the yankee and US domestic market, underwriters do not retain any of the stocks as investments for themselves whereas in the euromarkets this is a common practice and gives greater depth to the secondary market in the euro-securities.

For SEC purposes foreign issuers are defined as:

i)   foreign government issuers

ii) foreign private issuers, and

iii) Canadian private issuers who qualify as foreign private issuers.

The regulations and formalities relating to iii) above are generally treated as US domestic issues. Foreign government issuers are only required to disclose information as specified in Schedule 13 of the Securities Act. The details which follow relate solely to the requirements for foreign private issuers which fulfil the following criteria: less than half the outstanding equity (with voting rights) is registered in the names of US residents; less than half the issuer's assets are located in the USA; the issuer's business is not principally administered in the USA and not more than half the directors or executive officers are US citizens or residents.

The lead manager of a yankee bond appointed by the issuer is the representative of the syndicate of underwriters. He will advise the issuer and assist in the preparation of documents but he has an additional role and responsibility to investigate the issuer's affairs on behalf of the underwriters. In this regard they are expected to exercise "due diligence" in order to ensure that the registration statement does not contain any mis-statements or omissions. Under the Securities Act the lead manager and all underwriters who are potentially liable for any untrue statement of a material fact, or omission of such, may avoid such liability if it may be shown that reasonably diligent investigation (known as due diligence) had taken place. The issuer and every director thereof required to sign the registration certificate cannot avoid such liability. The due diligence investigation is normally conducted in a spirit of intensive enquiry, as court decisions have set a high standard for what is deemed to be "a reasonable investigation" and what constitutes "reasonable grounds for belief". There is no set checklist although each lead manager and their lawyers will have a very clear idea of areas to be examined and discussed. Pending litigation (if any), key board resolutions, details of significant contracts, and corroboration of statements made in the registration statement by the issuer, are certain to be discussed, reviewed and investigated in a due diligence examination.

The preparation period required before filing the registration statement will naturally vary from issuer to issuer, but it will normally take at least 30 to 60 days provided the financial information required can be prepared and audited in a manner satisfactory to the SEC within such a period. For new registrants the preparation of financial data in a completely new format may take many months to achieve.

A filing fee of $\frac{1}{50}$ of 1% of the issue offering price of the securities is payable to the SEC on filing the registration statement. The SEC's comments, and questions raised, must be answered either in writing and/or orally by the issuer in conjunction with the lead manager and their legal advisors. If any changes are required to be made to the registration statement they are normally filed as an amendment at the time the SEC declares it to be "effective". The issuer and lead manager decide (on the basis of market conditions) when they wish to agree on the pricing and the SEC is asked to declare the registration

536

statement effective from that day or the following day. Most yankee issuers prefer a "bought-deal" whereby the underwriters as principals buy the whole issue and thereby take the risk of not being able to resell the stock to investors. The terms of the underwriting agreement are negotiated between the issuer and lead manager acting for the underwriters before filing the registration statements and the agreement is normally executed immediately the issue is priced. In consideration of the underwriters purchasing the issue, the issuer will be expected to indemnify the underwriters against false or misleading statements or omissions in the registration statement, and will probably be required to provide a number of covenants and warranties, the inclusion of which in the agreement will depend on the issuer and the lead manager's negotiations. The underwriting agreement will specify the close date of the issue which is normally 8–14 days after the agreement is signed. At close, before the money is paid to the issuer, various legal opinions are required together with the issuer's certificate of no material adverse change in his circumstances. An auditor's letter of comfort for any unaudited financial information appearing in the registration statement is normally sought at this time as well. If the definitive securities (registered certificates) are not available to the underwriters at close, a temporary note issue must be available for distribution. This is a full note issue and each temporary note is exchangeable for a definitive engraved note when ready for delivery – temporary global note arrangements are not adopted in the US domestic or yankee capital markets.

Illustrations of a temporary note and a registered certificate are shown overleaf:

Private foreign issuers who tap the US domestic market for the first time will normally be required to complete the SEC registration statement on Form F.1; for subsequent issuers it may be possible to use shorter forms F.2 or F.3. The Form F.1 consists of 12 items of disclosure, the most important of which are items 3 and 11, the latter being subject to the completion of another 13 item document, Form 20.F. Both item 3 and 11 of Form F.1 refer to the more detailed financial statements and nature of the issuer's business and management.

538

Temporary Note

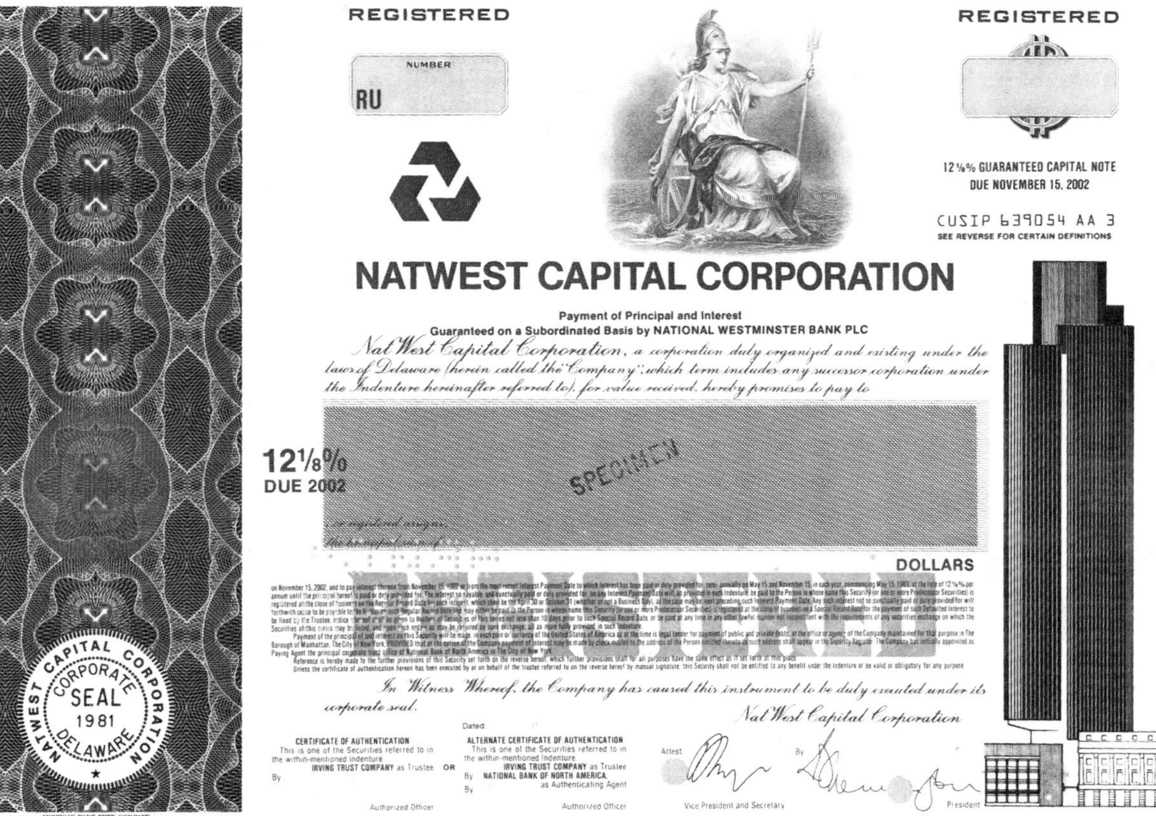

Registered Certificate

Yankee bond issues are subject to the Trust Indenture Act 1939. The trustee must be a US corporation being a commercial bank or trust company acting for the benefit of the investors. The Trust Indenture (trust deed) constitutes the terms and conditions of the issue and provisions relating to the trustee's independence and his duties, and is filed with the SEC with the registration statement so that it may be "qualified" as to the provisions of the Trust Indenture Act. The trust indenture, as with all trust deeds, is a lengthy document and it needs to be completed before the pricing of a yankee issue. In a euro-issue the trust deed must be executed by the closing of the issue and need only be in draft form at the time of the signing the subscription agreement. Rating of a yankee bond is not a legal requirement although it is certainly advisable for marketing reasons.

In addition to Federal legislation, several states in the USA have their own securities laws known as "Blue Sky" Laws. These laws may extend to prohibiting the sale of securities to investors resident in that state if the state regulators consider the offering "unfair" to investors. The underwriters need to ensure that their sales are legal and, therefore, additional information and/or certificates from the issuer may be sought.

Until 1982 foreign private issuers were unable to offer securities unless the registration statement contained financial statements not more than six months old. This requirement severely limited during the year the periods in which the yankee market could be approached if the borrower did not normally produce quarterly figures. The SEC Rule 415 permits the issuer to register the offering of securities "on the shelf", with a view to a later sale to take advantage of more propitious market conditions. Shelf registration is only available to foreign private issuers who are in a position to use Form F.3 for the registration statement. There is no doubt that the shelf registration route provides a much more flexible approach to the market and leads to marginally simpler documentation; however, it all depends upon the issuer's ability to comply with the conditions for registrants on Form F.3. These are:

    i)   to have filed all required reports to the SEC for the previous three years,

ii) to be eligible to file reports on Form 20.F,

iii) not to have failed to pay any dividend or materially default on loans or long-term leases, and

iv) to be world class issuers, or have debt rated in one of the four highest rating categories by a major rating organisation.

The listing of a yankee bond on a securities exchange such as the New York Stock Exchange or the American Stock Exchange is not mandatory, although for marketing reasons it may be considered advisable. There is, however, a large over-the-counter market for unlisted securities, and the National Association of Securities Dealers have an automated quotation system (NASDAQ) for displaying their prices so a "listing" on this may be obtained. The listing requirements of, say, the New York Stock Exchange are generally more stringent than those of the NASDAQ.

Maintenance of the required data flow to comply with the Securities Exchange Act 1934 requires the issuer to submit to periodic reporting under Section 15(d) of the Act. Yankee issuers must file annual reports on Form 20-F with the SEC, who also require other information published by the issuer, for its shareholders, to be submitted to them on Form 6-K.

Rating Agencies
In the United States there are three principal rating agencies, Standard & Poors Corporation, Moody's Investors Service Inc., and Fitch Investors Service, Inc. They provide guides to investors to enable them to determine the investment risk attaching to specifically rated securities. The rating represents the rating agencies' assessment of the issuer's creditworthiness in respect of a specific debt obligation and their assessment takes into consideration guarantors, insurers and lessees. The rating also considers special features of each issue rated, and where the rated debt ranks in relation to other debt issued by the same borrower. The economic and political scenario of the issuer's country, the currency of the obligation and the financial strength of the issuer, are also taken into account. The rating agen-

541

cies are always aware that every rating given must be credible to the investing public as well as the regulatory authorities (in particular the SEC). The SEC and other regulatory bodies, various government agencies in the US and elsewhere, trusts and corporations use the ratings as a yardstick for regulatory purposes, capital guidelines and investment policies. The US domestic investors in US domestic and yankee bond markets expect to find the securities offered rated, and are generally unused to evaluating foreign credit risks. Since 1974 only a couple of foreign institutions have issued unrated yankee paper and there is little doubt that an appropriate rating is a pre-requisite for successful entry to this market for marketing reasons, although it is not a legal requirement to do so. The US rating agencies usually rate all the SEC registered debt issued in the US and it is the normal procedure for a potential issuer to seek a preliminary rating before registration with the SEC. Ratings can be applied to existing or new eurobond issues, to commercial paper issues and to tranche CDs. The rating of a bond issue pending SEC registration will not be published until registration is made but having been made the rating will continue, subject to any necessary adjustments as perceived by the rating agency, until the issue is redeemed. If there is likely to be a change in the credit rating of an issue a sudden change of circumstances being announced or apparent and the agency has not had time to assess the impact on the rating, the borrower may be placed on "creditwatch". This will alert the investors, and others who use rating criteria, to a possible impending change of rating. The rating assessment of a corporation embraces the following key areas:

Relative country risk. It would be strange if a sovereign credit rating was lower than a corporate rating domiciled in the same country. Indeed, the sovereign credit rating (if there is one) will act as the highest rating any corporate borrower in that country can achieve. The corporation's exposure is assessed as to country risk, in its structure, earnings, cash flow, asset and liability spread on a multinational basis.

Management philosophy. Discussions take place annually between the agency and senior executives of the borrower to assess management performance not just on the company's earnings and financial position but also on its ability to achieve planned objectives and maintain sound financial strategies. The company's own policy in relation to country risk exposures and hedging techniques which the company has adopted to reduce or eliminate them is often discussed.

The degree of importance of the issuer in his own country. Will the authorities act as lender of last resort? Is the company of such importance to the national economy or to the industry in which it operates that a "life-boat" rescue operation would probably be mounted to avoid its liquidation?

The issuer's industry. Banks, from time to time, as issuers, have been affected by changes in the banking sector generally. A banking crisis in one country (indeed sometimes with one bank) may well be felt worldwide, or may just have a local impact within the country or market concerned. Labour relations, the size of workforce and strength of trade union representation in the industry and its vulnerability to industrial action are critical criteria: the industry, and therefore the company being rated, may be constrained in its flexibility to develop and, consequently, to maintain its profitability.

The issuer's operating efficiency and market position. Comparisons are made with competitors in the industry of profit margins; degree of integration; costs of production, and management strategies in different operating divisions and cost centres.

The accounting policies. These are analysed to assess how the issuer's statistics and ratios compare with competitors. The basic areas of difference between the UK and US accounting principles which the agency adjusts for comparative purposes are: foreign exchange and currency deposit treatment; goodwill and fixed asset evaluations.

Rating agencies give a rating to preferred stock issues, industrial revenue and pollution control bonds, municipal bonds, commercial paper and certificates of deposit in addition to the corporate bonds which have been described in this chapter.

543

Credit Ratings for Corporate and Municipal Bonds

Standard & Poor's	Moody's	Fitch	Canadian Bond Rating Service	Definitions
AAA	Aaa	AAA	A++	Highest quality minimum investment risk
AA	Aa	AA	A+	High quality little investment risk
A	A	A	A	Good quality. Favourable investment characteristics
BBB	Baa	BBB	B++	Medium quality, some speculative characteristics
BB	Ba	BB	B+	Lower medium quality speculative
B	B	B	B	Low quality. Lacks desirable investment characteristics
CCC	Caa	CCC	C++	Poor – predominantly speculative
CC	Ca	CC	C+	
C	C	C	C	
—	D	D	D	In default

Standard & Poor's and Fitch have modifications indicated by + or – signs against the ratings from AA to B and AA to BB respectively. These indicate whether the rated security ranks in the high end of its generic rating category or the lower end. Moody's apply numerical modifiers 1, 2 and 3 from classification Aa through to B.

544

CHAPTER TWENTY SEVEN

Regulation in the Securities Markets

In the interest of participants in the markets, fraud and abusive market practices have to be outlawed. As the markets in different countries, and internationally, have developed so have the undesirable techniques which will have a debilitating effect unless markets are efficiently and effectively regulated. It would seem that as the size of a market grows so does the degree of malpractice and fraud and therefore the need for greater regulation. Over-regulation can close a market entirely or drive it elsewhere where the participants can enjoy greater flexibility of action and possibly more favourable economic conditions. This is sometimes evidenced by the preference shown by participants for the international (euro market) over the correspondent domestic market. Perhaps the most important example is the Eurodollar market. A non-US borrower could, at the time of writing (1985), obtain a lower coupon on a euro-dollar FRN than on a yankee FRN. Yankee FRNs are generally priced at a margin over US short-term domestic money market instruments to attract American investors. Euro-dollar FRNs are priced at a margin over LIBOR, LIBID or their mean, which is both cheaper for the non-US borrower (despite the high front-end fees) and far quicker and simpler to obtain as no SEC submission is required. Fiscal legislation in the States in the Gibbons–Conable Bill 1984 abolished withholding tax on US domestic instruments for non-US citizen holders, yet the yield differential between Yankee and euro paper did not change as the international investor preference for euro-issues in bearer form does not require the investor to declare his domicile in order to achieve the same tax-free status.

The regulations (if any) which impact on the securities industry in any country may be imposed by:

* The fiscal authorities and tax legislation

- The monetary authorities and exchange control regulations (exchange control matters are developed in Chapter 7)

- The legal infrastructure relating to fraud prevention and company and commercial practices

- The market participants themselves in a self-regulating environment and market associations codes of conduct

- The stock exchange regulations

- The statutory regulators appointed for the industry (such as the SEC) as well as ombudsmen

To be effective, regulations have to be enforceable. The Division of Enforcement of the US Securities & Exchange Commission is concerned about the dual standards of enforcement which have developed in the treatment of US securities. Those which affect transactions entirely within the US are subject to strict supervision but anyone who chooses to deal in US securities through foreign based intermediaries can take advantage of foreign bank secrecy and blocking laws. It has been argued that the USA, in seeking forms of new co-operation in the policing of the world's capital markets, would not prejudice the sovereign right of each country to exercise jurisdiction effectively with respect to conduct within its own borders. On the other hand, any action or litigation construed as "interference" may well harden the attitudes of other governments and, at the same time, encourage a greater exodus of the US securities business to offshore centres. National views on another country's fiscal or exchange control regulations are naturally influenced by the regulations experienced at home. For example, the view that "one's own system is liberal, operates on a self-assessment basis and therefore, being self-regulating, is more conducive to honesty than 'police-state' fiscal laws and penal taxation exercised elsewhere", only provides evidence that such nationals do not perceive the need to regulate their markets to the extent required elsewhere. Any attempt to change such status quo would be likely to meet with resistance. There is little doubt that the USA has the world's most extensive regulatory framework for its financial markets and this centres on the Securities & Exchange Commission. The SEC was founded in 1934 under the US Securities & Exchange Act for the purpose of "maintaining just and equitable principles of trade which would be conducive to an open, fair and orderly market". In addition, the Commission aims to prohibit misrepresentation, manipulation and other financial malpractices in the markets. The six key provisions in the Act are:

- Every company with securities listed on an exchange must file, with the SEC, annual and periodic financial reports. The Securities Act Amendments of 1964 extended this reporting requirement to companies with securities traded over the counter if the company has at least $1 million in assets and 500 or more shareholders. The SEC makes these reports public in Form 10-K.

- "Insider" trading in listed securities must be reported regularly to the SEC. Insiders are officers, directors, and 10% owners (owners who hold at least 10% of the stock).

- The company's financial condition and other information must be contained in any solicitation for proxies (a proxy is a written authority by a shareholder for someone else – e.g. a company officer – to vote on his behalf).

- Dealers and broker-dealers on exchanges and the over-the-counter market must register with the SEC and are subject to given rules. Most rules are applied by the exchanges themselves.

- The SEC is empowered to police trading practices in the financial markets.

- The SEC has the power to subpoena books and records, to take testimony, and to obtain court orders of injunctions to prevent practices that violate the Securities Act of 1934.

The US Commodity Futures Trading Commission was formed in 1975 to protect individuals involved from irregular trading practices, fraud and misrepresentation.

The Federal Reserve Board sets stock margins and also shares with the SEC, the Comptroller of the Currency and the Federal Deposit

Insurance Corporation (FDIC), the supervision of banks acting as stock transfer agents.

In West Germany the Börsengesetz (Stock Exchange Law) is supplemented by the codes of practice of each of the seven different Stock Exchanges. As a result of serious irregularities in the German securities market during the period 1978–80, the principal regulatory authority for securities business, the Bundesaufsichtsamt fur das Kreditwesen issued the following Notice in April 1981 setting out the requirements concerning dealings in securities by banks:

"The following criteria will apply to security transactions of the banks:
1. Clear separation of functions into
    a) trading
    b) settlement, supervision and control
    c) accounting
    If it is not possible to separate the functions because of the size of the company, the management (if not available, persons authorised by them) must ensure that the transactions are carried out correctly.
    It must be possible for auditors to carry out a subsequent examination of each deal.

2. The traders must complete forms with the following minimum details for each completed deal: description of the principal, description of securities, amount, value, price and date of contract showing the hour.

    Forward deals and deals which are not settled immediately, also resale and repurchase commitments received, must be documented correctly.

    All deals concluded must be listed in numerical order; the settlement advice must be passed on immediately with all documents to sections separate from the dealing section for summarising and settlement.

A section separate from trading must make certain that the necessary written confirmations are received in time; these must contain all essential terms of the deal.

Confirmations received must pass through the correct channels, especially a neutral mail room. Claims must be taken up immediately.

No.2 does not apply to deals which are settled through the computer system of a stock exchange.

3. All deals, regardless of final accounting, must be listed daily.

   Forward deals, mentioned under No.2 paragraph 2, must in addition be listed by maturity dates.

   A section separate from trading must supervise execution and settlement of the deals.

4. The authorities responsible for taking measures to ensure liquidity and provision for risks must be informed at regular intervals of the forward deals mentioned under No.2 paragraph 2.

   In principle, there is no justification for concluding deals on terms which do not confirm with market trends. Documents for deals which for special reasons have been concluded on terms running counter to market trends must be submitted with all details to the management or to the person authorised by them.

5. Trading in one's own holdings of securities must only be carried out – with the exception of the acceptance and delivery of securities as is usual in daily trading – as part of the guidelines covering business policy and if necessary with the agreement of the authority responsible in the bank for controlling assets. Individual deals in the bank's own securities may only be carried out up to a limit fixed by the manage-

ment; the management or persons authorised by them must be informed of deals which exceed this limit.

6. Telexes and other advices which have led to the conclusion of a deal, must be filed completely as all other papers. They should be put in a binder at short intervals or be secured by some similar means.

7. The manager of the department responsible for security dealings must ensure that the regulations and internal instructions are being complied with; this must be checked by an internal audit.

8. Internal audits for the examination of the requirements contained in this notice must be carried out at irregular suitable intervals. The traders must declare on request, as part of this internal audit, that they have passed on all deals concluded by them for settlement.

   Entries on custodian accounts/deposit, on internal settlement accounts/deposit and settlements shown in secondary books must be included in the examination.

   Special attention should be paid to deals by staff of other banks and their relatives or persons authorised by them insofar as these are evident. The management must be informed of anything irregular.

9. At least once a year, the forward deals mentioned under No.2 paragraph 2 must be agreed between the principals and the banks' internal auditors.

   Internal bank rules must ensure that confirmations and claims as part of the agreement must be passed on immediately to the audit department.

10. The above requirements also apply to trading in borrowers' notes and registered bonds.

11. The above requirements must be covered within the bank by means of internal rules.

12. The bank has to make provision (e.g. in its labour contracts) on whether and how far their staff may carry out their own deals. This applies especially in those cases where there might be conflicts of interest with the bank's business for individual members of staff when carrying out deals for the investment and management of their own assets or for deals without risk and without using their own funds. The internal auditors must make certain that these rules are complied with."

Regulation of the UK securities market was reviewed in the Gower Report Part 1 published in 1984, the terms of reference being:

a) to consider the statutory protection now required by
   i) private, and
   ii) business investors in securities and other property including investors through unit trusts and open-ended investment companies operating in the United Kingdom;

b) to consider the need for statutory control of dealers in securities, investment consultants and investment managers; and

c) to advise on the need for new legislation

Coincidental with the publication of the Gower Report, major changes were being introduced in the structure of The Stock Exchange, London, brought about by commercial pressures following the abandonment of fixed commission charges on share transactions. The end of single capacity (functional separation of broking and stockjobbing) and the new dual capacity broker-dealer acting as agents, principals or both, led to a need for new regulations and a restructuring of the markets participants, and introduction of new technical systems.

551

The Gower Report makes 92 recommendations some of the more significant being:

- The Prevention of Fraud (Investments) Act, and relevant provisions in other legislation, should be replaced by a new Investor Protection Act providing a system whereby basic policy, overall surveillance and residual regulation of investment business (but not deposit-taking regulated under the Banking Act) would be undertaken by a governmental agency but day-to-day regulation so far as possible by self-regulatory agencies, initially based on existing professional bodies and organisations, recognised by the governmental agency.

- The Act should recognise that not all those who need to be regulated would be members of a recognised self-regulatory agency and that the governmental agency would have to regulate the admission to practice, and undertake the direct supervision, of those who were not.

- The Act should make it an offence to carry on investment business unless registered either directly with the governmental agency or through membership of a recognised self-regulatory agency.

- The Act to replace the Prevention of Fraud (Investments) Act should be called the Investor Protection Act and should, in principle, cover all forms of investments, other than those in physical objects over which the investor will have exclusive control, and all those whose business relates thereto. This principle should be given precision, coupled with the essential degree of flexibility.

- 'Investments' should be defined in the Act and the Secretary of State should be empowered to add to or subtract from those listed in the definition, either generally or for particular purposes, by regulations laid before Parliament and subject to an affirmative resolution in the case of additions.

- Contracts for commodity or financial futures or options and life insurance contracts should be included within the definition of investments.

- 'Securities' should be defined in similar manner but should be restricted to a narrower range of investments excluding the types of contracts referred to in the above recommendation.

- A clear distinction should be drawn between gaming contracts and investments.

- 'Investment business' should be defined in similar manner and should include all those professionally engaged in the marketing of investments including investment managers or advisers.

- Employees acting solely on behalf of employers registered for investment business should not, themselves, require to be registered; nor should employees (other than those who manage or advise on investments for pension fund trustees or public investment trust companies) who manage or advise only on their employers' investments.

- The definition of 'investment business' should not include bona fide investment clubs (but should include anyone professionally managing the club or its investments or advising its members on its investments).

- The Bank of England, on behalf of the Treasury, should retain its role of surveillance of the commodity and financial exchanges but the role of governmental regulator of commodity and financial brokers in the interests of investor protection should be vested in the government agency (or a self-standing commission).

- The Investor Protection Act should afford the same protection to both private and professional investors except that greater freedom should be allowed to communicate investment information to those carrying on investment business, banking or insurance.

- The Rules and Codes of Conduct of a self-regulatory agency recognised under the Investor Protection Act should, so long as the agency remains recognised, not be regarded as restrictive agreements within the meaning of the Restrictive Trades Practices Act 1976 and a course of conduct required or envisaged by such Rules or Codes should be excluded from the ambit of the Competition Act 1980.

- Recognised self-regulatory agencies should be empowered to apply to the courts for the issue of subpoenas to compel attendance of witnesses and production of documents required in connection with their disciplinary proceedings.

- Evidence given to such tribunals, reports of their findings and information interchanged between agencies in the exercise of their regulatory functions should be statutorily recognised as protected by qualified privilege for the purpose of the law of defamation and from actions for breach of confidence.

- The Act should empower the Department (or commission) to make regulations, relating to applications for registration, and rules for the conduct of business of those so registered. These should be based on The Dealers in Securities (Licensing) Regulations 1983 and The Licensed Dealers (Conduct of Business) Rules 1983 but substantially revised and re-arranged in the light of the expanded vires and coverage of the new Act.

- The statutory provisions in the Companies Acts relating to public issues, takeovers, and insider-dealing should be transferred in a revised and modernised form to the proposed Investor Protection Act.

- Invitations to the public, whether on a primary or secondary distribution or on a takeover, should be treated broadly on the same lines.

- Documents containing such invitations should be pre-vetted prior to distribution or publication and effective surveillance should be maintained over any market-makers in the securities concerned.

- Accordingly the Act should make it an offence to distribute or publish to the public an issue or takeover prospectus unless:

  a) it complied with the provisions of the Act and Regulations made thereunder, and
  b) permission to distribute and publish it had been granted (and not revoked) by the Department (or commission) or a self-regulatory agency recognised by it for this purpose.

- On transfer to the Investor Protection Act the present statutory provisions relating to public issues should be re-arranged and brought up-to-date, eliminating unnecessary differences between issues of the securities of domestic companies and those of foreign companies, between those of listed and unlisted securities and between those relating to primary and secondary distributions and should apply to any public offering of marketable securities not regulated under any other legal regime; and appropriate penalties, civil and criminal, should be prescribed in the event of breach.

- The Investor Protection Act should include provisions similar to Sections 13 (deceptive inducements) and 14 (investment circulars) of the Prevention of Fraud (Investments) Act but substantially re-drafted and clarified.

- The publisher of a newspaper or periodical should not escape liability for breach of the re-drafted Section 14 merely because he acted in the ordinary course of business in publishing an investment advertisement therein unless, in addition, he proved either that he had no reason to believe that it contained an invitation to enter into an investment transaction or that the material was placed by a person who was, or whom he believed on reasonable grounds to be, entitled under the Act or Regulations to issue the circular.

In January 1985, a White Paper entitled "Financial Services in the United Kingdom – A New Framework for Investor Protection" was presented to Parliament. The Government's intention is that the regulation of the financial services industry should be no more than the minimum necessary to protect the investor and that the arrangements will be in the interests of the industry itself as much as its customers. It recognises that regulation cannot eliminate risk and its aims are to reduce the scope of losses arising as a result of fraud or from the concealment of risk. The objectives are to foster: efficiency – competition – confidence – and flexibility. In order to achieve these objectives the following principles are envisaged:

- Ensuring that market forces operate effectively with specific regard to relevant disclosure of information and the forces of competition are applied to the practitioners and their institutions.

- That clearly understood, legally defined and established general principles and rules be created with regard to (i) the raising of capital in the United Kingdom (ii) investment and savings, and (iii) buying and selling investments.

- That fraud is less likely to occur with an efficient regulatory framework and that prevention is better than cure.

- That self-regulation by the practitioners themselves to foster high standards of integrity will minimise the opportunities of theft, fraud and deception occurring within the industry.

- That the law should not create artificial distinctions in that equal treatment be accorded between products and services competing in the same market.

The Regulatory System defines "investments" and "investment business" and makes it an offence to carry on the latter without authorisation. Investments for this purpose embrace inter alia securities covered by the Prevention of Frauds (Investments) Act 1958, and financial and commodity futures and options contracts.

The Secretary of State has the authority to delegate to a Regulatory Body the authorisation of investment business and the detailed requirements for such business to be conducted.

556

A degree of self-regulation is achieved in the international capital markets through membership of the AIBD. The Association of International Bond Dealers (AIBD) is an independent legal entity domiciled in Switzerland for the purposes of:

> promoting friendly relations between members' maintaining close liaison between primary and secondary markets in international securities, and establishing and maintaining mutually acceptable rules for the conduct and procedures carried out by participants in the international capital markets. The rules relate to all eurobond or note securities except those denominated in Deutschemarks, plus yankee bonds and all securities denominated in composite currency units.

Appendix 1 contains the AIBD rules and recommendations.

CHAPTER TWENTY EIGHT

What the Borrower Should Consider

Introduction

The various matters for a bank to consider prior to raising capital debt, as described in the following four chapters, commence with the identification of the need for such funds, assessment of market conditions, choice of currency, type and nature of debt instrument and selection of the appropriate borrowing vehicle. The factors which influence the selection of the management team, brokers, trustees, lawyers, tax officers and printers, are also discussed. Whether the stocks should be rated by a rating agency, and stock exchange listed, and the principal feature of the terms and conditions of a capital stock issue, which requires special consideration, such as subordination, pricing, redemption features, use of proceeds, etc. are also discussed in this Section.

Basic Framework for Potential Bank Borrowers

It is a Companies Act requirement that issuers of debt securities to the public must be public companies, and very careful consideration should be given to ensure that the company in whose name the debt is to be raised is an appropriate vehicle for such a purpose. Clearly there is a need to establish a vehicle which is legally competent to raise such funds and it is equally important that the banking operations of the group are not encumbered by restrictive covenants or constraints which might affect their future operations. Fiscal considerations are also of particular significance, for example, following the abolition of Exchange Control in the UK in 1979 and before the UK Finance Act in 1984, all securities issued by UK borrowers were subject to withholding tax. As it is a condition of the international capital market for coupon interest to be paid gross, it followed that no British company over that five year period could raise debt in its own name. Accordingly, offshore finance companies sprang up as wholly-owned subsidiaries of the British companies wishing to raise such debt. Companies such as National Westminster Finance B.V., Standard Chartered Finance B.V. and Midland International Financial Services B.V. were established in Holland, the debt raised in the offshore finance vehicle's name being guaranteed by the bank in the United Kingdom. Holland was a popular choice for such vehicles for the following reasons:

- it has a well established banking community

- it is geographically very close to the UK with excellent communications

- over the period it had a very similar level of corporation tax and a beneficial double taxation agreement with the UK

A detailed analysis must take place of the borrower's group tax consequences of raising long-term capital debt and the final choice of vehicle may well be determined as a result of fiscal implications because of the risk of incurring substantial costs. Sometimes such costs are not so immediately apparent, and they might be avoided or reduced with the full approval of all the interested fiscal parties provided sufficient planning and research is carried out before-hand.

Capital fund raising by a company in the UK must be authorised by the company's board. A special resolution of the board is also required when the company wishes to guarantee the indebtedness of a subsidiary company for the purpose of raising capital for the group. In order to take advantage of propitious market conditions, potential issuers are well advised to seek ways to establish a flexible system of operation which will avoid the necessity of calling together a full board to initiate the transaction at short notice and later to approve all matters relating to each issue as it progresses. The basic framework for a borrower might require the establishment of a board sub-committee with any two or more directors who are suitably empowered by the main board to approve the material details of the issues. If an offshore borrowing vehicle is also used, it is necessary to co-ordinate the functions of the board of that company with the guarantor, say, in the UK. It is also essential that the offshore com-

560

pany is run on an entirely "arms-length" basis and its directors fully understand the proposals and make their own decisions about all resolutions passed.

Identification of Long Term Funding Requirements
and Employment of Proceeds

Capital debt raising can be an expensive business and it is extremely important that potential raisers have an on-going policy of examining their present and anticipated future debt requirements. The primary consideration for raising loan capital is for balance sheet purposes in order to improve the gearing, maximise on debt equity headroom and enable the business of the company to develop. As time goes on, existing debt will come nearer to maturity and this will probably need to be replaced. Sinking funds and purchase agreements have to be considered in the context of the reduction of capital adequacy. Account must also be taken of the requirements of the regulatory authorities in determining the appropriate level of the company's capital adequacy. Banks in the United States, for example, would be aware of the Federal Reserve Board definition of capital as including: common stock, perpetual preferred stock, capital surplus, capital and contingency reserves, allowances for loan losses, mandatory convertible instruments, minority interests and undivided profits. Banks in the United Kingdom define capital as ordinary shares, preference shares, reserves, minority interests, qualifying subordinated loan stocks and provisions. The Bank of England takes the view that loan capital which has five years to run to maturity, will be amortised (in accordance with the Bank's perception of capital adequacy) on a straight line basis over the final five years of the debt. In the Bank of England's paper of 28th November 1984, "Subordinated loan capital issued by recognised banks and licensed deposit-takers", criteria were established for the supervisory treatment of issues of perpetual subordinated debt as qualifying primary capital and of issues of subordinated dated debt as qualifying secondary loan capital.

The funding of infrastructure in the form of long-term investments in subsidiary companies abroad may be considered in the context of capital debt raising. A major acquisition in the United States, West Germany or Switzerland, for example, will create in a UK company's balance sheet a fixed asset denominated in foreign currency. If the payment for such an investment was effected by an outright purchase of the foreign currency with, say, sterling, then the UK company would probably have created a substantial foreign exchange exposure. On the other hand, by borrowing the foreign currency relative to the asset, a matching liability will be achieved for balance sheet purposes. If the borrowing is acquired from the interbank or other short-term money market sources, then the company will run a maturity mis-match and may also create tax neutrality problems. A long-term "liability" in the form of a capital loan stock, hedging a long-term asset, if denominated in the same currency, has certain material benefits for a multinational company, particularly when the exposure would otherwise be significant. Many currencies are just not available in the international capital markets and, therefore, it is not always possible to borrow long-term funds in the same currency matching an acquisition abroad. Another purpose for long-term funding would be to provide finance for a specific major project or, perhaps, property development. This would be an unusual reason for a bank to consider in their assessment of long-term funding needs.

Consideration should be given to the nature of the debt itself. Whether it should be straight debt, convertible into equity or floating rate debt, will depend on a number of factors, very particularly market conditions. Convertible debt will tend to dilute the equity of the issuer if the conversion option is exercised and the cost of servicing the equity is usually substantially higher than the cost of servicing debt.

Improving the quality of the liability mix can be achieved by obtaining long-term funds at perceived relatively low interest rate levels and re-financing the short-term debt. The acquisition of long-term debt by way of floating rate notes may be an advantage to banks which are exposed on their balance sheet to falling interest rates in that particular currency. The acquisition on the other hand of a fixed-rate straight debt may be more appropriate for banks which are exposed to rising interest rates.

A very important point for a major bank or company to remember is to avoid the temptation of "jam potting". This phrase is sometimes used to describe the identification of liabilities with specific assets. The comments given above in this context are by way of illustration for ease of understanding rather than the more practical approach of a professionally managed corporate treasury function. Indeed, in the loan stock documentation it is normal to have a statement describing the use of proceeds of the issue. For banking purposes a general statement such as "the proceeds are employed in the international business of the group" is more appropriate than a specific statement advising that the proceeds are to be used for a particular purpose. One of the important aspects of banking is the fungibility of liabilities. It is important to maintain bank deposits and other liabilities in fungible form in order to defeat any attempt to trace the actual use to which the deposits may be put. Legal, accounting and practical considerations may demand that specific deposits are not identifiable and, therefore, the temptation to "jam pot" must be avoided even with material sums raised on the international or national capital markets.

Permission Required Precedent to a New Issue
The board resolutions of the borrowing company to authorise the issue and approve the terms and conditions thereof will be required. If the funds are to be raised through an offshore vehicle then the guarantor's board must also pass resolutions authorising the guarantee and terms and conditions of guaranteed indebtedness.

A UK guarantor of an issue made by a foreign subsidiary must obtain HM Treasury consent under Section 482 of the Income and Corporation Taxes Act 1970.

The structure of the debt raising may make it advisable to seek an advance ruling (in writing) from the borrower's local UK Inspector of Taxes and from the Inspector of Foreign Dividends in Somerset House.

If the issuer is a Dutch financing vehicle the prior ruling of the Inspector of Taxes in whose 'parish' the corporate seat of the Dutch finance vehicle is situated, should also be obtained. Terms of the agreement are normally established for all issues made over a given period in the future, and are not varied during the issue's life – therefore, with a new issue, it may be found that an earlier ruling may be applied.

No mandatory permissions are required from the Bank of England or the Dutch National Bank to make a new issue, although Dutch National Bank approval is required for the Dutch borrowing vehicle to up-stream the debt by way of loan to an offshore entity (usually the guarantor/parent or any other group company for capital adequacy purposes). If the borrower wishes to achieve capital adequacy the Bank of England's criteria for qualifying debt must be inherent in documentation submitted to the Bank for assessment before launch.

UK borrowers or guarantors must advise the UK Government Broker of their intention to make an issue.

The trustee of any outstanding loan stocks may have to approve the terms and conditions of all new capital fund-raising documentation prior to the close of the issue.

The stock exchange whereon a listing may be sought must approve the application and the requisite documents must be submitted 14 days before launch. For seasoned issuers however this period may be waived, provided that documentation is submitted prior to signing of the subscription agreement. If bearer stock is being issued, or guaranteed by a UK company and placed with a limited number of persons being banks and professional securities dealers, an application may be made for a Certificate of Exemption under Section 418 of the Companies Act 1948 to be issued by The Stock Exchange, London, for exemption from the Fourth Schedule of the Act as compliance may be considered unnecessarily burdensome.

For Guilder, Yen, Deutschemark and certain other foreign bond issues, local central bank approval is required.

**Lead Management and the Selection of Advisers,
Agents and other Parties involved in Capital Fund Raising**
Technical advisers who are familiar with market conditions should be encouraged to discuss developments and market conditions with the

issuer/guarantor frequently. This is particularly important when the borrower has a planned policy to raise debt on a regular basis to take full advantage of market conditions in different currencies when funds are available for appropriate amounts and on acceptable terms. Capital market conditions are so volatile that every advantage must be taken if borrowers are going to be successful in raising funds at the right time. For this purpose the technical advisers may well include directors from merchant or investment houses who are likely to be selected as lead or co-managers and, if the borrower is a bank, it is normal to involve the bank's in-house merchant bank, if there is one, and group treasury, to formulate recommendations to meet identified capital requirements and to implement policy decisions to raise funds in one capital market or another. Some advisers can sometimes be less aware of the tight time-frame of a capital debt issue than others. They do not always appear to have the necessary degree of urgency and understanding of the requirements of the market-place and it is essential for the borrower and lead manager to co-ordinate and maintain momentum to ensure the issue is completed in accordance with the timetable. The Dutch lunch hour can be quite annoying if time is of the essence!

Managers
Some corporate borrowers have put potential new issues out to tender. The advantage of this to the borrower is that he can obtain the best possible terms which the market would be likely to accept at the time of the tender. This approach is not popular with the investment and merchant bankers who generally like to work with a prospective borrower prior to an issue and by doing so be awarded the lead management role with the resultant lucrative front-end fees that this brings. If the borrower is a bank, then in practice it often happens that, if an innovatory and timely proposition is brought by an experienced and competent lead manager, and the borrower wishes to use the idea, then the investment house proposing it is involved in a lead or very prominent management position in the issue. Corporate treasurers are well advised to encourage creative ideas and attitudes from a number of investment houses and merchant bankers.

The choice of management team is sometimes left with the lead manager after the latter's appointment. In the case of banks as borrowers, the interbank relationships and business connections give rise to a greater than normal interest by the borrower in the involvement of participants in their issues. The lead bank must feel comfortable with its own management group as it will require its management team to perform effectively in the market place and have substantial placing power. Correspondent banking relationships between the borrower and the banks concerned in the issue are very important but at the end of the day it is necessary for the issue to be placed successfully. Lobbying by some banks for participation is inevitable and an even balance maintained by the borrower is imperative.

It is not sufficient to allow the lead manager to make all the decisions. After all, the lead manager has a conflict of interests which must be clearly recognised. Whilst employed by the borrower, the lead manager also has a duty to his investor clients and, in addition, is well aware that his continued good relationship with the selling and underwriting groups must be maintained for future deals. The authors have heard lead managers proudly announce after a new issue has been launched: "It has been a good issue – a lot of people are happy". One is left wondering whether, as the investors were so happy should the borrower have sought tighter terms? From the borrower's view-point, an easy ride should never be given to the management team and from a negotiation stance it should always be assumed that the managers represent not the borrower but the investors. On the question of negotiation of terms the lead manager must be presumed to be on the other side of the table. Having said this, the borrower should always seek a successful and well placed issue and if he is too hard nosed in his approach to the market, investor interest in any future issue may not be so easy to stimulate.

Legal Advisers
The selection of the right lawyer is vitally important to the borrower. It is the individual that matters not only so far as technical competence in his own discipline and experience in bond issues is concerned, but also that he can work to solve problems within a tight time-scale. These qualities do not automatically descend on every partner in every prestigious law firm. It is essential that the lawyer works with the borrower. After all, there will be lawyers representing

566

the lead manager and trustee, if there is one and, bearing in mind the very tight timing of debt issues, it is not sufficient to have a lawyer who will only provide answers to given questions. Objectivity and fast thinking are also essential qualities one should seek in a lawyer. However close to the ideal legal representative the borrower may be fortunate enough to engage, it is advisable that the borrower is able to validate the advice being given. This applies not only to legal advice but fiscal and other technical information sought from outside experts. By accepting technical advice without question or consideration, the borrower is abdicating his responsibilities of running the business. In addition to UK legal advice, a capital debt issuer normally requires legal advice from other countries, especially if the debt is a domestic issue in another country. German, Swiss and/or American lawyers would be required for domestic issues in those countries, for example, and if the borrower is a Dutch company a Dutch lawyer would naturally be required to represent the B.V. or N.V. financing vehicle. Lawyers need to work as an integral part of a closely knit team. They are required to help in the solving of problems and not just to advise, as many foreign lawyers do, that something cannot be done; what the borrower is interested in is 'how it *can* be done'.

The same principles apply to the selection of tax advisers as has been indicated above regarding lawyers. In many countries abroad there are tax lawyers as distinct from the tax accountants in the UK whose advice is often sought.

Fiscal Agents
Instead of a trustee a fiscal agent may be appointed for an issue where no trust documentation is required. A fiscal agent undertakes, inter alia, the duties of paying agents, but does not assume any fiduciary role. Although the fiscal agency agreement may identify various obligations of the issuer, the fiscal agent has no specific duties to act in the interest of or on behalf of investors.

A subordinated issue, or one guaranteed on a subordinated basis, requires the establishment of a trust and, therefore, the need for a trustee rather than a fiscal agent.

Trustee

For continuity, employment of the same trustee/trustees should be considered and, therefore, the initial choice should be right. A well established prestigious institution, normally being a bank or an insurance company, is the most popular choice for trusteeships. A trustee's remuneration is not excessive and should not, therefore, be the criterion on which a trustee is selected. It must be seen that the trustee is capable of, and has a track record of, effectively carrying out its functions, being to safeguard the interests of the note or bond holders.

Underwriting and Selling Group

Underwriting or selling group members are selected by the lead manager, although where a bank is the borrower, correspondent banking relationships invariably have to be considered and the comments under Lead Management above are relevant to this situation so far as a bank borrower is concerned. Once again, it should be stressed that the issue has to be placed with the investors and the team chosen must be one which will work effectively with the lead manager towards that common objective.

Printers

The choice of security printers is somewhat limited. It is advisable for a borrower to get quotations from at least two printing firms with a high reputation for quality and performance. The cost of producing the definitive issue will depend on the number of pieces of paper actually printed and whether there previously exists a plate from an earlier issue which can be used again. Naturally, the larger the denomination per bond the lower the printing costs. Security printers need to be advised of the denomination(s) of each bond, the number of coupons required, which will normally be the life of the issue times the frequency of the coupon per year. Any special protection which the borrower requires against possible forgery, particularly where bearer instruments are being printed, will naturally add to the cost but may be considered appropriate from the borrower's point of view, especially if the issue is likely to be around for a long time. Security printers are also interested to know what the timetable is and whether the issue can be made under a global note and when the definitive securities will be required. Later the security printer will need to liaise with the paying agent so far as delivery instructions are concerned. For yankee bonds, one of the requirements of the New York Stock Exchange (NYSE) is that a vignette appears on all registered certificates issued. A vignette is an engraved picture and for NYSE purposes the vignette must incorporate a human form. The securities printers do provide off-the-shelf vignettes but most borrowers would no doubt prefer to create their own in their corporate image, provided always that time permits.

The Stock Exchange, London, requires security printing of bearer bonds or notes to be entrusted to recognised security printers and that the paper used must be first-class bond or bank note paper, for which detailed records must be kept of the manufacture and consumption. Each coupon must bear the serial number of the bond and be numbered consecutively. The bonds must have at least one printing involving an engraved steel plate which includes the border. The design of each border is particular to the individual borrower and the same border will be used every time the issuer uses that printer.

Selection of an ordinary printer (for printing documentation other than the actual bonds) is normally made by the lead manager. However, costs can be alarming if there is no effective control exercised on the number of proofs, their distribution and the employment of printing staff overnight and week-ends etc. Borrowers may be advised to agree a price for ordinary printing with the lead manager and leave the responsibility to him to contain costs. Anything he saves is then for his own book and it is likely to make him more careful. Yankee bonds can be notorious in this connection.

Paying Agents

It is generally advisable to obtain quotations from several paying agents as there is sometimes a sizeable difference in their quotations. If time is short, paying agents' quotations may be obtained in a format suitable to the issuer so that the issuer can compare them without delay. A single price for the entire service over the given life of the issue, payable either annually or in a lump sum at the outset, for both paying agents and in the case of a floating rate note, the agent bank services combined as a comprehensive package, is easy to compare with similar quotes and to assimilate into the total calculation of the cost of the issue. Normally paying agents, unless asked to quote as suggested above, will break down their fees for every service provided, and it is therefore difficult to assess exactly what are the comparative costs. As with all advisers, excellence of service is presumed and quotations should only be sought from those agents who are capable of providing an efficient paying agency service. Some banks, when issuing debt, may decide to provide the paying agency and agent bank's services themselves or by a group company in order to save costs. Other banks consider it more appropriate in the interest of the investors and the general quality of the paper to place the paying agency arrangements at arms length with an independent bank.

Cost Considerations

Raising capital debt is often an extremely expensive method of obtaining funding. The costs involved can normally be segregated into structured fees and expenses. The fee structure varies considerably between euro-bonds, yankee bonds and other debt raised for foreign borrowers on domestic markets in different countries. A euro-bond, for example, can attract up to $2\frac{1}{2}\%$ structured fees, being $\frac{1}{2}\%$ for manager, $\frac{1}{2}\%$ for underwriting group and $1\frac{1}{2}\%$ for the selling group. For straight, fixed interest issues with a final maturity of seven years or less, the structured fees for a euro-bond might well be $\frac{3}{8}\%$ for manager, $\frac{3}{8}\%$ for underwriting and $1\frac{1}{2}\%$ for the selling group, totalling $2\frac{1}{4}\%$. By 1985 the fees for FRN issues had reduced considerably and, depending on the pricing structure, front end fees for such issues ranged between 10 basis points (0.1%) and 2% of the issue amount. The arithmetic example which follows is very much at the upper end of the fee range but nonetheless forms a useful example of fee calculations. The structured fees for a Swiss Franc issue may very well be as high as $4\frac{1}{2}\%$ and for a Deutschemark issue $3\frac{1}{2}\%$. There are smaller structured fees of about $1\frac{1}{4}\%$ for a yankee bond straight issue but the expenses are substantially higher than equivalent eurodollar bonds, and the coupon is payable semi-annually compared with annual payments on euro-bonds. Other expenses may be incurred initially and be payable front-end as are the structured fees, and there

570

are running expenses for the payment to the trustee, paying agent and possibly to the agent bank. It is sometimes possible to get the paying agent to waive the agent bank fee if he takes the dual role. The expenses incurred initially will include a lump sum (usually a substantial one) for printing costs, legal and other advisory costs and, in addition, there is also the cost of the borrower's own staff and administration involved in the issue.

It may be useful while on the subject of costs to illustrate how, for comparative purposes, the total costs of an issue may be assessed in terms of current coupon yields.

Take a eurodollar note issue on the following terms: (The fees are merely an illustration and not typical of those pertaining at the date of publication)

US$100 million – 10 year bullet FRN – interest payable semi-annually @ $\frac{1}{8}$% above the mean of the London bid and offered rates.

Structured fees	:	Managers	$\frac{3}{8}$%	
	:	Underwriters	$\frac{3}{8}$%	
	:	Selling group	$1\frac{1}{2}$%	
			$2\frac{1}{4}$% =	US$2,250,000

Expenses	:	Managers Legal Printing Listing Borrower and guarantor	say US$300,000
Fees	:	Paying agent/agent bank	US$ 50,000
			US$2,600,000 payable front-end

Trustee	US$ 2,000 p.a.
Net fiscal costs of the Dutch vehicle	US$135,000 p.a.
Annual administration costs	US$ 3,000 p.a.
	US$140,000 p.a.
	(assume semi annual cashflow)

Assuming an average six month LIMEAN (mean of London bid and offered rates) is estimated to be, say, 9% over the 10 years,

Present value   (PV) = Principal sum less front end expenses
$100 million − ($2,250,000 + $300,000 + $50,000) = $97,400,000

Future value   (FV) = $100 million

Number of semi
annual payments   (n) = 20

Payment flow (PMT) = $\dfrac{9\frac{1}{8}}{2}$ on $100 million + $\dfrac{140,000}{2}$ = $4,632,500
(semi annual)

Interest   (i) = 9.67656% p.a.

Deduct estimated
coupon

$$\underline{\begin{array}{l} 9.125 \quad \% \\ 0.55156\% \end{array}} = \text{cost of fees as a \% p.a. on the issue}$$

Such calculations are of value in establishing an assessment of the cost of funds and can be helpful when seeking ways of employing the proceeds profitably. It should be noted, however, that for accounting purposes the issue costs are invariably taken in the year in which they are incurred. If the issue happened to be redeemed one or two years early by the borrower exercising a call feature, naturally the costs expressed on a per annum basis would be more.

Need for a Debt Rating
Rating considerations are covered in greater detail in Chapter 26. However, in the context of this chapter it should be stressed that the initial objective of a rating is to enhance the ability of the issuer to raise proposed new debt as cheaply as possible. After a company has received a debt rating, maintenance of the rating often becomes a principal objective in itself. The fear of increased cost of funds to the

rated company, if down-rated, can lead to certain corporate action not being taken which would otherwise have long-term benefits for the company but in the short-term increase the company's risk exposure thereby making it vulnerable to a down-grading. A fine balance needs to be maintained and the corporate policy defined with regard to ratings. Ratings are often more visible to the issuer than perhaps to the market. Indeed, if a rated borrower experiences serious difficulties, the market will know all about it and have made their own judgment. They do not need to be told by a rating agency. Ratings *are* valuable, however, for the less sophisticated investor and, at the end of the day, much depends on the extent of distribution of an issue as to whether a rating is necessary. Clearly there is no point in having a private placement rated.

The following information would permit the US rating agencies to initiate an evaluation of the debt quality of bank liabilities.

- Detailed income statements for the last five years for the bank and major subsidiaries, reflecting revenues by asset origin or fee type, details of expense items including interest expense by type of liability instrument, and details of reserve provisions.

- Detailed balance sheets of the bank with schedules for major asset and liability accounts, and balance sheets for major subsidiaries.

- Loan portfolio details reflecting distribution geographically, whether corporate, financial institution, governmental or consumer, with a further break-down of corporate loans by industry and governmental loans geographically. Portfolio data of the most recent date possible is desirable.

- A list of loans in excess of 5% of equity, identified by type of borrower and nature of loan, i.e. term, security, etc.

- A reasonably comprehensive description of the organisation and management structure of the bank.

- Projections, including assumptions, for the next five years.

The above information would provide the basis for a series of in-depth discussions with appropriate management personnel. In addition to discussions of the basic structure and operations of the bank, extensive discussion in a number of other areas is to be expected. With respect to the loan portfolio, there would be discussions, in addition to the distribution of the portfolio, on lending policies and loan administration practices, particularly as they relate to externally imposed constraints and regulatory activities. Historical loss experience, write-off policies and practices, credit controls, collection procedures and similar matters would be reviewed as well.

To develop an understanding of the bank's liquidity, the liquidity aspects of its investment portfolio, balance sheet liability requirements, and the liquidity afforded by external resources available to the bank would be closely examined as well as the entire liability structure, investigating in particular the stability and diversity of fund sources, both domestically and internationally.

Exposures resulting from foreign exchange trading and other activities would be examined as well as the impact of such ancillary activities as guarantees of publicly issued debt outside the issuer's home base.

CHAPTER TWENTY NINE

Private Placements v. Public Debt Issues

A private placement is not easy to define precisely. The dividing line between a medium- or long-term bank loan and a private placement is as indistinct as the difference between a private placement and a public debt issue. Private placements may essentially be classified as part of the loan capital of a company provided it meets certain criteria. In the case of a bank it would need to be subordinated to differentiate between the medium- or long-term funds which, from time to time, may be taken by a bank as deposits. The legal requirements in different countries vary so far as private placements are concerned. In Switzerland, the maximum period for private placements is eight years, so debt raised in excess of eight years would have to be by way of public debt issue rather than a private placement. The number of participants so far as a Swiss private placement is concerned is unlimited. In the UK, private placements are limited to not more than 11 participants, otherwise it will be considered to be a public offering.

In the USA, private placements are not subject to the registration requirements of the US Securities Act of 1933 provided the debt is only offered to sophisticated investment institutions, and not more than 35 who are not so described. The definition of "sophisticated" is blurred and, in fact, hundreds of placees are possible, although the SEC will not be happy if paper is dumped on the market by more than, say, 35 institutions within a period of four months from launch. There is no prohibition on trading privately placed paper although the intention at the time of sale is for it to be held by the placees as investments rather than trading assets. A $\frac{7}{8}$% spread over the equivalent yield for publicly offered paper is normally expected for privately placed paper in the USA.

US privately placed domestic debt is arranged by way of note purchase agreement and similar facilities for managed issues of privately placed notes can be arranged in Holland, Germany and Switzerland. In each of these countries it is normal procedure for an actual issue of notes to be made. In the United Kingdom, however, any debt issue made by a UK resident, or any marketable instrument guaranteed by a UK resident, will not be construed as a private placement, but therefore be subject to the regulations/considerations of a public debt offering in the UK. All private placements for UK domiciled borrowers and/or guarantors, whether in sterling or foreign currencies, must be made by way of loan agreement, rather than the note purchase agreement facilities available in the Dutch, United States, West German and Swiss capital markets. In West Germany and Holland, private placements are normally subject to queueing procedures in just the same way as a public debt issue. Some private placements in the form of Schuldscheindarlehen, are not subject to the queue but there is still an unofficial control to the extent that advance information of such an issue must be given to the German authorities.

Some issues which have been listed on a stock exchange are, to all intents and purposes, private placements. These include some of the exotic issuers whose name or domicile would have limited appeal to investors internationally. Most private placements, however, are unlisted. Investors who participate in a private placement normally expect to receive a slightly higher return on the investment than they could expect to obtain from a more marketable security of comparable quality, maturity, etc. In other words, it is quite normal for the debt to remain with the initial placees for the entire duration until maturity. Documentation for private placements generally takes one of two routes – the loan agreement route or the note purchase agreement route. Loan agreements have similar procedures to a bank euro-credit or syndicated loan facility. Note purchase agreements involve the issue of securities with terms and procedures similar to a public debt issue but normally without the necessity for all the permissions of various authorities, publication of advertisements, listing arrangements or ratings.

When suitable investors have been identified, private placements can normally be arranged in a much shorter period of time than a

576

public debt issue generally takes. The costs are substantially less although the coupon yield is usually higher.

A typical Swiss Franc private placement involves the offering of bearer notes, normally denominated in amounts of SwFcs.50,000, with a maturity not less than three years but not more than eight years and, generally, five years. Whilst annual amortisation is possible, the earliest redemption would be after two years except where redemption is for tax reasons. Early redemption is normally subject to a premium. Only Swiss banks or Swiss branches of foreign banks may lead such an issue and the notes must be placed within 10 days of closing. If the placing is a straight issue, the interest rate will be fixed immediately before placement at current market rates. Floating rate notes and notes which are convertible into equity or bearer shares may also be issued by way of private placement.

Another form of semi-private placement is the euro-guilder note issue which may have a maturity of between five and seven years. These notes are not underwritten and are placed directly through financial institutions without a stock exchange listing or a prospectus. There is no limit on the number of institutions with whom the notes may be placed and distributed, as with the Swiss private placements, internally or with placees overseas. The size of the issue is normally between H.Fl.30-75 million and the denomination of the bearer notes is normally H.Fl.10,000. Euro-guilder note issues must be managed by a Dutch bank, although a limited number of foreign banks may co-manage. Fees for management and selling come to $\frac{1}{2}\%$ and 1% respectively. Application must be made for a euro-guilder note issue to the Dutch National Bank and the queue can be protracted at times. Apart from the absence of a prospectus and underwriting group, and with a limited secondary market, euro-guilder note issues nevertheless have greater similarity to a public debt issue than most private placements.

In Japan some of the Samurai issues are privately placed with financial institutions who recognise that the lesser known name of the issuer will result in the paper being less marketable than normal. By taking it, such investors realise that the investment will probably be held until maturity.

In Germany, Schuldscheindarlehen are debt certificates evidencing a participation in a loan agreement. In practice they are often treated as securities, although most banks who hold Schuldschein paper as "assets", will record them as "loans". Maturities range from one to fifteen years and there is no maximum amount applied to the size of an issue. Schuldschein may be assigned by a letter of assignment and a copy of the Schuldschein itself. The documentation is held by the first "lender". Non-residents of Germany may hold Schuldschein paper although sales to non-residents of paper with maturities of less than one year is prohibited. The marketability of Schuldschein, like many other instruments, depends on the issuer. Bundesrepublik paper is naturally very marketable but paper issued by lesser known names would be treated strictly as a private placement. Schuldschein are free from withholding tax, so far as non-residents of Germany are concerned.

Example of a private placement (see opposite) – subject to a note purchase agreement. Only two notes were issued in this case each for HK$1,250,000.

HK$1,250,000   No. C 000000

GRAND MARINE HOLDINGS LIMITED

(incorporated with limited liability in Hong Kong)

ISSUE OF HK$2,500,000 8½ PER CENT. NOTES DUE SEPTEMBER, 1980

Created and issued pursuant to the Articles of Association of Grand Marine Holdings Limited and to a resolution of its Board of Directors passed on 28th March, 1978.

GRAND MARINE HOLDINGS LIMITED ("the Company") HEREBY PROMISES to pay to the bearer of this Note the sum of ONE MILLION TWO HUNDRED AND FIFTY THOUSAND HONG KONG DOLLARS (HK$1,250,000) on the Interest Payment Date (as defined in Condition 1 (D) endorsed hereon) falling on or nearest to 28th September, 1980 (or on such earlier date as such principal sum may become payable in accordance with the terms and conditions endorsed hereon), together with interest on such principal sum at the rate of 8½ per cent. per annum (subject to Condition 2 (D) endorsed hereon) subject to deduction of interest tax (or any other Hong Kong tax for the time being payable by way of withholding or deduction) at the standard or other applicable rate for the time being in force as from and including 29th March, 1978 until payment has been duly made or provided for (as well after as before judgment) but, in the case of interest due on or before maturity, only upon the presentation of this Note for enfacement in accordance with such terms and conditions.

This Note forms one of a series of Notes of HK$1,250,000 each in the aggregate principal amount of HK$2,500,000 created and issued pursuant to a resolution of the Board of Directors of the Company passed on 28th March, 1978 and is subject to the terms and conditions endorsed hereon.

IN WITNESS WHEREOF the Company has caused this Note to be signed by its duly authorised representative.

GRAND MARINE HOLDINGS LIMITED

ISSUED: By:..
Hong Kong, as of 29th March, 1978.   *Director*

INTEREST PAYMENTS

No.	Interest payable on Interest Payment Date falling on or nearest to :—	Payment made			Date of Payment	Paying Agent	
		Gross HK$	Interest Tax (or other Hong Kong tax) HK$	Net HK$		Initials	Ex'd
1	28.9.1978						
2	28.3.1979						
3	28.9.1979						
4	28.3.1980						
5	28.9.1980						

Example of a private placement

CHAPTER THIRTY

The Principal Features of a Bank's Euro-Stock Conditions

For euro-public debt issues there are some 18 common clauses, which are listed below (whether the debt is a straight or a floating rate note). If the loan stock is raised by private placement, it is probable that some of these clauses will not be required. Issues on a domestic capital market for a foreign bank borrower will have very similar clauses to those for the same borrower for a public euro-currency debt issue. The clauses are:

Status of the bonds or notes - These usually rank pari passu with previous indebtedness of a similar type.

Subordination – In order to quality for balance sheet treatment as loan stock, it is necessary to differentiate between long-term debt raised in the ordinary course of banking business, either from customers or the interbank market.

In the event of a winding up of the issuing bank, the holders of the subordinated paper should not expect to receive payment from the liquidator until all ordinary creditors have been satisfied in full and therefore the rights of the holders of subordinated paper are subordinate to the rights of the ordinary creditors of the issuer. There may be several tiers of subordination. If the issue has been made in the name of an offshore financing vehicle and guaranteed by a bank or bank holding company, then the guarantee will be subordinated.

Negative Pledge – If at all possible no negative pledge should be given, and for the majority of borrowers it is doubtful if one is really necessary. Indeed if it is intended that the issue is to be considered as qualifying subordinated debt in the issuer's capital base by the Bank of England, then no negative pledge clause may be included. A negative pledge clause is an undertaking by the borrower that he will not offer security to investors in other bonds at a later stage which rank pari passu, thereby agreeing not to prefer investors in subsequent issues. It is extremely important that bank borrowers insist on wording which will not affect their ordinary course of banking business and, in practice the actual wording used in previous bank issues differs very considerably.

Interest – The interest clause for a fixed-rate issue is naturally uncomplicated. For a FRN, however, the definition of interest periods, interest determination dates and the ways in which the interest rate may be determined, lead to much more lengthy wording. The actual interest rate to be applied is one which is always subject to detailed negotiation with the lead manager and this also applies in the case of a FRN to the minimum interest rate, if any, and to the margin over the stated interbank or Treasury Bill rates.

Redemption – For bullet issues the notes and bonds will be redeemed at a specific date in the future. If there is a sinking fund or note purchase agreement, then the redemption clause will include such details. It is normal for a redemption option clause to be included for taxation reasons, the exercise of which by the issuer usually being subject to the satisfaction of the trustee that the borrower would be required to pay additional amounts owing to adverse changes in the tax position effecting the issue. Redemption may as a rule be made by way of "purchase" by the company, or the company's agent acting on their behalf in the market. If the issue is a straight issue, any optional redemption which may be exercised by the issuer is likely to be subject to a premium, normally a higher one for earlier years. With FRNs it is normal to have a call option redemption clause. The Bank of England requires the documentation of qualifying bank capital issues to state that no early repayment can be made without the Bank's consent.

Payments – Details of how and where the investor can obtain payment of interest and principal when due.

Taxation – A statement to the effect that payments of principal and interest on the securities are to be made without withholding tax.

582

Prescription – The bonds and notes normally become void unless presented for payment within 12 years for the principal, and 12 years for the coupons, from a specified relevant date in the terms and conditions of the security.

Events of Default – Borrowers are naturally keen that these are kept to a minimum. However, it is normal for non-payment of principal or interest within a reasonable time from the due date be an event of default. In such an event the terms may include the right to commence the winding up of the borrower or guarantor.

Other acts of default include the appointment of a receiver; evidence that the borrower or guarantor cannot pay its debts and the transfer or disposal of a substantial part of the borrower's or guarantor's assets to a subsidiary company without the trustee's approval. To qualify as capital indebtedness under Bank of England criteria the terms and conditions should not include default clauses which could trigger early repayment of the debt under any circumstances.

A definition of the form and denomination of the bearer or registered security.

Enforcement of Rights – If the securities are constituted under a trust deed rather than a fiscal agency agreement, then it is necessary to give the trustee some remedy in the event of an act of default having occurred. It must be possible for the trustee effectively to look after the interest of the note and bond holders for whom it has responsibility. The only effective remedy lies in the winding up of the borrower and/or guarantor in the event of a default and it is normally left to the discretion of the trustee whether such a course of action would indeed be in the collective interest of the investors. The Bank of England's criteria for qualifying capital documentation, tends to render the trustee toothless.

Details of replacement of bonds or notes and coupons in the event that they are lost, stolen, mutilated or destroyed, if not given under the "payments" clause, may be shown separately.

Notices relating to the issue must be published in a leading newspaper, the two most popular being the Financial Times and the International Herald Tribune for euro-currency issues. Common notices include:
- advice of new floating rate giving the amount of coupon
- interest payable for the next interest period
- advice of redemption of an issue
- advice of numbers of specific bonds drawn for redemption.

Meetings of noteholders, changes of terms and conditions and substitution of the principal debtor – So far as the substitution of the principal debtor is concerned, if a banking group wishes to make a structural change, then it may very well require a change to the principal debtor of the issue to be effected. An interesting point to consider here concerns taxation, in the event of a substitution of principal debtor, many tax authorities will treat the change as being a "disposal" so far as their resident investors for taxation are concerned. If the loan stock is denominated in foreign currency, such tax authorities will have calculated their home currency equivalent at the time of acquisition and will calculate the same currency equivalent again at the time of this "disposal". Any capital gain on these translation product differentials will be assessed for capital gains tax even though the investor has not actually sold the stock in the market. For example, if at the time the stock was purchased the US dollar sterling rate of exchange was $1.80 and at the time of "disposal" $1.10, the dollar denominated asset held by the investor will have appreciated in value making him liable for a substantial unrealised capital gain. The tax authorities in the UK are not, necessarily, the only fiscal authorities in the world likely to apply this principle. Accordingly, the trustee of loan stocks subject to a substitution of principal debtor clause would probably require the issuer and/or guarantor to indemnify the trustee on behalf of investors for any liability to capital gains tax which might be incurred. Careful consideration must be given before any substitution of principal debtor is made in the light of relative exchange rates for the currency debt against the investor's own currency. Bank borrowers may be well advised to devise formal wording in the loan terms which expressly state that they will incur no such liability to indemnify anyone for capital gains tax incidence which could arise from a substitution of the principal debtor.

Further issues – It is normal to insert a clause that the issuer may create further indebtedness without the consent of the note or bond holders.

Indemnification of the trustee

If subject to a trust deed the trustee will require indemnification which will include provisions relieving him from taking proceedings unless indemnified to his satisfaction and also to entitle the trustee to conduct other normal business transactions with the issuer and guarantor.

Governing law

For euro-issues the governing law is usually English Law. English law is a qualifying criterion for Bank of England approval so that the issue ranks as capital indebtedness for the issuing or guarantor bank. In the case of foreign debt issues the subordination clause must be subject to English law although other terms and conditions made subject to local foreign law may be acceptable to the Bank of England for qualifying bank capital debt.

CHAPTER 31

Capital and Funding Requirements for a Bank's Overseas Branch Affiliate or Subsidiary Investments

When establishing a branch operation abroad, the host country's capital requirements must be observed. In many countries the amount of quasi-capital injected will affect the level of business that can be undertaken. In West Germany, for example, the Banking Act contains rules on equity and liquidity. Branches of foreign banks are dealt with in Section 53 of the Banking Act and the quasi-capital donated by the head office abroad is referred to as Dotationskapital. Qualifying capital includes retained profits. All banks must maintain adequate equity or dotationskapital in accordance with Principles I, II and III. The first of these limits the aggregate loan assets and participations in subsidiaries to eighteen times its equity or dotationskapital. Principle IA, inter alia, limits the open positions in foreign currencies and precious metals to 30% of its total capital. Principles II and III are rules that govern the liquidity of the branch or bank. The Act also contains regulations relating to the size of loans a bank or branch can make under the Grosskredite requirement being large loans which are defined as exceeding 15% of capital. Loans to a single borrower are restricted to 75% of the capital, and the aggregate of the largest five loans must not exceed three times the amount of the equity, and the aggregate of all the Grosskredite loans eight times the amount of the equity. The capital base injected into a foreign branch can, therefore, be of considerable significance regarding its capacity to do business in accordance with the laws laid down in the host country.

Care, however, should be taken not to inject too much capital as taxes may be levied thereon. In Germany there is a 1% per annum tax on Dotationskapital or equity capital. In addition, any new capital will attract Stock Exchange transfer tax in Germany. In Switzerland the Banking Law Article 11 defines own resources of a foreign bank's branch as including share capital, open reserves, retained earnings and hidden reserves. Maximum lending limits to any one client are restricted under Article 21 of the Act to percentages of the lender's own resources which range from 160% for loans to Swiss public authorities and cantonal banks to 20% to unsecured borrowers. These limitations invariably mean that Swiss banks and branches of foreign banks, which have a slightly different definition of "own resources", have to have a large capital base. As in Germany, there is a capital tax which also applies to the Dotationskapital of branches of foreign banks.

In the UK the required amount of working capital injected into branches from the overseas head office will depend on the proposed amount of the branches' activities in London. So far as the taxing authorities are concerned, all funds emanating from head office are treated as free capital and interest which may be paid thereon will not be tax deductable. If a branch of a foreign bank in London receives deposits from its head office on the interbank market, so far as the Inland Revenue is concerned, this will be treated as working capital and therefore the interest payable thereon will not be tax deductable. There is a 1% capital duty on all issued share capital. The Bank of England's requirements regarding the measurement of capital is discussed in Chapter 5.

In the USA, under the International Banking Act of 1978 (IBA), there are limitations and restrictions based on a percentage of the amount of capital and retained reserves of branches and agencies of foreign banks. The US dollar equivalent of the capital and reserves of the foreign bank's parent is the basis on which the percentages are calculated. The IBA permits foreign banks to own Edge Act corporations, agreement corporations, national and state-chartered investment companies, representative offices, agencies and branches; indeed, all types of financial vehicle except securities corporations. In 1979 the Federal Reserve Board issued their Regulation K, called "International Banking Operations" which sets out the rules and regulations for lending limits and capital requirements of Edge Act companies and other regulatory restrictions on international operations of US banking institutions. It defines the rules relating to ownership of Edge Act corporations and their operation in the US and abroad. Offshore activities of Edge Act corporations, Federal Deposit Insurance Corporation (FDIC) member banks and domestic bank holding companies are also set out in Regulation K. The rules relating to capital requirements are based on "capital and surplus" which is defined as capital and reserves but does not include loan stocks. The capital requirement for holding companies is minimal and there are no capital requirements for agencies, offshore operations or International Banking Facilities (IBFs) and the regulations impose no lending limits for these three types of structure. Whilst there is no specifically allocated capitalisation required for branches, the regulation relating to lending limits per any one legal entity must not exceed 10% of the overseas parent bank's capital. For subsidiaries of national banks, state-chartered banks and for Edge Act corporations and agreement corporations, there exist similar maximum limits on lending to any one customer, i.e. 10% of the financial institution's capital and surplus.

In addition to the statutory and operational requirements relating to capital in the host country of an overseas branch or subsidiary, there are other matters which the parent company should also address. In most circumstances the host country's currency will be required for the purchase consideration of an outward direct investment abroad in the form of shares in an affiliate, or a controlling interest in a subsidiary, or quasi capital in respect of a branch. Aquisition of a subsidiary company can also be achieved by way of share exchange.

Quasi capital may be required for a branch abroad for the purchase of property and other start-up expenses. The foreign currency required may be bought or borrowed by the parent. The cost of borrowing must always be weighed up in the context of the exchange risk incurred in buying the currency. Depending on the domicile of the asset, the required currency may not be available for the parent to borrow on the interbank deposit market, particularly if the branch is situated in a country with a relatively exotic currency. In Chapter 16 on Foreign Exchange reference is made to currencies which are widely traded and others which are less tradable or those where no market exists. The less tradable currencies are sometimes called "exotics". The question that then arises would be against which currency should the purchase consideration or quasi capital be purchased; should it be the home currency or perhaps US dollars? If the home currency is not US dollars, to fund the purchase consideration out of US dollars may involve the parent in a double exchange risk rather than a single exchange risk. Many companies take the view that, when foreign currency cannot be borrowed for a reasonable period of time and at an acceptable level of interest, then the funding should take place in the home currency, albeit with the attendant exchange exposure. When matching foreign currency funds are available on the long-term fixed interest capital markets, any underlying infrastructure in the form of material subsidiaries, should be hedged with long-term liabilities when market rates reach an acceptably low level. A major consideration must be the amount of funding the parent company needs to consider. At the outset it may be argued that the purchase consideration is the appropriate sum to consider. If there is an element of goodwill to be written off, then it is arguable whether supporting funding in a foreign currency is required to hedge a lower asset value in the same currency as this would create a balance sheet exposure. As the company or branch activities develop and the asset value of the investment abroad increases, the parent should consider whether the funding is sufficient to avoid balance sheet distortion on translation exposure. Sometimes an aggressive funding policy is adopted where the projected asset values of all material overseas subsidiary companies at the end of the next financial year is assessed, and the potential translation exposures are hedged.

Whether profits made by overseas subsidiaries are up-streamed to the parent or distributed depends first of all on the repatriation regulations in the host country. Many countries closely regulate repatriation and in some countries the parent may be required to ensure that profits are repatriated. Initially the correct selection of the country of the parent's domicile must be a very important primary consideration.

Finally, consideration must be given to tax neutrality in the balance sheet, especially as regards the level of foreign currency loan stocks and long-term assets in the form of investments in subsidiary companies abroad. Accounting practice and taxation treatment varies from country to country. It is essential to endeavour to achieve tax neutrality if the bank has subsidiaries and/or loan stocks domiciled abroad or expressed in foreign currency.

Principles of International Accounting

This chapter is concerned with accounting principles in general, and in particular their relevance to Treasury activities. Taxation issues and any special accounting treatment related thereto are not addressed.

International Accounting Standards

Through its own regulatory and/or professional accounting bodies, each country has established its own criteria for the presentation of financial statements and, in particular, disclosure requirements. For example, the United States has developed specific legal requirements in respect of the presentation and disclosure of the financial statements of US incorporated banks and bank holding companies. These are required to be prepared in accordance with the promulgations of the Financial Accounting Standards Board and regulations of the Securities and Exchange Commission. The United Kingdom does not have specific statutes related to banks' financial reports. Within the United Kingdom the financial statements and disclosure requirements of UK incorporated banks and other companies are governed by the Companies Acts and prepared and presented in accordance with the Statements of Standard Accounting Practice (SSAPs) as promulgated by the Accounting Standards Committee which comprises representatives from the major accountancy bodies in the United Kingdom and Ireland.

An International Accounting Standards Committee (IASC) was established during 1973, as a result of an agreement by accounting bodies in Australia, Canada, France, Germany, Ireland, Japan, Mexico, the Netherlands, the United Kingdom, and the United States of America. The objectives of IASC are:

- To formulate and publish in the public interest accounting standards to be observed in the presentation of financial statements and to promote their worldwide acceptance and observance.

- To work generally for the improvement and harmonisation of regulations, accounting standards and procedures relating to the presentation of financial statements.

The members of the IASC agreed to support these objectives by publishing in their respective countries every International Accounting Standard (IAS) approved for issue by the board of the IASC, and by using their best endeavours to:

- ensure that published financial statements comply with IAS's in all material respects and disclose the fact of such compliance.

- persuade governments and standard-setting bodies that published financial statements should comply with IAS's in all material respects.

- persuade authorities controlling securities markets and the industrial and business community that published financial statements should comply with IAS's in all material respects and disclose the fact of such compliance.

- ensure that the auditors satisfy themselves that the financial statements comply with IAS's in all material respects.

- foster acceptance and observance of IAS's internationally.

The IASC have published a total of 24 standards. These are listed below:

    IAS1 – Disclosure of accounting policies
    IAS2 – Valuation and presentation of inventories in the context of the historical cost system
    IAS3 – Consolidated financial statement
    IAS4 – Depreciation accounting
    IAS5 – Information to be disclosed in financial statements

IAS6 – "Superseded by IAS15"
IAS7 – Statement of changes in financial position
IAS8 – Unusual and prior period items and changes in accounting policies
IAS9 – Accounting for research and development activities
IAS10 – Contingencies and events occurring after the balance sheet date
IAS11 – Accounting for construction contracts
IAS12 – Accounting for taxes on income
IAS13 – Presentation of current assets and liabilities
IAS14 – Reporting financial information by segment
IAS15 – Information reflecting the effects of price changes
IAS16 – Accounting for property, plant and equipment
IAS17 – Accounting for leases
IAS18 – Revenue recognition
IAS19 – Accounting for retirement benefits
IAS20 – Accounting for government grants and disclosure of government assistance
IAS21 – Accounting for the effects of changes in foreign exchange rates
IAS22 – Accounting for business combinations
IAS23 – Capitalisation and borrowing costs
IAS24 – Related party disclosures

In the UK and Ireland SSAPs incorporate in all material respects 12 of the above statements. Of the remaining 11 IAS5, 13 and 16 are covered by the requirements of the Companies Acts. IAS14 is partly incorporated in the Companies Acts and, where applicable for Stock Exchange listed companies, partly in Stock Exchange requirements. The content of IAS18 is generally accepted practice and IAS17, 19 and 22 are proposed to be introduced. IAS23 and 24 are not covered. IAS15 is comparable to SSAP16, the contents of which are no longer mandatory and this SSAP has been cancelled.

The accounting requirements of the Companies Act 1981 implementing the provisions of the EEC 4th Directive, which is now consolidated into the Companies Act 1985 does not generally apply to banks and licensed deposit taking institutions, and consequently accounting standards and the format of presentation and disclosure requirements for banks in the UK, as in many other countries, have been defined through recommended and practical interpretation of accounting standards and on the basis of best accepted practices which have evolved as custom and practice within the Banking Industry. The most relevant International Accounting Standards which require consideration in relation to the activities of banks discussed in this publication are IAS1, 7 and 21 which relate respectively to:

SSAP2 – Disclosure of accounting policies
SSAP10 – Statement of source and application of funds
SSAP20 – Accounting for currency translation

There are four fundamental accounting assumptions addressed in IAS1 and SSAP2 which are expected to be complied with in the preparation of financial statements and disclosure requirements, and consequently their implications are evident throughout established accounting procedures and practices. These are "going concern", "consistency", "accruals" and "prudence". It is assumed that:

- the reporting institution is treated and viewed as a going concern.

- accounting policies remain consistent from one period to another.

- revenues and costs are accrued as they are earned and incurred, and not when they are received or paid.

If the above three points do not pertain then disclosure is required. It is also expected that "prudence, substance over form, and materiality should govern the selection and application of accounting policy" i.e. the "prudence concept" prevails over the "accruals concept". This implies that:

- uncertainties which may apply to any transactions should be recognised by exercising prudence in preparing financial statements.

- transactions should be accounted and presented in accordance with their substance and financial reality and not merely with their legal form.

- financial statements should disclose all items which are materially bad enough to affect evaluation or decision.

- financial statements should disclose a true and fair view.

Both IAS1 and SSAP2 require, inter alia, that financial statements should include clear and concise disclosure of all significant accounting policies which have been used and that any change in an accounting policy that has material effect in the current period, or may have a material effect in subsequent periods, should be disclosed together with the reasons. The effect of the change, if material, should be disclosed and quantified.

The recommended presentation of source and application of funds as presented in IAS7 and SSAP10 is not appropriate to the presentation of a bank's assets and liabilities. However, there have been various developments which have taken place in recent years which may impact ultimately upon requirements for banks either internationally or just within the EEC. On the 1st May 1980 the IASC issued a discussion paper on the specific subject of bank's financial statements and disclosure requirements. This paper followed discussions with the Basle Committee of Banking Supervisors and, inter alia, suggests that a bank's published accounts should incorporate:

- Classification of assets and liabilities by nature,

- Analysis of assets and liabilities by maturity

- Concentration of assets and liabilities,

- Commitments

In addition the EEC issued a proposed directive in 1981 on the subject of disclosure and financial reporting by member country banks. This directive includes, among other things, requirements for disclosure of the maturity analysis of assets and liabilities.

IAS21 and SSAP 20 "Accounting for foreign currency translation" provides guidance for banks on the subject of accounting for its net investment/asset position in overseas operations (i.e. infrastructure investments) and procedures to be adopted when accounting for the effects of changes in their value. Although these standards are concerned with translation issues related to monetary assets and liabilities, the nature of a bank's assets and liabilities, being monetary (i.e. its stock in trade), are not conducive to treatment in accordance with these standards. Also the subject of the methods of calculating profits and losses arising from dealing in foreign currencies is specifically excluded.

Treasury Accounting

The asset and liability structure of the Treasury operations of a multi-national bank, together with the range of products and instruments in which it trades, is both wide ranging and complex. However, irrespective of this complexity, the main elements of a treasury's income will accrue from:

- Assets
- Loans and Advances – commercial and interbank
- Portfolio Investments
- Liquidity Investments
- Dealing Assets – e.g. various financial instruments
- Foreign Exchange Trading
- Financial Futures Trading
- Options Trading
- Bullion Trading

Other than its day to day operational costs, a treasury's most significant expense will be related to funding requirements. These will include:

- Liabilities
- Deposits
- Certificates of Deposit and other related debt paper
- Commercial Paper
- Capital Debt

598

In total the main elements of a treasury's income and expense will relate to:

- Interest receipts and payments
- Portfolio investment income
- Liquidity investment income
- Discount received and Discount paid
- Fee income and expense
- Provision for frauds, losses and doubtful debts
- Normal running expenses, including staff costs, premises, furniture, machines, equipment, etc.
- Hedge income and expense related to –
    Futures
    Options
    Interest and foreign currency liability swaps
    Forward rate agreements
- Dealing and trading income from –
    Foreign exchange
    Futures
    Options
    Bullion

Each asset and liability and item of income and expense must be accounted and recorded completely and accurately. This must be undertaken in accordance with accepted accounting standards and practices. It must conform with both the legal or promulgated reporting and disclosure requirements that are applicable to the domicile of each separate banking operation within a group, and also provide information in accordance with the parent country's reporting and disclosure requirements.

Aside from formal disclosure and financial reporting, it is also desirable for the management of individual banks to establish separate returns, and develop systems, which are better suited for internal management and processing purposes. Therefore, when considering an appropriate accounting system, which for a major treasury operation must of necessity be computerised, such system must be conducive to:

- the generation of accounting and recording entries in accordance with the bank's accounting procedures and practice

- the submission of mandatory external reports (including those of its supervisory and regulatory bodies)

- the provision of desired internal financial budgetary and profit reporting requirements in accordance with its group chart of accounts

- the provision of detailed management, trader and dealer information which is perceived to be required to control its business and safeguard its assets

- the provision of confirmations and other documentation required by counterparties.

There are three accounting methods for recording foreign currency transactions. These are single, dual and multi-currency accounting systems. Under a single currency accounting system all foreign currency items are translated at their value dates and recorded in the base currency. Dual currency provides for every currency transaction to be recorded in its base and foreign currency amounts. A multi-currency system records each transaction in the subject currency.

A single currency system does not provide for the identification of individual currency items or positions. The dual currency system involves unnecessary duplication of effort and does not readily facilitate differentiation between currency assets and liabilities and identification of foreign exchange exposure. A multi-currency system which is, in the authors' view, the only appropriate system for a sizeable treasury operation, forms the basis upon which subsequent comment in this chapter is made. A multi-currency system provides for current assets and liabilities to be recorded in general ledgers, by currency. It also records contingent assets and liabilities including not-in-value forward, futures, option and forward rate agreement contracts and provides for cash flows related to interest and foreign currency liability swaps to be properly recorded and accounted. As contingent assets and liabilities, not-in-value forward, futures, option and forward rate contracts, each of which is commonly referred to as "off-balance sheet", may be recorded in general ledger contra accounts with supporting journals. Alternatively, these records may be maintained in separate memoranda and journals with automated interfaces to the General Ledger. Similar procedures may also be adopted for interest rate and currency liability swaps.

Within a multi-currency system, each nostro account will constitute the "bank" account in its appropriate currency general ledger and the balance thereon will, after reconciliation, be equal and opposite to that reflected or the actual correspondent account related thereto. All external in-value transactions will reflect over this or, when more than one nostro is maintained in a currency, these accounts.

Where a treasury area is responsible for the control of a bank's main nostro account in a currency, each of its branches and other operating areas will be in account with the treasury area. Conversely where another area of a bank has responsibility for nostro account maintenance control, the treasury's nostro account will be represented by its account with that area, and not the correspondent bank account.

Other than when a bank is buying or selling a currency or where it has a net currency exposure, for example through its net overseas investment/asset position or dealing activities, the base or reported currency equivalents of underlying assets and liabilities in each currency are, in profit and loss terms, of little consequence.

Where a bank buys or sells one currency for another currency it normally creates exchange risk exposure and also makes profits and losses, which must be measured. Within a multi-currency system the measurement of profit and loss is achieved by establishing a common unit of account. The measurement of exposure is attained by segregating general ledger balances which are related to foreign exchange exposure risk from those which are simply an asset or liability in that currency.

The common unit of account which is applied may comprise the base currency of the domicile of the operation, the reported currency of the bank or the major currency of its activities. Irrespective of which currency is used, it is for the purpose of this chapter referred to as the "base" currency. The subject of the valuation of both dealing positions and net investment/asset positions are discussed in detail later, but now it may be useful to clarify the accounting treatment of purchases and sales within a multi-currency system.

The basic principle of recording foreign currency purchases and sales within a multi-currency system is by reference to the base currency as the common unit of account. It is important to remember that, as discussed in Chapter 16, each sale or purchase of a currency is in itself a purchase and sale, i.e. the payment of one currency against the receipt of another. Let us first consider the transaction:

> Where the base currency is not a subject currency of a transaction, a base currency equivalent is established by applying an appropriate mid-market rate of exchange for the base currency against either of the subject currency amounts. Where US dollars is a subject currency and not the base currency that rate will normally be used. This procedure creates a cross currency value for the other currency and this will usually be verified as a double check of accuracy. This can be illustrated by the following:

> Let us assume a base currency of sterling and a sale of US$5 million against Deutschemarks @ 3.0195 = DM15,097,500 with a mid rate of US$/£1.3070

> US$5,000,000 @ 1.3070   = £3,825,554.71
> DM15,097,500 @ a cross rate of
> 3.9464865 (3.0195 × 1.3070) also   = £3,825,554.71

> For recording purposes the rate applied to the first currency thereby establishing a cross currency value for the second is irrelevant, but for revaluation purposes and profit measurement by currency traded, it is very important. Therefore it is essential that the rates used are at or near market.

Now let us consider the accounting records:

> Within a multi-currency accounting system a "dealing" account, more commonly known as an "exchange dealing account" is

established in each currency general ledger. As is appropriate or desired, separate general ledger exchange accounts are also established for any net investment/asset and open position accounts, together with any other transaction, or series of transactions, in a currency which may contain foreign exchange exposure and which is required to be separately identified. In addition, *separate* accounts are opened within the base currency general ledger for *every* exchange account which is opened in each of the currency general ledgers. Thereafter all sales and purchases of foreign currency for whatever purpose are processed as sales or purchases respectively against the base currency and recorded in the appropriate exchange accounts.

Taking the example above, the book-keeping entries would be:

<pre>
    US$ General Ledger
        CR Nostro   5,000,000
        DR Exchange Dealing A/c   5,000,000

    DM General Ledger
        DR Nostro   15,097,500
        CR Exchange Dealing A/c   15,097,500

    Sterling General Ledger
        CR US$ Exchange Dealing A/c   3,825,554.71
        DR DM Exchange Dealing A/c   3,825,554.71
</pre>

As will be noted the net result is nil in the sterling nostro account. As these "nostro" transactions are not external payments or receipts, they will not reflect on the sterling correspondent account, therefore in practice they may for convenience of reconciliation be passed over separate control accounts. Where transactions include the base currency as a subject currency they will, in the normal course of events, impact upon the appropriate exchange accounts. The above procedures will be similarly applied to all not-in-value forward exchange transactions with their respective values reflecting on separate not in value exchange dealing contra accounts within the general ledger or separate memoranda control accounts in each currency and in the base currency. Thereafter, in book-keeping terms, as at their respective value date, the subject currency of each sale and purchase will move from the not in value records to be recorded over the appropriate general ledger exchange dealing accounts with corresponding entries being passed from the not in value records to their respective exchange dealing accounts in the base currency general ledger, as described above.

The net overbought or oversold outright dealing positions in each currency will comprise the balance on the respective exchange dealing account adjusted by the net of not in value translation within that currency.

Although, as previously stated, for profit and loss purposes, the base currency amounts of most underlying currency assets and liabilities are of little relevance to a treasury function, they will require to be calculated for translation purposes as at financial reporting dates. Consequently a multi-currency accounting system will have the facility to convert each currency balance into both the reported and/or base currency equivalents.

To digress slightly from the main theme of accepted accounting standards and practices, it may be helpful briefly to consider the detailed analysis which may be achieved within a computerised multi-currency accounting system if it is used to its full potential in relation to:

- Profit centre accounting within a treasury area

- Management, trader and dealer information

- Control procedures

- Internal and external reports

- Processing and accounting

Although it is not usual or recommended that any pressure be placed upon dealers with regard to profit performance it is equally important that a large Treasury operation is able to safeguard its assets and measure its performance properly. All too often a situation exists where profits are made but no one knows exactly and precisely from where they are generated. This can only be achieved if responsibilities are clearly defined, and accounting and reporting procedures are developed to identify transactions and functions with these responsibilities.

- As discussed in Chapter 15, a primary responsibility of a deposit trader in both domestic and international currency markets is to fund or utilise all shortfall/surplus cash requirements on a daily basis to maximise advantage, or minimise cost. Subject to any adjustments for items in the course of collection, the balance of the nostro account or nostro accounts in each currency, in conjunction with the actual balances and account detail advised by the correspondent banks, will form the basis for each day's cash management process. It follows therefore, that the impact of all interest receipts and payments resultant from the deployment and funding of these balances comprise part of that dealer's profit measurement.

- Within a multi-currency system the balance of each nostro account (or the net balance of the nostro accounts where more than one is maintained in a currency) is resultant from the totality of all external in-value payments and receipts in that currency. Therefore the nostro balance represents the net of the gross positions as reflected on each general ledger account (exclusive of contingencies and not-in-value transactions). In turn each of the other general ledger balances represent the negative and positive cash flow positions resultant from the underlying activity which they represent, i.e. loans and advances, foreign exchange dealing, hedging, asset portfolio, overheads impersonal accounts, etc.

- Therefore, first by operating on a value dated basis and second, by calculating interest upon each general ledger account, which is not directly related to the deposit and loan portfolio controlled by the deposit trader, actual interest to and from each profit and cost centre may be accurately calculated and applied. Where management of a separate profit or cost centre or asset portfolio, which is subject to separate measurement, chooses to fund or utilise resources other than maintaining, what is effectively, a current account balance with the deposit trader, such transactions are normally arranged as though they were fixtures or call accounts with an external client, and separately recorded and priced. When this procedure is adopted the rate of interest applied to the "current account" balances and other sections of a treasury area and, as appropriate, branches, will usually constitute the overnight average funding/lending rate achieved by the deposit dealer which is, in theory, where these balances are utilised or funded.

• Nostro accounts do usually require compensating credit balances or are subject to fee charges. As the deposit dealers are not the sole users of these accounts it will be necessary to consider the impact of any free balances which are required to be maintained, or specific transaction charges imposed on the use of these accounts by the correspondent bank. These should be charged to a central cost unit and thereafter applied proportionately on a transaction basis to the profit centres which originate transactions and use the accounts.

• A further advantage of a multi-currency system is the separate identification of the absolute amounts of funds being used and/or generated by each foreign currency trader, both in terms of currency (as represented by the exchange dealing account in the currency general ledger) and also in terms of the base currency (on the appropriate currency exchange dealing account in the base currency general ledger). As discussed in Chapter 16, a foreign exchange trader is either able to fund or utilise day to day cash requirements by utilising cash or rolling them forward by using swap transactions. The effect of this latter form of funding will, as measured by premium discounts within exchange rates, be included within the overall revaluation process which is discussed later in this chapter. Through the application of interest related to a dealers day to day cash positions on both the currency and base currency elements, it is possible to establish the impact of funds upon trading results properly.

Through the above procedures gross profits for each type of activity can be established. Treasury operations are both cost and labour intensive areas. A dealer's full potential can only be achieved if the infrastructure is provided to support those activities and his success is therefore very dependent upon the quality of people providing these services. Consequently, in the measurement of the profit performance of individual sections of a treasury area cognizance must be taken of these support functions. It is therefore equally important that attention is focused upon costs and that they are carefully analysed and recorded by each profit, cost and support section. This will include both direct and indirect costs together with the application of brokerage, commission, fees, communications and computer facilities provided. Thereafter, within the parameters of subjective views and agreed methodology, it is relatively simple to establish vertically a time cost factor for each area's involvement in each type of transaction, and to establish horizontally an average transaction cost for each area of activity. The integration of these two factors will assist in the apportionment of cost from support functions to profit functions. This will both identify a meaningful bottom line working profit for each area and provide a basis for product costing and efficiency measurement within the support areas.

Each general ledger account and, as appropriate, all forward transaction control accounts will be supported by account/transaction journals. These journals will comprise detailed data bases, which incorporate all information which may be required for operational, financial, accounting, mandatory and management reporting purposes. Inter alia, these records will provide for the preparation and/or identification of:

Management, trader and dealer information:

- the bank's exposure position reports

- counterparty exposure position reports

- liquidity profiles

- asset and liability maturity profiles by final maturity

607

- asset and liability maturity profiles by interest rate period

- forward foreign exchange maturity profiles

- cash flow projections

- liquefiable assets, by type and transaction

- interest rate mis-match and interest rate sensitivity profiles

- eligible or reservable liabilities

- MLAs

Control:

- counterparty limits and utilisation

- dealing limits and utilisation

- limit excess reports

- production and verification of confirmations

- reconciliation information

- product pricing and internal profit/cost centre control and monitoring

Internal and external reports:

- financial reporting in terms of a bank's group chart of accounts

- profit reporting and analysis

- budgetary control and product costing

- source of funds

- utilisation of funds by type

- loan classification by type and final maturity

- country exposure returns

- central bank reporting requirements

- translation to base and/or reporting currency

Processing and accounting:

- exchange exposure positions by type:
    dealing
    net investments/asset positions
    structural positions

- deposit swap transactions

- interest accruals and amortisation of premia, discounts and fee income

- amortisation of due to/from interest rate and foreign currency liability swaps

- margins received and paid

- amortisation of specific hedges

- contingent accounts

- statements of account, positions, margins, etc.

- options premiums paid and received, differentiating between trading, dealing and hedging portfolios

- revaluation/mark to market

- currency translation to base or reporting currency

- pay and receive and delivery information

- value dating transactions

It is essential that within the accounting records, all client positions and a bank's own trading, dealing, investment and any other asset portfolio, together with related hedge and funding transactions, which may be the subject of special accounting treatment and separate management control, and profit performance measurement are separately identified and recorded. As previously discussed, this is usually achieved by maintaining separate subsidiary general ledger accounts and supporting journals for each functional operation. In practice, each net investment/asset position, structural position and any other exchange transaction which requires to be separately identified will be initiated by a foreign exchange transaction undertaken within the dealing portfolio. Segregation of these items is achieved by establishing them as internal contracts with the relative functional area of operation. Thereafter within the dealing portfolio they are simply treated as though they were normal contracts with another counterparty and will, within agreed dealing policy, be part of a dealer's overall position or covered specifically in the market.

The necessity for properly accounting, recording, and undertaking control procedures together with the ability to identify profit performance accurately cannot be over-emphasised. Weaknesses within these procedures have over the years proved to be a significant contributory factor to many large potential losses and unidentified risks being existent, without the knowledge of management, until it was too late to take corrective action.

Profit Reporting
When applying the four fundamental accounting concepts of going concern, accruals, prudence and consistency to treasury activities, items of income and expense, asset value, foreign exchange, futures,

options and any other traded subject matter should be considered separately although in practical terms they are all closely related.

Income and Expense

When considering individual items of income and expense, the concept of accruals requires that, where ultimate cash realisation can be assessed with reasonable certainty, the accrual concept should apply. Income and expense should be recorded in the period in which it accrues and not when it is paid or received. However, the concept of prudence, which takes precedence over the concept of accruals, requires that where items of income and expense are not able to be reasonably assumed, they should be deferred until they are received or incurred.

Interest

Exclusive of those transactions which are perceived to be bad or doubtful and management have decided, or statute dictates, that it would no longer, for prudential reasons, be correct to do so, it is accepted practice within banks for interest accruals to be recorded to current income irrespective of whether the amounts have been paid or received. This will include all interest bearing assets and liabilities inclusive of loans and deposits, funding instruments, dealing and investment portfolios and capital debt issues, irrespective of whether they are calculated on the basis of a fixed, floating, or discounted rate.

Interest income and interest expense for each reporting period will be represented respectively by interest received and interest paid during the period, adjusted by the difference between the accrued interest receivable and payable as at the last date of the period and the accrued interest receivable and payable as at the last date of the previous period. For example for the month of January gross interest income will comprise.

Interest Received During January

+ accrued interest receivable as at 31st January

− accrued interest receivable as at 31st December

Gross interest expense will be similarly calculated. In book-keeping terms interest accrued, but not due, is recorded on impersonal accounts over the end of the reporting period.

Within a multi-currency operation interest received and interest paid accounts must be monitored – like all other impersonal accounts – very, very closely. It is common practice for foreign currency interest received and interest paid accounts to be netted off at regular intervals and any shortfall or surplus being bought or sold with, or for, the base currency. Under normal circumstances a net interest received situation will emerge since this represents a profit element on the part of the bank's business. The timing of interest payments and receipts, however, needs to be closely recorded and monitored before any decisions are taken to switch an apparent surplus into the home currency. Anticipated currency receipts can and should be hedged if it is felt that a particular currency will weaken by the time it is expected to be available for realisation. A specific area to be aware of is any mismatch in the underlying funding of, for example, an investment portfolio. The timing of interest payments on the funding cover may not match the income from the asset in respect of an investment portfolio where coupon interest is usually paid either annually or semi-annually but not necessarily during the same months or on the same dates as the funding cover. There are distinct benefits to be received from having a computerised system of management information to assist with an effective management of currency income and payment. If a net interest paid situation should arise in any particular currency it is essential that this is not allowed to be rolled up by borrowing currency in order to fund the situation. This can give rise to a concealed foreign exchange exposure which, if allowed to continue, may prove costly. It is also important to remember that on an accruals and a cash basis negative net interest flows are a cost factor, positive net interest flows generate income.

Hedge Transactions and Fees
In accounting on an accruals basis, it is important that the true rate of return/expense is recorded and consideration will require to be given to the impact of both hedges and fees.

Hedges

Hedge transactions may comprise specific or general hedges. Specific hedges relate to identified underlying transactions or positions; for example, to hedge the interest rate on an identified deposit or loan with futures contracts. In the UK the recording of any profits or losses on specific hedges should be consistent with the accounting principles being applied to the underlying transaction. To qualify for this treatment, the hedging instrument should have a high degree of correlation in price movement with the underlying subject and be similar in terms of maturity and amount. Where a specific hedge is taken in anticipation of a transaction in the future it must be reasonably expected that that transaction will come to fruition. Specific hedges require to be documented and related to the underlying purpose for which they were taken in order to satisfy both internal and external auditors.

A general hedge relates to a composite risk, for example interest rate sensitivity, which is perceived to exist within an asset and liability portfolio. All general hedges and specific hedges which are no longer required for the purpose for which they were established, should be accounted and recorded as general trading positions which are discussed separately. By their nature most interest rate and currency liability swaps and forward rate agreements together with an element of forward, futures and option contracts will comprise specific or general hedges.

Swap Deposits

The forward exchange legs of swap deposits are specific hedges and should be accounted as such. The accounting procedures for recording swap deposit transactions therefore do require special consideration for the calculation of interest revenue and expense. Both accruals and paid and received amounts for both the interest and premium/discount elements of swap deposits should be applied as interest accruals. As discussed in Chapters 15 and 16 swap (switch) deposits comprise the funding of a loan in one currency from a deposit taken in another currency. The exchange risk is eliminated by covering the spot sale of the funding currency and spot purchase of the lending currency by establishing forward contracts to sell the lending currency and buy the funding currency. These sales and purchases are arranged to coincide with the maturity of the underlying advance and deposit. As the interest receivable and payable is accruing in different currencies either the exact interest receivable or the exact interest payable must also be sold or bought forward to the same date. This procedure effectively transfers the net profit or loss on the entire transaction into one currency. However, the interest receivable or payable, which has been sold or bought forward, will require to be offset by the impact of the relative premium or discount and amortised over the life of the underlying deposit and loan transactions.

Front End Fees

It is now common practice for banks to incorporate front end fees as a requirement of negotiated facilities, and the negotiated interest margin of return on the commitment is priced accordingly. As with the concept of accruals such fees should be amortised over the life of the underlying obligation. The imprudent accounting practice of taking all front end fees into current income immediately they are received has been the cause of embarrassment to several banks as returns on assets declined in subsequent years.

Fees, Commission & Expenses

With the exception of fee income, which specifically relates to current and contingent commitments, it is usual to record all fee and commission income as it is earned. Banks also usually provide for all expenses inclusive of brokerage, front end, underwriting and management fees as they become due, irrespective of the period of the underlying transaction or liability to which they may relate.

Interest on Bad and Doubtful Debts

It is not unknown for treasury areas to incur bad and doubtful debts resultant from their wholesale interbank and corporate lending activities. In most countries interest on doubtful loans and advances may continue to accrue to profit and loss accounts until such time as a judgement or act of default occurs or management consider it is no longer appropriate on prudential grounds. However, in other countries regulative criteria is established within which, in the event of specific circumstances, banks are precluded from continuing to accrue interest. For example in the United States, a loan is deemed to be non-performing if interest due is not paid within a period of 90 days from the date when it became due. Thereafter, no further interest may be accrued to current income and all previously recorded but still outstanding unpaid interest on that account or transaction must be reversed from P and L until such time as it is received. Although interest may continue to be calculated and accrue on each account it will be treated as interest in suspense and not current income until such time as payment is received.

Revaluation

In considering asset value the prudence concept requires that all losses should be recognised as they occur, but profits should only be accrued when they are realised. However, it also requires that substance over form and materiality should govern the selection and application of accounting policy. Let us now consider these issues in relation to accepted standards and practices within banks and how they may be related to dealing assets, foreign exchange, futures, options, bullion and other instruments traded.

A bank's asset structure, together with the "off balance sheet" instruments in which it trades, is different from those of most other types of business. A bank's stock in trade comprises, in the main, monetary items or the exchange of one unit of measure for another. Therefore, in applying the four fundamental accounting concepts to a bank's assets and trading activities, primary considerations are not related to placing an historic monetary value on an asset but in assessing first the current market value of that monetary asset, and secondly, the purpose for which it is held. Also, when reviewing a bank's dealing and trading activities, considerations are related to the profits and losses accruing and the impact of subsequent price movements thereon.

A bank's objective in maintaining dealing portfolios of whatever nature is both to provide services and maximise profits from dealing opportunities. The results of these activities must be frequently and carefully monitored and reported. It is now generally accepted that the only realistic basis of valuation and profit assessment is by a full comparison of all dealing portfolios, including as appropriate, both in-value and not-in-value transactions, with the appropriate current market rates at which such positions could be closed out. This is necessary:

- for management control purposes,
- to measure profit performance
- to avoid profit manipulation

This procedure is commonly referred to as 'revaluation'. A revaluation exercise is the process of valuing open positions at their current market price or prices. A revaluation exercise is applied to all dealing portfolios including dealing assets, foreign exchange, futures, options and bullion. Thereafter, the result of each valuation is accounted in accordance with each bank's individual accounting policies, which must be consistently applied. In practice for management control purposes a treasury operation will revalue its dealing portfolios on a more frequent time cycle than is required for profit accounting and reporting purposes, and these procedures are often implemented on a daily basis.

Accounting policy for recording profits and losses resultant from a revaluation exercise continue to be a subject of considerable discussion and deliberation. Although several authoritative documents have been issued on this subject, it is not covered by any specific IAS or SSAP and there continues to be a variance of views, practice and regulation in relation to the manner in which the resultant figures are recorded and reported within financial accounts. Accounting and reporting policy for the revaluation of both current and contingent assets and liabilities is open to subjective judgements related to providing a true and fair view, prudence, and accruals concepts together with accepted standards and practices with the banking industry in each country. It is now generally accepted accounting practice within the UK and many other countries that banks may either:

- value dealing assets at the lower of cost or market value, thereby recognising losses but deferring the recognition of profit until realisation – in accordance with the prudence concept and to provide a true and fair view, or

- value dealing assets at a full mark to market by recording all profits and losses resultant from a revaluation exercise immediately they are identified - in accordance with the accruals concept and the principle of providing a true and fair view.

It is pertinent, however, to mention that in some countries, for example West Germany, this choice is not available as statutory regulations require that the first method is adopted. Where the alternative is available and consideration is given to the adoption of the second method of accounting noted above, it is important that the prudence concept is fully considered and in this regard cognizance must be taken of both the liquidity of the market available to dispose of, or cover, dealing exposure and the size of portfolio held in relation to the overall size of the market in each type of instrument.

The authors support the view that, in the absence of any regulatory constraint and if the prudence concept is satisfied, the second method should be adopted for all dealing and trading portfolios and both profits and losses resultant from a revaluation of all in-value and not-in-value transactions should be recorded to current income. In this context it is considered that the impact of managements' decisions not to close out open dealing positions should be recorded in the accounting period during which these decisions are taken. Also, many trading portfolios incorporate inter-related transactions which are unable to be individually paired and identified, and therefore a true and fair view is not obtained unless the totality of the portfolio is considered. Although it is accepted that the accounted profit may not always be realised ultimately, the opportunity for profit distortion, either intentional or unintentional, will be reduced and any subsequent change will be properly measured. Additionally, substantial differentials will be avoided, from profit period to profit period, which will occur in many portfolios if the first method is adopted. However, irrespective of the accounting treatment adopted, it is essential that, for management control and monitoring purposes, together with profit performance measurement, the effect of all profits and losses are considered. Control procedures must also exist to ensure that the basis of the revaluation is properly applied to ensure that the possibility of intentional or unintentional profit distortions is excluded. In particular it is essential that rates and prices utilised are either checked or provided independently of the dealing room.

Assets

A treasury's asset portfolio, which will include fixed rate and floating rate investments, is held for a variety of reasons and prior to considering accounting treatment, it is necessary to establish the purpose for which assets are held and distinguish between those which comprise:

- Portfolio investments
- Dealing Assets
- Liquid Assets

Portfolio investments are those assets which a bank purchases with the immediate intention to hold until their final maturity, albeit that in practice sometimes these decisions may be subsequently reversed. Dealing assets are held with a view to taking advantage of short-term changes in market prices. Both portfolio and dealing assets constitute, and are properly considered to represent, liquid assets to a bank. However, a bank often buys and sells short-term instruments which, whilst in theory are either portfolio investments or dealing assets, in practice are not so defined at the outset of a transaction. These assets are held as short-dated liquid assets which may be realised as required or held until maturity. They normally have a final maturity of less than six months and include treasury bills, local authority bills, certificates of deposit and bankers acceptances.

The separation of assets between portfolio investments, dealing and liquid and, as discussed below, the different accounting treatments which may be related thereto are considered to be appropriate in terms of best accepted practices. However, as the division of individual assets between investment and dealing and liquidity portfolios is often, in practice, a function of subjective decisions, it is important that a bank is consistent in its approach to these decisions and exercises prudence in its application. Although portfolio investments usually comprise those assets which a bank intends to hold until final maturity, situations, requirements, and perceived objects do change. Therefore, assets held as portfolio investments need not necessarily be held until maturity and it is at the discretion of management as to whether they sell or switch such investments. Realised profits and losses on investment portfolios are usually taken to current income immediately they are incurred on the basis of an average cost price of the respective stock held. In practice it may also be desirable for securities to be transferred from an investment to a dealing portfolio. In these instances, transfers are normally made on the basis of the underlying securities' current market value.

Portfolio Investments
Portfolio investments are, in accordance with the basic concept of prudence, normally recorded at the lower of cost or market value with losses immediately recorded, but profits only taken into income when they are realised. However, this policy may differ according to the nature of the investment. Income on fixed rate, fixed redemption date assets may, through one method or another, accrue over the period of their life as an alternative to accounting on a lower of cost or market value. This method of accounting is usually adopted by the treasury function of a bank as most of their portfolio investments will fall into this category. This may be achieved by either:

- Accounting the initial investment at cost, accruing interest on a yield basis related to the coupon value and purchase price, and subsequently writing the cost up or down by the amortisation of the premium or discount to P and L through to redemption and accordingly adjusting the yield.

  or

- Retaining the investment at cost throughout its life at a yield related to the coupon value and separately amortising premium or discount to profit and loss to the debit or credit of a suspense account through to redemption.

or

- Writing the investment up or down to its redemption value by immediately debiting or crediting a suspense account with the full amount of premium or discount and subsequently amortising the suspense account to P and L through to redemption.

Both the first and second methods only record the current assessed value at any point in time which will ultimately be equal to the redemption value, whilst the third records the redemption value from the outset.

Care must be exercised with portfolio and dealing investments regarding segregation of any substantial cum-dividend or interest payments discounted in the price, and also to record separately any accrued interest paid at the time of purchase pending its receipt or sold at the time of sale. None of these amounts should have an effect upon current income other than through the cost of carry or return thereon. In the UK, this latter consideration is particularly relevant to gilt edged securities with less than five years to redemption, where quoted prices do not include interest accruals.

All floating rate investments and, if held, any undated securities, will accrue interest as a yield on cost calculated by reference to the current note rate. For revaluation purposes they will be compared to their current market price with any resultant loss recorded and un-realised profits ignored. In book-keeping terms any adjustment to current income will normally be passed to the credit of an impersonal account with the original cost value continuing to be recorded as the prime record of account. The impersonal balance will be incorporated with the cost for the purpose of further revaluations. For the purposes of this exercise each security is compared with the mid-market price at the appropriate profit dates. Accounting standards recommend that all losses on each investment type should be recorded. However, as close correlations frequently exist between many of the instrument types held, many banks only record any net resultant shortfall related to particular groups of investment.

Dealing Assets

Large international banks maintain a wide variety of dealing assets across a broad spectrum of currencies and instruments. These may include a mix of fixed rate, fixed redemption date government securities and bonds, undated or floating rate government securities and bonds, together with various money market instruments including CDs, treasury bills, local authority and municipal bonds, bankers acceptances, etc.

The interest return on dealing assets will normally be accrued on a yield basis, calculated through reference to the net asset cost against the interest return on the nominal or face value of the instrument. The impact of premiums and discounts will not be considered other than in calculation of the yield against the coupon or discounted return. The revaluation of a dealing asset portfolio will be similar to that discussed in regard to portfolio investments. Each security is compared with the mid-market price at the appropriate profit dates. In applying the lower of cost or market value only realised profits and losses, together with any projected losses on each type of security will be recorded, but projected profits will not. Under the mark to market procedure the net overall result of the revaluation will be taken into account.

Liquid Assets

Liquid assets which will normally comprise fixed rate instruments, may be recorded and accounted as either portfolio investments or dealing assets as described above, their essential feature being that they are readily realisable.

Foreign Exchange Revaluation

The revaluation of a foreign exchange dealing portfolio is achieved by the application of current rates to both current and contingent assets and liabilities in each currency.

As previously discussed in the context of a multi-currency system, both the subject currency amount and the base currency contract amount, or in the case of a cross currency deal both currencies concerned, of all in value deals, are respectively recorded over "exchange dealing accounts" within the appropriate foreign currency and base currency general ledgers. By this means the current asset or liability balance of each currency "exchange dealing account" is represented by a current asset or liability balance on that currency's "exchange dealing account" in the base currency general ledger.

For revaluation purposes the exchange dealing account in each currency will be revalued at current market rates and the resultant base currency equivalent compared with the base currency amount outstanding on the appropriate exchange dealing account within the base currency general ledger. As at profit reporting dates any surplus or shortfall between these two amounts will be credited or debited, as the case may be, to profit and loss.

The revaluation of a bank's forward foreign exchange transactions is achieved by notionally closing out the net overbought or oversold position for each value date in the future, by applying the appropriate current market rates of exchange at which these positions could be closed out. Thereafter the net base currency contract amounts for each forward period of the revaluation, at their contracted rates, are compared to the revalued amounts. The net difference for each value date represents the notional profit or loss for that date and, when combined by currency, the profit or loss per currency of the not-in-value deals. As the dealing position is represented by both past-value and not-in-value transactions, substantial movements will be apparent between realised and forward profits and losses. From a management view-point, profits for any accounting period will be the net of profits and losses realised during the month plus or minus the improvement or deterioration in net forward profits and losses as reflected by a comparison of the revaluation exercise for the end of the current reporting period with the end of the previous reporting period. However, as these movements do represent cash movements which are being carried either as a cash balance or in swap costs they must be closely monitored.

Within the lower of cost or market value method of accounting only realised profits and losses together with forward losses by currency would be recorded. Forward profits by currency are ignored. Under the mark to market method of accounting all resultant profit

622

and losses as reflected by the revaluation for both in-value and for-ward value contracts will be applied to current income. All not-in-value contracts will continue to be recorded at their original contract values and, as appropriate in the case of cross currency deals, the original assessed base currency values. In book-keeping terms losses and/or profits will be recorded through an impersonal account. Consideration should be given to the following when revaluing a foreign currency portfolio:

- Market rates are not readily available for each value day on which a bank has an open position. Consequently it is usual for a computerised system to take the same day value rate, as the basis of revaluing the "exchange dealing account" balances, and specific one day value, spot and other short dated exchange rates, which are available. Thereafter to amortise monthly rates on a straight line basis across the intervening days between rate periods. This helps with the realistic identification of short dated mis-matches in future months which would otherwise distort the resultant figures, if one monthly rate was applied across a whole month period. The application of current market rates differs from bank to bank. Whilst most banks apply mid-market rates to both long and short positions for each day, others apply the appropriate bid or offered rate separately to each net position.

- In undertaking a revaluation exercise of a foreign exchange dealing portfolio, it is important to ensure that only those transactions which comprise part of that portfolio are revalued. It is also equally important to ensure that when netted out, each days overbought or oversold positions as calculated for the revaluation exercise, together with the "exchange dealing account" balance for each currency, are in agreement with the outright positions, and that internal accounting and recording entries do not distort the true dealing positions. In this latter regard special attention will, for example, require to be given to swap deposit transactions.

- The spot leg of a swap deposit transaction will affect the "exchange dealing account" balance and the forward leg for both principal and interest as a long or short position on its value

623

dates. However, these are hedging transactions which should not be allowed to impact upon the revaluation exercise and arrangements must be made to ensure they are excluded from this exercise. Segregation may be achieved through the generation of equal but opposite "dummy" or reversing entries which effectively negate these transactions from the exchange dealing account and forward positions, or separately record them in the accounting records. Similarly any other hedging or internally generated foreign exchange transactions for specific purposes other than exchange dealing positions should not in themselves affect the results of this exercise. As previously discussed it is customary to establish formal contracts with other areas or profit segments of a bank's operations for these transactions and thereafter include them within the revaluation exercise as though they were an extant transaction with an outside counterparty.

Special care will also be required to be given to variable delivery foreign exchange contracts, i.e. where a customer has an option **on the time of take up** not on the right of take up. These transactions can have a distorting effect upon the revaluation exercise if they are not separately assessed. It is desirable to revalue these items separately and thereafter amalgamate their affect with the overall results of the revaluation exercise. There is no ready formula for the accurate revaluation of these items but the authors suggest they should be revalued, in order of preference either:

- as at the date to which the dealer has swapped the underlying cover for such transactions (if this can be identified) or

- based on current rate structures at a worst possible scenario during the option period or

- at the next month revaluation date during which they can be taken up but following the criteria of "worst scenario" within that month.

A dealer will normally retain each dealing position against the base currency and therefore profits and losses are sold or purchased as they are accrued. Where this procedure is not adopted exchange exposure will result and the selling or covering of profits and losses will require separate consideration.

Net Investment Assets

In accordance with IAS21 when a bank has a net investment/asset position (infrastructure) in a foreign currency it should be translated as at the close of business on reporting dates at the current rate of exchange which is applicable between the investment currency and base currency. Any resultant difference should be applied to the reserves and not treated as current income. Where a specific hedge has been arranged that is similarly accounted to reserves.

Open Positions (other than dealing portfolios)

The basis of revaluation and reporting for open positions is the same as that applied to foreign exchange dealing positions discussed above. Each position will be measured against current market rates with any identified difference between the revalued base currency amount and as appropriate the open dealing position account being adjusted to current income.

Futures

As developed in detail in Chapter 17 the daily realisation of profits and losses on closed out futures contracts, and the settlement of unrealised profits and losses on the basis of a mark to market of all open positions at the daily futures exchange settlement price, is an integral part of the financial futures markets. That chapter also explains both the original and variation margin requirements and procedures related to futures. Although futures contracts are contingent assets and liabilities, margins and profits and losses on closed out deals are current assets and liabilities and will be recorded accordingly. A bank's transactions on or through a futures exchange will usually comprise a mix of its own dealing portfolio, internal hedge transactions and underlying commercial interest. The accounting records will therefore require to distinguish and, where regulations require, segregate these transactions. First between a bank's activities and those transactions undertaken on behalf of its customers. Second, within a bank's own transactions, between those contracts which relate to a dealing portfolio and those which relate to specific hedges, or other purposes, unrelated to futures trading. These will include any transactions undertaken for deposit or foreign exchange dealers and traders. Both initial and variation margins related thereto will be similarly segregated. Thereafter the revaluation figures for the dealing portfolio as at the close of business on the profit reporting date, as established by reference to the appropriate exchange closing daily settlement price of that day for each contract, will be utilised as the basis of profit reporting.

Gross dealing profit performance for each reporting period will be measured by actual profits and losses on open and closed contracts together with the net cost or benefit resultant from both initial and variation margins. Trading profit will be represented by net profits/losses on contracts closed during the reporting period adjusted by profits and losses on open contracts at the end of the period, less profits and losses on open contracts at the end of the last reporting period. To establish gross trading profits or losses the resultant figure will then require to be adjusted by the net of interest paid and received on margin positions during the reporting period. Where the margin is satisfied by letters of credit or other forms of collateral any costs related thereto will require to be measured similarly. Profits and losses on specific hedges and other separately identified transactions will be calculated, and thereafter be recorded in accordance with the appropriate accounting principles already discussed. Exchange and clearing house fees are recorded as current expenditure by banks as they are incurred.

Financial recording and reporting of profits and losses arising from futures trading is also the subject of a variety of views and practices and is not covered by any specific accounting standard, although in the United States the OCC, FRB and FDIC issued on 20th March 1980 revised guidelines for banks that engage in futures, forward and standby contracts on US government and agency securities. Inter alia these guidelines require that banks determine the market value of all open contracts at least monthly, and thereafter account consistently for such transactions on the basis of the mark to market or at lower of cost or market.

Unlike open positions in forward foreign exchange contracts, where considerations relate to unrealised profits and losses, futures provide two different situations. First, most contracts are closed out and profits and losses are realised prior to the delivery date of the underlying contract; and second, although for recording purposes open contracts are contingent assets and liabilities, all profits and losses are realised through the daily variation margin procedures. Consequently a case may be made for deferring or amortising profits on closed out contracts until, or over a period up to, the underlying contracts settlement date. However it is not considered that this would be consistent with the accruals concept or providing a true and fair view. The accounting of specific hedges should be consistent with the accounting principles being applied to the underlying transaction and general hedges treated as general trading positions.'

As described in Chapter 17 different factors affect the cash and futures markets, and the futures basis frequently moves. These movements may create sizeable swings in profit accruals from month to month but should correct themselves over time. They must be closely monitored.

Options

As relatively new financial instruments, and bearing in mind their unique features, there are no promulgated accounting standards for the reporting of options. However, the authors suggest that the procedures outlined below would appear to satisfy the four fundamental accounting concepts discussed in this chapter with premium payments and premium receipts being separately considered.

The accounting and reporting principles related to traded and over the counter options should be based upon the substance rather than form of the underlying transactions. As discussed in Chapter 18, options may among other things be purchased or granted by a bank as principal, for an underlying commercial customer's requirement to hedge, to generate additional income on an underlying object, or as part of an overall dealing strategy as a market-maker in the instrument. The general accounting principles of prudence, consistency, accruals, and going concern must be applied. The characteristics of an option contract are:

- unlike foreign exchange and futures contracts, it is a unilateral contract which provides the purchaser of the option with the right, but not the obligation, to buy or sell the underlying subject matter at a predetermined price during or at a specified time in the future.

- from the point of view of the option buyer the premium is a non-refundable payment, rather than a down payment applied to the purchase price of the underlying commodity.

- the purchaser's profit on a call option is determined by the extent to which any rise in the price of the underlying subject matter over the strike price exceeds the cost of the premium and on a put option the extent of any fall in price. The purchaser's loss is limited to the amount of the premium.

- the grantor's profit potential is limited to the amount of premium (and fees) he receives whilst his loss on an uncovered option is virtually unlimited.

- option premiums comprise both time value and intrinsic value.

Although options are unilateral contracts they are regarded as assets or liabilities and should be recorded as such. Premiums are usually required to be paid at the commencement of an option, but sometimes, as is the case on LIFFE, payment may be deferred until an option is exercised or expires. Where premiums are received or paid at the commencement of the contract they will be utilised to record the value of the asset or liability and be recorded in premium suspense accounts. These accounts require segregation first between those relating to general trading, hedging, specific hedges, income generation and dealing portfolios, and second, by premium receipts and premium payments. Where premium payments are deferred they should be recorded as contingent assets and liabilities and similarly segregated. Premium receipts and payments related to a dealing portfolio should form the basis of the revaluation exercise as discussed

628

below. Premium receipts should for all other options granted be considered on a net basis and revalued as discussed below. Premiums paid on options purchased other than on those comprising a dealing portfolio should:

- when related to general trading and general hedging, be amortised to current expense on a straight line basis over the life of the option, or

- when established as a specific hedge, be accounted in accordance with the accounting criteria applied to the underlying asset or liability.

As explained in Chapter 18, as appropriate and in accordance with each exchange's rules, profit and losses on exchange traded options are, like futures contracts, subject to daily settlement through the margin procedures. These margins will be recorded suitably on margin suspense accounts as current assets or liabilities. The terms and conditions of over-the-counter options may also incorporate margin requirements and similar procedures should be adopted in these situations.

The value of an option is measured by its premium value which includes both intrinsic and time value. Consequently, the revaluation of options must be based upon the current premium value of each option. The basis of the establishment of current premium value will, in the case of exchange traded options, be by reference to the daily exchange settlement price as at the reporting date. Over-the-counter options may be priced against current premium prices as calculated with an option pricing model or at the premium value at which an equal and opposite transaction could be consummated either in the traded or over-the-counter market. Alternatively they may be assessed by recourse to the grantor of the option to establish the rate at which they would repurchase and settle the option.

All options purchased irrespective of the portfolio to which they belong should be revalued on this basis. Thereafter, resultant profits and losses should be recorded in accordance with the accounting procedures relative to the type of option and activity they represent:

- General trading and general hedges –
  all realised profits on purchases and profits and losses on grants
  will be recorded in accordance with the underlying accounting
  policy of each bank. i.e. either lower of cost or market or mark
  to market .

- Specific hedges –
  for purchases the profits arising from the revaluation, and for
  sales any resultant profit or loss net of premium value should be
  recorded in accordance with the accounting policy related to the
  underlying asset or liability against which it was taken.

Options Dealing Portfolios

The income potential in a dealing portfolio depends on a bank's
ability to meet its obligations by managing its hedging strategy within
the parameters of net premium payments and receipts. Consequently
the overall results of these activities inclusive of all hedges will require to be measured through a revaluation exercise. Hedges will
include futures and spot and forward cash market transactions,
together with any carry costs related thereto. Each of these will be
separately revalued. The revaluation of carry costs is through a revaluation of actual interest rates for the current term of the deposit or
loan against interest rates for the remaining period of the deposit or
loan as at the date of the revaluation, i.e. the interest costs which
would be incurred to close the position. The net result of all of these
revaluations will be compared with the net of premium receipts and
premium payments and thereafter the net result is recorded in
accordance with the underlying accounting policies of the bank.

Interest Rate and Currency Liability Swaps

The initial exchange, or value of a currency swap should be recorded
at the same rate as the final exchange and therefore revaluation issues
related thereto, need not be considered. Each interest rate and currency liability swap should be recorded as an off balance sheet asset
and liability. This procedure will both establish their existence within
the accounting records and also facilitate accrual of the payment
amounts as though they were interest. As interest rate and currency

liability swaps will by their nature comprise either specific or general hedges, both incoming and outgoing cash flows will normally be accrued to current income. If, for any reason, the underlying liability of a specific hedge is not treated on an accruals basis nor will the cash flows related to the hedge be accrued to current income. In monitoring the profitability of Swaps care is required to measure the impact of any inherent time gaps between cash flows.

Forward Rate Agreements

Upon the establishment of a forward rate agreement it should be recorded as a contingent asset. This will be necessary to establish its impact on future maturity diaries etc. Upon receipt or payment of the settlement fee, these contingent accounts should be closed and an asset or liability account established for the cash settlement amount. Thereafter where taken as a specific hedge this sum should be amortised on a straight line basis to the portfolio in which the underlying asset(s) or liability against which it was established is recorded.

Gold Dealing

Where a bank has gold holdings for its own account it will simply revalue them at current market prices for that form of gold. However, as discussed in Chapter 21, the activities of a large gold dealing operation will involve various gold positions both spot and forward, inter-related advances and deposits in several currencies, foreign exchange and futures transactions. Also it may include a sizeable option trading portfolio, together with business undertaken on a fee and commission basis. The procedures and systems for recording and revaluing the monetary items is the same as those related to banking which have already been discussed. Similarly, the revaluation of a gold option dealing portfolio will be based on the principles of option business already discussed.

As with foreign exchange, the revaluation of a gold portfolio requires both in-value and not-in-value transactions to be valued against their respective current market rates. In-value gold stocks are recorded over inventory accounts as ounces and decimals thereof by type of gold in its gross and net weight or in the case of grammes, ounces, tolas, taels and coins as pieces. The gold content of each bar is individually assayed and recorded from its date of assay and the gold content of all other stocks is known and also recorded. Thereafter all bars and pieces are converted to fine troy ounce weights and the resultant figure marked to current market value. The basis of this revaluation is normally the loco London price for that date. All "added value" existent in gold coins or other form of polished instrument is ignored for the purpose of this exercise. The gold and currency amounts and all forward deals are thereafter revalued on the basis of net daily open positions in accordance with the current value for those contracts.

In addition, all monetary, foreign exchange and option transactions together with assets and liabilities, both current and not-in-value which are established and related to the dealing portfolio, are revalued in accordance with the procedures already outlined in this chapter. Thereafter the combined effects of the results of these revaluations are taken together to assess recorded profits for the period under review. Subsequently in accordance with normally accepted prudence and accruals concepts, those profits related to forward transactions may be either included or excluded from the reported figures.

Translation Exposure
As discussed within this chapter it is normal for a bank's exposure positions whether created by net asset value structural or dealing positions to be separately identified, revalued and accounted, and foreign currency earnings to be protected and hedged. Translation exposure in any currency can impact upon either assets and liabilities, and affect the balance sheet in terms of volumes and ratios. As discussed in Chapter 2, these ratios are important and unless a bank's capital mix of currencies is similar to the underlying mix of currencies of its assets and other liabilities, substantial distortions can be created as exchange rate fluctuations impact upon the published accounts.

Transaction flow analyses for foreign exchange, currency deposits, financial futures, foreign currency options and gold provide an overview of the inter-relationships between the various functions within a dealing environment. These are illustrated on the following pages.

Foreign exchange transaction flow analysis

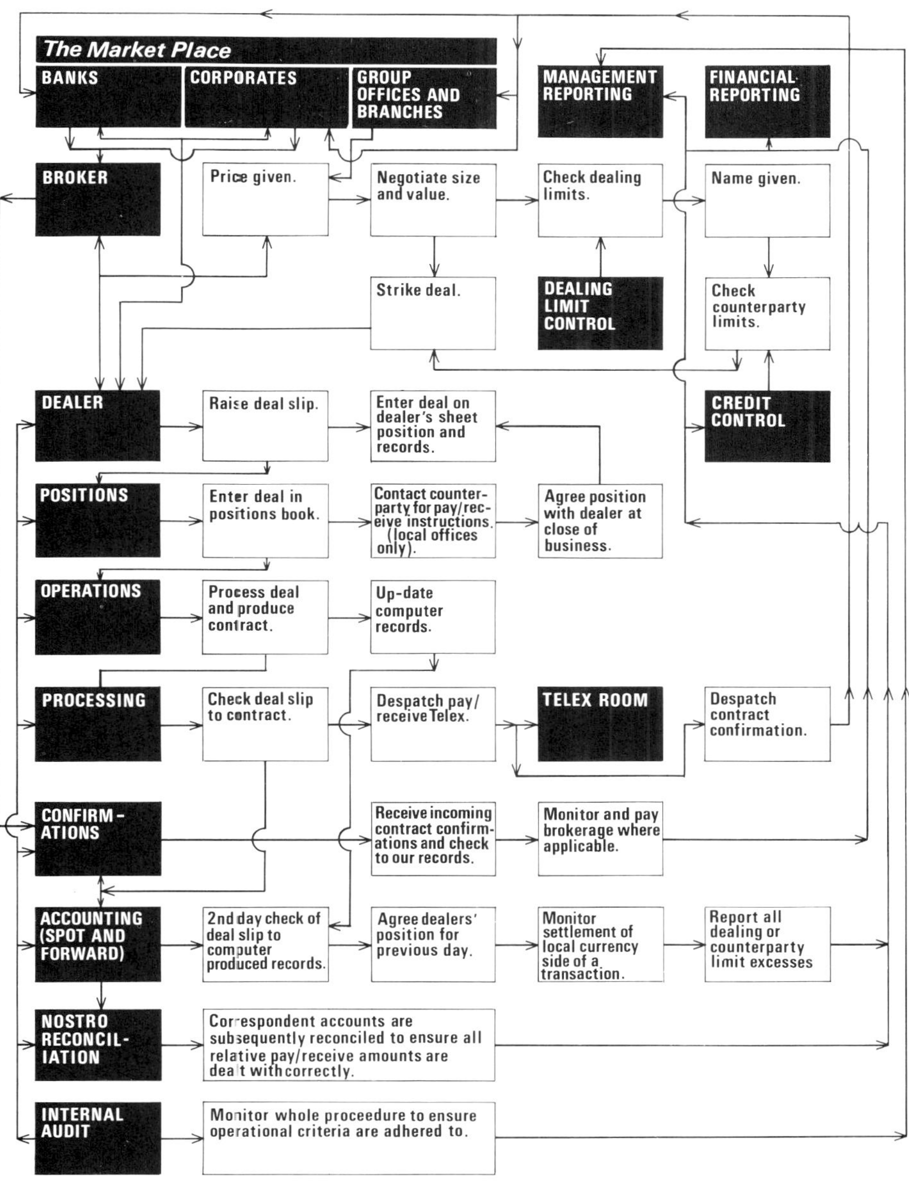

Currency deposit transaction flow analysis

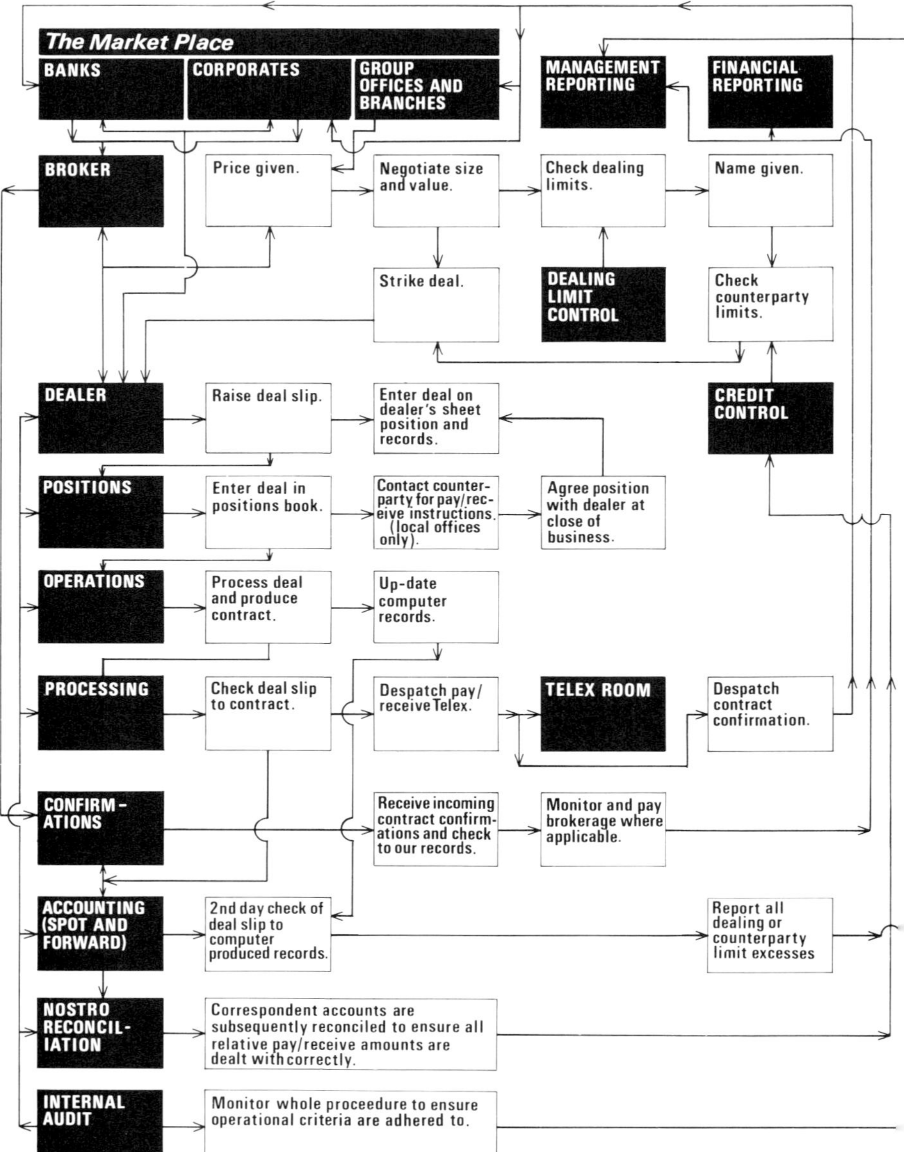

Financial futures transaction flow analysis

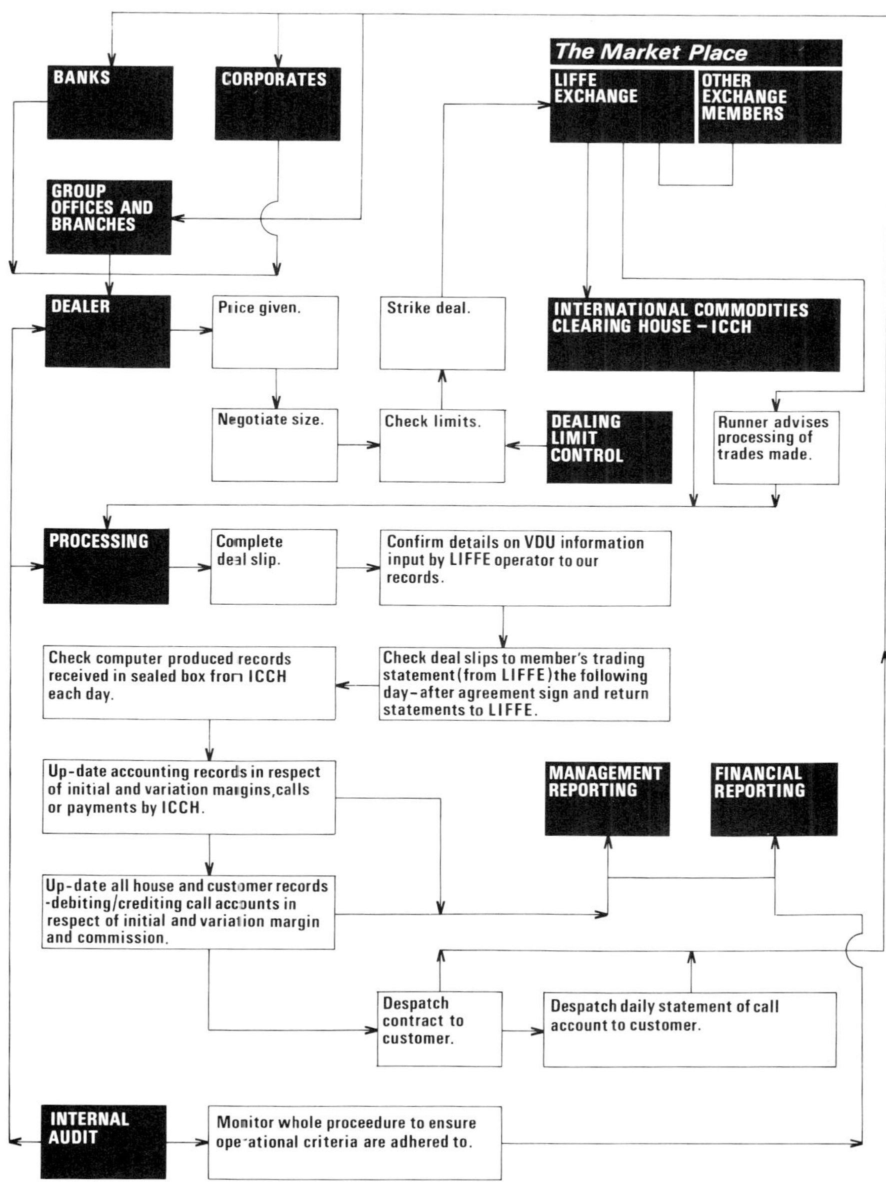

OTC foreign currency option transaction flow analysis

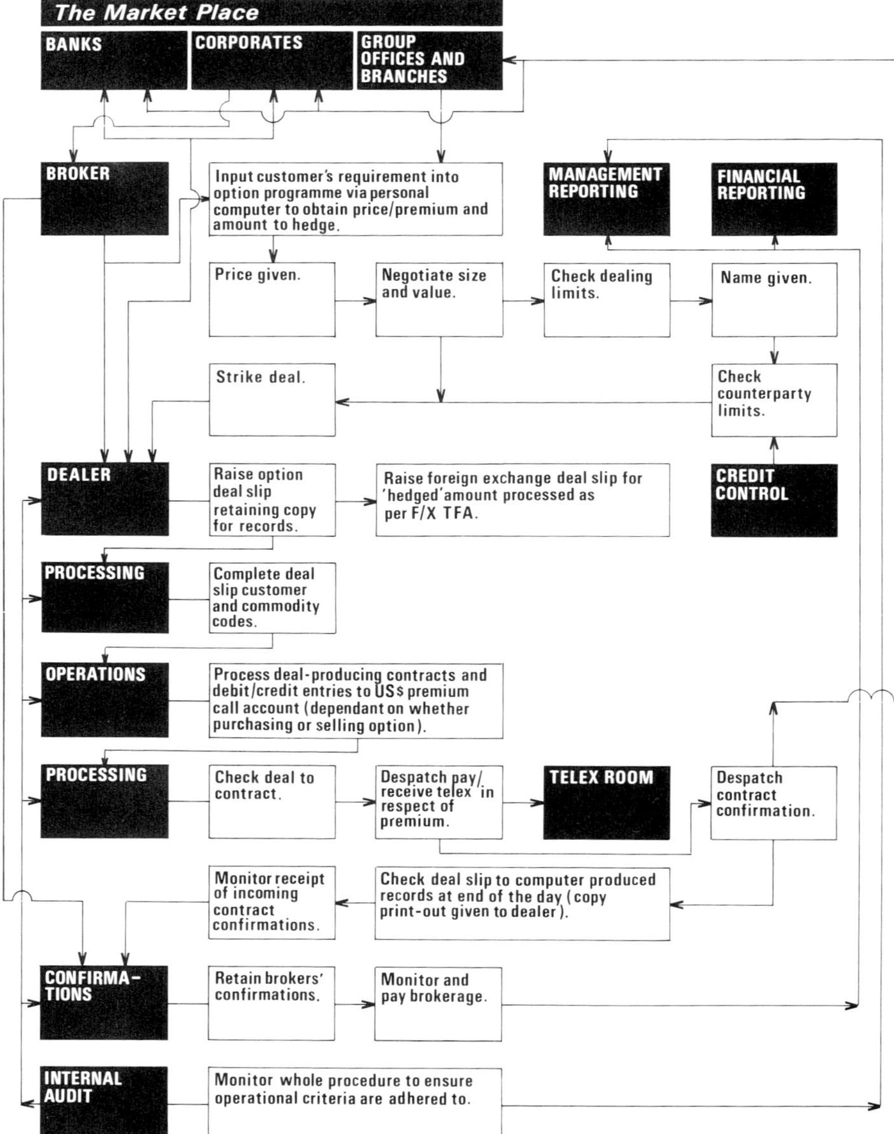

Gold transactions flow analysis

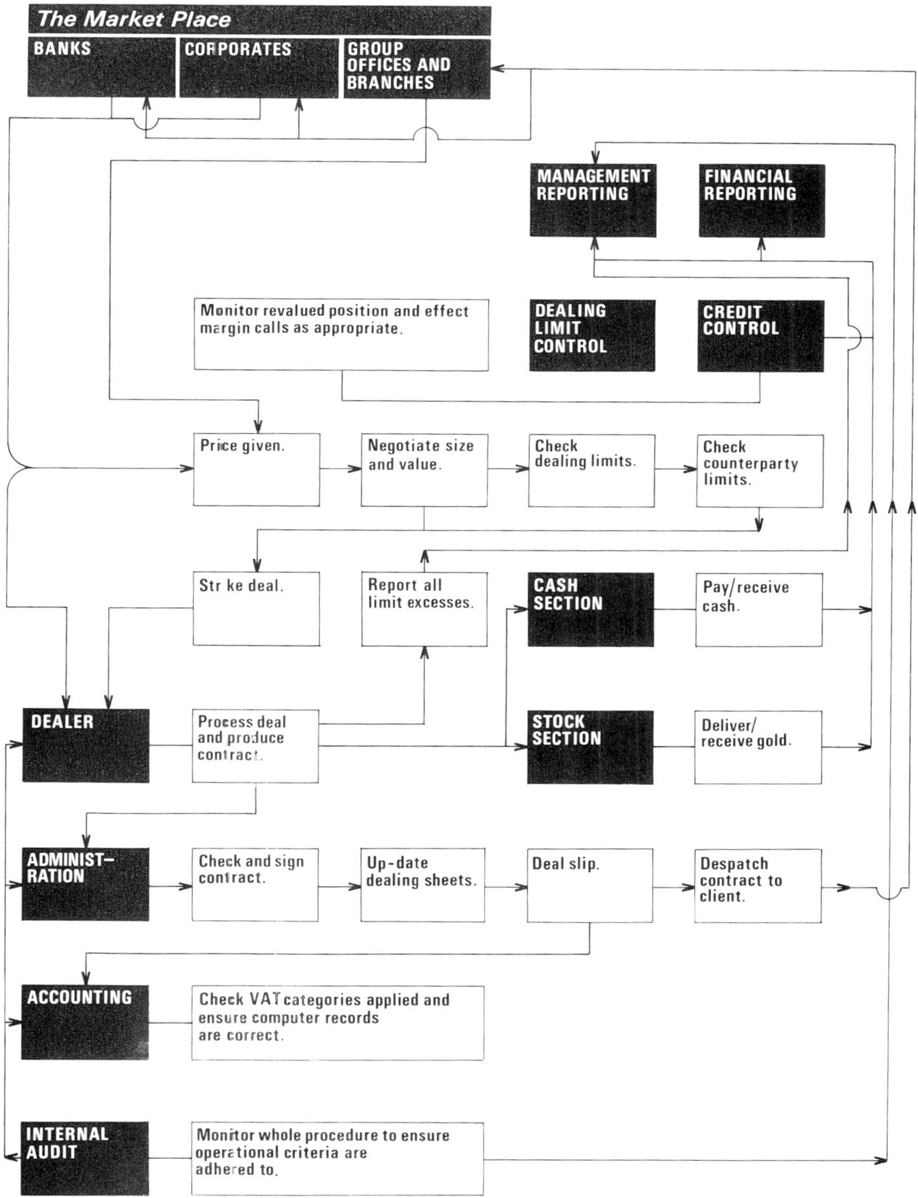

CHAPTER THIRTY THREE

Foreign Notes and Coin – Procedures and Practice

Introduction

Cash settlement for a wide variety of domestic commercial transactions is still the normally accepted practice – for other transactions, credit cards, cheques, giro payments and interbank transfers, are being adopted on an ever increasing scale. In the USA where credit cards are probably used more widely than in any other country, hotels, for example, will not be happy if the traveller has no acceptable plastic whether or not he offers to pay cash in advance. Filling stations and restaurants in America may wish to record your name and address if you tender a US$100 bill or a larger denomination. Perhaps this reflects the diminishing reliance on cash as a settlement method as well as an awareness of an increased level of bank note forgery and money laundering. The risk of violent crime is also growing annually in many countries and it is just not safe to carry about a lot of cash – indeed people who do in some countries are often treated with a degree of suspicion. It is, perhaps, worth considering that if the nationals of certain countries tend to be cautious of their own legal tender, with which they must, of course, be extremely familiar, the traveller and those handling these currencies abroad should be even more careful. Travellers tend to accept unfamiliar notes with absolute faith from the bank or bureau dispensing them.

The counterfeit problem

Bankers and bureau operators need to take care to ensure that any foreign notes and coin deposited or exchanged are genuine. To pass on a counterfeit note to someone else is an offence in any country. Banks and bureaux are considered to be money experts, and there is an inherent need for their staff to exercise *special* care in handling foreign notes, as there is no exemption from the legal consequences of passing forgeries to others. In most of the larger banks there is a central foreign notes and coin department within which, inter alia, specialised skills to identify forgeries can be developed. Nevertheless, once a branch has bought such a note or notes, the money may have been paid away one or two days before the forgery is discovered. If the note(s) came from a customer, it is generally possible for the branch to recover the loss; but in the majority of cases, counterfeit notes have been taken by a branch of a bank where they were exchanged for someone they are unlikely ever to see again. Great care must, of course, be exercised by bankers and bureau officers if large amounts of foreign notes are offered by non-customers unknown to them. After all, to carry a lot of cash is not normally a sensible thing to do and, whilst the real reason for so doing may be harmless enough, on the other hand it may be to pass counterfeit notes or, perhaps, evade the monetary or fiscal regulations of another country. Indeed the US Authorities are particularly concerned about the volume of cash transactions which takes place both within and outside the USA. The recycling of cash arising from the sale of drugs in order to conceal those involved and to obtain "clean" money from a "reputable" source is a form of money laundering of the greatest concern to law enforcement agencies worldwide. Tax avoidance activities and breaches of exchange control regulations undoubtedly give rise to substantial money laundering techniques often involving noticeably large amounts of notes being tendered or requested. In the authors' opinion banks should be on their guard whenever any exceptionally large cash transaction is proposed. If, after enquiry, the banker is still not satisfied that the proposition is one with which the bank would wish to be associated, then commonsense dictates that the business offered or service requested must be turned aside, even though there may be nothing illegal in the bank providing the service requested. Bankers should also remember that no reason *must* be given for rejecting a proposition or a new account other than to indicate that it is not the type of business that they wish to do. There are certain countries which tend to generate an above-average volume of forged documentation and, as a result, some nationals of such countries occasionally carry large amounts of cash with them to enable them to enter into business commitments which otherwise might not be possible. As a rule, however, foreign currency in the form of bank notes and coin is *not* used to settle international trade.

The most forgery-prone currency is the US dollar – indeed the passing of counterfeit US dollar bills is a daily occurrence in London and in most European countries. All denominations are subject to a vast number of counterfeits covering a very wide variety of different plate numbers. *Every* US dollar note to be purchased must be carefully scrutinised before-hand, particularly the US and Canadian $50 and $100 notes, and most banks will have well established lines of communication to draw on for expert advice and instructions on the detection of forgeries and action to be taken.

In the UK it is a felony for a person to possess a forged bank note, without lawful excuse and knowing it to be forged. This applies equally to bank notes issued within the UK and to foreign bank notes. The relevant statutes are the Forgery Act 1913 Section 8(1) and the Counterfeit Currency (Convention) Act 1935 Section 1. The sections mentioned provide for circumstances where the presenter of a forgery does not wish to part with it – the bank or bureau should draw his attention to his legal position.

It is normal procedure for all forged foreign notes to be handed to the local police immediately against a formal receipt. Under no circumstances should the notes be returned to the presenter. As it is quite probable that the police would wish to know the name and address of the presenter, banks are advised to obtain a customer's written authority before divulging this information. However, so far as strangers are concerned, it is normal practice for all details to be automatically disclosed on request.

Where any doubt exists as to the genuineness of notes presented to branches of banks with a centralised department specialising in foreign notes, then no money should be paid over to the presenter and the branch may send the notes "for collection" to their specialised unit for expert examination.

Country regulations and convertibility
There is a popular school of thought, to which the authors of this book subscribe, which differentiates foreign bank notes from foreign exchange – the latter being claims to foreign currency payable abroad

641

in the form of currency accounts with banks as well as bills of exchange, cheques, and certificates of deposit payable abroad in foreign currency. In the narrowest sense "foreign exchange" may be defined as "bank balances denominated in foreign currency". While foreign exchange is nearly always convertible into foreign currency notes, the reverse is not always permitted or there are restrictions as to the amounts that may be converted per transaction. Convertibility is the ability of the owner of the asset to exchange it from one currency into another. The currencies of the exchange control-free countries, for example, Sterling, US Dollars, Deutschemarks and Swiss Francs, are fully convertible. Exchange control regulations tend to limit convertibility and are discussed in the context of Chapter 7.

Currency and exchange control regulations are always subject to changes as the economic and/or political environment of the country of issue dictates. At the time of writing the following regulations existed for the countries listed:

1. **Total prohibition on the import or export of notes into or out of:**

*Albania	*Guinea Republic	*Nepal
Algeria	Hungary	*North Korea
*Angola	India	Peoples Republic of
Bulgaria	Jamaica	China
*Burma	*Kenya	Poland
*Cape Verde	*Khymer	Romania
Islands	Republic	Sudan
*Cuba	*Laotian Democratic	
Czechoslovakia	Republic	*Tanzania
Dominican	Libya	Tonga
Republic	Mauretania	Tunisia
Ethiopia	*Mongolian	*USSR
	People's	Vietnam
East Germany	Republic	*Western Samoa
Ghana	*Morocco	Zaire
	Mozambique	

2. Restrictions on import of notes into:

Bangladesh
Belize
Botswana
*Burundi
Colombia
Cyprus
Egypt
El Salvador
Faroe Islands
Gambia
Greece

Guyana
Iceland
Indonesia
Iran

Iraq
Italy
Lesotho
Malawi
Malta
Mauritius
*Nigeria
Pakistan
Peru
Philippines
Peoples
   Republic of
   Yemen
Portugal
*Rwanda
Sierra Leone
Somali
   Democratic
   Republic

South Africa
South Korea
Spain
Sri Lanka
Surinam
Swaziland
Syria
*Taiwan
Thailand
*Trinidad &
   Tobago
Turkey

*Uganda
Yugoslavia
*Zambia
Zimbabwe

3. Restrictions on export of notes from:

Afghanistan
Australia
Austria
Bahamas
Bangladesh
Barbados
Belize
Bermuda

Botswana
Brunei
*Burundi
Colombia
Cyprus

Egypt
El Salvador
Faro Islands

Fiji
Finland
France
French Polynesia
Gambia
Greece

Guyana
Iceland
Indonesia
Iran

Iraq
Ireland
Israel
Italy
Japan

Jordan
Lesotho
*Malagasy
   Republic
Malawi
Mali Republic
Malta
Mauritius

(continued)

3 (continued) Restrictions on export of notes from:

Netherlands	*Portuguese	Swaziland
Antilles	Timor	Sweden
New Zealand	*Rwanda	Syria
*Nigeria	Seychelles	
Norway	Sierra Leone	*Taiwan
Pakistan	Solomon Islands	Thailand
Papua New	Somali	*Trinidad &
Guinea	Democratic	Tobago
*Peoples	Republic	Turkey
Republic of	South Africa	*Uganda
Yeman	*South Korea	Yugoslavia
Peru	Spain	
Philippines	Sri Lanka	*Zambia
Portugal	Surinam	Zimbabwe

The market in London or elsewhere offshore for the currencies of the countries above *marked with an asterisk* is either extremely limited or non-existent. In addition, virtually no market exists for Lebanese, Chilian, Oman or Uruguayian currencies either. For other countries' currency a free market may exist, whether or not there is a prohibition on the cross-frontier movement of notes imposed by the country of issue as per (1) above.

In the UK the purchase or sale of any notes for currency against sterling have been unrestricted since exchange control was abolished in 1979. When selling foreign currencies banks generally alert the traveller if note import restrictions exist in the countries to be visited. Indeed, banks should advise clients that any currency bought which is in excess of the permitted amount must be at the client's own risk if he still wishes to take it with him. A written statement from the client to this effect is obtained by some banks and this is a procedure to be recommended.

Market operations
Apart from London as an international dealing centre for notes, banks in Austria, Portugal, Spain and Switzerland also participate. In

1983 the estimated foreign notes turnover in London was equivalent £2½ billion and in world terms £5 billion.

The professional market is small indeed; in London there are only some 10 banks participating, although many of the 600 or more banks and licensed deposit taking institutions and several hundred bureaux de change provide travellers with foreign note and coin exchange services. The London interbank market exists primarily to service the foreign note requirements of travellers and also to reduce the need for each participating institution to import or repatriate notes to meet, or surplus to, immediate or anticipated requirements.

The larger banks in the market have a natural flow arising from one or more of the following sources: facilities provided for individual travellers by their own branch network; bureaux and travel agents who are in account or with whom direct note facilities have been agreed; and the larger companies whose executives frequently travel abroad on business. The UK clearing banks have approximately one branch in six which has a foreign till. Notes can be provided immediately over the counter at such branches in modest amounts of the more popular currencies. It is normal for banks to be able to buy foreign notes on the spot, and to provide the less common currencies as well as the larger quantities of popular ones within a couple of days.

The major banks in the market are likely to keep stocks in, or be able to obtain upwards of, 150 different currencies. Naturally, the size of stocks of notes held in each currency needs to be carefully controlled. Notes cannot earn interest when held in stock. The timing of bulk orders to meet future tourist demand in the popular currencies, which, in the UK, is invariably well in excess of similar notes sold by returning travellers or incoming tourists, is crucial for the bank to maximise not only on beneficial exchange rates but also to minimise the cost of retaining such non interest-bearing assets. Banks are not alone in this context – tourists may also accelerate or delay the purchase of foreign notes they require and hold back the disposal of surplus foreign notes on their return. Travel agencies and bureaux often take strategic decisions of this nature, and cumulatively the effect can have a significant impact on the supply of, or demand for, foreign notes at various times.

Exchange rates for foreign notes

The extract from the Financial Times reproduced below, compares the principal foreign note rates with the spot sterling rates for 13th March 1984.

13th March		**The Pound Spot**	
	£		
	Note Rates	*Day's Spread*	*Close*
Austria	26.45–26.75	26.42–26.72	26.62–26.67
Belgium			
(convertible)	79.25–80.05	76.90–77.50	77.25–77.35
Denmark	13.76–13.89	13.75–13.84	13.81–13.82
France	11.60–11.72	$11.58\frac{1}{2}$–$11.66\frac{1}{2}$	11.63–11.64
Germany	$3.76\frac{1}{4}$–$3.80\frac{1}{4}$	$3.75\frac{1}{2}$–$3.79\frac{1}{2}$	$3.77\frac{1}{2}$–$3.78\frac{1}{2}$
Italy	2335–2365	2334–2352	$2344\frac{1}{2}$–$2346\frac{1}{2}$
Japan	324–329	325–329	327.50–328.50
Netherlands	4.25–4.29	4.24–4.28	$4.26\frac{1}{2}$–$4.27\frac{1}{2}$
Norway	10.87–10.98	10.86–10.96	$10.94\frac{1}{2}$–$10.95\frac{1}{2}$
Portugal	186–196	189.50–192.00	191.00–191.50
Spain	$212\frac{1}{4}$–$222\frac{1}{2}$	217.80–219.40	219.00–219.20
Sweden	11.21–11.32	11.20–11.30	$11.28\frac{1}{4}$–$11.29\frac{1}{4}$
Switzerland	3.11–3.14	3.10–$3.13\frac{1}{2}$	$3.11\frac{1}{2}$–$3.12\frac{1}{2}$
United States	$1.44\frac{1}{2}$–$1.46\frac{1}{2}$	1.4535–1.4705	1.4685–1.4695

The pound had a weak start in the currency markets that day but recovered later on in the mid and late afternoon as the UK budget announcements were being made. The foreign exchange (FX) rates started the day well within the foreign notes spread, and the apparently favourable rates at which the market was prepared to buy notes (the high side) was probably still within the FX spread at 3.30 p.m. when the banks closed for customer business.

Notes and coin rates are calculated on the basis of the current foreign exchange rate plus a margin for transportation, insurance handling and retention.

Coins are normally purchased at a greater discount because of the additional cost of handling and transportation in proportion to their value. Not all coins are automatically accepted and, indeed, the smaller denominations of foreign coins will not normally be purchased by banks or bureaux.

Foreign currency accounts maintained by customers outside the country of issue may have foreign notes, in the same currency, credited and withdrawn from such accounts. Even though the same currency is involved, there is, however, a rate differential between the note rate and the foreign exchange rate. This further highlights the difference between foreign exchange and foreign notes referred to at the beginning of this chapter. By way of example, assume a US dollar account maintained with a bank in London is to receive US$1,000 in notes. The notes will be sold to the bank at the note rate and bought from the bank with the sterling proceeds at the foreign exchange conversion rate. Using the note rates quoted above, US$1,000 at $1.46\frac{1}{2}$ equals £682.59 assuming that the spot foreign exchange rate at the time was 1.46. £682.59 at 1.4600 equals US$996.59 which will be credited to the account. On the other hand if the spot selling rate for US dollars at the time was 1.4675, the customer's account would have been credited with US$1,001.70. These figures do not take into account any commissions or handling charge that banks usually make in connection with foreign note transactions and this, of course, will be deducted from the figures given in the example above. Similarly, if notes are required from such an account they will normally have to be purchased at the bank's selling rate for notes.

The following criteria are taken into account when determining notes rates:

- denomination of currency

- time of the year, particularly if there is a seasonal demand or offering for the currency.

- the period of time the currency may have already been held in stock.

- the ruling spot foreign exchange rates.

- if changes in the foreign exchange rate are anticipated, especially during the course of the day. This will also be taken into account when assessing the note rate which, in practical terms, cannot be varied as quickly or as regularly as the interbank foreign exchange rates.

- any forward price that may have been entered into for bulk purchases of a particular currency.

- any natural set-off for a particular currency which may be required and has recently been offered with matching value dates.

- if there is not a direct courier system operating on a regular daily basis, the physical delivery of notes is likely to be delayed on occasions by postal delays before it reaches a bank abroad for the credit to the note trader's account. Accordingly, the cost of losing a day or more's interest should be computed into the rates.

- shortages of a particular denomination in a specific currency may well give rise to deviations from the normal spread of foreign notes rates which would tend to lie either side of the opening spot foreign exchange rate, other factors being equal.

- as with all items of value foreign notes require to be specifically insured whilst they are in transit and the premium costs related thereto will be considered within the rate pricing structure.

It goes without saying that before a customer can be given any foreign notes he may wish to purchase, the bank must previously have obtained physical delivery of them from elsewhere. Very careful control must be exercised in the sale of notes for collection at a later date which are not actually held in stock at the time the sale price is agreed.

Finally, on the subject of rates, foreign notes as well as travellers cheques may be exchanged for local currency in many places including camp sites, hotels and a proliferation of bureaux and money changers, and of course in a variety of banks. However, travellers often find that the rates quoted by banks are substantially better than those obtainable elsewhere, particularly with some of the back street money changers, whose rates are set to include a substantial margin to cover basic operating costs, owing to the absence of alternative services offered. A number of banks in different countries will provide bureau de change operations functioning outside the normal banking hours applicable in that country.

Control of Note Dealing Operations

All banks having a sizeable note dealing operation should have very clearly defined written instructions for both dealers and those engaged in the settlement of dealing transactions similar to those of any other trading operation. These instructions may be conveyed in a separate dealing manual, by way of a bank policy document, or just by way of senior management memoranda. As with all dealing operations there should be a complete segregation between the dealers on the one hand and on the other those people involved in the handling of cash, processing of entries and any correspondence or complaints arising from dealing transactions.

Apart from this fundamental segregation of duties, it is a sensible precaution to forbid all dealing personnel to have powers to sign anything on behalf of the bank. They should also have no access to electronic means of payment switching, or to testing devices. Dealing personnel should never be allowed to deal for their own account in the bank's name. Indeed, if they or their family wish to have foreign note facilites for, say, holiday purposes, then they should apply for them just as any other ordinary member of the public or employee of the bank. If the afore-going principles are observed it means that no dealing personnel will be able to issue any form of payment, perform any settlement function, write any letters relating to deals, pass any entries, or give any instructions, other than those deals conveyed in the dealing slips, to staff engaged in the settlement of the transactions.

The only people authorised to quote rates should be the dealers and strict limits for the maximum size of deal each dealer may authorise should be clearly established to ensure that each dealer's ability is commensurate with his level of responsibility, and is recognised and controlled. It is vital to establish an overall limit for a bank or branch's foreign currency note holdings. The currency in which all limits are written must be determined and the stocks of foreign notes will need to be revalued on a daily basis on a determined and consistent formula.

Suitable checks by management experienced in the technical aspect of foreign note business, as well as independent checks by internal auditors, is an essential feature of a properly structured control system. The management information arising from dealing transactions is all important and needs to be in accordance with the scale of operations of the dealing function. Telex machines in a dealing or settlement area should be closely scrutinised by management.

Depending on the size of the dealing operation, settlements staff should not be allowed to handle the receipts and deliveries of cash. Confirmations of all deals must be sent to the counterparty on the day that the deal is done and all dealing slips should be checked by the settlements staff immediately and processed without any delay. It is advisable to maintain a daily reconciliation of all notes purchased and not yet received, and include any outstanding forward exchange contracts.

Receipts and Deliveries of Foreign Notes
Many countries have regulations which prohibit the import or export, or both, of large denomination notes. Care must be exercised not to repatriate such notes in contravention of local regulations. In certain circumstances, it is unwise to consider purchasing notes on which such restrictions are imposed and, in any other circumstances where limited numbers may be purchased, they would normally attract a deep discount owing to the lack of demand. For the physical movement of foreign notes an approved security transport firm is normally employed for the larger consignments. The smaller consignments are sometimes despatched by registered mail, although so far as the postal authorities in the UK are concerned, the maximum insurable amount of one package is £1,000.

It is a sensible policy to retain a register of packets despatched with foreign bank notes either to satisfy the requirements of a branch network or sent to a correspondent bank abroad, giving full details of the notes contained therein. When receiving notes in the mail, special care is necessary to ensure that notes are not thrown away with the envelopes. Depending on the size of the operation, inward and outward mail for notes should be segregated from the normal mail received by the bank and handled in a suitable, secure area.

Finally there are some 22 currencies which are denominated in dollars and seven currencies denominated in rupees. Care needs to be exercised to ensure that these currencies are not confused.

CHAPTER THIRTY FOUR

Interbank Agency Agreements

Introduction

A variety of written and informal agreements with banking institutions abroad is essential to every bank which engages in international business. There are basically two ways by which these arrangements may be made. Correspondent banking relations may be established with other banks usually indigenous to the host country abroad. Such banks may offer reciprocal business despite the intense competition between banks for profitable business. The other course adopted is to channel the overseas business through a branch, subsidiary or affiliate organisation with appropriate representation in the overseas country. The operating costs involved in providing many of the services required are high, and in order to cover the overheads there is considerable competition between banks within each major financial centre to attract the high volumes required to achieve optimum employment of expensive automated equipment and sophisticated systems. Individual banks' philosophy in this context varies from total reliance on correspondent bank relations to total independence through an international branch and subsidiary network. By far the majority of international banks, however, use some of the required services provided by correspondent banks even in centres where they do have representation, and rely totally on correspondent banks where no local representation has been established. Reciprocity, quality and price of the services provided by correspondent banks are the main criteria on which decisions to direct specific business are made, and although long-standing relationships tend to be an influence, the diminishing profitability of many banks has focused greater attention on the above three prime criteria. Moreover, in order to satisfy customer demand for the widest range, highest quality, lowest price and adaptability of services, banks in an ever increasing competitive environment are conscious of the need to be duly selective with their choice of correspondent banks. Indeed, customers often have firm ideas as to the choice of overseas correspondent for specific types of business and it is essential for banks to be able to cater for such 'directed business' if their customer's wishes are to be satisfied.

An illustration of a simple agency agreement:

SUMMARY OF AGENCY ARRANGEMENTS BETWEEN

OVERSEAS BANK   AND   UK BANK PLC
HEAD OFFICE   LONDON
TOKYO

1) Control Documents

Each bank to provide the other with its signature lists/books covering all the offices which are included in the arrangements.

UK Bank PLC is to provide its telegraphic test key for reciprocal use for the authentication of cable and telex messages between all participating offices listed under Paragraph 2 below.

2) Offices included in the arrangement

OVERSEAS BANK   UK BANK PLC

1. Head Office, Tokyo   Overseas Branch, London
2. Hong Kong   International Department, Manchester
3. Singapore
4. Manilla
5. Kuala Lumpur
6. Jakarta

3) Drafts and mail transfers

All drafts will be advised by airmail on the date of issue. Drafts issued by UK Bank PLC may be paid without advice only on the responsibility of the paying bank. Drafts issued by Overseas Bank cannot be paid without advice if over £10,000 or US$20,000.

Offices of UK Bank PLC mentioned in Paragraph 2 above, may draw drafts on, and send mail transfers to, any of the offices listed under Paragraph 2) provided they are properly authenticated.

Overseas Bank and its branches may draw drafts on, and send mail tranfers to, UK Bank PLC, Overseas Branch, London and International Department, Manchester.

4) Telegraphic transfers

Offices of UK Bank PLC, mentioned in Paragraph 2) above, may send properly authenticated telegraphic payment orders direct to any of the offices of Overseas Bank listed under Paragraph 2).

Overseas Bank and its branches may send authenticated telegraphic payment orders to the two UK Bank PLC branches listed under Paragraph 2).

5) Currencies and Reimbursement

Cover for all telegraphic payment orders must be sent by telex or cable.

In respect of all sterling transfers initiated by UK Bank PLC, cover will be credited to the sterling account No 88872371 held in the name of Overseas Bank, Head Office, Tokyo. Reimbursement for all sterling transfers initiated by Overseas Bank will be debited to their Head Office Account No 88872371 held with UK Bank PLC. •

Cover for all U S dollar transactions directed to UK Bank PLC is to be credited to their U S dollar account with UK Bank USA Inc. New York. Cover for all U S dollar transactions directed to Overseas Bank, Tokyo is to be credited to their U S dollar account with First National Bank, New York.

6) Documentary Credits

The offices of each bank included in the arrangement may open documentary credits direct with those offices listed under Paragraph 2) above. Credits may be opened by way of airmail or telex and reimbursement instructions are to be included with the credit. Credits issued by both banks shall guarantee to honour the drafts drawn under and in compliance of the terms and conditions of their credits on presentation and delivery of documents to the designated parties. These credits shall be subject to Uniform Customs and Practice for Documentary Credits (1983 Revision) International Chamber of Commerce, Publication 400.

7) Collections

All offices of both banks listed under Paragraph 2) above may send collection orders direct to each other for collection as per their tariffs. Instructions covering the disposal of the proceeds must accompany each remitting schedule. Collections emanating from both banks shall be subject to the Uniform Rules for Collection of Commercial Paper (1978 Revision) International Chamber of Commerce Publication No 322.

_______________________________________   Date _______________
FOR UK BANK PLC

_______________________________________   Date _______________
FOR OVERSEAS BANK

The Nature of Agency Agreements

The written agreements vary from simple documents setting out arrangements between two offices to provide international transfer services, to the more detailed arrangements agreed between two major banking groups involving a wide range of services to be provided for the specified branches and subsidiaries.

The Range of Services

Many services carried out by one bank on behalf of another do not, necessarily, feature in agency agreement documents. Foreign exchange facilities, placing and standby lines are usually the subject of separate arrangements which, like any credit facilities selectively granted, will be carefully controlled and kept under constant review. The initial correspondent relationship involves a discussion of the services the two banks (or their groups) can offer each other and the fees involved, where applicable. If any relationship is contemplated each bank and their involved branches and subsidiaries must be able to authenticate messages by mail, telex or electronic transfer systems purporting to have originated from the other bank. An exchange of authorised signatures and testing cyphers is, therefore, a fundamental requirement, whether or not any mutual account-holding relationship is sought.

The list of services offered and sought by correspondent banks given below is by no means comprehensive. New technology gives rise to new systems and enhancements of existing services. Development and diversification of banking business in various countries and the creation of new markets continue to add to the list. The detailed break-down of trade related services such as documentary credit (opening, advising, confirming, transferring, amending, accepting, negotiating, paying) are not developed here since they form part of the fundamental subject of "Finance of International Trade" and are adequately covered in the Institute of Bankers' textbook of that title.

Subject to relevant current exchange control requirements services may be provided for facilities denominated in local currency, foreign currency and composite currency units such as SDRs and ECUs.

655

The services are

- Accounting and transfer facilities including clearing, transmission of funds, and settlement of international payment instructions. The maintenance of accounts in local currency and third country currencies.

- Trade related services involving the handling and processing of shipping documentation and contract guarantees, particularly collection and documentary credit services.

- Financial facilities including temporary resultant overdrafts, overdrafts, loans, acceptances, various financial facilities provided for local branches and subsidiaries, and syndications.

- Cash management facilities, automated balance reporting and vostro account investment schemes.

- Money market and treasury facilities including foreign exchange lines, placing lines, gold trading, futures, options, interest rate swaps and foreign exchange swaps.

- Securities facilities including – purchase and sale, custodian, clearing, registrar, paying and fiscal agency, underwriting, advisory, futures and options, new issue management and advisory services.

- Travel services including – foreign notes and coin, travellers cheques, drafts, travellers letters of credit, eurocheque encashment facilities, local drawing and cheque encashment facilities, local borrowing supported by banker's guarantee.

- Commercial and economic advisory services including status reports, industry surveys, and economic reports on countries and international matters and markets.

- Other facilities – insurance, trustee, advisory services on mergers and acquisitions.

The most common services offered are documentary credits, foreign exchange, settlement services (particularly SWIFT transfers), clearing, collections and account facilities. The size and nature of the banking institution's business and its country of domicile will give rise to variations and other preferences, although the services indicated in this paragraph are widely considered profitable and reciprocal business is generally sought on the basis of facilities offered.

Correspondent banks are not only customers but in the main are an essential corner-stone to the provision of international banking services for all the other customers of the bank. It is essential, therefore, to maintain an efficient and cordial working relationship. Quality of service has been cited earlier as one of the prime criteria a bank should seek in choosing its banking correspondents. Errors will be made from time to time however efficient a banking operation may be and it is essential that errors, when made, are effectively and swiftly corrected, that the error rate itself is low, and that where loss has been occasioned, the bank responsible compensates without argument or delay. The quality of service is also measured by the time taken to process operational transactions. In this context, correspondents which offer the required services with electronic/automated/computerised systems, capable of processing transactions more quickly than perhaps traditional methods offered by other banks, are likely to be successful (always provided of course that they work), the error rate is low, and that there also exists accurate and prompt communication of statements and systems for communicating advices of transactions which have been effected. In order to maintain a good working relationship with correspondents, mutual visits of well briefed account officers and senior managers is essential. The list of services which may be offered can exceed well over a 100, the principal ones being listed above. Account officers, when offering services to correspondent banks, will previously define which services the bank wishes to promote and be aware of the relative return to the bank, if any, likely to be achieved from each service. It is easy to give away someone else's money.

AIBD Rules and Recommendations for Operations in the Eurobond Secondary Market

Reprinted from the International Association of Bond Dealers *Statutes, By-laws, Rules and Recommendations 1985/86*, May, 1985

The AIBD rules and recommendations apply to operations in the secondary market only, unless otherwise stated.

Section 100 Clients' orders
Rule 101 Alteration or cancellation of order
In the event that a client places an order to buy or to sell bonds at the best possible market price or at a price limit and wishes thereafter to alter or cancel his order before expiration of the order's time limit, he may do so provided that no part of his order has been executed prior to his notification of alteration or cancellation. The execution of part of the order must be accepted by the client unless the order had been placed with the specification "all or none".

Section 120 Dealing practices
Rule 121 "Odd lot" transactions
The minimum "round lot" trade effected between members of the Association shall be US$25,000 nominal or its equivalent in other currencies for transactions in non-dollar denominated bonds. Prices for transactions in amounts of less than US$25,000 nominal or its equivalent shall be discretionary.

Section 140 Multiple currency unit bonds
Rule 141 Choice and indication of currency
Marketmakers quoting prices in multiple currency unit bonds must indicate the currency in which the transaction is to be settled. This can be one of the currencies by which the multiple currency is defined, at the fixed rate of exchange established by the definition, or any other currency, at a rate of exchange agreed at the time of dealing.

Section 160 Dealing in new issues
Rule 161 Aftermarket transactions
All transactions in the aftermarket shall be settled in accordance with normal market practices, except where the buyer and the seller expressly agree to deal at issue terms.

Recommendation to section 160
Transactions in bonds being publicly offered through a new issue should not be entered into prior to the signing of the underwriting subscription agreement of such issue, nor on an "if, as and when issued" basis.

Section 180 Special deals and situations
Rule 181
(1) Special deals – reference on contract note or confirmation note
Special terms and conditions, agreed between the buyer and the seller at the time of the conclusion of a transaction, must be clearly stated and described as such by both parties on their contract note or confirmation note.

(2) Except in the case of a "buy-in" execution (where rule 427 applies), where a member firm issues a contract note or confirmation note at a price different from the quoation prevailing at the time of the conclusion of the transaction, the contract note or confirmation note must clearly identify such as a special transation.

Recommendation to rule 181
Where a member firm concludes a transaction in international securities at a price significantly different from the prevailing quotation it is

recommended that the reason for the price difference be noted on the contract note or confirmation note.

Rule 182 Special deals – settlement instructions
If special terms and conditions attaching to a transaction necessitate special settlement instructions, both parties shall notify their clearing agents accordingly.

Rule 183 Special deals – non fulfilment
Where the special terms and conditions described as per rule 181 are not fulfilled by one party, its counterparty shall have the right to either cancel the transaction or obtain reimbursement in full for any loss incurred due to such non-fulfilment of the special terms and conditions.

Rule 184 Special situations – exercise of rights attached to securities or public offers
(1) Where two parties have entered into a transaction in securities which are subject to a public offer or which have terms providing that certain rights may be exercised up to a fixed deadline, the seller shall deliver such securities in time for the buyer to exercise such rights.
(2) The seller being unable to deliver in time shall promptly obtain from the buyer appropriate instructions as to the rights, and shall act upon such instructions. Where no such instructions can be obtained from the buyer, the seller shall use his best judgment and make every effort to protect the interests of the buyer. The seller shall immediately inform the buyer of any action taken. In this case the buyer will have no recourse against the seller.
(3) Where the seller fails to deliver in time, and does not take appropriate action relative to the rights for the benefit of the buyer, the buyer shall have the right to claim from the seller indemnification for any direct loss sustained as a result of such failure. These provisions shall however not apply if the failure to deliver in time was attributable to the buyer.
(4) If the seller exercises the rights on behalf of the buyer, the original contract shall be replaced by a contract in the new securities resulting from the exercise of the rights. Such contract(s) shall include any cost incurred by the seller in exercising such rights on behalf of the buyer.

Recommendations to rule 184

When the deadline is approaching for the exercise of any rights attached to securities, for example in connection with warrants, partial or final redemption, lapse date, conversion, instalment payment, exchange, share or cash offer, transactions should only be concluded for guaranteed delivery on a date to be decided by the buyer, with attention to the timing set forth in paragraph 2 of rule 184.

Rule 185 Special situations – multi-currency issues with coupon record dates

(1) In multi-currency issues where coupons have to be lodged or listed on a prescribed record date in order to obtain payments at a preferential rate of exchange, a seller shall deliver such bond(s), owed from a transaction with a value date prior to such record date, in time for the buyer to benefit from such a situation. Failing this, rule 333 will be applicable.
(2) Transactions in securities described in this rule shall be concluded "ex coupon" if the value date of the transaction falls between the record date and the payment date of such coupon.
(3) Securities described in this rule do not constitute good delivery if presented "cum coupon" after the record date of such coupon.

Recommendation to rule 185

Where a seller is unable to deliver bond(s) in accordance with rule 185(1), he shall himself cash the coupon(s) in the most advantageous currency in order to protect himself against rule 333.

Rule 186 Special situations – called/drawn bonds

Where part of an issue is called for redemption, the buyer shall have no claim against the seller for any undelivered bonds, unless:
a) the transaction has been effected for guaranteed delivery or
b) the numbers of the bonds traded in have been submitted prior to the date of availability by publication or otherwise of the numbers of the bonds drawn.
Such exceptions fall under rule 181.

Rule 187 Bonds in default

Where a debtor fails to pay the interest or principal of a bond on the due date such bond must henceforth be traded at a "flat" price and contracts must be marked accordingly. Bonds which are traded at a "flat" price must have all unpaid or partly paid coupons attached.

Rule 188 Change in basis from "plus accrued" to "flat"
When a change in the basis of trading in bonds from "plus accrued" to "flat" becomes effective, limited selling orders shall be raised in price by the amount of the accrued interest. This shall be done by the party to whom the selling order has been entrusted for execution. The party who gave the order to sell shall be immediately notified that his order to sell at a price "plus accrued" is no longer valid and has, for his protection, been replaced by an equivalent order at a "flat" price, pending his further instructions.

Rule 189 Change of name of borrower
Where a company changes its name, its outstanding bonds shall continue to be traded under the original name shown on the bearer certificates.

Section 200 Contract note and confirmation note

Rule 201 Issue of contract note or confirmation note
(1) Each member of the AIBD shall issue a contract note or telex a confirmation note as per rule 202 for every transaction in an international security as regulated by the AIBD.
(2) Contract notes or confirmation notes shall be dispatched to the counterparties not later than on the business day following the trade date.

Recommendations to rule 201
(1) A contract note or a confirmation note issued by a member of the AIBD should be marked as follows:
   "This contract/confirmation note is issued in accordance with the rules of The Association of International Bond Dealers."
(2) Contract notes or confirmation notes should be in English or include an English translation of the original text.
(3) Where a contract note or a confirmation note is transmitted by mail, members are recommended to issue a preliminary telex confirmation.

(4) Where a confirmation note issued as per rule 202 is transmitted by telex but is not going to be confirmed by mail, this should be stated in the telex.

Rule 202 Contents of contract note or confirmation note
A contract note or a confirmation note issued as per rule 201 shall include the following information:
a) name and address of counterparty,
b) clear and unmistakable description of the bond including interest rate and year of maturity and, where necessary, month and day of maturity, as well as reference to share purchase warrants or similar features, if any,
c) principal amount of bonds bought or sold and price at which the transaction was effected, interest amount, if any, currency and net amount of the transaction,
d) trade date and value date of the transaction,
e) detailed instructions where the countervalue is to be paid or where the securities are to be delivered and what method of settlement is to be applied.

Rule 203
Checking the counterparty's contract note or confirmation note
Each member of the AIBD shall on receipt of a contract note, a confirmation note or a preliminary telex confirmation from a counterparty check the contents of such communication and advise the counterparty by telex or cable of any disagreements, errors or omissions within two business days of receipt of such communication.

Rule 204 Amendment and cancellation
(1) Where a recipient of a contract note or confirmation note advises his counterparty of a disagreement, error or omission in accordance with rule 203, both parties shall immediately examine the matter and the party at fault shall issue an amended contract note or confirmation note or a note of cancellation.
(2) A contract note or confirmation note issued in accordance with rules 201 and 202 need not be amended or cancelled unless advice of a disagreement, error or omission has been received in accordance with rule 203 or unless an important error of typographical, mathematical or technical nature is discovered and reported subsequent to the two day period prescribed by rule 203.

664

Rule 205

Confirmation of transaction through communication system
Where members of the AIBD have agreed to confirm their transactions through a communication system, the rules and regulations of such system may supersede all other rules in this section 200.

Section 220 Value date and calculation of accrued interest
Rule 221 Normal value date
The value date for a transaction in international securities as regulated by the AIBD shall be the seventh calendar day following the trade date, regardless of any local or generally recognised holidays.

Rule 222 Special value date
A special value date may be mutually agreed between the buyer and the seller at the time of dealing.

Rule 223 Value date on non-settlement day
Where the value date coincides with a bank holiday in the centre where the payment and/or the delivery is to be effected, the first business day in that centre following that bank holiday shall be accepted by both parties as the date for payment and/or delivery. No adjustment of accrued interest shall be made.

Rule 224 Value date and coupon due date
Where the due date of an interest coupon coincides with the value date of a transaction, the buyer shall not acquire such coupon and no accrued interest shall be calculated on such a contract. With the exception of floating rate notes, a transaction with a value date on the thirty-first calendar day of the month and a coupon due date on the first calendar day of the following month, accrued interest shall correspond to the full value of the coupon.

Rule 225 Accrued interest calculation
(1) With the exception of floating rate notes, accrued interest on a contract shall be calculated on a 360 days per year basis from and including the day following the due date of the last paid interest coupon or the day following the day from which interest is to accrue for a new issue up to and including the value date of the transaction.

(2) With the exception of floating rate notes, a full month being counted as thirty days, accrued interest to a value date on the thirty-first calendar day of a month shall be the same as to the first calendar day of the following month.

(3) Accrued interest on a contract for floating rate notes shall be calculated on actual days, divided by 360 (or by 365 in the case of a Euro-sterling issue) from and including the day following the due date of the last paid interest coupon or the day following the day from which interest is to accrue for a new issue up to and including the value date of the transaction.

(4) No accrued interest shall be calculated where rule 224 applies or where the value date coincides with the date of issue or where a transaction has been concluded at a "flat" price.

Rule 226 Accrued interest computation – fractions
In all transactions involving the payment of interest, fractions of a cent equalling or exceeding five mills shall be regarded as one cent and fractions of a cent less than five mills shall be disregarded. Examples:
$137.625 accrued interest has to be increased to $137.63
$137.624 accrued interest has to be decreased to $137.62

Rule 227 Value date of secondary market transactions in new issues of international securities
The value date of secondary market transactions in new issues of international securities, as regulated by the AIBD will be the business day at the recognised international clearing system following the closing date or seventh calendar day following the trade date, whichever is the later.

Section 300 Settlement instructions
Rule 301 Phrasing of settlement instructions
Instructions to a clearing agent to receive or to deliver securities shall conform to the operating procedures promulgated by such clearing agent. *Note: Rules 302–3 are deleted.*

Rule 304 Discretion on countervalue
(1) Each member of the AIBD shall give a standing discretion to its clearing agent(s) that they may accept bonds against payment of

666

the amount claimed by the presenting party provided the difference in countervalue does not exceed US$500 or equivalent in other currencies, per transaction.

(2) The clearing agent(s) shall be asked to report to the buyer any such difference on the advice of settlement.

(3) Such difference shall be examined and settled between the buyer and the seller without delay.

Rule 305

Settlement instructions transmitted through communication system
Where a member of the AIBD and his clearing agent or system have agreed that such member shall transmit and such agent or system shall accept settlement instructions through a communication system, the rules and regulations of such communication system may supersede all other rules in this section.

Section 320 Settlements

Rule 321 Method of settlement

(1) Each member of the AIBD shall settle all transactions concluded with another member of the AIBD in those securities which are regulated by the AIBD, by clearance through the recognised international clearing systems. Exceptions fall under rule 181.

(2) Where a buyer and a seller are members of the same clearing system and settle a transaction between themselves through such system, the rules and regulations of such system shall apply to such settlement in lieu of the AIBD rules on settlement instructions.

(3) Similarly, where a buyer and a seller are members of distinct clearing systems and settle a transaction between themselves through an intersystems link organised by such clearing systems, the terms and conditions governing such intersystems link shall apply to such settlement in lieu of the AIBD rules on settlement instructions.

Rule 322 Initiative for settlement

(1) It is the responsibility of the seller or his clearing agent to present the securities to the buyer or his designated clearing agent, thereby indicating:

a) by whose order the bonds are being delivered (the seller),
b) for whose account the bonds are being delivered (the buyer),
c) the value date of the transaction as contained in the settlement instructions,
d) the amount of funds, if any, to be paid in exchange for the securities.

(2) It is the responsibility of the seller or his clearing agent to collect the countervalue of the securities from the buyer or his clearing agent in the case of a delivery against payment.

Rule 323 Timing of settlement

The settlement of a transaction shall not be effected prior to the value date of the transaction.

Rule 324 Partial settlement

A partial settlement of a transaction shall only be effected after having obtained the express agreement of the buyer. This rule shall apply to free deliveries and deliveries against payment.

Rule 325 Called/drawn bonds

(1) Bearer bonds called for redemption, which are received by a recognised international clearing system on or after the value date, or which, if no value date is specified, are received by such clearing system, do not represent good delivery on or after the official publication of the numbers of the bonds drawn, except when an entire issue is called for redemption and except in respect of transactions in called bonds dealt in specifically as such.

(2) Certificates of registered bonds which are called for redemption do not represent good delivery on or after the record date fixed for the purpose of the drawing for redemption or the date of the closing of transfer books, except when an entire issue is called for redemption and except in respect of transactions in called bonds dealt in specifically as such.

(3) Where the buyer or his agent has caused the failure of settlement, the seller shall have the right to claim from the buyer any loss incurred.

(4) Where the buyer requires physical delivery of bonds outside of the recognised international clearing systems and such delivery is being made by the seller or his agent, any called/drawn bonds

shall constitute good delivery if the seller can provide proof of dispatch dated prior to the official publication of the numbers of the bonds drawn.

(5) Where bonds are delivered which do not constitute good delivery under this rule, the buyer may claim replacement of the bonds within 30 days of the date of receipt. If the buyer does not claim replacement in the specified period, he shall be deemed to have accepted the delivery as it was effected.

Rule 326 Mutilated securities

(1) Mutilated securities and/or securities with mutilated coupons attached do not constitute good delivery.

Mutilation is any damage to pertinent information contained in bonds and/or coupons such as certificate number, dates, signature or details of the indenture.

(2) The receiving party shall determine whether a security is in sufficiently good condition to constitute good delivery under observations of (1) above.

(3) It is the responsibility of the delivering party to have mutilated bonds and/or coupons authenticated by the trustee or fiscal agent or by any paying agent acting on behalf of the trustee or fiscal agent.

Rule 327 Temporary certificates not good delivery after issue of definitive certificates

Where temporary certificates have been issued, these shall not constitute good delivery on or after the date when definitive certificates are available. Temporary certificates in transit on such date shall be exempt from this rule.

Rule 328 Shipment advice

It is compulsory that shipment advices contain a full description of the securities, including the certificate numbers and a specification of the attached coupons.

Rule 329 Coupon bonds/bonds with warrants

(1) A bond shall have securely attached the proper coupon sheet of the same certificate number as the bond.

(2) A bond whose warrants have been detached prior to the date stipulated in the issue prospectus shall not constitute good delivery. Deliveries subsequent to the official detachment date of the warrants shall be governed by the terms of the prospectus.

Rule 330 Erroneous or bad delivery of bonds
The member having caused erroneous or bad delivery shall bear the cost for return or transfer of such shipment and cover its insurance.
Note: Rules 331–2 are deleted.

Rule 333 Missing coupons
(1) The buyer shall have no claim to physical delivery of coupons unless specifically dealt as such under rule 181. The seller shall promptly settle the countervalue of the missing coupons with the buyer.
(2) Missing coupons payable in a specific currency –
(a) European and Asian delivery
Where a bond is delivered without the coupon(s) required by the contract, the seller or his agent shall compensate the buyer for the countervalue of such coupon(s) in the currency in which the coupon is denominated.
(b) New York delivery
Where a bond is delivered without the coupon(s) required by the contract, it shall be accompanied by a cheque for the equivalent amount of such coupon(s).
(3) Missing coupons where a choice of currency exists –
Where a bond of this type is delivered without the coupon(s) required by the contract, the seller, unless he has received specific instructions from the buyer in due time, shall settle the countervalue of such coupon(s) with the buyer in accordance with the provisions relating to the financial servicing of that bond.

Rule 334 Claim to coupon proceeds prior to delivery
(a) In the case of delivery of the securities against payment, the buyer shall not be entitled to claim the countervalue of coupon(s) due prior to the settlement of the transaction.
(b) In the case of delivery of the securities free of payment, the buyer shall be entitled to claim the countervalue of the coupon(s) only if he has paid for the securities on the value date.

Rule 335 Shipping and insurance costs
Shipping and insurance costs for transactions in the secondary market in bonds traded for delivery in the recognised delivery centre shall be paid by the seller. Expenses incurred in delivering such securities outside of such centres can be charged to the buyer. Instructions relating to the insurance coverage shall always be the responsibility of the seller unless other arrangements have been made under rule 181.

Section 400 Refusal of delivery
Rule 401 Reasons for refusal of a delivery against payment
A clearing agent, acting on behalf of a buyer, may refuse to accept against payment the securities presented to him for the account of the buyer for one or several of the following reasons:
a) absence of instructions from the buyer,
b) insufficiency of cash or credit in buyer's account,
c) difference in description of securities,
d) money difference of more than US$500 or equivalent in other currencies, per transaction,
e) coupon(s) or compensation missing,
f) warrant(s) missing or not conforming to terms of prospectus,
g) mutilated securities not properly authenticated,
h) registered bonds not properly endorsed,
i) called bonds in accordance with rule 325,
j) multi-currency bonds "cum coupons" after record date as per rule 185(3),
k) account unknown.

Rule 402 Reasons for refusal of a free delivery
A clearing agent, acting on behalf of a buyer, may refuse to accept a free delivery of securities presented to him for the account of the buyer for one or several of the following reasons:
a) difference in description of securities,
b) mutilated securities not properly authenticated,
c) registered bonds not properly endorsed,
d) warrant(s), missing or not conforming to terms of prospectus,
e) called bonds in accordance with rule 325,
f) multi-currency bonds "cum coupons" after record date as per rule 185(3),

g)   account unknown,
h)   coupon(s) or compensation missing.

Rule 403 Advice of refusal
Each member of the AIBD shall instruct the clearing agent(s) acting on his behalf
a)   to advise him and the presenting party in writing whenever securities presented for his account are refused and the reason for such refusal according to rules 401 and 402.
b)   to advise him in writing whenever securities delivered on his behalf were refused by the counterparty and the reason for the refusal according to rules 401 and 402 that was given by the counterparty,
c)   not to allow a refusal of securities by a counterparty unless a reason according to rules 401 and 402 is given in writing.

Appendix to rules 401 to 403
Specimen letter of instructions re refusal of deliveries.
By registered mail
To XYZ Bank
Custody Department
Permanent instructions regarding refusal of deliveries in accordance with AIBD rules 401 to 403.
We herewith ask you to kindly follow rules 401 to 403 of the AIBD when acting on our behalf in the settlement of international bonds. A photocopy of these rules is attached to this letter.
It is of particular importance that you advise us in writing whenever a delivery by our order is being refused by the counterparty or whenever you refuse a delivery presented to you for our account and that you state the exact reason for the refusal.

Rule 404 Examination of refusal of delivery
Following refusal of delivery, the seller shall take up the matter immediately and all parties involved shall co-operate in resolving the problem.

Rule 405 Fault of buyer or his clearing agent
Where the buyer or his clearing agent has caused the failure of the settlement, the buyer must issue corrected instructions to his clearing agent or repeat the original instructions if necessary.

Rule 406 Interest claim against buyer

Where the buyer or his clearing agent has caused the failure of settlement, the seller shall have the right to claim from the buyer loss of interest on the net amount of the transaction, calculated at the prevailing euro call money rates from the date of presentation of the securities until the date that settlement takes place.

Rule 407 Fault of seller or his clearing agent

Where the seller or his clearing agent has caused the failure of settlement, the seller must by cable or telex issue corrected instructions to his clearing agent or repeat the original instructions, if necessary.

Section 420 "Buy-in"

Rule 421 "Buy-in" timing

(1) If a delivery is not made within twenty-one calendar days following the value date, the buyer shall have the right to telex or cable to the seller a "buy-in" notice.

(2) Where a delivery has been refused through the fault of the buyer or his clearing agent, the timing for the "buy-in" shall commence on the date on which instructions are corrected or re-submitted as per rule 405.

(3) The buyer shall not lose his right to effect a "buy-in" after the expiration of the timing prescribed in this rule.

(4) The board shall have the authority to alter the timing for a "buy-in" as prescribed in this rule, if and when the delivery situation permits or requires such alteration.

Rule 422 "Buy-in" notice

A "buy-in" notice shall state:

a) the buyer's intention to close out the contract by means of a "buy-in",

b) the date when the "buy-in" will be executed which shall be the fourteeth calendar day from the date of such notice,

c) full details of the original contract note or confirmation note including the settlement instructions,

d) the principal amount of bonds to be bought-in,

e) the name of the AIBD member who will be instructed to effect the "buy-in".

Rule 423 "Buy-in" execution

On failure of the seller to effect delivery on or before the business day preceding the date of the "buy-in", the buyer shall instruct the third party to purchase on the "buy-in" day in the best available market for guaranteed delivery on the normal value date all or any part of the securities.

Recommendation to rule 423

Between receipt of the "buy-in" notice and the "buy-in" date, the seller, in order to avoid the execution of the "buy-in" and if he cannot otherwise arrange the delivery, can either buy bonds for guaranteed delivery from another counterparty and use these bonds as settlement or agree a transaction and subsequent compensation with the buyer to whom he owes the bonds.

Rule 424 "Buy-in" completion

In the event that a "buy-in" cannot be completed by the party named under 422e) on the "buy-in" date specified in the "buy-in" notice, this agent may be substituted with another AIBD member by the buyer. Such substitution must be advised to the seller under one business day's telex notice.

Any appointed agent may complete the "buy-in" of the securities on any subsequent business day until completed or until the buyer relieves him of his function as agent.

Rule 425 Partial delivery

a) While a "buy-in" notice is in force, or an uncompleted "buy-in" is in force, a partial settlement of the "buy-in" shall only be effected after having obtained the explicit agreement of the buyer.

b) However, on the execution date of the "buy-in", the buyer must accept during his regular business hours any portion of the securities outstanding and the seller must advise the buyer by cable or telex of such partial delivery 24 hours in advance.

c) Such bonds received shall be deducted from the principal amount of bonds stated in the "buy-in" notice or from the balance of bonds still to be "bought-in".

674

d) Settlement as prescribed in this rule will take place free or against payment or the pro rata countervalue depending on the terms of the original contract.

Rule 426 Securities in transit – physical delivery

If prior to the close of business preceding the day of "buy-in" or during an uncompleted "buy-in" operation, the buyer receives from the seller a cable or telex notice declaring that all or part of the securities are being physically delivered or airmailed that day in accordance with the settlement instructions and stating the certificate numbers, then the buyer may not execute the "buy-in" of those securities for a period of seven calendar days.

Should such securities not arrive at their destination within the seven calendar day period, the "buy-in" on those securities shall be executed or continued.

Rule 427 Notice of execution ("Buy-in")

The buyer shall immediately on receipt of advice of execution from the third party, notify the seller by cable or telex of the quantity purchased and the price contracted, and shall promptly issue a contract note or confirmation note to be accompanied by the third party's confirmation note which shall state: "we have executed this trade for guaranteed delivery as nominated 'buy-in' agent."

Rule 428 "Buy-in" settlement

The money difference between the original contract and the close-out contract, taking into consideration possible interest coupon due dates, shall be settled between the seller and the buyer without any delay.

Rule 429 Securities exempt from "buy-in"

The provisions of the "buy-in" procedure as set forth in this section shall not apply to contracts for any issue of securities which has been entirely called for redemption.

Rule 430 "Buy-in" primary market

Where bonds are allotted in the primary market at net issue terms or less reallowance, delivery to the subscriber must be made immediately after the individual bonds or a global certificate have been released for delivery by the trustee or agent of the issue.

In the event that the subscriber has not received delivery of the bonds, or, in the case of a global certificate, has not been notified of a book entry at one of the recognised international clearing systems within seven calendar days following the date of such release, the subscriber shall have the right to telex or cable to his counterparty a "buy-in" notice.

The execution of the "buy-in" by the third party shall be effected on the seventh calendar day following the date of the "buy-in" notice.

The board shall have the authority to alter the timing for a "buy-in" as prescribed in this rule.

Other relevant regulations of section 420 shall apply.

Section 440 "Sell-out"

Rule 441 "Sell-out" timing

(1) Where a delivery against payment has been refused through the fault of the buyer or his clearing agent and if no instruction has been corrected or re-submitted as per rule 405 by the close of the seventh calendar day following the date of the refusal, the seller shall have the right to telex or cable to the buyer a "sell-out" notice.

(2) If a payment due on the value date of a transaction or a payment requested by a telex pre-advice of delivery has not been received during the two business days following such value date or telex date, the seller may telex or cable to the buyer a "sell-out" notice.

(3) The seller shall not lose his right to effect a "sell-out" after the expiration of the timing prescribed in this rule.

Rule 442 "Sell-out" notice

A "sell-out" notice shall state:

a) the seller's intention to close-out the contract by means of a "sell-out",

b) the date when the "sell-out" will be executed, which shall be the seventh calendar day following the date of such notice,

c) full details of the original contract note or confirmation note including the settlement instructions,

d) the principal amount of bonds to be sold-out,

e) the name of the AIBD member who will be instructed to effect the "sell-out".

676

Rule 443 "Sell-out" execution

On failure of the buyer to effect payment or accept delivery prior to the date of the "sell-out, the seller shall instruct the third party to sell on the "sell-out" day in the best available market all or any part of the securities.

Rule 444 "Sell-out" completion

In the event that a "sell-out" cannot be completed on the "sell-out" date specified in the "sell-out" notice the named agent may be substituted with another AIBD member by the seller. Such substitution must be advised to the buyer under one business day's telex notice. Any appointed agent may complete the "sell-out" of the securities on any subsequent business day until completed or until the seller relieves him of his function as agent.
No partial settlement shall be admitted during such period.

Rule 445 Notice of execution ("Sell-out")

The seller shall immediately on receipt of advice of execution from the third party, notify the buyer by cable or telex of the quantity sold and the price contracted and shall promptly issue a contract note or confirmation note to be accompanied by the third party's confirmation note which shall state: "we have executed this trade as nominated 'sell-out' agent."

Rule 446 "Sell-out" settlement

The money difference between the original contract and the close-out contract, taking into consideration possible interest coupon due dates as well as the loss of interest to the seller on the countervalue of the securities, calculated at prevailing euro call money rates, shall be settled between the seller and the buyer without any delay.

Rule 447 Securities exempt from "sell-out"

The provisions of the "sell-out" procedure as set forth in this section shall not apply to contracts for any issue of securities which has been entirely called for redemption.

Section 600 Primary market

Rule 601 Shipping and insurance costs in the primary market

Shipping and insurance costs for bonds obtained from underwriting or selling group allotment shall be paid by the allottee. Instructions relating to the insurance coverage shall always be the responsibility of the underwriting or selling group member unless any other arrangements have been made with the delivery agent in writing.

Section 800 Miscellaneous

Rule 801 Lost, stolen or forged bonds

As soon as a member has knowledge of lost, stolen or forged securities, he shall impart this information without delay to the trustee or fiscal agent responsible for the issue in question, either directly or through his insurance company.

Recommendation to rule 801

(1) As soon as a member or his agent has knowledge of lost, stolen or forged securities, he shall advise immediately by registered mail:
  a) the trustee or fiscal agent of the issue, requesting publication of the information,
  b) the board of the AIBD, which shall notify the members.
(2) In such circumstances all necessary action under national legal regulations and practices must be taken immediately.
(3) As soon as a member or his agent has the necessary written evidence confirming the resolution of the problem, he shall immediately forward such evidence by registered mail:
  a) to the trustee or fiscal agent of the issue,
  b) to the board of the AIBD which, after consultation with the trustee or fiscal agent, shall inform the members.
(4) The board may recommend to AIBD members to cease trading as soon as possible any issue where forged securities are known to be in circulation.

Rule 802 Shortages and/or discrepancies arising from
security shipments

The liability of the seller, for any shortage and/or discrepancy of a security shipment, terminates when he or his agent has received written, dated and officially signed acknowledgement from the buyer or his agent of the acceptance of securities.

Recommendation to rule 802
The seller or his agent should forward the original shipping advice under separate cover, whereas a duplicate of such advice should be enclosed with the shipment. Such duplicate should be issued as form of acknowledgement.

Rule 803 Standard maturity yield definition
(1) The standard AIBD method of calculating maturity yields shall be based on the definition of annual interest compounding, i.e. a bond with a 7% coupon, payable annually, priced at 100%, yields 7% per annum and the same bond paying interest semi-annually yields more.
(2) A member of the AIBD calculating maturity yields by a method other than the one described above shall state exactly what method has been used for the calculation.

Rule 804 Agent's authority on conversion
Issuers of convertible debentures shall have agents in Europe, New York and Asia with the authority to cancel bonds presented to them for conversion and to instruct by cable or telex release of the shares to the order of the party presenting the bonds. The appointed conversion agent(s) for any convertible bond issue must be fully conversant with all the relevant conversion requirements as laid down in the final prospectus for such issue.

Recommendations to issuing houses
Recommendation 1 Distribution of issues
New issues, whether in definitive or global certificate form should be initially distributed through a recognised clearing agent.
In all instances, the issue manager should state clearly in the underwriting and selling group invitation telexes as well as in the preliminary and final prospectus, the place, time and other material conditions relating to the initial distribution of the issue.

Recommendation 2 – deleted

Recommendation 3 Regular coupons

The issue date, the maturity date and the interest due dates of a loan should be so co-ordinated that interest is payable semi-annually or annually but never for an irregular period of time. In choosing coupon dates, issuers should avoid February 28 in any year including a leap year.

Recommendation 4 Place of delivery

The manager of a new issue should state in the issue documentation (such as invitation telex, allotment telex and issue prospectus) whether the bonds will be traded for delivery in Europe, New York or Asia. For Asian deliveries the manager should also specify the city where delivery will take place.

The availability of an issue should be limited to one centre only.

The respective security code numbers of the clearing systems should be given in the allotment telexes.

Any derogation from this recommendation should be discussed before hand with the AIBD.

Recommendation 5 Accrued interest calculation

Issuing houses should conform to rule 225 of the AIBD in their calculation of accrued interest, if any, payable on the allotment of bonds by the underwriters, selling group members, agents and clients.

Recommendation 6 – deleted

Recommendation 7 Redemption drawing – method

When bonds are drawn for redemption for sinking fund requirements or other reasons, the certificate number of each bond to be drawn should be chosen through a random selection throughout the entire range of outstanding certificate numbers.

Every Eurobond issue prospectus should clearly state the manner in which drawings of bonds will be conducted.

Recommendation 8 Public notices

When the publication of the details of full and/or partial redemption and sinking fund drawings of bond issues is required to be made in the press, the trustee or fiscal agent should simultaneously supply such details to a central agency and the clearing systems for distribution to interested parties who could subscribe to this service.

Recommendation 9 Floating rate note interest rate fixing
The agent bank or other institution responsible for fixing the new rate on a floating rate note should communicate on the same day such new rate is fixed, the interest rate for the new interest period, the starting and the ending days of such period, and the exact number of days for such period to the stock exchanges where the issue is listed, to the clearing systems, to the board of the AIBD and to the press.

Recommendation 10 Floating rate note availability
The availability date of floating rate notes should be one and the same as the issue payment date.

Recommendation 11 Floating rate notes – no fixed coupon dates
The interest payment dates on floating rate notes should not be fixed dates, but should be determined as in the following example (of a semi-annual payment):

The interest payment date is the date falling six calendar months after the closing date and each date thereafter which falls six calendar months after the preceding interest payment date. If any interest payment date would otherwise fall on a day which is not a business day, it shall be postponed to the next business day unless it would thereby fall in the next calendar month. In the latter event, the interest payment date shall be the immediately preceding business day and each subsequent interest payment date shall be the last business day of the sixth calendar month after the month in which the preceding interest payment date shall have fallen.

General recommendation 1
(1) Where the general indebtedness of a borrower is the subject of a rescheduling any changes in the terms and conditions governing international securities (as defined by article 2 of the statutes) can only be accomplished with the necessary degree of consent of the holders of such securities as provided for in the terms and conditions of the said securities and procedures followed to gain

the necessary level of consent of such holders must be those laid down by the terms and conditions; and
(2) no attempt should be made to cause any holders of bearer securities to identify themselves via affidavits or other methods as a condition of the continued servicing of such securities or in order to permit separate negotiations with some holders except as provided for in the terms and conditions of said securities.

General recommendation 2
(1) When a member firm is a contributor to one of the on-screen price services, that firm has a responsibility to the market to indicate accurate prices and should make every effort to keep its prices up-to-date.
(2) Contributors who quote prices on the screen for issues in which they do not make a market should also indicate on the screen whether prices are 'firm' or 'subject' and the size of the offering and/or the bid.

The above rules and recommendations were last amended by the members at the general meeting at Helsinki on May 24, 1985.

Licom Terms and Conditions for Foreign Currency Options

Reprinted from the booklet *Foreign Currency Options ("LICOM" terms)*, published by the British Bankers' Association (in assocition with the Foreign Exchange and Currency Deposit Brokers' Association), August, 1985

Recommended Terms and Conditions

1. The Option

1.1 The Grantor grants the Option to the Purchaser and in consideration the Purchaser agrees to pay the Grantor the Premium on the Premium Payment Date.

1.2 Payment of the Premium shall be made in immediately available and freely transferable funds to a bank in the principal banking centre in the country of the currency concerned, and, in the case of United States Dollars, settled through the New York Clearing House Interbank Payments System (CHIPS).

1.3 The Option granted provides the Purchaser with the right but not the obligation to exchange a predetermined amount of one currency, the 'Underlying Currency', for a predetermined amount of a second currency, the 'Counter Currency', at a specified rate of exchange on one specific date or between two specified dates as determined by the Option contract.

1.4 At the time that the Option is granted, the Grantor and the Purchaser shall agree whether, in the event of the Option being exercised, settlement will be on a Principal Settlement or Net Cash Settlement basis.

1.5 Net Cash Settlement Options under these terms can be established only in currencies for which there is a published Settlement Price.

1.6   Unless otherwise specified at the time the Option is granted, it will be assumed that the Option is an American Option.

2.   Non-Payment of Premium

2.1   Without prejudice to any other rights of the Grantor under the Option contract, the Grantor shall have the right to decline to accept exercise of the Option until the Premium has been paid in full.

2.2   To the extent that the Purchaser pays later than for good value on the Premium Payment Date the Grantor will charge interest on the premium amount in the same manner as done for any other late payment in the interbank foreign exchange market.

3.   Confirmations

3.1   The Grantor and the Purchaser shall each issue a confirmation to the other as designated in Section D. Failure by either party to issue such a confirmation will not alter the rights and obligations of either party under the Option.

4.   Assignment

4.1   The Purchaser or Holder may assign an Option to a subsequent Holder only with the consent of the Grantor in writing.

4.2   The assignor shall advise the Grantor of the name and address of the new Holder and the effective date of the assignment and shall also furnish the new Holder with a copy of the Grantor's original confirmation specifying the particulars of the Option assigned.

4.3   All costs, taxes and duties which may arise on the assignment of an Option shall be for the account of the assignor.

5.   Surrender

5.1   If the Grantor and the Holder so agree the Holder may surrender the Option to the Grantor and in consideration the Grantor will pay to the Holder a surrender premium in such amount as may be agreed between them.

Upon surrender, the Holder surrenders all rights contained in the Option and releases the Grantor from all obligations therein save only the payment of the agreed surrender premium.

5.2   Surrender may be negotiated at any time in normal London Business Hours during the life of the Option up until Expiration Time on the Expiration Date. The conditions regarding the payment of the surrender premium shall be determined in the same manner as for a new Option.

5.3   Surrender shall be arranged with the Grantor by telex or by telephone. The telex or subsequent written confirmation shall include sufficient data covering the Option so that it can be positively identified. The information should include:

Date of original transaction;
Grantor's reference number;
Underlying Currency and amount;
Strike Price;
Counter Currency and amount;
Whether Call or Put;
Expiration Date;
Settlement instructions for surrender premium.

6.   Exercise

6.1   At any time up until the Expiration Time on the Expiration Date the Holder may give Notice of Exercise to the Grantor. No exercise is possible on the Business Day immediately prior to 25th December.

6.2   Expiration Time for Notice of Exercise of any Option to be settled on a Principal Settlement basis is 1500 hours London Time. Expiration Time for Notice of Exercise of any Option to be settled on a Net Settlement basis is 1430 hours London time. No exercise is possible after the Expiration Time on the Option's Expiration Date.

6.3   Notice of Exercise of American Options received by the Grantor *before* the Expiration Time on a Business Day in London on or before the Expiration Date will be for settlement as stated in paragraph 7.3 below. Notice of Exercise of American Options received by the Grantor *after* the Expiration Time on a Business Day in London before the Expiration Date, will be for settlement at the earliest on:

i)   the First Settlement Date; or,

ii) if later, the third Business Day immediately following the Notice of Exercise which (together with the two preceding Business Days) shall be a Business Day in New York and the countries of the respective Underlying and Counter Currencies of the Option concerned.

6.4   It is the responsibility of the Holder to give Notice of Exercise and all such Notices of Exercise must be given by the Holder to the Grantor during Business Hours and before the Option's Expiration Time by telex or telephone, subject to the provisions of paragraph 9.7 in respect of Net Cash Settlement Options.

6.5   The telex or subsequent written confirmation of Notice of Exercise shall include sufficient data covering the Option so that it can be positively identified. The information should include:

> Date of original transaction;
> Grantor's reference number;
> Underlying Currency and amount;
> Strike Price;
> Counter Currency and amount;
> Whether Call or Put;
> Expiration Date;
> Settlement instructions.

6.6   Options shall be exercised in whole and not in part; unless otherwise agreed between the parties.

7.   Settlement Date

7.1   Exercise shall be effected for value on the Settlement Date.

7.2   For a European Option, the Settlement Date will be the second Business Day immediately following the Expiration Date which (together with the preceding Business Day) shall be a Business Day in New York and the countries of the respective Underlying and Counter Currencies of the Option concerned.

7.3   For an American Option, the Settlement Date may be specified by the Holder as follows:

(a) At the earliest:
   i)   the First Settlement Date, or

   ii) if later, the second Business Day immediately following the Exercise Date which (together with the preceding Business Day) shall be a Business Day in London, New York and the countries of the respective Underlying and Counter Currencies of the Option concerned.

(b) At the latest, the second Business Day immediately following the Expiration Date which (together with the preceding Business Day) shall be a Business Day in London, New York and the countries of the respective Underlying and Counter Currencies of the Option concerned.

8. Principal Settlement

8.1   In the case of a Call, the Holder pays the Counter Currency amount to the Grantor at the bank designated by the Grantor for value on the Settlement Date; and the Grantor pays the Underlying Currency amount to the Holder at the bank designated by the Holder, also for value on the Settlement Date.

8.2   In the case of a Put, the Holder pays the Underlying Currency amount to the Grantor at the bank designated by the Grantor for value on the Settlement Date; and the Grantor pays the Counter Currency amount to the Holder at the bank designated by the Holder, also for value on the Settlement Date.

8.3   Payments shall be made in immediately available and freely transferable funds to a bank in the principal banking centre in the country of the currency concerned and, in the case of United States Dollars, settled through the New York Clearing House Interbank Payments System (CHIPS).

8.4   Once settlement as above has been effected the Option shall be deemed to have been fulfilled and no further rights or obligations shall exist in respect of such Option contract.

9   Net Cash Settlement

9.1   It would normally be expected that a Net Cash Settlement Option would be terminated by surrender. In the event that a surrender premium cannot be agreed by the parties, then the Holder retains the right to exercise the Option, as set out in paragraphs 9.2 to 9.8 below.

9.2   The Grantor shall pay the Net Settlement Amount to the Holder for value on the Settlement Date.

9.3   The Net Settlement Amount shall be paid in the same currency as that in which the original premium was paid to the Grantor.

9.4   Payments shall be made in immediately available and freely transferable funds to a bank in the principal banking centre in the country of the currency concerned and, in the case of United States Dollars, settled through the New York Clearing House Interbank Payments Systems (CHIPS).

9.5   The Net Settlement Amount shall represent the price difference in the Holder's favour, if any, between the Strike Price and the Settlement Price.

Example:

DM Call Option against US$1 million at Strike Price 3.30

Settlement Price 3.2120

Net Settlement Amount, in US$

$$= \frac{(3,300,000 - 3,212,000)}{3.2120}$$

$$= \quad US\$27,397.26.$$

9.6   It shall remain the responsibility of the Holder to notify the Grantor at any time during the period of five business days prior to the Expiration Date, but in any event before the Expiration Time on the Expiration Date, of the existence of his expiring Option and to give payment instructions for any Net Settlement Amount which may become due to him. In the absence of such notification and payment instruction and notwithstanding paragraph 9.7 below the Option will be deemed to have lapsed.

9.7   Assuming that the required notification under paragraph 9.6 has been duly given, on the Expiration Date any Net Cash Settlement Option having a positive value to the Holder, as reckoned by reference to the Strike Price and the Settlement Price, as above, shall be deemed to have been exercised by the Holder, and the Grantor shall pay the Net Settlement Amount to the Holder's order.

9.8   Once settlement as above has been effected the Option shall be deemed to have been fulfilled and no further rights or obligations shall exist in respect of such Option contract.

10.   Lapse

10.1   Failing Surrender or Exercise under Clauses 5 – 9 above, the Option shall lapse at the Expiration Time on the Expiration Date.

10.2   Other than the original confirmation issued to the Purchaser the Grantor shall not be required to notify or pre-notify the Holder of Expiration of the Option.

11.   London Interbank Foreign Exchange Market Practice

11.1   Options entered into under these arrangements shall be subject to the normal conditions of business for transactions in the London interbank foreign exchange markets and also to the specific conditions of the London Interbank Currency Options Market Recommended Standard Terms and Conditions, "LICOM TERMS" herein.

12. Governing Law

12.1   Options entered into under these Terms and Conditions shall be governed by and construed in accordance with the laws of England.

APPENDIX THREE

BBAIRS Terms and Conditions for Currency and Interest Rate Swaps

Reprinted from the booklet *Interest Rate Swaps ("BBAIRS" terms)* published by the British Bankers' Asociation (in association with the Foreign Exchange and Currency Deposit Brokers' Association), August, 1985

D. SINGLE CURRENCY FIXED/FLOATING INTEREST RATE SWAPS

Swaps in which one party exchanges payments determined by reference to a fixed rate of interest in return for payments from the other determined by reference to market deposit rates.

Recommended Terms and Conditions

1. Scope

Unless expressely agreed to the contrary, these Terms and Conditions (known as "BBAIRS Terms") shall apply to all London interbank single currency fixed/floating Interest Rate Swap transactions with maturity dates not exceeding two years from the Commencement Date. BBAIRS terms can be adopted for longer dated transactions provided both parties agree.

2. Definitions (denoted by initial capital letters in all texts)

"BBA Designated Banks" means the panel of not less than twelve banks currently designated by the British Bankers' Association for the purpose of establishing the BBA Interest Settlement Rate.

"BBA Interest Settlement Rate"	means, in respect of any Calculation Period, the rate calculated, and published, by the information vendor for the time being designated by the British Bankers' Association to make such calculation. The information vendor shall calculate such rate by taking the rates quoted to it by eight BBA Designated Banks as being in their view the offered rate at which deposits in the Currency for such Calculation Period are being quoted to prime banks in the London interbank market at 11.00 a.m. on the relevant Calculation Date and eliminating the two highest (or, in the event of equality, two of the highest) and the two lowest (or, in the event of equality, two of the lowest), taking the average of the remaining four rates and then (if necessary) rounding the resultant figure upwards to five decimal places.
"Business Day"	means a day (other than a Saturday or Sunday) on which banks are open for business (including dealings in foreign exchange and foreign currency deposits when the Currency is not Pounds Sterling) in London and in the Financial Centre of the Currency.

With regard to a non-Business Day:
In the event that the Commencement Date, the Maturity Date, any Fixed Rate Payment Date or any Floating Rate Payment Date would otherwise fall on a day which is not a Business Day then the relevant date shall be extended to the next suceeding Business Day (unless the effect thereof would be to extend it into the next calendar month, in which case the relevant date shall be the immediately preceding Business Day).

"Calculation Date" means, in respect of each Calculation Period, for currencies other than Pounds Sterling, two London Business Days prior to the first Business Day of the Calculation Period and, in the case of Pounds Sterling, the first Business Day of the Calculation Period.

"Calculation Period" means the period from and including the Commencement Date to but excluding the first Floating Rate Payment Date and each period from and including the immediately preceding Floating Rate Payment Date to but excluding the following Floating Rate Payment Date.

"Commencement Date" means the designated Business Day on which interest will first begin to accrue with respect to the Notional Principal.

"Contract Date" means the date on which the parties enter into this agreement.

"Currency" means the currency in which the Notional Principal is designated, being a currency for which, on the Contract Date, a BBA Interest Settlement Rate is available.

"Financial Centre" of a particular currency means the recognised principal financial centre of the country whose lawful currency for the time being is such currency and, in the case of Pounds Sterling, means London; of US Dollars, New York; of Deutschemarks, Frankfurt; of Yen, Tokyo and of Swiss Francs, Zurich.

"Fixed Rate" means the rate of interest agreed between the parties, expressed as a per cent per annum, which shall remain constant from the Commencement Date until the Maturity Date.

"Fixed Rate Days Fraction"	means, in respect of each Fixed Rate Payment Date, a fraction being the actual number of days elapsed from the next preceding Fixed Rate Payment Date (but, in the case of the first Fixed Rate Payment Date, from the Commencement Date) divided by 360 or (if the Currency is Pounds Sterling) 365.
"Fixed Rate Payer"	means the party who agrees to make the Fixed Rate Payments.
"Fixed Rate Payer's Account"	means the account specified as such in the Confirmation, or such other account as the Fixed Rate Payer may notify in writing to the Floating Rate Payer.
"Fixed Rate Payment"	means, in respect of each Fixed Rate Payment Date, the amount agreed between the parties and specified as such in the Confirmation or, if no such amount has been agreed and specified, an amount equal to the product of the Notional Principal, the Fixed Rate and the Fixed Rate Days Fraction.
"Fixed Rate Payment Date(s)"	means the date(s) specified as such in the Confirmation.
"Floating Rate"	means, in respect of any Calculation Period, the BBA Interest Settlement Rate expressed as a per cent per annum, applicable to such Calculation Period.
"Floating Rate Days Fraction"	means, in respect of each Floating Rate Payment Date, a fraction being the actual number of days elapsed from the next preceding Floating Rate Payment Date (but, in the case of the first Floating Rate Payment Date, from the Commencement Date) divided by 360 or (if the Currency is Pounds Sterling) 365.

"Floating Rate Payer"	means the party to the transaction who agrees to make the Floating Rate Payments.
"Floating Rate Payer's Account"	means the account specified as such in the Confirmation, or such other account as the Floating Rate Payer may notify in writing to the Fixed Rate Payer.
"Floating Rate Payment"	means, in respect of each Floating Rate Payment Date, an amount equal to the product of the Notional Principal, the Floating Rate and the Floating Rate Days Fraction.
"Floating Rate Payment Date(s)"	means the date(s) designated as such and specified in the Confirmation.
"London Business Day"	means a day (other than a Saturday or Sunday) on which banks are open for business (including dealings in foreign exchange and foreign currency deposits) in London.
"Maturity Date"	means the day on which this Agreement is to end.
"Notional Principal"	means the amount of Currency on which interest is accrued with respect to both the Fixed Rate Payments and the Floating Rate Payments.

3. Exchanges

On the Calculation Date in respect of each Calculation Period, the Fixed Rate Payer shall determine the Floating Rate Payment payable on the relevant Floating Payment Date and the date of such Floating Payment Date (if appropriate) and as soon as reasonably practicable notify the Floating Rate Payer thereof. The Fixed Rate Payer agrees to pay to the Floating Rate Payer on each Fixed Rate Payment Date the relevant Fixed Rate Payment; and the Floating Rate Payer agrees to pay to the Fixed Rate Payer on each Floating Rate Payment Date the relevant Floating Rate Payment.

4. Payments

i) If the Fixed Rate Payer is obliged to pay any sum to the Floating Rate Payer under Clause 3 on the same day as the Floating Rate Payer is obliged to pay any sum to the Fixed Rate Payer under Clause 3 such sums shall not be paid and instead the party liable to pay the greater of such sums shall on such day pay to the other party in the same manner a sum in the same currency equal to the excess of such greater sum over the other sum.

ii) Each payment to be made hereunder by either party shall be made for value on the day when such payment is due in immediately available freely transferable funds and shall be made, if to the Fixed Rate Payer, at the Fixed Rate Payer's Account or, if to the Floating Rate Payer, at the Floating Rate Payer's Account.

5. Deductions, Default and Termination

The provisions set out in Section G relating inter alia to Representations and Warranties, Deductions and Withholdings, Default and Termination shall form part of this Agreement.

6. Confirmation

As soon as practicable after conclusion of this Agreement each of the principal parties shall submit to the other a confirmation of particulars substantially in the form set out opposite.

7. (a) **Example of Confirmation to be Exchanged between the Parties**

FIXED RATE PAYER BANK PLC,
Main Street,
LONDON, E.C.2.

To: Floating Rate Payer Bank Inc.,
Moorgate,
London, E.C.2.

Date: 26th September, 1984
Our Ref: XYZ0001

CONFIRMATION OF SINGLE CURRENCY FIXED/FLOATING
INTEREST RATE SWAP AGREEMENT

We hereby confirm particulars in respect of the following single currency fixed/floating Interest Rate Swap Agreement entered between us subject to the British Bankers' Association's Recommended Terms and Conditions ("BBAIRS Terms") dated August, 1985.

Contract Date:	26th September 1984
Fixed Rate Payer:	Fixed Rate Payer Bank PLC
Floating Rate Payer:	Floating Rate Payer Bank Inc.
Direct/Broker:	Broker
Commencement Date:	28th September 1984
Maturity Date:	30th September 1985
Currency:	U.S. Dollars
Notional Principal:	U.S. $20 Million
Fixed Rate Payments:	
Fixed Rate:	12.12500% per annum
Floating Rate:	First period 11.50000%, thereafter 3 months BBAIRS Settlement Rate
Fixed Rate Payment Dates:	Maturity Date
Floating Rate Payment Dates:	19/12/84 - 20/03/85 - 19/06/85 - 30/09/85
Variation to BBAIRS Terms:	None
Fixed Rate Payers Account:	ABC Bank, New York
Floating Rate Payers Account:	XYZ Bank, New York

PLEASE TELEPHONE OR CABLE US IMMEDIATELY SHOULD THE PARTICULARS OF THIS CONFIRMATION NOT BE IN ACCORDANCE WITH YOUR UNDERSTANDING.

For ___________

____
(title)

(b) **Example of Broker's Telex Notification**

```
To:   Fixed Rate Payer Bank PLC,
      Main Street,
      LONDON, E.C.2.

      and

To:   Floating Rate Payer Bank Inc.,        Date:    26th September, 1984
      Moorgate,
      LONDON, E.C.2.
```

NOTIFICATION OF SINGLE CURRENCY FIXED/FLOATING
INTEREST RATE SWAP AGREEMENT

We hereby notify particulars in respect of the following single currency fixed/floating Interest Rate Swap Agreement arranged by us and entered into between you subject to the British Bankers' Association's Recommended Terms and Conditions ("BBAIRS Terms") dated August, 1985.

Contract Date:	26th September 1984
Fixed Rate Payer:	Fixed Rate Payer Bank PLC
Floating Rate Payer:	Floating Rate Payer Bank Inc.
Commencement Date:	28th September 1984
Maturity Date:	30th September 1985
Currency:	U.S. Dollars
Notional Principal:	U.S. $20 Million
Fixed Rate Payments	
Fixed Rate:	12.12500% per annum
Floating Rate:	First period 11.50000%, thereafter 3 months BBAIRS Settlement Rate
Fixed Rate Payment Dates:	Maturity Date
Floating Rate Payment Dates:	19/12/84 - 20/03/85 - 19/06/85 - 30/09/85
Variation to BBAIRS Terms:	None
Fixed Rate Payers Account:	ABC Bank, New York
Floating Rate Payers Account:	XYZ Bank, New York
Brokerage	

PLEASE TELEPHONE OR CABLE US IMMEDIATELY SHOULD THE PARTICULARS OF THIS CONFIRMATION NOT BE IN ACCORDANCE WITH YOUR UNDERSTANDING.

Regards,

Broker

E. CROSS CURRENCY INTEREST RATE SWAPS

Swaps in which either the two parties exchange payments determined by reference to fixed rates of interest in two currencies, or one party makes payments by reference to a fixed rate of interest in one currency and the other in US dollars by reference to market deposit rates.

Recommended Terms and Conditions

1. Scope

Unless expressly agreed to the contrary, these Terms and Conditions (Known as "BBAIRS Terms") shall apply to all London interbank Cross Currency Interest Rate Swap transactions with maturity dates not exceeding two years from the Commencement Date. BBAIRS terms can be adopted for longer dated transactions provided both parties agree.

Normally the principal amounts involved in a transaction are agreed at the outset. In the case of swaps arranged more than two days prior to the Commencement Date, the principal amount is fixed in one currency and the exchange rate reference for calculating the equivalent amount in the second currency is agreed. The parties have the option to agree to an initial exchange of the principal amounts on the Commencement Date, but, even if there is no initial exchange of principal, the parties will always undertake a reverse exchange on maturity.

2. **Definitions** (denoted by initial capital letters in all texts)

"BBA Designated Banks"	means the panel of not less than twelve banks currently designated by the British Bankers' Association for the purpose of quoting deposit rates in the Currency concerned.
"BBA Interest Settlement Rate"	means, in respect of any Calculation Period, the rate calculated, and published, by the information vendor for the time being designated by the British Bankers' Assocation to make such calculation. The information vendor shall

calculate such rate by taking the rates quoted to it by eight BBA Designated Banks as being in their view the offered rate at which deposits in US Dollars for such Calculation Period are being quoted to prime banks in the London interbank market at 11.00 a.m. on the relevant Calculation Date and eliminating the two highest (or, in the event of equality, two of the highest) and the two lowest (or, in the event of equality, two of the lowest), taking the average of the remaining four rates and then (if necessary) rounding the resultant figure upwards to five decimal places.

"Business Day"

means a day (other than a Saturday or a Sunday) on which banks are open for business, (including dealings in foreign exchange and foreign currency deposits) in London and the Financial Centres of Currency A and Currency B.

With regard to a Non-Business Day:
In the event that the Commencement Date, the Maturity Date, any Currency A Payment Date or any Currency B Payment Date would otherwise fall on a day which is not a Business Day then the relevant date shall be extended to the next succeeding Business Day (unless the effect thereof would be to extend it into the next calendar month, in which case the relevant date shall be the immediately preceding Business Day).

"Calculation Date"

means, in respect of each Calculation Period two London Business Days prior to the first Business Day of the Calculation Period.

"Calculation Period"

means, if Currency A is US Dollars and the Currency A Rate is the BBA Interest Settlement Rate, the period from and including the Commencement Date to, but excluding, the first Currency A Payment Date and each period from and including the immediately preceding Currency A Payment Date to, but excluding, the following Currency A Payment Date.

"Commencement Date" means the designated Business Day on which interest will first begin to accrue with respect to the Currency A Amount and the Currency B Amount.

"Contract Date" means the date on which the parties enter into this Agreement.

"Currency A" means US Dollars or such other currency as may be agreed between the parties.

"Currency A Amount" means the amount of Currency A agreed between the parties on which interest is to accrue with respect to the Currency A Payments or if no such amount is specified, means an amount denominated in Currency A, such amount being established by reference to the Foreign Exchange Rate Reference.

"Currency A Days Fraction" means, in respect of each Currency A Payment Date, a fraction being the actual number of days elapsed from the next preceding Currency A Payment Date (but, in the case of the first Currency A Payment Date, from the Commencement Date) divided by 360 or (if Currency A is Pounds Sterling) 365.

"Currency A Payer" means the party who agrees to make the Currency A Payments.

"Currency A Payer's Account"	means the account specified as such in the Confirmation, or such other account as Currency A Payer may notify in writing to Currency B Payer.
"Currency A Payment"	means, in respect of each Currency A Payment Date, the amount agreed between the parties and specified as such in the Confirmation or, if no such amount has been agreed and specified, an amount equal to the product of the Currency A Amount, the Currency A Rate and the Currency A Days Fraction.
"Currency A Payment Date(s)"	means the date(s) designated as such and specified in the Confirmation.
"Currency A Rate"	means either a fixed rate (which shall remain constant from the Commencement Date until the Maturity Date) agreed between the parties or, if Currency A is US Dollars, either a fixed rate or the BBA Interest Settlement Rate, as agreed between the parties.
"Currency B"	means such currency as may be agreed between the parties.
"Currency B Amount"	means the amount of Currency B agreed between the parties on which interest is to accrue with respect to the Currency B Payments or, if no such amount is specified, means an amount denominated in Currency B, such amount being established by reference to the Foreign Exchange Rate Reference.

"Currency B Days Fraction"	means in respect of each Currency B Payment Date, a fraction being the actual number of days elapsed from the next preceding Currency B Payment Date (but, in the case of the first Currency B Payment Date, from the Commencement Date) divided by 360 or (if Currency B is Pounds Sterling) 365.
"Currency B Payer's Account"	means the account specified as such in the Confirmation, or such other account as Currency B Payer may notify in writing to Currency A Payer.
"Currency B Payment"	means, in respect of each Currency B Payment Date, the amount agreed between the parties and specified as such in the Confirmation or, if no such amount has been agreed and specified, an amount equal to the product of the Currency B Amount, the Currency B Rate and the Currency B Days Fraction.
"Currency B Payment Date(s)"	means the date(s) designated as such and specified in the Confirmation.
"Currency B Rate"	means the rate of interest agreed between the parties, expressed as a per cent per annum, which shall remain constant from the Commencement Date until the Maturity Date.
"Financial Centre"	of a particular currency means the recognised principal financial centre of the country whose lawful currency for the time being is such currency and, in the case of Pounds Sterling, means London; of US Dollars, New York; of Deutschemarks, Frankfurt; of Yen, Tokyo and of Swiss Francs, Zurich.

"Foreign Exchange Rate Reference"	means the Foreign Exchange Rate Reference agreed between the parties for determining the exchange rate to be used for the purposes of calculating the Currency B Amount by reference to the Currency A Amount in the case that the Currency B Amount is not specified or the Currency A Amount by reference to the Currency B Amount in the case that the Currency A Amount is not specified.
"London Business Day"	means a day (other than a Saturday or a Sunday) on which banks are open for business (including dealings in foreign exchange and foreign currency deposits) in London.
"Maturity Date"	means the day on which this Agreement is to end.

3. Exchanges

If the parties agree that there shall be an initial exchange, Currency A Payer agrees to pay to Currency B Payer, on the Commencement Date, the Currency B Amount, and Currency B Payer agrees to pay to Currency A Payer, on the Commencement Date, the Currency A Amount.

If Currency A is US Dollars and the Currency A Rate is the BBA Interest Settlement Rate, on the Calculation Date in respect of each Calculation Period, Currency A Payer shall determine the Currency A Payment and as soon as reasonably practicable notify Currency B Payer thereof.

Currency A Payer agrees to pay to Currency B Payer on each Currency A Payment Date the relevant Currency A Payment; and Currency B Payer agrees to pay to Currency A Payer on each Currency B Payment Date the relevant Currency B Payment.

On the Maturity Date Currency A Payer agrees to pay to Currency B Payer the Currency A Amount, and the Currency B Payer agrees to pay to Currency A Payer the Currency B Amount.

4. Payments

Each payment to be made hereunder by either party shall be made for value on the day when such payment is due in immediately available freely transferable funds and shall be made, if to Currency A Payer, at Currency A Payer's Account or, if to Currency B Payer, at Currency B Payer's Account.

5. Deductions, Default and Termination

The provisions set out in Section G relating inter alia to Representations and Warranties, Deductions and Withholdings, Default and Termination shall form part of this Agreement.

6. Confirmation

As soon as practicable after conclusion of this Agreement each of the principal parties shall submit to the other a confirmation of particulars substantially in the form set out overleaf.

7. (a) Example of Confirmation to be Exchanged between the Parties

CURRENCY A PAYER BANK PLC
Main Street,
LONDON, E.C.2.

To: Currency B Payer Bank Inc.,   Date: 12th October, 1984
     London Branch,   Ref: XYZ 002
     Moorgate,
     LONDON, E.C.2.

CONFIRMATION OF A CROSS CURRENCY INTEREST RATE SWAP AGREEMENT

We hereby confirm particulars in respect of the following Cross Currency Interest Rate Swap Agreement entered into between us subject to the British Bankers' Association's Recommended Terms and Conditions ("BBAIRS terms") dated August, 1985.

Contract Date:	12th October, 1984
Currency A:	Dollars
Currency B:	Swiss Francs
Currency A Payer:	Currency A Payer Bank PLC
Currency B Payer:	Currency B Payer Bank Inc.
Direct/broker:	Broker
Commencement Date:	18th October, 1984
Maturity Date:	18th October, 1986
Currency A Amount:	U.S. $9,797,775.00
Currency B Amount:	Sw.Fr. 25,000,000.00
Foreign Exchange Rate Reference:	N/A
Initial Exchange:	Yes/~~No~~
Currency A Rate:	6 months BBAIRS Settlement Rate
Currency A Payment:	N/A
Currency A Payment Dates:	18/4/85 - 18/10/85 - 18/4/86 - 18/10/86
Currency B Rate:	N/A
Currency B Payment:	equal annual amounts of Sw.Fr. 1,475,000.00
Currency B Payment Dates:	18/10/85, 18/10/86
Variation to BBAIRS Terms:	None
Currency A Payer's Account:	A/c 000123 with X Bank - Zurich
Currency B Payer's Account:	A/c 000456 with Y Bank - New York

PLEASE TELEPHONE OR CABLE US IMMEDIATELY SHOULD THE PARTICULARS OF THIS CONFIRMATION NOT BE IN ACCORDANCE WITH YOUR UNDERSTANDING.

For ____________

    (title)

7.   (b) **Example of Broker's Telex Notification**

To: Currency A Payer Bank PLC,
Main Street,
LONDON, E.C.2.

and

To: Currency B Payer Bank Inc.,   Date: 12th October, 1984
London Branch,   Ref: PQR 001
Moorgate,
LONDON, E.C.2.

NOTIFICATION OF A CROSS CURRENCY INTEREST RATE SWAP AGREEMENT

We hereby notify you of particulars in respect of the following Cross Currency Interest Rate Swap Agreement arranged by us and entered into between you subject to the British Bankers' Association's Recommended Terms and Conditions ("BBAIRS terms") dated August, 1985.

Contract Date:	12th October, 1984
Currency A:	Dollars
Currency B:	Swiss Francs
Currency A Payer:	Currency A Payer Bank PLC
Currency B Payer:	Currency B Payer Bank Inc.
Commencement Date:	18th October, 1984
Maturity Date:	18th October, 1986
Currency A Amount:	U.S. $9,797,775.00
Currency B Amount:	Sw.Fr. 25,000,000.00
Exchange Rate Reference:	N/A
Initial Exchange:	Yes/~~No~~
Currency A Rate:	6 months BBAIRS Settlement Rate
Currency A Payment:	N/A
Currency A Payment Dates:	18/4/85 - 18/10/85 - 18/4/86 - 18/10/86
Currency B Rate:	N/A
Currency B Payment:	equal annual amounts of Sw.Fr. 1,475,000.00
Currency B Payment Dates:	18/10/85, 18/10/86
Variation to BBAIRS Terms:	None
Currency A Payer's Account:	A/c 000123 with X Bank - Zurich
Currency B Payer's Account:	A/c 000456 with Y Bank - New York
Brokerage:	

<u>PLEASE TELEPHONE OR CABLE US IMMEDIATELY SHOULD THE PARTICULARS OF THIS CONFIRMATION NOT BE IN ACCORDANCE WITH YOUR UNDERSTANDING.</u>

Regards,

Broker

F.   CROSS CURRENCY FLOATING RATE SWAPS

Swaps in which the two parties exchange payments in two different currencies with both amounts being determined by reference to market deposit rates.

Recommended Terms and Conditions

1.   Scope

Unless expressly agreed to the contrary, these Terms and Conditions (known as "BBAIRS Terms") shall apply to all London interbank Cross Currency Floating Rate Swap transactions with maturity dates not exceeding two years from the Commencement Date. BBAIRS terms can be adopted for longer dated transactions provided both parties agree.

Normally, the principal amounts involved in a transaction are agreed at the outset. In the case of swaps arranged more than two days prior to the Commencement Date, the principal amount is fixed in one currency and the exchange rate reference for calculating the equivalent amount in the second currency is agreed. The parties have the option to agree to an initial exchange of the principal amounts on the Commencement Date, but, even if there is no initial exchange of principal, the parties will always undertake a reverse exchange on maturity.

2.   Definitions (denoted by initial capital letters in all texts)

"BBA Designated Banks"	means the panel of not less than twelve banks currently designated by the British Bankers' Association for the purpose of quoting deposit rates in the Currency concerned.
"BBA Interest Settlement Rate"	means, in respect of any Currency A Calculation Period or, as the case may be, Currency B Calculation Period, the rate calculated, and published, by the information vendor for the time being designated by the British Bankers' Association to make such calculation. The in-

formation vendor shall calculate such rate by taking the rates quoted to it by eight BBA Designated Banks as being in their view the offered rate at which deposits in the relevant currency for such Calculation Period are being quoted to prime banks in the London inter-bank market at 11.00 a.m. on the Currency A Calculation Date or, as the case may be, the Currency B Calculation Date and eliminating the two highest (or, in the event of equality, two of the highest) and the two lowest (or, in the event of equality, two of the lowest), taking the average of the remaining four rates and then (if necessary) rounding the resultant figure upwards to five decimal places.

"Business Day" means a day (other than a Saturday or a Sunday) on which banks are open for business (including dealings in foreign exchange and foreign currency deposits) in London and in the Financial Centres of Currency A and Currency B.

With regard to a non-Business Day:
In the event that the Commencement Date, the Maturity Date, any Currency A Payment Date or any Currency B Payment Date would otherwise fall on a day which is not a Business Day then the relevant date shall be extended to the next succeeding Business Day (unless the effect thereof would be to extend it into the next calendar month, in which case the relevant date shall be the immediately preceding Business Day).

"Commencement Date" means the designated Business Day on which interest will first begin to accrue with respect to the Currency A Amount and the Currency B Amount.

"Contract Date"	means the date on which the parties enter into this Agreement.
"Currency A"	means US Dollars, or such other currency as the parties may agree, being a currency for which, on the Contract Date, a BBA Interest Settlement Rate is available.
"Currency A Amount"	means the amount of Currency A agreed between the parties on which interest is to accrue with respect to the Currency A Payments or, if no such amount is specified, means an amount denominated in Currency A, such amount being established by reference to the Foreign Exchange Rate Reference.
"Currency A Calculation Date"	means, in respect of each Currency A Calculation Period for currencies other than Pounds Sterling, the day which is two London Business Days prior to the first Business Day of the Calculation Period or, in the case of Pounds Sterling, the first Business Day of the Currency A Calculation Period.
"Currency A Calculation Period"	means the period from and including the Commencement Date to, but excluding, the first Currency A Payment Date and each period from and including the immediately preceding Currency A Payment Date to, but excluding, the following Currency A Payment Date.
"Currency A Days Fraction"	means, in respect of each Currency A Payment Date, a fraction being the actual number of days elapsed from the next preceding Currency A Payment Date (but, in the case of the first Currency A Payment Date, from the Commencement Date) divided by 360 or (if Currency A is Pounds Sterling) 365.

"Currency A Payer" means the party who agrees to make the Currency A Payments.

"Currency A Payer's Account" means the account specified as such in the Confirmation, or such other account as Currency A Payer may notify in writing to Currency B Payer.

"Currency A Payment" means, in respect of each Currency A Payment Date, an amount equal to the product of the Currency A Amount, the BBA Interest Settlement Rate in respect of the relevant Currency A Calculation Period and the Currency A Days Fraction.

"Currency A Payment Date(s)" means the date(s) designated as such and specified in the Confirmation.

"Currency B" means such currency as may be agreed between the parties, being a currency for which, on the Contract Date, a BBA Interest Settlement Rate is available.

"Currency B Amount" means the amount of Currency B agreed between the parties on which interest is to accrue with respect to the Currency B Payments or, if no such amount is specified, means an amount denominated in Currency B, such amount being established by reference to the Foreign Exchange Rate Reference.

"Currency B Calculation Date" means, in respect of each Currency B Calculation Period, for currencies other than Pounds Sterling, the day which is two London Business Days prior to the first Business Day of the Calculation Period or, in the case of Pounds Sterling, the first Business Day of the Currency B Calculation Period.

"Currency B Calculation Period"	means the period from and including the Commencement Date to, but excluding, the first Currency B Payment Date and each period from and including the immediately preceding Currency B Payment Date to, but excluding, the following Currency B Payment Date.
"Currency B Days Fraction"	means, in respect of each Currency B Payment Date, a fraction being the actual number of days elapsed from the next preceding Currency B Payment Date (but, in the case of the first Currency B Payment Date, from the Commencement Date) divided by 360 or (if Currency B is Pounds Sterling) 365.
"Currency B Payer's Account"	means the account specified as such in the Confirmation, or such other account as Currency B Payer may notify in writing to Currency A Payer.
"Currency B Payment"	means, in respect of each Currency B Payment Date, an amount equal to the product of the Currency B Amount, the BBA Interest Settlement Rate in respect of the relevant Currency B Calculation Period and the Currency B Days Fraction.
"Currency B Payment Date(s)"	means the date(s) designated as such and specified in the Confirmation.
"Financial Centre"	of a particular currency means the recognised principal financial centre of the country whose lawful currency for the time being is such currency and, in the case of Pounds Sterling, means London; of US Dollars, New York; of Deutschemarks, Frankfurt; of Yen, Tokyo and of Swiss Francs, Zurich.

"Foreign Exchange Rate Reference"	means the foreign exchange rate reference agreed between the parties for determining the exchange rate to be used for the purposes of calculating the Currency B Amount by reference to the Currency A Amount in the case that the Currency B Amount is not specified or the Currency A Amount by reference to the Currency B Amount in the case that the Currency A Amount is not specified.
"London Business Day"	means a day (other than a Saturday or a Sunday) on which banks are open for business (including dealings in foreign exchange and foreign currency deposits) in London.
"Maturity Date"	means the day on which this Agreement is to end.

3. Exchanges

If the parties agree that there shall be an initial exchange, Currency A Payer agrees to pay to Currency B Payer, on the Commencement Date, the Currency B Amount, and Currency B Payer agrees to pay to Currency A Payer, on the Commencement Date, the Currency A Amount.

On the Currency A Calculation Date in respect of each Currency A Calculation Period, and on the Currency B Calculation Date in respect of each Currency B Calculation Period, Currency A Payer shall determine respectively the Currency A Payment and the Currency B Payment and as soon as reasonably practicable notify Currency B Payer thereof.

Currency A Payer agrees to pay to Currency B Payer on each Currency A payment Date the relevant Currency A Payment and Currency B Payer agrees to pay to Currency A Payer on each Currency B Payment Date the relevant Currency B Payment.

On the Maturity Date Currency A Payer agrees to pay to Currency B Payer the Currency A Amount, and Currency B Payer agrees to pay to Currency A Payer the Currency B Amount.

4. Payments

Each payment to be made hereunder by either party shall be made for value on the day when such payment is due in immediately available freely transferable funds and shall be made, if to Currency A Payer, at Currency A Payer's Account or, if to Currency B Payer, at Currency B Payer's Account.

5. Deductions, Default and Termination

The provisions set out in Section G relating inter alia to Representations and Warranties, Deductions and Withholdings, Default and Termination shall form part of this Agreement.

6. Confirmation

As soon as practicable after conclusion of this Agreement each of the principal parties shall submit to the other a confirmation of particulars substantially in the form set out opposite and overleaf.

7. (a) **Example of Confirmation to be Exchanged between the Parties**

CURRENCY A PAYER BANK PLC
Main Street,
LONDON, E.C.2.

To: Currency B Payer Bank Inc., Date: 12th October, 1984
London Branch, Ref: XYZ 002
Moorgate,
LONDON, E.C.2.

CONFIRMATION OF A CROSS CURRENCY FLOATING RATE SWAP AGREEMENT

We hereby confirm particulars in respect of the following Cross Currency Floating Rate Swap Agreement entered into between us subject to the British Bankers' Association's Recommended Terms and Conditions ("BBAIRS terms") dated August, 1985.

Contract Date:	12th October, 1984
Currency A:	Dollars
Currency B:	Sterling
Currency A Payer:	Currency A Payer Bank PLC
Currency B Payer:	Currency B Payer Bank Inc.
Direct/Broker:	Broker
Commencement Date:	18th October, 1984
Maturity Date:	18th October, 1986
Currency A Amount:	U.S. $10,000,000
Currency B Amount:	£ equivalent
Exchange Reference:	mid/~~bid/offer~~ £/$ rate quoted by IWB & Citibank at 11.00 a.m. on 16.10.85
Initial Exchange:	Yes/~~No~~
Currency A Rate:	6 months BBAIRS Settlement Rate
Currency A Payment Dates:	18/4/85 - 18/10/85 - 18/4/86 - 18/10/86
Currency B Rate:	6 months BBAIRS Settlement Rate
Currency B Payment Dates:	18/4/85 - 18/10/85 - 18/4/86 - 18/10/86
Variation to BBAIRS Terms:	None
Currency A Payer's Account:	A/c 000123 with X Bank - London
Currency B Payer's Account:	A/c 000456 with Y Bank - New York

PLEASE TELEPHONE OR CABLE US IMMEDIATELY SHOULD THE PARTICULARS OF THIS CONFIRMATION NOT BE IN ACCORDANCE WITH YOUR UNDERSTANDING.

For ___________

(title)

7. (b) **Example of Broker's Telex Notification**

To: Currency A Payer Bank PLC,
Main Street,
LONDON, E.C.2.

and

To: Currency B Payer Bank Inc.,   Date: 12th October, 1984
London Branch,   Ref: PQR 001
Moorgate,
LONDON, E.C.2.

NOTIFICATION OF A CROSS CURRENCY FLOATING RATE SWAP AGREEMENT

We hereby notify you of particulars in respect of the following Cross Currency Floating Rate Swap Agreement arranged by us and entered into between you subject to the British Bankers' Association's Recommended Terms and Conditions ("BBAIRS terms") dated August, 1985.

Contract Date:	12th October, 1984
Currency A:	Dollars
Currency B:	Sterling
Currency A Payer:	Currency A Payer Bank PLC
Currency B Payer:	Currency B Payer Bank Inc.
Direct/Broker:	Broker
Commencement Date:	18th October, 1984
Maturity Date:	18th October, 1986
Currency A Amount:	U.S. $10,000,000
Currency B Amount:	£ equivalent
Exchange Reference:	mid/~~bid/offer~~ £/$ rate quoted by IWB & Citibank at 11.00 a.m. on 16.10.85
Initial Exchange:	Yes/~~No~~
Currency A Rate:	6 months BBAIRS Settlement Rate
Currency A Payment Dates:	18/4/85 - 18/10/85 - 18/4/86 - 18/10/86
Currency B Rate:	6 months BBAIRS Settlement Rate
Currency B Payment Dates:	18/4/85 - 18/10/85 - 18/4/86 - 18/10/86
Variation to BBAIRS Terms:	None
Currency A Payer's Account:	A/c 000123 with X Bank - London
Currency B Payer's Account:	A/c 000456 with Y Bank - New York
Brokerage:	

PLEASE TELEPHONE OR CABLE US IMMEDIATELY SHOULD THE PARTICULARS OF THIS CONFIRMATION NOT BE IN ACCORDANCE WITH YOUR UNDERSTANDING.

Regards,

Broker

716

G. CLAUSES COMMON TO ALL TRANSACTIONS

The following provisions shall form part of the Recommended Terms and Conditions for Single Currency Fixed/Floating Interest Rate Swaps, set out in Section D, for Cross Currency Interest Rate Swaps, set out in Section E, and for Cross Currency Floating Rate Swaps set out in Section F.

1. Representations and Warranties

1.1 Each party represents and warrants to the other that:

i) it has full power and authority (corporate and otherwise) to enter into this Agreement and to exercise its rights and perform its obligations hereunder and has obtained all authorisations and consents necessary for it so to enter, exercise rights and perform obligations and such authorisations and consents are in full force and effect;

ii) the obligations expressed to be assumed by it under this Agreement are legal and valid obligations binding on it in accordance with their terms; and

iii) it is not required to make any such deduction or withholding as is contemplated in Clause 2 on or in respect of any payment to be made by it under this Argeement.

1.2 The representations and warranties contained in sub-Clause 1.1 shall be given as at the Contract Date and those in paragraphs i) and ii) shall be deemed to be given again by each party on each date on which that party is required to make any payment under this Agreement.

2. Deductions and Withholdings

2.1 Each payment to be made hereunder by either party ("Payer") to the other ("Payee") shall (except to the extent required by law) be paid free and clear of and without any deduction or withholding for or on account of any present or future tax, duty or charge ("Taxes") and without deduction or withholding for or on account of any other amount, whether by way of set-off or otherwise, other than a set-off or counterclaim arising from a default by the Payee in the performance of its obligations hereunder which are due prior to the relevant payment date.

2.2   If the Payer is required by law to make any deduction or withholding for or on account of any Taxes or otherwise from any sum paid or payable under this Agreement:

i)   the Payer shall pay such Taxes or other amounts before the date on which penalties attach thereto;

ii)   the sum payable by the Payer, in respect of which the relevant deduction or withholding is made or is required to be made, shall be increased to the extent necessary to ensure that, after making such deduction or withholding, the Payee receives on the due date and retains (free from any liability in respect of any such deduction or withholding) a net sum equal to that which the Payee would have received and so retained had no such deduction or withholding been required or made; and

iii)   within 30 days after paying any sum from which it is required by law to make any deduction or withholding, and within 30 days after the due date for payment of any Taxes or other amount (which it is required by this sub-clause 2.2 to pay), the Payer shall deliver to the Payee an official receipt or other official documentation evidencing such payment.

3.   Default Interest

Any payment required to be made hereunder which is not made when due shall (insofar as permitted by applicable law) bear interest, payable in the currency of such payment. Such interest shall accrue and be calculated from the date when the relevant payment was due to the date of its final payment in full. Such interest shall be calculated at the rate certified by the Payee as being one per cent above the effective cost to it of funding such sum from such sources and for such periods as the Payee may from time to time decide. Such interest shall be due on the last day of each such period decided by the Payee and, if not then paid, shall itself bear interest hereunder.

4.   Termination

If in respect of either party (the "Affected Party") (i) the Affected Party shall be or become liable pursuant to Clause 2 above to pay additional amounts as set forth therein or (ii) it becomes unlawful for the Affected Party to perform its obligations hereunder as a result of existing or future laws or regulations, directives or requirements of any regulatory authority or agency of any relevant jursidiction and unless the Affected Party could avoid such requirement or such illegality by making reasonable alternative arrangements which may (but shall not necessarily) include, without limitation, having this Agreement relate to another office or changing to alternative sources or applications of funds or by assigning (with the prior consent of the other party ("the Injured Party")) its rights hereunder to any other person, which other person shall at the same time assume the obligations of the Affected Party; the Affected Party may, on giving notice to the Injured Party, terminate this Agreement with effect from the date specified in such notice (the "Termination Date"), being not less than 14 and not more than 30 days after the date of service of such notice.

5. Events of Default

The occurrence of any one or more of the following circumstances in respect of either party (the "Defaulting Party") shall be an Event of Default:

i) failure by the Defaulting Party to pay any sum due and payable hereunder within three Business Days of receipt of written notice from the other party (the "non-Defaulting Party") that such sum is overdue; or

ii) an order of a competent court is made or an effective resolution is passed for the winding up or dissolution of the Defaulting Party other than for the purpose of a reconstruction or amalgamation previously approved in writing by the non-Defaulting Party, such approval not to be unreasonably withheld; or

iii) the initiation of proceedings under any applicable bankruptcy, reorganisation, composition or insolvency law by (in respect of itself) or against the Defaulting Party, provided that such proceedings have not been discharged or stayed within 30 days, or the appointment of a receiver over all or any part of the undertaking or any property, asset, or revenues of the Defaulting Party; or

iv) any representation made or warranty given by the Defaulting Party pursuant to Clause 1 is or proves to have been materially incorrect or misleading when made.

At any time after an Event of Default has occurred and while such event is continuing unremedied, the non-Defaulting Party may, by giving telex notice to the Defaulting Party, terminate forthwith this Agreement.

6. Currency of Account

Each party shall be bound to make every payment in respect of its obligations hereunder in the currency in which such obligation is denominated. If any sum due from either party ("Payer") hereunder or any order or judgement given or made in relation hereto has to be converted from the currency ("the first currency") in which the same is payable hereunder or under such order or judgement into another currency ("the second currency") for the purpose of (i) making or filing a claim or proof against the Payer, (ii) obtaining an order or judgement in any court or other tribunal or (iii) enforcing any order or judgement given or made in relation hereto, the Payer shall indemnify and hold harmless the other party ("Payee") from and against any loss suffered as a result of any discrepancy between (a) the rate of exchange used for such purpose to convert the sum in question from the first currency into the second currency, and (b) the rate or rates of exchange at which the Payee may in the ordinary course of its business purchase the first currency with the second currency upon receipt of a sum paid to it in satisfaction, in whole or in part, of any such order, judgement, claim or proof.

7. Compensation on Termination

7.1 The Defaulting Party shall fully indemnify (and keep indemnified) the non-Defaulting Party from and against any and all expense, cost, loss, damage or liability, reasonably incurred by the non-Defaulting Party arising out of the termination of this Agreement pursuant to Clause 5 by the non-Defaulting Party which the non-Defaulting Party incurs as a consequence (directly or indirectly) of the occurrence of any Event of Default in respect of the Defaulting Party and/or such termination including, but without limitation, any reasonable legal or out of pocket expenses, and any reasonable amount required to compensate the non-Defaulting Party for any losses sustained and/or costs incurred by the non-Defaulting Party in making reasonable alternative arrangements to secure the financial equivalent of the payments and receipts contemplated by Clause 3 of Section D, E, or F, as the case may be. In each case, a certificate of the non-Defaulting Party as to the amount of any such costs and/or losses shall be conclusive in the absence of manifest error. Each party expressly recognises that the other is or may become party to one or more transactions which are the reverse of the transactions contemplated in this Agreement to which that party may refer for the purpose of computing its expenses, costs, losses, damage or liability.

7.2   If the obligations of the parties are terminated under Clause 4 and:

a)   only one party is the Affected Party and the other party has estimated that it will incur losses, the Affectd Party shall pay to the other party the amount of such estimated losses; or

b)   only one party is the Affectd Party and the other party has estimated that it will make profits, the other party shall pay to the Affected Party the smaller of such profits and the estimate by the Affected Party of its losses; or

c)   both parties are Affected Parties, and either party has estimated that it will incur losses, the party which has estimated that it will make profits or incur smaller loses shall pay to the other party an amount equal to half the difference between such profits and losses (losses being treated as a negative number) or between such losses;

provided that if neither party estimated losses, no payment shall be made. For the purpose of estimating losses, each party shall be entitled to have regard to those matters to which it would have had regard under sub-Clause 7.1 if it had been a non-Defaulting Party.

Each party shall, within 60 days of the Termination Date, deliver to the other a written computation of all such losses, costs and expenses, setting out the basis upon which such figures have been calculated and such details as may be necessary of any underlying transactions which are or may be affected by such termination.

7.3   If either party fails, within 60 days of the Termination Date, to provide a statement as required by sub-Clause 7.2 then sub-Clause

7.1 shall apply as if the party which did so provide a statement was the non-Defaulting Party.

8. Governing Law

Any agreement entered into under BBAIRS Terms shall be governed by and construed in accordance with the laws of England.

FRABBA Terms and Conditions for Forward Rate Agreements (FRA)

Reprinted from the booklet, *Forward Rate Agreements ("FRABBA" terms)*, published by the British Bankers' Association (in association with the Foreign Exchange and Currency Deposit Brokers' Association), August 1985

Recommended Terms and Conditions

1. Scope

1.1 These recommended Terms and Conditions shall apply to all forward rate agreements (FRAs) between participants operating in the UK interbank market and shall be deemed to be incorporated in any contract, whether oral or written, entered into relating to a FRA. Unless otherwise stated all FRA deals will be regarded as having been written on "FRABBA" terms. ANY VARIATION FROM THESE RECOMMENDED TERMS AND CONDITIONS MUST BE CLEARLY AGREED AT THE TIME OF THE DEAL AND SPECIFIED IN THE DOCUMENTATION.

1.2 A FRA is an agreement between any two banks seeking to protect themselves against a future interest rate movement in the currencies listed in the Appendix, for an agreed Contract Amount, for a specified Contract Period at an agreed Contract Rate; and requires that settlement is effected between the parties in accordance with Section D.4. For the purpose of the FRA there is no commitment made by either party to lend or borrow the Contract Amount.

1.3 It is understood that both parties have entered into this FRA in accordance with normal banking practice.

2. Representations and Warranties

Each party represents and warrants to the other that:-

i)   it has full power and authority (corporate and otherwise) to enter into this FRA and to exercise its rights and perform its obligations hereunder and has obtained all authorisations and consents necessary for it so to enter, exercise rights and perform obligations and such authorisations and consents are in full force and effect;

ii) the obligations expressed to be assumed by it under this FRA are legal and valid obligations binding on it in accordance with their terms; and

iii) as of the date of this FRA all payments to be made by it hereunder may be made free and clear of, and without deduction for or on account of, any taxes whatsoever.

3. Confirmation/Notification

FRAs may be entered into either orally or in writing and any demand may be made orally or in writing. Each of the parties shall be bound (but without prejudice to the binding nature thereof) to give confirmation in writing of any FRA or demand concluded or made orally. Where such confirmation or demand is made or confirmed by letter it shall be deemed to have been properly made or confirmed to the counterparty, if posted, addressed to the counterparty's registered office or such other address as may be notified and shall be deemed to have been given or made at the time at which it would, in the ordinary course of post, have been delivered. Where such a confirmation or demand is made by telex (or other agreed telegraphic means) it shall be deemed properly made at the time of transmission provided the telex (or other transmission) was sent to the last published number of the recipient and, in the case of telex, the last published answer back of the recipient appears thereon.

4. Settlement (for contract periods in excess of one year)

4.1   Wherever two parties enter into a FRA the Buyer will agree to pay to the Seller on the Settlement date (if the Contract Rate exceeds the BBA Interest Settlement Rate) and the Seller will agree to pay to the Buyer on the Settlement Date (if the BBA Interest Settlement

Rate exceeds the Contract Rate) an amount calculated in accordance with the following formula:

a) when L is higher than R

$$\frac{(L - R) \times D \times A}{(B \times 100) + (L \times D)}$$

or

b) when R is higher than L

$$\frac{(R - L) \times D \times A}{(B \times 100) + (L \times D)}$$

where L = BBA Interest Settlement Rate (expressed as a number and not a percentage, e.g. 10.11625 and not 10.11625%)

R = Contract Rate (expressed as a number and not a percentage)

D = Days in Contract Period

A = Contract Amount

B = 360 except where the Contract Currency is Pounds Sterling (or any other currency where the contract rate is calculated on 365 days according to market custom) when 'B' = 365.

4.2 Broken dates

In the event that no BBA Interest Settlement Rate is available for the Contract Period, then it will be the responsibility of both parties to agree both the basis for establishing an alternative rate and the reference banks to be used for this purpose; and to specify the Settlement Date and the Maturity Date at the time of dealing.

4.3 Subsequent Declaration of Non-Business Day

If a Contract Period ceases to be eligible for settlement under recommended FRABBA terms owing to circumstances where the original Settlement Date ceases to be a normal business day (e.g the announcement, subsequent to the contract date, of a public holiday and/or a market closure in London or in the other relevant financial centre) the settlement rate will be obtainable for the revised Fixing Date from a member of FECDBA (in liaison with members of the Sterling Brokers Association) as specified from time to time by their Hon.Secretary.

5. Payment

Any payments shall be made for value on the Settlement Date when due in the Contract Currency and be immediately available, freely transferable and freely convertible by credit to the counterparty's specified account.

6. Cancellation/Compensation

Subject to mutual agreement between both parties, an existing FRA can be cancelled, at which time the method of calculating the Settlement Sum must be agreed by both parties. In the event that agreement cannot be reached there will be no cancellation.

7. Events of Default

7.1   The occurrence of any one or more of the following circumstances in respect of either party (the "Defaulting Party") shall be an Event of Default:

i)   an order of a competent court is made or an effective resolution is passed for the winding up or dissolution of the Defaulting Party other than for the purpose of a reconstruction or amalgamation previously approved in writing by the other party, such approval not to be unreasonably withheld; or

ii)   the initiation of proceedings under any applicable bankruptcy, reorganisation, composition or insolvency law by (in respect of itself) or against the Defaulting Party, provided that such proceedings have not been discharged or stayed within 30 days, or the appointment of a receiver over all or any part of the undertaking or any property, assets or revenues of the Defaulting Party; or

iii)   any representation made or warranty given by the Defaulting Party pursuant to Clause 2 is or proves to have been materially incorrect or misleading when made.

7.2 Notice of Event of Default

Each of the parties undertakes with the other that it will promptly notify the other of any occurrence which constitutes an Event of Default by it. Upon an Event of Default occurring in respect of either party, the other (the "non-Defaulting Party") may, by notice to the

Defaulting Party, elect to terminate this FRA immediately whereupon each party shall be released and discharged from its obligations hereunder, providing always that the foregoing shall be without prejudice to any rights, obligations or liabilities under this FRA of the parties hereto which may have accrued up to and including the date of such notice.

8. **Indemnity**

The Defaulting Party shall fully indemnify (and keep indemnified) the non-Defaulting Party from and against any and all expense, cost, loss, damage or liability, incurred by the non-Defaulting Party arising out of the termination of an FRA pursuant to Clause 7 by the non-Defaulting Party which the non-Defaulting Party incurs as a consequence (directly or indirectly) of the occurrence of any Event of Default in respect of the Defaulting Party and/or such termination including, but without limitation, any legal or out-of-pocket expenses, and any amount required to compensate the non-Defaulting Party for any losses sustained and/or costs incurred by the non-Defaulting Party in making alternative arrangements to secure the financial equivalent of the payments and receipts contemplated by Clause 4. In each case, the certificate of the non-Defaulting Party as to the amount of any such costs and/or losses shall be conclusive in the absence of manifest error. Each party expressly recognises that the other is or may become party to one or more transactions which are the reverse of the transactions contemplated in this FRA to which that party may refer for the purpose of computing its expenses, costs, losses, damage or liability.

9. **Rights and Remedies**

9.1   These Terms and Conditions shall be binding upon and enure to the benefit of both parties and their respective successors and assigns. The rights and obligations of each party may not be assigned (whether by way of charge or other wise) or transferred without the prior written consent of the other party.

9.2   No delay or omission by either party in exercising any right, power or privilege conferred upon it by this FRA shall impair the same nor shall any single or partial exercise thereof preclude any further exercise thereof or the exercise of any other right power or privilege. The rights and the remedies herein provided are cumulative and not exclusive of any rights or remedies provided by law.

10. Governing Law

FRAs entered into under these Terms and Conditions shall be governed by and construed in accordance with the laws of England.

Index

730

745